Archaeology and Prehistory

Pam J. Crabtree
New York University

Douglas V. Campana
New York University and National Park Service

Boston   Burr Ridge, IL   Dubuque, IA   Madison, WI   New York   San Francisco   St. Louis
Bangkok   Bogotá   Caracas   Kuala Lumpur   Lisbon   London   Madrid   Mexico City
Milan   Montreal   New Delhi   Santiago   Seoul   Singapore   Sydney   Taipei   Toronto

McGraw-Hill Higher Education

A Division of The **McGraw-Hill** Companies

ARCHAEOLOGY AND PREHISTORY
Published by McGraw-Hill, an imprint of the McGraw-Hill companies, Inc., 1221 Avenue of the Americas, New York, NY 10020. Copyright © 2001 by The McGraw-Hill Companies, Inc. All rights reserved. No part of this publication may be reproduced or distributed in any form or by any means, or stored in a database or retrieval system, without the prior written consent of The McGraw-Hill Companies, Inc., including, but not limited to, in any network or other electronic storage or transmission, or broadcast for distance learning.

Some ancillaries, including electronic and print components, may not be available to customers outside the United States.

This book is printed on acid-free paper.

1 2 3 4 5 6 7 8 9 0 DOW/DOW 0 9 8 7 6 5 4 3 2 1

ISBN 0-07-840516-5

Vice president and editor in chief: *Thalia Dorwick*
Editorial director: *Phillip A. Butcher*
Senior sponsoring editor: *Carolyn Henderson*
Developmental editor: *Katherine Blake*
Project manager: *Laura Ward Majersky*
Production supervisor: *Susanne Riedell*
Designer: *Matthew Baldwin*
Senior photo research coordinator: *Keri Johnson*
Lead supplement coordinator: *Cathy L. Tepper*
Compositor: *Shepherd Incorporated*
Typeface: *10.5/12 New Aster*
Printer: *R. R. Donnelley & Sons Company*

Library of Congress Cataloging-in-Publication Data
Crabtree, Pam J.
   Archaeology and prehistory / Pam J. Crabtree, Douglas V. Campana.
     p. cm.
   ISBN 0-07-840516-5 (alk. paper)
   1. Prehistoric peoples. 2. Antiquities, Prehistoric. 3. Anthropology, Prehistoric. I. Campana, Douglas V. II. Title.

GN740 .C727 2001
930.1—dc21
                            00-066434

www.mhhe.com

To Mike, Tom, and Robby,
with love.

About the Authors

Pam J. Crabtree

Pam J. Crabtree, who received her Ph.D. in anthropology from the University of Pennsylvania in 1982, is an Associate Professor of Anthropology at New York University, where she has worked since 1990. Professor Crabtree was an Assistant Professor of Anthropology at Princeton University from 1985 to 1990 and a research fellow at the Museum Applied Science Center for Archaeology of the University of Pennsylvania from 1982 to 1984. She has written many scholarly articles on zooarchaeology and animal domestication, co-edited *Animal Use and Culture Change* (with Kathleen Ryan), and edited *Medieval Archaeology: An Encyclopedia*. Professor Crabtree has conducted archaeological research in England, Ireland, Germany, India, the West Bank, and the United States. She is currently engaged in an archaeological study of forts of the French and Indian War period in the Delaware Water Gap area. Professor Crabtree is a member of the Hopewell Township (New Jersey) Historic Preservation Commission.

Douglas V. Campana

Douglas V. Campana is a Research Associate in Anthropology at New York University and an archaeologist for the National Park Service at the Valley Forge Center for Cultural Resources. He received his Ph.D. in Anthropology from Columbia University in 1981. Dr. Campana has published scholarly articles on Near Eastern prehistory and bone tool technology, and edited *Before Farming: Hunter-Gatherer Society and Subsistence*. He has conducted archaeological research in Israel, the West Bank, and Europe; his research has been sponsored by the National Science Foundation, the Wenner-Gren Foundation, the Leakey Foundation, and the National Geographic Society. As an archaeologist for the federal government, Dr. Campana has directed archaeological excavations throughout the Mid-Atlantic states. He is currently excavating a portion of George Washington's Revolutionary War encampment at Valley Forge.

Although Dr. Campana is a federal archaeologist, the positions and conclusions expressed in this text are his own and do not reflect any official position of the National Park Service, the Department of the Interior, or the government of the United States. Dr. Campana is not involved in the administration of NAGPRA or the decisions involving the Kennewick remains.

Brief Contents

v

Contents

Acknowledgments

Writing an introductory textbook in archaeology and prehistory is a daunting undertaking. This project could not have been completed without the help of colleagues, friends, and family members, and we would like to thank all of them.

We are grateful for the support of our colleagues at New York University and the National Park Service who have provided help and encouragement throughout the project. In particular, we would like to thank Jim Boyle and Heather Heineman, who researched the permissions for many of the figures that are included in this text. Special thanks are due to Laurie Tedesco, who went above and beyond the call of duty. We would also like to thank our many colleagues who provided photographs and line art for this text.

We are especially grateful to the reviewers of this textbook, whose helpful and insightful suggestions improved the content and presentation of the text in many ways. We owe a special debt of gratitude to Bernard Wailes (University of Pennsylvania), Richard Lesure (University of California, Los Angeles), Terry Harrison (New York University), and Francis McManamon (National Park Service), who read and commented on various chapters. We are also very grateful to David Bernstein (State University of New York at Stony Brook), David Carlson (Texas A & M University), Christopher DeCorse (Syracuse University), James Enloe (University of Iowa), Michael Jochim (University of California at Santa Barbara), Mary Lou Larson (University of Wyoming), Deborah Olszewsky (The Bishop's Museum, Hawaii), Alan Osborn (University of Nebraska, Lincoln), Rene Peron (Santa Rosa Junior College), Gerald Schroedl (University of Tennessee), and Tammy Stone (University of Colorado at Denver).

The editorial and production staff at McGraw-Hill has been wonderfully supportive and patient throughout the long development of this textbook. We are especially grateful to our developmental editor, Kathy Blake; to our project manager, Laura Majersky; and to our photo researcher, Barbara Salz, all of whom have worked diligently on our behalf to see this project to completion.

Finally, we want to thank our family and friends for their support throughout the long process of writing and revising this textbook. Special thanks go to our sons, Michael, Thomas, and Robert Campana, for their patience and understanding.

Pam J. Crabtree
Douglas V. Campana

Preface

Because archaeology is rarely taught in high schools, many students first encounter archaeology during their first or second year in college. By that time, however, many students already have some preconceived ideas about what archaeologists do for a living.

We might envision archaeologists exploring ancient Egyptian tombs, searching for traces of early human activity in East Africa, or studying Mayan ruins in the jungles of Guatemala. The romance of discovery is unmistakable. But, what are archaeologists really looking for? How do they know where to dig? How do they interpret what they find? We have designed this text to answer these questions by providing a concise, yet comprehensive, introduction to both archaeology and prehistory.

What Are Prehistory and Archaeology?

Prehistory is the chronicle of all that human beings accomplished before the advent of written records. While humans and their direct ancestors have lived on earth for about five million years, it was just over 5,000 years ago that writing was developed. During the many millennia before the invention of writing, prehistoric humans spread to every continent except Antarctica. They developed farming and permanent villages; they even built cities that housed complex, class-stratified societies. In this text, we will trace human history in many different parts of the world, from its earliest beginnings up to the appearance of writing.

Archaeology is the collection of methods, techniques, and analytical procedures that scholars use in their attempts to understand the events that took place in the past. These events are evidenced today by material remains buried in the earth, from simple fragments of pottery and stone tools to elaborate burial sites and temples. To study these remains, archaeologists make use of ideas, methods, and techniques derived from geology, biology, chemistry, physics, the social sciences, and other fields, as well techniques developed by archaeologists themselves. We will explore the techniques that archaeologists use to understand and interpret the past in the absence of written records.

Approach

Most traditional textbooks on world prehistory include a few brief introductory chapters on archaeological methods and then go on to recount a detailed world prehistory, paying very little attention to how archaeologists actually study the past. Textbooks on archaeological methods tend to be cookbooks, with very few examples of how these methods are applied in the real world.

Our approach is very different. We wrote *Archaeology and Prehistory* because we wanted to integrate archaeology and prehistory into a single introductory text so students could really begin to understand how archaeologists do their work. We believe that students need to understand that archaeological methods are not simply a bag of scientific tricks. The methods used by archaeologists are designed to answer specific questions about how real people lived in the past. In *Archaeology and Prehistory*, we integrate relevant aspects of archaeological method into almost every chapter on prehistory. We do this in boxes entitled "Archaeology in Practice." For example, our chapter on the earliest human ancestors (Chapter 3) includes an "Archaeology in Practice" on the methods used to date these very early sites. Our chapter on the earliest farmers in the Old World (Chapter 18) includes "Archaeology in Practice" boxes describing how archaeologists try to distinguish early domesticated or farm animals and plants from their wild relatives. The chapter on cities, states, and empires in the Andes (Chapter 26) includes an "Archaeology in Practice" on the preservation of organic materials such as the beautiful textiles that have been recovered from many prehistoric sites in Peru.

Complementing the "Archaeology in Practice" boxes, many chapters include a Case Study focusing on a major archaeological issue or site discussed in the chapter. These case studies are set in a broad archaeological context to allow students to understand why the sites are important. In Chapter 3, for example, a case study examines the evidence and controversy concerning the question of whether the *australopithecines* were hunters, or were themselves the hunted. Chapter 12 includes a case study of the site of Lake Mungo in Australia, which first revealed that the Australian continent had been settled by hunter-gatherers more than 25,000 years ago. Another case study (Chapter 21) describes the spectacular discoveries of Sir Leonard Woolley in the Royal Cemetery of Ur, while another (Chapter 27) describes the achievements of Native Americans in the great Mississippian site of Cahokia. A final case study (Chapter 28) discusses the discovery of the Kennewick skeleton and the controversy over whether these remains should be returned to the Native American tribes that have claimed them under the provisions of the Native American Graves Protection and Repatriation Act.

Organization

Archaeology is a rapidly growing field, and no simple textbook can provide a comprehensive survey of all of world prehistory. In *Archaeology and Prehistory*, we have chosen to focus on the major issues, questions, and controversies that archaeologists and prehistorians have tackled in the past and that continue to occupy their attention today. We will introduce students to such "big picture" questions as:

- What can archaeology tell us about the lives of human ancestors?

- When did modern humans first appear, and how did they spread throughout the world?

- How did human hunter-gatherers respond to the climatic changes that took place at the end of the ice age, and why did certain peoples begin to practice agriculture at about that time?

- How and why did cities and states develop in both the Old World and the Americas?

Our organization is essentially chronological. Part I provides background and context to present-day viewpoints. Chapter 1 offers a brief history of earlier thoughts about human antiquity and about the ways in which archaeology developed in both the Old World and the Americas. In Chapter 2, we provide a basic introduction to archaeological data and examine the kinds of questions that archaeologists ask about the past.

Part II focuses on the early evolution of humans. We begin with an overview of the fossil evidence for human evolution and then examine the beginnings of the archaeological record and the earliest archaeological sites in Africa. We look at the ways in which archaeology can be used to study the behavior of early human ancestors, creatures who were very different in terms of biology and behavior, from ourselves.

Part III centers on the movement of ancient humans out of Africa and into the subtropical and temperate areas of the Near East, East Asia, and Europe. We focus on the ways in which simple stone tools were made and used, and on the questions raised by evidence of hunting and scavenging in the archaeological record and by the evidence of the first controlled uses of fire. The final chapter in Part III is devoted to the archaeology of the Neanderthals, one of the most intriguing issues in all of world prehistory.

Part IV begins with the critical question of where, when, and how modern humans first appeared. In an attempt to answer this important question, we draw on evidence from archaeology, molecular biology, and human skeletal remains. An "Archaeology in Practice" is devoted to the molecular evidence for human evolution. We discuss the latest archaeological evidence for the replacement of the archaic Neanderthals by anatomically modern humans. The remainder of Part IV is devoted to the archaeological study of early modern humans, including the appearance of art and the initial human settlement of Australia and the Americas.

Part V examines the changes that human societies experienced at the end of the ice age, just over 10,000 years ago. We focus on the techniques—for example, pollen analysis—that archaeologists use to study past environments and the ways in which human societies in North America and Europe responded to these changes.

Until just over 10,000 years ago, all humans everywhere in the world made their living by some combination of hunting, fishing, and plant collecting. Farming was unknown. Beginning about 10,000 years ago, humans began to experiment with planting crops and keeping animals. Farming developed independently in several areas of the world, including the Near East, Southeast Asia, West Africa, Mesoamerica, highland South America, and eastern North America.

Part VI examines the origins and spread of farming in both the Old and New Worlds. In the final chapter in Part VI, we explore some of the consequences of agriculture, including population growth, the development of new technologies, and increasing incidences of certain diseases such as anemia.

One of the most interesting consequences of the advent of farming is the development of complex, urban societies. Extensive archaeological research in both the Old World and the Americas has shown that agriculture provided the economic basis for the development of urban societies such as the Maya of Central America and the Egyptians of North Africa. We will examine how and why these large-scale, class-stratified societies developed.

Part VII examines the origins and growth of urban societies in the Old World, focusing on Egypt, Mesopotamia, the Indus Valley, and Europe before the Romans, while Part VIII explores the rise of complex societies in the Americas, and includes chapters on Mesoamerica, highland South America, and eastern North America.

The final chapter explores the future of archaeology. We consider such questions as the looting and destruction of archaeological sites, the issues of archaeology and nationalism, and the ways in which archaeological data have been used for political purposes. We also discuss the relationship between archaeologists and Native Americans in North America, including the return of excavated human remains to Native American tribes. These are some of the critical ethical questions that surround archaeology today.

Special Features

In addition to the Case Studies and "Archaeology in Practice" boxes, this text includes a number of other pedagogical elements to enhance learning and make the presentation more engaging.

- **Maps:** Maps help students locate the major sites discussed in the chapter and provide a sense of the prehistoric landscape and landforms.

- **Key Terms:** Key terms are boldfaced within the text.

- **Glossaries:** End-of-chapter glossaries provide capsule definitions of important terms and sites, and also serve as chapter reviews.

- **Further Reading** and **Other Bibliography** sections: Each chapter includes a short, annotated list of references that students and instructors should find helpful in searching for additional material on the respective chapter contents. Selected readings include easy-to-read, accessible articles and books. In addition, each chapter includes a more comprehensive bibliography.

Experience Archaeology Firsthand

We hope that this text will spark your interest in archaeology, and we encourage you to become a volunteer on an archaeological excavation. The best way to learn about archaeology is to experience it firsthand. Both of us decided to become archaeologists after working as volunteers on archaeological excavations while we were undergraduates. Doug Campana's first archaeological experience was working as a volunteer on the early Paleolithic site of 'Ubeidiya in Israel (see Chapter 5), while Pam Crabtree first worked as a volunteer at the excavation of the medieval city of Winchester in England.

The Archaeological Institute of America publishes an annual *Archaeological Fieldwork Opportunities Bulletin,* which should prove a valuable reference for students searching for archaeological excavations that accept volunteers. The Internet is also a valuable resource.

Part I

Introduction to Archaeology and Prehistory

What is archaeology, and what is it that archaeologists actually do? In the popular imagination, archaeologists lead glamorous and romantic lives, digging up mummies and ancient treasures in exotic lands, like the swashbuckling Indiana Jones in the films of the 1970s. In reality, archaeology has much more in common with scientific laboratory research than with the exploits of Indy and his cronies. Archaeologists carefully excavate and record mundane objects such as fragments of broken pottery and butchered animal bones in an attempt to understand how people lived in the past.

The first two chapters of this textbook provide a brief introduction to the field of archaeology and to archaeological excavation. We begin with a history of archaeology, showing how the modern discipline of archaeology developed from a seventeenth- and eighteenth-century interest in ancient objects and old monuments. In Chapter 2 we introduce some of the basic terms and concepts used in archaeological research. These terms and concepts will be used throughout the text. In our introduction we hope to show that archaeology is an exciting and intellectually challenging field of study, even if archaeologists do not usually face the physical dangers that Indiana Jones confronted in his movie exploits.

Chapter 1

What Is Prehistory?
The World before the Written Word

Introduction

In October 1992, the cover of *Time* magazine, a space usually reserved for celebrities and politicians, displayed the face of a man about whom virtually nothing was known, not even his name, and who had died more than 5,000 years ago **(Figure 1.1)**. The discovery of the Iceman, as he was called, generated a press sensation. Scores of newspaper and magazine articles and several books on the Iceman soon appeared, including one denouncing the find as a fraud. Most scientists, however, are quite convinced that he is genuine. The body was discovered in September 1991, high in the Tyrolean Alps between Italy and Austria. The summer had been warm, and a deposit of dust on the glacier resulted in an unusual degree of melting. The Iceman's frozen body, entombed in the glacial ice for millennia, was finally released. German tourists hiking though the pass came upon his remains just poking through the ice. Had they not found him, within a few days he would have been covered with a fresh fall of snow and returned once more to the glacier.

Why should the Iceman, whose possessions were humble in the extreme, who hailed from a time scarcely known to the average person, have aroused such excitement? Much was made of the claim that the Iceman was the oldest completely preserved human, but, in truth, some Egyptian mummies were older. For some Europeans, surely, the fact that the Iceman was himself a European provided a tie to their past. Most likely, though, he was so interesting because he was a common man, the antithesis of the pharaohs of Egypt or the emperors of China. Possibly, he was a shepherd, not so different from the Tyrolean shepherds of today. He carried with him only the equipment that served him in his everyday life. His garments, equipment, and weapons buried with him in the ice told of an ordinary man.

The methods of archaeology tell us all we know about who the Iceman was. (Physical anthropologists and biologists study the man's body itself.) The Iceman carried with him a metal

Figure 1.1

The 5,000-year-old body of the Iceman, recovered from a glacier in the Tyrolean Alps.

Figure 1.2

A copper axe and a flint knife, a few of the numerous items in the Iceman's equipment.

axe **(Figure 1.2)**, at first believed to be bronze, because it closely resembled the axes found in sites dated to the early Bronze Age of the region (starting about 2200 B.C.). When samples from the Iceman, however, were dated using radiocarbon (to be discussed in detail in Chapter 10), he was found instead to have died between 3500 and 3000 B.C.—the early Copper Age. The blade of the axe was analyzed chemically; it turned out to be copper. Its flanged form, though, was unusually sophisticated for that early date. The early Copper Age from this part of the Alps is so poorly known that the local occurrence has not even been given a name. The closest analog to the flanged axe comes from a nearby cemetery at Remedello, but about 500 years later. The rest of the Iceman's equipment has even fewer parallels, and much of it is unique, because objects of wood and leather are very rarely preserved. It was a remarkable set of equipment. His leather clothing, although crudely patched, perhaps by the Iceman himself, had been finely stitched together by a practiced hand from the contrasting skins of several animals. His shoes were well made, grass-insulated against the cold, and he wore a fur-lined cap on his head. He carried his supplies in a wood-framed backpack, including a quiver filled with arrows, a few of which still had feathers attached. Around his waist he wore a leather pouch that contained some flint tools and tinder for fire making. He had a birch-bark container as well, blackened on the inside as if it had contained fire. Very likely, the Iceman was making himself a new bow when he met his death, for he carried an unfinished longbow made from yew, the best wood known for that purpose. There were other items as well, some 20 in all. Particularly interesting are some bits of fungus threaded on a thong. Known to have antibiotic value, they perhaps served as a first-aid kit. The sophistication of the Iceman's clothing, his tools, and his evident knowledge of the natural world all came as a surprise.

The European Copper Age, or Chalcolithic, is an age known only from archaeology. All that we know of the people of the European Copper Age comes from the material traces they left behind. **Archaeology** means, literally, the study of ancient things; it refers in practice to the study of the material remains created by past human beings. Archaeologists use a wide range of techniques to puzzle out the past, and they enlist the aid of many specialists from other fields. Archaeology is more, though, than the collection of methods and techniques needed to uncover individual facts about the past. As we will see in Chapter 2, archaeology provides a variety of ways for integrating these isolated facts into a broad picture of the world of the past and a framework for understanding how that world developed and changed.

In Europe, the people of the Copper Age did not write. Indeed, we can only speculate about what sort of language they may have spoken. More than 2,000 years would pass before the epics of Homer would mark the beginning of written history in Europe. The events of the Copper Age are the stuff of prehistory, as are all the events in which humans participated before the advent of written records. **Prehistory** (as archaeologists use the word) is the sum of all that we know of the activities of humans before the beginning of written history, and archaeology is the means by which we have gained almost all this knowledge.

Prehistory

Homer and the classical authors of ancient Greece and Rome, the writers of the Old Testament of the Bible, the scribes of ancient Egypt and Mesopotamia, the historians of ancient China, and the carvers of Mayan inscriptions, among others, have given us the names of kings, told us of the adventures of heroes, and set down for us their understanding of the place of humanity in the natural and spiritual worlds. But what do we know of prehistory—the vast expanse of time before humanity learned to write? During that long, silent era, people evolved from their prehuman ancestors, learned to make tools, captured fire, and spread into almost every habitable region of the earth. Humans learned to till the soil for crops, domesticated animals, and settled into villages. We know the names of none of these people. The human story begins millions of years in the past, but recorded history begins only about 5,000 years ago, with the growth of cities and the rise of the ancient civilizations of the Old World. In the New World the recording of history is more recent still, beginning about 2,000 years ago.

Written records, which range from literature and history to the humble account books of ancient clerks and merchants, can provide an irreplaceable window into the minds of ancient people. Through them, we may see how the people of earlier societies viewed their world, how they ranked and categorized what was important to them, and how they understood the workings of the social universe in which they lived. Written records, though, are available for only a minute fraction of past human societies. Writing is the exception rather than the rule. For most of humanity's time on earth, all that is left to us are material remains: stone tools and potsherds, skeletons and animal bones, trash pits, structures, stains in the soil. All that we know of our most ancient roots has been dug from the earth. Yet the material vestiges of past human behavior have much to tell us about how these ancient human societies subsisted, developed, and interacted, and even, through careful inference, something of their ideas and beliefs. The challenge of archaeology is to "read" the unwritten material record in the soil and to use these data to write prehistory.

Archaeology

Archaeology, as noted earlier, is the study of the material remains of past societies. If we are to understand the forces that shaped human society, we must try to interpret these remains, to understand what they were and how they came to rest where they were found, and to infer from them human behavior, social organization, and the relationship between early humans and their environment. This is the basic challenge faced by the prehistoric archaeologist. It is a bit like a detective story in which an unseen crime must be pieced together from often elusive clues. Like Sherlock Holmes, the prehistoric archaeologist must exercise careful logic in interpreting the archaeological data and then formulate likely hypotheses to account for what is observed. These hypotheses must then be tested against further observations so that unsatisfactory explanations can be eliminated. Archaeologists try, in the end, to arrive at the most likely explanation for events in the past.

The Issues and Problems of Prehistory

This text will concentrate on the prehistoric periods around the globe and on archaeology as it is applied to the study of prehistory. Many of the crucial events that have shaped humanity and human society have left behind no record other than stone tools, some food remains, and the skeletons of our predecessors. Prehistoric archaeologists find themselves with some fascinating and challenging problems to solve. Some of the most important issues are the following:

- Who were our earliest human ancestors? What were their lives like? Did they hunt for their food, or did they obtain it by scavenging kills left behind by more powerful carnivores? How were early human societies organized? We will address these questions in Chapters 3 through 7.

- How, when, and where did modern humans evolve? How did they come to replace more ancient forms of human beings, and when and how did they spread throughout the world? These questions will be addressed in Chapters 8 through 12.

- When, where, and why did farming replace hunting and gathering? When did the first permanent villages appear in the Old World and in the Americas? Chapters 13 through 20 will address these issues.

- Can we trace the development of the great civilizations of the Old World? How did the pre-Columbian civilizations of the New World develop? These questions will be addressed in Chapters 21 through 27.

Today archaeologists believe they have some answers to some of these questions, but many basic problems are yet unresolved. Many alternative hypotheses have been offered concerning these issues, and much lively (and sometimes rancorous) debate continues among archaeologists. There is much work for the future.

The methods and archaeological viewpoints to be discussed in this book are primarily those developed in the West, specifically Europe and North America, in the wake of the explosive growth in the natural sciences during the eighteenth and nineteenth centuries. In the early twentieth century the political dominance of the West led to the adoption of Western archaeological practices and prehistoric frameworks throughout much of the world. Some peoples outside Europe, however, held quite distinctive views of their own most ancient times. The Chinese, in particular, have recorded their own history for millennia, and even in the earliest writings they took notice of the material remains from bygone ages. Chinese historical writings were sometimes supplemented with detailed descriptions (with a distinctly archaeological flavor) of objects belonging to ancient periods. Like the ancient Greeks, the early Chinese were aware that their own use of metals was preceded by a time when people depended on stone tools.

The modern-day search for our early human ancestors, however, surely found its impetus in the scientific and humanistic developments in Europe during the eighteenth and nineteenth centuries. In the late nineteenth and early twentieth centuries, Western scholars journeyed to Africa, Southeast Asia, and China in search of the antecedents of humanity. They took Western science with them, particularly the methods of geology and the concepts of biological evolution. National scholars in Africa and Asia by and large accepted these ideas. The methods of European archaeology and the prehistoric framework originally developed for Europe came to be applied in many areas of the world. Archaeologists soon came to realize, though, that the prehistory of most of the world could not be forced into the European mold. Today archaeologists from China, Japan, Africa, South America, and elsewhere are hard at work refining the unique prehistories of their regions; in so doing, they are expanding the horizons of scientific archaeology as a whole.

The Historical Growth of Archaeology in Europe

Until a few hundred years ago almost no one could conceive of the great antiquity of human presence on the earth. The medieval European universe, for example, was short-lived and firmly centered, both physically and

Figure 1.3

A plate from the Nuremberg Chronicle *of 1493. At the center is the earth, as pictured by Ptolemy. The circles of the sun, moon, planets, and stars surround it. Outside the sphere of stars are heaven's angels.*

philosophically, on the earth and humanity. The medieval European worldview was soon to change radically. In the next few centuries the foundations of the natural sciences as we now know them were laid, including the concept of human evolution. Before we turn to a detailed discussion of the issues facing prehistorians today and of modern archaeological methods, we must summarize how the scholarly world came to accept the idea of human antiquity.

The universe of fifteenth-century Europe was circumscribed by the sphere of the fixed stars, beyond which lay the heavens **(Figure 1.3)**. The age of the universe was perceived to be short and its duration strictly limited. For European Christendom the world began shortly before the creation of Adam and Eve, and Armageddon lay not very far in the future. In the sixteenth and seventeenth centuries, new astronomical discoveries brought a better understanding of the size and complexity of the physical universe, but, in the popular mind at least, the life span of this universe was derived from a reading of the Bible. In 1636, the Irish archbishop James

Figure 1.4

Seventeenth-century architect Inigo Jones's interpretation of Stonehenge as a Roman temple.

Ussher calculated, on the basis of the text of the Bible, that the world had been created in 4004 B.C. Together with the works of classical antiquity, the Bible provided all that was known of history.

During the seventeenth century, however, scholars began to examine the world of nature ever more closely. As the telescope had revealed the universe, the invention of the microscope opened up the world of the very small. The sciences of chemistry and physics were developing, and the earth's array of plants and animals began to be classified. This growing interest in the natural world also drew the curiosity of many to the mysterious monuments scattered across the European countryside—earthworks, stone chambers and rings, and standing stones. Among the most well known of these ancient monuments were the standing stones that make up Stonehenge. In the twelfth century the English chronicler Geoffrey of Monmouth ascribed the construction of Stonehenge to the magical activities of King Arthur's legendary wizard, Merlin. The seventeenth-century scholar no longer accepted magic, but the explanation of such structures had to fit into a short historical chronology beginning with the biblical account of the Creation. Most commonly, the building of Stonehenge was ascribed to the Celts or Britons or other peoples known from the classical writers. In 1620 the royal architect Inigo Jones concluded that Stonehenge was a Roman temple **(Figure 1.4)**. John Aubrey (1626–1697) was the first to undertake a detailed study of the great stone circle: "The celebrated antiquity of Stonehenge . . . I affirme to have been temples, and built by the Britons [the inhabitants of Britain at the time of the Roman conquest of the island in the first century A.D.]" (Aubrey in Daniel 1967: 37). Aubrey believed Stonehenge was the work of Druid priests living in Britain before the Roman conquest of the island. This myth was popularized in the eighteenth century and remains imbedded in popular culture even today. Neo-Druids congregate at Stonehenge on the summer solstice (June 21) to celebrate this popular myth. Stonehenge, in fact, far antedates the Britons; its earliest phases were probably erected before 2000 B.C.

Medieval farmers frequently encountered stone axes in their fields; such things were usually attributed to magic or to the "little people" (leprechauns) or to the action of lightning. The sixteenth-century voyages of discovery brought a better answer: These objects were stone tools made in the absence of metals, not unlike the tools and weapons used by many native New World peoples. Still, the true antiquity of these stone tools could not be imagined. Not until the nineteenth century, in fact, was it possible to appreciate how very old these objects were. In 1802 the Danish archaeologist Rasmus Nyerup could still lament that

> everything which has come down to us from heathendom is wrapped in a thick fog; it belongs to a space of time we cannot measure. We know that it is older than Christendom but whether by a couple of years or a couple of centuries, or even by more than a millennium, we can do no more than guess. (Nyerup in Daniel 1967: 36)

For this fog to be lifted, the chronology of the earth had to be recast, and the evidence for this new chronology was to come from the developing science of geology.

The New Geology

Archbishop Ussher had set the date not only of the creation of the world but also of the Great Flood in the time of Noah—2501 B.C. Everything that followed the flood was history; that which preceded it was from an unknown antediluvian epoch. Eighteenth-century geologists were becoming increasingly aware that a complex history of the earth was recorded in the succession of strata, or rock layers, that make up the earth's crust. Today we take it for granted that the many meters of consecutive rock layers (which can be seen clearly in places like the Grand Canyon) were laid down layer by layer over many ages. At the start of the eighteenth century, this concept was not so clear. The prevailing idea at that time was that the rocks of the earth had precipitated all at once from a world-encircling ocean.

The key figure in refuting this **hypothesis,** or explanation, was the Scotsman **James Hutton** (1726–1797). Hutton would not accept that the geological features of the earth were laid down by the Great Flood. Instead, he argued, we must look to processes still at work on the earth today, such as soil erosion and volcanic activities, to explain what happened in the past. This view was later called the uniformitarian principle, or **uniformitarianism.** The crust of the earth, according to Hutton, was constantly being uplifted and eroded, and the deep layers of sedimentary rock had been laid down over many millennia from the sediment carried from the uplands to the sea, a process that may be observed today. The layers of rock are immensely thick,

and such processes are very slow. The earth, therefore, must be far older than the 6,000 years calculated by Ussher.

Hutton published his work in 1785 and 1788, but it did not fit in with the tenor of the times. Early geologists recognized that the successive rock strata of the earth often held fossils of many varied species that appeared and then disappeared with the passage of time. Most scholars, however, saw the fossil record as a series of catastrophes that, like the Great Flood, had swept away the living species, after which new species would appear. Some scientists pictured these upheavals as local phenomena, but others saw the catastrophes as worldwide in scope, implying that the new species appearing after the catastrophe had been newly created. This theory, known as **catastrophism,** was more in keeping with the early nineteenth-century worldview; Hutton's ideas were practically forgotten.

Between 1830 and 1833, however, **Charles Lyell** (1797–1875) published a textbook, *Principles of Geology,* that revived the uniformitarian principles introduced by Hutton, but which was bolstered by much additional evidence. Lyell argued his position extremely convincingly; the textbook saw many editions, and the uniformitarian view of geology came to be practically universally accepted. By the mid-nineteenth century most scientists had come to accept the deep antiquity of the earth, an earth shaped by the slow, gradual effects of ordinary geological processes—the erosion of the rocks and soil by wind and water and the slow buildup of sediments by rivers and streams. Among those scientists was **Charles Darwin** (1809–1882). During the 1830s Darwin signed on as natural history officer aboard the HMS *Beagle* and began his famous voyage of discovery down the coast of South America and through its offshore islands. (Darwin had read Lyell's book before embarking.) During this trip he made the crucial wildlife observations that would lead to his publication of *On the Origin of Species* in 1859 (for a more detailed discussion, see Eiseley 1958). The mechanism proposed by Darwin for the evolution of new species, natural selection, proceeded by the extremely slow accumulation of minute changes; only the time depth provided by Lyell's geology could make evolution possible.

Human Antiquity

During the nineteenth century the evidence for the true antiquity of humans began to pile up (Daniel 1959; Daniel and Renfrew 1988; Grayson 1983). In 1797, **John Frere** (1740–1807) recognized that humans had lived on earth for a very long time based upon his discoveries at Hoxne, Suffolk, in eastern England. Many flint tools, including chipped flint axes **(Figure 1.5)**, and the bones of extinct animals were found buried in a layer some 4 meters (12 ft.) below the ground surface. As Frere noted:

> The situation in which these weapons were found may tempt us to refer them to a very remote period indeed, even beyond that of the present world. (Frere in Daniel 1967: 47)

Could humans really have lived at the same time as extinct animals? In the 1830s, at a cave known as Kent's Cavern in England, flint tools were found together with the bones of extinct animals, sealed beneath a layer of limestone that had been deposited by the percolating water in the cave. The scientific establishment of the time, however, would not accept the contemporaneity of the tools and extinct animal bones. It could not be proved that the limestone layer had not been broken and the tools introduced much later than the fossil bone. Yet, further associations of flint tools and ancient animals continued to come to light. In 1832 the Frenchman **Jacques Boucher de Perthes** (1788–1868) found a flint **handaxe,** a stone tool, in a gravel pit at Abbeville in the Somme Valley. Over the years Boucher de Perthes collected thousands of stone artifacts, found in the company of the bones of mammals long extinct in Europe, such as mammoths and rhinoceroses. They came from a layer of gravel 12 meters (40 ft.) below the surface, known as the drift. Boucher de Perthes published extensively on antediluvian humans, but his ideas were met mostly with disdain.

The turning point was an excavation conducted by **William Pengelly** (1812–1894). Pengelly was a natural science teacher and a talented amateur geologist. In 1846 he decided to reexamine the finds from Kent's Cavern; he became convinced that the simple stone tools were indeed contemporary with the bones of extinct animals, implying that humans had lived at the same time as those prehistoric beasts. He could not, however, convince the members of the English scientific societies, who pointed out that the cave had been extensively disturbed by the earlier excavations. Their minds were no longer closed, however, and Pengelly was given an opportunity to prove his point. In 1858 Pengelly undertook the excavation of Brixham Cave, near Windmill Hill, Torquay, in southwest England. His work was closely observed by a group of prominent scientists, including Charles Lyell, from the Royal Society (a highly influential, learned scientific society) and the Geological Society of London. The cave contained an unbroken floor of stalagmite. Pengelly broke through the floor, and beneath it were stone tools in the company of the bones of mammoth, woolly rhinoceros, cave bear, cave lion, and other ancient mammals. The learned societies were convinced; ancient humans had lived at the same time as extinct animals. Later that year two of Pengelly's observers visited Abbeville. They came back assured that Boucher de Perthes's obser-

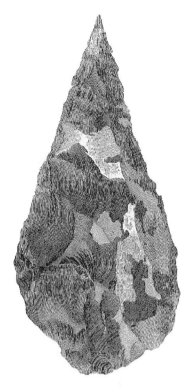

Figure 1.5

Flint handaxe found by John Frere at Hoxne, Suffolk, in 1797, which he realized came from the remote past.

vations too were correct. In 1859 these conclusions were presented to the Royal Society. Many questions were still unresolved, but from then on, most scientists would accept the antiquity of humanity.

What, though, of Stonehenge, the stone tombs, and the many objects of bronze and iron found scattered throughout Europe? These things were obviously far later than the stone tools in the Somme gravels and the English cave sites, but they too could not be accounted for within the time of written history. Scandinavia was particularly rich in such finds, and by the early 1800s many such artifacts had been collected to form the core of the Danish National Museum. **Christian J. Thomsen** (1788–1865), the first curator of the museum, had an idea about how this large collection could be organized logically. Thomsen had experience in organizing ancient coins in chronological order. When dates were not present on the coins, stylistic similarities suggested which coins were closest in time. He applied the techniques he had learned to the objects in the museum. Thomsen grouped the objects into those of stone, bronze, and iron. He went further, however, and suggested that they represented three successive ages: the Stone Age, the Bronze Age, and the Iron Age. Thomsen recognized that bronze and stone objects, for instance, might continue to be made in the Iron Age. He used stylistic similarities among the objects, as he had with coins, to sort out which of them were likely to be contemporary. This straightforward ordering of Scandinavian antiquities became known as the **Three Age System** and was soon extended to much of Europe north of the Alps.

Thomsen was assisted in his research and later succeeded by **Jens Worsaae** (1821–1885), who is now recognized as one of the founders of the discipline of archaeology. Worsaae examined the burial mounds and other ancient sites of Denmark. It was Worsaae who recognized that a bronze or an iron object found in isolation would do little to unravel the chronology of prehistory. It was critically important to observe which kinds of objects were regularly found together, and which were associated with particular burial practices and monuments. Groups of objects usually found together could be assumed to be contemporary, and if one group of objects was found to overlie another, the overlying group was clearly later in time. When the successive groups of artifacts were taken all together, a pattern emerged that could be interpreted as gradual change. Worsaae's careful excavations established the chronological validity of the Three Age System. He was able to show that sites and burials containing artifacts only of stone were older than those that also contained bronze artifacts. Worsaae published his work in 1843. He was far ahead of his time; only many years later would an appreciation of his methods reach beyond Scandinavia to the rest of the world. Many problems remained, but today the emergence of scientific dating methods has done much to clarify the chronology of the European Bronze and Iron Ages (see Chapter 24).

The Beginnings of Archaeology in the Americas

While the beginnings of archaeology in Europe were closely linked to growing European nationalism, the beginnings of archaeology in the Americas were linked to colonialism and the relationships between Europeans and Native American peoples. In the wake of Columbus's voyages, and the European explorers, conquerors, and settlers that followed, the fate of the native peoples of the Americas was inextricably caught up in the course of European history. Native American peoples, for the most part, were never afforded the opportunity to write down their own history, and most of the newly arrived Europeans assumed that the native peoples knew no history. Today, scholars realize that this view was not accurate. Many nonliterate Native American groups had rich traditions of oral history; the literate Maya (Chapter 25), we now know, recorded historical events for future generations.

Still, archaeology as it developed in the Americas, and as it has been practiced until recently, has had a fundamentally European perspective. Although change is on the horizon (see Chapter 28, "The Future of Archaeology"), the role of Native American perceptions and insights has been relatively minor. American archaeology has its academic roots in the European scientific developments we have just discussed. Seen less positively, Native Americans have been viewed largely as they appear to European eyes.

The first Europeans to encounter Native American peoples had considerable difficulty fitting them into the traditional European worldview, since American Indians held no obvious place in either classical history or religious teaching. Some speculated that they were the descendants of the Ten Lost Tribes of Israel. Others saw the American natives as scarcely human and thus rationalized the Europeans' right to displace them from their lands. In Mexico and Peru, the Spanish conquerors sought to consolidate their own colonial power and suppress the native religion. They did what they could to cut off the native peoples' contact with their history by destroying their monuments and burning their texts. In North America, Native Americans were commonly viewed as simple, unchanging savages, and many years of strife and warfare between the colonists and natives exacerbated such beliefs.

Not all Europeans, however, shared these attitudes toward Native Americans. The most notable exception was surely Thomas Jefferson, who would ultimately become president of the United States. Jefferson was a member and eventually president of the American Philosophical Society. He shared the society's interest in scientific debate, including the ongoing controversy over the nature of the ancient mounds found in many areas of eastern America. In 1784 Jefferson undertook the excavation of several of the burial mounds he found on his Virginia plantation. Jefferson did this work carefully. He took note of the distinctive layers in the soil and how some graves overlay others, indicating a long series of burials over time. Most important, Jefferson excavated these mounds to try to learn something of the Native American past.

Thomas Jefferson sometimes has been called the father of American archaeology. As Willey and Sabloff (1980: 38) have pointed out, however, he was a parent without intellectual offspring. Very little notice was taken of his archaeological endeavors. In the climate of the times, it is not likely that many European colonists would have favored research that demonstrated the antiquity of Native Americans' claim to the land. The most impressive ancient features on the North American landscape, the great mounds of the Ohio Valley, were assumed to be the work of a vanished Mound Builder people, who had been driven away by the savage Indians. Throughout the nineteenth century a majority of scholars stereotyped Native American cultures as uniformly simple and unchanging. Even the achievements of the Inca and Aztec civilizations were explained away as simply the products of Spanish exaggeration, intended to heighten the glory of their conquest.

Eventually, the accumulation of evidence would sweep away that point of view. A series of travelers and explorers penetrated the jungles of the lowland Maya homeland and brought home stirring tales of their adventures and magnificent images of the hidden, ancient cities they found there. These popular accounts suited the public tastes of the time and were read avidly. New scientific expeditions of discovery were mounted, and by the end of the nineteenth century a variety of surveys and studies of the antiquities of Middle and South America had been completed or were under way.

Archaeology, in close association with anthropology, continued to develop in the United States during the late nineteenth century. It was recognized that much of the diversity of Native American culture was fast disappearing, including many Native American languages and traditions. In 1879 the Smithsonian Institution formed the Bureau of Ethnology (later called the Bureau of American Ethnology) to record the vanishing languages and traditions. Archaeology was seen as a part of those studies, but archaeological findings were interpreted largely as projections of modern Native American societies into the past. Only in the twentieth century have archaeologists recognized the depth, diversity, and complexity of the North American archaeological record. Nineteenth-century efforts to describe and classify Native American antiquities gave way to the establishment of prehistoric sequences and chronologies (Willey and Sabloff 1980), and more recently, to attempts to explain the events of American prehistory.

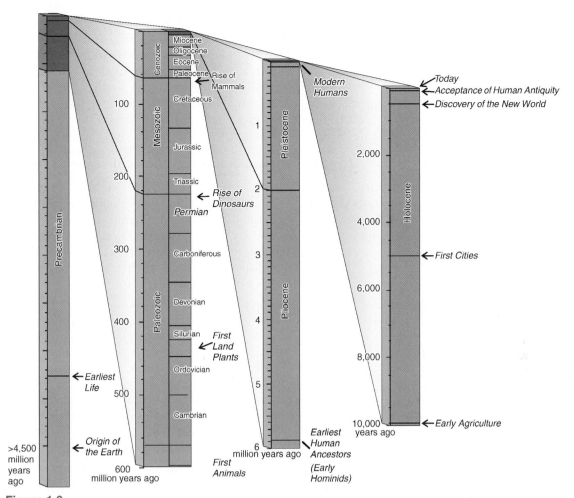

Figure 1.6

The geological ages and a perspective on human antiquity. If the 3.8 billion years of life on the earth were represented as 1 year, modern humans would have come into existence less than 15 minutes ago, and literacy and urbanism would have begun about 40 seconds ago.

A Twentieth-Century Perspective

Modern science has cast the human experience into a far wider perspective than that of the nineteenth-century archaeologists. Geologists now know that life has existed on the earth for approximately 3.8 billion years. In comparison, the few million years of human evolution has been a short time indeed (**Figure 1.6**). Yet the full span of human evolution was more than a thousand times longer than the roughly 5,000 years of recorded history.

The work of the founders of archaeology has been extended and expanded on by the generations of archaeologists that followed them. Today, archaeological research is being undertaken by scholars of many nationalities around the world. The contributions of many of these researchers will be described, in the context of their research, throughout the following chapters. Worsaae's basic principles still hold, but excavation methods, recording techniques, and archaeologists' methods of analysis have been greatly refined. Other fields of science have come to archaeology's aid; geology, paleontology, zoology, botany, chemistry, physics, computer science, and mathematics all play a part in modern archaeological research. Many of these special studies and techniques will be discussed throughout this text in the Archaeology in Practice boxes. Chapter 2 will introduce the basic methods and techniques of modern archaeology and describe the ways today's archaeologists think about the past.

 Glossary

Archaeology. The study of the material remains of past human behavior. The nature of modern archaeology is discussed in detail in Chapter 2.

Boucher de Perthes, Jacques (1788–1868). French customs agent of aristocratic birth whose discoveries of ancient stone tools along with the bones of extinct animals in the Somme Valley, north of Paris, provided key evidence for the antiquity of humans.

Catastrophism. The idea that the succession of layers seen in the earth's crust was the result of a series of catastrophes (such as universal floods) that wiped out many of the plant and animal species in existence, which were then replaced by new species.

Darwin, Charles (1809–1882). One of the key figures in the development of our modern understanding of biological evolution. Darwin proposed that new plant and animal species arise as a consequence of natural selection—as organisms are confronted by new circumstances, only individuals that are well adapted to their environments survive to reproduce. He published his theory in *On the Origin of Species* (1859).

Frere, John (1740–1807). English scholar who was one of the first to suspect the antiquity of human beings. He discovered flint tools buried deep below the surface, in the company of the bones of unknown animals, at Hoxne, Suffolk, in eastern England, and concluded that the flint tools must have been made in the very remote past.

Handaxe. A stone implement characteristic of the early Stone Age (the Lower Paleolithic), generally oval or elliptical and about the right size to fit in the hand. It was made by removing flakes from either side of a stone nodule. Handaxes are discussed in greater detail in Chapter 5.

Hutton, James (1726–1797). Scottish geologist who contended that the earth underwent a continuous cycle of mountain uplift, erosion, and the deposition of sediments to form new layers of rock. Hutton introduced

the doctrine of uniformitarianism (see below).

Hypothesis. A tentative explanation to account for an observed set of facts or events. A hypothesis is provisional and unproved, and its acceptance depends on the gathering of further evidence. A hypothesis often suggests specific consequences so that it can be tested by an attempt to observe those consequences.

Lyell, Charles (1797–1875). English geologist whose extremely influential textbook *Principles of Geology* (1830–33) revived and expanded the uniformitarian principles introduced by James Hutton. Lyell's work helped stimulate the young Charles Darwin in the development of his theory of the origin of species by natural selection.

Pengelly, William (1812–1894). English schoolteacher with a deep interest in natural history. Pengelly reinvestigated Kent's Cavern and later excavated Brixham Cave, near Windmill Hill, Torquay, in southwest England, under the close observation of a committee of prominent scientists. His discovery of flint tools together with the bones of ancient animals was a turning point in the acceptance of the antiquity of humans.

Prehistory. The reconstruction of the human events that occurred before the advent of writing.

Thomsen, Christian J. (1788–1865). First curator of the Danish National Museum of Antiquities. Thomsen grouped the objects in the museum according to the material from which they were made and asserted that they represented three successive ages: the Stone Age, the Bronze Age, and the Iron Age. This organizational scheme is known as the Three Age System.

Three Age System. A system initially developed by C. J. Thomsen as a way of organizing the collections in the Danish National Museum. He sorted the tools according to the materials they were made of—stone, bronze, and iron—and suggested that they represented three successive ages: the Stone Age, the Bronze Age, and the Iron Age.

Uniformitarianism. The view of the earth's geological history, introduced by James Hutton and further developed by Charles Lyell, that the geological processes that operated in the past were similar in nature to those that are observable today.

Worsaae, Jens (1821–1885). Successor to Christian Thomsen as director of the Danish National Museum. Worsaae is sometimes called the father of modern archaeology; he was the first professional archaeologist. He excavated extensively throughout Denmark and established many of the basic methods used by modern archaeologists.

 Further Reading

Daniel, Glyn
1959. The Idea of Man's Antiquity. *Scientific American* 201 (5): 7–11.
A very readable, brief introduction to how human antiquity came to be recognized.

Daniel, Glyn, and Colin Renfrew
1988. *The Idea of Prehistory.* Edinburgh: Edinburgh University Press.
An updated version of Daniel's account of the beginnings of prehistoric archaeology, including the contributions of recent workers in the field.

Eiseley, Loren
1958. *Darwin's Century: Evolution and the Men Who Discovered It.* Garden City, NY: Doubleday.
A detailed account of the geological and biological discoveries and thinking that led up to, and followed, Darwin's publication of *On the Origin of Species.*

Grayson, D. K.
1983. *The Establishment of Human Antiquity.* New York: Academic Press.
An in-depth discussion of the early evidence for human antiquity.

Willey, G. R., and J. A. Sabloff
1980. *A History of American Archaeology,* 2d ed. London: Thames and Hudson.
A comprehensive history of archaeology as practiced in the Americas.

 Other Bibliography

Daniel, Glyn
1967. *The Origins and Growth of Archaeology.* Harmondsworth, England: Penguin.

Chapter 2

What Is Prehistoric Archaeology?
A Window on the Past

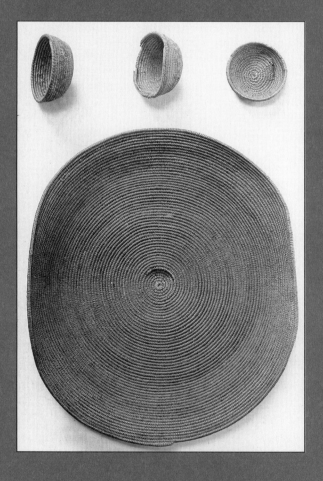

Introduction

Archaeology is a changing and growing discipline. Archaeologists may ask many questions about the past, but which questions *should* they ask? Archaeologists are often quite contentious about the "right" way to interpret the past, as evidenced by the many publications on issues of archaeological theory that appear in scientific journals. Yet in actual archaeological practice, there is wide consensus regarding the methods and techniques used in archaeological studies and the basic goals of archaeological research. In this chapter we will examine the modern discipline of archaeology and the research goals that are shared by archaeologists working in different time periods and different areas of the world. We will then examine the issues of archaeological explanation—how modern archaeologists have come to think about their data and how this information should be interpreted.

The Field of Archaeology Today

Archaeology as it is practiced today is broad and varied. Archaeologists study a wide range of ancient peoples and work in a broad variety of settings, from universities and museums to federal and state governments and private companies. All the different varieties of archaeology, however, share a basic premise: that the material remains left behind by people in the past can be interpreted to yield an understanding of past human behavior.

In America, archaeology has developed as part of the broader discipline of **anthropology.** As noted in Chapter 1, during the early years of archaeology, the Americas were home to numerous Native American peoples whose languages and traditional ways of life were fast disappearing. The new social science of anthropology was growing up, and early anthropologists saw themselves in a race against time to record native languages, traditions, and religious practices. They approached their topic along four fronts, which were to become the four major branches of American anthropology. American **cultural anthropology** began with the **ethnography** of Native American peoples—the detailed recording of these peoples' societies and lifeways. **Anthropological linguistics** started with comparative studies of Native American languages, and **physical anthropology** involved comparative anatomical studies of the people themselves. American **anthropological archaeology** was concerned with the material remains of the Native Americans' predecessors. All these fields have since grown far from their original roots as the discipline of anthropology has evolved. Today, cultural anthropologists study contemporary human societies around the world; biological anthropologists study human evolution, primate biology and behavior, and modern human biological adaptations; and anthropological linguists are interested in languages and the social context of language throughout the world.

Until about 25 years ago, most American archaeologists, particularly those interested in prehistory, were trained as anthropologists and held appointments in college and university departments of anthropology. While most U.S. archaeologists are still trained as anthropologists, the majority of American archaeologists today work outside the academy. Since the early 1970s, federal environmental legislation has required that any federally funded construction include environmental impact statements describing the effects that the new construction will have on existing archaeological resources. Later legislation was directed specifically toward the preservation and protection of archaeological resources, and similar laws were enacted by the states. More recently, the Native American Graves Protection and Repatriation Act (NAGPRA) was enacted to help protect Native American cultural heritage. These topics will be discussed further in Chapter 28. As a result of these laws, many archaeological surveys and excavations have been conducted in advance of highway, bridge, and building construction in the United States. For example, the Five Points site **(Figure 2.1)**, a nineteenth-century immigrant neighborhood in downtown New York City, was discovered and excavated in advance of construction carried out at the New York federal courthouse building. Today, many archaeologists are employed within cultural resource management (CRM) divisions of federal, state, and local government agencies, within similar CRM departments of large private engineering

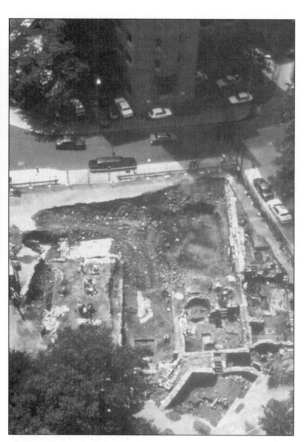

Figure 2.1

Excavations on the site of a new courthouse at Foley Square in lower Manhattan exposed the remains of tenements that were part of the infamous Five Points neighborhood. The excavation was done by Historic Conservation and Interpretation (HCI) in 1991; artifact analysis and interpretation were completed by John Milner Associates under contract to the U.S. General Services Administration.

and architectural firms, or within independent archaeological firms providing their services to government agencies under contract.

In Europe the development of archaeology took a somewhat different path. Archaeology grew up as part of the desire to understand local cultural and national origins. As we saw in the previous chapter, it grew up too in the company of the developing natural sciences of geology and paleontology. As a result, depending on the period of interest, most European archaeologists see themselves closely linked with the disciplines of history and geology, and they frequently hold university appointments in these departments. Many European universities now include independent departments of archaeology that accommodate archaeologists with a diversity of interests. This same interest in local culture history and national origins has encouraged the growth of archaeology in Latin America, Africa, and South and East Asia, especially in the postcolonial period. In India, for example, the end of British colonial rule in 1947 was followed by an explosive growth in indigenous Indian archaeology. A striking example is the excavation of the major port city of Lothal **(Figure 2.2)** in northwest India by the Indian archaeologist S. R. Rao between 1954 and 1958 (for a more complete discussion of Lothal and the Indus Valley civilization, see Chapter 22). As in America, in many other nations today, much archeology is conducted following the mandates of archaeological preservation laws.

In North America until about 20 years ago, archaeologists who studied literate societies were found in departments of classical archaeology, biblical archaeology, Egyptology and Assyriology (the studies of ancient Egypt and Mesopotamia, respectively), art history, and history. In recent years, however, North American archaeologists have applied the methods and techniques of prehistoric archaeology to historically documented societies. Historical archaeologists in North America study the changes that have occurred in the New World since Columbus's voyages 500 years ago. They have used archaeology, for example, to provide new insights into the lives of enslaved African Americans in the antebellum South (Orser 1990). In the Old South many slaves were prevented

Figure 2.2

The site of Lothal in northwest India. The excavation of this important Indus Valley site was sponsored by the Indian government in the 1950s.

from learning to write, and the available historical records were written mostly by and about the white planters. Archaeological evidence can provide unique information about the daily lives of enslaved people and about the institution of slavery itself.

In Europe, the methods and techniques of prehistoric archaeology have been used to cast new light on historical periods such as the early medieval Dark Ages. The end of the Western Roman Empire in the fifth century A.D. led to profound changes in settlements, farming technologies, and trade. For much of the Roman Empire, there are very few documents that provide information about daily life after the end of Roman rule. Archaeological excavations of Dark Age sites, such as the early Anglo-Saxon site of West Stow **(Figure 2.3)** in eastern England (West 1985), have provided information about post-Roman settlements and subsistence practices in the former Western Roman Empire.

Goals of Archaeological Interpretation

Medieval and historic North American archaeologists share both methods and approaches with prehistoric archaeologists. Like prehistoric archaeologists, they are interested in using material remains to study the ways humans lived in the past and to explore changes in human societies through time and space. Today, archaeologists generally share five goals for research and interpretation. First, *they aim to build a time and space framework for the past.* Archaeologists want to answer the basic who, what, where, and when questions of human prehistory. Second, *archaeologists try to understand how humans lived in the past.* What kinds of houses did they build? What kinds of food did they eat? How did they make their living? Third, *archaeologists want to be able to answer the why questions of human prehistory,* that is, to try to explain why change takes place in human societies. These first three goals have formed the basis of archaeological research for over 30 years. Two additional goals have come to the forefront in recent years. The first is the goal of *understanding the nature of the archaeological record itself.* Archaeologists want to understand the relationship between material remains, such as pieces of pottery and house foundations, that are discovered through excavations and the actual prehistoric behavior that produced those remains. Second, *archaeologists are*

Figure 2.3

The early Anglo-Saxon village of West Stow. Excavations carried out at this Dark Age site provided information on day-to-day life in Britain after the collapse of the Western Roman Empire. The photograph shows reconstructions of the early Anglo-Saxon houses that were built between the fifth and seventh centuries A.D.

interested in preserving the past for the future. Each of these goals will be examined in detail below.

Reconstructing Culture History: Archaeology as History without Writing

During the early years of the discipline, archaeologists were concerned primarily with gathering the data needed to fill in the vast span of time before writing began—to develop histories without written records. In Europe much of the early impetus for research came from the desire to know more about national and cultural origins. In Scandinavia, as we have seen, it was the formation of the Danish National Museum that led Thomsen and Worsaae to undertake their pioneering work. The antiquities of Denmark in particular were of interest to the museum; the goal was a better understanding of the origins and early history of the Danish people. Nationalistic motivations played a strong role in the development of archaeology in Germany, Italy, and England as well. At the

same time, the discovery of ancient stone tools, fossil humans of archaic form (to be discussed in Chapters 3 through 7), and the general intellectual climate following Darwin's *On the Origin of Species* soon led many archaeologists into a search for human origins. While anatomists and paleontologists studied the fossil humans themselves, archaeologists concentrated on the objects those early humans made and what those objects could tell us about the lifeways of early humans and the relationships among the peoples who made them. Archaeologists sought, and have continued to seek, the origins of new technologies and the beginnings of major changes in social life: the first stone tools, the earliest use of fire, the beginning of farming, the first cities. The finding of a new, earlier date for an invention or event still captures the popular imagination, but today archaeologists agree that it is far more important to try to understand *how* and *why* such changes occurred.

Culture history is the chronicle of the changes that occur within an archaeological culture over time. In Europe, in the early

Figure 2.4

An example of an archaeological culture: the Linear Pottery culture of central Europe. Large rectangular timber houses and pottery marked with curvilinear designs are typical of the Linear Pottery culture.

twentieth century, the eminent prehistorian V. Gordon Childe used the term **archaeological culture** to denote widespread and regularly associated occurrences of archeological finds. For example, the Linear Pottery, or Linearbandkeramik, culture, the material remains of the earliest farmers of central Europe, is characterized by distinctive pottery with curvilinear decorations; rectangular, timber longhouses; the cultivation of emmer wheat; and livestock husbandry, principally cattle **(Figure 2.4)**. Commonly, an archaeological culture can be subdivided into a number of successive periods based on relatively minor temporal changes in the constellation of characteristics that typify the culture. One archaeological culture may also succeed and replace another. Culture history chronicles these kinds of changes.

Anthropologically trained archaeologists working in the Americas have preferred to avoid the restricted usage of the term *archaeological culture* because it conflicts with anthropology's broader definitions of culture. The concept of culture is central to anthropological research. Although it has been defined in numerous ways, **culture** refers to the system of values, beliefs, customs, behaviors, and artifacts that the members of a particular society share and that allows those individuals to cope with their world and with each other (Bates and Plog 1990: 7). Although this terminology is still widely used in Old World archaeology, an archaeological culture, which is defined on the basis of artifacts and features alone, is not necessarily the same thing as a system of shared beliefs and values. American archaeologists, notably Gordon Willey and Philip Phillips (1958), have introduced a culture-historical terminology that consciously avoids semantically loaded terms like *culture* **(Figure 2.5)**. This terminology recognizes a time dimension on one hand and a spatial dimension on the other. (*Artifact, site*, and other archaeological terms will be defined later in this chapter.)

Phase	A short segment of time within the continuum of change at a site (or a group of related sites) that is sufficiently distinctive to be treated as a unit.
Period	A sequence of related phases.
Tradition	A group of regularly associated artifacts, usually of a single kind that persists and develops for an extended length of time. The sequence of phases and periods in a given area may be united by their sharing of a distinctive tradition.
Culture area	A wide geographical region occupied by a number of archaeological sites with broadly similar cultural characteristics.
Horizon	A contemporaneous group of broadly similar artifacts and traits that is spread over a wide geographic area. The widespread and highly distinctive Chavin art style of Peru (about 900 B.C.) is a marker of such a horizon.

Figure 2.5

Culture-historical terminology introduced by Gordon Willey and Philip Phillips (1958), in which both time and spatial dimensions are recognized. The Willey and Phillips terminology has been applied primarily in the New World.

The Investigation of Prehistoric Lifeways

By the 1950s archaeologists in both the Old World and the Americas had established a temporal and spatial framework for prehistory. A sequence of successive archaeological periods had been developed, and the location and geographic extent of various archaeological culture areas had been delineated. At the same time, there was great interest in both the Old and New Worlds in interpreting what life had been like in ancient times. Such interpretations were stimulated initially in Europe by the mid-nineteenth-century discovery of the Swiss lake villages. In 1853 an uncommonly dry year led to an unusual lowering of the Swiss lakes' waters, revealing remarkably well preserved wooden structures built on pilings. These proved to be the dwellings of late Stone Age and early Bronze Age farmers, dating from approximately 4000 to 1500 B.C. The water had preserved a wealth of materials that normally would have disappeared: wooden utensils, basketry, matting, ropes, fishnets, balls of linen thread, and fabrics, as well as plant foods such as wheat and barley, hazelnuts, and apples **(Figure 2.6)**. These things provided a rich visual image of daily village life.

American archaeologists working in the southwestern United States enjoyed some similar advantages. The prehistoric pueblo dwellers of the Southwest had lived in a desert climate that also preserved much of their organic material culture, notably plant foods and basketry **(Figure 2.7)**. Even more important, the direct descendants of these peoples lived on in the area. Much in the prehistoric

Figure 2.6

Organic materials preserved from the Swiss lake dwellings include wooden items, textiles, and plant foods.

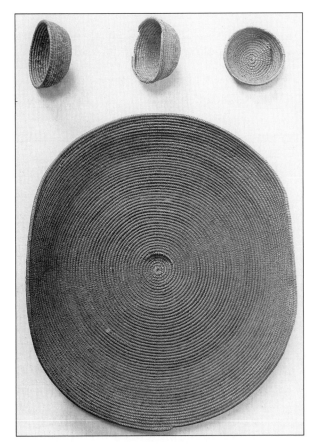

Figure 2.7

Coiled baskets recovered from Broken Roof Cave in Arizona.

culture that might not have been interpretable otherwise became comprehensible when compared with modern practices. The prehistoric sites, for example, contain features that are similar to kivas, subterranean religious structures still in use today. This interpretive approach, the projection of the present into the past, is known as **direct historical analogy.** It is meaningful only if a direct historical relationship can be demonstrated between a historically known and a prehistoric people. For most of prehistory, there are no such links.

In the early 1950s the British archaeologist J. G. D. Clark investigated the waterlogged site of Star Carr, in East Yorkshire, England. Star Carr was a campsite of hunters who lived at the very end of the Stone Age. Clark's work went beyond the simple description of the way of life of these hunters to attempt to sort out how they functioned within their natural environment. A major goal of the excavation was the recovery of the well-preserved organic remains, which an interdisciplinary team of botanists and zoologists helped analyze. One of Clark's major aims was the interpretation of the subsistence pattern of the Star Carr hunters—the range of foodstuffs on which they lived and the means used to procure them **(Figure 2.8)**. J. G. D. Clark trained many students while at Cambridge University. He and

Figure 2.8

Life *magazine (from the 1950s) illustration of daily life at Star Carr.*

his work have been a major factor in shaping British archaeology today. The results of Clark's work at Star Carr will be discussed in greater detail in Chapter 15.

Eric Higgs, one of Clark's students, focused even more directly on the **paleoeconomy** of prehistoric societies. Higgs's method involved a detailed investigation of the natural resources available within the region of an archaeological site and an analysis of the exploitation of those resources. A number of Higgs's own students have followed his lead, but the paleoeconomic approach frequently has been criticized for assuming that the subsistence economy was the major factor in shaping prehistoric societies. Paleoeconomic approaches often take no account of religion, ideology, social structure, and other noneconomic variables that may also play important roles in governing past human behavior.

Today, all archaeologists would agree that human societies are much more than economic and technological systems. An effort to gain an understanding of social life, religion, and ideology is critical in the study of prehistoric societies. For example, archaeologists have used differences in house forms, burials and grave goods, and even diets to study dif-

ferences in social status. In an archaeological study of medieval nunneries, Roberta Gilchrist (1994) showed that wealthy medieval nuns feasted on venison, porpoise, and crane, while poorer religious women ate chicken, goose, and conger eel, supplemented by bread, beer, and vegetables. Gilchrist's study also showed that gender is an important structuring principal for premodern social systems. She found significant differences between nunneries and male monasteries that reflect differences between male and female roles in medieval society.

Archaeology as the Study of Culture Change

Archaeologists must do more than reconstruct the ways of life of a particular historical period. They need to understand how and why lifeways changed in the past. The approaches that archaeologists have taken to the study of culture change have varied dramatically over the past 50 years (see Trigger 1989). This section presents a brief historical overview of differing approaches to the study of culture change and the ways those changes are explained by archaeologists.

It is the process of fitting a particular site or group of sites into a wider context that lies at the heart of archaeological interpretation. Even within the framework of culture history, archaeologists attempted to explain why cultures change. Until the 1950s archaeologists explained change in essentially historical terms—in terms of the movement of peoples from one region to another or the exchange of ideas between one group and another. The wholesale replacement of the artifacts and features typifying one archaeological culture with an entirely different set was often interpreted as evidence of the **migration** into the region of people with new traditions. For example, during the first few hundred years A.D. the stone tool–using hunters of much of southern Africa were largely displaced by the southward migration of iron-using farmers, probably related to today's Bantu speakers. Most of the changes that are observed in archaeological cultures are less pervasive. A new trait—a technological innovation or a new artistic style, for example—may appear within a region. If the new technology or artistic style is known from an earlier time in an adjacent region, the acquisition of the new trait is usually ascribed to **diffusion.** Diffusion is the spread of cultural traits, such as artistic styles or technological methods, from one culture to another. Diffusion may mean that some new item of material culture, such as a pottery style or a metalworking technique, may be introduced bodily from an outside source, perhaps through trade. Diffusion might also occur if new individuals with a special skill, such as skilled potters, should enter the group, perhaps through a marriage. Finally, if no outside source for a new trait or technology is apparent, its appearance may be attributed to **independent invention.**

During the 1950s and 1960s archaeologists became increasingly dissatisfied with historical explanations of culture change. All the culture-historical "explanations" were essentially descriptive; they provided little insight into how and why a new trait developed, or why it should be accepted from an outside source. Why should a culture develop in a particular way? Why, too, did some unrelated cultures come to follow similar courses of development? Anthropologist Julian Steward (1955) suggested that the answer lay in the complex relationship between a culture and its environment. He termed the study of this relationship **cultural ecology,** an extension of the biological study of ecology that examines the mutual relationships among various organisms and their environments. Culture change, Steward argued, could come about as a given culture adapts to changes in the environment. Change arises through the interplay of the culture (as determined by its previous history), its physical habitat (climate and geography), the animals and plants on which it depends, and the influence of neighboring cultures.

The 1950s and 1960s saw several major archaeological projects that incorporated a broadly ecological approach. These projects were also distinguished by their explicit problem orientation. The excavators set out to answer a specific set of questions. For example, several projects focused on the investigation of the beginning of farming in the Old and New Worlds. The Iraq-Jarmo Project, directed by Robert Braidwood, investigated a wide range of archaeological sites in Iraqi Kurdistan (northern Iraq). This region, because of its topography, its climate, and the availability of the wild ancestors of sheep, goats, wheat, and barley, was a very likely location for the appearance of the earliest Old World farmers. Braidwood's research will be discussed in some detail in Chapters 17 and 18. In highland Mexico Richard S. MacNeish undertook the Tehuacán Archaeological-Botanical Project. This project investigated the beginnings of food production in the New World, as well as the ways in which the landscape was utilized, both seasonally and over the longer term (see Chapter 19). Both Braidwood's and MacNeish's projects brought together large teams of geologists, biologists, and archaeologists to lend their particular insights to the research. While these projects set out to attempt to explain the process by which agriculture came into being, they were far more successful in describing how early farmers functioned in relation to their environment.

Ecological approaches continue to play a major role in archaeological interpretation. Today the environment is defined broadly to include not just the physical and the biological environments but also the social environment, that is, the relationships with other people. Modern ecological explanations emphasize the interrelations between humans and their environment. Archaeologists investigate the effects of human behavior on the environment as well as environmental constraints on human behavior.

Archaeology as a Science

Is archaeology a science? In the 1960s the American archaeologist Lewis Binford, introducing what has come to be known as the **New Archaeology,** contended that archaeology, as a part of anthropology, should be a science, and that archaeological research should follow the methods of science (Binford 1962). This view of archaeology was most fully articulated as an explicitly scientific approach by P. J. Watson, S. LeBlanc, and C. Redman (1971, 1984). Julian Steward had called for archaeologists to look beyond the goals of culture history and to begin to investigate the *processes* by which cultures changed. Binford took up this cause. He further argued that if archaeologists were to discover the reasons cultures function as they do and why cultures change, they must try to find broadscale regularities in the way cultures function and develop. Binford and others argued that the ultimate goal of archaeological research should be the formulation of **covering laws,** similar to the laws of physics, to explain ancient human behavior and the process of culture change.

If archaeology were to develop such a set of laws, that is, to take on a theoretical structure similar to that of the physical sciences, then archaeological research would have to be conducted according to the rules of scientific method. The use of the scientific method was not simply a matter of incorporating the findings of other scientific disciplines, such as scientific dating methods, into archaeological interpretation. The use of the scientific method, as recommended by the new archaeologists, required archaeologists to begin research by formulating hypotheses (models) to explain past human behavior. They then had to develop research designs to test those hypotheses against real archaeological data. Only hypotheses that could withstand repeated rigorous testing could be accepted as theory. The application of scientific methods to study the processes of culture change has

been termed the **processual approach** to archaeological interpretation.

In attempting to understand how and why cultures change, processual archaeologists often viewed human cultures as systems of behaviors that allowed humans to adapt to the constraints of their natural and social environments. Processualists emphasized the dynamic relationship between human cultures and their environments, and cultural changes were often seen as adaptive responses to changes in the biological, physical, or social environments.

While the goals of the New Archaeology were admirable, in practice, archaeologists found it difficult to develop meaningful general laws to explain past human behavior. As yet we have no archaeological equivalent of the laws of thermodynamics. Archaeology today is probably no closer to uncovering significant cultural covering laws than it was when the goal was first conceived. Human societies are too varied, and the limitations of the archaeological record have proved a much higher hurdle than was once hoped.

Contemporary Approaches to Archaeological Interpretation

While many contemporary archaeologists continue to rely on a processual approach to archaeological interpretation, others have grown increasingly wary of the optimistic outlook of the New Archaeology. Processual models and hypotheses have been drawn, for the most part, from the natural sciences, particularly from ecological models for animal behavior. Such models, it is argued, are too simplistic to explain how and why human cultures change. Culture provides humans with a wider range of available responses to change than is available to other animals. On the other hand, the cultural beliefs or values of a specific human group may restrict and shape that group's response to a new situation. Further, processual models do not allow for the effect on a society of the sometimes unpredictable and idiosyncratic actions of individuals.

Reaction to the limitations of the processual approach led to the beginnings of the **postprocessual movement** in archaeology approximately 15 years ago. While archaeologists recognize that the processual approach brought scientific rigor to archaeological method, some contemporary archaeologists are not satisfied with processual explanations for cultural change. They argue that the processual approach failed to appreciate the dynamic roles that ideology and social and political structures can play in the process of social transformation. Moreover, the post-processualists argue that the processualists viewed human societies as made up of a series of "faceless blobs" (Tringham 1991), rather than seeing societies as made up of individual actors. Members of different political factions, different social classes, and even different genders may think and act in very different ways. In order to understand how and why cultural changes come about, archaeologists must begin to examine the social, political, and economic diversity that characterized ancient societies. In order to do this, postprocessual archaeologists have drawn on social theories that were developed by cultural anthropologists and scholars in other social sciences and the humanities. Today postprocessual archaeologists are drawing alternative models for the interpretation of culture change from perspectives as diverse as feminist theory, literary criticism, and Marxist economic interpretations (see, for example, Hodder 1992).

The Archaeological Record

All the structure of interpretation we have discussed—culture history, explanation of culture change, descriptions of ancient lifeways—rests on a fundamental foundation: the discovery, recording, and decoding of the archaeological record. Survey, excavation, cataloging, the analysis and interpretation of finds, as well as the integration of data from history, geology, biology, and other fields, are the essential first steps that archaeologists must pursue in their attempt to understand the past.

The attention of the general public is often captured by spectacular discoveries such as the Iceman or a gold-filled tomb, but the vast bulk of archaeological research is focused on the prosaic. The gradual accumulation of archaeological knowledge is the result of extensive preparation, patient and persistent fieldwork, and careful analysis of what is found. Discoveries are not usually made purely by chance. Our knowledge of the pre-

historic past is compounded from the posing and answering of many limited research questions. Archaeologists undertake surveys and excavations with well-defined research goals in mind. Research is usually designed to address a specific hypothesis or competing hypotheses about events in the past. An archaeologist, usually with the assistance of others in the sciences and humanities, must interpret the data that result from fieldwork and decide whether these data provide new insight into his or her research goals. Such interpretation can be very difficult and must be approached in the full light of peer review and criticism.

Wresting an understanding of the past from what remains in the earth can be a daunting task. Nearly all our knowledge of the prehistoric past comes from the study of ordinary things, usually small fragments of such materials as stone tools and pottery that have been preserved because of their chemical stability. Almost everything that was made or used by humans in the distant past has disappeared. Except under the most fortuitous circumstances (in the extreme aridity of a desert or a perennially waterlogged peat bog, for instance), organic materials such as wood, hides, horn, and fabric soon rot away. Most metals corrode and are gone as well. Bone, too, can sometimes disintegrate, depending on the nature of the soil. The skeletons of ancient humans, though, are sometimes preserved, as are the bones of the animals they ate. Stone tools have been preserved in vast numbers, and they are by far the most common finds from early prehistory. Pottery, which was first invented about 14,000 years ago, is a common find in later archaeological sites. Whole vessels are rare; most pottery is found broken into small fragments. All these things together can provide only a dim reflection of the lives of ancient humans, but this is the evidence that is available to prehistoric archaeologists. The challenge for the archaeological detective is to extract from these data as much understanding as is possible of the world of the distant past.

Artifacts, Ecofacts, and Features

Before we can move on to our discussion of archaeology and prehistory, we must first define some of the fundamental terms used

STONE TOOLS and the waste from their manufacture are by far the most common artifacts found in the archaeological sites preserved from the first few million years of human evolution. As time passed their forms and the techniques for their manufacture became increasingly sophisticated.

ANIMAL BONES, usually food remains, are ecofacts found at many sites from the most ancient to the most recent. Animal bones provide information about diet and the methods used for obtaining food.

POTTERY appears to have been independently invented several times in both the Old and New Worlds during the last several thousand years. With the appearance of settled villages, pottery (usually broken into small fragments) becomes the most widespread of artifacts, varying distinctively from culture to culture.

PLANT REMAINS are far less frequently recovered ecofacts than are animal bones. Plants are usually only preserved if they are charred, desiccated, or waterlogged. When they are found, however, they provide much information about ancient diet as well as the natural environment and climate.

Figure 2.9

Artifacts and ecofacts.

by archaeologists. The basic unit of archaeological analysis is the **artifact** (Figure 2.9), which is any object made, modified, or utilized by humans. A stone axe, a pottery vessel, a bronze sword, and a marble statue are all artifacts. Broadly speaking, a stone tomb or a discarded soup bone is also an artifact. In practice, however, archaeologists frequently use the term *artifact* to refer to a portable, intentionally manufactured or used object. Structures, modifications of the landscape, and animal and plant remains left behind by humans are dealt with separately. Artifacts are sometimes found singly, but more commonly, artifacts of varying kinds are found grouped together. Any such group of artifacts found together, and which appear to have been deposited together, is known as an **assemblage.** Sometimes an artifact grouping was intentional, as in the case of offerings that were placed with a body in a grave. These might include, perhaps, a bronze dagger and a distinctive pottery vessel used for a food offering, as well as personal items of adornment on the body, such as pins, bracelets, and earrings. Other assemblages are unintentional, such as those in a trash pit, which might include food wastes, broken pottery fragments, and other worn-out and cast-off items. Another example of an unintentional assemblage is the small objects, such as coins, pins, and bits of pottery and glass, that frequently accumulate beneath the wooden floor of a house.

Ecofacts (a term introduced to archaeology in the 1960s) are those remains deriving from the natural environment that, while not intentionally made or manufactured by humans, become incorporated into archaeological deposits. They can provide information about past environments or ways of life. Ecofacts include the products of human activities such as the preparation and consumption of food. Food wastes may include animal bones or charred plant fragments and seeds. The analysis of these materials can provide insight into what was eaten, as well as how it was obtained, prepared, and distributed. Other ecofacts may enter the deposit purely accidentally. Pollen may be blown in by the wind or carried in on people's feet. Various kinds of insects and small mammals such as mice may take up residence in people's houses. Pollen, insect remains, and the bones of small mammals can yield much valuable information about climate, local plant and animal communities, and the degree to which the local environment has been altered by human interference.

Features are the immovable products of human activities that are affixed to or imbedded in the landscape. Buildings are features, as are trenches and earthworks. Smaller features include such things as burials, hearths, and stone pavements. The soil discoloration left behind by the rotting away of a timber post (a post mold) or the filling in of a storage pit are also features. Movable artifacts are frequently, but not necessarily, included within features. Archaeologists expend a good deal of effort in working out the spatial, functional, and chronological relationships among archaeological features.

Sites

Artifacts, ecofacts, and features found together constitute an archaeological **site.** A site is a rather loosely defined entity that may range from a few stone flakes scattered on the ground to an entire ancient city. It is an area where artifacts and features indicate that human activity has taken place. There are a multitude of types of sites. Some sites result from only a short period of human activity, such as a butchery site where a game animal was cut up for transport, leaving behind only some waste bone and a few worn-out stone tools. Another site might represent an encampment of a few days or weeks, including, perhaps, debris from the making of stone tools, some food remains, traces of a hearth, or a ring of stones where a tent was pitched. Sometimes a favored camping place was revisited time after time, creating a cluster of superimposed and partially overlapping campsites. Other sites are formed by long-term, continuous or nearly continuous occupations. In settled villages dwellings are built and abandoned, walls constructed and torn down or weathered away, and new structures built over the rubble of the old dwellings and the refuse of the previous inhabitants. Layer by layer these sites grow thicker, the older occupations buried below the more recent. The great artificial mounds, called tells, of the Middle East, often many meters high, were formed in just this fashion. At the base may lie a tiny farming village; above it many layers, or **strata,** of refuse, decaying walls, and silt were deposited through hundreds or thousands of years of occupation. The superimposed strata in an archaeological site are frequently compared to a layer cake, but this comparison is an oversimplification. The disentangling of the complicated relationships among the strata in a site, the art and science

Archaeology in Practice

Stratigraphy and Stratigraphic Analysis: How Do Archaeologists Reconstruct the Sequence of Events at an Archaeological Site?

Archaeologists are often asked how they trace the sequence of events that occurred at an archaeological site. How do they know that one building or structure was built before another? How can they be sure that two buildings were in use at the same time, or that one grave is older than another? The answers to these questions depend on detailed stratigraphic analyses, the critical interpretation of the layers and features that make up an archaeological site. In practice, this interpretation involves many complexities and subtleties, but the fundamental principles involved are simple and straightforward.

The simple **principle of superposition of strata,** first widely applied by geologists in the eighteenth century, states that if the strata in a geological deposit are piled up like the layers in a cake, the oldest must be at the bottom. Archaeologists also use this principle, but the deposits in an archaeological site may derive from a wide variety of sources. An individual stratum or layer may be distinguished by its distinctive color, texture, and composition. Often inclusions such as pebbles or charcoal help define strata. A fine greenish clay stratum, for instance, may be easily distinguished from a layer of coarse yellow sand. Frequently, however, stratigraphic boundaries are difficult to perceive, and they can tax the skill of the field archaeologist in following them.

Some of the strata are purely geological in nature. The underlying soil or bedrock is, of course, of geological origin. Later, the debris of human activities may be covered by soils and silts carried by natural agencies such as the wind and running water. Soils and deposits near the tops of hills may be washed down by rainstorms to collect in the hollows of the landscape (slopewash). Fine silts may be carried by the wind to cover broad areas of the landscape, including archaeological sites. The most dramatic of natural deposits to cover or intrude on archaeological sites are the products of volcanic eruptions, such as ash and pumice. Pompeii, magnificently preserved by the fall of ash from nearby Mount Vesuvius, is the most famous of such sites, but others will be discussed in this text.

Archaeologists are most interested in the deposits of anthropogenic origin—the products of human activities. Humans disturb natural soils (and older archaeological deposits) in a multiplicity of ways. Holes and pits may be dug for food storage, trash disposal, and burials. Trenches and pits may be dug during construction activities. Those features cut through earlier strata, and the soils they contained (including artifacts) may be displaced. Later, when dwellings are occupied, debris from everyday life accumulates, including artifacts and food remains. Some of those deposits may be trampled into dirt floors; other trash may be spread around dwellings or be carried to trash dumps (middens). Fireplaces or hearths for heating and food preparation, often containing charcoal and food remains, are another such localized deposit. When a structure is abandoned, it may be intentionally destroyed and the rubble spread around to make a base for a new structure. If a site is no longer occupied, the forces of rain and wind may accomplish that dispersal. Many sites show alternating phases of occupation and abandonment, with strata of human origin alternating with naturally deposited silts or sands.

Archaeological sites that are repeatedly reoccupied or occupied for a long time will contain many interdigitated layers, small localized deposits (called lenses), and features (Figure 2.10). Some strata may extend across the site; others may be very limited in extent. At the start of an excavation, archaeologists frequently dig a small test trench to ascertain the nature and duration of the occupation and the sequence of occupations, from earliest to latest. A **stratigraphic cross section** of the test trench is prepared to serve as a guide for further excavation. This is a carefully prepared measured drawing, supported by photographs, of one or more of the vertical faces of the trench. The face is made as clean, flat, and vertical as possible so that subtle changes in the stratigraphy may be seen and recorded. Distinctive characteristics of each of the strata and lenses, such as color, texture, and inclusions, are noted on the cross section. These data may prove helpful in correlating (provisionally, at least) the stratigraphy in different parts of the site. Because test trenches are frequently misleading, good judgment must be exercised in their placement and interpretation. The earliest, the latest, or intermediate phases of occupation might not be represented in the place where a particular test is dug. If, for example, the eastern portion of a large site was occupied during the earliest and latest phases of

A1 — Structure belonging to Period A
A2 — Recent soil, deposited since the abandonment of the Period A structure
A3 — Artifact-bearing layer, formed during the habitation of the Period A structure
A4 — Trench cut through underlying strata while building Structure A1
A5 — Water-deposited soils, containing artifacts of Period A, but pre-dating the construction of Wall A1
A6 — Cross section of a deep trench, dug before the formation of layer A5
A7 — A deep layer of wind-deposited silt, containing no artifacts (archaeologically sterile)
B1 — A packed-earth structure belonging to the middle period, Period B

B2 — Debris from the collapse of Structure B1
B3 — Artifact-bearing layer, formed during the habitation of Structure B1
B4 — Burial containing artifacts characteristic of Period B, dug before the occupation of Structure B1
B5 — Archaeologically sterile silt
C1 — A stone paving belonging to the earliest period C; The paving on the left is later than that on the right, as it overlies a layer of occupation debris, C5
C2 — Superimposed hearths belonging to Period C
C3 and C5 — Strata formed during earlier and later phases of occupation of period C
C4 — Burial dug between the earlier and later phases of Period C

Figure 2.10

A simplified, imaginary cross section of an archaeological site, illustrating some of the typical strata and features that are encountered. Three main periods of occupation are represented: A, B, and C. A structure belonging to the latest phase, Period A, still stands at the surface.

occupation and the western portion was occupied only during the middle and latest phases, tests placed in these different areas would give quite different impressions of the site's contents. A small test can easily be misplaced within the boundaries of a feature or into soil that was disturbed in ancient times, leading to difficulties in interpretation. Only when a reasonably extensive area of the site is excavated can these difficulties usually be resolved.

Archaeologists today often attempt to expose large areas of a site to try to trace activity areas and to interpret functional relationships within the site. The occupants of a dwelling may manufacture their pottery in an area nearby, use these vessels to cook their food on a hearth within the house (where a few broken fragments fall through the floor), and dispose of broken pottery, along with food remains, in a trash pit

out of the way of daily traffic. They may bury their dead in a grave adjacent to their dwelling or even beneath its floor. All these activities produce distinctive features and artifacts. A structure, burial, or hearth might belong to any of the periods of occupation represented at a site. A functional interpretation of the features and artifact distributions within a site is meaningful only if we are certain that the features and artifacts were actually in use at the same time. Within an individual site, archaeologists need to determine which of the various deposits and features are contemporary. They must be sure that artifacts and features interpreted as a unit were found within the same or demonstrably contemporary strata, a procedure known as maintaining **stratigraphic control.**
Archaeologists must follow stratigraphic distinctions over broad areas and find ways to correlate the

stratigraphic cross sections in different parts of the site, which is rarely easy to do. The excavators need sharp eyes and a sensitive touch to follow subtle color and texture changes and to expose a single layer over a broad horizontal area. This work is guided by constant cross-checking against vertical cross sections that are preserved at the margins of the excavated area.

Features and artifacts that are found within the same layer are said to be associated, and, if they are not greatly displaced from their original locations, can be assumed to be contemporary. Great care must be taken, however, to ensure that the artifacts found in a layer are not intrusive. Many processes can result in the intrusion of younger or older artifacts into an archaeological deposit. Pits, ditches, and burials from later periods penetrate the strata laid in earlier times, carrying more recent materials downward and bringing earlier materials upward. Burrowing animals, such as mice, rats, and porcupines, do the same. Often these problems can be controlled for by careful recording of the features and the locations of animal burrows.

Geological forces can also move artifacts. Very ancient archaeological sites may have been subjected to the same geological forces that have modified the rest of the earth's surface. Archaeological strata may have been eroded, or even folded or tilted. Alternating periods of freezing and thawing may have churned the soil. Stream actions, in particular, can mix artifacts from many different strata and locations, creating artifact associations that have little to do with human activities. The stratigraphic interpretation of such sites often requires a thorough knowledge of soil formation processes and the geology of wind- and water-laid sediments. It has been especially difficult to unravel the complicated relationship between geologic forces and human activities that formed the sites associated with our earliest human ancestors. We shall return to this problem in Chapters 3 and 4.

of **stratigraphic analysis,** is one of the principal preoccupations of the field archaeologist. In this analysis, the sequence of events that created the site can be worked out.

Understanding How the Archaeological Record Was Formed

The Archaeology in Practice box reveals some of the difficulties that archaeologists face in trying to interpret complex archaeological sites. Most archaeological sites result from a combination of human activities and natural processes such as sedimentation. Archaeologists must be able to distinguish traces of human activity from deposits that result from geological or biological processes. In addition, archaeologists seek to identify the human behaviors that produce specific combinations of artifacts, ecofacts, and features. The American archaeologist Lewis Binford has been in the forefront of the development of a series of theories that are intended to explain specific archaeological phenomena. These theories, known as **middle-range theories,** are designed to serve as bridging arguments, establishing relationships between the archaeological record and the dynamic behavioral processes that produced it. Hypotheses and data can be drawn from a variety of sources, including experiments and the observations of modern peoples. The field of **ethnoarchaeology,** the study of the behavior of modern peoples and of the material remains of that behavior, has developed as part of the search to develop middle-range theories that can establish links between the static archaeological record and the dynamic behaviors that produced those material remains.

An example of such research had been carried out by C. K. Brain, a specialist in the study of archaeological animal bone remains. Working in South Africa, Brain (1967, 1981) examined the bone remains of domestic goats that had been eaten by Hottentot herders and discarded outside their camp. These bones were later scavenged by numerous dogs. Brain found that the dogs destroyed certain kinds of bones and left others, producing a distinctive pattern of bone survival. Brain could then hypothesize that similar patterns of animal bones found in the archaeological record might also be the result of carnivore scavenging. These observations have been of great importance. Carnivores may have actually created certain sites that had been attributed to the activities of early human ancestors. Brain's research will be discussed further in Chapter 3.

Preserving the Past

One of the biggest challenges facing all archaeologists today is the preservation of the world's archaeological heritage. Each archaeological site is unique and contains information that may not be available anywhere else. Every year hundreds of sites are damaged and destroyed as a result of development, vandalism, and looting. For every one site that is excavated by a team of professional archaeologists, many are destroyed and the information that they contained is lost forever. Archaeologists have an obligation to preserve the world's archaeological heritage for future generations.

This obligation can take a number of different forms. At the most basic level, archaeologists work to pass laws that protect archaeological sites and to end the trade in artifacts that have been removed illegally from archaeological sites. In addition, archaeologists have a responsibility to educate the public about our shared past. All archaeological excavation involves destruction. If archaeologists fail to publish and publicize their results, they are no better than the looters and pot hunters who destroy archaeological sites. Since many excavations today are funded by public monies, archaeologists have an obligation to share their research with the taxpayers who funded it. Moreover, an educated public is more likely to support archaeology and historic preservation legislation. We will return to these important issues in Chapter 28.

Conclusion

Although archaeologists study many different time periods and work in many different areas of the world, all archaeologists share common goals and methods. Archaeologists are interested in reconstructing culture history, in studying the ways people lived in the past, and in understanding why human cultures change through time. Modern archaeologists also seek to understand the complex nature of the archaeological record and to preserve our common cultural heritage for future generations. In the following chapters we will begin to explore our common human past, starting with the earliest human ancestors who appeared in Africa over 4 million years ago.

Glossary

Anthropology. The study of the biology, evolution, and culture of human beings, both in the past and in the present. In the United States, anthropology includes four subfields: **cultural anthropology**—the study of modern human cultures, both of specific cultures and of the character of human cultures in general; **physical anthropology**—the study of the biology and evolution of human beings and their close primate relatives; **anthropological linguistics**—the study of the nature, development, and social functions of language; and **anthropological archaeology**—the study of the material remains of cultures and peoples in the past.

Archaeological culture. A widespread and regularly occurring association of artifact types and features, usually assumed to belong to a specific human group.

Artifact. Any object made, modified, or utilized by humans.

Assemblage. A group of artifacts found together within a specific feature or layer, and which appear to have been deposited together.

Covering laws. General laws that describe and explain a broad range of phenomena, similar to the basic laws of chemistry and physics.

Cultural ecology. The study of the interrelationships between humans and their environment. The environment is defined broadly to include the physical environment, the plants and animals that make up the biological environment, and the social environment, which includes other social groups.

Culture. The system of shared ideas, beliefs, and practices of a group of people that permits them to relate to each other and to give meaning to their everyday lives. Archaeologists generally include the tangible products of these practices—artifacts—within their definition of culture.

Culture area. A wide geographical region occupied by a number of archaeological sites with broadly similar cultural characteristics.

Culture history. The chronicle of the successive cultures within a region, and the description of the character and relationships of those cultures.

Diffusion. The spread of cultural traits, such as technologies, practices, and artistic styles, from one culture to another.

Direct historical analogy. The interpretation of archaeological artifacts or features by comparing them to similar artifacts or features in use today, where a direct historical relationship is known to exist between the archaeological remains and the present-day culture.

Ecofacts. Those natural remains that, while not made or manufactured by humans, become incorporated into archaeological deposits and can provide information about past environments and/or human behavior.

Ethnoarchaeology. The study of the behavior of modern peoples and of the material remains of that behavior. This subfield of archaeology has developed since 1970.

Ethnography. The recording and study of the culture, including social relationships and lifeways, of a specific group of people.

Features. The immovable products of human activities that are affixed to or imbedded in the landscape, such as buildings, earthworks, pits, ditches, burials, hearths, and postholes.

Horizon. A contemporaneous group of broadly similar artifacts and traits that is spread over a wide geographic area. A distinctive art style, for instance, may serve as a marker of a specific horizon.

Independent invention. The independent development of a new trait or technology within a region without the influence of an outside source.

Middle-range theories. Hypotheses and theories of a limited nature intended to explain specific archaeological phenomena.

Migration. The physical movement of a people from one geographical area to another.

New Archaeology. The view, advocated by such workers as L. Binford, P. J. Watson, S. LeBlanc, and C. Redman, that archaeology should focus on processes of culture change rather than the compilation of culture histories, and that archaeologists should attempt to develop archaeological and cultural laws, similar to those of the natural sciences, through the formulation and testing of hypotheses.

Paleoeconomy. The archaeological study of the means by which a prehistoric people gained their livelihood, that is, by hunting, gathering, fishing, farming, and so on.

Period. An interval of time that includes archaeological occurrences that are sufficiently similar and distinctive to be treated as a unit. A period may be further subdivided into a number of **phases.**

Postprocessual movement. The postprocessual movement is unified by its critique of processual archaeology of the 1960s and 1970s. Postprocessual archaeologists make use of models developed in the social sciences and the humanities to study social and cultural change in the archaeological record.

Principle of superposition of strata. A principle, derived from geology, that if the strata in a geological deposit are piled as layers from bottom to top, the oldest must be at the bottom.

Processual approach. An archaeological approach that focuses on the processes of culture change. The variables that influence culture change are studied using scientific methods that include the formulation and testing of specific archaeological hypotheses.

Site. An area where artifacts and features indicate that human activity has taken place. A site may range from a few artifacts scattered on the ground to an entire ancient city.

Strata. Distinct layers within an archaeological deposit formed through either cultural or natural processes. Strata can be distinguished by their color, texture, or the materials included within them.

Stratigraphic analysis. The recording and analysis of the layers within an archaeological site, by which the sequence of events that led to the formation of the site is worked out.

Stratigraphic control. The use of stratigraphic analysis to determine whether artifacts and features found in separated areas of a site are contemporary.

Stratigraphic cross section. A carefully excavated and carefully recorded vertical profile of an archaeological excavation, intended to delineate the sequence of layers and features in the site.

Tradition. A group of regularly associated artifacts, usually of a single kind, that persists and develops for an extended length of time.

 Further Reading

Binford, L. R.

1962. Archaeology as Anthropology. *American Antiquity* 28: 217–225.

Lewis Binford's classic paper introduces his concepts of scientific, processual archaeology.

Hodder, I.

    1992. *Reading the Past: Current Approaches to Interpretation in Archaeology,* 2d ed. Cambridge: Cambridge University Press.

    An alternative, contemporary view of the interpretation of the archaeological record. This book is the most readable introduction to the postprocessual movement in archaeology.

Trigger, Bruce G.

    1989. *A History of Archaeological Thought.* Cambridge: Cambridge University Press.

    A detailed history of archaeology, focusing on the changing approaches to the interpretation of the archaeological record.

Watson, P. J., S. A. LeBlanc, and C. L. Redman

    1984. *Archaeological Explanation: The Scientific Method in Archaeology.* New York: Columbia University Press.

    A detailed argument for the application of the methods of scientific reasoning to archaeology.

Other Bibliography

Bates, D. G., and F. Plog

    1990. *Cultural Anthropology,* 3d ed. New York: McGraw-Hill.

Brain, C. K.

    1967. Hottentot Food Remains and Their Bearing on the Interpretation of Fossil Bone Assemblages. *Scientific Papers of the Namibian Desert Research Station* 32: 1–11.

    1981. *The Hunters or the Hunted? An Introduction to African Cave Taphonomy.* Chicago: University of Chicago Press.

Gilchrist, Roberta

    1994. *Gender and Medieval Culture: The Archaeology of Religious Women.* London: Routledge.

Orser, Charles E., Jr.

    1990. Archaeological Approaches to New World Plantation Slavery. In *Archaeological Method and Theory,* vol. 2, edited by M. B. Schiffer, pp. 111–154. Tucson: University of Arizona Press.

Steward, Julian

    1955. *Theory of Culture Change: The Methodology of Multilinear Evolution.* Urbana: University of Illinois Press.

Tringham, Ruth

    1991. Households with Faces: The Challenge of Gender in Prehistoric Architectural Remains. In *Engendering Archaeology: Women and Prehistory,* edited by J. R. Gero and M. W. Conkey, pp. 93–131. Oxford: Blackwell.

Watson, P. J., S. A. LeBlanc, and C. L. Redman

    1971. *Explanation in Archaeology: An Explicitly Scientific Approach.* New York: Columbia University Press.

West, S. E.

    1985. *West Stow: The Anglo-Saxon Village.* East Anglian Archaeology, Report No. 24. Ipswich, England: Suffolk County Planning Department.

Willey, G. R., and P. Phillips

    1958. *Method and Theory in American Archaeology.* Chicago: University of Chicago Press.

Part II

Who Were Our Earliest Ancestors?

Questions about human origins and human evolution have intrigued scholars for over a century. This part of the text examines the role that archaeology can play in the study of our earliest human ancestors. Chapter 3 begins with a brief history of research on human origins, highlighting the discovery of the Taung child by Raymond Dart and Louis Leakey's work at Olduvai Gorge. This is followed by a brief overview of the earliest-known human ancestors, the australopithecines. These early human ancestors walked upright, but they did not leave an archaeological record because they did not manufacture and use stone tools.

The main focus of Part II is on the archaeology of early members of the genus *Homo,* who made and used simple stone tools. Chapter 4 examines the archaeological record of early human behavior at East African sites, including Olduvai Gorge in Tanzania and Koobi Fora in Kenya. We consider how these ancient sites are excavated, how they are dated, and what can be learned about early human behavior from the study of simple stone tools and butchered animal bones.

Chapter 3

Our Earliest Human Ancestors
The Australopithecines and the Earliest Humans

Introduction

Most of this chapter will discuss a topic that, strictly speaking, is neither archaeology nor prehistory. It deals with the earliest members of the human family, who inhabited Africa between 6 million and 2 million years ago. These early human ancestors did not make or use stone tools and therefore did not leave an archaeological record. We must understand the nature of these early human ancestors, however, to appreciate the pattern and tempo of early human evolution and the relationship of our early ancestors to later humans, who did make and use stone tools.

In 1856, three years before the publication of Darwin's *On the Origin of Species*, a skull was found in a cave in the Neander Valley, near Düsseldorf, Germany. It was of a being like, and yet unlike, modern humans—heavily built, with a protruding face, a sloping forehead, and thick ridges above the eyebrows—the skull of an ancient form of human that has come to be called Neanderthal. In the decades to follow, with interest piqued by Darwin's theory of evolution, scientists soon embarked on a search for human origins. So began a long trail of discoveries that has led ever backward in time, from Europe to Asia and, ultimately, back to Africa. To tell the story of human evolution as it was discovered would be to tell it in reverse, for over the last 150 years, ever older human and prehuman fossils have come to light. This text will begin where human evolution appears to have begun, in Africa. The earliest human ancestors have been found only in the last few years. It will be easier to understand the significance of these fossils if we follow the trail of African discoveries beginning in the 1920s. First, though, we must make clear how modern humans are classified among the animal species of today.

Humans as Primates and Hominids

Humans are members of the order **Primates,** which also includes the prosimians (lemurs, tarsiers, lorises, aye-ayes, and indris), the Old and New World monkeys, and the apes. The apes include the lesser apes—gibbons and siamangs—and the great apes—orangutans, gorillas, and chimpanzees—who are humans' closest living relatives. Humans and the great apes evolved from a common ancestor. The line that would lead to *Homo sapiens,* known as the Hominidae, or **hominids,** split off sometime between 6 million and 10 million years ago. The hominids include modern humans and the immediate ancestors of humans, plus several very closely related forms. Just when this split occurred has proved very difficult to document. While quite a number of early hominid fossils are now known, there are no fossils at all available of the early ancestors of the gorillas and chimpanzees, and very few fossils of either hominids or great apes dating to between 6 million and 10 million years ago have been recovered.

How should a hominid be defined? It is not difficult to set down how modern humans differ from the other primates. Modern humans are **bipedal;** that is, they walk upright on two legs. Theories for the origins of bipedalism are varied; they include freeing the hands for using tools or carrying objects, or even for a wider range of climbing activities. Modern humans also possess large brains, which provide the capacity for language and culture. A large brain and erect posture are reflected by the human skeletal form. Of great importance to paleontologists are the less obvious differences in the shape of the teeth, because teeth are among the most common fossils. In contrast to humans, male and female great apes often differ

Figure 3.1

Map of southern Africa showing locations of australopithecine sites.

markedly, with the males having large, projecting canines. Human canines in both males and females are very small. These characteristics, though, represent the end point of human evolution. How would we recognize a primitive hominid who was not far removed from the common ancestor of chimpanzees and humans? Did all the uniquely human traits develop together, or did different traits develop at different times? At the start of the twentieth century most scientists were convinced that it was the enlargement of the brain, with the consequent growth of human intelligence, that was the primary event that preceded and led to all the other human evolutionary changes. It was also generally believed that the earliest human ancestors would be found in Asia. *Pithecanthropus*—the so-called Java Man—had been found by Eugene Dubois in 1891 in what is now Indonesia. Beginning in the 1920s, however, a remarkable series of discoveries made in Africa would radically challenge these views.

Australopithecus and the South African Discoveries

Raymond Dart, an anatomy professor at the University of Witwatersrand, South Africa, had an avid interest in fossils. In 1924 Dart learned of a nearby limestone quarry at a place called **Taung (Figure 3.1)** that had been producing many interesting fossils; he made an arrangement with the quarry owner to be

allowed to study them. In the box of fragments sent to him, Dart soon made a riveting discovery. It was a very small skull imbedded in limestone, rather like that of a chimpanzee but yet definitely not a chimpanzee. After painstakingly freeing the skull from the limestone matrix, Dart found that the skull was indeed unique. It was the skull of a child; the deciduous (milk) teeth were still in place, with the permanent molars just coming in. The teeth, especially the canines, were very different from those of an ape. Apes and monkeys have large canines, but the canines in this skull were small, more like those of humans. The face was flatter too, and the forehead was higher than those of apes or monkeys. Most striking of all, however, was the position of the foramen magnum, the hole at the base of the skull through which the spinal cord passes. In apes and monkeys, as in most quadrupeds, the foramen magnum is near the back of the skull, but in the Taung fossil, the foramen magnum was directly beneath the skull. Unlike the skull of a quadruped, which is in front of its body, this skull had been balanced vertically above the vertebral column. The Taung child, Dart concluded, had walked erect.

Dart quickly published his discovery. He named it ***Australopithecus africanus*** **(Figure 3.2)**, which means "southern ape of Africa." Dart asserted that *Australopithecus* was on or close to the human ancestral line. In the public eye the Taung child was an im-

Figure 3.2

The Taung child: The first Australopithecus africanus *fossil, discovered by Raymond Dart in 1924.*

Figure 3.3

Robust and gracile australopithecines.

mediate sensation, but the scientific world greeted Dart's claims with skepticism. There were numerous problems. The fossil did not fit the early twentieth-century ideas of what an early human ancestor should look like. The Taung fossil had a very small **cranial capacity,** the volume enclosed within the braincase. It has been estimated that if the Taung child had grown to be an adult, it would have had a cranial capacity of only about 440 milliliters, compared with an average of about 1,350 milliliters for modern humans. Dart's analysis suggested that upright walking had preceded the expansion of the brain, contrary to the notion prevalent in the 1920s. In any case, the Taung skull was immature, and because immature skulls of humans and apes are rather similar, many scientists argued that this skull might have been a young ape rather than a young hominid.

Eventually, though, new specimens were found that helped support Dart's position. In 1936 Robert Broom, a Scottish physician who had gained prominence for his paleontological studies of African reptiles and mammals, made a major find at the cave of **Sterkfontein,** near the site of Taung. The Sterkfontein skull was very similar to the one from Taung, but this specimen was mature; it was clearly not an ape. Still, few workers felt comfortable placing these fossils on the human family line, and Broom's finds the next year confused the situation even more. He discovered another hominid site at **Kromdraai,** about a kilometer from

Sterkfontein. The Kromdraai fossils were quite different from the previous finds. The Taung and Sterkfontein skulls were lightly built, or gracile; the Kromdraai skull was much more robust, with bony attachments for much larger chewing muscles. The cheek teeth (the molars and premolars) were much larger than those of Taung and Sterkfontein **(Figure 3.3)**. The robust forms may have had a very different diet from the gracile australopithecines. The large teeth and strong chewing muscles of the robust australopithecines would have been well adapted to the consumption of tough plant materials such as tubers and seeds. The gracile forms probably had a more generalized, omnivorous diet, similar to that of chimpanzees. Today, the robust forms are generally assigned to a separate species, **Australopithecus robustus.** As will be discussed below, some workers would separate them even further and assign the robust forms to a separate genus, **Paranthropus.**

After the Second World War, Broom and his assistant, John T. Robinson, resumed work at these sites, which yielded many more fossils. Broom soon found further specimens of the robust form both at Kromdraai and at another nearby site, **Swartkrans.** Sterkfontein produced a nearly complete gracile skull and additional bones, including a pelvis, vertebrae, and part of a femur. Additional gracile australopithecines were discovered by Dart in 1948 at the cave of **Makapansgat.** In all, nearly 150 early hominid fossils have been recovered in South Africa.

All the South African sites are caves, dissolved into the limestone bedrock. The caves were never actually occupied by hominids; instead, the hominid bones, along with the bones of many other animals, fell or were washed into the caves through long vertical shafts in the caves' roofs. Later, the surface above the caves eroded away, exposing the caves' contents. The stratigraphy of these sites is difficult to interpret, and the fossils themselves are encased in a hard limestone concretion that forms in caves, called **breccia.** Currently, there is no method available to date any of these sites accurately; the best evidence for the relative age of these sites is provided by the kinds of extinct animals associated with the hominid fossils. (See the Archaeology in Practice box later in this chapter.) The animal bones suggest that the *Australopithecus africanus* sites are the earliest, with Makapansgat perhaps as old as 3 million years. The *Australopithecus robustus* sites of Kromdraai and Swartkrans are younger, possibly 2 million years old or less.

Figure 3.4

The Great Rift Valley in East Africa, showing the locations of the most important archaeological and paleontological sites.

The Leakeys and Olduvai Gorge

Because the South African sites have been so difficult to interpret and date, much recent research has focused on other areas of Africa. Nearly all the finds of the past 40 years have come from the **Great Rift Valley** of East Africa, which runs from Mozambique in the south to the Red Sea in the north, enclosing Olduvai Gorge in Tanzania, Lake Turkana, and ending in the Afar Triangle of northern Ethiopia **(Figure 3.4)**. The Great Rift Valley is a giant geological fault; the land to the east of the rift is slowly pulling away from the rest of Africa. At the time when the early hominids were evolving, the Rift Valley contained numerous volcanoes, which frequently showered the landscape with pumice and ash. These ashfalls have been a boon to paleontologists. Volcanic rock can be dated in absolute terms by a scientific dating method known as potassium-argon (K-Ar) dating (which will be discussed in detail below). **Tuffs,** layers formed from falls of volcanic ash, serve as chronological markers for the fossils contained within them or between them. The land of the Rift Valley has been in constant motion. In some areas, such as at Olduvai, the land was uplifted. Fast-running rivers cut deep canyons through the sediments, revealing deposits laid down over millions of years. In other areas, the sediments were tilted and deformed by the moving rift, bringing ancient deposits to the surface where their contents could be revealed by erosion. The geology of the Great Rift Valley is complex but interpretable, and vast areas within it are littered with fossils.

Louis Leakey and archaeologist Mary Leakey first began their search for early humans at **Olduvai Gorge,** Tanzania, in the early 1930s. Louis Leakey was convinced that the earliest human ancestors were to be found in Africa. Olduvai Gorge was an ideal place to look for them. The gorge is a deep valley cut down through the sediments laid down by an ancient lake. Animals of many kinds had visited the shores of the lake, and many had died there. Fossil bones of all sorts had eroded from the beds at Olduvai. So had stone tools, including very simple forms—stone flakes and pebbles with just a few flakes knocked off—which came from the lowest beds. Yet for all their conviction and many years of searching, the Leakeys found only a few hominid fragments. Only in 1959 did Mary Leakey happen upon the first major hominid find at Olduvai. It was a relatively complete, although fragmentary, skull of a robust australopithecine, even more robust than the ones from South Africa. Louis Leakey named it *Zinjanthropus boisei;* today it is usually classified as **Australopithecus boisei,** but the original specimen is commonly referred to as Zinj **(Figure 3.5).** Zinj's cheek teeth were even larger than those of the South African robust fossils, and the chewing

Figure 3.5

Zinjanthropus—Australopithecus boisei. *An extremely robust australopithecine fossil, discovered by Mary and Louis Leakey at Olduvai Gorge.*

muscles must have been larger too. Running front to back at the top of the skull was a high bony ridge, the sagittal crest, to which enormous temporal muscles used in chewing had been attached.

Australopithecus boisei appeared even farther from the human line than the South African fossils, but it provided a crucial piece of evidence: a firm, geophysically derived date. The shores of the ancient Olduvai lake had been showered at intervals by falls of volcanic ash from the nearby volcano, Mt. Ngorongoro. The Zinj skull was found in the lowest bed at Olduvai Gorge, Bed I, sandwiched between ashfalls dated at 1.8 million years ago below and 1.7 million years ago above. It was clear now that by 1.75 million years ago there were at least two, perhaps three, different kinds of hominids. A common ancestor for these forms had to be sought farther back in time.

Australopithecus afarensis: Lucy and the First Family

American anthropologist Donald Johanson, together with French geologist Maurice Taieb, found a possible human ancestor at **Hadar,** in the Afar Triangle of Ethiopia, during the 1970s. The Hadar deposits hold many well-preserved fossils that can be closely dated through a variety of geological and physical methods (described below). An exceptional series of hominid fossils have been recovered from Hadar. The earliest, dating to around 4 million years ago, consists of only an australopithecine knee joint. The shape, however, suggests that even at this time *Australopithecus* walked erect.

The best-known find from Hadar dates from later in time, about 3 million years ago. It is the partial skeleton of a small australopithecine, nicknamed Lucy, after a popular Beatles song of the 1960s. The skull is only fragmentary, but about 40 percent of the body skeleton was recovered. Since the right and left sides of the body are symmetrical, enough bone was recovered to permit a quite complete reconstruction of how Lucy's skeleton appeared **(Figure 3.6)**. Lucy stood about 1 meter ($3\frac{1}{2}$ ft.) tall, and walked upright. Generally similar to that of the South African gracile australopithecines, Lucy's cranial capacity was even smaller (about 400 milliliters). A number of other features appear more primitive: The canine teeth, for example, are larger than those of the South African gracile australopithecines. Many additional fossils, including numerous skull fragments, have been recovered from Hadar. Lucy and many of the other Hadar hominids have been placed into a separate species, ***Australopithecus afarensis,*** which was probably ancestral to the other later australopithecine forms.

Shortly after the discovery of Lucy, another very important find was made at Hadar: A collection of nearly 200 hominid bones, all belonging to *A. afarensis,* were found together, in circumstances suggesting that they may have all died together as a group. At least 13 individuals are represented, including four children. How they were killed is not clear, although the excavators speculate

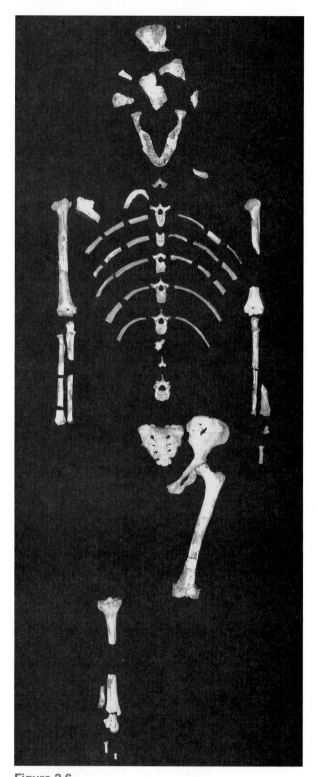

Figure 3.6

Lucy—Australopithecus afarensis. *One of the most complete australopithecine skeletons, Lucy appears to have stood 1 meter ($3\frac{1}{2}$ ft.) tall and walked erect.*

that they may have been caught in a flash flood. This group has come to be called the First Family, although whether the individuals were actually related is not known. Dating to about 3.5 million years ago, the find provides the earliest evidence for the range of variation that was present within an early hominid population. Including Lucy, the Hadar adult australopithecines vary greatly in size, from 1 meter (3½ ft.) (Lucy) to about 1.5 meters (5 ft.) tall. Some of this variation may be accounted for by a considerable size difference between the sexes.

In 1992 and 1993 T. White, G. Suwa, and B. Asfaw uncovered a group of fossils that are even earlier. Found at Aramis, near Hadar, and dating to around 4.4 million years ago, these fossils include some teeth, some skull fragments, and several arm bones. The Aramis specimens appear even more primitive than *A. afarensis,* and some of the dental and other characteristics approach those found in apes such as the chimpanzee. The forward position of the foramen magnum, however, suggests that this species may be an early hominid. The discoverers initially proposed the name ***Australopithecus ramidus*** for these finds **(Figure 3.7)**. *Ramidus* means "root" in the Afar language; the name was suggested because these fossils seem to be very near the root of the hominid line (White et al. 1994). These fossils have recently been reclassified as ***Ardipithecus ramidus*** (White et al. 1995).

A clearly bipedal hominid that is even older the *A. afarensis* has recently been discovered in Kenya (Leakey et al. 1995). ***Australopithecus anamensis*** fossils have been dated to about 4.2 million years ago. The tibia (shin bone) of this species indicates that it walked upright, and the fossils share many other similarities with *A. afarensis.* However, the lower jaws of *A. anamensis* are U-shaped, like those of modern apes. As a result, these early hominid fossils have been placed in a separate species.

The Laetoli Footprints

While Johanson and his team were at work at Hadar, Mary Leakey had begun excavating a new site, **Laetoli,** in Tanzania. Laetoli is quite early, dating to about 3.7 million years

Figure 3.7

Arm bones from Australopithecus (Ardipithecus) ramidus, *found at Aramis, near Hadar, in Ethiopia. Dating to 4.4 million years ago, A.* ramidus *shares some features with both the hominids and the apes such as the chimpanzee.*

ago. Several hominid fossils were found, similar to the *A. afarensis* finds from Hadar. Initially, the assignment of the Hadar and Laetoli hominids to the same species was questioned because the two sites are widely separated geographically, but a number of new fossil finds from areas lying between Hadar and Laetoli indicate that *A. afarensis* was widely distributed in East Africa. Laetoli, however, has preserved other fossil information in addition to animal and hominid bones. An extremely unusual and fortuitous series of events during the formation of the Laetoli deposits created a matrix in which thousands of animal footprints have been preserved. A nearby volcano produced a series of ashfalls, which, when wet by the rain, formed a cementlike mud in which the tracks were impressed. Soon after the mud dried, another ashfall sealed the layer, preventing the tracks from being washed away again. In 1975 a unique discovery was made. Among the multitude of animal tracks were the footprints of at least two, probably three, bipedal hominids, one larger than the others, probably walking together **(Figure 3.8)**. The trail of footprints extends in a straight line across the level ground for nearly 25 meters (80 ft.). It

Figure 3.8

The footprints of an erect-walking hominid, discovered by Mary Leakey and her colleagues in a volcanic ash deposit at Laetoli.

is assumed that they were made by *Australopithecus afarensis.* Their gait was much like that of modern humans. The shape of the prints is humanlike too, with the big toe pointing farther forward than in the apes. The Laetoli tracks capture a moment of hominid behavior of nearly 4 million years ago; they also prove conclusively that these hominids easily walked erect (Hay and Leakey 1982).

The Branching Tree of Hominid Evolution

How do the australopithecine fossils relate to the human ancestral line? In a number of ways (particularly the dentition) the earlier gracile forms seem more like modern humans than do the later robust types. Most anthropologists consider *A. robustus* and *A. boisei* to be side branches of hominid evolution and not direct ancestors of modern humans. In 1985 a new fossil, discovered on the west bank of Lake Turkana, shed considerable light on the evolution of the robust australopithecines. Known as the Black Skull (KNM-WT 17000, its museum accession number), the nearly complete cranium dates from about 2.5 million years ago (Walker et al. 1986). The skull bears a combination of traits reminiscent of *Australopithecus afarensis* and robust features much like those of *A. robustus* and *A. boisei.* The antiquity of the Black Skull indicates that the divergence of the evolutionary line leading to the robust australopithecines took place very early. This evidence has led some workers to separate all the robust forms, including the Black Skull, from the australopithecines, placing them in the genus *Paranthropus,* which means "beside man." The Black Skull itself **(Figure 3.9)** has been given the name ***Paranthropus aethiopicus.*** It is unlikely that *A. africanus* evolved into the robust forms. It remains an open question whether *Australopithecus africanus* is ancestral to later humans **(Figure 3.10)**.

The Earliest Humans

Louis Leakey never accepted the australopithecines as human ancestors. He was convinced that more humanlike fossils would be found, and in the early 1960s several new fossil skull fragments came to light from the lower beds of Olduvai. Leakey believed that the fossils filled this gap. He considered these fossils very primitive humans, and he and his colleagues gave them the name **Homo habilis** (handy man). The average cranial capacity of the skulls was about 640 milliliters, larger than the australopithecines, but this estimate was in doubt because the fossils were very fragmentary and in poor condition. Very few other anthropologists accepted Leakey's attribution of the fossils to *Homo*. Better evidence was needed.

Richard Leakey, Louis and Mary Leakey's son, began work in 1969 at a site near Lake Turkana (formerly Lake Rudolf) in Kenya, known as **Koobi Fora.** Koobi Fora is a very large, well-preserved site that has produced many thousands of fossils, including numerous hominids. In 1972 Richard Leakey announced the discovery of a new skull of unique importance. Known as KNM-ER 1470, this skull was relatively complete, although it was badly fragmented and required painstaking reconstruction. It was strikingly different from the australopithecines, with a notably higher, more rounded braincase, and a much larger cranial capacity of 775 milliliters. Today, most anthropologists accept KNM-ER 1470, along with a number of other more recent finds from Koobi Fora and elsewhere, as representative of the genus *Homo*. There is, in fact, considerable diversity in the group of fossils now assigned to early *Homo*.

Figure 3.9

KNM-WT 17000: the Black Skull—Paranthropus aethiopicus. *A very early robust form.*

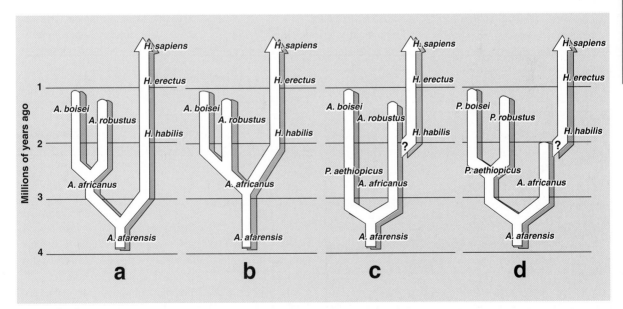

Figure 3.10

Some of the different possible family trees that have been proposed for the early hominids. (a) Johanson and White 1979; (b) Skelton et al. 1986. More recent schemes that take P. aethiopicus *into account include (c) Walker et al. 1986; (d) Grine 1988. The most important difference is whether* Australopithecus africanus *is placed in the human ancestral line or not.*

Source: Adapted from Grine 1993.

Archaeology in Practice

Dating the Earliest Hominids

Which fossil hominid came first? The dating of fossil finds is critical to any understanding of human evolution; earlier fossils may potentially be ancestral to later fossils. Placing them in chronological order is a matter of **relative dating.** A variety of physical and chemical methods have also permitted scientists to assign actual calendar dates to archaeological and fossil deposits. This process is known as **absolute dating.** Together, these methods have permitted paleontologists and archaeologists to construct a temporal framework for the early fossil hominids. Unfortunately, for this early time period, there are no methods currently available that can be used to date the fossils themselves. Instead, the fossils must be dated indirectly, by determining the dates of the geological strata in which they lie. More often than not, even this is not possible, so the date of a fossil is usually estimated by dating deposits that lie above or below the fossil. The fossil may be

presumed to be younger than a dated deposit lying below it and older than a dated deposit found above it **(Figure 3.11)**. If datable deposits can be located both above and below a fossil, its date can be fixed within well-defined limits.

Depending on the geological circumstances and time frame involved, certain absolute dating methods may be amenable to a given site, while others may not be applicable. In practice, each of the physical dating methods has potential sources of error, so cross-checking using several dating methods is the best course of action. In some instances no absolute dates are possible; for these sites relative dating techniques may help fix their place in time. The following discussion introduces the basic principles behind the most important methods used to date the early hominid sites.

Absolute Dating

Radiometric Clocks

Fixing an absolute date depends on finding a suitable clock. A variety of physical and chemical processes can be called on to serve as clocks.

These processes all consist of measurable changes that occur in a regular way over an extended period of time. Among the best such clocks are those that depend on changes in the atomic nucleus. Nuclear processes are virtually unaffected by environmental

variables, such as temperature and pressure, that might otherwise affect the rate of ticking of the clock. Most of the clocks so far devised depend on the spontaneous radioactivity of certain atoms, known as radioactive **isotopes.** Most chemical elements found in nature include several isotopic forms, some of which may be radioactive. The nuclei of radioactive isotopes may also gradually break down to produce other chemical elements, known as daughter nuclei. The radioactivity of a given isotope and the rate at which a nucleus breaks down can be precisely determined. The period of time required for one-half of the nuclei of a radioactive isotope to break down (to form daughter products) is known as its **half-life.** All the radiometric dating methods in use measure just how much of a specific radioactive isotope in a sample has broken down since the sample was formed; the more that has broken down, the older the sample. The actual technique for measuring this quantity takes a number of forms, depending on the method used.

Potassium-Argon Dating

The **potassium-argon dating method** (Aitken 1990) is one of the most important for the dating of the early hominid sites, and provides an illustration of the basic principles of radiometric dating. The very long half-life of potassium-40 (1.25 billion years) permits the dating of very ancient rocks, while advances in analysis techniques have made it possible to obtain dates younger than 100,000 years. The potassium-40 isotope makes up about 0.01 percent of naturally occurring potassium, which is found in substantial quantities in igneous rocks such as volcanic lavas, ashes, and tuffs. As the potassium-40 decays,

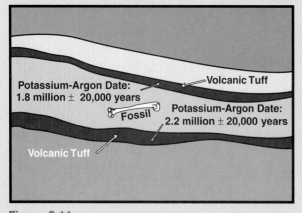

Figure 3.11

The fossil bone must be older than 1.8 million years and younger than 2.2 million years. Estimated age is about 2 million years.

Figure 3.12

The principle of potassium-argon dating. The more argon-40 accumulated in the sample, the older it is.

Source: After Aitken 1990: 121.

a small proportion (about 0.06 percent every million years) is converted into the inert gas argon-40. The argon gas remains trapped within the structure of the mineral crystals until the rock is melted, releasing the argon gas. This occurs during a volcanic eruption; at that time the potassium-argon clock is "set to zero." As soon as the rock solidifies, the argon begins accumulating again. In principle, to ascertain the date of the volcanic eruption, it is necessary to determine only how much potassium-40 is present and how much argon-40 has accumulated in the intervening span of time (Figure 3.12). The argon-40 gas is released by melting the rock sample, and is measured in a mass spectrometer, a sensitive instrument for separating atoms of differing weights.

Potassium-argon dating is straightforward, but if reliable dates are to be obtained, the samples used must be uncontaminated by older or younger inclusions. The method is further complicated because some

Figure 3.13

Fission tracks.

minerals may leak argon gas and therefore give an incorrect age. A new technique that uses a laser to melt individual mineral grains has helped alleviate some of these problems.

Fission-Track Dating

Fission-track dating (MacDougall 1976) is an alternative method that has also been used to date the early hominids. It is a more limited method in that it is practical for only a few minerals, of which zircon is the most frequently used. These minerals include small quantities of uranium-238 as an impurity. In addition to being radioactive, uranium-238 will occasionally spontaneously fission, forming two smaller daughter atoms. As the two atomic nuclei recoil from one another, they disrupt the structure

of the mineral crystal, leaving behind fission tracks that can be made visible by appropriate chemical treatment. When viewed under the microscope, the fission tracks appear as short, dark lines scattered over the crystal's surface. If the crystal is heated, the tracks anneal, causing them to disappear. The number of fission tracks, therefore, is proportional to the time elapsed since the mineral was last heated. The technique can be used to date igneous rocks such as lava that contain suitable mineral grains. The age is proportional to the ratio of the number of fission tracks to the amount of uranium-238 present. The age of the sample is determined by chemically etching the fission tracks to make them visible and counting them under a microscope (Figure 3.13). The amount of uranium-238 present is found by irradiating the sample in a nuclear reactor to induce a known proportion of the uranium atoms to fission, and then counting the newly formed fission tracks.

Geomagnetic Reversals

The earth's magnetic field is not static; the magnetic poles of the earth are in constant movement. The past location of the magnetic poles can be found through the examination of rock formations. When volcanic rock solidifies, or when a sedimentary rock hardens, magnetic particles in the rock that had aligned themselves with the earth's magnetic field become frozen in position. The rock acquires a weak magnetic field that may be used to determine the orientation of the earth's field in the past.

The earth's magnetic poles wander continuously. In addition, at irregular intervals, the magnetization of rock formations indicates that the earth's poles have abruptly exchanged positions, with the North pole becoming the South pole and vice versa. These interchanges are termed **geomagnetic reversals.** Through the use of radiometric dating methods, such as potassium-argon dating, the dates of many of these reversals have been determined. The pattern that has emerged is of extended epochs (or chrons) during which the field is either normal (as it is today) or reversed. These epochs are interrupted by short periods (called events, or subchrons) during which the field temporarily has the opposite polarization. **Figure 3.14** shows the major reversals of interest to archaeologists.

Geomagnetic reversals do not directly provide a date for a site. If the orientation of the earth's magnetic field during the formation of a site can be determined, however, it can help resolve difficult situations where the dates provided by absolute dating methods are ambiguous or in conflict.

Figure 3.14

Major geomagnetic reversals.

Source: Based on data in Aitken 1990 and Butler 1992.

Relative Dating

Correlation of Faunal Assemblages

The animals that inhabit a given location change over the course of geological time as some species become extinct and others evolve to take their place. Paleontologists have long used the associated group of animals found at a site, the **faunal assemblage,** to help temporally correlate rock strata found at different locations. Two strata containing very similar types of fossils can usually be presumed to be close in age. During the age of mammals, the Cenozoic, animal species evolved rapidly, so a distinctive faunal assemblage can often be quite accurately placed within the evolutionary sequence. Only areas that are not too distant geographically and have similar environments, however, may be expected to have supported similar faunas. Further, an isolated area may have seen a course of evolution different from that of other areas. With the environment taken into account, however, faunal correlations have proved very useful for tying together the early hominid sites.

A number of African archaeological sites dating to the time of the early hominids have provided assemblages of animal bones that can be used as chronological guides. The site of **Omo** in Ethiopia, studied under the direction of F. C. Howell, has produced an extensive sequence of animal bone assemblages as well as a number of hominid remains. The sequence of deposits at Omo can also be anchored in time through the potassium-argon dating of key strata. Olduvai Gorge and Hadar have also produced good animal bone sequences with some absolute dates. Several kinds of animals, including horses, elephants, and particularly, various types of pigs, appear, diversify, and become extinct in turn. At any given time period, the faunal assemblage at a site can be expected to include a characteristic group of species that differs from that of earlier or later periods. The various species of pigs have proved to be particularly important temporal indicators. Today three species of pigs remain in sub-Saharan Africa: the bushpig, the giant forest hog, and the warthog. About 1 million years ago 10 different species were to be found, 7 of which are now extinct. About 2 million years ago yet another set of pig species was present, and so on back through the last several million years. **Figure 3.15,** derived from the sequence proposed by H. B. S. Cooke (1985), shows the associations of pig species characteristic of each distinctive faunal period. Horses and elephants can also be used to produce similar temporal associations of species (Cooke 1983). The strata at Omo, Olduvai Gorge, Hadar, and a number of other African sites have been correlated through the application of these faunal data.

Dating in Practice

How Were the Earliest Hominids Dated?

None of today's physical dating methods were available when the South African australopithecine fossils were first discovered. The approximate dates of Taung and Sterkfontein were estimated on the basis of the species of animals found at the sites. Even today the dating of the South African sites has proved difficult because there are no volcanic deposits suitable for potassium-argon dating. The animal species present in the South African sites differ from those in East Africa, but the group of species present at Makapansgat, Taung, and Sterkfontein is different from those found in Kromdraai and Swartkrans. The faunal evidence suggests that Makapansgat, Taung, and Sterkfontein (the *A. africanus* sites) were roughly contemporary, while Kromdraai and Swartkrans (the *A. robustus* sites) were later in time (Cooke 1966: 106; see also White and Harris 1977). Faunal correlations with East African sites have proved very uncertain because the environments of the two areas are quite different, and it is possible that some species survived longer in South Africa.

In East Africa the potassium-argon method has provided dates for a number of key strata (primarily volcanic tuffs), and these dates have frequently been cross-checked through the application of fission-track dating, determinations of geomagnetic polarity, and faunal correlations. The dating of the fossil finds at Hadar provides an example (Johanson and Edey 1981). A key date was provided by the potassium-argon dating of a volcanic ash dated at 2.8 ± 0.04 million years that overlay the principal australopithecine finds. This date was confirmed by a fission-track date of 2.7 ± 0.23 million years. Another basalt layer below the fossils was at first potassium-argon dated to about 3 million years, but because of the nature of the test material this dating was doubtful. The magnetization of the basal layer indicated that it was laid down during a period when the earth's poles were reversed. This occurred between 3 million and 3.1 million years ago (the Mammoth event) and, previously, between 3.4 million and 3.8 million years ago (at the end of the Gilbert reversed epoch). The later date of 3 million years was initially accepted, making Lucy and the other *A. afarensis* fossils about 2.9 million years old. The fossil pigs in the assemblage,

Figure 3.15

The temporal relationship among the various species of pigs found in East Africa during the Pliocene and Pleistocene, as proposed by H. B. S. Cooke (1985). Several distinct chronological groups of species can be distinguished. A similar scheme, differing only in details and some of the species names, has been proposed by J. M. Harris and T. D. White (1979).

however, seemed too primitive for that date. Cooke (1978) thought an age of 3 million to 3.5 million years was more likely. The basalt layer, therefore, probably formed in the earlier period of geomagnetic reversal, about 3.75 million years ago.

The dating of the *Homo habilis* (*rudolfensis*) fossil KNM-ER 1470 at Koobi Fora is another example of the difficulties encountered in absolute dating. KNM-ER 1470 had been found below a volcanic stratum, known as the KBS tuff, that served as a critical chronological marker. The first potassium-argon dates for the KBS tuff placed it at about 2.6 million years old. The *Homo habilis* (*rudolfensis*) skull, therefore, would have had to be older, perhaps 2.9 million years old. That would have been far too old for *Australopithecus africanus* to be a human ancestor. The other animal species in the deposit, particularly the fossil pigs, however, suggested that it was considerably younger, correlating with deposits from Omo of about 2 million years of age. The reexamination of rock samples from the KBS tuff complex revealed that they were contaminated by older minerals; new potassium-argon determinations of carefully purified samples have given a date of 1.88 ± 0.02 million years ago (Feibel et al. 1989), and KNM-ER 1470 is now dated to about 1.9 million years.

Figure 3.16

KNM-ER 1470: Homo habilis (rudolfensis). *An early human skull from Koobi Fora.*

Some specimens, such as KNM-ER 1470, possessed relatively large brains, and rather large teeth as well. Others had smaller brains and also smaller, human-sized, teeth. Some workers today recognize two species of early *Homo: Homo habilis,* which includes the finds from Olduvai Gorge, and *Homo rudolfensis,* which includes KNM-ER 1470 and similar fossils **(Figure 3.16)**.

The dating of the deposits at Koobi Fora has been an issue of critical importance for the understanding of the early stages of human evolution. Potassium-argon dating has been applied to the volcanic tuffs present at the site, and comparative studies of the associated animal species have also played an important role. At present, the best estimate for the age of KNM-ER 1470 is about 1.9 million years. The first appearance of *Australopithecus africanus* is earlier than that of *Homo habilis. Australopithecus africanus* and *Homo habilis* are rather similar, and at present *Australopithecus africanus* cannot be ruled out of the direct line of human evolution. Some of the current hypothetical hominid family trees are illustrated in Figure 3.10.

Case Study
The South African Australopithecines: Did They Hunt or Were They Hunted?

Stone tools have never been found associated with australopithecines except in sites in which early *Homo* may also have been present. Still, the earliest hominids may have used tools made from other materials: wood, bone, teeth, or horn. This was the suggestion of Raymond Dart, based on his investigations of the South African australopithecine sites. The use of bone tools by the australopithecines has proved very difficult to verify, and Dart's suggestion was widely challenged. Further, Dart coupled his hypothesis with some rather startling assertions concerning australopithecine behavior. The australopithecines, he said, were violent, aggressive hunters, violent not only toward their prey but also toward each other. Dart's evidence for this scenario and its refutation by the careful observations and experiments of C. K. Brain (1981) are detailed below.

The South African sites at which *Australopithecus africanus* has been found—Taung, Sterkfontein, and Makapansgat—contained no stone tools associated with the fossil hominids. Instead, each of these cave sites held large quantities of fragmentary animal bones belonging to a variety of species. Earlier researchers had interpreted similar deposits as the work of large carnivores, notably hyenas, but on the basis of his experience and some limited research, Dart rejected hyenas as likely bone-collecting agents. At an early stage in his researches Raymond Dart became convinced that the South African bone accumulations came into the caves as the result of hominid activities. The deposit at Taung, he noted, was similar to known archaeological sites belonging to early modern humans (Dart 1929: 648). Dart reasoned that the animal bones must have been brought into the caves for a purpose. At Makapansgat the proportions of the various skeletal parts recovered were markedly different from their proportions in a complete animal skeleton, suggesting to Dart that certain bones had been selected for use as tools. He thought he could identify pointed tools made by twisting and cracking long bones, scoops and spatulate bone tools, and composite tools made by forcing one bone into another or by wedging stone fragments into the ends of bones. Dart envisioned uses for practically all the bone that was found at Makapansgat. He termed this technology the **osteodontokeratic** (bone, tooth, and horn) industry.

Among the bones from Taung, Sterkfontein, and Makapansgat were numerous baboon skulls. Dart noted that many of these skulls, as well as six australopithecine skulls, bore depressed fractures, as if they had been struck on the head. Dart concluded that these fractures must have been caused by violent attacks by the australopithecines, and, in the absence of stone artifacts, that the weapon used must have been a large animal bone, possibly an antelope humerus (upper arm bone). Examining the bone collection from Makapansgat, Dart observed that there was a high proportion of antelope skulls present, but very few neck vertebrae or tailbones. This suggested to him that the game animals had been intentionally decapitated, and that the australopithecines were headhunters. The australopithecines were, in Dart's reasoning,

> confirmed killers: carnivorous creatures that seized living quarries by violence, battered them to death, tore apart their broken bodies, dismembered them limb from limb, slaking their ravenous thirst with the hot blood of victims and greedily devouring livid writhing flesh. (Dart 1953: 209)

The idea that the human lineage is innately violent soon penetrated into popular culture. Dart's lurid view of early hominid behavior was popularized by science writer Robert Ardrey in a best-selling book *African Genesis* (1961). Stanley Kubrick's classic 1969 film *2001: A Space Odyssey* opens with a series of scenes of violent, club-wielding australopithecines.

Dart's enticing hypotheses, however, have not stood up to closer scrutiny. A series of observations and experiments, primarily the research of C. K. Brain, presented in his 1981 book *The Hunters or the Hunted?* have shown that some of Dart's fundamental premises were incorrect.

Dart was convinced that the bone accumulations were the work of hominids and that large carnivores had played no part. Later research has shown, however, that large carnivores such as hyenas and leopards can and do carry meat into their lairs, resulting in large accumulations of food bone. A number of observers have reported bone accumulations by African hyenas. Particularly interesting are the observations made by G. Ilani (1975) of a striped hyena den in the Negev Desert of southern Israel. Within the den were hundreds of skulls of domestic dogs, camels, donkeys, sheep, and goats, including two human skulls, presumably from a nearby Bedouin cemetery. On the basis of his own observations, Brain has demonstrated that leopards too will collect the bones of their prey in

feeding lairs. Vegetarian porcupines also collect bones, which they chew to wear down their incisors. Any or all of these animals may have contributed to the South African bone assemblages.

What of the fractures and depressions in the animal and hominid skulls? Brain points out that fossil bones frequently become deformed and marked from the pressure of stones in the deposit in which they lie and that such markings can easily imitate the results of injuries. Since the nature of the deposit is unknown for all the fossils showing depressions, the actual cause of these markings cannot be demonstrated. The question is largely moot for the site of Taung. The Taung cave, from which the hominids were recovered, was destroyed by mining operations in the late 1920s, so the exact context of the Taung fossils is unknown. Recently, however, geological examinations of the Taung area and of the sediments adhering to the fossils have indicated that the geological history of the Taung cave was more complicated than Dart realized, and that the hominid fossils actually came from a later time period than the game they had presumably hunted. Further, Brain was able to examine a preserved block of limestone breccia from Taung containing a number of baboon skulls and other bones. He confirmed that the bones had been damaged by gnawing and that they were very likely the food bone accumulation of a large carnivore such as a leopard.

What of the odd distribution of bone types at Makapansgat, attributed by Dart to conscious selection by hominids? Brain's observations of the food remains left behind by Hottentot goat herders provide an alternative explanation. The Hottentots butcher and eat numerous goats, scattering the bones in the area of their huts, where they are gnawed on by dogs. Brain noted that many of these bone fragments look like bone tools, even though the Hottentots deny that they ever made bone tools. The wear that appeared on the pseudotools that Brain collected apparently came from the abrasion of the bone fragments in the sand as they were trodden underfoot. Over two years Brain collected several thousand discarded goat bones from the Hottentot villages. By counting the numbers of each of the different skeletal parts present (femurs, humeri, mandibles, etc.), it was possible to determine the minimum number of goats that must originally have been present, and from that number to calculate how many of each kind of bone should have been found had all the bones been preserved. The proportions of bone types that actually remained after the Hottentot butchers and the ravaging dogs had done their work proved to be markedly different from the proportion that had originally existed. Mandibles (lower jaws) were the best preserved; most of them still remained. Most other bones fared far more poorly. The sample should have contained 1,224 caudal vertebrae (tailbones), but there were none. Unchewable bones survived best; young, soft bones survived the worst.

When Brain compared the Hottentot data to the bone assemblage from Makapansgat, the similarity was immediately apparent. Although minor differences existed, in general, those skeletal parts found in large numbers in the modern goat bone sample were also common in Makapansgat. Conversely, those bones that had been destroyed in the goat bone sample were also missing from Makapansgat. The most likely explanation for the bone collection at Makapansgat, therefore, is that it was probably collected, and greatly modified, by the activities of large carnivores.

The events at Sterkfontein have proved more difficult to interpret, largely because the collections of animal bones from the site may have been biased and incomplete. The great majority of specimens from the site are skulls, with very few other skeletal parts represented. Nevertheless, the collection is remarkable. The most common animals at the site were baboons, followed in turn by *Australopithecus africanus,* and then by large carnivores such as saber-toothed cats. Brain's reexamination of the skulls supposedly damaged by violent blows showed little that could not equally be attributable to compressional effects, and the preponderance of skulls strongly suggests that Sterkfontein too is a collection created by large carnivores.

How did so many baboons and hominids find their way into the Sterkfontein deposit? Clues may be found in the examination of other South African hominid sites. The cave of Swartkrans, which contained both *Australopithecus robustus* and fossils of early humans, shows some interesting similarities to Sterkfontein. Skulls are preponderant in the lower layer of Swartkrans, where nearly all the hominids were found. Baboons and hominids are the most common species and about equally frequent. Large herbivores follow, and large carnivores are also common. The distribution of skeletal parts at Swartkrans, as at Makapansgat, and frequent evidence of carnivore gnawing make it clear that this collection of bones was created by the activities of large carnivores. The bone assemblage in the *Australopithecus robustus* site of Kromdraai shows many similarities to that of Swartkrans, although the bones are very fragmentary and the case is not so clear.

Brain concludes, therefore, that the australopithecines in Sterkfontein, Swartkrans, and Kromdraai did not inhabit the sites where they were found but rather were dragged there as food by large carnivores, such as leopards, saber-toothed cats, or perhaps hyenas. Rather than being the vicious predators envisaged by Dart, the australopithecines were instead the prey of more powerful creatures. How did the bones end up in the caves? Brain presents an intriguing hypothesis **(Figure 3.17)**. Today the openings to limestone caves are

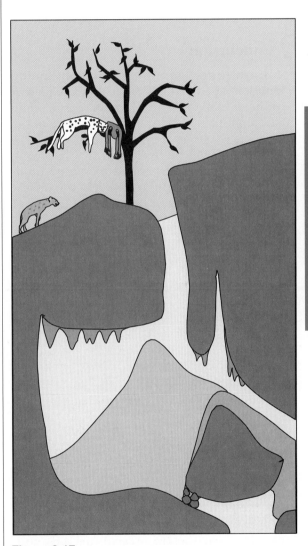

Figure 3.17

The Swartkrans leopard hypothesis: A leopard has carried an australopithecine into a tree to protect it from scavengers such as hyenas. Later the remains will fall to the ground and the bones will be washed into the cave.

Source: After Brain 1981.

frequently surrounded by groves of trees that grow readily because of the abundance of groundwater. Leopards often carry their prey onto the branches of trees, where they can feed undisturbed by hyenas. Brain speculates that leopards may have carried the unfortunate australopithecines up into the trees growing above the Swartkrans shaft, and that their remains ultimately dropped down into the cave. Brain supports this hypothesis by a fascinating piece of evidence. The skull of an australopithecine child from Swartkrans shows two holes pierced through it, 33 millimeters (1.3 in.) apart. This spacing exactly fits the canine teeth of a leopard also found in the deposit.

 ## Conclusion

Brain himself found a few convincing bone tools at Swartkrans, but they could well have been made by early humans rather than australopithecines. With the appearance of the genus *Homo*, stone tools also appear in large numbers. As will be discussed in Chapter 4, scatters of stone artifacts and the waste products from their manufacture are the surest signs of the presence of humans. A number of archaeological sites, including concentrations of stone artifacts, animal bones, and sometimes hominid fossils as well, have come to light at Olduvai, at Koobi Fora, and elsewhere in Africa. Unlike the South African australopithecine sites, these sites are much more likely to be the result of early human activities: places where animal foods, obtained through scavenging or hunting, were butchered, possibly shared, and consumed. The interpretation of these sites has been the subject of much controversy, but they provide the first clues to the lifeways of our earliest ancestors. The nature and interpretation of these sites will be the subject matter of Chapter 4.

 ## Glossary

Absolute dating. Dating methods that provide dates in calendar years, usually expressed as years before present (B.P.). By convention, *present* is defined as A.D. 1950, about the time when radiometric dating methods first came into use.

Australopithecus afarensis. A small-brained, fully bipedal hominid found at a number of East African sites extending from Hadar in Ethiopia to Laetoli in Tanzania. The earliest certain hominid, *A. afarensis* dates from perhaps as early as 5.6 million to 2.9 million years ago.

Australopithecus africanus. A lightly built hominid found in South Africa, dating to between 3 million and 2 million years ago. Although *A. africanus* probably evolved from *A. afarensis,* it is not yet clear whether *A. africanus* falls in the line of human evolution.

Australopithecus anamensis. A recently discovered bipedal human ancestor dated to about 4.2 million years ago. Although *A. anamensis* shows many similarities to *A. afarensis,* the shape of the jaws of *A. anamensis* is more like that of modern apes.

Australopithecus boisei. A massively built hominid found in East Africa, even more robust than *A. robustus. A. boisei* dates from 2 million to 1 million years ago, continuing in existence even after the appearance of *Homo erectus* (see Chapter 6). Today it is classified by some scholars as *Paranthropus boisei.*

Australopithecus ramidus. The name proposed by White, Suwa, and Asfaw for the hominid fossils found at Aramis, Ethiopia, that have some characteristics typical of both hominids and great apes. The fossils, dating from about 4.4 million years ago, have recently been reclassified as *Ardipithecus ramidus.*

Australopithecus robustus. A heavily built hominid with large rear teeth, found in South Africa, appearing somewhat later in time than *A. africanus,* from 2 million to 1.5 million years ago. *A. robustus* appears to have diverged significantly from the human ancestral line. Today it is classified by some scholars as *Paranthropus robustus.*

Bipedal. Walking upright on two legs.

Breccia. A hard limestone concretion formed from percolating cave water, in which ancient artifacts and fossils are frequently imbedded.

Cranial capacity. The volume of the braincase in milliliters, reflecting the size of the brain.

Faunal assemblage. The group of associated animal bones found together at an archaeological or paleontological site. In East

Africa, a distinctive group of animal species, particularly the various species of pigs, is characteristic of a particular period of time, and the faunal assemblages have been used effectively to chronologically correlate the East African early hominid sites.

Fission-track dating. An absolute dating method that relies on the counting of the visible trails left behind in mineral crystals by the fission products of uranium-238.

Geomagnetic reversals. Abrupt interchanges of the earth's North and South magnetic poles, reflected in the magnetization of the earth's rocks, and useful for estimating the possible ages of geological deposits.

Great Rift Valley. The great valley system of East Africa, extending from Mozambique in the south to the Red Sea in the north, which includes most of the early hominid sites of East Africa. The Great Rift Valley was formed by the movement of the geological rift that separates the continental African plate from the Somali plate to the east.

Hadar. Site located in the Afar Triangle, Ethiopia, that has produced an extensive series of fossils of *Australopithecus afarensis*.

Half-life. The time required for one-half of a radioactive element to decay.

Hominids. Members of the family within the Primates that includes humans and their closest bipedal relatives. The hominids include the genera *Homo* and *Australopithecus*.

Homo habilis. The earliest members of the genus *Homo*. *Homo habilis* was first found at Olduvai Gorge. The best known of the Koobi Fora finds, KNM-ER 1470 is now classified by some scholars as belonging to a second genus, **Homo rudolfensis.** *H. habilis* has been identified at Omo and at Sterkfontein in South Africa as well, and dates from 1.5 million to 1.9 million years ago.

Isotopes. Forms of a chemical element, distinguished by differences in atomic weight.

Koobi Fora. Locality in Kenya that has produced many early hominid fossils, including fossils of *Australopithecus boisei* and *Homo erectus*, as well as some of the best-preserved specimens of *Homo habilis*.

Kromdraai. Site in South Africa that has yielded fossils of *Australopithecus robustus*.

Laetoli. Site in Tanzania that has produced fossils of *Australopithecus afarensis*. It is best known for the trail of footprints of an erect-walking hominid discovered there.

Makapansgat. Site in South Africa that has yielded many fossils of *Australopithecus africanus*.

Olduvai Gorge. Locality in Tanzania that includes numerous fossil and archaeological sites and that has produced many early hominid fossils. *Australopithecus boisei* and *Homo habilis* were first identified at Olduvai Gorge, and *Homo erectus* has also been found there.

Omo. Site in southern Ethiopia, investigated by F. C. Howell and Y. Coppens, that includes, in addition to a number of early hominid fossils, a broad range of animal fossil assemblages in a particularly well-dated context. These animal bone data have been very useful in chronologically correlating the fossil hominid sites in eastern Africa.

Osteodontokeratic. A technology based on bone, teeth, and horn that Raymond Dart ascribed to the australopithecines, in the absence of any clear evidence for the use of stone tools by these hominids.

Paranthropus aethiopicus. A fossil hominid found at West Turkana, dating to about 2.5 million years ago, that combines primitive features with features similar to those of the robust australopithecines. Known as the Black Skull, this fossil indicates that the evolutionary line of robust hominids is very ancient.

Potassium-argon dating method. An absolute dating method, generally applied to volcanic rocks, that relies on the determination of the relative proportion of potassium-40 to argon-40, the product of its radioactive decomposition.

Primates. The mammalian order to which humans and the other hominids belong, and which also includes the prosimians, the Old and New World monkeys, and the great and lesser apes.

Relative dating. Dating methods that do not provide dates in calendar years, but can be used to determine whether two sites are the same age or whether one site is older or younger than another.

Sterkfontein. Site in South Africa that has yielded fossils of *Australopithecus africanus*, as well as (in a different area) *Homo habilis*.

Swartkrans. Site in South Africa that has yielded fossils of *Australopithecus robustus*, as well as (in a different, later area) *Homo erectus*.

Taung. Site in South Africa where Raymond Dart found the Taung child, classified as *Australopithecus africanus*, the first australopithecine to be discovered.

Tuffs. Geological layers formed from falls of volcanic ash.

 ## Further Reading

Aitken, M. J.
1990. *Science-Based Dating in Archaeology*. London and New York: Longman.

An up-to-date, concise summary of the principles, applications, and limitations of the physical dating methods currently in use in archaeology. Recommended for the advanced student.

Johanson, Donald, and Maitland Edey
1981. *Lucy: The Beginnings of Humankind*. New York: Simon and Schuster.

A very readable, popular book recounting the history of early hominid research in Africa as well as the discovery of the early australopithecine Lucy. Chapter 9, "How Old Is Lucy?" presents a simple description of the potassium-argon dating method and a discussion of the complexities involved in dating the Hadar deposits.

MacDougall, J. D.
1976. Fission-Track Dating. *Scientific American* 235 (6): 114–122.

An older but clear explanation of the principles and procedures of fission-track dating.

Tattersall, I., E. Delson, and J. Van Couvering
1988. *Encyclopedia of Human Evolution and Prehistory*. New York: Garland.

A concise reference source, suitable for students, covering the major topics in human evolution.

 ## Other Bibliography

Ardrey, R.
1961. *African Genesis*. New York: Atheneum.

Brain, C. K.
1981. *The Hunters or the Hunted? An Introduction to African Cave Taphonomy*. Chicago and London: University of Chicago Press.

Butler, Robert F.
1992. *Paleomagnetism: Magnetic Domains to Geologic Terrains*. Boston: Blackwell Scientific Publications.

Cooke, H. B. S.
1966. Pleistocene Mammal Faunas of Africa, with Particular Reference to Southern Africa. In *African Ecology and Human Evolution*, edited by F. C. Howell and F. Boulière, pp. 65–116. Chicago: Aldine.
1978. Pliocene-Pleistocene Suidae from Hadar, Ethiopia. *Kirtlandia* 29: 1–63.
1983. Horses, Elephants and Pigs as Clues in the African Later Cainozoic. In *Late Cainozoic Palaeoclimates of the Southern Hemisphere*, edited by J. C. Vogel, pp. 473–482. Rotterdam: A. A. Balkema.
1985. Plio-Pleistocene Suidae in Relation to African Hominid Deposits. In *L'Environment des Hominidés au Plio-Pléistocene*, edited by M. Michel Beden et al., pp. 101–117. Paris: Masson.

Dart, R. A.
1929. A Note on the Taung Skull. *South African Journal of Science* 26: 648–658.
1953. The Predatory Transition from Ape to Man. *International Anthropological Linguistics Review* 1: 201–218.

Feibel, C. S., F. H., Brown, and I. McDougall
1989. Stratigraphic Context of Fossil Hominids from the Omo Group Deposits: Northern Turkana Basin, Kenya and Ethiopia. *American Journal of Physical Anthropology* 78: 595–622.

Grine, F. E.
1988. Evolutionary History of the "Robust" Australopithecines: A Summary and Historical Perspective. In *Evolutionary History of the "Robust" Australopithecines*, edited by F. E. Grine, pp. 509–519. New York: Aldine de Gruyter.
1993. Australopithecine Taxonomy and Phylogeny: Historical Background and Recent Interpretation. In *The Human Evolution Source Book*, edited by R. L. Ciochon and J. G. Fleagle, pp. 198–210. Englewood Cliffs, NJ: Prentice Hall.

Harris, J. M., and T. D. White
1979. Evolution of the Plio-Pleistocene African Suidae. *Transactions of the American Philosophical Society* 69 (2): 1–128.

Hay, R. L., and M. D. Leakey
1982. The Fossil Footprints of Laetoli. *Scientific American* 246 (2): 50–57.

Ilani, G.
1975. Hyenas in Israel. *Israel—Land and Nature*. October: pp. 10–18.

Johanson, D. C., and T. D. White
    1979. A Systematic Assessment of Early African Hominids. *Science* 202: 321–330.

Leakey, M. G., C. S. Feibel, I. McDougall, and A. Walker
    1995. New Four-Million-Year-Old Hominid Species from Kanapoi and Allea Bay, Kenya. *Nature* 376: 565–571.

Skelton, R. R., H. M. McHenry, and G. M. Drawhorn
    1986. Phylogenetic Analysis of Early Hominids. *Current Anthropology* 27: 21–35.

Walker, A. C., R. E. F. Leakey, J. M. Harris, and F. H. Brown
    1986. 2.5 Myr *Australopithecus boisei* from West of Lake Turkana, Kenya. *Nature* 322: 517–522.

White, T. D., and J. M. Harris
    1977. Suid Evolution and Correlation of African Hominid Localities. *Science* 198: 13–22.

White, T. D., G. Suwa, and B. Asfaw
    1994. *Australopithecus ramidus,* a New Species of Early Hominid from Aramis, Ethiopia. *Nature* 372: 306–312.
    1995. *Australopithecus ramidus,* a New Species of Early Hominid from Aramis, Ethiopia. Corrigendum. *Nature* 375: 88.

Chapter 4

The Earliest Archaeological Sites
The First Stone Tools

Introduction: Understanding the Behavior of Our Earliest Ancestors

How do archaeologists recognize the earliest archaeological sites? The earliest, simplest sites have presented archaeologists with a major challenge. How can we distinguish the evidence for specifically human activities from the remains left by other animals, such as the bone accumulations of scavenging carnivores, or from natural accumulations created by running water or other geological forces?

For most archaeologists, the first appearance of stone tools marks the beginning of the archaeological record—the record of specifically human activities. Stone tools within an archaeological site are one clear marker that the site resulted, at least in part, from human rather than nonhuman activity. The evidence, however, for the use of the simplest stone tools by our remote human ancestors is usually quite ambiguous and difficult to interpret. How do archaeologists determine that a stone object is really an artifact made and utilized by humans?

How are archaeologists to interpret the accumulations of stone tools and bones that form the earliest sites? What can the remaining material evidence tell us about the lives and activities of the proto-humans and humans that created these sites? What can we learn of how the earliest humans behaved, obtained the food they needed to survive, and related to other members of their species? These questions have proved tantalizing, difficult, and contentious.

The Beginnings of the Archaeological Record

All modern humans make and use tools. While it is known that other species, most notably chimpanzees (Figure 4.1), also use tools occasionally, the use of tools is fundamental to all human societies. Did the earliest hominids make and use tools? In the localities where only australopithecine fossils are found, the stone tools that are so common at later sites are missing.

The oldest stone tools known at present have been found in Ethiopia, from deposits near Hadar, dating to about 2.5 million to 2.7 million years ago, older than any known fossils of *Homo*. No hominid remains are associated with these artifacts, which include a number of very simple stone tools from which only a few flakes have been removed, as well as flakes and flake fragments. Most archaeologists assume, however, that these tools were made by early humans, rather than australopithecines.

The simplest stone tools can be difficult to distinguish from fragmented stones resulting from natural geological processes. Two lines of evidence indicate to the archaeologist that a specific object is the result of human activity. The first is *location:* If no known natural process can account for the occurrence of an object in the place where it is found, the archaeologist may suspect that the object, even an unworked stone, was brought there by human agency. It is not always easy, though, to determine whether or not natural forces (notably water action and the activities of animals) played a role in the location of artifacts. The importance of this problem will be discussed later in this chapter.

The second line of evidence that an artifact is of human origin is the degree to which a natural object, such as a stone nodule, has been *modified*. If an artifact has clearly been *intentionally changed*, the archaeologist may conclude that it is a product of human activity. The very earliest assemblages of stone tools were scarcely worked. When the degree of modification of a stone is minimal, it can be very difficult to ascertain whether the object was the product of natural agencies or intentional manufacture. As the degree of modification is increased (as more flakes are removed), the archaeologist may be more confident that the object is of human origin.

Figure 4.1

A chimpanzee making use of a tool.

Figure 4.2

Olduvai Gorge, Tanzania. The circles mark archaeological sites.
Source: After M. Leakey 1971.

The Earliest Forms of Stone Tools

An assemblage of stone tools made and used together is termed a **lithic industry,** from the Greek word for stone, *lithos.* The earliest lithic industries generally resemble that found in the lowest level at Olduvai Gorge, Bed I, where several important archaeological sites have been discovered. This industry is named the **Oldowan** (after an alternate name for Olduvai). The Oldowan is

typified by the assemblage from the site DK, which lies near the base of the long sequence at Olduvai Gorge **(Figure 4.2)**, in Bed I, and dates to approximately 1.8 million years ago. DK will be discussed in some detail later in this chapter. The most common stone tools at DK are choppers and chopping tools **(Figure 4.3)**, chipped, for the most part, from locally available basalt pebbles (see the Archaeology in Practice box). A few were made from quartzite. Some pebble tools, flaked in several directions to form intersecting edges, are classified as **polyhedrons,** while others, made of flattened pebbles, are termed **discoids.** Other tools have been classed as **scrapers.** All these artifacts are crude and grade from one form to another. Rather enigmatic artifacts found in the Oldowan are the **spheroids**—pebbles flaked over their entire surface to a roughly spherical form. The functions of these objects are unknown, but many of these tools show edges that are chipped and battered from use. Numerous flakes, both of basalt and quartzite, are found in the assemblage, and some of them show signs of utilization. Experiments by archaeologist Nicholas Toth have demonstrated that flakes such as these would have been quite suitable for butchering animals, and traces of wear on flakes of similar age from Koobi

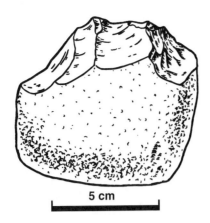

Figure 4.3

A typical chopping tool made from a basalt pebble from the site of DK, Olduvai Gorge.

5 cm

Fora do suggest that they were used for cutting meat (Toth 1987; Keeley and Toth 1981).

The Nature of the Early Archaeological Sites

The lower layers of Olduvai Gorge and the approximately contemporary deposits at Koobi Fora have produced a variety of sites that include artifacts and bones evidencing hominid activity. Attempts to understand and interpret the nature of these sites have proved challenging and frequently controversial. The true nature of the earliest African archaeological sites has been the subject of intense debate.

When the archaeological deposits at Olduvai Gorge and Koobi Fora were first discovered, archaeologists attempted to interpret them in terms of modern human behavior. Those sites containing concentrations of artifacts and animal bones resembled archaeological sites from later periods that have ordinarily been interpreted as **base camps**—areas occupied by a human group for a period of weeks or months in which a variety of domestic activities took place. Were the similar-appearing sites at Olduvai and Koobi Fora very early examples of base camps?

The widespread scatters of artifacts had clearly accumulated over a long period of time and had often been redistributed by geologic factors such as erosion. The artifacts and bones in most of the accumulations, however, were concentrated in thin layers and showed little evidence of having been eroded or moved by running water. The excavators, therefore, accepted these deposits as relatively undisturbed evidence for human

behavior. Mary Leakey interpreted sites containing the bones of a single animal associated with a small number of artifacts as **butchery** or **kill sites.** Sites that included a concentration of artifacts associated with the bones of a number of different animals, usually representing several species, were interpreted as **living floors.** If these interpretations are accepted, further inferences about early human subsistence and social behavior may follow.

The Interpretation of Proto-Human Behavior

What do the earliest archaeological sites tell us about early human behavior? In the 1970s the early African archaeological sites were widely accepted as primarily the product of proto-human activity, but what function did these sites serve? The interpretation that had gained the most widespread acceptance, advanced by archaeologist Glynn Isaac (1978), was known as the **food-sharing hypothesis.** According to the food-sharing hypothesis, the well-preserved artifact and bone concentrations at Olduvai and Koobi Fora were evidence for home bases, to which proto-human hominids, presumably hunter-scavengers and gatherers, carried meat and other foods for consumption. The most prominent examples of such sites included FLK at Olduvai (the Zinjanthropus floor) and FxJj 50 at Koobi Fora. In its most elaborated form, the food-sharing hypothesis envisaged the hunters (probably males) sharing their quarry with other members of their social group, including juveniles and females, who presumably also contributed to the diet through the gathering of vegetal foods and small animals. Features characteristic of modern human societies, therefore, such as family organization and the sexual division of labor, were seen as having their roots in this very early period.

Archaeologists believed they were justified in creating this scenario because they perceived a trail of similar archaeological evidence leading backward from the present into the past. Concentrations of artifacts and food refuse can be observed accumulating around the camps of modern hunter-gatherers. Similar features are commonly found in relatively

Archaeology in Practice

The Basics of Working Stone

Stone artifacts (along with bones) are without doubt the most important evidence available for the archaeology of early humans. Unlike many of the materials that may have been used by early hominids, stone is practically indestructible. Early archaeological sites often include artifacts left from every stage of the procurement, manufacture, and use of a stone

When a projectile such as a BB strikes a pane of plate glass, the force of the impact spreads out as a conical wave, known as the cone of percussion. The glass fractures along this cone, dislodging a conical fragment, and leaving behind a conical hole in the glass. The same effect occurs when a sharp blow is delivered to a homogeneous material such as flint.

The simplest form of stone working is direct percussion. A nodule of a homogeneous stone such as flint or basalt is struck with a hammerstone to remove a flake or a series of flakes. The stone from which the flake was removed is known as a core. Both the flakes and the core may be used as tools or further worked into other artifacts.

As ripples spread from a rock thrown into a pool of water, ripples may form along the plane of fracture, radiating away from the point of impact. The surface formed resembles a clamshell. This kind of breakage is known as choncoidal fracture.

Proximal end

Point of impact

Bulb of percussion

Scar

Ripple marks

Distal end

Edge

A typical flake, showing some of the terms used to describe it.

Figure 4.4

The basic principles of stone flake production.

implement. Archaeologists can recover the raw materials from which the objects were made, waste products from the manufacture process, and the stone tools themselves in every stage from new, through modification and reuse, to final discard. Through many years of analysis, ethnographic observations, and experimentation, archaeologists now know much about the processes of stone tool manufacture.

Initially, early humans must have made use of whatever stone was conveniently at hand that was suitably sized and shaped for a hammer, pounder, or the like. No one knows how early humans learned that certain types of stone could be flaked, yielding useful fragments with sharp cutting edges. It is evident, however, that the special suitability of certain types of stone was recognized early on and that these stones were intentionally sought out as tool-making materials.

A stone appropriate for being made into flaked stone tools must possess certain characteristic properties: It must be hard enough to produce effective cutting edges; it must break relatively easily when struck with a sharp blow; and it must be sufficiently homogeneous that the breakage can be controlled to produce thin flakes. Stones such as slate or calcite that break, or cleave, along well-defined **planes of cleavage** (planes along which the rocks split easily) or that tend to shatter when struck are far more difficult to work. Usually, stones that are deficient in any of these properties were only used when better materials were not readily available.

By far the most widely used materials for the manufacture of flaked stone tools belong to a closely related group of fine-grained siliceous stones that includes chalcedony, jasper, flint, and chert. These materials generally were deposited from silica-containing groundwaters into the seams and hollows of limestone bedrock. Erosion may reveal seams of blocky **tabular chert,** while **flint nodules** commonly accumulate in the beds of streams where they may readily be collected. Flint and its relatives exhibit excellent properties for flaking, or knapping. Their constituent mineral, silica, is very hard, and flint edges will cut or scratch almost all other natural materials, including bone. They break very easily when struck with a hammer, yielding large, thin flakes. A skilled flint-knapper can easily control the character of the flakes produced because good-quality flint is very homogeneous. Instead of breaking irregularly or along cleavage planes, flint fractures along a cone, or portion of a cone, radiating from the point of impact (Figure 4.4). Concentric ripple marks usually form so that the surface resembles a seashell. This phenomenon is called **conchoidal fracture** (from the Greek word for mussel, *konché*).

At its simplest, a stone striker, known as a **hammerstone,** may be used to detach a flake, or a few flakes, from one side of another stone, such as a flint nodule or a basalt pebble. The stone from which the flakes are detached is called the **core.** It may serve as a source of flakes, or it may itself be used as a **core tool.** A pebble with only a few flakes removed from one side is said to be **unifacially** worked, and is called a **chopper** (Figure 4.5). The core may then be turned over and flakes struck from the opposite side, using the surface from which the flake was detached as a **striking platform.** The ridge between the two opposing sets of flakes forms a sharp edge. Such tools are said to be **bifacially** worked, and they are sometimes distinguished from choppers as **chopping tools.**

Figure 4.5

The earliest stone tools: choppers and chopping tools.

First blow:
A flake is detached

Unifacial
Chopper

Second blow:
Another flake is detached
from the opposite side
of the core

Bifacial
Chopping Tool

recent archaeological contexts, such as in Native American sites in North America or in late Stone Age sites in Africa or Europe. That these latter-day sites represent encampments has not been questioned. Sites such as DK and FLK strongly resemble these later campsites, and they were initially accepted by their excavators as similar in nature. The bone refuse within the sites, including the skeletal remains of a wide variety of animals, large and small, was assumed to be primarily the result of hominid activities. These hominids clearly ate meat, and since the food remains were concentrated at what appeared to be a home base, the hominids very likely shared the meat among the members of their group.

In the early 1980s Lewis Binford (1981) sharply criticized the food-sharing hypothesis. Much of his criticism, and most of the extended debate that followed, has centered on the site **FLK** at Olduvai Gorge, where the Zinjanthropus fossil was found. FLK is one of the most fully studied of the living floor sites. Binford challenged the interpretation of FLK along two lines. First, according to Binford, the *integrity* of FLK as an undisturbed archaeological site had not been established, and further, the period of time during which the deposit at FLK had accumulated (the *resolution* of the site) was unknown. Therefore, the relationships among the artifacts and the bones were suspect. Second, Binford performed a statistical analysis of the animal bones based on the preliminary data included in Mary Leakey's 1971 report. Binford concluded that the assemblage of animal bones did not resemble what would be expected of a hunter's refuse, but rather that of "a hominid scavenging the kills and death sites of other predator-scavengers for abandoned anatomical parts of low food utility" (Binford 1981: 282). In effect, Binford has turned the humanlike depiction of the food-sharing hypothesis on its head, and instead describes the FLK hominids as, at best, marginal scavengers.

How Were the Olduvai and Koobi Fora Sites Formed?

Many of Binford's points were well taken, but the implications of the food-sharing hypothesis as well as the character of the Olduvai and Koobi Fora sites had been coming under close scrutiny well before the publication of Binford's critiques. The most crucial question to be resolved was whether or not these sites had been formed by the activities of hominids. Several alternative explanations were possible:

- The sites may have been created by natural forces, particularly the action of running water.
- The accumulations of artifacts and bones may have been accidental associations that built up over a very extended period of time.
- The accumulations of bones may have been created by scavenging carnivores and later utilized by hominids.
- The bone and artifact accumulations may have been created by hominids and later acted upon by scavenging carnivores.

Taphonomy is the study of the processes by which bones and artifacts finally become incorporated into a site and of the factors that modify the composition of those assemblages. **Figure 4.6** illustrates some of the processes that influenced the buildup of the combination of bones and artifacts that eventually characterized the Olduvai and Koobi Fora sites. In the 1970s a number of archaeologists began detailed taphonomic studies of these sites. From this work (Kroll and Isaac 1984; Bunn 1982; Bunn and Kroll 1986), the following points may be drawn:

- Although the sites had been moved about slightly by gently moving water and covered by waterborne deposits, none of the sites showed any geological evidence of water that moved swiftly enough to account for the observed accumulation.
- The densities of artifacts and bones are much greater in the site areas than in surrounding areas.
- The layers containing artifacts and bones are quite thin, generally less than 10 centimeters (4 in.), and many fragments of stone tools and pieces of animal bone can be fitted back together (see the Archaeology in Practice box in Chapter 5), indicating that those bones were deposited at the same time, and that the stone tools were manufactured on the spot.

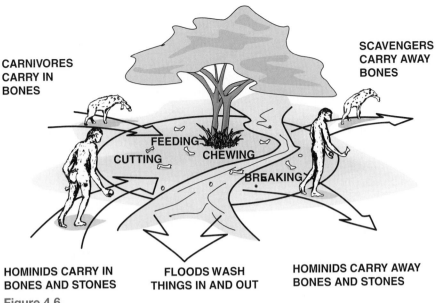

CARNIVORES CARRY IN BONES

SCAVENGERS CARRY AWAY BONES

FEEDING

CUTTING

CHEWING

BREAKING

HOMINIDS CARRY IN BONES AND STONES

FLOODS WASH THINGS IN AND OUT

HOMINIDS CARRY AWAY BONES AND STONES

Figure 4.6

A variety of processes result in the adding, rearrangement, modification, and removal of bones and artifacts at an archaeological site.
Source: Adapted from an illustration by Isaac 1983.

- The degree of weathering on the bones indicates that they were exposed on the surface for varying times up to about 10 years. There are differing opinions as to whether this represents the time during which the site was occupied (Potts 1988) or the time it took for a very brief occupation to be completely covered (Bunn and Kroll 1986), but the period of accumulation appears to have been short in geological terms.

Taken together, this evidence makes a good case that the Olduvai and Koobi Fora sites were not chance phenomena, long-term accumulations, or accidental water-laid deposits. Who, then, created them?

Who Created the Sites? The Roles of Carnivores and Hominids

As discussed in Chapter 3, scavengers such as hyenas are known to have collected accumulations of food bones in their dens. Could these sites have been primarily the product of scavenging carnivores such as hyenas? Richard Potts (1988) examined this possibility in some detail. When the assemblage of animal bones from the Olduvai sites was compared with that recovered from a known hyena den, there were some similarities, but there were also differences, notably in the proportions of the ends versus the shafts of bones. Bunn and Kroll (1986) noted that at FLK the proportion of gnawed bones is far lower than that observed in carnivore accumulations. Further, the presence of stone artifacts points unambiguously to hominid involvement; it is rather difficult to picture early hominids confronting scavenging carnivores in their den to obtain a few remaining scraps of food. The weight of the evidence, therefore, seems to point to the Olduvai and Koobi Fora sites as primarily the result of hominid activities, and today most investigators accept this interpretation.

If hominids carried the animal bones (and, presumably, the surrounding meat and/or marrow) into the sites, how did they obtain them? There is clear-cut evidence that both hominids and carnivores acted on the bone assemblage. The initial assumption, underlying the food-sharing hypothesis, was that hominids hunted the animals, or at least most of them. Binford's assertion, on the contrary, was that carnivores killed the animals and hominids merely collected the scavenged remnants. The implications of these opposing interpretations were in marked contrast:

- If hominids were the primary hunters, large portions of meat were being brought to the sites—too much for a single meal, but enough to be shared among the other members of the social group.

- If, on the other hand, only the meat-stripped remnants of carnivore kills were being carried in by the hominids, all that would be available would be some scraps of meat and the marrow that could be obtained by cracking open the long bones—enough to feed a single individual. There would be no food sharing.

Does the truth lie at either of these extremes, or somewhere between? Differences of opinion are almost as numerous as there are scholars in the field. Lewis Binford still holds to his interpretation based primarily on the published data. Other workers have extended the analyses of the Olduvai and Koobi Fora animal bones. These more detailed studies include a complete analysis of the fauna from FLK by H. T. Bunn as well as studies by several workers, including Bunn, R. Potts, and P. Shipman, of **butchery marks** appearing on the bones. These butchery studies have provided the primary evidence for the relative roles of hominids and carnivores.

Cut Marks on Bone: Butchery at Olduvai and Koobi Fora

When hunters or herders skin an animal for its pelt, dismember it, or remove meat for food, cuts and scrapes are left on the bones. Bone may be intentionally broken too, most often for the removal of marrow. Archaeologists have long been aware that cut marks on bones and the way bones are fragmented can yield clues to the activities that produced the bone assemblage.

In addition to butchery there are, of course, other sources for the marks found on bone surfaces, and sometimes those marks can be quite difficult to distinguish from cuts. Such marks include certain natural features

of the bone, marks left by rootlets on the bone surface, scratches caused by trampling on the bone, and marks left during the course of excavation. Of particular interest are the tooth marks left behind when carnivores gnaw on bones.

Henry Bunn (1983) examined the animal bones from FLK (and some roughly contemporary sites at Olduvai and Koobi Fora), relying for the most part on observations at low magnifications. He observed that several hundred of the bones bore cut marks on their surfaces. A methodologically different approach had been taken by Richard Potts and Pat Shipman (1981), who chose to study a sample of about 20 cut-marked bones from several Olduvai sites using the scanning electron microscope (SEM). Bones were also experimentally cut and scored in a variety of ways, and the results documented with the SEM. Their goal was to establish a set of criteria for unambiguously identifying cut marks (**Figure 4.7 and Figure 4.8**). Shipman (1986) has since followed up on this work with an SEM study of about 200 bones from Olduvai with cutlike markings. Shipman's criteria for accepting a mark as a stone tool cut are considerably more conservative than those of Bunn.

Not too surprisingly, Bunn, Shipman, and Potts reached some quite different conclusions about the meaning of the Olduvai bones. All these investigators, however, agree

Figure 4.7

Cut-marked bone.

that many of the bones show unambiguous cut marks from stone tools as well as numerous tooth marks from carnivore gnawing. In several cases tooth marks and cut marks overlap—sometimes the tooth marks came after the cuts; somewhat more frequently, the tooth marks were there first.

Were these early hominids hunters, or did they scavenge the meat brought down by other carnivores? It is clear that both carnivores and hominids had access to the bones. Sometimes the carnivores had them first; at other times carnivores chewed the bones after the hominids left them. Unfortunately, the cut-mark evidence has been ambiguous, and it has been interpreted in diametrically opposing ways.

Bunn and Kroll (1986) emphasize the frequent cut marks they found on the shafts of meaty bones, as well as the presence of cuts around the ends of bones. The marks near the ends of bones, they argue, indicate that the bones were cut apart (presumably for transport away from a carcass), and that the cuts on the bone shafts indicate that substantial portions of meat were available on the bones. This evidence implies that the hominids had access to the meat before it had been consumed by other carnivores, and therefore the early hominids were either hunters or they scavenged meat so aggressively that they drove away other animals before they had an opportunity to eat their kill (Bunn 1991). Shipman (1986), on the other hand, argues that the proportion of cuts near the ends of bones is too low to indicate the regular disarticulation of the limb bones. She suggests instead that bones were largely free of meat when they were obtained—that is, the bones were scavenged.

Potts (1988) takes an intermediate position. He argues that hominids scavenged from carnivores' kills at a fairly early stage, while there was still substantial meat available. Potts (1988: 202; 218) points out that not all the marrow-bearing bone was smashed to obtain the last bit of nourishment and enough food was left to attract carnivores back to the bones.

While the cut marks and tooth marks on bones have provided some intriguing evidence, how this evidence can be applied to the hunting-versus-scavenging controversy remains to be resolved. It is clear that hominids had begun to eat meat; what is less clear is how it was obtained and just how much meat was available. The assumption that these early hominids were either hunters or marginal scavengers is probably an oversimplification. They may have both hunted and scavenged as the opportunity presented itself, or they may have scavenged aggressively enough to obtain carcasses with a substantial amount of meat. The disentangling of these complex possibilities has proved extremely difficult.

Explaining the Sites: Alternative Hypotheses

Regardless of how they were obtained, animal carcasses appear to have been transported by hominids to limited locations, where they were further processed. Why were certain locations chosen? It is difficult to find much in the setting of the archaeological sites that sets them apart from the surrounding area. One possibility is that these locations represented shady spots or even groups of trees into which the hominids could climb for protection from competing carnivores (Isaac 1983). Still, dangerous carnivores would likely be attracted to the accumulations of bone in such areas.

Richard Potts (1984) has suggested instead that the availability of stone for the making of tools determined the site locations.

Figure 4.8
Bone gnawed by a carnivore.

Suitable stone would have been difficult to transport; instead, according to his hypothesis, it would have been cached at various locations on the landscape. The carcasses, however acquired, would then be brought to the caches for processing. This activity would be carried out as expediently as possible, and the site would be abandoned before competing carnivores put in their appearance. Potts's hypothesis accounts for the overlapping of tooth and cut marks, and it also helps explain the occurrence of the bones of many other animals surrounding the main skeleton at the so-called butchery sites. According to Potts's scenario, the discovery of the large carcass would have led the hominids to bring the needed stone tools to the location. These tools were then left there, and other animals were gathered to the spot for butchery. The **stone cache hypothesis** has been criticized as crediting these hominids with an unlikely degree of foresight and planning (Binford 1985). Potts (1988) has countered that it is merely a matter of remembering where the caches of stone are.

 ## Successful Scavengers?

The interpretation of the animal bone data offered by Bunn and Kroll suggests that early sites were indeed created by hominids that hunted and obtained substantial amounts of meat—a view supportive of the food-sharing hypothesis. Binford's and Shipman's views suggest that meat was obtained from scavenged carnivore kills. Some archaeologists have seen scavenging as marginal activity, unlikely to provide the abundance of food resources that might have encouraged food sharing. Recent studies, however, have shown that under certain conditions natural mortality can provide scavengers with large amounts of meat.

Robert Blumenschine (1986) has carried out extensive studies of the activities of scavengers in the modern Serengeti and Ngorongoro. His work has made clear that an abundance of scavenging opportunities can be found in the woodlands bordering lakes and streams, the kinds of environments in which the Olduvai and Koobi Fora sites were located. Food resources vary depending on the time of year. During the dry season, starva-

tion leaves numerous carcasses accessible to scavengers. Lions kill large animals, mostly during the dry season, and sometimes abandon their carcasses for extended periods of time. These resources would have been available to early hominids, but at some risk on the open plain. A safer resource, available all year round, would have been the carcasses of mid-sized animals that leopards frequently store in trees, where they are hidden from competing scavengers such as hyenas and vultures. As pointed out by Blumenschine and Cavallo (1992), hominids could have exploited these opportunities, filling out their normally vegetarian diets with meat and marrow during the dry season, when suitable plants were less available. By beating out competitors, they might well have carved out a niche that could provide them, as scavengers, with sufficient surplus to make food sharing possible.

Case Study
The Interpretation of Early Hominid Behavior: The DK Controversy

In 1962 Mary Leakey undertook the excavation of the site **DK** (the *K* stands for *Korongo*, meaning "gully" in Swahili) in Bed I of Olduvai Gorge. The site lies below a volcanic tuff dated to 1.75 million years ago, and rests on a layer of lava. DK contains numerous stone artifacts, mostly of basalt, plus a wide variety of animal bones. Stone artifacts and bones were found throughout the deposit.

A unique feature at DK, however, sets it apart from all the other very ancient sites. As reported by Mary Leakey (1971), a rough circle of blocks of basalt about 4 meters (13 ft.) in diameter lay on the old soil surface **(Figure 4.9)**. Most of these stones were 10 to 15 centimeters (4 to 6 in.) in diameter, and some of the stones were piled in heaps about 30 centimeters (12 in.) in height. Some stone was also scattered within the circle. The circle, in fact, was not immediately recognized, and a portion of it was destroyed before the excavators realized what it was. The positions of the removed stones had all been previously recorded, however, so the plan of the entire circle could be restored.

Mary Leakey suggested that the piles of stone at DK may have anchored wooden poles or branches to form a crude shelter or windbreak. The circle was very reminiscent of features commonly

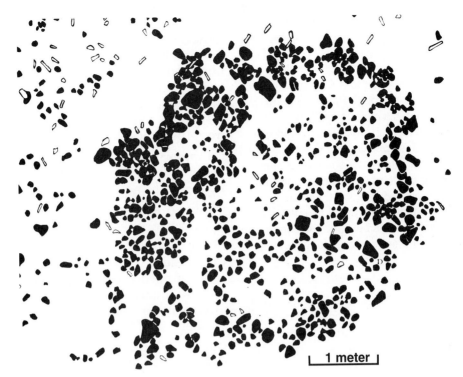

Figure 4.9

The circle of basalt stones at DK, Olduvai Gorge.
Source: After M. Leakey 1971, Figure 7.

found in sites of much later periods, and, as illustrated in the Olduvai site report, the present-day Okombambi people of Namibia build branch and grass shelters held down by a ring of stones at the base. If the DK circle had been found in a late Stone Age site, its acceptance as an architectural feature would likely be unquestioned.

The Reinterpretation of DK   Today, few archaeologists accept the DK circle as representing an ancient structure. The controversy surrounding the site, however, serves to illustrate the difficulty of interpreting the behavior of the earliest hominids, and how greatly a scientist's preconceptions can influence his or her interpretation of what is observed. Lewis Binford (1981: 254), in particular, has vigorously challenged Mary Leakey's interpretation of DK on two grounds. First, Binford questions whether DK, among other sites, can realistically be considered a living floor. The designation "living floor" implies a relatively undisturbed site including the remains from a brief, well-defined period of occupation. Binford argues that the deposits at DK probably built up over a long period of time. Binford's principal evidence for this

contention is the large number of crocodile teeth found in the site. DK was located on a lake margin. The teeth were gradually shed by the crocodiles living in the lake; a long period of time must have passed for the more than 4,600 teeth found at DK to have accumulated. Binford concludes, therefore, that the interpretation of DK as a living floor cannot be supported by the evidence. Second, Binford argues that the interpretation of the stone circle as human-constructed was influenced by the excavator's acceptance of the DK deposit as primarily the product of human activity. The South African windbreaks that had been offered as parallels were created by modern humans, not early members of the genus *Homo* who lived nearly 2 million years ago. It is problematic to project the behavior of modern humans onto *Homo habilis,* especially since *H. habilis* lacked fire. Fire, which can be used for warmth, protection from predators, and the preparation of food, is one of the principle features of modern human campsites. Without fire for protection, the concentration of food in a home base would have been very attractive to predators; it might have been a very dangerous place indeed for early humans.

Binford offers no alternative interpretation of the circle, which he concedes is enigmatic. One alternative, suggested by Richard Potts (1984: 345), is that the stones were thrust up from the underlying lava layer by the action of tree roots. This possibility is yet to be investigated. Although Binford had no alternative explanations, his critique has been strongly influential. While archaeologists remain sharply divided about his specific conclusions, they generally agree that the interpretation of early sites must include a broad range of alternatives, and that any hypotheses put forward must be rigorously tested against the evidence. Moreover, we cannot assume that ancient hominids behaved the same way as anatomically modern humans do.

 ## Conclusion

Although archaeologists may disagree on the interpretation of the very early archaeological sites, the archaeology of early humans has revealed several important aspects of the behavior of early members of the genus *Homo*. It is clear that early humans made and used stone tools. One way these early stone tools were used was to remove meat from animal carcasses. This use demonstrates that meat played a role in the diet of these early humans. Finally, it is clear that the behavior of these early humans differed from the behavior of both modern humans and nonhuman primates such as chimpanzees. It is only through detailed archaeological investigations that we can begin to reconstruct the behavior of the ancient hominids.

 ## Glossary

Base camps. Areas occupied by a human group for some time, in which a variety of domestic activities took place, such as the preparation, distribution, and consumption of food and the manufacture and use of artifacts such as stone tools. Later base camps commonly show indications of some form of shelter and the use of fire in hearths.

Bifacial flaking. The removal of flakes alternately from both sides of a stone core (or larger flake) to form an artifact worked on both sides.

Butchery marks. The marks left on animal bones during the processes of skinning, carcass disarticulation, and meat removal.

Butchery sites. Sites where meat is removed from the bones of one or more animals. The animal may have been either hunted or scavenged. These sites are marked by the bones of one or more animals plus cutting, chopping, and cleaving tools used to disarticulate the carcass and to remove meat from the bones.

Chopper. Pebble tool with only a few flakes removed from one side.

Chopping tools. Pebble tools with flakes removed alternately from two sides. The ridge between the two opposing sets of flakes forms a sharp edge.

Conchoidal fracture. Flint fracture along a cone, or portion of a cone, radiating from the point of impact. Concentric ripple marks usually form so that the surface resembles a seashell.

Core. A stone from which flakes are detached. Either the core itself or the flakes removed may be used as tools.

Core tool. A tool shaped by removing a series of flakes from a stone core.

Discoids. Oldowan stone tool types made by removing flakes from flattened pebbles.

DK. An early hominid archaeological site found in 1962 in Lower Bed I of Olduvai Gorge by Mary Leakey. DK dates to greater than 1.75 million years ago. It contains an enigmatic and controversial circle of stones, which has variously been interpreted as the remains of a shelter and as the result of natural phenomena.

Flint nodules. Rounded lumps of flint (a very fine-grained form of silica) originally deposited by silica-containing groundwater into hollows in limestone bedrock. Erosion commonly leaves deposits of flint nodules in the beds of streams, where they form a convenient source of flint for toolmaking.

FLK. An early hominid archaeological site in Lower Bed I of Olduvai Gorge and dating to about 1.75 million years ago. FLK is the site where the *Zinjanthropus* fossil was found by Mary Leakey in 1959. FLK is one of the most intensively studied of the early Olduvai archaeological sites, and it has figured prominently in the debate concerning hunting versus scavenging by early hominids.

Food-sharing hypothesis. Hypothesis proposed by Glynn Isaac to account for the function of the early hominid sites at Olduvai Gorge and Koobi Fora. According to the food-sharing hypothesis, sites such as FLK served as home bases, to which hunter-scavengers (presumably males) brought meat and to which other group members (presumably females) brought gathered plant foods and small game. At the home base these foods were shared and redistributed among the group. The food-sharing hypothesis makes the organization of early hominid groups seem very much like that of later humans.

Hammerstone. A stone used as a striker to remove flakes from a stone core.

Kill sites. Archaeological sites where an animal or animals were hunted and killed. These sites are usually marked by the bones of one or more animals plus weapons such as spear points.

Lithic industry. A set of artifacts, primarily tools, made from stone.

Living floors. Ground surfaces on which an assemblage of artifacts and (frequently) food remains is found. The term implies a relatively undisturbed site including the remains from a brief, well-defined period of occupation.

Oldowan. The very early stone industry, first described by Mary Leakey, originally found in the archaeological sites in Bed I at Olduvai Gorge but since found elsewhere in Africa. The characteristic artifacts of the Oldowan are choppers and chopping tools made from pebbles. Other artifact forms present include flakes, cores, polyhedrons, scrapers, spheroids, and discoids.

Planes of cleavage. Planes along which rocks or minerals split easily.

Polyhedrons. Oldowan stone tool types consisting of pebbles that have been flaked in several directions to form intersecting edges.

Scrapers. Stone tool types shaped to include an edge prepared so that the implements would be suitable for scraping activities (although these artifacts may not have functioned in this way). In the Oldowan, the tools classed by Mary Leakey as scrapers grade into the polyhedrons.

Spheroids. Oldowan stone tool types consisting of a core from which numerous flakes have been removed from the entire surface, forming a roughly spherical shape.

Stone cache hypothesis. Hypothesis proposed by Richard Potts as an alternative explanation for the function of the early hominid sites at Olduvai Gorge and Koobi Fora. According to this hypothesis, sites such as FLK were simply places where caches of stone tools were stored. Animals were taken to these places and quickly butchered; then the site was abandoned before competing carnivores were attracted to the spot.

Striking platform. The point near the edge of a stone core that is struck to remove a flake.

Tabular chert. A fine-grained silica (suitable for making into stone tools) that is deposited between the layers of limestone bedrock. Tabular chert usually must be obtained by digging or quarrying.

Taphonomy. The study of the processes by which bones and artifacts finally become incorporated into a site and of the factors that modify the composition of those assemblages.

Unifacial flaking. The preparation of a stone artifact by the removal of flakes from only one side of a stone core (or larger flake).

Further Reading

Blumenschine, R. J., and J. A. Cavallo
     1992. Scavenging and Human Evolution. *Scientific American* 267 (4): 90–96.
     The authors argue that early hominids may have succeeded as efficient scavengers rather than as hunters.

Isaac, G. L.
     1978. The Food-sharing Behavior of Protohuman Hominids. *Scientific American* 238 (4): 90–106.
     A clear description of Isaac's food-sharing hypothesis as it was originally formulated. In later years Isaac accepted that this version of the hypothesis made early hominids seem too much like modern humans.

Potts, R.
     1984. Home Bases and Early Hominids. *American Scientist* 72: 338–347.

Potts's criticism of the interpretation of the early Olduvai and Koobi Fora sites as home bases, and his formulation of his stone cache hypothesis.

Toth, Nicholas
1987. The First Technology. *Scientific American* 256 (4): 112–121.

A description of the experimental replication and use of Oldowan-type stone tools in an effort to understand the nature and function of the Olduvai and Koobi Fora stone tool assemblages.

 Other Bibliography

Binford, L. R.
1981. *Bones, Ancient Men and Modern Myths.* New York: Academic Press.
1985. Human Ancestors: Changing Views of Their Behavior. *Journal of Anthropological Archaeology* 1: 5–31.

Blumenschine, R.
1986. *Early Hominid Scavenging Opportunities.* Oxford: British Archaeological Reports, International Series 283.

Bunn, H. T.
1982. *Meat-eating and Human Evolution: Studies on the Diet and Subsistence Patterns of Plio-Pleistocene Hominids in East Africa.* Ph.D. Dissertation. Department of Anthropology, University of California, Berkeley.
1983. Evidence on the Diet and Subsistence Patterns of Plio-Pleistocene Hominids at Koobi Fora, Kenya, and Olduvai Gorge, Tanzania. In *Animals and Archaeology: I. Hunters and Their Prey,* edited by J. Clutton-Brock and C. Grigson, pp. 21–30. Oxford: British Archaeological Reports, International Series 163.
1991. A Taphonomic Perspective on the Archaeology of Human Origins. *Annual Review of Anthropology* 20: 433–467.

Bunn, H. T., and E. M. Kroll
1986. Systematic Butchery by Plio-Pleistocene Hominids at Olduvai Gorge, Tanzania. *Current Anthropology* 27: 431–452.

Isaac, G. L.
1983. Bones in Contention: Competing Explanations for the Juxtaposition of Early Pleistocene Artifacts and Faunal Remains. In *Animals and Archaeology: I. Hunters and Their Prey,* edited by J. Clutton-Brock and C. Grigson, pp. 3–19. Oxford: British Archaeological Reports, International Series 163.

Keeley, L., and N. Toth
1981. Microwear Polishes on Early Stone Tools from Koobi Fora, Kenya. *Nature* 293: 464–465.

Kroll, E., and G. Isaac
1984. Configurations of Artifacts and Bones at Early Pleistocene Sites in East Africa. In *Intrasite Spatial Analysis in Archaeology,* edited by H. J. Hietala, pp. 4–31. Cambridge: Cambridge University Press.

Leakey, M. D.
1971. *Olduvai Gorge,* vol. 3. Cambridge: Cambridge University Press.

Potts, R.
1988. *Early Hominid Activities at Olduvai.* New York: Aldine de Gruyter.

Potts, R., and P. Shipman
1981. Cutmarks Made by Stone Tools on Bones from Olduvai Gorge, Tanzania. *Nature* 291: 577–580.

Shipman, P.
1986. Scavenging or Hunting in Early Hominids: Theoretical Framework and Tests. *American Anthropologist* 88: 27–43.

Part III

What Were Archaic Humans Like, and How Did Their Society Differ from Our Own?

Over 1 million years ago human ancestors began to move out of Africa and into the subtropical and temperate regions of the Old World, including East Asia, Southeast Asia, the Near East, and Europe. *Homo erectus,* a human ancestor that initially appeared in Africa about 1.8 million years ago, was the first ancient human to migrate widely outside Africa. While fossils of *Homo erectus* are rare, many early archaeological sites have been found in Asia, North Africa, the Middle East, and Europe (Chapters 5 and 6).

These sites allow us to trace the spread of humans out of Africa and to examine the role that fire played in this expansion. Stone tools allow us to study the technological capacities of these early humans, and butchered animal bones can shed light on the ways they made a living. Were these early humans big-game hunters, or did they survive by scavenging, or by some combination of scavenging and hunting? Sites such as Torralba and Ambrona in Spain have traditionally been seen as evidence for large-mammal hunting by *Homo erectus,* with important implications for archaic humans' use of language, technological sophistication, and social cooperation. Modern reanalyses of these sites have challenged traditional ideas about "man the hunter."

In Chapter 7, we examine the most intriguing and enigmatic of all archaic humans, the Neanderthals. The chapter begins with a history of the discovery of Neanderthal fossils. In the remainder of the chapter we focus on the role that archaeology can play in studying Neanderthal behavior, including Neanderthal burials and the question of whether the Neanderthals were hunters or scavengers.

Chapter 5

Homo erectus and the Lower Paleolithic in Africa and the Near East

Introduction

About 1.6 million years ago a new form of stone tool appeared in Africa alongside the simple choppers that typified the Oldowan stone industry. The Oldowan choppers had required little more than a moment's thought and a few blows from a hammerstone to produce the sharp cutting edge needed to butcher an animal. The new tool, the **handaxe,** was very different (Wynn 1995). A handaxe is a large stone tool, usually oval, with a flattened cross section (see Figure 5.1a). The tool was made by removing a series of flakes from both sides of a stone core to produce a length of relatively straight cutting edge. Usually, one end was relatively pointed; the other, more rounded so that it could be held in the hand. Early archaeologists called these tools handaxes, because they presumed that the tools were unhafted hacking implements held in the hand.

The first truly standardized tool form, the handaxe was the result of a definite, preconceived idea in the mind of its maker. Planning and considerable stoneworking skill were required to make a handaxe. Most important, the making of handaxes became a tradition, passed from maker to maker, down through the millennia. With the appearance of the handaxe, culture—the transmission of shared ideas from generation to generation—becomes evident as a dominant force in the shaping of human development.

The Acheulian Industry

The handaxe is the hallmark of the **Acheulian industry** (Clark 1994), named after the **type site** at Saint-Acheul, a suburb of Amiens in northern France, where the industry was first described. At first, handaxes were irregular and crudely made. Over the many thousands of years during which they were made, they gradually became thin, symmetrical, and skillfully crafted, and they were made in a wide variety of forms. At the start of the Acheulian, other large forms usually accompanied the handaxes. Some typical forms, such as **trihedral picks** and **cleavers,** are shown in **Figure 5.1.** Tool types characteristic of the Oldowan persisted, such as choppers, spheroids, and polyhedrons. The true function of the Acheulian handaxe is not really known; it may have served as a weapon, a chopper, or a digging tool. When archaeologists have looked closely, they have found that Acheulian sites contain numerous flakes along with the large tools. Flakes would have been produced during tool manufacture, but would also have served as very effective cutting implements in themselves.

The Acheulian industry was to be one of the longest-lasting and one of the most geographically widespread technological traditions in all of prehistory. It persisted for almost 1.5 million years, giving way to new forms of stone tools only within the last 200,000 years. Today archaeologists have found Acheulian stone artifacts throughout all of Africa, most of western Europe, and much of western Asia as well.

The Makers of the Acheulian Industry

Who created the Acheulian industry? While *Homo habilis (rudolfensis)* seems to have been responsible for the artifacts of the Oldowan industry (Chapter 4), the Acheulian handaxe is associated with the appearance of a new, more advanced hominid form, *Homo erectus.* *Homo erectus* was the immediate successor to *Homo habilis* (and related forms). The oldest known representative of *Homo erectus* comes from East Turkana and is approximately 1.8 million years old (Rightmire 1990). The earliest Acheulian assemblage known so far was found at the base of the deposits at **Konso-Gardula** in Ethiopia, dated to 1.6 million years ago. A mandible attributed to *Homo erectus* has recently been found at Konso-Gardula in deposits dated to about 1.4 million years ago.

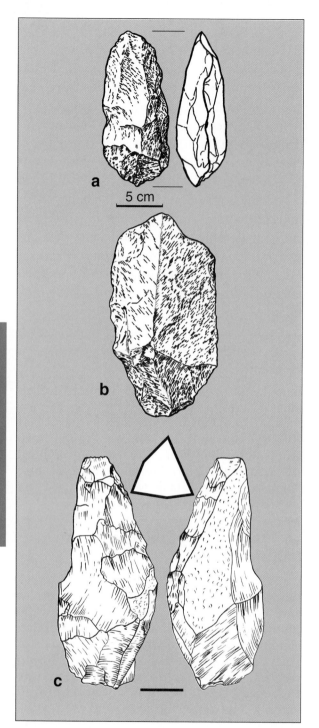

Figure 5.1

(a) Acheulian handaxe (basalt) from Olduvai Gorge; (b) Acheulian cleaver (quartzite) from MNK, Olduvai Gorge; (c) trihedral pick (basalt) from 'Ubeidiya, Israel.

The fossils are closely associated with a rich stone tool assemblage belonging to the Acheulian industry, suggesting that *H. erectus* may have made them (Asfaw et al. 1992).

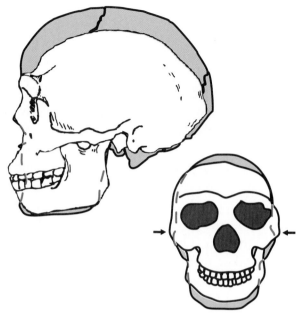

Figure 5.2

Skull shape of Homo erectus *(front) compared with* Homo sapiens *(rear). Arrows point to location of greatest breadth of* Homo erectus *skull.*

Homo erectus supplanted the earlier forms of hominids, and, as we will discuss in the next chapter, soon expanded out of Africa into Europe and Asia. The Acheulian industry spread along with *Homo erectus.*

Currently included under the name *Homo erectus* is a somewhat variable group of fossils that have been found in Africa, Indonesia, and China. Related fossils have also been found in Europe. Most of the distinguishing characteristics of *Homo erectus* are in the skull. *Homo erectus* possessed a brain considerably smaller than that of modern humans, accounting for many of the differences in the shape of the skull. The top of the thick-boned skull is flattened rather than rounded. A heavy bar of bone surmounts the eye sockets; behind the orbits of the eyes the skull is markedly narrower (constricted) compared with that of modern humans **(Figure 5.2)**. When viewed from behind, the widest part of the skull of *Homo erectus* is set much lower than in modern humans, again due to the smaller brain size. From the rear, the skull appears angular, roughly pentagonal in shape, with a distinct ridge at the top of the skull. The cranial capacity ranges from 650 to 1,250 milliliters, compared with an average of 1,350 milliliters for modern humans. The

Experimental Archaeology: How Were Stone Tools Made and Used?

For almost the entirety of human existence, stone has been the primary raw material for the manufacture of weapons and tools. Before the discovery of metallurgy, much of the history of technology consisted of the development of new ways to shape and use stone. Archaeologists, therefore, have a great interest in understanding these processes. Today, however, with only rare exceptions, the knapping, or flaking, of stone to produce useful objects has become a lost art.

Fortunately, the art was not completely unknown. In the late nineteenth century, the English antiquarian John Evans was interested in trying to replicate the handaxes he had seen coming from archaeological sites. At that time, at Brandon in eastern England, workers were still mining and knapping flint (Figure 5.3). They were shaping the flints into gunflints—small, square fragments of flint that were fixed into the mechanism of flintlock pistols and muskets. When the trigger was pulled, the flint struck steel, creating a shower of sparks to ignite the gunpowder. Flintlock guns were first invented in the seventeenth century, and they were the principal weapon of the American Revolution. Gunflints, often of English flint, are one of the common artifacts found in American Revolutionary War sites. In some places flintlocks continued in use through the nineteenth and even into the twentieth century.

Evans observed and described the gunflint workers' techniques, and he applied what he observed to an attempt to replicate ancient stone tools. Over the years since Evans's time, a number of archaeologists have concentrated on replicating the techniques by which stone tools were made. Sometimes ethnographic sources have provided some clues. Although stone tools had long since ceased to be made in Europe and the Americas, some Pacific Islanders still made and used stone implements though the eighteenth and nineteenth centuries. A few rare groups even continued to make them in the twentieth century. Nicholas Toth and his co-workers (Toth et al. 1992) were able to observe a group of New Guinea highlanders making and using stone axes for woodcutting, using techniques much like those that must have been used throughout the Old and New Stone Ages (Figure 5.4).

More often, the experiments are a matter of guessing the most likely practical technique. The results of these trials are then compared with the ancient artifacts to see how closely the finished products match in form, sequence of flake removal, and details of flake characteristics. Sometimes the flakes removed during the manufacture of an ancient stone tool can be found and fitted back together. This provides another source of evidence for the sequence of flake removal that the experimenter needs to duplicate. If the match is very close, the experimental

Figure 5.3

Nineteenth-century flint workers at Brandon, England, making flints for use in firearms. Such flints were used to create the spark that fired a flintlock musket or pistol.

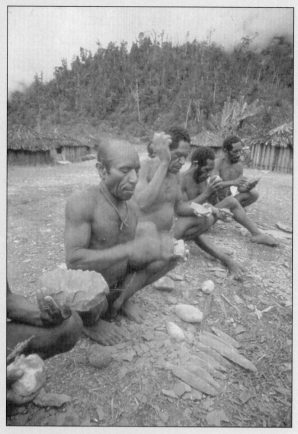

Figure 5.4

New Guinea highlanders making stone axes.

technique may be much like that used in the past.

In recent years the **refitting** of artifacts, particularly lithics, has become an increasingly important archeological technique (Figure 5.5). Although the technique is simple, it is not easy. Reassembling a lithic jigsaw puzzle demands the extensive examination and painstaking manipulation of large assemblages of artifacts. Artifact refitting can yield information about past behavior that goes well beyond the reconstruction of flint-knapping techniques. Reassembling the trimming flakes onto a stone core, for instance, illustrates the sequence of flake removal from the core. If a core and its trimming flakes are all found in a single area of the site, that area may represent the workshop area where a stone tool was made. (Depending on what is found, it might also represent an area in which waste materials were dumped.) Sometimes cores and flakes and finished tools that can be refitted, or **conjoined,** are found in separate areas of a site. This might represent the separation of areas of stone tool manufacture and use, or the circulation or exchange of artifacts within an encampment. Artifact refitting can also yield very valuable information about the processes by which a site was formed. Broad scatters of conjoinable artifacts, especially if they are distributed through several vertical layers, are strong evidence that the site was disturbed after it was originally deposited. Conversely, providing that site stratigraphy is clear and unambiguous, conjoinable artifacts spanning two or more artifact scatters are a strong indication that the scatters were formed contemporaneously.

Archaeologist Nicholas Toth has performed some interesting experiments in attempting to duplicate and use some of the characteristic Oldowan and early Acheulian stone tools found in the earliest African sites (Toth 1987). Toth made choppers and chopping tools as well as Acheulian-like handaxes. He noted that the ancient tools were asymmetrical in the way that the flakes were removed from the core. This is a result of which hand held the core and which hand held the hammerstone. Comparing these tools with his experiments, Toth determined that the ancient African hominids were predominantly right-handed, just as people are today.

Toth then used these tools, as well as the flakes produced in making them, to butcher a wide variety of animals ranging from goats and sheep through wildebeests, up to the butchery of an elephant. He found that simple, unretouched flakes were most effective for cutting up a large animal carcass. Toth suggested that too much emphasis has been placed on core tools, and that the importance of simple flakes in these early sites must be taken into account. Choppers do serve well, however, for breaking up bones, and Toth found that an Acheulian handaxe was effective in disarticulating the joints of very large animals (Figure 5.6).

Experiments like these can show that certain types of stone implements were usable for a variety of butchery tasks, but they do not prove that the ancient tools were actually used in these ways. Further evidence can come from the marks left by tools on the ancient bones, as was discussed in Chapter 4. The use of stone tools for various tasks may also leave distinctive wear patterns on the tool itself. These patterns can sometimes tell how, and on what material, a tool was used. Some specialists concentrate on experiments designed to determine the distinctive patterns of microscopic chipping, scratches, and polish left on the edges and surfaces of flint tools when the tools are used to cut meat, work wood, dig in the earth, and so on. They can then apply those observations to prehistoric artifacts, and sometimes it has been possible to determine how the ancient tools were used. Although most of the African Oldowan and Acheulian tools were made of basalt, which is too coarse-grained for such analysis, a few finer-grained tools did show wear consistent with cutting meat, working wood, and cutting vegetation (Toth 1987).

The refittable fragments of a stone core are plotted on a site plan to illustrate their horizontal distribution. Lines connect the flakes to the core from which they were struck.

A similar cross-section diagram might be constructed to show the vertical distribution of refittable artifacts.

Plan (in meters)

Figure 5.5
The technique of artifact refitting.

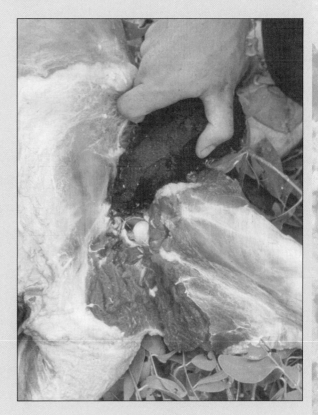

Figure 5.6
Nicholas Toth butchering a large game animal using a handaxe he replicated. The animal died of natural causes.

face projects forward, and the heavy lower jaw lacks a chin. The teeth of *Homo erectus* are larger than those of modern humans.

Nariokotome: The Turkana Boy

Until recently, little was known of the stance, stature, or appearance of early *Homo erectus* in Africa. Most of the fossil finds were skull fragments, with only a few bones from below the neck to provide clues. Then, in the summer of 1984, a group of investigators led by Richard Leakey, working in a deposit approximately 1.6 million years old at **Nariokotome III** near Lake Turkana, Kenya, uncovered the skeleton of a young boy. Soon nicknamed the Turkana Boy, it proved to be the most complete specimen of *Homo erectus*[1] yet discovered (Walker and Leakey 1993). The skeleton lacked only its hands and feet **(Figure 5.7)**.

The teeth and limb bones indicate that the boy was approximately 11 years old. He died among the reeds growing in the still, shallow water at the banks of a lake or slow-moving river. Little evidence survives to indicate how he died; nothing on the bones suggests that he was attacked by an animal. No tools or other artifacts were found with the body. The only clue to possible ill health was some resorption of the jawbone around his teeth, the result of periodontal infection. Without modern antibiotics, infections of this kind can lead to very serious consequences, even death. Usually, when the earliest humans died, their bodies fell prey to the same fate as those of any other animal, to be consumed by scavengers, the bones destroyed or scattered far and wide. The circumstances of the Turkana Boy's death must have resulted in the rapid burial of the body, hiding it from the view of scavengers. The body lay facedown in the water, where it was soon covered with silt. Apart from some trampling and water transport of the bones, the skeleton suffered little disturbance until very recently—when the bones were discovered, a large tree was growing among them.

Figure 5.7

*The Turkana Boy—Nariokotome III—*Homo ergaster *(originally* H. erectus).

---

[1]Some workers now consider the Nariokotome find to be sufficiently different from the Asian *Homo erectus* finds (to be described in Chapter 6) to warrant assigning it to a separate species, **Homo ergaster,** which may be more directly ancestral to modern humans than the Asian fossils.

Typical of *Homo erectus*, the Turkana Boy possessed a low, sloping skull without a forehead, which housed a brain about two-thirds the size of a modern human's brain. The post-cranial (body) skeleton, however, although differing in some details, was much like that of modern humans. Had the boy grown to be an adult, he would have been quite tall, perhaps 180 centimeters (6 ft.) in height. Comparison of this complete skeleton with the other, more isolated, finds of *Homo erectus* limb bones from Africa and Asia shows that his height was not atypical—as a group *Homo erectus* was much taller than the preceding *Homo habilis* (around 150 centimeters [5 ft.] in height). The Turkana Boy's tall and slender body type, which maximizes the ratio of heat-radiating surface to body bulk, would have been well adapted to coping with the heat of the tropics. Some modern African peoples have similar body builds. Some of the details of the boy's pelvis and femurs (thigh bones) retain some traits characteristic of earlier hominids, but the overall configuration suggests that he was a very effective walker and runner, perhaps better at those activities than modern humans. Physically, *Homo erectus* was well equipped to be an effective hunter, gatherer, or active scavenger.

The Control of Fire

Some scant, but tantalizing, evidence suggests that *Homo erectus* may have achieved an important technological breakthrough even before expanding out of Africa. The control of fire (although not necessarily the ability to create it) would have greatly improved human chances to thrive and expand in the harsher, colder world north of sub-Saharan Africa.

The recognition of the earliest use of fire in the archaeological record is not easy. The remnants of burning—charcoal, ashes, burned bones, or burned and baked soil—may be found, but may be the result of natural fires, which occurred frequently. The least ambiguous evidence for the control of fire is a constructed hearth, but hearths do not appear until relatively late in the archaeological record. Burned clay was found at the Oldowan site of **Chesowanja,** Kenya, dated to 1.4 million years ago, in a concentration that might represent a hearth, with a skull belonging to *A. boisei*

nearby (Gowlett et al. 1981). This fire, though, might have been the result of natural causes.

Clearer evidence comes from Swartkrans Cave, South Africa, estimated to date between 1 million and 1.5 million years ago. Although no hearths have been found, one of the layers does contain evidence of fire. Of nearly 60,000 animal bones found in the layer, 270 bones, mostly of antelope, were burned (Brain and Sillen 1988; Sillen and Brain 1990). Experiments indicate that the bones were heated to the temperatures found in campfires. The only hominid found in the layer containing burned bones was *Australopithecus robustus,* but earlier deposits in the cave contain fossils of both *A. robustus* and *Homo erectus.* The burned bones were scattered through many different levels, indicating that fires were a repeated occurrence. The evidence does not indicate, though, whether the fire was used for heat, cooking, or protection from predators, or which of the hominids used the fire.

When and Why Did the Hominids Expand Out of Africa?

The movement out of Africa may predate the appearance of the Acheulian industry. The site of '**Ubeidiya,** dated to about 1.4 million years ago, lies within the Jordan Rift Valley, just south of the Sea of Galilee **(Figure 5.8)**. Geologically, the Jordan Rift Valley is a continuation of the Great Rift Valley of Africa. The conditions in the Jordan Rift Valley 1.4 million years ago were much like those in Africa. The region of the present Jordan Valley was then filled with a number of freshwater lakes, providing an environment that could support large herds of animals. With an abundance of game animals, the Jordan Valley would have been attractive to early humans. 'Ubeidiya may be the first stop of *Homo erectus* along the route out of Africa. The site was discovered by accident when the land was graded to plant a vineyard. Numerous fossil bones were uncovered, including a few tiny fragments of hominid skull. Numerous pebble tool artifacts were also found. The fauna indicated that the

---

[2]The Pleistocene geological epoch began about 1.6 million years ago and ended about 10,000 years ago. In the northern latitudes, the Pleistocene was characterized by alternating cold periods (ice ages) and warmer intervals.

Figure 5.8

The major archaeological sites discussed in this chapter. The arrow traces the initial expansion of Homo erectus *out of Africa and into the Middle East.*

site dated to the earliest part of the Pleistocene.[2] Excavated first by the Israeli archaeologist M. Stekelis and later by his student O. Bar-Yosef of the Hebrew University of Jerusalem, 'Ubeidiya has proved to be a remarkable site. 'Ubeidiya lies in a portion of the Rift Valley that has experienced marked geological shifting and folding since the archaeological layers were deposited. Today the strata at 'Ubeidiya are tilted nearly perpendicular to their original position **(Figure 5.9)**. This odd circumstance had some advantages for the excavators: A horizontal trench could expose a long series of strata.

The deposits at 'Ubeidiya indicate that people camped near the shore of a lake that occupied the Jordan Valley at the time. Fifteen layers yielded major assemblages of artifacts and animal bones. Some of the layers consist of very compact expanses of large pebbles and cobbles separated from adjacent layers by layers of silt. The bones and artifacts lie among the cobbles. The bones of many species of fish, amphibians, birds, and mammals have been found at 'Ubeidiya. The 80 or so species of mammals range in size from rodents to hippopotamuses and elephants. The large assemblage of animal bones provides the means for dating the site. The range of species present correlates well with European assemblages of known age— between 1 million and 1.4 million years ago. The many species present indicate that this is a naturally accumulated fossil assemblage rather than the remains of human hunting, although some of the large deer, bovines, and hippos appear to have been butchered and eaten by the human inhabitants of 'Ubeidiya,

Figure 5.9
Tilted strata at 'Ubeidiya.

because stone tool cut marks are visible on some of the bones.

The lowest layers at 'Ubeidiya contain stone tool assemblages resembling those of the African Oldowan, including choppers made from flint, polyhedrons, and limestone spheroids, as well as flakes. The later layers include **bifaces,** made mostly from basalt, but also of limestone and flint. These assemblages, with thick bifaces and heavy trihedral and quadrahedral (four-sided) picks, are characteristic of the early Acheulian (Bar-Yosef and Goren-Inbar 1993).

Farther north and east, **Dmanisi,** in the Caucasus of Georgia (in the former Soviet Union), is of similar age. At Dmanisi the stone industry also lacks handaxes, consisting primarily of choppers (Bar-Yosef 1994). While the very fragmentary hominid fossils from 'Ubeidiya can only be presumed to be *Homo erectus,* Dmanisi has yielded a *Homo erectus* mandible (Gabunia and Vekua 1995). Recent excavations at this site are continuing to yield fossils, including two crania dated to about 1.7 million years ago. The crania closely resemble *Homo*

ergaster specimens from Africa (Gebunia et al. 2000). These sites demonstrate that by 1.7 million years ago, *Homo erectus* had penetrated far into the Near East and Asia. Perhaps these sites represent an early wave of people, soon to be overtaken by other groups bearing the Acheulian industry. At 'Ubeidiya the chopping tools are soon joined by an early Acheulian industry much like that in Africa.

Why did *Homo erectus* expand out of Africa? At present there is no sure answer to this question, nor is it clear whether the expansion was a continuous process or consisted of several discrete episodes. Perhaps the movement was the result of the natural increase in human population and the desire of intelligent humans to see what lay beyond their boundaries. Perhaps the emigration from Africa was the result of a climatic change. About 1.8 million years ago Africa was experiencing a shift to a markedly more arid climate. Food resources would have been more limited than before, and early humans would have found themselves in increased competition with the large African predators,

Figure 5.10

Gesher Benot Ya'aqov elephant with wooden log.

the lions, leopards, and hyenas. The promise of richer food resources may have drawn early humans from their homeland into Southwest Asia and beyond.

The Later Acheulian in the Near East: Gesher Benot Ya'aqov

Handaxe-using peoples probably followed the northward route up the Rift Valley and through the extension of the rift that forms the Jordan Valley. Many later Acheulian sites have been found in the areas of Southwest Asia bordering the Mediterranean Sea, particularly Israel, Jordan, Lebanon, and Syria. Many of these sites are scatters of stone tools on the surface, but several deep Acheulian deposits have been found in the caves and rock shelters common in the mountainous regions of Israel, Lebanon, and Syria. Only a very few Acheulian sites are known in Iraq, Iran, and the Arabian Peninsula, but to some extent this is due to the limited research that has been conducted in those areas.

Somewhat later in time is the site of **Gesher Benot Ya'aqov** (meaning "Bridge of Jacob's Daughters," in Hebrew), located north of the Sea of Galilee in the Jordan Valley of Israel (see Figure 5.8). Gesher Benot Ya'aqov, although its strata have been tilted by geological movements, includes several occupations that seem relatively intact. Preserved organic remains are extremely rare in the oldest archaeological sites. Gesher Benot Ya'aqov is a unique exception. In this Lower Paleolithic site, wood, seeds, fruits, and bark are found in abundance. Potassium-argon and geomagnetic reversal data indicate that the site must date to between 240,000 and 730,000 years ago. Like 'Ubeidiya, the site represents an occupation along the shores of a lake that occupied the Jordan Valley at that time. As at 'Ubeidiya, the layers at Gesher Benot Ya'aqov have been tilted, to about a 45-degree angle. Seven archaeological occupations were found, yielding assemblages that included Acheulian basalt bifaces and cleavers. The cleavers were made using a distinctive technique first seen in Africa. The assemblage as a whole seems to have African affinities; perhaps Gesher Benot Ya'aqov was an encampment of a group of people moving up the Rift Valley from Africa.

The artifacts appear to lie in their original locations. Among these artifacts the excavators found the skull of an early straight-tusked elephant, lying bottom-side up in the deposits. The entire base of the skull had been removed. Fragments of the skull were scattered around it. Beneath the skull lay an oak log about 1 meter (3 ft.) long **(Figure 5.10)**. A large basalt core, 32 centimeters (13 in.) long, and a basalt boulder were also found beneath the skull. A number of basalt handaxes lay nearby. On the basis of the condition of the deposits, the excavators do not think it is likely that the skull came to the site by natural means. They offer the possible explanation that the elephant's skull was deliberately opened to extract its brain, a very desirable food. The log may have been used to turn the skull base-side up, and the boulder and core used to prop it up while it was being broken open (Goren-Inbar et al. 1994).

Another remarkable find at Gesher Benot Ya'aqov was a fragment of a plank of willow wood. This object, a small piece about 25 cm (10 in.) long of something originally larger, appears to have been intentionally flattened and polished on one side. If this object is what it seems, the range of Acheulian technology may have included wood and other perishable materials not often preserved in archaeological sites.

 ## Conclusion

In this chapter we have discussed the appearance of *Homo erectus* (or *H. ergaster*) in Africa. *Homo erectus'* new technologies, including the probable control of fire, facilitated the movement of early humans out of Africa. They were able to settle much of the subtropical and tropical and even some of the temperate zones of Asia. The Acheulian handaxe industry appears in Africa shortly thereafter, to become the most widespread and long-lasting prehistoric technological tradition. The earliest emigrants from Africa appear to have been users of simple choppers and chopping tools. Later, they were followed into western Asia and Europe by people who made and used handaxes. The colder climate of Europe presented a significant challenge. Just when early humans reached western Europe remains an open issue. The earliest settlement of eastern Asia and Europe will be discussed in the following chapter.

 ## Glossary

Acheulian industry. A stone tool industry characterized by bifacially worked core tools, primarily handaxes and cleavers. The Acheulian industry first appeared in Africa about 1.6 million years ago and lasted until about 200,000 years ago (and in some areas as late as 100,000 years ago). The human fossils associated with the Acheulian industry are generally *Homo erectus*, or, in Europe, transitional fossils between *Homo erectus* and very early *Homo sapiens*.

Bifaces. Tools made by removing flakes from both sides of a stone core. Acheulian handaxes and cleavers are usually bifaces.

Chesowanja. An open site located in the Rift Valley of Kenya, dated to 1.4 to 1 million years ago. The stone industry is Oldowan, including choppers and flakes. Areas of burned clay suggest that fire may have been in use. An *Australopithecus boisei* skull was found in the same formation.

Cleavers. Bifacially worked tools similar to handaxes, but with flat, hoelike edges rather than a point.

Conjoined artifacts. Artifacts that can be fitted back together.

Dmanisi. A site in the Caucasus of Georgia, dated to about 1.7 million years ago. In 1991, a *Homo erectus* mandible was found at the site. Recently, two additional crania have been found at Dmanisi that closely resemble the *Homo ergaster* specimens from Africa. The stone industry consists primarily of choppers and is lacking in handaxes.

Gesher Benot Ya'aqov. An Acheulian site in the Jordan Valley of Israel, dated roughly between 240,000 and 730,000 years ago. The site includes well-preserved organic remains (wood, seeds, fruits, and bark). An elephant skull at the site may have been manipulated with the help of a log that was found beneath it.

Handaxe. A large stone tool, usually bifacially worked and ovoid, with a flattened cross section. Handaxes are characteristic of the Acheulian industry, but they are found in later industries as well.

Homo erectus. The successor to *Homo habilis*. *Homo erectus* includes a variable group of fossils with brain sizes generally greater than those of *H. habilis* but less than those of modern humans. *Homo erectus* generally had a low, sloping forehead with a thick bar of bone over the eyes and a forward-projecting face.

Homo ergaster. Classification used by some scholars for African specimens such as the boy at Nariokotome III. These scholars, arguing that the African fossils are more closely related to later *Homo sapiens*, reserve the term *Homo erectus* for the Asian fossil humans.

Konso-Gardula. One of the very earliest Acheulian sites. Konso-Gardula, in Ethiopia, is dated to about 1.6 million years ago. A *Homo erectus* mandible was found at the site.

Nariokotome III. A site near Lake Turkana, Kenya, dating to about 1.5 million years ago.

A very nearly complete skeleton of a young *Homo erectus* (or *H. ergaster*)—Turkana Boy—was found at the site.

Refitting.   The process of piecing together the matching portions of artifacts, particularly lithics, bones, and pottery. Matches of refitted artifacts between features or between layers provide information about activity areas, site formation processes, and the degree of integrity of a site.

Trihedral picks.   Large, thick bifaces with sharp points and a triangular cross section, characteristic of the early Acheulian industry.

Type site.   The site after which an archaeological occurrence, such as a stone industry, is named.

'Ubeidiya.   A site in the Jordan Valley of Israel, dated to approximately 1.4 million years ago, with an Oldowan industry in its lowest layers and an early Acheulian industry in the later layers. 'Ubeidiya is one of the earliest archaeological sites outside Africa.

 Further Reading

Bar-Yosef, Ofer
    1994. The Lower Paleolithic of the Near East. *Journal of World Prehistory* 8: 211–265.
    An up-to-date review of the Near Eastern evidence by one of the leading scholars in the field.

Clark, J. Desmond
    1994. The Acheulian Industrial Complex in Africa and Elsewhere. In *Integrative Paths to the Past: Paleoanthropological Advances in Honor of F. Clark Howell,* edited by R. S. Corruccini and R. L. Ciochon, pp. 451–469. Englewood Cliffs, NJ: Prentice Hall.
    An excellent overall review of the Acheulian industry and the principal Acheulian sites.

Sillen, A., and C. K. Brain
    1990. Old Flame: Burned Bones Provide Evidence of an Early Human Use of Fire. *Natural History* 4: 6–10.
    A brief description of the evidence for the use of fire at Swartkrans.

Toth, Nicholas
    1987. The First Technology. *Scientific American* 256 (4): 112–121.
    A clear description of Toth's stone tool replication and butchery experiments using Oldowan- and Acheulian-like tools.

Toth, Nicholas, Desmond Clark, and Giancarlo Ligabue
    1992. The Last Stone Ax Makers. *Scientific American* 267 (1): 88–93.

A description of the making and use of stone axes by New Guinea highlanders using techniques much like those of the Stone Ages.

Wynn, Thomas
    1995. Handaxe enigmas. *World Archaeology* 27 (1): 10–24.
    A discussion of the possible functions of handaxes and their significance to an understanding of the development of language.

 Other Bibliography

Asfaw, Berhane, Yonas Beyenne, Gen Suwa, Robert C. Walter, Tim D. White, Giday Woldegabriel, and Tesfaye Yemane
    1992. The Earliest Acheulian from Konso-Gardula. *Nature* 360: 732–735.

Bar-Yosef, O., and N. Goren-Inbar
    1993. *The Lithic Assemblages of 'Ubeidiya: A Lower Paleolithic Site in the Jordan Valley.* Jerusalem: Qedem 34.

Brain, C. K., and A. Sillen
    1988. Evidence from the Swartkrans Cave for the Earliest Use of Fire. *Nature* 336: 464–466.

Gabunia, L., and A. Vekua
    1995. A Plio-Pleistocene Hominid from Dmanisi, East Georgia, Caucasus. *Nature* 373: 509–512.

Gabunia, L., A. Vekua, D. Lordkipanidze, C. Swisher, R. Ferring, A. Justus, M. Nioradze, M. Tvalchrelidze, S. C. Antón, G. Bosinski, O. Jöris, M. de Lumley, G. Majsuradze, and A. Mouskhelishvili
    2000. Earliest Pleistocene Hominid Cranial Remains from Dmanisi, Republic of Georgia: Taxonomy, Geological Setting. *Science* 288: 1019–1025.

Goren-Inbar, N., A. Lister, E. Werker, and M. Chech
    1994. A Butchered Elephant Skull and Associated Artifacts from the Acheulian Site of Gesher Benot Ya'aqov, Israel. *Paléorient* 20 (1): 99–112.

Gowlett, A. J., J. W. K. Harris, D. Walton, and B. A. Wood
    1981. Early Archaeological Sites, Hominid Remains and Traces of Fire from Chesowanja, Kenya. *Nature* 294: 125–129.

Rightmire, G. Philip
    1990. *The Evolution of Homo erectus: Comparative Anatomical Studies of an Extinct Human Species.* Cambridge: Cambridge University Press.

Walker, Alan, and Richard Leakey, eds.
    1993. *The Nariokotome Skeleton: Homo erectus.* Cambridge, MA: Harvard University Press.

Chapter 6

The Lower Paleolithic in Asia and Europe

Introduction

Historically, the first fossils of *Homo erectus* were uncovered in Asia, long before any such finds had been made in Africa. They were the result of nineteenth-century science's search for a so-called missing link—an intermediate fossil form between modern humans and their presumed apelike ancestors. In the last quarter of the nineteenth century our knowledge of early human fossils was meager at best. Several Neanderthals (a form of fossil human that lived about 100,000 to 30,000 years ago) and some fossils of anatomically modern humans were all that had been found. Scientists, however, had become convinced of the reality of evolution, including human evolution. Somewhere, it was argued, might be found the fossils of the common ancestor of humans and the apes. Anatomists argued that such a creature should be intermediate in form between modern humans and the great apes, and even gave it a name: *Pithecanthropus*, literally, "ape-man."

The Appearance of *Homo erectus* in Asia

In the 1890s a young Dutch anatomist, Eugene Dubois, set off with the express purpose of finding the ape-man, or "missing link." Convinced that the most likely place to find him was in the tropics, Dubois succeeded in getting himself posted as a doctor in the Dutch army in Sumatra and later in Java. In Java he began a series of excavations at the site of **Trinil,** on the Solo River **(Figure 6.1).**

Figure 6.1

The island of Java in Indonesia, where Eugene Dubois found the first evidence of Homo erectus *(originally named* Pithecanthropus erectus*) at Trinil on the Solo River. Later discoveries at Mojokerto and Sangiran have recently been dated to as early as 1.8 million years ago.*

Figure 6.2

Trinil Homo erectus *fossils.*

Amazingly, within a year, and among a stream of fossil mammal finds, he found what he was looking for. Dubois found the top portion of a humanlike skull, but it was far too thick and robust to be that of a modern human. Later, at some distance from the skullcap, he found a human femur, or thighbone **(Figure 6.2)**. The femur, though, was very much like that of a modern human. Dubois was convinced that both fossils came from a single individual, and that individual must have walked erect. He named his discovery **"*Pithecanthropus erectus,*"** the erect-walking ape-man.

At first, Dubois's ideas were met with skepticism and even derision. Few scholars accepted his claim that the Java fossils were an intermediate form between apes and humans, and many doubted that the fossils were actually associated with one another. Discouraged, Dubois withdrew from academic society and for many years refused to show or discuss his finds. Fortunately, other scholars eventually followed up his work in Java. Other fossil-bearing sites were discovered in Java at **Mojokerto** in 1936 and at **Sangiran** in the 1970s. These fossils have been assigned to *Homo erectus*, broadly defined. Dubois's *Pithecanthropus* is now also assigned to the species *Homo erectus*, and Dubois is universally recognized as the discoverer of *Homo erectus*.

The Mojokerto and Sangiran fossils from Java have recently been dated to 1.6 to 1.8 million years ago, making them the oldest known examples of *Homo erectus* outside Africa (Swisher et al. 1994). These dates, however, are derived from the geological formations in which the fossils are believed to have been found. Unfortunately, the locations of the original find spots are somewhat uncertain, so some doubt has been cast on the accuracy of the dating. The meaning of such early dates, if they can be demonstrated to be accurate, would be dramatic. It would imply that within a paleontologically imperceptible time after the first appearance of *Homo erectus* in Africa, the species had spread from its homeland across the breadth of the Old World, traversing the Middle East, India, and Indonesia en route to Java **(Figure 6.3)**. This interpretation has received some support by finds of simple stone tools at Riwat, Pakistan, and some hominid teeth and jaw fragments from Longuppo, China, both sites possibly dating to about 1.9 million years ago. These recent finds are still being evaluated. (For up-to-date reviews of the movement of *Homo erectus* out of Africa, see Larick and Ciochon 1996 and Tattersall 1997.)

Stone Industries with and without Handaxes: The Movius Line

Acheulian-like handaxe industries spread to cover Southwest Asia and as far east as the Indian subcontinent. Ultimately, the Acheulian industry reached most of western Europe. Handaxe industries, however, have not been found in eastern Europe or in Russia north of the Caucasus. The Acheulian seems never to have reached eastern Asia. Instead, a broad area of the Old World came to be dominated by industries lacking in handaxes **(Figure 6.4)**. In eastern Europe and southern Russia these industries are Oldowan-like, while distinctive chopper–chopping tool industries are found in China, Southeast Asia, and Indonesia. The abrupt demarcation between areas with handaxes and those without handaxe industries was first noted by archaeologist Hallam Movius in the 1940s. This boundary has come to be called the **Movius Line.** Despite a half-century of continued research and reevaluation, this basic distinction still appears valid.

The archeological evidence suggests that the earliest wave of emigrants from Africa (eventually reaching Java) did not make handaxes. A later wave of handaxe makers overtook them, and handaxe industries spread into

Figure 6.3

The spread of Homo erectus *from sub-Saharan Africa into North Africa, across Asia, and into Europe.* Homo erectus *may have appeared in Java as early as 1.8 million years ago. The major sites discussed in this chapter are also indicated.*

western Europe and as far east as India. Why did handaxes spread no farther? Several hypotheses have been offered to explain the phenomenon of the Movius Line (Schick 1994):

- It has sometimes been suggested that eastern Asia lacked suitable raw materials for making bifaces, and that therefore the Acheulian tradition was lost. However, this lack of materials cannot really be demonstrated for the vast area of Asia.

- Perhaps other raw materials were used instead of the stone handaxe in the east, especially if stone suitable for biface

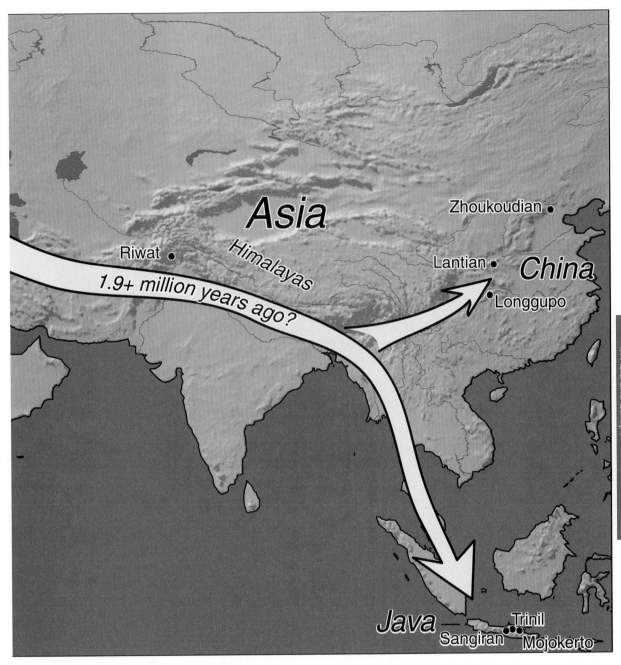

production was hard to obtain. Bamboo would have been readily available and could have been fashioned into tough, sharp cutting and stabbing implements.

- Perhaps at the time of the spread of the Acheulian industry, geographical barriers such as mountains or rain forests cut

these peoples off from the populations to the east. According to this scenario western and eastern populations continued to develop separately.

- It is unknown whether *Homo erectus* possessed any spoken language. If, as is likely, this species did not, then the

Figure 6.4

The Movius Line, the demarcation between areas with handaxes and those without handaxes, first proposed by archaeologist Hallam Movius in the 1940s.
Source: After Schick 1994.

transmission of the Acheulian tradition must have depended on nonverbal demonstration and observation. Toth and Schick (1993) have suggested that the handaxe-making tradition may have been lost if, during early humans' spread out of Africa, suitable materials for making bifaces were to be unavailable for more than a generation.

Beyond the Movius Line: The Lower Paleolithic of East Asia

Late Acheulian sites appear as far east as Pakistan and India, where handaxe industries, fashioned largely from quartzite, are found in several deeply stratified sites. On the Indian subcontinent, Acheulian sites are found as far north as Nepal.

A vast area of Asia, however, including China and Southeast Asia (and extending west as far as eastern Europe) lay beyond the boundaries of the Acheulian industry (see Figure 6.4). In China and Southeast Asia the stone assemblages consist of flakes and simple core tools, termed chopper–chopping tool complexes.

By far the most important of the Chinese Lower Paleolithic sites, and the earliest discovered, is **Zhoukoudian,** near Beijing **(Figure 6.5)**. (The discovery of Zhoukoudian and a description of the site, its inhabitants, and their material culture are discussed below.) More recently, other important sites have come to light, notably the **Lantian** area in central China, which has produced both *Homo erectus* fossils and an assemblage of quartz and quartzite artifacts.

Figure 6.5
Zhoukoudian cave site.

⚱ Dragon Bones, Zhoukoudian, and the Discovery of Peking Man

According to traditional Chinese medicine, dragon bones, when finely powdered and brewed into a tea, were a cure for fever, dysentery, malaria, and numerous other diseases. In the early twentieth century these so-called dragon bones could be found readily in the apothecary shops of China. Farmers discovered the ancient bones and brought them to the shops for sale. As paleontologists working in China were aware, the bones were, in reality, fossils of ancient birds and mammals. One place from which large numbers of dragon bones were known to have come was called Chicken Bone Hill (Zhoukoudian), near Beijing. By the 1920s the richness of the site led paleontologists, headed by J. G. Andersson, to begin excavating it for the ancient mammal fossils to be found there. Then, in 1926, two teeth were found. They were turned over to Davidson Black, a Canadian anatomist, of the Peking Union Medical College, for identification. Black identified them as definitely hominid. On the basis of the associated fauna, Black realized that the teeth were proof of the antiquity of humans in China. Encouraged by the finds, and with Black in charge of the hominid studies, the excavation of Zhoukoudian was renewed in earnest. Another tooth was found, and Black named the fossils *Sinanthropus pekinensis,* roughly, "Chinese man of Peking." (Today we would classify these specimens as ***Homo erectus pekinensis***). Finally, in 1929, a skull was found. In the years that followed, until 1937 when the excavations were halted by the events leading up to World War II, many more fossils were found representing at least 40 individuals that became familiar to the public as Peking Man.

Zhoukoudian was the first, and remains the most important, early hominid site in China. The Zhoukoudian sites are actually a number of limestone caves, just west of Beijing (see Figure 6.3). The most important is Locality 1, Lung Ku Shan (Dragon Bone Hill). This is a very large cave including more than 40 meters (130 ft.) of deposits. It is estimated that the cave was occupied for about 200,000 years, between 460,000 and 230,000 years ago. It was initially excavated in the 1920s and 1930s under the direction of the Chinese archaeologist Pei Wenzhong. Younger Chinese scholars studied the site anew during the 1970s (Wu Rukang and Lin Shenlong 1983). Fourteen skulls, plus many teeth and other bones, belonging to about 45 individuals were recovered from this cave. They all belonged to the Chinese variety of *Homo erectus* **(Figure 6.6)**. Below the neck they were fully erect and not very different from modern humans. The Zhoukoudian skulls were much like those from Java, with a thick skull, a receding chin, and heavy bars above the eyes, but the brain size was larger, averaging about 1,075 milliliters. Far more skulls than postcranial bones were found at Zhoukoudian, and many of the skulls had their bases broken in, perhaps to extract the brains. This circumstance led the excavators to infer that the inhabitants of the Zhoukoudian cave were probably head-hunters and likely to have been cannibals as well. Some scholars, however, have questioned this interpretation and prefer to attribute the breakage to the activities of other carnivores, such as hyenas, whose bones are also found in the cave (see Binford and Stone 1986).

Vast numbers of animal bones were recovered from the sites, including many deer. It remains a matter of some contention what proportion of these bones may have been left by the carnivores who also occupied the cave, particularly in the earliest phases, but many, surely, were the food remains of the human occupants. It is not known whether they hunted or scavenged this game. Very large

Figure 6.6
Zhoukoudian H. erectus *skull.*

numbers of charred hackberry seeds were also recovered. They too may have been a food source.

Zhoukoudian is located in northern China; thus the cave dwellers there would have experienced very cold winters. The cave is one of the earliest sites with extensive evidence for the use of fire. The excavators found four thick layers of ashes in the cave, ranging from 1 to 6 meters (3 to 20 ft.) in depth. Perhaps the Zhoukoudian inhabitants obtained fire from a natural source, such as a lightning strike, and having brought it to the cave, kept the fire burning for a very long time, resulting in the thick ash accumulation.

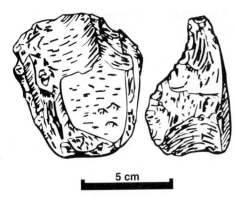

Figure 6.7

Chopper from Zhoukoudian.

The stone tools at Zhoukoudian include no handaxes. Instead, the industry includes choppers **(Figure 6.7)** and numerous flakes, which were often retouched into other tools. Quartz, flint, and sandstone were used. Many flakes were made by striking a core directly with a hammerstone. Another technique, characteristic of Zhoukoudian, was to place the stone to be flaked on a larger stone, which served as an anvil. The stone to be flaked was then struck with a hammerstone, knocking off flakes that had bulbs of percussion at both ends. This technique is call **bipolar percussion.** The stone industry at Zhoukoudian slowly changed during the long history of occupation at the site. Bipolar percussion becomes increasingly common in the latest levels at Zhoukoudian.

The fossils found at Zhoukoudian were a treasure trove of information about early humans in China. Unfortunately, during the turmoil of the Second World War, the ancient bones disappeared under mysterious circumstances as they were about to be loaded on board a ship that was to take them to the United States for safekeeping. The story of the discovery, disappearance, and renewed search for the Peking Man fossils is a fascinating one, and is described in detail in *Peking Man*, by Harry L. Shapiro, from which much of this account has been drawn.

The Initial Settlement of Europe

The research and discoveries of pioneers such as Pengelly and Frere in Britain and Boucher de Perthes in France helped establish the antiquity of humanity, but just when

Europe was initially settled is still an open question. Some scholars would date the first entry of humans into Europe as early as 2 million years ago, or even before. The evidence for such early settlement, however, is very sparse and contested. Numerous sites throughout western Europe have potentially early dates (before 500,000 years ago), but most are surface finds, stratigraphically insecure or poorly dated (Gamble 1994). Absolute dating has proved a problem for very early sites in western Europe. Potassium-argon (K-Ar) dating is the most reliable dating technique for sites of this age, but it is dependent on the presence of volcanic deposits that can be related to the archaeological sites. Only a few such sites are found in Europe. The site of **Isernia La Pineta,** in central Italy, is one of the best-dated early sites (see Figure 6.3). A volcanic tuff there directly overlies an archaeological level containing stone tools and animal bones. The tuff has been K-Ar dated to 730,000 years. (Some authors argue, however, on the basis of faunal evidence, that the site should be dated to after 500,000 years ago.)

The dating of most other early sites has depended on a combination of faunal correlations and paleomagnetic studies, which attempt to place the site within the known sequence of geomagnetic reversals (see Chapter 3). Such data are open to a broad range of interpretations, so the dates of such sites are frequently debatable. A particularly controversial site is the cave of **Vallonet,** near Nice on the southern coast of France. The stone tools there are simple choppers and flakes, and the fauna is similar to that of the late Villafranchian (early Pleistocene). The magnetic polarity of the deposits, however, is normal. Because of the primitive character of the lithics and the fauna, the excavator (H. de Lumley) has advocated dating the site to the time of the Jaramillo event, a brief magnetically normal period during the Matuyama epoch, 900,000 years ago. Other scholars, however, would place the site much later in time.

The Earliest Inhabitants of Europe: The Gran Dolina Site, Spain

Spain, just across the Strait of Gibraltar from North Africa, was likely a way station on one of the probable routes of early humans

Figure 6.8
Atapuerca area, showing Gran Dolina.

into Europe. Numerous early sites have been found in Spain, but, for the most part, they have been unstratified surface finds. The cave site of **Gran Dolina** (Figure 6.8), in the Atapuerca mountain range, northern Spain, is an exception. It contains a long stratigraphic sequence with a potentially early date and is rich in artifacts, fauna, and human remains.

At the end of the nineteenth century, during the construction of a railroad, a deep cut was made through the limestone beds at Atapuerca, revealing a number of caves and cavities filled with sediment. The importance of those caves was not recognized at the time. From 1978 onward, however, a number of excavations have been undertaken in the area. Excavation began at the cave of Gran Dolina in the 1980s (Carbonell et al. 1995; Carbonell and Rodriguez 1994). Gran Dolina contains more than 16 meters (50 ft.) of stratified deposits, divisible into 11 distinct geological layers. Five of these layers contain bones, both human and animal, as well as stone tools. The stone assemblages of the three upper layers include bifaces, but the lower two include only pebble cores and flakes.

The lowest layer in which artifacts were found contained only three quartzite cores and two flakes, although it also held the bones of bear, deer, and rhinoceros, as well as other smaller animal species. A layer about 4 meters, (13 ft.) higher proved considerably richer in artifacts. During the 1994 excavation season, one of the archaeological strata in that layer yielded more that 30 human bones within a 6-square-meter (64-sq.-ft.) exposure. About 100 stone artifacts were found as well, including cores and flakes of limestone, quartzite, sandstone, and flint. There are no bifaces. The bones of numerous mammals, large and small, were also recovered.

The human bones belonged to at least four individuals, including adults, an adolescent, and a child. The form of these fossils suggests that they differ significantly from Asian *Homo erectus* and are perhaps most similar to a mandible found in 1907 at Mauer, just outside Heidelberg, Germany. The **Mauer mandible** has features suggestive of both *Homo erectus* and an early form of *Homo sapiens*, and is sometimes given a separate name, ***Homo heidelbergensis.***

The Gran Dolina site has been dated through a combination of faunal associations and paleomagnetic measurements. The long stratigraphic section within the cave has provided a long series of samples for paleomagnetic dating. Although initial analysis had suggested a considerably younger age, new studies (Parés and Pérez-Gonzales 1995) now indicate that the rich upper stratum was laid down near the time of the Brunhes-Matuyama geomagnetic reversal (see Chapter 3). This would date that stratum to older than 780,000 years and would make the Gran Dolina fossils among the oldest in Europe.

The Later Lower Paleolithic in Europe

While the issue of the earliest settlement of Europe remains unresolved, it is clear that after 500,000 years ago, Europe saw a large influx of settlers. Many of those in the western portion of Europe carried with them the Acheulian industry. A second group of sites is lacking in handaxes. The assemblages in that group, dominated by flakes, are termed **Clactonian,** after the site of Clacton-on-Sea, in southern England. The Acheulian and Clactonian appear to be separate industries.

Acheulian sites are widespread in France, Spain, southern England, and northern Italy. A notable group of sites is found in the Somme Valley in northwest France, including Abbeville, excavated by Boucher de Perthes, and St. Acheul, for which the Acheulian is named. Historically, the French Acheulian sequence has been divided into Lower, Middle, and Upper Acheulian **(Figure 6.9)**, but this sequence cannot readily be extended to the rest of western Europe. Moreover, these divisions do not correspond to the early, middle, and late Acheulian of the Near East and Africa.

The Levallois Technique

In the course of the Middle Acheulian, a special technique became increasingly important. In the **Levallois technique** (named for a Paris suburb), a stone core was specially shaped (prepared) so that, ultimately, a flake or series of flakes could be struck from it that would be essentially preformed to the desired shape, requiring little further working **(Figure 6.10)**. The use of the technique implies considerable forethought and knowledge of the worked material. Prepared-core techniques become increasingly important through the Middle and Upper Paleolithic.

5 cm

Figure 6.9

Characteristic handaxes from the French Middle Acheulian (left, from Commont's Workshop, in the Somme Valley) and Upper Acheulian (right, from La Micoque, a cave site in the Dordogne).

Acheulian Lifeways: Elephant Hunters or Scavengers? The Evidence from Torralba and Ambrona

At the twin sites of **Torralba and Ambrona** in central Spain, Acheulian handaxes and other artifacts lie amid the bones of dozens of elephants, as well as horses, deer, wild cattle, and other large animals. The sites appear to date to sometime between the early and middle Acheulian, perhaps 420,000 to 450,000 years ago. First discovered and partially excavated in 1909, the sites were studied by F. C. Howell and L. Freeman over a number of seasons between 1961 and 1981. The excavations were extensive; over 1,000 square meters (0.25 acre) at Torralba and about 2,800 square meters (0.7 acre) at Ambrona were excavated. At both sites, which were originally wet or were even marshlands, numerous archaeological strata point to a lengthy series of events.

The finds at Torralba and Ambrona were highly suggestive. At Torralba stone tools and flakes were associated with the partial skeleton of an ancient elephant, and at Ambrona elephant bones and tusks were also accompanied by stone tools. Fragments of apparently

The Levallois Technique

Using the Levallois technique, a series of flakes requiring little or no further shaping could readily be struck from a stone core. Before the first desired flake was struck from the core, the core was prepared, or pre-shaped, in a very standardized way:

1. A series of flakes are removed from around the periphery of the core. (The arrows indicate the direction and point of impact of the blow used to detach the flake).

2. The core is then turned over, and a second series of flakes are struck on the other side of the core, converging at the center.

3. This results in one fully-worked surface on the core. The core now resembles the shell of a tortoise.

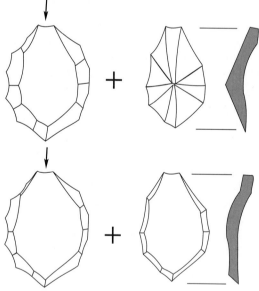

4. A carefully placed blow at the edge of the core detaches a characteristically-shaped Levallois flake.

5. Subsequent blows detach further fully-formed Levallois flakes, until no more can be made. The core is then said to be exhausted.

Figure 6.10
The Levallois technique.

Figure 6.11

Elephant bone alignment at Ambrona.

worked wood were also found. Bits of charcoal were scattered in the deposits. A particularly intriguing and enigmatic feature at Ambrona is a linear arrangement of elephant bones, with limb bones lined up end to end and other bones lying perpendicular to the alignment **(Figure 6.11)**.

In keeping with the views current in the 1960s and 1970s, Howell and Freeman initially interpreted the finds at Torralba and Ambrona as evidence for the killing and butchering of elephants by bands of Lower Paleolithic big-game hunters. A number of imaginative reconstructions were put forward. One scenario, picked up in the popular press, pictured bands of ancient hunters, armed with torches, driving a herd of elephants into the marsh to be slaughtered.

Lewis Binford, in the same 1981 volume in which he attacked the interpretation of the Olduvai Gorge living floors (Chapter 4), leveled a similar set of criticisms at the interpretation of Torralba and Ambrona (Binford 1981). He questioned the assumption that the bone accumulations at these sites were primarily the result of human activities. Considering the long period of time during which these deposits accumulated, he proposed that the animals may have met their deaths there

naturally and that the role of humans may have been marginal. In a later publication, Binford (1987) made some further suggestions concerning Torralba. Using previously published data, he statistically reanalyzed the relationships among stone tool types and the various animal bones. On the basis of this analysis, Binford came to the conclusion that not only were the elephants at Torralba not hunted, but the archaeological evidence there pointed to, at most, the opportunistic scavenging of animal leftovers. This conclusion was bolstered by some studies of the Torralba bones that pointed to only a very low frequency of butchery marks.

Binford's assessment was widely accepted. P. Villa, in her 1990 study of the site of **Aridos,** near Madrid, accepted the characterization of Torralba as a highly disturbed site but questioned Binford's conclusion that only marginal scavenging was involved. Aridos (actually two adjacent sites) is a more recently excavated Acheulian site, quite similar to Torralba and Ambrona. At Aridos, too, elephant bones are closely associated with an assemblage of stone tools **(Figure 6.12)**. Many of the stone artifacts could be refitted, indicating that they resulted from a single episode. The lithics found at the site appear

Figure 6.12

Plan showing location of elephant bones (in outline) at Aridos, Spain. Lines show refitted artifacts.

to represent the remains from the manufacture and resharpening of tools used by a small group of humans specifically for butchering the elephants there. Whole carcasses seem to have been involved, not just leftovers.

In his recent review of the Torralba and Ambrona sites, Freeman (1994) readily admits that the early interpretations of these sites had been overdrawn. He argues, however, that Binford's statistical analysis of his data is invalid, because the data Binford used were flawed and because the methods were

inappropriate. Freeman also argues that the deposition at Torralba and Ambrona did not occur continuously over a long period, but instead, represented a series of discrete events, separated by lengthy hiatuses. Further, he states that contrary to some analyses, a substantial number of bones bear gross butchery marks and quite a few of the lithics could be refitted.

In short, Torralba and Ambrona do not seem too different in nature from Aridos (and recall as well Gesher Benot Ya'aqov, Chapter 5). Real evidence for big-game hunting is lacking, but these sites clearly indicate that the Acheulian people regularly butchered and ate elephants, even if they may not have hunted them.

Terra Amata: A Hunters' Encampment?

While Torralba, Ambrona, and Aridos appear to be butchery sites, the site of **Terra Amata** in southern France has been interpreted as an Acheulian habitation. According to the excavator, Henri de Lumley, the site of Terra Amata preserves the remains of a series of wooden huts. These would be the earliest-known structures in Europe. This interpretation, however, has been seriously questioned; the data from the site present numerous difficulties. Terra Amata, however, is a rare example of an in-place Acheulian encampment in the open air, rather than within a cave. It remains, therefore, one of the most important Acheulian sites in Europe.

The digging of Terra Amata was, in fact, an example of urban rescue archaeology. A large apartment building was under construction in downtown Nice in southern France. In the alleyway named Terra Amata, after which the site is named, the builders came upon a sandy beach deposit, containing Acheulian artifacts. Once the importance of the find was appreciated, the construction work was halted, and in 1966, Henri de Lumley, with the help of a large crew of volunteer workers, began a major archaeological salvage excavation. Today, the site is preserved in a museum in the building's lower floor. Over a period of five months more that 200 cubic meters (262 cu. yds.) of soil were excavated.

The site is dated to 230,000 ± 40,000 years ago, based on thermoluminescence dating of burnt flints (see the Archaeology in Practice box on the next page). At that time the Mediterranean Sea level was much higher than it is today. Although the site is now inland, a series of ancient beaches were found at Terra Amata; the inhabitants of the site occupied the youngest of the beaches, not far from the Mediterranean shore.

When the excavation was completed, de Lumley (1969) distinguished 21 separate Acheulian living floors at Terra Amata, 4 on a sandbar, 6 near the shore, and 11 on an inland dune. According to de Lumley's reconstruction, these floors held evidence for a series of oval huts, ranging in length from 8 to 15 meters (26 to 49 ft.) and from 4 to 6 meters (13 to 20 ft.) in width, outlined by stakes driven into the sand. Ash and organic material filled the interior of the structure. Large holes within some of the huts suggest that sturdy poles may have been used to support the roof. Each hut had a hearth at its center, with a little wall on the northwest side, probably to act as a windbreak.

Animal bones found at Terra Amata include those of elephants, deer, wild cattle, and wild boar; the fragments of a rhinoceros jaw; plus some rabbit bones. A few shellfish were also found. At the time of the excavation it was assumed that these animals were the prey of the Terra Amata big-game hunters. Whether the animals were acquired by hunting or scavenging is not known.

De Lumley interpreted the superimposed huts (particularly the 11 found on the dune) as very brief seasonal encampments, perhaps yearly visits to the spot by the same group of individuals. This interpretation has since been called into question. In particular, P. Villa (1983) has cast doubt on whether the site can really be divided into distinct living floors, based on a refitting study of the Terra Amata lithics (see Chapter 5, Archaeology in Practice box). Lithics that frequently were vertically separated by up to 30 centimeters (12 in.), often across different levels, could be refitted. Trampling, geological processes, and movement by animals are some of the possible causes of the up-and-down movement of artifacts (see Chapter 2). The deposits at Terra Amata might also have been more finely divided vertically than was really justifiable. The thickness of the levels there was frequently only a few centimeters; segments of different levels might also have inadvertently been confused.

De Lumley's interpretation of the site as a series of well-defined structures has also been questioned, as only a few actual stake holes were found and recorded, rather than the many suggested by early site descriptions (Villa 1994: 54–55). The site data have been published only in a preliminary fashion. A real assessment of the site must await the final publication of the data.

Archaeology in Practice

Dating the Past: Thermoluminescence (TL) and Electron Spin Resonance (ESR)

Potassium-argon dating methods are limited to sites that include or are in close relationship with volcanic deposits (see Chapter 3). Radiocarbon dating methods (Chapter 10) are limited to relatively recent times (later than 60,000 to 70,000 years ago). Archaeologists have long been in need of dating methods applicable to a wider variety of sites and suitable for dating deposits formed between 100,000 and 1 million years ago.

Two new methods have come into use to fill this need. **Thermoluminescence (TL) dating** is an absolute dating technique applied originally to the dating of pottery. The underlying principle can also be applied to the dating of burnt flint, and this newer application is becoming increasingly important. **Electron spin resonance (ESR) dating** is a closely allied measurement technique. These methods can be used to date materials as old as 500,000 years and can sometimes be extended as far back as 1 million years.

From the time they are first formed, the mineral crystals within a ceramic fragment or within a piece of flint receive a constant low-level flow of radiation from adjacent minerals and deposits. Some minerals can absorb the energy from this radiation in the form of entrapped electrons within their crystal structure. This energy accumulates slowly over time, and if the rate of accumulation can be determined, it can serve as an absolute clock. Thermoluminescence and ESR dating are alternative techniques for measuring the energy trapped in the crystal grains. When a ceramic object is fired or when a flint is heated in a fire, the energy entrapped in the crystals is released; in effect, the mineral clock is set to zero. The energy then begins to accumulate anew.

Thermoluminescence dating measures the energy trapped in crystal grains by the slow heating of the mineral within a highly sensitive light sensor. As the crystal heats up, the stored energy is released as a pulse of light, superimposed on the normal red-hot glow of the sample. The age of the sample is proportional to the amount of light released.

ESR directly measures the number of electrons trapped in the crystal. The sample is placed in a magnetic field and exposed to a high-frequency electromagnetic field. Under these conditions the electrons will precess, or spin rather like tops, and at a certain combination of frequency and field strength, they will suddenly resonate with the electromagnetic field, drawing power from it, which can be measured. In this case the age of the sample is proportional to the amount of energy absorbed from the electromagnetic field.

Both thermoluminescence and ESR dating present many practical difficulties. Both depend on accurate measurement of the amount of radiation reaching the sample as well as an accurate measurement of the sensitivity of the sample to radiation. Various physical and chemical effects complicate the measurements. When these methods are used to date burned flint, one must be certain that the sample was sufficiently heated in antiquity to set the clock to zero.

The Distribution of Early Humans in Europe

The earliest humans seem never to have reached beyond southern and central Europe. Premodern humans probably did not possess the skills and technology needed to cope with the harsh environments of Scandinavia and the northern borders of Europe.

Archaeologists still have much to learn about the lifeways of Lower Paleolithic people in Europe. It is unclear whether these early inhabitants were hunters or scavengers. The role of plant foods in the diet is also unknown owing to the absence of preserved plant materials. Although these early Europeans may have constructed simple shelters, their degree of seasonal mobility is also unknown. Did they move their campsites on a seasonal or periodic basis, or did they occupy a single site for an extended portion of the year? Sites such as Terra Amata have provided some clues, but the interpretation of this excavation has been controversial. These topics all await further research.

Conclusion

Archaeological data indicate that early humans had reached the Middle East and Southeast Asia well before 1 million years ago. Acheulian industries never reached eastern Asia. In East and Southeast Asia increasingly sophisticated chopper and flake industries persisted throughout the Middle Pleistocene. While southern Europe appears to have been colonized somewhat later than the Far East, new data from Gran Dolina suggest that this colonization may have begun before 780,000 years ago. The earliest emigrants from Africa, who penetrated as far as Southeast Asia, were followed by handaxe makers, who would reach western Asia and Europe. In those regions, the Acheulian industry dominated until the appearance of the Middle Paleolithic industries about 130,000 years ago.

Glossary

Aridos. An Acheulian site near Madrid, Spain, where bones and stone tools indicate that an elephant was butchered.

Bipolar percussion. A stoneworking technique, characteristic of Zhoukoudian, in which the piece to be worked is placed on a stone anvil and then struck with a hammerstone. The resulting flakes have bulbs of percussion on both ends.

Clactonian. A stone tool industry, named after Clacton-on-Sea in southern England, dominated by flakes and without handaxes. The Clactonian appears to be a separate industry from the Acheulian.

Electron spin resonance (ESR) dating. An absolute dating method related to thermoluminescence (TL) dating, based on the electronic measurement of energy trapped in the mineral crystals of a sample. The method is suitable for dating sites of the Lower Paleolithic period and later.

Gran Dolina. Cave site in the Atapuerca mountain range in northern Spain, containing a long sequence of strata with stone artifacts and numerous human fossils. The lower layers contain pebble tools and flakes as well as fossils of early *Homo*, possibly similar to that found at Mauer, Germany. The site may date to greater than 780,000 years ago.

Homo erectus pekinensis. Originally called *Sinanthropus pekinensis*. The variety of *Homo erectus* found in China at Zhoukoudian.

Homo heidelbergensis. A form of early human, named after the mandible found at Mauer, near Heidelberg, that is intermediate in some respects between *Homo erectus* and early *Homo sapiens*.

Isernia La Pineta. Site in central Italy containing stone tools and animal bones, dated by K-Ar to greater than 730,000 years ago, although faunal evidence suggests that the age of this site may be considerably younger.

Lantian. An area in central China where *Homo erectus* fossils have been found.

Levallois technique. A technique in which a stone core was specially shaped so that flakes of a predetermined shape and size could be struck from it.

Mauer mandible. Mandible found at Mauer, near Heidelberg, Germany, with features suggestive of both *Homo erectus* and an early form of *Homo sapiens*. It is sometimes given a separate name, *Homo heidelbergensis*.

Mojokerto. Site in Java at which *Homo erectus* fossils have been found and recently redated to 1.6 million to 1.8 million years old.

Movius Line. The line of demarcation between those parts of the Old World with handaxes (Africa, western Europe, the Near East, and India) and those areas with Oldowan-like, or chopper–chopping tool, industries without handaxes (eastern Europe, China, Southeast Asia, and Indonesia). This distinction was first proposed by Hallam Movius in the 1940s.

"Pithecanthropus erectus." The name originally given by Eugene Dubois to the fossils he found in Java, now classified as *Homo erectus*.

Sangiran. Site in Java at which *Homo erectus* fossils have been found and recently redated to 1.6 million to 1.8 million years old.

Terra Amata. A beachfront early Acheulian open site, now in the city of Nice, France. A series of superimposed huts has been claimed as the earliest evidence for structures in Europe.

Thermoluminescence (TL) dating. An absolute dating method related to electron spin resonance (ESR) dating, based on the measurement of energy trapped in the mineral crystals of a sample. The energy is measured as light, which is released when the sample is heated. The method is suitable for dating sites of the Lower Paleolithic period and later.

Torralba and Ambrona. Nearby sites in central Spain where Acheulian artifacts have been found among the bones of numerous elephants, horses, deer, wild cattle, and other large animals. Many of the animals were clearly butchered; whether they had been hunted or scavenged is not known.

Trinil. Site on the Solo River of Java where in the 1890s Eugene Dubois found the fossils that he named *Pithecanthropus erectus* and that are now assigned to *Homo erectus*.

Vallonet. A cave site near Nice on the southern coast of France, with simple choppers and flakes and early Pleistocene fauna. The actual age of the site is controversial.

Zhoukoudian. A cave site near Beijing, China, occupied for about 200,000 years, between 460,000 and 230,000 years ago. The bones of about 45 *Homo erectus* individuals were found there, along with a stone industry without handaxes. Deep layers of ash in the cave have usually been interpreted as indicative of the extensive and prolonged use of fire.

 Further Reading

de Lumley, H.
  1969. A Paleolithic Camp at Nice. *Scientific American* 220: 42–50.
  A readable description of de Lumley's interpretation of the Acheulian structures found at Terra Amata. The reader should be aware of Villa's criticisms (see Villa 1983).

Gamble, Clive
  1986. *The Paleolithic Settlement of Europe.* Cambridge: Cambridge University Press.
  An extensive analysis and synthesis of the evidence for the Paleolithic settlement of Europe, based on a regional model. Although a very demanding text, this is one of the most important current studies of this topic.
  1999. *The Paleolithic Societies of Europe.* Cambridge: Cambridge University Press.
  An important new book that examines the nature of Paleolithic societies in Europe from 500,000 years ago until the end of the Upper Paleolithic.

Larick, Roy, and Russel L. Ciochon
  1996. The African Emergence and Early Asian Dispersals of the Genus *Homo. American Scientist* 84 (6): 538–551.
  A clear discussion of the possible causes for the movement of *Homo* from Africa into Asia.

Shapiro, Harry L.
  1974. *Peking Man: The Discovery, Disappearance and Mystery of a Priceless Scientific Treasure.* New York: Simon and Schuster.
  A very readable narrative about the discovery of the Zhoukoudian fossils, their disappearance during World War II, and the search for them.

Schick, Kathy D.
  1994. The Movius Line Reconsidered: Perspectives on the Earlier Paleolithic of Eastern Asia. In *Integrative Paths to the Past: Paleoanthropological Advances in Honor of F. Clark Howell,* edited by R. S. Corruccini and R. L. Ciochon, pp. 569–596. Englewood Cliffs, NJ: Prentice Hall.
  A clear overview of the geographical relationships between handaxe and non-handaxe industries during the Lower Paleolithic. Various hypotheses are offered to explain why handaxe industries never reached beyond the Movius Line.

Tattersall, Ian
  1997. Out of Africa Again . . . and Again? *Scientific American* 276 (4): 60–67.
  A concise and up-to-date discussion of the evidence for repeated waves of hominid migration out of Africa into Asia and Europe.

Villa, Paola
  1990. Torralba and Aridos: Elephant Exploitation in Middle Pleistocene Spain. *Journal of Human Evolution* 19: 299–309.
  Villa's interpretation of the evidence for elephant butchery at Aridos, with a discussion of the quality of the evidence from Ambrona as well as a criticism of Binford's arguments for elephant scavenging.

Wu Rukang and Lin Shenlong
  1983. Peking Man. *Scientific American* 248 (6): 86–94.
  Although some of the interpretations have been disputed, a clear description of the Zhoukoudian site and of the archaeological research that has been conducted since the 1960s.

 Other Bibliography

Binford, Lewis R.
  1981. *Bones, Ancient Men and Modern Myths.* New York: Academic Press.
  1987. Were There Elephant Hunters at Torralba? In *The Evolution of Human Hunting,* edited by M. H. Nitecki and D. V. Nitecki, pp. 47–183. New York and London: Plenum Press.

Binford, Lewis R., and Nancy M. Stone

1986. Zhoukoudian: A Closer Look. *Current Anthropology* 27 (5): 453–475.

Carbonell, E., J. M. Bermúdez de Castro, J. L. Arsuaga, J. C. Diez, A. Rosas, G. Cuenca-Bescós, R. Sala, M. Mosquera, and X. P. Rodriguez

1995. Lower Pleistocene Hominids and Artifacts from Atapuerca-TD6 (Spain). *Science* 269: 826–830.

Carbonell, Eudald, and Xosé Pedro Rodriguez

1994. Early Middle Pleistocene Deposits and Artifacts in the Gran Dolina Site (TD4) of the "Sierra de Atapuerca" (Burgos, Spain). *Journal of Human Evolution* 26: 291–311.

Freeman, Leslie G.

1994. Torralba and Ambrona: A Review of Discoveries. In *Integrative Paths to the Past: Paleo-anthropological Advances in Honor of F. Clark Howell,* edited by R. S. Corruccini and R. L. Ciochon, pp. 597–637. Englewood Cliffs, NJ: Prentice Hall.

Gamble, Clive

1994. Time for Boxgrove Man. *Nature* 369: 275–276.

Parés, Josep M., and Alfredo Pérez-Gonzales

1995. Paleomagnetic Age for Hominid Fossils at Atapuerca Archaeological Site, Spain. *Science* 269: 830–832.

Swisher, C. C., III, G. H. Curtis, T. Jacob, A. G. Getty, A. Suprijo, and Widiasmoro.

1994. Age of the Earliest Known Hominids in Java, Indonesia. *Science* 263: 1118–1121.

Toth, N., and K. Schick

1993. Early Stone Industries and Inferences Regarding Language and Cognition. In *Tools, Language and Cognition in Human Evolution,* edited by K. R. Gibson and T. Ingold, pp. 346–362. Cambridge: Cambridge University Press.

Villa, Paola

1983. *Terra Amata and the Middle Pleistocene Archaeological Record of Southern France.* Berkeley: University of California Press.

1994. Europe: Lower and Middle Pleistocene Archaeology. In *History of Humanity: Volume I, Prehistory and the Beginnings of Civilization,* pp. 44–61. London and New York: Routledge; Paris: UNESCO.

Chapter 7

The Middle Paleolithic and the Appearance of the Neanderthals

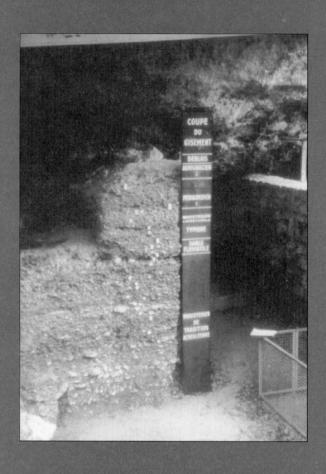

Introduction

The name Neanderthal conjures up vivid and varied images in the popular imagination. The popular image of the Neanderthal is a rather brutish form of cave-dwelling subhuman with limited intellectual powers. Neanderthals have also been subjects of popular works of fiction, including Jean Auel's *Clan of the Cave Bear*. This novel paints a more sympathetic portrait of the Neanderthals, depicting them as capable of, among other things, caring for the infirm and elderly members of their community. Auel's work of fiction is based on data recovered from the excavations of Shanidar Cave in Iraq. In this chapter we will examine the archaeological record of Neanderthal behavior. We begin, however, with the initial discovery of Neanderthal fossils 150 years ago.

Humans unlike Ourselves: The Discovery of the Neanderthals

In the year 1830, in the **Engis** cave in Belgium, the skull of a young child with an anatomy quite unlike our own came to light (**Figure 7.1**). Although its excavator was convinced of the skull's antiquity, the scientific community took little notice. A similar skull, that of an adult, was found by military builders at **Forbes' Quarry, Gibraltar,** in 1848. As with the Engis discovery, few were interested in the meaning of this skull; Western science was not yet ready to accept the antiquity of humanity. By 1856, though, just three years before Darwin would publish *On the Origin of Species*, scientific ideas about human evolution were beginning to change. In that year workers quarrying for limestone in a German grotto called **Feldhofer** happened upon the skull and the skeleton of a strange, robust human, with thick ridges over his eyes and thick, curved limb bones. The valley, the Neander Tal (Neander Valley) near Düsseldorf, where the cave is located, would give its name to these new humans. Unlike the Engis and Gibraltar skulls (now known also to be **Neanderthals**), the Feldhofer fossils created an immediate sensation. The bones had been delivered to a local schoolteacher, who recognized their importance and engaged an anatomy professor from the University of Bonn to help study them. Together they presented their findings to the scientific world, with the conclusion that these bones represented a form of human of the greatest antiquity. Their conclusions were by no means generally accepted, but the debate about the nature of the Neanderthals, which continues to this day, had begun.

To date, the remains of several hundred Neanderthal individuals have been found, although usually an individual is represented by just a few bones. A small number of fairly complete skeletons have been found. The Neanderthal anatomy is markedly different from that of modern humans (**Figure 7.2**). Although different individuals show considerable variation, in general, Neanderthal skulls have thick, bony ridges over each eye and a low, sloping, rather than upright, forehead. The lower jaw lacks a chin. The face projects forward and must have been dominated by a remarkably large, broad nose. The limb bones are thick and robust and often slightly curved to support a powerful, muscular physique. The skull, however, encloses a brain as large as or slightly larger than that of modern humans.

Could such beings have been the ancestors of modern humans? In 1913, when the French paleontologist Marcellin Boule set out to describe the Neanderthals, such an idea was very difficult to accept. Boule based his study primarily on the most complete Neanderthal skeleton so far discovered, an individual found in 1908 at **La Chapelle-aux-Saints** in central France. The portrait Boule reconstructed was hardly flattering. Boule painted the Neanderthals as more apelike than human, with bent knees, a slouching posture, and a forward-thrusting face. Such a creature

Figure 7.1

The location of the sites mentioned in this chapter. St. Césaire will be discussed in Chapter 8. The light shading on the smaller map shows the region inhabited by the Neanderthals.

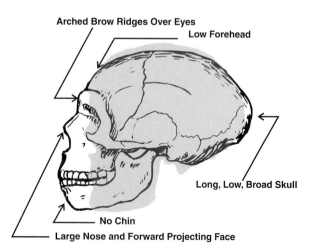

Figure 7.2

A Neanderthal skull, showing its distinctive anatomical features, including the low, sloping forehead; massive brow ridges; projecting face; and absence of a chin. Shading shows modern human skull.

The Pleistocene and Its Chronology

The environment of the Neanderthals was the Ice Age world of the Pleistocene epoch. The Pleistocene began about 1.6 million years ago and ended about 10,000 years ago, at the end of the last great glaciation. The Pleistocene Epoch was characterized by a series of episodes of worldwide cold climate, known as **glacials,** during which average temperatures were considerably lower than today (perhaps 6 to 8 degrees Celsius [11 to 14 degrees Fahrenheit]). Current evidence indicates that as many as 30 such episodes occurred during the Pleistocene epoch, alternating with extended periods when temperatures were as high as or higher than those today, periods known as **interglacials.** During the cold phases great glaciers covered much of northern Europe, the northern portion of Eurasia, and northern North America as far south as New York State. Glaciers grew in the high mountain ranges as well, notably the Alps.

The movements of the glacial ice left distinctive features on the landscape. European geologists in the early twentieth century could identify the traces left behind by the advances of the Alpine glaciers. These great glaciations were named after the Alpine valleys where the evidence was found: the Günz (the earliest), the Mindel, the Riss, and the Würm (the latest). The Neanderthals first appear in Europe between the Riss and the Würm, and are replaced by modern humans well before the Würm comes to an end. Until recently, the Alpine sequence of glaciations (and related sequences elsewhere in Europe) had formed the chronological framework for

European prehistory during the Pleistocene. Archaeological sites were tied to the glacial and interglacial periods by means of a wide variety of geological phenomena and observations. These correlations always proved extremely difficult because the geological record is, unfortunately, very incomplete. **Figure 7.3** presents an approximate chronology of the Alpine and North American Pleistocene glaciations. The Alpine glacial terminology appears in many older publications, and some workers continue to use those terms as a matter of convenience.

A New Chronology: Deep-Sea Cores and Oxygen Isotope Ratios

A new approach has provided geologists and archaeologists with a far better understanding of the climatic fluctuations of the Pleistocene. Terrestrial geology has preserved evidence from just the last few glaciations; deep-sea cores, however, provide a record of sediments accumulated throughout the Pleistocene. Deep-sea cores indicate a long series of cold-warm oscillations during the Pleistocene epoch.

The mechanism by which deep-sea cores have captured a record of ancient temperatures is quite indirect, but it has proved very reliable. Consistent results have been obtained from hundreds of cores. The deep-sea cores take samples of the calcitic ooze made up of the skeletons of marine microorganisms that settled to the ocean floor in a constant rain throughout the Pleistocene. When these organisms were alive, they absorbed oxygen from the ocean water. When they died and settled to the bottom, that

oxygen was incorporated into the sediment. Oxygen occurs in several forms, or isotopes. The lighter isotope, oxygen-16 (^{16}O), is the common form; the heavier isotope, oxygen-18 (^{18}O), is much rarer. The ^{16}O isotope, being lighter, tends to evaporate from the surface of the oceans more readily than does the heavier form. During glacial periods, water containing an excess of ^{16}O evaporates from the oceans and becomes trapped in the glaciers, leaving the oceans enriched in ^{18}O; therefore a higher percentage of ^{18}O is incorporated into the marine microorganisms. During warm periods, glacial water runs into the oceans, raising the proportion of ^{16}O. This change too is reflected in the microorganisms. Sediments relatively rich in ^{18}O, therefore, indicate a colder climate; sediments with a higher proportion of ^{16}O indicate a warmer climate.

A record of climatic oscillations without a time scale would be of little use. Fortunately, the ocean sediments preserve a record of the orientation of the earth's magnetic field at the time of their deposition. This sequence can be correlated with the sequence of the earth's magnetic reversals, which have been well dated by absolute dating techniques, such as potassium-argon dating (see Chapter 3, Archeology in Practice box).

Today the preferred chronological framework for the Pleistocene is expressed in terms of the fluctuations seen in the deep-sea cores. Each distinctive period of warm or cold climate is referred to as a numbered **oxygen isotope stage,** which may be further divided into substages. In general, each major glacial-interglacial oscillation is represented by a cold stage and a warm stage. The exception is the Late

Figure 7.3 — The Alpine and North American glacial chronology

AGE IN YEARS	OXYGEN ISOTOPE STAGE	ALPINE GLACIATION	SOME KEY SITES	NORTH AMERICAN GLACIATION
10,000	1 / 2 / 3	HOLOCENE WÜRM	UPPER PAL. — Monte Verde; Grotte Chauvet; Upper Swan; La Chapelle-aux-Saints	HOLOCENE WISCONSAN
75,000	4		MIDDLE PAL.	
	5	RISS-WÜRM INTERGLACIAL	Klasies River Mouth	SANGOMON INTERGLACIAL
	6			
200,000		RISS	Kabwe	ILLINOISIAN
250,000	7			
	8			
	9		Zhoukoudian	
	10			
	11	MINDEL-RISS INTERGLACIAL	Torralba / Ambrona	YARMOUTH INTERGLACIAL
	12 / 13 / 14			
600,000	15			
	16 / 17 / 18 / 19	MINDEL		KANSAN
750,000	20			
	21 / 22	GÜNZ-MINDEL INTERGLACIAL	Gran Dolina	AFTONIAN INTERGLACIAL
900,000				
		GÜNZ	AFRICA — EUROPE — ASIA — AUSTRALIA — AMERICA	NEBRASKAN

(Center column spanning label: LOWER PALEOLITHIC)

Figure 7.3

The Alpine and North American glacial chronology, which was in widespread use until recently.

Pleistocene, which is represented by more stages because the data are better. In the time between the human fossils at Gran Dolina (see Chapter 6), 780,000 years ago, and today, at least eight major glacial-interglacial cycles have occurred. The earliest Neanderthals appeared in Europe during isotope stage 7, which began 250,000 years ago (the latter part of the Riss glaciation). They disappeared during isotope stage 3, ending 30,000 years ago, in the midst of the Würm glaciation (**Figure 7.4**).

While the deep-sea core studies have greatly improved our knowledge of the Pleistocene climate, it remains difficult to tie individual archaeological sites into the new chronology. Absolute dating methods such as thermoluminescence and electron spin resonance (see Chapter 6, Archaeology in Practice box) will gradually change this picture.

surely could not have been in the direct line of human ancestry. Today we realize that the posture and gait of the Neanderthals were not very different from our own. Boule's interpretation may have been skewed by the La Chapelle-aux-Saints Neanderthal, known as the Old Man, who suffered from severe arthritis. More likely, though, Boule (who was an excellent anatomist and quite aware of the fossil's arthritic condition) was led astray by his own preconceptions. Scientists, strive as they may for objectivity, are inevitably caught in the conceptual framework of their time. Nevertheless, Boule's reconstruction

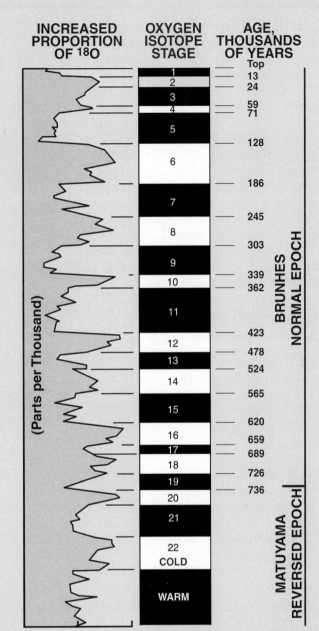

Figure 7.4

The oxygen-isotope stages for the Pleistocene and their approximate dates.

became the dominant image of the Neanderthals for decades to come.

Humans with the full range of Neanderthal features lived throughout Europe south of the areas covered by the glaciers. They have been found in the Near East (in Israel and Iraq) and as far east as Uzbekistan in Central Asia. The Neanderthals may be descended from a population represented by fossil finds at **Ehringsdorf,** near Weimar, Germany, dated to 230,000 years ago (Stringer and Gamble 1993: 66). These fossils, including a skull, show the characteristic Neanderthal features, such as heavy brow ridges, but in a less extreme form than in later Neanderthals. During the Neanderthals' long existence, the earth's climate oscillated from warm to cold several times. The Neanderthals developed in a world growing increasingly cold and harsh. Their stocky bodies and short limbs were probably an adaptation helping them conserve body heat under those challenging conditions. The short and stocky bodies of the Inuit who live in Alaska, northern Canada, and Greenland are a modern-day example of such an adaptation. The Neanderthals survived an extended period of severely cold climate and continued into a time of milder temperatures. The last Neanderthals, who lived about 28,000 years ago, saw the world growing cold again.

Middle Paleolithic Archaeology: The Mousterian Industry

As the Neanderthal people came to dominate the European landscape, the characteristic stone tools found in the associated archaeological sites gradually changed. The Acheulian industry, typified by bifacially flaked handaxes made on stone cores, was replaced by another industry, known as the **Mousterian,** in which most of the stone tools were made from large, thick flakes. Traditionally, this shift denotes the end of the Lower Paleolithic period and the beginning of the **Middle Paleolithic.** The Mousterian is named for the stone tool industry discovered in the nineteenth century within the cave of **Le Moustier,** near Les Eyzies in the Dordogne region of southern France **(Figure 7.5)**. In 1908, in another shelter just below Le Moustier, a skeleton of an adolescent Neanderthal was found. Until recently, it had appeared the Neanderthal people and the Mousterian stone tool industry were invariably interlinked—Neanderthals were often referred to as possessors of a Mousterian culture. Today, it is clear that the reality was more complex. In Europe, some later Neanderthals have now been shown to have used more advanced types of stone tools. In the Near East, as in Europe, Neanderthals are associated with Mousterian artifacts, but recent evidence shows that another form of human—the early anatomically modern humans—was using Mousterian stone tools

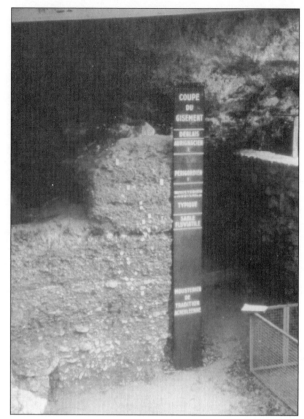

Figure 7.5

The site of Le Moustier (Dordogne), France, the type site for the Mousterian stone tool industry.

as well. (These issues will be discussed in greater detail in Chapter 8.)

The Bordes Typology of Middle Paleolithic Stone Tools

The Mousterian stone tool industry remains a primary source of evidence for the activities of the inhabitants of Europe and adjacent areas during the long duration of the Middle Paleolithic. While the Acheulian industry includes only a limited variety of stone tool forms, the Mousterian includes many more types of stone artifacts. An artifact **typology** is the systematic classification of those artifacts according to clearly defined characteristics. The French archaeologist François Bordes (1968, 1984) systematized the typology of the Mousterian industry in the early 1960s, and his typology continues in use today. Bordes subdivided the Mousterian stone artifacts into 63 distinctive tool types (Bordes and de Sonneville-Bordes 1970). Many of these tool types were various kinds of **scrapers:** flakes **retouched** into a number of shapes by the removal of a series of small flakes from one or more edges. The tools presumably were used for tasks such as scraping hides, but might have served many other purposes. Other types included several kinds of points and knives, **borers** (pointed stone tools suitable for making holes), and **burins** (tools with a sharp facet suitable for cutting or engraving materials such as wood or bone). **Notches** were tools with a notch retouched into an edge, perhaps for shaping wood. **Denticulates** were flakes heavily retouched to have a saw-toothed edge. Levallois flakes and points were also tabulated.

Bordes quantified the proportions of different tool types he found in the Middle Paleolithic assemblages. He also constructed proportions (indexes) that reflected the technological characteristics of the assemblage. One standard measure was the **Levallois Index,** essentially the proportion of artifacts in the assemblage made using the Levallois technique. Bordes used the proportions of artifact types and the indexes he devised to compare a large number of French Middle Paleolithic stone tool assemblages. He found that tool proportions were not random, but instead, clustered into five distinctive groups. Bordes named these groups the Typical Mousterian, Denticulate Mousterian (with many denticulates and notches), Mousterian of Acheulian Tradition (includes handaxes, in greater or lesser proportion), and a Charentian Group, divided into two subgroups after the sites where they were found: Quina Mousterian (with a high proportion of Levallois artifacts), and Ferrassie Mousterian (with a low proportion of Levallois artifacts).

◖ Explaining the Variability in Mousterian Assemblages: Tribes, Activities, and Tool Manufacture

These groups were not geographically separated, nor were they separated in time. Instead, at cave sites such as **Pech de L'Azé** and **Combe-Grenal** (Figure 7.6), strata bearing the different Mousterian groups interdigitate,

seemingly at random. Bordes interpreted the differing groups of Mousterian artifacts as the products of distinct, separate tribes of Mousterian people, coexisting in the French countryside, but scarcely interacting. It is hard to imagine such distinctive groups living together in close proximity for many millennia while maintaining their individual identities. Bordes, however, stressed the conservatism of primitive societies: "If one supposes that a Mousterian of Acheulian tradition man married a Quina woman, she might have gone on using the thick scrapers to which she was accustomed, but we doubt that her daughters would have done the same" (Bordes 1972: 147).

Bordes's viewpoint was immediately challenged. Lewis and Sally Binford (Binford and Binford 1966) subjected the data from some of Bordes's excavations, as well as data from Sally Binford's own excavation in the Near East, to a series of statistical analyses. From this analysis they produced a number of groups of artifacts, called factors, that tended to be correlated. They interpreted the various factors as representing differing activities. The different Mousterian assemblages, they suggested, were the result of whether the site was a base camp (where people slept, ate their meals, and carried on routine activities) or a hunting camp or work camp (where food or other raw materials were procured). The Binfords' interpretation drew fire in its turn. Bordes did not accept the Binfords' site classification as applicable to southwest France; he believed a wide range of activities took place in the sites. Others questioned the Binfords' statistical methods and their functional interpretation of the correlated groups of artifacts. The debate continued for some years.

Recently, a new approach has been offered to account for some of the variability in Mousterian stone assemblages. Departing from the conventional typology of Bordes, Harold Dibble (Dibble and Roland 1992) has focused instead on **lithic reduction sequences.** Stone tool types are not fixed, according to Dibble's research, but instead pass through a number of forms during the extended history of their use. As a scraper, for instance, is dulled by use, its edge must continually be resharpened by retouching. Over time the shape of the tool changes, and a large side scraper may eventually be reduced to become a small transverse scraper. Mousterian

Typical Mousterian

Denticulate Mousterian

Quina Mousterian

Ferrassie Mousterian

Mousterian of Acheulian Tradition

Figure 7.6

Diagram of stratigraphic section from Combe-Grenal, showing the stratigraphic positions of the various Mousterian variants.

toolmakers did not, therefore, set out to make a specific kit of scrapers with preconceived forms. The proportion of tool forms in an assemblage has much to do with how those tools were made, used, and reused over time.

The Culture of the Middle Paleolithic

For the Neanderthal people living in Europe during the height of the Ice Ages, life must have been very hard indeed. For much of the year, plant foods must have been scarce or nonexistent. At times the Neanderthals' diet must have consisted almost entirely of animal foods, either hunted or scavenged. To the south and east, the Neanderthals living near the Mediterranean in what is now Israel and in the mountains of what is now northern Iraq enjoyed somewhat less challenging conditions. Archaeologists generally agree that the Neanderthals were successful

hunters of small to medium-large animals. Philip Chase (1986, 1988) has studied the animal bone remains from the site of Combe-Grenal, France, closely. Many of the horses eaten at Combe-Grenal were in the prime of life. Large, meat-bearing bones, often with marks of butchery, are common in the assemblage. The ages at death of the animals and the butchery marks on the bones strongly indicate that the Mousterian inhabitants of this cave were hunting rather than scavenging horses (Chase 1986). The animal food remains found in European sites are dominated by the bones of red deer, wild cattle, horses, and reindeer. In the Near East, fallow deer, gazelle, and wild sheep and goats are the common food animals.

Mary Stiner's (1994) work on Mousterian faunas from Middle Paleolithic sites in west central Italy sheds important new light on Neanderthal subsistence practices and ecology. Stiner found that Neanderthals, like modern humans, obtained food both by hunting and by scavenging. However, she found that after about 55,000 years ago, there was a shift toward ambush hunting, focusing on prime-age adults. What is most interesting is that this change in foraging behavior does not correspond to a change in stone tool technology or to the replacement of one human form by another.

Whether the Neanderthals successfully hunted very large mammals, such as mammoth and hippopotamus, or simply scavenged them when they were available is an open question. A site that seems to illustrate at least one, perhaps exceptional, example of the hunting of large mammals has been found at **La Cotte de Sainte-Brelade,** on the Isle of Jersey in the English Channel. Found beneath a rock cliff, two large piles made up from the bones of numerous mammoths and woolly rhinos have been interpreted as the result of a Middle Paleolithic hunting drive (Scott 1980). Another find suggesting the hunting of large mammals is a spear made of yew wood, 2.5 meters (8 ft.) long, found beneath the skeleton of an elephant at the early Middle Paleolithic site of **Lehringen,** Germany.

Middle Paleolithic open-air sites are rare. Most of the sites discovered so far have been within caves and rock shelters, and archaeological exposures of horizontal surfaces in these sites have been limited. With the exception of a few sites at the very end of the Middle Paleolithic, shelters and other structures are unknown. Mousterian sites typically consist of scatters of stone tools and chipping debris along with bones from the animals eaten there. Many sites include hearths, presumably for protection and warmth, and perhaps for cooking food. These were simply large scatters of charcoal and ash without any additional structure. Constructed hearths with stone walls appear only at the very end of the Middle Paleolithic. In addition to the stone tools, hearths and animal bone food remains are the only significant evidence of everyday life during the Middle Paleolithic.

In the Near East, the Middle Paleolithic is typified by a variety of the Mousterian, known as the **Levalloiso-Mousterian,** that includes many Levallois flakes and points. Recent excavations in the cave of **Kebara,** in northern Israel, have produced one of the broadest exposures of a Mousterian site to date and have also provided new insights into the nature of the Neanderthals.

Case Study
The Excavations in Kebara Cave, Israel

The cave of Kebara, in the limestone hills overlooking the coastal plain of northern Israel, has been in use by humans for more than 60,000 years. In recent times, until the cave was first investigated by archaeologists in the 1920s, the cave continued in use by local pastoralists for penning their sheep and goats. The top several meters of the site, containing extensive remains from more recent periods, were excavated almost completely in the 1930s. Beneath lay Levalloiso-Mousterian deposits. In 1982, Israeli archaeologist Ofer Bar-Yosef and French anthropologist Bernard Vandermeersh began an interdisciplinary study of the cave, a project that included many other scholars as well (Bar-Yosef et al. 1992).

A principal goal of the excavation was a clarification of the absolute dating of the Middle Paleolithic of the region. Better dating was crucial for understanding the temporal relationship between the Neanderthal and more modern-appearing hominids in the area, both of whom produced Mousterian industries. (This issue will be discussed in detail in Chapter 8.) Other goals were studies of the distribution of the features, artifacts, and animal bones in the site, and of the processes that formed those deposits. The excavators also hoped to find new human fossils.

The excavation continued through nine field seasons. During this time many excavation units and soundings were placed in the cave. At the center of the cave, an area of about 12 square meters (130 sq ft.) was excavated with the greatest of care. This entire area was excavated horizontally, following the site's stratigraphy as closely as possible. A number of circular hearths containing charcoal and ashes were exposed. The positions of the many flint artifacts and animal bones were carefully recorded. Other Middle Paleolithic hearths were revealed in the carefully prepared stratigraphic cross sections elsewhere in the cave. The excavation was capped by the discovery in a deep sounding of a Neanderthal burial of great importance **(Figure 7.7)**.

As had been the case elsewhere, the hearths contained no stones or other trace of structure. They were merely roughly circular deposits of

Figure 7.7
Neanderthal burial from Kebara Cave in northern Israel.

charcoal, usually less than a meter across—fires built from oak wood and grasses. Above the charcoal was a layer of white ash, which appeared to have been spread about after the fire was extinguished. The hearths were ranged toward the front of the cave. Against the back wall of the cave was what appeared to be a refuse dump of artifacts and animal bones—gazelle, deer, horses, wild cattle, and many others, including even a few bones of rhinoceros. Many of the bones were burned or showed cut marks from butchery. The evidence indicates that the human inhabitants of the cave consumed this game, although carnivores such as hyenas clearly ravaged the bones during the intervals when the cave was not occupied. No animal bones were in the hearths, but carbonized seeds, particularly wild peas, were found among the charcoal. Kebara, therefore, contains evidence for the consumption of both animal and plant foods.

The burial in the deep sounding proved to hold the most complete Neanderthal skeleton yet discovered. The burial was dated by thermoluminescence and electron spin resonance to between 64,000 and 59,000 years ago. Although the skull itself was missing, the lower jaw and hyoid bone remained. Because the hyoid bone anchors the muscles of the tongue, it plays a role in the ongoing debate over whether or not Neanderthals were fully capable of speech. The Kebara hyoid, the first Neanderthal specimen discovered, was shaped much like that of modern humans, suggesting that the anatomy of the Neanderthal throat could probably have supported speech.

The Kebara Neanderthal was intentionally buried; the wall of the burial pit could clearly be discerned. The body of a male, lying on his back,

appeared to have been placed intact into his grave shortly after death. Only later, after the body had decayed, was the skull removed. The manner of removal argues that humans, rather than animals, removed the skull. Their purpose, of course, remains unknown.

The Issue of Neanderthal Burials

No human fossil from before the Middle Paleolithic shows any signs of having been intentionally buried. Early hominid remains are generally sparse and fragmentary, because they were preserved by the same processes that preserved any other animal fossil. Middle Paleolithic human remains, especially Neanderthals, are far more common and often more complete. In part, this is because at least some Neanderthals were quickly interred beneath the earth, and thus protected from scavengers and other natural processes that scatter and destroy bones. Because burials were made in caves, they were preserved where they could readily be found by archaeologists.

One of the first Neanderthals discovered, at Le Moustier, appeared to have been purposely buried. The find at La Chapelle-aux-Saints may also have been a burial. Seven burials were found in 1934 at the nearby site of **La Ferrassie.** Sometimes interpreted as a family cemetery, the graves included a man and woman, two children, and three infants. The skull of one of the children was buried separately from the body, under a stone.

Although Neanderthal burials have been a subject of controversy (Gargett 1989), most prehistorians accept that these people did bury at least some of their dead. A more difficult question is what Neanderthal burials imply about these people's concepts of religion and ritual. Stringer and Gamble (1993: 160) argue that these burials were not related to symbolic behavior at all, but were merely "corpse disposal." One Neanderthal burial difficult to fit into this description is the child's grave at **Teshik-Tash,** Uzbekistan. This burial was surrounded by a ring of goat horns driven point-down into the ground.

The huge cave of **Shanidar** in the Zagros mountains of Iraq, excavated in the 1950s by Ralph S. Solecki, has produced one of the largest samples of Neanderthal individuals found so far in any site (Solecki 1971; Trinkaus 1983). In all, nine Neanderthals were found in the cave. Four of them met their deaths beneath giant boulders falling from the roof of the cave. The remaining five were purposefully buried. One of these burials, Shanidar IV, seemed quite remarkable.

As Shanidar Cave was excavated, numerous soil samples were collected. Later, these samples were subjected to a **palynological** (pollen) **analysis** by specialist Arlette Leroi-Gourhan (1975). Pollen is resistant to decomposition and can provide much information about past environments and the human uses of plants (see Chapter 13). The pollen produced by flowering herbs and trees is quite distinctive in shape and can often be identified as to species. The plant species found in the Shanidar Cave samples that Leroi-Gourhan analyzed were all very consistent, with the exception of two samples that were quite different. Those samples contained very large numbers of flower pollen, many of them grouped into clumps indicating that they must have come from complete blossoms. Those samples (and later a third) proved to have come from the soil beneath the Neanderthal burial, Shanidar IV. Solecki and Leroi-Gourhan concluded that Shanidar IV must have been laid to rest in a grave lined with flowers. Their interpretation has been questioned, and the presence of the flower pollen has been attributed to contamination, perhaps borne in on workers' clothing. It is difficult to explain, however, why the approximately 6,000 other pollen determinations from the cave showed no sign of contamination.

If the evidence for flowers in the grave of Shanidar IV is accepted, it demonstrates a concern among the Neanderthals for the dead (or at least for the individual buried in that grave). Another of the Shanidar Neanderthals, Shanidar I, shows that these people could also show concern for the living. The Neanderthals lived a very harsh existence; many skeletons show signs of broken bones and other wounds. Life had been especially hard for Shanidar I. At some time, a blow to his body had damaged his right arm so badly that it withered away. The lower arm and hand either dropped off or were amputated. He was blind in one eye, and his legs were partially crippled. Yet this unfortunate individual probably lived into his forties—old age for a Neanderthal. It is difficult to imagine how this man could have survived the rigors of life for so long had he not been cared for by others. While the Shanidar Neanderthals may well have shown compassion, interpersonal violence was likely also a part of life. One of the ribs of another Shanidar Neanderthal shows a partially healed wound, probably caused by a thrusting weapon that may well eventually have cost him his life.

The Middle Paleolithic–Middle Stone Age in Africa

Neanderthals, strictly speaking, have not been found in Africa. Middle Paleolithic sites, however, are widespread across northern Africa. South of the Sahara a similar time span is filled by assemblages belonging to the African **Middle Stone Age.** A number of human fossils from this time have been found in Africa, most notably **Kabwe (Broken Hill),** from Zambia (formerly Northern Rhodesia, leading to the name Rhodesian Man). The skull, with massive brow ridges, in some ways resembles the Neanderthals, but today most scholars place it closer to the line leading to modern *Homo sapiens*. (This topic will be discussed in greater detail in Chapter 8.)

In North Africa the Acheulian was followed by a Mousterian industry similar to those of Europe and the Near East. At some time, perhaps as early as 70,000 years ago, the Mousterian was then replaced by a distinctive North African industry known as the **Aterian.** The Aterian stone tools possessed distinctive tangs (narrowed projections at the base) to facilitate hafting. Just who made the Aterian industry is not yet clear, but at the site of **Dar-es-Soltan,** Morocco, Aterian artifacts are associated with robust but modern-looking humans (Stringer and Gamble 1993: 131).

South of the Sahara, in broad regions of central and west Africa, the Acheulian industry developed into a characteristic African Middle Stone Age industry called the **Sangoan,** named after Sango Bay in Uganda. The Sangoan shows a very clear likeness to the Acheulian and is typified by large core scrapers and large, bifacially worked core tools, particularly a slender picklike form. Until recently the Sangoan industry was thought to

Figure 7.8
Middle Stone Age tools from the Klasies River Mouth, South Africa.

5 cm

be relatively late, dating to after 50,000 years ago. New date estimations, however, place the beginning of the Sangoan, at least at some sites, as early as 100,000 years ago, making it contemporary with the other industries discussed in this chapter. The Sangoan industry has sometimes been described as an adaptation to a forest environment, but this connection has never been clearly demonstrated. Since human fossil evidence is lacking, the makers of the Sangoan industry are unknown.

In South Africa, however, a new Middle Stone Age industry (sometimes called **Pietersburg**) appears that shows a complete break with the preceding Acheulian. Although numerous sites have been investigated, some with very deep deposits and long archaeological sequences, very little is known of the transition to this new industry. One of the best-known of these sites is **Klasies River Mouth** on the southern coast of South Africa **(Figure 7.8)**. The new industry appears with initial occupation of the site, dated to greater than 120,000 years ago. It is a flake-blade industry, with characteristic long, parallel-sided flakes struck from specially made cores. This industry persisted at Klasies River Mouth for perhaps 80,000 years. The site is rich in animal bone remains, indicative of the hunting and/or scavenging of a wide range of species (Klein 1976; Binford 1984). Shellfish were also gath-

ered throughout the occupation, the earliest example of exploitation of marine resources.

Human remains recovered at Klasies River Mouth have been interpreted as *Homo sapiens sapiens*—modern humans. This very early appearance of modern human forms is of great importance to our understanding of how anatomically modern humans spread throughout the Old World. Klasies River Mouth will be discussed in more detail in the following chapter.

Conclusion

For much of the latter part of the Pleistocene, until about 30,000 years ago, Europe and the Middle East were occupied by the Neanderthals, a form of human distinctly different from ourselves. They made and used stone tools that were quite different from and more varied than those of the preceding Acheulian. Neanderthals began to intentionally bury their dead, but what this implies about their worldview has been the subject of much debate. In the meantime, by about 100,000 years ago, modern *Homo sapiens sapiens* is appearing in southern Africa. In the next chapter we examine the replacement of the Neanderthals by anatomically modern humans.

Glossary

Aterian. A stone tool industry that replaced the Mousterian in North Africa, perhaps as early as 70,000 years ago. Aterian stone tools have distinctive tangs to facilitate hafting onto wooden shafts.

Borers. Stone tools retouched to create an extended projection used for drilling holes in materials such as wood and bone.

Burins. Stone tools with a chisel-shaped facet, used for engraving and sometimes cutting apart material such as bone and antler.

Combe-Grenal. A Middle Paleolithic cave site along the Dordogne River in southwestern France illustrating the interstratification of layers containing Typical Mousterian, Denticulate Mousterian, and Quina-type Mousterian industries.

Dar-es-Soltan. A site in Morocco that contained the remains of robust but modern-looking humans associated with an Aterian stone tool industry.

Denticulates. Flake tools with a series of sawlike teeth retouched onto the edges.

Ehringsdorf. A site located near Weimar in Germany that is dated to about 230,000 years ago and yielded the human fossils that show many of the characteristics of later Neanderthals, including heavy brow ridges.

Engis. A cave site in Belgium where the skull of a Neanderthal child was discovered in 1830. This was the first Neanderthal fossil to be discovered, although its importance was not recognized at the time.

Feldhofer. The site in the Neander Tal, a valley near Düsseldorf, Germany, where a Neanderthal skeleton was discovered in 1856.

Forbes' Quarry, Gibraltar. A site where in 1848 a Neanderthal skull was discovered during military construction.

Glacials. Episodes of worldwide cold temperatures during which much of the earth's water was trapped in large ice masses (glaciers) that covered large parts of northern Eurasia and North America.

Interglacials. Warmer periods that alternated with the glacials, when temperatures were often as high as or higher than they are today.

Kabwe (Broken Hill). A human skull discovered in Zambia (formerly Northern Rhodesia) that may be an ancestor of modern humans. This robust skull dates to perhaps 200,000 years ago and was formerly known as Rhodesian Man.

Kebara. A site in northern Israel that has yielded the remains of a nearly complete Neanderthal skeleton as well as extensive evidence for hearths, faunal remains, and Middle Paleolithic stone tools.

Klasies River Mouth. A site in South Africa where Middle Stone Age tools appear before 120,000 years ago associated with the remains of early anatomically modern humans.

La Chapelle-aux-Saints. A site in central France where a relatively complete Neanderthal skeleton was discovered in 1908. The Old Man of La Chapelle suffered from severe arthritis.

La Cotte de Sainte-Brelade. A site on the Isle of Jersey in the Channel Islands where

the bones of numerous woolly rhinos and mammoths have been found beneath a cliff. The site has been interpreted as the remains of a hunting drive.

La Ferrassie. A site in the Dordogne region of southwestern France that yielded seven Neanderthal burials. The site has sometimes been interpreted as a family cemetery.

Lehringen. An early Middle Paleolithic site in Germany that has produced the remains of a wooden spear found beneath the skeleton of an elephant.

Le Moustier. A site in the Dordogne region of southwestern France that gave its name to the Mousterian stone tool industry. The cave site has yielded Neanderthal skeletal remains in addition to a wide range of Middle Paleolithic stone tools.

Levallois Index. A measure of the proportion of Middle Paleolithic stone tools in an assemblage made using the Levallois technique (see Chapter 6).

Levalloiso-Mousterian. The term used to describe the Middle Paleolithic stone tool industry in the Near East. These assemblages generally include large numbers of Levallois flakes and points.

Lithic reduction sequences. Sequences of steps used to produce stone tools. Using refitting techniques, archaeologists can describe the steps used to produce a finished stone tool from an unmodified flint nodule. The ways in which a tool was resharpened and reused can also be determined.

Middle Paleolithic. The term used to describe the stone tool industries of Europe, the Middle East, and North Africa that date between about 130,000 and 40,000 years ago. They generally include a wider range of tool forms than the earlier Lower Paleolithic industries and often include large numbers of tools made using the Levallois technique.

Middle Stone Age. The term used to describe the African stone tool industries that are roughly contemporary with the Middle Paleolithic industries of Europe and the Near East. Middle Stone Age industries often include large numbers of parallel-sided flakes or blades, often produced using the Levallois technique.

Mousterian. A term used to describe the Middle Paleolithic (130,000 to 40,000 years ago) industries of Europe, North Africa, and the Middle East. These industries are named for the type site of Le Moustier in southwestern France.

Neanderthals. Archaic form of *Homo sapiens* found in Europe and the Middle East between about 130,000 and 30,000 years ago. The Neanderthals are characterized by massive brow ridges; sloping foreheads; long, low skulls; and the absence of a chin.

Notches. Stone flake tools with a notch retouched into one edge, possibly for woodworking.

Oxygen isotope stage. One of a series of alternating warm and cold climatic periods defined by the relative proportions of ^{18}O and ^{16}O in deep-sea cores.

Palynological analysis. Analysis of fossil plant pollen recovered from archaeological and geological sediments.

Pech de L'Azé. A deeply stratified cave site in southwestern France that illustrates the apparently random interstratification of different types of Mousterian industries such as Typical Mousterian and Denticulate Mousterian.

Pietersburg. A Middle Stone Age industry of southern Africa that is characterized by the production of parallel-sided flake-blades from prepared cores.

Retouch. Removal of a series of small flakes from one or more edges of a stone tool.

Sangoan. A Middle Stone Age industry of central and west Africa characterized by the presence of large core scrapers and bifacially worked core tools. It may represent an adaptation to forested environments.

Scrapers. Tools that may have been used to scrape hides. Various shapes of scrapers have been identified in Middle Paleolithic stone tool assemblages. The edges of these tools are generally modified by steep retouch.

Shanidar. A cave site in northern Iraq that produced the remains of nine Neanderthal individuals, including five that appear to have been intentionally buried.

Teshik-Tash. A Middle Paleolithic site in Uzbekistan that included a child's grave surrounded by a ring of wild goat horns, providing clear evidence for intentional burial of Neanderthals with grave goods.

Typology. The systematic classification of artifacts according to their shape or form.

Further Reading

Mellars, P.
   1996. *The Neanderthal Legacy: An Archaeological Perspective from Western Europe.* Princeton, NJ: Princeton University Press.
   An important new book on the archaeology of the Neanderthals in Europe.

Stringer, Christopher, and Clive Gamble
   1993. *In Search of the Neanderthals.* New York: Thames and Hudson.
   A readable introduction to the archaeology and physical anthropology of the Neanderthals written by two of the foremost authorities on the subject.

Trinkaus, Erik, and Pat Shipman
   1992. *The Neandertals: Of Skeletons, Scientists, and Scandal.* New York: Vintage Books.
   This book presents a detailed history of the discovery of the Neanderthals and shows how interpretations of Neanderthal behavior and phylogeny have changed through time.

Wong, Kate
   2000. Who Were the Neanderthals? *Scientific American* 282 (4): 98–107.
   An up-to-date summary of recent research on the Neanderthals and their relationship to anatomically modern humans.

Other Bibliography

Bar-Yosef, O., B. Vandermeersh, B. Arensburg, A. Belfer-Cohen, P. Goldberg, H. Laville, L. Meignen, Y. Rak, J. D. Speth, E. Tchernov, A-M. Tillier, and S. Weiner
   1992. The Excavations in Kebara Cave, Mt. Carmel. *Current Anthropology* 33 (5): 497–550.

Binford, Lewis R.
   1984. *Faunal Remains from the Klasies River Mouth.* New York: Academic Press.

Binford, Lewis, and Sally Binford
   1966. A Preliminary Analysis of Functional Variability in the Mousterian of Levallois Facies. *American Anthropologist* 68 (2): 238–295.

Bordes, F.
1968. *The Old Stone Age.* New York: McGraw-Hill.
1972. *A Tale of Two Caves.* New York: Harper and Row.
1984. *Leçons sur le Paléolithique II: Le Paléolithique en Europe.* Paris: Êditions du CNRS, Cahiers du Quaternaire 7.

Bordes, F., and D. de Sonneville-Bordes
1970. The Significance of Variability in Paleolithic Assemblages. *World Archaeology* 2: 61–73.

Chase, P. G.
1986. *The Hunters of Combe Grenal: Approaches to Middle Paleolithic Subsistence in Europe.* Oxford: British Archaeological Reports, International Series 286.
1988. Scavenging and Hunting in the Middle Paleolithic: The Evidence from Europe. In *Upper Pleistocene Prehistory of Western Eurasia,* edited by H. L. Dibble and A. Montet-White, pp. 226–232. Philadelphia: University Museum, University of Pennsylvania.

Dibble, H. L., and N. Roland
1992. On Assemblage Variability in the Middle Paleolithic of Western Europe: History, Perspectives, and a New Synthesis. In *The Middle Paleolithic: Adaptation, Behavior, and Variability,* edited by H. L. Dibble and P. Mellars, pp. 1–28. Philadelphia: University Museum, University of Pennsylvania.

Gargett, R.
1989. Grave Shortcomings: The Evidence for Neanderthal Burial. *Current Anthropology* 30: 157–190.

Klein, R. G.
1976. The Mammalian Fauna of the Klasies River Mouth Sites, Southern Cape Province, South Africa. *South African Archaeological Bulletin* 31: 75–98.

Leroi-Gourhan, Arlette
1975. The Flowers Found with Shanidar IV, a Neanderthal Burial in Iraq. *Science* 190: 562–564.

Scott, K.
1980. Two Hunting Episodes of Middle Paleolithic Age at La Cotte de Sainte-Brelade, Jersey (Channel Islands). *World Archaeology* 12: 137–152.

Solecki, Ralph S.
1971. *Shanidar—The First Flower People.* New York: Knopf.

Stiner, M. C.
1994. *Honor among Thieves: A Zooarchaeological Study of Neanderthal Ecology.* Princeton, NJ: Princeton University Press.

Trinkaus, Erik
1983. *The Shanidar Neanderthals.* New York: Academic Press.

Part IV

The Origins of Modern Human Society: Archaic versus Modern Cultures

Part IV examines the problem of the evolution of modern humans. Since early modern humans were the first hominids to inhabit the Arctic and sub-Arctic regions of both the Old and New Worlds, the chapters in this section examine the subsistence practices and settlement patterns of early modern humans in Eurasia, as well as the peopling of the New World and Australia. Chapter 8 examines both the molecular evidence and the hominid fossil record for the appearance of early modern humans. Chapters 9 and 10 examine the archaeological evidence for early modern human settlement and subsistence in the Near East and Europe. Chapter 11 focuses specifically on the art of the Upper Paleolithic and its implications for communication, social organization, and religion. In Chapter 12 we examine the migration route that modern humans may have used to enter the New World and Australia, as well as new evidence for the dating of those migrations.

Chapter 8

The Appearance of Modern Humans

Introduction

Shortly after 28,000 years ago, the last of the European Neanderthals disappeared. Anatomically modern humans, essentially like ourselves, took their place. In 1868 a group of skeletons much like those of modern humans was discovered in the cave of **Cro-Magnon,** in southern France. The artifact assemblage associated with those skeletons was quite different from the Mousterian tool kits usually associated with the Neanderthals. The appearance of the Cro-Magnon people coincided with the beginning of the **Upper Paleolithic** period in western Europe. Upper Paleolithic assemblages are far more varied than those of the Middle Paleolithic. A wide range of stone implements, many for specialized tasks, were retouched from stone **blades** struck from specially prepared **blade cores.** Blades are long, narrow, parallel-sided flakes, at least twice as long as they are wide. Upper Paleolithic assemblages also include large numbers of tools made from bone and antler. All these artifacts reflect an increasingly elaborate technology and material culture. Upper Paleolithic assemblages display many more regional and temporal differences than before, as will be discussed in Chapters 9 and 10. Art, virtually nonexistent before, arrives early in the Upper Paleolithic. The most notable examples are the spectacular cave paintings of western Europe (Chapter 11).

This swift transition has caught both scholarly and popular imaginations since the early years of the twentieth century. The slouching, primitive Neanderthal pictured by Marcellin Boule could scarcely be seen as an ancestor of modern humans, and the contrast between the limited range of the Mousterian culture and the richness of the Upper Paleolithic strongly reinforced that view. Fictional literature soon picked up the theme, building on the imagined conflict between the simple Neanderthals and the sophisticated, technologically superior modern humans who replaced them. Modern fiction, notably Jean Auel's *Clan of the Cave Bear,* has continued this tradition, albeit with more sympathy for the cultural and emotional capacities of the Neanderthals.

The Origins of Modern Humans

When and where did anatomically modern *Homo sapiens* originate? During the early years of the twentieth century the predominant view was that modern humans must have arrived from outside Europe and that the Neanderthals had little, if any, role in modern human ancestry. Some scholars, such as Boule, saw the Neanderthals as so different that the divergence of modern humans from the Neanderthal line must have occurred far in the past. Others, such as the American anthropologist W. W. Howells (1976), argued that the split occurred much more recently, and that modern humans and the so-called classic Neanderthals both derived from more generalized, although Neanderthal-like, ancestors.

A few scholars held a very different view. Ales Hrdlicka (1927) and later, Franz Weidenreich contended that certain anatomical traits seen in the fossil evidence suggested that the races of modern humans found in Europe, Asia, and Africa could be traced backward to the earliest inhabitants of those areas. According to this model, which emphasized regional continuity, the Neanderthals were direct ancestors of the modern human inhabitants of Europe, while the modern human inhabitants of East Asia and Africa found their roots in the peoples represented at Zhoukoudian and Kabwe, respectively. Milford Wolpoff (1989) championed a more recent version of this perspective, known as the **multiregional hypothesis.** Wolpoff emphasized the unity of modern *Homo sapiens.* He

Archaeology in Practice

Biochemical Evidence of Heredity and the Molecular Clock

How closely related are the living races of modern humans? In recent years techniques for the analysis of DNA have provided a new, quantitative measure of how closely any two individuals are related. DNA (deoxyribonucleic acid) is the molecular basis for heredity. In DNA, four different bases are strung together in a multitude of different ways. These combinations constitute the genetic code, which in turn determines the characteristics of an organism. Mutations, which provide the new variation that permits organisms to evolve, are random changes in the base sequences of DNA.

The millions of genes that determine the characteristics of an individual are enclosed in the nucleus of each cell. The mitochondria, located in the body of the cell, provide the cell with energy. The mitochondria, however, have a separate heredity from the remainder of the cell. Each mitochondrion encloses its own loop of DNA, encoding just 37 genes. While the DNA in the nucleus of the cell is derived from the fusion of sperm and egg during fertilization, **mitochondrial DNA (mtDNA)** is inherited from the mother alone. Mutations occur constantly in this DNA, but only mutations that cause no change in the mitochondrion's function are preserved. Since natural selection does not affect these mutations, they continue to accumulate indefinitely.

Observations have indicated that mutations occur frequently in mitochondrial DNA. Consequently, this DNA provides a good measure of how closely two individuals are related. The farther back in time they descended from a common maternal ancestor, the more different their mtDNA will be. Since all humans are related, ultimately, all modern people must share a common maternal ancestor at some time in the past. The question is how far back in time this common ancestor is to be found.

Mitochondrial DNA appears to mutate at a fairly constant rate. It can be used, therefore, as a kind of clock—the more variable a population's DNA, the farther back in time it diverged from its common ancestor. The difficulty lay in calibrating the clock. Rebecca Cann and her co-workers used two events with established dates to do this. The mtDNA of humans and chimpanzees, which diverged about 5 million years ago, are about 25 times more different than the variability seen in modern human populations. At the other end of the scale, Australian and New Guinea aboriginals, who reached those areas about 50,000 to 60,000 years ago, are only about one-third as variable as are modern humans as a whole. These considerations suggest that modern humans diverged from a common maternal ancestor roughly 200,000 years ago.

Recently, the mitochondrial DNA studies have been joined by new studies of certain genes found within the nuclear DNA (Tishkoff et al. 1995). One set of studies has concentrated on genes found on the Y chromosome (Dorit et al. 1995), making it possible to track human ancestry back through the paternal as well as the maternal line. The nuclear DNA studies agree rather well with mtDNA findings, suggesting that living humans descended from a common ancestor between 100,000 and 200,000 years ago.

The mtDNA data can also be used to construct family trees, using a statistical technique known as cluster analysis. Individuals with the greatest similarity are first grouped together; these groups are in turn linked to other groups, and the process is repeated until all the individuals are linked to a common ancestor. When this was done, individuals with the most closely similar mtDNA generally came from the same geographic region, and the pattern suggested that the earliest ancestor of modern humans came from Africa. The conclusion seemed clear: About 200,000 years ago (give or take 100,000 years) modern humans migrated out of Africa, completely displacing the preexisting inhabitants of Europe and Asia.

proposed that, while the African, Asian, Australian, and European populations evolved simultaneously, sufficient gene flow always occurred among these groups to maintain *Homo sapiens* as a single, if variable, species.

 ## The Biochemical Evidence

In recent years new fossil evidence, new absolute dates, and new biochemical evidence have strongly challenged the multiregional hypothesis. One of the most important new lines of research has been developed by molecular biologists, using a body of data totally separate from the fossil and archaeological evidence. In 1987 Rebecca Cann, Mark Stoneking, and Allan Wilson published a study comparing the mitochondrial DNA (see the Archaeology in Practice box) from 147 individuals from around the world (Cann et al. 1987). A statistical analysis of these data led them to conclude that the most likely origin for modern *Homo sapiens* lay in Africa. Later studies involving larger samples led them to suggest that all modern humans have descended from an ancestral population that spread out from Africa about 200,000 years ago. In the opinion of these molecular biologists, the preexisting populations of Europe and Asia, including the Neanderthals and the Asian representatives of *Homo erectus*, played no role at all in the ancestry of modern humans. This scenario, known as the **Out-of-Africa model,** was readily accepted by those anthropologists who had reached similar conclusions based on the fossil evidence (Stringer and Andrews 1988). More recently, however, the statistical methods used in these DNA studies have been questioned, and the proposed dating has been questioned as well. According to critics, the data can be interpreted to support points of origin other than Africa, and if Africa was the origin, the date of departure might be early enough to represent the initial spread of the hominids into Europe and Asia. While these issues remain unresolved, recent analyses of mitochondrial DNA (mtDNA) recovered from Neanderthal skeletons have cast additional doubt on the multiregional model.

In 1997 a team of German and American researchers (Krings et al. 1997) reported their analyses of mtDNA extracted from the Neanderthal type specimen from Feldhofer Cave in Germany. They found that the Neanderthal mtDNA was outside the range of variation of modern humans and concluded that Neanderthals contributed little, if anything, to modern human mtDNA. Three years later, another team of researchers (Ovchinnikov et al. 2000) reported the extraction and sequencing of mtDNA from a second Neanderthal individual, a 29,000-year-old infant from **Mezmaiskaya Cave** in the Caucasus of Georgia. That individual's mtDNA was also outside the

range of variation of modern humans. Moreover, the Mezmaiskaya mtDNA is strikingly similar to the mtDNA from the Feldhofer specimen, even though Feldhofer is located approximately 2,500 kilometers (1,550 mi.) from Mezmaiskaya.

Fossil Evidence: The Appearance of Modern Humans in Africa

The evidence from mtDNA is supplemented by a rich record of fossils from Africa, the Near East, and Europe **(Figure 8.1)**. Fossil evidence that has gradually accumulated is interpreted today as demonstrating the early evolution of African *Homo erectus* into anatomically modern *Homo sapiens*. The Kabwe (Broken Hill) skull from Zambia appears to date to near the beginning of this process, perhaps 200,000 years ago **(Figure 8.2)**. This robust skull is problematic, with a mixture of *erectus*-like and Neanderthal-like features. Limb bones found nearby somewhat resemble more modern *Homo sapiens*. Some scholars (Stringer and Gamble 1993: 127) would group the skull with *Homo heidelbergensis* (Chapter 6) and consider it a possible ancestor of both the Neanderthals and modern humans.

Fossil skulls dating to between 200,000 and 100,000 years ago that are regarded as transitional to modern *Homo sapiens* have been found in several parts of Africa. **Omo 2,** from Omo Kibish in Ethiopia, dated to about 130,000 years ago, is particularly notable. The rear of this skull resembles *Homo erectus*, but the face looks quite modern, with practically no brow ridge. A rather similar specimen was found at **Jebel Irhoud** in Morocco, although the dating is not so certain. A skull from the site of **Ngaloba,** Laetoli, Tanzania, dating to about 130,000 years ago, was found along with Middle Stone Age artifacts. This skull also has a mixture of ancient and modern features, but housed a fully modern-sized brain.

Fully modern humans seem to appear about 100,000 years ago in Africa. An anatomically modern skull and long bones found at **Omo Kibish,** not far from the spot where Omo 2 was found, may date to about 100,000 years ago. At Dar-es-Soltan in Morocco, a modern-looking skull was found in

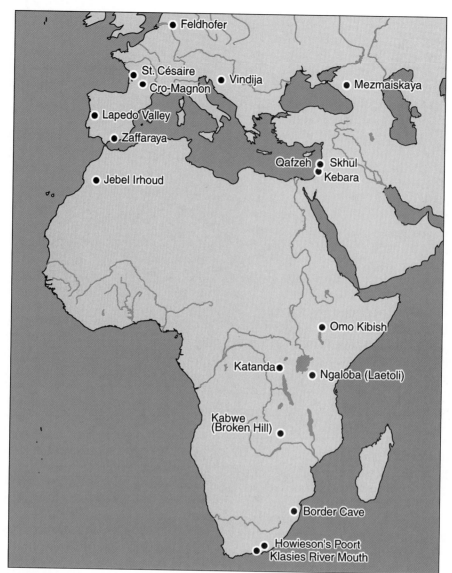

Figure 8.1

Location of sites mentioned in this chapter. The cave of Tabun is immediately adjacent to Skhul.

association with Middle Stone Age Aterian artifacts (Chapter 7). Modern-appearing humans' fossils have been found in the Middle Stone Age levels of **Border Cave** in Natal, South Africa, but it is possible that those fossils may be intrusive from later deposits.

Of greatest interest, however, is a series of skull fragments and limb bones from Klasies River Mouth, South Africa (mentioned in Chapter 7). These fragments, which closely resemble those of modern humans, are associated with the Middle Stone Age assemblages at the site, and date from 70,000 to

120,000 years ago (Rightmire and Deacon 1991). The site is rich in animal bone remains indicative of the hunting and/or scavenging of a wide range of species. Klasies River Mouth, which is very near the coast, provides the earliest example for the exploitation of marine resources (Klein 1979). Although no evidence for fishing was recovered, seals made up a substantial part of the diet, and shellfish were also gathered throughout the occupation.

The elongated flake-blade Pietersburg-like Middle Stone Age stone industry at Klasies River Mouth somewhat resembles the blade

Figure 8.2

Kabwe (Broken Hill) skull, formerly known as Rhodesian Man.

Figure 8.3

Typical tools, including microliths, of the Howieson's Poort industry.

industries that make their appearance with the Upper Paleolithic (see Chapter 9), although no direct relationship is likely. This stone industry persists through the entire Middle Stone Age occupation of the site complex, except for a brief interruption that occurred about 70,000 years ago. For a short time the flake-blade industry was displaced by an industry that included very small stone blades, often trimmed into tiny geometric forms known as **microliths** (very tiny stone tools). This industry, called **Howieson's Poort,** is known from a number of sites in the region (**Figure 8.3**). The Howieson's Poort industry is by far the earliest known occurrence of a microlithic stone industry; it anticipates by 50,000 years the microlithic assemblages that would characterize the Epi-paleolithic and

Mesolithic cultures of the Near East and Europe (Chapters 15 and 18). The makers of the Howieson's Poort industry are unknown, as no associated human remains have been found.

Even more unusual are the finds made by Alison Brooks and John Yellen at some Middle Stone Age sites at **Katanda,** in the Upper Semliki Valley, Zaire (Brooks et al. 1995; Yellen et al. 1995). In close association with Middle Stone Age artifacts, these sites contained a series of finely worked bone points, many with barbs along one or both edges (**Figure 8.4**). In general form and sophistication of manufacture, these bone points resemble artifacts typical of the European Upper Paleolithic of 15,000 years ago. Surprisingly, thermoluminescence and electron spin resonance measures have dated the deposits to approximately 90,000 years ago. Numerous bones of large catfish were found along with the bone points. The people at Katanda probably camped there to fish in the nearby streams—perhaps the bone points served as fishing implements. If the early

Figure 8.4

Example of a finely worked bone point from Katanda, Zaire.

10 cm

dates hold true, the Katanda sites may provide evidence for much greater technological sophistication at this early time than had previously been thought possible.

New finds and new, much earlier, dates assigned to African stone industries strongly support Africa as the original home of modern *Homo sapiens*. New absolute dates have also changed our picture of the relationship of modern *Homo sapiens* to the Neanderthals in the Near East.

Case Study
Skhul, Qafzeh, and Kebara: Anatomically Modern Humans and Neanderthals in the Levant

In the period between the First and Second World Wars a series of excavations was conducted in the Near East that did much to establish the prehistory of the area. The research done by the British archaeologist Dorothy Garrod, along with an international, interdisciplinary team, in the Mount Carmel region of northern Israel was particularly important. Garrod excavated a number of caves and rock shelters in the Wadi Mughara (Valley of the Caves) near the coast of the Mediterranean. The deposits in these caves spanned much of the Paleolithic and helped define the sequence of archaeological industries of the Levant (Garrod and

Bate 1937). Two of these caves, the **Mugharet es Skhul** (the cave of the kids) and the **Mugharet et Tabun** (the cave of the oven) contained Middle Paleolithic layers filled with artifacts belonging to the Levalloiso-Mousterian industry (Chapter 7). Both caves also contained a number of human skeletons. The cave of Skhul held the remains of 10 individuals, including a child, apparently intentionally buried. Several lay in what is known as a flexed posture, with their knees drawn up to their chests. One male held the jaw of a wild boar in his arms. In the cave of Tabun a skeleton of a woman was found, plus a separate large jawbone.

All these skeletons had features more or less reminiscent of the European Neanderthals, but the fossils differed greatly from one another. The Skhul skeletons, particularly, looked far more like modern humans than did those from Tabun. All, however, were associated with Mousterian tools. Initially, the entire group of Mount Carmel skeletons was regarded as a highly variable Neanderthal population.

The cave of **Qafzeh,** near Nazareth, was also initially excavated between the wars by the French archaeologist René Neuville. Neuville found five skeletons in the Middle Paleolithic Mousterian levels, but he died before the data could be published. In the 1960s Bernard Vandermeersch took over the excavation of the cave. The remains of 24 more individuals were found. Among them was a burial of a young woman with a 6-year-old child buried across her feet. Another child was buried with the skull of a deer, complete with antlers. The Qafzeh skeletons, accompanied by Mousterian tools, looked very much like the skeletons from Skhul.

Vandermeersch undertook an extensive study of the Qafzeh remains (Vandermeersch 1981). He demonstrated that the Qafzeh people (and the very similar Skhul population) were actually early anatomically modern humans rather than Neanderthals **(Figure 8.5)**. Their stone industry, however, was Levalloiso-Mousterian, essentially the same as that of other undoubted Neanderthals who also lived in the region. This finding shattered the old belief that only Neanderthals were associated with the Mousterian. Contrary to the expectations of archaeologists, two very different groups of people were making and using the same kinds of tools.

More surprises were to come. Dating of the Near Eastern Middle Paleolithic deposits had long been a problem, as their dates lay well beyond the limits of radiocarbon age determination (Chapter 10). Some scholars assumed that because the Skhul and

Figure 8.5

Early modern human skull from Qafzeh, northern Israel.

Qafzeh people were closer to modern humans, they must necessarily be later than the Neanderthals of Tabun. Israeli zoologist Eitan Tchernov (1981, 1989) argued otherwise. On the basis of his studies of the small mammal remains found in the deposits, Tchernov argued that the Qafzeh hominids were much earlier than had been supposed. This idea was greeted with skepticism, but when electron spin resonance and thermoluminescence dating became available, these methods confirmed Tchernov's inference. Qafzeh was dated by thermoluminescence to 92,000 years ago, and by electron spin resonance to between 100,000 and 120,000 years ago. Somewhat later, Skhul was found to have similarly early dates. (See Schwarcz 1994 for a summary of the dating evidence from these sites.)

At the same time, the Neanderthal skeleton from Kebara Cave was securely dated to between 64,000 and 59,000 years ago. (The excavation of the Neanderthal skeleton from the cave of Kebara in northern Israel has been described in some detail in Chapter 7.) This dating evidence means that Neanderthal people were inhabiting the Levant about 40,000 years *after* modern humans lived there. New dates for the Neanderthal layers at Tabun, on the other hand, have placed them at about the same time as Qafzeh and Skhul.

The relationship between modern humans and the Neanderthal people in the Levant remains very unclear. It is difficult to imagine such dissimilar groups living side by side, producing essentially the same material culture. Although the stone tool assemblages used by the Neanderthals and early modern humans in the Near East are quite similar, detailed studies of the stone tool assemblages and the fauna from these sites have pointed up some subtle but intriguing differences in the ways these two groups made a living (Lieberman and Shea 1994; Shea 1993). The faunal data indicate that the sites occupied by anatomically modern humans were occupied for only one season, while those occupied by Neanderthals were occupied for more than one season. On the other hand, the stone tool assemblages associated with the Neanderthals include a slightly higher percentage of projectile (spear) points, indicating that the Neanderthals may have hunted somewhat more frequently than anatomically modern humans did. The increased intensity of hunting by the Neanderthals might have been a strategy for coping with the animal resource depletion that resulted from multiseasonal occupation of sites over a long period of time (Lieberman and Shea 1994).

The Levant is an ecological crossroads where African and European flora and fauna intermingle and alternate according to changes in climatic conditions. Perhaps Neanderthal and modern human groups alternated in the region, with Neanderthal groups moving in during times of harsh glacial conditions in the north (Tchernov 1992).

From Africa to Europe

In broad terms the African and Near Eastern fossil evidence and the new dates provided by thermoluminescence and electron spin resonance accord well with conclusions drawn by the DNA specialists: Modern humans left Africa about 100,000 years ago. The early modern humans living in the caves of the Levant may well have been among that first wave of emigrants. Modern humans, however, are unknown in central and western Europe before the appearance of the Cro-Magnon people, about 32,000 years ago. The Aurignacian stone tool industry, which is generally associated with modern humans, appears in Europe a few thousand years earlier than the earliest modern human fossils. The movements of early modern humans in the intervening 60,000 years are currently unclear. Perhaps they continued pushing eastward into Asia, leaving Europe to the Neanderthals. Modern humans spread into western Europe at a relatively late date, probably at first coexisting with the Neanderthals and then displacing them.

Saint Césaire and the Last Neanderthals

It is clear that some Neanderthals lingered on in western Europe even as modern humans were appearing. In 1979, construction workers discovered an archaeological site near the base of a cliff called La Roche à Pierrot, near the village of **Saint Césaire,** in western France (Lévêque et al. 1993). A salvage excavation was quickly organized. When the site was dug, the archaeologists (led by François Lévêque) discovered the skeleton of the most recent Neanderthal then known. Thermoluminescence dates on flints near the skeleton placed its age at about 36,300 ± 2,700 years ago. The Saint Césaire skeleton was a nearly complete, tightly flexed burial. What was most remarkable, though, was the stone industry with which it was associated. All previous European Neanderthals had been found along with Mousterian tools. The Saint Césaire Neanderthal was associated with a stone industry known as the **Châtelperronian.** Actually, the Châtelperronian contains many Mousterian artifact types, including Levallois flakes and Mousterian-like scrapers and points. What distinguishes the Châtelperronian industry is the prevalence of a pointed blade implement with a curved, blunted back, known as a Châtelperron knife. Although François Bordes had argued that the Châtelperronian evolved from the Mousterian of Acheulian Tradition (Chapter 7), the Châtelperronian had always been considered an Upper Paleolithic industry, and it had tacitly been assumed to have been the work of modern humans.

How should this surprising discovery be interpreted? For those archaeologists who held to a multiregionalist view, the Saint Cé-

saire find lent support to the idea that the Neanderthals were independently evolving to an Upper Paleolithic way of life. Those who argued that the Neanderthals were replaced by modern humans from elsewhere saw in the Saint Césaire Châtelperronian industry an example of the last Neanderthals borrowing ideas from the modern humans with whom they were now coming into contact.

During the past 20 years, even more recent Neanderthal fossils have been discovered in Europe. Neanderthal bones dating to 32,000 years ago were found at Zafarraya in Spain (Smith 2000). A Neanderthal fossil from **Vindija** in Croatia has been dated to 28,000 to 29,000 years ago (Smith et al. 1999), and the infant from Mezmaiskaya Cave in the Caucasus is of similar age. Since modern humans were established in Europe by 32,000 years ago, these new dates clearly indicate that Neanderthals and modern humans coexisted in Europe for several thousand years.

In 1998 an even more intriguing fossil discovery was made when a child's skeleton was found in Portugal's Lapedo Valley. The 24,500-year-old skeleton appears to be a modern human, but it shares some characteristics with Neanderthals, including short lower limbs. Some anthropologists have seen the **Lapedo Child** (Figure 8.6) as a hybrid between a Neanderthal and a modern human.

Conclusion

Although the Neanderthals and modern humans seem to have coexisted in Europe for several millenia, shortly after 28,000 years ago the last Neanderthals were replaced by modern humans. These modern humans carried with them the more advanced tools of the Aurignacian industry, which marked the beginning of the Upper Paleolithic period (Chapter 10). The nature of this replacement remains a matter of great debate. As Erik Trinkaus, a biological anthropologist from Washington University, recently noted:

> The extinction of the Neanderthals by early modern humans, whether by displacement or population absorption, was a slow and geographically mosaic process. The differences between the two groups in basic behavior and abilities must have been small and rather subtle. (UniSci 1999: 1)

Figure 8.6

The Lapedo Child, seen by some as a possible Neanderthal–modern human hybrid.

While Neanderthals ultimately became extinct, recent multidisciplinary research has shed new light on the biology and behavior of this archaic form of humanity.

 Glossary

Blades. Long, narrow stone flakes with parallel sides. Blades are generally at least twice as long as they are wide.

Blade cores. Cores from which blades are struck. Blade cores are generally prismatic (faceted), and blades are struck off in sequence all around the core (see Chapter 10).

Border Cave. A site in the Natal region of South Africa that has produced the remains of anatomically modern humans.

Châtelperronian. A European stone tool industry that shows both Middle Paleolithic and Upper Paleolithic features. The industry includes Levallois flakes, Mousterian-like scrapers, and backed knives made on blades. This industry was associated with the Saint Césaire Neanderthal.

Cro-Magnon. A cave site in the Dordogne region of southwestern France that has produced the remains of early anatomically modern humans.

Howieson's Poort. A Middle Stone Age industry, dating to about 70,000 years ago, characterized by the presence of microliths.

Jebel Irhoud. A site in Morocco that yielded a skull whose features are transitional between *Homo erectus* and modern humans.

Katanda. A site in Zaire, dated to approximately 90,000 years ago, that has produced Middle Stone Age artifacts and a number of finely worked bone points, many with barbs along one or both edges.

Lapedo Child. A skeleton from Portugal of a 4-year-old child dated to 24,500 years ago. The skeleton shows morphological features of both modern humans and Neanderthals. Some anthropologists have interpreted the child as a hybrid.

Mezmaiskaya Cave. A cave in Georgia (in the Caucasus) that has yielded the remains of a 29,000-year-old Neanderthal infant. Recent studies have shown that the infant's mtDNA is outside the range of modern human variation but is quite similar to that of the Feldhofer Neanderthal from Germany.

Microliths. Very small stone tools, often hafted or used as barbs for arrowheads.

Mitochondrial DNA (mtDNA). DNA (or units of heredity) that is located in the body, not the nucleus, of the cell and is inherited from the mother only.

Mugharet es Skhul. A cave site in the Mount Carmel region of northern Israel that has produced the remains of 10 human individuals associated with a Levalloiso-Mousterian industry. The human fossils appear to be early anatomically modern people.

Mugharet et Tabun. A cave site in the Mount Carmel region of northern Israel that has yielded the skeleton of a woman in addition to a Levalloiso-Mousterian stone tool assemblage.

Multiregional hypothesis. The hypothesis proposing that modern human populations in Africa, Asia, and Europe are descended from earlier (*Homo erectus*) populations in each area. Sufficient gene flow would have occurred among these groups to maintain *Homo sapiens* as a single, variable population.

Ngaloba. A site in Tanzania that yielded a skull that shows a mix of modern human and archaic (*Homo erectus*-like) features. It was found associated with a Middle Stone Age stone tool assemblage.

Omo 2. A skull from Omo Kibish, Ethiopia, dating to about 130,000 years ago. The face looks quite modern, but the rear portion of the skull resembles earlier *Homo erectus* fossils.

Omo Kibish. A site in Ethiopia that yielded an anatomically modern skull and limb bones dating to about 100,000 years ago as well as Omo 2, a skull resembling *Homo erectus*.

Out-of-Africa model. The model proposing that all modern populations descended from an anatomically modern human ancestor that evolved in Africa between 100,000 and 200,000 years ago.

Qafzeh. A cave site in northern Israel that has produced the remains of anatomically modern humans associated with a Levalloiso-Mousterian stone tool industry.

Saint Césaire. A site in western France where the remains of a Neanderthal, dated to about 36,000 years ago, were found in association with Châtelperronian tools.

Upper Paleolithic. A term used to describe the Late Pleistocene (ca. 35,000 to 10,000 years ago) industries of Europe, the Near East, and North Africa. These industries are generally characterized by a high proportion of blade tools.

Vindija. A cave site in Croatia yielding a Neanderthal skeleton that has recently been radiocarbon dated to between 28,000 and 29,000 years ago.

 ## Further Reading

Klein, R. G.

   1995. Anatomy, Behavior, and Modern Human Origins. *Journal of World Prehistory* 9 (2): 167–198.

   This article provides a comprehensive overview of the problem of the origins of modern humans and includes an extensive and up-to-date bibliography.

Other Bibliography

Brooks, Alison S., David M. Helgren, Jon S. Cramer, Alan Franklin, William Hornyak, Jody M. Keating, Richard G. Klein, William J. Rink, Henry Schwarcz, J. N. Leith Smith, Kathlyn Stewart, Nancy E. Todd, Jacques Verniers, and John E. Yellen

   1995. Dating and Context of Three Middle Stone Age Sites with Bone Points in the Upper Semliki Valley, Zaire. *Science* 268: 548–553.

Cann, R., M. Stoneking, and A. Wilson
   1987. Mitochondrial DNA and Human Evolution. *Nature* 325: 31–36.

Dorit, R. L., H. Akashi, and W. Gilbert
   1995. Absence of Polymorphism at the ZFY Locus on the Human Y Chromosome. *Science* 268: 1183.

Garrod, D. A. E., and D. M. A. Bate
   1937. *The Stone Age of Mount Carmel,* vol. I. Oxford: Clarendon Press.

Howells, W. W.
   1976. Explaining Modern Man: Evolutionists versus Migrationists. *Journal of Human Evolution* 5: 477–495.

Hrdlicka, A.
   1927. The Neanderthal Phase of Man. *Journal of the Royal Anthropological Institute* 67: 249–269.

Klein, R. G.
   1979. The Mammalian Fauna of the Klasies River Mouth Sites, Southern Cape Province, South Africa. *South African Archaeological Bulletin* 31: 75–98.

Krings, M., A. Stone, R. W. Schmitz, H. Krainitski, M. Stoneking, and S. Pääbo
1997. Neanderthal DNA Sequences and the Origin of Modern Humans. *Cell* 90: 19–30.

Lévêque, F., M. Backer, and M. Guilbaud
1993. *Context of a Late Neanderthal.* Madison, WI: Prehistory Press, Monographs in World Prehistory 16.

Lieberman, D. E., and John J. Shea
1994. Behavioral Differences between Archaic and Modern Humans in the Levantine Mousterian. *American Anthropologist* 96 (2): 300–332.

Ovchinnikov, I. V., A. Götherström, G. P. Romanova, V. M. Kharitonov, K. Lidens, and W. Goodwin
2000. Molecular Analysis of Neanderthal DNA from the Northern Caucasus. *Nature* 404: 490–493.

Rightmire, G., and H. Deacon
1991. Comparative Studies of Late Pleistocene Human Remains from Klasies River Mouth, South Africa. *Journal of Human Evolution* 20: 131–156.

Schwarcz, H. P.
1994. Chronology of Modern Humans in the Levant. In *Late Quaternary Chronology and Paleoclimates in the Eastern Mediterranean,* edited by O. Bar-Yosef and R. S. Kra, pp. 21–31. Tucson, AZ: Radiocarbon.

Shea, J.
1993. Lithic Use-Wear Evidence for Hunting by Neanderthals and Early Modern Humans from the Levantine Mousterian. In *Hunting and Animal Exploitation in the Later Paleolithic and Mesolithic of Eurasia,* edited by G. L. Peterkin, H. M. Bricker, and P. Mellars, pp. 189–197. Washington, DC: Archaeological Papers of the American Anthropological Association 4.

Smith, Fred H.
2000. The Fate of the Neanderthals, pp. 106–107 in Who Were the Neanderthals, by Kate Wong, *Scientific American* 282 (4): 98–107.

Smith, F. H., E. Trinkaus, P. B. Pettitt, I. Karavanić and M. Paunović
1999. Direct Radiocarbon Dates for Vindija G and Velika Pecina Late Pleistocene Hominid Remains. *Proceedings of the National Academy of Sciences* 96 (22): 12281–12286.

Stringer, C., and P. Andrews
1988. Genetic and Fossil Evidence for the Origin of Modern Humans. *Science* 239: 1263–1268.

Stringer, C., and C. Gamble
1993. *In Search of The Neanderthals.* New York: Thames and Hudson.

Tchernov, E.
1981. The Biostratigraphy in the Middle East. In *Préhistoire du Levant,* edited by J. Cauvin and P. Sanlaville, pp. 69–97. Paris: Êditions du CNRS.
1989. The Middle Paleolithic Mammalian Sequence and Its Bearing on the Origin of *Homo sapiens* in the Southern Levant. In *Investigations in South Levantine Prehistory,* edited by O. Bar-Yosef and B. Vandermeersch, pp. 25–42. Oxford: British Archaeological Reports, International Series 497.
1992. Biochronology, Paleoecology, and Dispersal Events of Hominids in the Southern Levant. In *The Evolution and Dispersal of Modern Humans in Asia,* edited by T. Akazawa, K. Aoki, and T. Kimura, pp. 149–188. Tokyo: Hokusen-sha.

Tishkoff, S. A., E. Dietzsch, W. Speed, A. J. Pakstis, J. R. Kidd, K. Cheung, B. Bonné-Tamir, A. S. Santachiara-Benerecetti, P. Moral, M. Krings, S. Pääbo, E. Watson, N. Risch, T. Jenkins, and K. K. Kidd
1995. Global Patterns of Linkage Disequilibrium at the CD4 Locus and Modern Human Origins. *Science* 271: 1380–1387.

Trinkaus, E., and C. Duarte
2000. The Hybrid Child from Portugal, pp. 102–103 in Who Were the Neanderthals, by Kate Wong, *Scientific American* 282 (4): 98–107.

UniSci
1999. Neanderthals, Modern Humans, Coexisted, Likely Cohabited. Daily University Science News, October 26, 1999. http://unisci.com/stories/19994/102699.htm

Vandermeersch, Bernard
1981. *Les hommes fossiles de Qafzeh (Isräel).* Paris: Êditions du CNRS.

Wolpoff, M. H.
1989. Multiregional Evolution: The Fossil Alternative to Eden. In *The Human Revolution: Behavioural and Biological Perspectives on the Origins of Modern Humans,* vol. I, edited by P. Mellars and C. Stringer, pp. 62–108. Edinburgh: Edinburgh University Press.

Yellen, John E., Alison S. Brooks, Els Cornelissen, Michael J. Mehlman, and Kathlyn Stewart
1995. A Middle Stone Age Worked Bone Industry from Katanda, Upper Semliki Valley, Zaire, *Science,* 268: 553–556.

Chapter 9

Late Paleolithic Cultures of the Near East and Africa

Introduction

As we saw in the previous chapter, the relationship between archaic and early modern humans is complex. While early modern humans appeared in Africa 100,000 or more years ago, modern humans did not replace the European Neanderthals until around 30,000 years ago. The relationship between archaic and modern humans is even more complicated in the Near East, where modern humans appeared at such sites as Qafzeh and Skhul over 90,000 years ago, but Neanderthals are known from more recent sites, including Kebara and Shanidar. Moreover, there is no simple correlation between fossil humans and the kinds of artifacts they left behind. In the Middle East both Neanderthals and early modern humans made Mousterian tools. In addition, the differences between Neanderthal and modern behavior in the Near East are subtle; early modern humans appear to have been somewhat more mobile, while Neanderthals used more spear points, perhaps indicating that they hunted more frequently (Lieberman and Shea 1994).

In this chapter we will examine the late Pleistocene cultures of the Near East and Africa, from about 40,000 years ago to the end of the Ice Age, about 10,000 years ago. We will be looking at the archaeological record of early modern humans, although human skeletal remains are few in both areas. The stone tool industries we will discuss are termed **Upper Paleolithic** in the Near East and northern Africa, while in sub-Saharan Africa, the term **Late Stone Age** is used. In addition to examining the development of stone tool technologies in these areas, we will also look at changes in settlement patterns and subsistence strategies. That is, we will ask how these early human populations made a living by hunting, gathering, and other activities, such as fishing.

Although identifying artifacts such as spear points as hunting weapons provides some information about these early humans, examining faunal remains (archaeologically recovered animal bones) plays a crucial role in the study of prehistoric subsistence. Bones are preserved with increasing frequency in late Pleistocene sites. The ways in which animal bones can be used to reconstruct hunting practices are described in the Archaeology in Practice box.

The Upper Paleolithic in the Near East

Until the 1960s, excavations of Upper Paleolithic sites in the Near East had focused on a limited number of caves and rock shelters. In the past 30 years, however, our knowledge of Upper Paleolithic sites in the Near East has expanded dramatically. Many new sites have been discovered as a result of archaeological survey projects in the Negev Desert, in the Sinai, and in southern Jordan. New caves and open sites have been excavated, and artifactual and faunal materials from old excavations have been reanalyzed. These efforts have resulted in a revised picture of life in the Near East in late Pleistocene times.

During the cold phases of the Pleistocene glaciations, ice sheets covered many of the northerly parts of Eurasia and North America. Although the Near East was not covered by glacial ice, the glaciations in the northern latitudes had significant effects on the climate of the region. In general, periods of glacial advance in the northern latitudes correspond to relatively cold and dry eras in the Levant (the regions of the Near East bordering on the Mediterranean). The period between 75,000 and 45,000 years ago was a relatively dry period in the Near East, and relatively dry conditions continued until about 32,000 years ago. The climate became more humid between 32,000 and 22,000 years ago, but very cold and dry conditions prevailed between 22,000 and 13,000 years ago.

Archaeology in Practice

Animal Remains as Archaeological Evidence

Zooarchaeology (Brewer 1992, Reitz and Wing 1999), or faunal analysis, is the study of animal remains, primarily bone and shell, recovered from archaeological sites. It is one of the fastest-growing specializations in modern archaeology. Until the 1950s animal bones and shells were rarely collected from archaeological sites in a systematic way. Fine screens were not always used, so the remains of small vertebrates such as birds, fish, and rodents were often lost during excavation. In addition, excavators often saved only complete or identifiable bones, abandoning many bone fragments in the field. Animals bones were identified by zoologists, whose interests were not always the same as those of prehistoric archaeologists.

As archaeologists have become increasingly interested in the dynamic relationship between past human cultures and their environments, faunal studies have come to play a major role in archaeological analysis and interpretation. Faunal remains can provide valuable information on prehistoric subsistence strategies, hunting practices, and diets. Zooarchaeology also plays an important role in the study of animal domestication and animal husbandry practices (Chapter 18).

At the most basic level, faunal analysts can identify the animal species that were killed by prehistoric hunters. Since most archaeological animal bones have been butchered and broken, they are more difficult to identify than complete specimens. Bone fragments are identified using a **comparative collection** of modern reference specimens. Taphonomic studies (Chapter 4; see also Lyman 1994) can be used to distinguish the remains of hunted and scavenged animals from fauna that may have entered the deposit naturally.

Archaeologists want more than just a laundry list of the animal species present in an archaeological deposit; they want to know which animals were most important in prehistoric economies. A number of methods of quantification (Grayson 1984) have been developed to estimate the relative importance of the various animal species in an archaeological assemblage. The two most widely used techniques are the fragment count, or **NISP (number of identified specimens per taxon)** method, and the **MNI (minimum number of individuals).** Using the NISP method, species frequencies are based on the counts of bones identified to each species of animal. For an assemblage that included 400 reindeer bones and 100 bison bones, the ratio of reindeer to bison would be 4 to 1. The MNI method is used to calculate the minimum number of animals that are needed to account for all the bones of a given species in an archaeological bone collection. For example, a minimum of 8 reindeer are needed to account for 8 left reindeer femurs (thigh bones). Thus, a minimum of 8 reindeer and 2 bison would also produce a reindeer-to-bison ratio of 4 to 1. Zooarchaeologists have debated endlessly over the relative merits of these two methods (see, for example, Grayson 1984; Marshall and Pilgrim 1993), but both are commonly used by faunal analysts.

Zooarchaeologists can also identify the ages of the animals that were killed by prehistoric hunters. Aging data can allow archaeologists to determine whether hunters were preying on whole herds of animals, whether they were focusing on mature adults, or whether they were killing only immature and elderly animals. Both teeth and limb bones can be used to estimate the ages of mammals. In mammals, the deciduous, or milk, teeth are replaced by permanent teeth in a known sequence. The degree of tooth wear can be an approximate indicator of age in older animals. The limb bones of mature mammals can also be distinguished from those of juvenile mammals. In juvenile animals, the ends of the long bones are separated from their shafts by plates of cartilage. When the animal nears bodily maturity, the plates of cartilage ossify, joining the bone ends to their shafts.

Zooarchaeologists can use a variety of techniques to determine the season or seasons in which animals were killed (Monks 1981). These data can indicate whether animals were being killed throughout the year, or whether they were killed during only one season. The data have important implications for studies of settlement patterns and seasonal mobility (Lieberman 1994). In addition, large seasonal kills may have necessitated some form of meat preservation, such as drying, smoking, or freezing.

Butchery marks on bone can indicate the techniques used to dismember the carcass and to remove the meat from the bones. Limb bones may also have been broken for the extraction of marrow (Figure 9.1). In addition, careful identification and matching of the bones can allow the archaeologists to trace the distribution of a single animal across a site.

Figure 9.1

Animal long bones broken for the extraction of marrow.

Figure 9.2

Location of Near Eastern sites mentioned in this chapter in relationship to the distribution of the Mediterranean climatic zone.

site of **Boker Tachtit** (Marks and Kaufman 1983), located near a spring-fed lake at the mouth of a narrow box canyon, was occupied between about 45,000 and 38,000 years ago. The occupation floors at Boker Tachtit provided evidence of core stone tool production, use, and discard. By careful refitting of the stone tool fragments, archaeologists were able to reconstruct the process by which stone tools were manufactured at the site. In the early phases of the site, points and blades were produced using a specialized Levallois technique, a typically Middle Paleolithic method of stone tool production. By the end of the occupation, blades were produced from single striking platform blade cores, a strategy that is more typical of later Upper Paleolithic sites. The Upper Paleolithic blade core technology is more efficient than the Levallois technique; that is, more cutting edge can be produced from the same amount of flint using the blade core technology. The excavator of the site, Anthony Marks of Southern Methodist University, argues that this change in stone tool technology is related to increasing mobility during the early Upper Paleolithic. As human populations moved more frequently, they would not always have had access to high-quality flint. The adoption of an Upper Paleolithic blade technology was one facet of adaptation to a more mobile way of life in the late Pleistocene.

Faunal data also suggest that Upper Paleolithic populations in the Levant were highly mobile. Daniel Lieberman (1993, 1994) has used gazelle teeth to determine the seasons at which Middle and Upper Paleolithic sites in the Near East were occupied. The cementum, or connective tissue, that surrounds gazelle teeth forms alternating translucent and opaque bands. The opaque and translucent bands alternate seasonally and reflect seasonal differences in diet **(Figure 9.3)**. In the winter wet season, gazelles eat mainly grasses, while in the summer, their diet includes a higher percentage of browse (Lieberman 1994: 533). By examining the outermost layer of cementum, Lieberman was able to determine the season in which prehistoric gazelles were killed. Lieberman's (1993) research showed that at Middle Paleolithic sites such as Kebara, gazelles were killed during more than one season, indicating that many of the Middle Pale-

These climatic fluctuations would have had some impact on vegetation in the Near East, although the changes may not have been dramatic. The lusher areas of the Near East are characterized by a Mediterranean climate with short, mild winters and hot, dry summers. The vegetation is a mix of trees and maquis (shrubs), including oak, pistachio, cedar, pine, cypress, olive, laurel, and juniper (Gilead 1991: 112). The more marginal areas, including the Sinai, the Negev, southern and eastern Jordan, and the Syrian desert are generally drier, with annual rainfalls of between 100 and 350 millimeters (4 and 14 in.). These marginal areas are characterized by steppe and desert vegetation. During the drier phases of the Pleistocene, areas of steppe and desert may have expanded at the expense of Mediterranean forests **(Figure 9.2)**.

Recent archaeological excavations in the Negev area suggest that the transition from Middle to Upper Paleolithic stone tool technology may have been a very gradual one in the Near East (Marks and Ferring 1988). The

Figure 9.3

Cementum or connective tissue in gazelle teeth forms seasonally alternating translucent and opaque bands. Studies of these cementum bands suggest that Upper Paleolithic sites in the Near East were occupied for one season only.

olithic sites may have been occupied for an extensive portion of the year. Upper Paleolithic sites included the remains of gazelles that were killed during only one season, suggesting a pattern of seasonal movement.

The stone tool industries of the Near East and Europe that date between 35,000 to 40,000 and 10,000 years ago are usually termed Upper Paleolithic. Upper Paleolithic stone tool assemblages generally include large numbers of tools made on blades that are often struck from prismatic (regularly faceted) blade cores. The Near Eastern Upper Pale-

olithic sites that date between 38,000 and 22,000 years ago are termed Early Upper Paleolithic (Gilead 1991: 121). The earliest Early Upper Paleolithic stone tool assemblages from Near Eastern sites generally contain a very high proportion of blades (long, slender flakes that are more than twice as long as they are wide) and bladelets (small blades). The term **Ahmarian tradition** is used to refer to these blade and bladelet assemblages. Other Early Upper Paleolithic sites have produced fewer blades and bladelets and more flakes, end scrapers, and burins. These assemblages are

Figure 9.4

Excavations at the Kebaran site of Ein Gev I overlooking the Sea of Galilee in eastern Israel. The site appears to have been a seasonal hunters' encampment.

termed **Levantine Aurignacian.** Similar Aurignacian industries have been identified from as far east as Iran and Iraq (Olszewski and Dibble 1994). The relationship between the Ahmarian and the Levantine Aurginacian is unclear. Was the Levantine Aurignacian a local development from the earlier Ahmarian industry, or was it introduced from the outside? Who developed these stone tool industries? While it is likely that both industries were made by early modern people, no human remains have been recovered from any Early Upper Paleolithic sites in the Near East.

A number of different lines of evidence suggest that the Upper Paleolithic population of the Near East was relatively small, especially in the core areas of Mediterranean vegetation. Surveys in the Mount Carmel area of northern Israel have revealed few Upper Paleolithic sites (Olami 1984). Most Upper Paleolithic sites are small, Upper Paleolithic levels in cave sites are usually thin, and the area occupied is limited (Ronen 1975: 242). These data suggest that the Near East was occupied by small, highly mobile hunting and gathering bands during the Upper Paleolithic.

The Early Upper Paleolithic economy of the Levant appears to be based on the hunting of a number of medium to large mammals, such as gazelles, fallow deer, and ibex. There

is little evidence for the use of small mammals, reptiles, fish, and invertebrates. The role of plant foods in the Upper Paleolithic diet in the Near East remains unknown, but it is likely that plant foods did play a significant role in the diet. Plant foods such as acorns and pistachios would have been available in the core Mediterranean areas.

This pattern of small, mobile hunter-gatherer bands continued into the later part of the Upper Paleolithic. The term **Kebaran Complex** has been used to describe the stone tool industries from the Levant dated between approximately 19,000 and 14,000 years ago. The Kebaran Complex is named after the type site of Kebara Cave where the industry was first found in the uppermost layers. Traditionally, the Kebaran was distinguished from earlier Upper Paleolithic industries by the presence of microliths, very small stone implements that would have formed parts of **composite tools,** or tools made of more than one material. The microliths, for example, could have served as barbs for projectile points.

The site of **Ein Gev I** in eastern Israel typified the way of life of the Kebarans. The site overlooks the Sea of Galilee (Lake Kinnaret) and appears to have been occupied on a seasonal basis by a small band of hunters **(Figure 9.4)**. It has been suggested that the Ke-

sickle or knife

adze

transverse arrowhead

barbed spear

Figure 9.5

Reconstructions of the ways backed microliths from Late Stone Age South African sites were hafted.

barans practiced a circulating settlement pattern (Mortenson 1972), making use of a variety of different areas on a seasonal basis during the course of a single year.

About 13,000 years ago, the world's climate began to change. In the Near East this final Pleistocene warming trend is associated with the expansion of the zones of Mediterranean vegetation. These climatic changes, which had profound effects on systems of human settlement and subsistence in the Near East, will be discussed in detail in Chapter 17.

The Late Stone Age in Africa

Similar trends are apparent in the archaeology of the African Late Stone Age. In sub-Saharan Africa there is a great deal of continuity between the Middle Stone Age and the Late Stone Age industries, perhaps because both were made by anatomically modern hu-

mans. Late Stone Age industries generally show an overall reduction in artifact size, including a large number of microliths. These tools were often fitted into hafts or handles, or used as barbs or tips for arrows **(Figure 9.5)**. The edges of the microliths were steeply trimmed in order to blunt them so that they would not split the hafts (Phillipson 1993: 60–61). Late Stone Age industries also show increased evidence for regional diversification. During this period nearly all areas of the African continent were occupied, some for the first time. Clearly some of the regional variability that is apparent in Late Stone Age industries reflects adaptation to different environments.

A number of Late Stone Age sites in South Africa have provided evidence for changes in hunting and subsistence practices. Of particular interest is the Late Stone Age site of **Nelson Bay Cave** in South Africa **(Figure 9.6)**. The site is dated to between 19,000

Figure 9.6

Location of Nelson Bay Cave in relation to other Middle and Late Stone Age sites in southern Africa.

and 12,000 years ago and is associated with a stone tool industry that includes many tiny bladelets and few standardized retouched tools. As noted in Chapter 8, the Middle Stone Age levels at Klasies River Mouth provide evidence for the use of marine foods, including molluscs, seals, and penguins. The faunal data from Nelson Bay Cave indicate that coastal resources were exploited even more effectively during the Late Stone Age (Klein 1979). The Nelson Bay faunal assemblage includes large numbers of bones of fish and flying seabirds such as cormorants, gulls, and gannets. The artifactual assemblage from Nelson Bay Cave includes two types of artifacts that may have been used in fishing: stone net or line sinkers and bone gorges, small bone slivers with points on both ends, which may have been used to bait a line.

Differences between the Middle and Late Stone Ages are also apparent in the hunting of terrestrial mammals. The Middle Stone Age faunal assemblage from the Klasies River Mouth is dominated by the remains of the relatively docile eland; remains of wild pigs are rare. In the Late Stone Age at Nelson Bay Cave, wild pigs, including bushpigs and warthogs, are far more common. Wild pigs are dangerous when attacked, so the intensive hunting of these animals must have required sophisticated technology such as snares and possibly the bow and arrow.

As we will see in Chapter 10, there is also faunal and artifactual evidence for increasingly sophisticated hunting technology in the Upper Paleolithic of Europe. In addition, coastal resources were increasingly exploited at some late Upper Paleolithic sites in western Europe.

 Conclusion

In the Near Eastern Upper Paleolithic we see the emergence of small, highly mobile bands of hunters and gatherers who made use of plant and animal resources on a seasonal basis. The contemporary Late Stone Age sites in Africa reveal an increasing sophistication in hunting and gathering technology, including the use of bird and fish resources.

 Glossary

Ahmarian tradition. The term used to refer to early Upper Paleolithic assemblages in the Levant, which are dominated by blades and bladelets.

Boker Tachtit. A site in the Negev Desert in southern Israel dated to between 45,000 and 38,000 years ago. The site shows a technological transition from tools produced from Levallois cores to tools produced from single striking platform blade cores.

Comparative collection. A collection of well-documented modern animal skeletons that can be used to identify fragmented archaeological animal bones.

Composite tools. Tools made of more than one material. Examples include a stone spear point attached to a wooden spear and small flint microliths used as barbs for wooden arrows.

Ein Gev I. A Kebaran hunters' campsite overlooking the Sea of Galilee. The site appears to have been used on a seasonal basis and was undoubtedly part of a broader circulating settlement pattern.

Kebaran Complex. The term used to describe the later Upper Paleolithic industries in the Levant, dated between 19,000 and 14,000 years ago. Microliths typically form a major part of Kebaran stone tool assemblages.

Late Stone Age. The term used to describe the late Pleistocene stone tool industries of sub-Saharan Africa. These industries are broadly contemporary with the Upper Paleolithic cultures of Europe, the Near East, and Northern Africa.

Levantine Aurignacian. The term used to describe Early Upper Paleolithic sites that have produced relatively few blades and bladelets and greater numbers of flakes, end scrapers, and burins. Similar assemblages, termed Zagros Aurignacian, have been identified from Upper Paleolithic sites in Iran and Iraq.

MNI (minimum number of individuals). A technique for estimating the relative proportions of different species in a faunal assemblage. It is based on an estimation of the number of animals needed to account for all the bones in the assemblage.

Nelson Bay Cave. A Late Stone Age (19,000 to 12,000 years ago) site in South Africa that has yielded evidence for late Pleistocene hunting, fowling, and fishing practices.

NISP (number of identified specimens per taxon). A method for calculating the relative portions of various animals in a faunal collection. It is based on the total number of bones identified for each species.

Upper Paleolithic. The late Pleistocene (between 35,000 to 40,000 and 10,000 years ago) stone tool industries of Europe, North Africa, and Asia, generally characterized by a high proportion of tools made on blades.

 Further Reading

Gilead, I.
1991. The Upper Paleolithic Period in the Levant. *Journal of World Prehistory* 5 (2): 105–154.
An up-to-date and comprehensive review of the Levantine Upper Paleolithic by one of the foremost authorities in the field.

Phillipson, David W.
1993. *African Archaeology,* 2d ed. Cambridge: Cambridge University Press.
A comprehensive overview of African archaeology and prehistory from the earliest humans to the complex societies of the second millennium A.D.

Other Bibliography

Brewer, Douglas T.
1992. Zooarchaeology: Method, Theory, and Goals. In *Archaeological Method and Theory,* vol. 4, edited by M. B. Schiffer, pp. 195–244. Tucson: University of Arizona Press.

Grayson, D. K.
1984. *Quantitative Zooarchaeology.* New York: Academic Press.

Klein, Richard G.
1979. Stone Age Exploitation of Animals in Southern Africa. *American Scientist* 67: 151–160.

Lieberman, D. E.
1993. Variability in Hunter-gatherer Seasonal Mobility in the Southern Levant: From the Mousterian to the Natufian. In *Hunting and Animal Exploitation in the Late Pleistocene Old World,* edited by G. Peterkin, H. Bricker, and P. Mellars, pp. 207–219. Washington; DC: Archaeological Papers of the American Anthropological Association.
1994. The Biological Basis for Seasonal Increments in Dental Cementum and Their Application to Archaeological Research. *Journal of Archaeological Science* 21: 525–539.

Lieberman, D. E., and John J. Shea
1994. Behavioral Differences between Archaic and Modern Humans in the Levantine Mousterian. *American Anthropologist* 96 (2): 300–332.

Lyman, R. Lee
1994. *Vertebrate Taphonomy.* Cambridge: Cambridge University Press.

Marks, A. E., and C. R. Ferring

1988. The Early Upper Paleolithic in the Levant. In *The Early Upper Paleolithic, Evidence from Europe and the Near East,* edited by J. F. Hoffecker and C. A. Wolf, pp. 43–72. Oxford: British Archaeological Reports, International Series 437.

Marks, A. E., and D. Kaufmann

1983. Boker Tachtit: The Artifacts. In *Prehistory and Paleoenvironments in the Central Negev, Israel,* vol. III, edited by A. E. Marks, pp. 69–125. Dallas: Southern Methodist University Press.

Marshall, F., and T. Pilgrim

1993. NISP vs. MNI in Quantification of Body-Part Representation. *American Antiquity* 58 (2): 261–269.

Monks, G.

1981. Seasonality Studies. In *Advances in Archaeological Method and Theory,* vol. 4, edited by M. B. Schiffer, pp. 177–240. New York: Academic Press.

Mortenson, P.

1972. Seasonal Camps and Early Villages in the Zagros. In *Man, Settlement and Urbanism,* edited by P. J. Ucko, R. Tringham, and G. W. Dimbleby, pp. 293–297. London: Duckworth.

Olami, Y.

1984. *Prehistoric Carmel.* Jerusalem and Haifa: Israel Exploration Society and M. Stekelis Museum of Prehistory.

Olszewski, D. I., and H. L. Dibble

1994. The Zagros Aurignacian. *Current Anthropology* 35 (1): 68–75.

Reitz, E. J., and E. S. Wing

1999. *Zooarchaeology.* Cambridge: Cambridge University Press.

Ronen, A.

1975. The Palaeolithic Archaeology and Chronology of Israel. In *Problems in Prehistory: North Africa and the Levant,* edited by A. E. Marks, pp. 229–248. Dallas: Southern Methodist University Press.

Chapter 10

The Industries and Cultures of the Upper Paleolithic in Europe

Introduction

Living in the information age, we marvel at the speed of the technological and social changes that are going on around us. Today's laptop and desktop computers are more powerful than many mainframe computers that were in use just 30 years ago. We can hop on a commercial passenger jet in New York and arrive in London 6 hours later. Our family cars are made up of parts that are manufactured in a dozen different countries. At the same time, many older Americans who now take refrigerators for granted grew up in a world where ice for iceboxes was delivered in horse-drawn vans. While it is hard to imagine a world without cable television, VCRs, and video rentals, most Americans over age 50 remember their family's first purchase of a TV set. Although the nineteenth century was marked by the invention of the steam engine, railroads, the telephone, the phonograph, and the lightbulb, to name just a few examples, the speed of technological change in the twentieth century far outstripped that of the nineteenth.

The same kind of comparison can be made between the speed of change during the Lower and Middle Paleolithic periods in Europe and the more rapid and dramatic changes that took place during the Upper Paleolithic period, between about 35,000 and 10,000 years ago. The Acheulian stone tool industry lasted for over 1 million years. Although Acheulian technology spread from Africa to Europe, the Middle East, and South Asia, the Acheulian industry remained essentially unchanged for hundreds of thousands of years. While there is clear evidence for the development of the Levallois technique during the later part of the Lower Paleolithic, the pace of technological innovation was slow at best. During the late Pleistocene, however, it appears that the rate of technological change was accelerating throughout the world. The changes can be seen in many areas of human activity, including the appearance of art (Chapter 11), improvements in hunting and foraging technology, and the spread of humans to Australia and the New World (Chapter 12). This acceleration in the rate of cultural and technological change was especially marked in Europe, because the Middle to Upper Paleolithic transition appears to correspond to the replacement of Neanderthals by anatomically modern humans. In this chapter, we will examine the development of stone tool technology, subsistence practices, and settlement patterns during the late Pleistocene in Europe. The following chapters will discuss the appearance of art and symbolic communication (Chapter 11) and the archaeological record of the settlement of Australia and the New World (Chapter 12).

This chapter focuses on the stone tool industries that developed in Europe between about 35,000 and 10,000 years ago. In Europe, as in Asia and North Africa, these stone tool traditions are termed Upper Paleolithic. During this period we see increasing evidence for regional differences in stone tool technology, often accompanied by variations in settlement patterns, subsistence technology, and other aspects of material culture. As described in the Archaeology in Practice box, radiocarbon dating became available to provide accurate absolute dates for sites and industries in this time period.

Radiocarbon Age Determination

The development of **radiocarbon dating** in 1949 revolutionized the archaeology of the Upper Paleolithic and later periods. Before Willard Libby (Libby et al. 1949) developed the radiocarbon dating method, there were no dating methods available that could provide absolute dates (in years before the present) for the Upper Paleolithic period. Sites and industries could often be placed in a relative sequence based on their geological context and stratigraphic position, but it was nearly impossible to determine how old those sites really were. The radiocarbon revolution provided a chronological framework that allowed archaeologists to examine the rate of technological and cultural changes during the Upper Paleolithic.

The radiocarbon dating method is based on carbon, an element that is present in all living things. The most common isotope of carbon is a light, stable isotope, carbon-12 (^{12}C); however, all living plants and animals also contain trace quantities of a heavier, radioactive isotope of carbon, carbon-14 (^{14}C). Small quantities of radioactive ^{14}C are constantly being formed in the earth's upper atmosphere. Both ^{14}C and ^{12}C combine with oxygen to form carbon dioxide, one of the most common gasses in the earth's atmosphere. Carbon dioxide (CO_2) is absorbed by plants during photosynthesis, a process by which plants convert CO_2 and sunlight into food and oxygen. When plants absorb CO_2 from the atmosphere, they absorb large quantities of ^{12}C and trace amounts of ^{14}C. As these plants are eaten by animals who are, in turn, eaten by other animals, radiocarbon is spread throughout the food chain. Therefore, living plants and animals will contain the same small proportion of ^{14}C that exists in the earth's atmosphere. (The ratio of ^{12}C to ^{14}C in the earth's atmosphere is about 8 hundred billion to 1.)

When an organism dies, it ceases to take up any new radiocarbon. The radioactive carbon that is present in the organism's tissues decays at a known rate, called the half-life, or the amount of time needed for half the radioactive atoms to decay. The half-life of radiocarbon is 5,730 ± 30 years. Thus, by measuring the amount of radioactive carbon that remains in a sample of organic material, archaeologists can estimate the amount of time that has elapsed since that organism died. This is the principle that underlies radiocarbon age determination. (See Renfrew 1973 for a detailed summary of the assumptions that lie behind the radiocarbon dating method.)

The advantage of radiocarbon dating over other methods is that it can be used on a wide range of organic materials: charcoal, wood, bone, shell, and the like. Traditional radiocarbon dating requires about 25 grams (about 1 oz.) of the organic material for laboratory analysis. The material is cleaned and then converted to a gas by burning; its radioactivity is measured over a period of 2 weeks. This measure is used to estimate the amount of radiocarbon remaining in the sample. A newer procedure known as the **AMS (accelerator mass spectrometry)** method uses an accelerator and a mass spectrometer to measure directly the amount of ^{14}C remaining in the sample (Hedges and Gowlett 1986). The AMS technique, which allows much smaller samples to be dated, has been used to date the charcoal wicks in Upper Paleolithic lamps and the charcoal used as a colorant in ancient wall paintings (Chapter 11).

With conventional radiocarbon dating techniques, organic materials as old as about 40,000 years can be dated. After about seven half-lives, the amount of ^{14}C remaining in the sample is so small that it becomes difficult to measure. The AMS technique may allow somewhat older samples to be dated, but the samples must be entirely free of modern organic contamination.

Radiocarbon age determinations are expressed in years B.P., or before present. The present has been defined arbitrarily as A.D. 1950. Radiocarbon dates always include a plus-or-minus factor, for example, 2,550 ± 50 years B.P., because radiocarbon dates are not absolute ages; they are statements of probability. The date of 2,550 ± 50 B.P. means that there is approximately a 66 percent (2 out of 3) chance that the true age of the archaeological sample will fall between 2,500 and 2,600 years B.P. The "± 50 years" is a statistical measure known as a standard deviation.

Upper Paleolithic Industries: General Characteristics

When compared with the Middle Paleolithic industries that preceded them, Upper Paleolithic industries in Europe are characterized by the use of a wider range of stone tool types. Many of those tools were made on blades—long and narrow flint flakes. By definition, blades must be at least twice as long as they are wide. Blades are often removed from prismatic (regularly faceted) cores using a **punch technique (Figure 10.1)**. The punch technique is one of a number of methods of **indirect percussion** used to manufacture stone tools. The hammerstone does not contact the flint core directly; instead, the hammerstone strikes a punch, usually made of bone or antler. A blade is detached at the point where the punch contacts the flint core. This technique allows a large number of long, thin blades to be removed from a single flint core. The main technological advantage of this method over the Levallois technique is that it allows the knapper to produce much more cutting edge per kilogram of flint. The blade technology makes efficient use of available resources. The blades serve as blanks for the production of a wide range of stone tools, including spear points and burins, tools with a sharp, chisel-shaped edge that can be used to work bone or antler.

Upper Paleolithic industries are generally characterized by a much wider use of bone and antler as raw materials. In western Europe, bone spear points and antler harpoons appear for the first time during the Upper Paleolithic. The Upper Paleolithic also is characterized by an increasing use of composite tools, or tools made of more than one material. Examples of composite tools include bone spear points hafted onto wooden shafts and bows and arrows.

The Upper Paleolithic Sequence in Europe

Much of the research on the Upper Paleolithic period has focused on western Europe, particularly on the Dordogne region of southwestern France. The fascination with the Upper Paleolithic cultures of southwestern France can be explained, at least in part, by historical factors. In the Dordogne region of France, the Vezère River cuts through an area of limestone caves and rock shelters that were attractive to Paleolithic people. In 1863, Edouard Lartet, a French lawyer and amateur geologist, and Henry Christy, an English banker of independent means, began a series of excavations in the Dordogne region that were to change the course of Paleolithic archaeology. They began work at a time when scholars had just begun to recognize the great antiquity of the human presence on earth. Lartet and Christy excavated many important French Upper Paleolithic sites, including La Madeleine and Laugerie-Haute; they also began excavation at the site of Le Moustier, which was to become the type site for the Mousterian industry in Europe. Lartet and Christy's pioneering work established a strong tradition of Paleolithic research in the Dordogne region that continues to the present day. Because of the wealth of archaeological data

Figure 10.1

The use of the punch technique to remove blades from a blade core.

available from southwestern France, François Bordes (1968, 1984) based his typological studies of Upper Paleolithic stone tools primarily on data from France. However, recent research in eastern Europe, the Near East, sub-Saharan Africa, and eastern Asia has revealed great regional variation in late Paleolithic stone tool industries from around the world (Chapter 9). Nevertheless, the rich archaeological record from western Europe provides important information on how early modern humans coped with the cold, periglacial environments of the late Pleistocene period.

Until perhaps 30 years ago, much of the research on the European Upper Paleolithic focused on the typological study of stone, bone, and antler implements to develop a chronological sequence of Upper Paleolithic industries. The western European Upper Paleolithic sequence is briefly summarized in **Table 10.1**.

These industries were originally defined on the basis of a series of type fossils (artifacts deemed typical of a particular period); typical tools from each period are illustrated in **Figure 10.2**. The **Aurignacian** period in southwestern Europe is characterized by the presence of a range of stone and bone tools, including nosed and carinated (shaped like a ship's keel) end scrapers made on thick flakes and blades, large blades with continuous retouch around their edges, strangulated blades (with a central constriction), and bone points, including those with split bases. Typical **Gravettian** (or Upper Perigordian) tools include gravette points, microgravette bladelets, tanged points, and burins made on truncations (snapped-off ends). The **Solutrean** is characterized by the presence of large, flat spear points known as laurel leaves. Producing these points required that the flint first be heat-treated, or "cooked,"

for an extended period to facilitate the initial removal of flakes from the cores. The laurel leaves were shaped using a technique known as **pressure flaking,** in which a flint knapper presses a piece of a hard material such as antler or wood against the edge of the tool to detach a small, flat flake. Eyed needles also make their first appearance during the Solutrean (Stordeur-Yedid 1979). These needles may have been used to produce tailored, or fitted, clothing made of hides, skins, and leather. Sinew (animal tendons) may have been used as thread. The **Magdalenian** period is characterized by the appearance of barbed points made of antler, known as harpoons. Typical stone tools include bladelets, a variety of borers, small blades with abrupt retouch, and increasing numbers of microliths (small stone tools, generally less than 1 centimeter [1/2 in.] in maximum dimension).

Since the 1960s, the focus of archaeological research has shifted away from typological studies toward questions of human subsistence and settlement. Specifically, archaeologists have tried to understand how Upper Paleolithic people made a living in the cold climates that characterized late Pleistocene Europe. Archaeologists have used paleoenvironmental data such as pollen cores and oxygen isotope analyses to reconstruct the late Pleistocene environment; faunal remains and artifacts have been used to reconstruct hunting practices; and increasingly precise methods of excavation have been used to study Upper Paleolithic settlements.

The Upper Paleolithic period in Europe was a time of full glacial conditions. The Alpine ice sheet covered much of Alpine central Europe, while the Scandinavian sheet covered Scandinavia as well as northern Germany, northern Poland, the Baltic states, and parts of Russia **(Figure 10.3)**. In general, Europe's climate was dry and very cold. In southwest France, July temperatures are estimated to have been about 5 degrees Celsius (9 degrees F.) colder than at present (White 1985: 41). At the height of the last glaciation, about 18,000 years ago, the earth's sea levels dropped by about 100 to 150 meters (330 to 490 ft.). While many parts of Europe experienced steppic or even tundra-like conditions during this period, the vegetation in southwest Europe (southwestern France and

Table 10.1

Major periods of the southwest European Upper Paleolithic and their approximate dates.

Period	Approximate Dates
Aurignacian	34,000–30,000 B.P.
Gravettian	30,000–22,000 B.P.
Solutrean	22,000–18,000 B.P.
Magdalenian	18,000–11,000 B.P.

MAGDALENIAN
a - borer
b - bladelet
c, d - harpoons

SOLUTREAN
laurel leaf point

GRAVETTIAN
a - gravette
b - Noailles burin
(arrow points to burin facet)
c - Font Robert point
d - microgravette

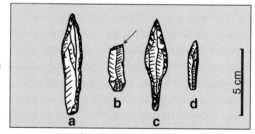

AURIGNACIAN
a - nosed scraper
b - carinated scraper
c - retouched blade
d - strangulated blade
e - split based bone point

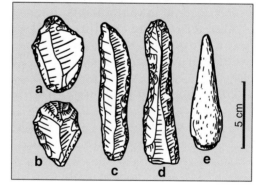

Figure 10.2

Typical tools from each phase of the European Upper Paleolithic.

Figure 10.3

Extent of the Alpine and Scandinavian ice sheets and the locations of the sites mentioned in this chapter.

northern Spain) appears to have been much more diverse. The varied topography in this region supported different plant and animal communities at different elevations. Pollen data suggest that sheltered, south-facing areas with adequate water may have supported warm-loving trees, such as hazel and oaks, even during the glacial maximum (see, for example, Straus and Clark 1986: 371). The varied vegetation would have supported a large and diverse animal community, which, in turn, may have supported a large human population (White 1985: 49–51).

Subsistence Strategies in the European Upper Paleolithic

Artifactual evidence from a wide range of European Upper Paleolithic sites suggests that increasingly sophisticated hunting technologies were developing throughout the period. Stone, bone, and antler projectile points are common throughout the Upper Paleolithic. Spear throwers, which would have increased both the speed and the accuracy of thrown spears, appear in Upper Paleolithic assemblages by 20,000 B.P. (White 1986: 43). The presence of barbed and tanged arrowheads at Solutrean sites in Spain provides indirect evidence for the use of the bow and arrow at that time (Davidson 1974). However, zooarchaeological evidence is required to study the kinds of animals that were hunted during the Upper Paleolithic and the techniques that were used to hunt them. For example, archaeologists want to know whether large herds of animals were hunted on a seasonal basis or whether individual animals were hunted as they were encountered throughout the year.

Recent studies by Françoise Audouze and James Enloe (1991) have shown that both types of hunting can be documented in the European Upper Paleolithic. Audouze and Enloe contrasted the pattern of hunting seen at the Magdalenian site of Verberie in the Paris basin with the hunting techniques seen at the site of Le Flageolet in the Perigord region of southwestern France. Both sites are overwhelmingly dominated by the remains of reindeer; at Le Flageolet reindeer make up 95 percent of the animals hunted. At Verberie the large size of the reindeer kill and the ages of the animals suggest that the reindeer were killed in large numbers during the autumn migration. During the fall the reindeer would have been at their nutritional peak because the best forage would have been available during the summer months. Moreover, the reindeer would have been available at a predictable time and place during the fall migration. By killing large numbers of reindeer in the fall, the hunters at Verberie would have obtained large amounts of high-quality, fat-rich meat, which would have been stored for use throughout the winter (Audouze and Enloe 1991: 64).

The pattern of hunting seen at Le Flageolet is quite different. At Le Flageolet, many of the reindeer that were hunted were adults, especially adult females. In the winter, female reindeer are generally in better condition than the males. The high numbers of adult female reindeer at Le Flageolet suggest that the hunters at the site were hunting individual or small groups of reindeer throughout the winter, a pattern known as encounter hunting. The different patterns of hunting seen at Verberie and Le Flageolet point to the varying hunting strategies and techniques used by Upper Paleolithic hunters in Europe.

Case Study
Paleolithic Subsistence: La Riera Cave

The excavations at the Upper Paleolithic site of **La Riera** (Straus and Clark 1986) in northern Spain demonstrate how hunting and foraging practices changed through time. La Riera Cave is located in the Cantabrian region of northern Spain, halfway between the cities of Santander and Oviedo. The cave offered its Paleolithic inhabitants shelter and proximity to fresh water. From the cave, prehistoric people could have made use of the coastal plain, the coastal estuaries, local rivers, and the slopes and cliffs of the coastal mountain ranges. The location of La Riera Cave meant that ancient people had access to a wide variety of terrestrial and marine food resources. La Riera produced a long sequence of occupations and a large number of radiocarbon dates. Initially occupied over 20,000 years ago, the site was inhabited during the Solutrean (20,500 to 17,000 B.P.), Lower Magdalenian (17,000 to 16,000 B.P.), Upper Magdalenian (12,400 to 11,000 B.P.), and later periods. Detailed studies of the faunal and artifactual remains from the cave reveal the ways that hunting and foraging techniques changed throughout these periods.

The principal game species throughout the occupation of La Riera Cave was red deer (*Cervus elaphus*), an animal closely related to the American elk. Beginning in the Solutrean period, there is evidence that La Riera hunters were using techniques such as drives or surrounds to capture a large number of animals of all ages and both sexes at one time. The highly fragmented state of the mammal bones indicates that they were probably used for marrow and grease in addition to meat. There is also evidence for the increasing use of marine and estuarine resources through time. Limpets and, later, marine fish such as sea bream are added to the diet during the Upper Magdalenian period. Thus the record reflects both an intensification of large mammal hunting and a diversification of the subsistence base through the addition of marine fish and shellfish. As we shall see (Chapter 17), this pattern of intensification and diversification of the subsistence base is seen in the late Pleistocene of the Near East as well. The excavators of La Riera Cave, Lawrence Straus and Geoffrey Clark, attribute these changes to a growing imbalance between population and available food resources.

Meat, fish, and shellfish made up only part of the diet during the Upper Paleolithic period in Europe. While very few plant foods would have been available during the cold winter months, plant foods must have played a role in the diet during the warmer summer season. There is little clear evidence for the use of plant foods at La Riera Cave. However, the nearby early Magdalenian site of El Juyo (Freeman et al. 1988) has produced evidence of 51 different genera of plants from 21 different families. The plant remains include fragments of acorns, beechnuts, and raspberry pits.

It is difficult to assess the relative importance of animal and plant foods in the European Upper Paleolithic diet. Clearly, relatively few plant foods would have been available in the colder, drier areas of eastern Europe, especially during the coldest periods of the Pleistocene. A greater variety of plants may have been available in the summer months during the warmer periods of the Pleistocene and in areas such as southwestern France that supported a diverse mixture of grassland and forested environments.

Upper Paleolithic Settlement Patterns

Studies of Upper Paleolithic subsistence practices are closely related to questions of settlement patterns, or how prehistoric people distributed themselves across the landscape. In studying prehistoric settlement patterns, archaeologists want to know how sites are distributed in relationship to natural landscape features such as rivers and lakes, the sizes of sites and their locations in relationship to other sites, and how houses and other structures are distributed within the sites themselves. The rich archaeological record for Upper Paleolithic Europe allows archaeologists to begin to answer some of these questions.

As noted above, environmental data suggest that the rich late Pleistocene environments of southwestern France and northern Spain would have supported comparatively large human populations. The varied landscape, with a mosaic of steppe and forest environments, would have supported a rich and diverse range of animal resources on which those human populations depended (White 1985: 51). For example, the site of Le Flageolet has produced the animals that lived in woodland, forest, steppe, and montane environments, including the reindeer, red deer, horse, and ibex (Boyle 1990: 276). The valley-side locations of many of the sites in southwestern France allowed hunters to make use of several different environmental zones during the course of a season or a year. These locations also provided ready access to water.

Upper Paleolithic sites in Europe vary greatly in size. Ethnographic studies of modern hunter-gatherer populations indicate that group size varies throughout the year. At certain seasons of the year, large groups of perhaps 50 to 100 people congregate to make use of seasonally available plant and animal resources. During much of the rest of the year, the population breaks up into small bands, sometimes as small as individual families. A similar pattern may be reflected in the archaeological record of the European Upper Paleolithic. Excavations at caves, rock shelters, and open sites have revealed a pattern of many small sites and a few much larger occupations. Many of the smaller sites may have been occupied by individual hunting bands on a seasonal basis. The larger sites have produced greater quantities of artwork (see Chapter 11). They probably represent seasonal aggregation sites where large social groups came together for initiation rites, marriage ceremonies, and other ritual activities, in addition to hunting and plant collecting.

While many of the sites in southwestern France and northern Spain are located in caves and rock shelters, some of the most impressive evidence for the layout of individual settlements comes from open-air sites. One of the most famous is the site of **Pincevent** in the Paris basin (Leroi-Gourhan and Brézillon 1972). The site, which was excavated by André Leroi-Gourhan, not only has provided a wealth of new information on the structure of late Paleolithic hunters' camps, but also has served as a laboratory for the development of new methods and techniques of excavation.

Excavators at Pincevent used a program of horizontal excavation. The goal of horizontal excavation is to open up a broad area of the site so that the spatial relationship of artifacts, ecofacts, and features to one another can be seen clearly. Not only was the precise location of each artifact and animal bone recorded; but the artifacts and bones were left in place so that their relationship to each other could be seen clearly. The distribution of these artifacts was documented using both drawings and photography, and the location of each piece of charcoal and each fragment of red ochre (an iron-based red pigment) was also indicated on the plans and drawings. Once each excavation unit had been drawn and photographed, a mold was made of the living surface using latex rubber. A plaster

Figure 10.4

One of the habitations at Pincevent. The photograph illustrates how the distribution of stone tools, bones, charcoal, and other artifacts can be used to define the size and shape of the huts.

cast of the living surface could be made from the mold, thus preserving the spatial relationships of the artifacts even after they were removed from the ground.

The excavations at Pincevent revealed the remains of several small, circular huts **(Figure 10.4)**. Although nothing remained of the huts themselves (they were undoubtedly made of perishable materials such as skins or hides), the stone tools and animal bones formed distinctive circular concentrations. Asymmetrical, hollow hearths were located outside the huts (Audouze and Enloe 1991: 64). These habitations would have been occupied by reindeer hunters for a short period in September and October (Enloe et al. 1994: 106). Detailed studies of the animal bones revealed how the individual reindeer carcasses were shared among the different huts (Enloe and David 1989).

Similar methods of excavation were used to document the nearby Magdalenian quarry site of **Étiolles** (Pigeot 1987) **(Figure 10.5)**. At this site workers were manufacturing stone tools from flint nodules that were up to 50 centimeters (20 in.) long. The difficulty of working these large cores led to an increased flexibility in stone tool manufacture. Workers needed to adapt their techniques to the shape

of the raw material and the accidents of the knapping process. Detailed spatial and refitting studies have been carried out at one of the habitations at Étiolles. They reveal that the expert flint knappers worked around the central hearth, striking a large number of blades from the best cores, which had been preshaped before they reached the habitation. Farther away from the hearth, novice knappers practiced their skills on partly worked-out cores. At Étiolles detailed spatial studies allow the excavators to reconstruct the organization of stone tool production.

Some of the most spectacular evidence for Upper Paleolithic living sites has come from open-air sites in eastern Europe. Among the most unusual are the mammoth-bone dwellings found at sites on the East European Plain in the Ukraine and adjacent areas of Russia and Belarus. An example is the site of **Mezhirich** (Gladkih et al. 1984), located near the Dnieper River in the Ukraine. At least five mammoth-bone dwellings are known from the site, and four have been excavated **(Figure 10.6)**. These small, circular huts are between 4 and 7 meters (13 and 23 ft.) in diameter, providing an interior floor area of 8 to 24 square meters (86 to 258 sq. ft.). Inside the

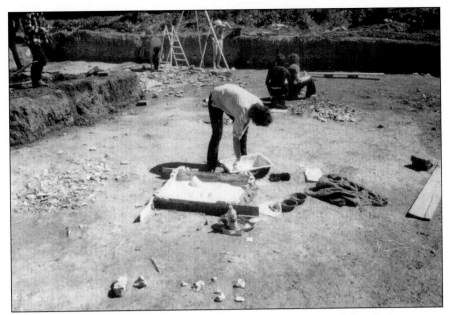

Figure 10.5
Étiolles: the use of latex rubber to make a mold of the living surface.

Figure 10.6
A mammoth-bone dwelling from Mezhirich, Ukraine.

dwellings are the remains of hearths where bone was used as a fuel. Timber would have been very scarce in the steppe environment of the Russian plain during the Pleistocene. The foundations and walls of these huts were constructed of carefully assembled mammoth bones. The outer portion of the wall of one hut was made of 95 mammoth mandibles (lower jaws) placed chin down to form a herringbone pattern. These mammoth-bone dwellings were probably occupied during the 9-month cold season; during the summer, the inhabitants would have moved to temporary warm-season camps. Radiocarbon dates suggest that these

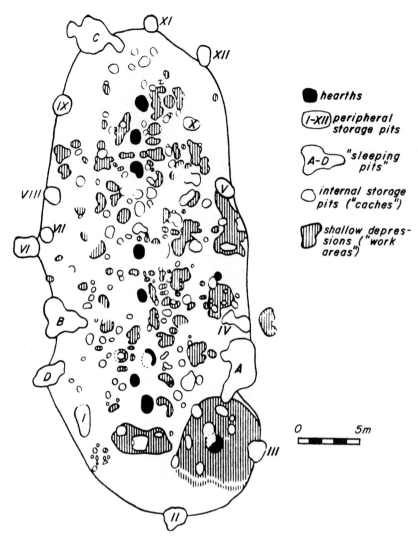

Figure 10.7

Plan of Kostenki I-1, showing location of storage pits, activity areas, sleeping pits, and the central hearths.

mammoth-bone dwellings were occupied about 15,000 years ago. The presence of these huts on the Russian plain indicates that Upper Paleolithic hunters were able to adapt successfully to the cold, glacial climates of the eastern European periglacial steppes where winter temperatures may have reached –35° to –40° Celsius (–31° to –40° F.).

Substantial dwellings of a different form have been recovered from the site of **Kostenki I** (Klein 1973: 103) on the Don River in the eastern Ukraine. Kostenki I-1 **(Figure 10.7)** revealed a large complex of features covering an area of roughly 18 by 40 meters (60 by 130 ft.). The outside was

surrounded by a series of storage pits that appear to have been used to store mammoth bones as fuel. The feature complex included a central line of hearths, as well as sleeping pits, internal storage pits, and work areas. It is not clear how this complex structure may have been roofed, but it appears to have housed a sizable population.

Conclusion

How do the settlement patterns, subsistence practices, and technological systems of the inhabitants of Upper Paleolithic Europe compare with what is known from the preceding Middle Paleolithic period? The artifactual evidence, including spear throwers and bows and arrows, suggests an increasingly sophisticated hunting technology. This impression of hunting success is confirmed by the animal bone evidence, which indicates that Upper Paleolithic people in Europe were successfully hunting a wide range of herbivores, including reindeer, bison, wild cattle, mammoth, wild swine, horse, ibex, chamois, and red deer. The settlement evidence from both eastern and western Europe indicates that Upper Paleolithic people had successfully adapted to the cold, dry climates of the late Pleistocene period. In both eastern and western Europe, the density of settlements increased in the Upper Paleolithic. In Russia, Upper Paleolithic settlements extend as far north as the Arctic Circle, while Mousterian sites are found no farther north than 54° north latitude (Klein 1973: 122). Clearly, innovations such as fitted clothing must have played an important role in the successful occupation of the Arctic Zone during the Upper Paleolithic. Moreover, it is during the late Pleistocene that we see the expansion of northeast Eurasian populations into the New World, a topic we will address in greater detail in Chapter 12.

Glossary

AMS (accelerator mass spectrometry). A method of radiocarbon dating that uses an electrostatic accelerator and a mass spectrometer to measure the amount of radiocarbon (^{14}C) that remains in a sample of organic material. The technique allows small samples of organic materials to be dated using the radiocarbon method.

Aurignacian. Industry (ca. 34,000 to 30,000 B.P.) that is characterized by the presence of nosed and carinated end scrapers made on thick flakes and blades, large blades with continuous retouch, strangulated blades, and bone points, including those with split bases.

Étiolles. A Magdalenian site located in the Paris basin, where huge flint nodules were used to manufacture stone tools. Careful excavation and recording allowed the process of stone tool manufacture to be recorded.

Gravettian. Industry (ca. 30,000 to 22,000 B.P.) that is characterized by the presence of gravette points, microgravette bladelets, tanged points, and burins made on truncations. Also referred to as Upper Perigordian.

Indirect percussion. A method of producing stone tools in which the hammerstone never makes direct contact with the flint core. The hammerstone strikes an intermediate object, such as a punch, which is in contact with the stone core.

Kostenki I. An Upper Paleolithic site on the Don River in eastern Ukraine that has yielded evidence for a large complex of habitation features, including storage pits, sleeping pits, work areas, and central hearths.

La Riera. A Solutrean, Magdalenian, and later site in northern Spain that reveals changes in Upper Paleolithic subsistence through time. The data suggest that marine and estuarine resources played an increasingly important role in the diet.

Magdalenian. The term used to describe late Upper Paleolithic sites in western Europe, about 18,000 to 11,000 years ago. Magdalenian sites are characterized by the presence of bone and antler harpoons.

Mezhirich. A late Upper Paleolithic site near the Dneiper River in Ukraine that has yielded evidence for several small dwellings constructed of mammoth bone. The site is dated to about 15,000 B.P.

Pincevent. A late Magdalenian hunters' encampment in the Paris basin of France. The site was occupied by reindeer hunters for a short period in the autumn.

Pressure flaking. A method of stone knapping in which pressure is applied to the edge of a stone tool, usually with a flaker made of wood or bone, in order to detach a small, flat flake. Pressure flaking was used to shape the Solutrean laurel leaf points.

Punch technique. A method of indirect percussion used to strike a large number of long, narrow blades from a prismatic core. The hammerstone strikes a punch—a tapered piece of bone, wood, or antler—which is placed near the edge of a blade core. The resultant force detaches a long, slender blade. Moving the punch around the core makes it possible to detach many blades from a single piece of flint.

Radiocarbon dating. A method for dating organic materials (e.g., charcoal, bone, shell, wood) based on the decay of a radioactive isotope of carbon, ^{14}C.

Solutrean. The period in western European prehistory that corresponds to the coldest phases of the late glacial period, about 22,000 to 18,000 B.P. Solutrean assemblages are characterized by the presence of finely flaked points shaped like laurel leaves.

 ## Further Reading

Gamble, Clive
1986. *The Palaeolithic Settlement of Europe.* Cambridge: Cambridge University Press.
A comprehensive review of the Paleolithic settlement of Europe from the initial occupation of the continent to the end of the Pleistocene. While this is undoubtedly the most comprehensive volume available in English on the Paleolithic in Europe, it is written at a high level and recommended for serious students only.

Renfrew, Colin
1973. *Before Civilization: The Radiocarbon Revolution and Prehistoric Europe.* Cambridge: Cambridge University Press.
Although this excellent volume focuses primarily on the impact of the radiocarbon revolution on later European prehistory (see Chapter 24), it provides an authoritative and readable explanation of radiocarbon age determination.

 ## Other Bibliography

Audouze, Françoise, and James Enloe
1991. Subsistence Strategies and Economy in the Magdalenian of the Paris Basin. In *The Late Glacial in North-West Europe: Human Adaptation and Environmental Change at the End of the Pleistocene,* edited by N. Barton, J. Roberts, and D. A. Roe, pp. 63–71. London: Council for British Archaeology Research Report No. 77.

Bordes, F.
1968. *The Old Stone Age.* New York: McGraw-Hill.
1984. *Lecons sur le Paléolithique II: Le Paléolithique en Europe.* Paris: Éditions du CNRS, Cahiers du Quaternaire 7.

Boyle, K. V.
1990. *Upper Palaeolithic Faunas from South-West France.* Oxford: British Archaeological Reports, International Series 557.

Davidson, I.
1974. Radiocarbon Dates for the Spanish Solutrean. *Antiquity* 48: 63–65.

Enloe, J., and F. David
1989. Le remontage des os par individus: Le partage du renne chez les Magdaléniens de Pincevent (La Grande Paroise, Seine-et-Marne). *Bulletin de la Société Préhistorique Française* 86 (9): 275–281.

Enloe, J., F. David, and T. S. Hare
1994. Patterns of Faunal Processing at Section 27 of Pincevent: The Use of Spatial Analysis and Ethnoarchaeological Data in the Interpretation of Archaeological Site Structure. *Journal of Anthropological Archaeology* 13: 104–124.

Freeman, L. G., J. Gonzáles Echegaray, R. G. Klein, and W. T. Crowe
1988. Dimensions of Research at El Juyo. In *Upper Pleistocene Prehistory of Western Eurasia,* edited by H. L. Dibble and A. Montet-White, pp. 3–39. Philadelphia: University Museum Monograph 54, University of Pennsylvania.

Gladkih, M. I., N. L. Kornietz, and Olga Soffer
1984. Mammoth-Bone Dwellings on the Russian Plain. *Scientific American* 251(5): 164–175.

Hedges, R. E. M., and J. A. J. Gowlett
1986. Radiocarbon Dating by Accelerator Mass Spectrometry. *Scientific American* 254 (1): 100–107.

Klein, Richard G.
1973. *Ice-Age Hunters of the Ukraine.* Chicago: University of Chicago Press.

Leroi-Gourhan, André, and M. Brézillon
1972. *Fouilles de Pincevent: Essai d'analyse ethnographique d'un habitat magdalénien.* Paris: Éditions du CNRS, Supplément à *Gallia Préhistoire,* 7.

Libby, W. F., E. C. Anderson, and J. R. Arnold
1949. Age Determination of Radiocarbon Content: World-wide Assay of Natural Radiocarbon. *Science* 109: 227.

Pigeot, Nicole
1987. *Magdaléniens d'Etiolles: économie de debitage et organisation sociale: (l'unité d'habitation U5).* Paris: Éditions du CNRS, Supplément à *Gallia Préhistoire,* 25.

Stordeur-Yedid, D.

1979. *Les aiguilles à chas au Paléolithique.* Paris: *Gallia Préhistoire,* Supplement 13.

Straus, Lawrence G., and Geoffrey A. Clark

1986. *La Riera Cave: Stone Age Hunter-Gatherer Adaptations in Northern Spain.* Tempe: Arizona State University, Anthropological Research Papers No. 36.

White, Randall

1985. *Upper Paleolithic Land Use in the Périgord.* Oxford: British Archaeological Reports, International Series 253.

1986. *Dark Caves, Bright Visions: Life in Ice Age Europe.* New York: Norton.

Chapter 11

Art and Cognition in the Upper Paleolithic

Introduction

The Upper Paleolithic art of Europe, including both cave paintings and small sculptures, represents one of the most interesting and enigmatic subjects in all of Paleolithic archaeology. For both archaeologist and layperson alike, these works of art provide a link to the ideas, thoughts, and beliefs of the long-vanished people of the Paleolithic. Yet this feeling of communication with the past is in large measure illusory. While the paintings and sculptures of animals and symbols surely had meaning to their creators and evoke an emotional response in the modern viewer, millennia of cultural change separate the artists from us. Our intuitive reaction to this art, shaped by thousands of years of social, religious, and artistic tradition, is likely to be far afield from the artwork's meaning to its ancient makers.

How do we know that this art was produced by Paleolithic artists? How was this art produced, and how has it been preserved for tens of millennia? This chapter will seek to answer those questions. Why did the hunters and foragers of late Ice Age Europe paint naturalistic images on the almost inaccessible walls and ceilings of caves? What meaning did those works of art have within the cultures that produced them? This chapter will address those issues as well. While numerous hypotheses have been offered, we can probably never fully understand the intended meaning of Paleolithic art.

Historical Background: The Discovery of the Painted Caves

In Europe, there are two major forms of Paleolithic art: **parietal** (cave wall) **art** and **mobiliary,** or portable, **art.** Cave paintings are known primarily from three areas in western Europe—southwestern France, northern Spain, and the Pyrenean region. Small carvings and sculptures are known from a much broader area across Ice Age Europe. The locations of the major southwest European sites discussed in this chapter are shown in **Figure 11.1**. Parietal art includes both the paintings (**Figure 11.2**) and engravings or low-relief carvings (**Figure 11.3**) that were used to decorate the walls and ceilings of caves. Mobiliary, or portable, art includes a range of small carved or engraved objects made of bone, antler, or stone. The famous statuettes sometimes referred to as Venuses (**Figure 11.4**) were sculptures of women, often depicted with protruding breasts and buttocks. Other examples of mobiliary art include engraved plaques, as well as carved and decorated items such as spear throwers deco-

rated with animal figures (**Figure 11.5**). Examples of mobiliary art were first recovered from archaeological sites in the mid-nineteenth century, along with stone tools and the bones of Ice Age animals. Because these small plaques and carvings were found along with Stone Age tools, their authenticity as products of Paleolithic craftworkers was never seriously questioned. The acceptance of the painted caves as the work of Paleolithic artists, however, was a longer and more complicated process.

One of the great milestones in the history of Paleolithic cave art was the discovery of painted bison on the ceiling of the Spanish cave of **Altamira** in 1879. The excavator of the cave was a Spanish nobleman, Don Marcelino Sanz de Sautuola. The previous year he had visited an exhibition of Paleolithic mobiliary art and artifacts in Paris. In November of 1879 de Sautuola was excavating the floor of the cave at Altamira, searching for artifacts, while his young daughter Maria was running wildly around the cave. Suddenly, she recognized the figures of a group of bison on the roof of the cave. De Sautuola recognized that the style of the

Figure 11.1

Location of sites mentioned in this chapter.

Figure 11.2

Naturalistic painted bison from the ceiling of the cave at Altamira (Santander), Spain.

Figure 11.3

Low-relief carving of a salmon from the Abri de Poisson (Dordogne), France, 105 centimeters (41 in.) in length.

Figure 11.5

Elaborately decorated spear thrower (9 centimeters [3.5 in.] in length by 7 centimeters [3 in.] in height) made of reindeer antler. The carving depicts two headless ibexes locked in an embrace (possibly playing or fighting). The heads of the two animals may have been attached separately.

Figure 11.4

Carved stone female figurine known as the Venus of Willendorf, Austria, approximately 11 centimeters (4 in.) in height.

bison was similar to the style of carving used on the portable art he had seen in Paris. In 1880 he published a short booklet on his discoveries at Altamira, cautiously asking whether the painted bison might be contemporary with the Paleolithic deposits from the cave floor. Unfortunately, his suggestions were greeted with skepticism and derision by the archaeological community.

The discovery of another series of cave paintings and engravings around the turn of the twentieth century led to the eventual acceptance of Paleolithic cave art. When, in 1895, the owner of La Mouthe cave in France removed some debris, he exposed a previously unknown gallery containing painted images. Another important discovery was the painted and engraved images at the cave of Pair-non-Pair near Bordeaux. The acceptance of the authenticity of cave art in the early twentieth century led, in the first two decades of the century, to the search for and discovery of a number of painted caves in the Dordogne region of France, the Cantabrian region of Spain, and the Pyrenees.

The most spectacular find, however, was that of **Lascaux Cave** (Arlette Leroi-Gourhan 1982) in France at the very beginning of World War II. The discovery of the cave has often been attributed to French schoolboys, who found the cave after their dog had fallen into a deep hole. In fact, the boys were using stones to test the depth of a hole created by a fallen pine tree. Once the opening had been enlarged, they slid down a tunnel of wet clay. Within the cave they were met by a spectacular array of horses, cattle, and other animals painted in bright colors along the walls and ceiling of the cave. They reported the discovery to their schoolmaster. The cave was subsequently inspected by the Abbé Henri Breuil, an important French prehistorian, whose *Four Hundred Centuries of Cave Art* (1952) remains an important sourcebook for the study of Paleolithic art in Europe. The beauty and mystery of this site for the general public led to its becoming a major tourist attraction. The popularity of Lascaux threatened the images, which had been preserved as a consequence of the naturally stable temperature and humidity in the cave. Visitors introduced dust, dampness, and fungi, causing the paintings to deteriorate. Lascaux is now closed to

all but a very small number of visitors, but Lascaux II, a three-dimensional reproduction of the paintings made using original techniques and completed in 1984, still attracts many tourists.

The discovery of several new painted caves in the past few years has put Ice Age art back on the front pages of newspapers around the world. For example, the discovery in 1994 of the **Grotte Chauvet** in Vallon-Pont-d'Arc (Ardèche) in southern France revealed an unusual range of Ice Age images (Chauvet et al. 1996; Clottes and Courtin 1996). In addition to painted pictures of horses, bovids, and other common animals, the Grotte Chauvet included depictions of woolly rhinos and carnivores such as cave bears and felines. In fact, rhinos, felines, mammoths, and bears make up 60 percent of the images from Grotte Chauvet (Clottes 1996).

The 1991 discovery of the **Grotte Cosquer** (Clottes and Courtin 1996), a painted cave near Marseilles whose entrance lies 37 meters (120 ft.) underwater, has also attracted worldwide attention. At the time the cave was painted, between 19,000 and 27,000 years ago, the cave entrance would not have been underwater; the entrance was submerged as a result of rising sea levels at the end of the Pleistocene. The paintings within the cave date to two distinct periods. The earlier paintings include 46 hand outlines, while the later paintings and engravings include images of horses, ibex, bison, and deer, as well as unique representations of seals and great auks.

Parietal Art: The Images on the Walls

The subjects represented in parietal art include both figurative and nonfigurative motifs. Most of the figures are naturalistic representations of animals, including horses, wild cattle, bison, ibex, reindeer, red deer (an animal similar to the American elk), mammoths, woolly rhinos, birds, fish, and occasional carnivores such as cave lions. Horses, wild cattle, and bison are the most common images. Human figures are relatively rare; they are generally far less naturalistic than the animal images. Positive and negative images of hands have also been recovered from caves such as Gargas **(Figure 11.6)**. Nonfigurative

Figure 11.6

Hand stencils from Gargas (Hautes Pyrenées), France. Some appear to have missing digits.

images include a number of signs, which range from simple fingerprints to complex quadrilateral images. Some are shaped like arrows, while others appear to resemble female genitalia.

Earth tones predominate in the cave paintings. The reds, yellows, oranges, and browns were produced using iron oxides such as hematite, limonite, and especially, red ocher (Martin 1993: 261). Manganese dioxide and occasionally charcoal were used to produce the black pigments, while porcelain clay was used for the whites. At Lascaux, cave water, which is naturally high in calcium, was mixed with the ground mineral pigments to ensure both durability and adhesion to the cave wall surface (Arlette Leroi-Gourhan 1982: 109–110). Experiments suggest that the paint may have been applied by a number of different techniques. It may have been applied with the fingers or by using animal-hair brushes. Pieces of red ocher may also have been used as crayons. The negative hand impressions must have been produced using a spray painting technique. Experiments suggest that dry pigment could have been blown through a tube, or wet pigment could have been blown directly from the mouth.

Since paintings were often placed in remote areas of dark caves, lighting would have been a major challenge for Ice Age artists. De Beaune and White (1993) studied approximately 300 stone lamps that have been recovered from over 100 different Upper Paleolithic sites, mostly in southern France. Most of the lamps are made of limestone or sandstone, and investigations of the chemical residues remaining in the lamps indicate that they would have been used to burn animal fats (De Beaune and White 1993: 111). Experiments indicate that suitable wicks could have been made out of dried lichen, moss, or juniper twigs. Juniper twigs have been identified as one of the wick materials used at Lascaux (Arlette Leroi-Gourhan 1982: 107).

Scaffolding would have been necessary for painters to reach the upper parts of the walls and ceilings of the caves. At Lascaux recesses cut into the cave walls about 2 meters (6 ft.) above the floor have been identified. The recesses were packed with clay and could have supported heavy branches that served as the foundation for a platform.

Incised designs and low-relief carvings could have been made with flint burins and other sharp flint tools. Deep engravings, such

Figure 11.7

An early Aurignacian baton de commandement *made of reindeer antler, from the site of Abri Blanchard (Dordogne), France, 15 centimeters (6 in.) in length.*

as those found on the walls of Pair-non-Pair Cave in France, could have been made with stone picks (Bahn and Vertut 1988: 91). The artists often made use of natural irregularities in the cave walls to indicate parts of the animals' bodies. For example, a bulge in the cave wall might be used to indicate a shoulder or hip.

 Mobiliary (Portable) Art

Small, decorated objects were commonly made of antler, stone, ivory, and bone. Animals are often represented in mobiliary art, appearing as decorations on spear throwers and other items that would have been used for an extended period of time. Carved or incised decoration often appears on enigmatic objects termed **batons (or *batons de commandement*) (Figure 11.7)**. These objects are generally made of reindeer antler and are perforated near one end. The function of these objects is unknown, but hypothesized uses range from spear-shaft straighteners to tent pegs to symbols of authority (White 1986: 47). Other engraved items include small plaques, often decorated with rows of incised dots. Microscopic examination has revealed that these dots were often made by a number of different tools, suggesting that they were made over a period of time (Marshack 1972). Traditionally, these dots have been seen as tally marks, perhaps representing individual kills, similar to the notches on a cowboy's gun. Alexander Marshack (1972) argued in-

stead that the patterning of these marks showed some correlations with the phases of the moon and suggested that they may represent a primitive calendar. Whether these dots represent tally marks, a primitive calendrical system, or something entirely different remains a matter of debate.

The so-called Venus figurines are among the most well known examples of prehistoric art. Many of these female figurines date from the Gravettian period, approximately 30,000 to 22,000 years ago. They are made from a variety of materials, including ivory, steatite, and calcite (White 1986: 114). The Venuses often have exaggerated breasts and buttocks, and some appear to be pregnant. Bahn and Vertut (1988: 138) note that the fleshier ones appear to represent "bodies worn out and altered by age and childbearing." The heads of the figurines are often small, and the legs frequently taper to a point. The function of these figures and their role in Upper Paleolithic ritual and religion remain unknown. While the Venuses have often been viewed as fertility goddesses, only a minority (17 percent) can plausibly be interpreted as pregnant (Rice 1981). Moreover, as will be discussed in Chapter 14, many modern hunter-gatherer populations work to limit their fertility rather than increase it.

 Dating and Chronology

The chronological development of Upper Paleolithic art has presented several methodological challenges for archaeologists. Unlike the Middle Stone Age in Africa, where decorated bone objects are known from recent excavations in Zaire (Yellen et al. 1995), there is relatively little evidence of art or decoration in the European Middle Paleolithic (Chase and Dibble 1987). The appearance of art in the Upper Paleolithic in Europe has been seen as a kind of creative explosion (Pfeiffer 1983). Understanding the origins and development of the art of Upper Paleolithic Europe necessitates some kind of chronological framework.

While mobiliary art is usually found in archaeological layers in association with materials such as charcoal that can be dated using the radiocarbon method, it is far more difficult to date the cave paintings. Early attempts at developing a chronology for Upper Paleolithic parietal art were based primarily on stylistic changes (see, for example, André Leroi-Gourhan 1968). Unfortunately, stylistic changes cannot provide an absolute chronology for artistic developments. Recent developments in radiocarbon dating (Chapter 10), including the use of the AMS method for the dating of very small samples of organic materials, are beginning to provide a more detailed chronology for the development of Paleolithic art. The radiocarbon method has been used to date the carbonized wicks remaining in lamps, the torch marks on cave walls, and sometimes even the organic materials within the pigments themselves. At least 80 percent of the known Upper Paleolithic art from Europe dates to the latest phase of the Upper Paleolithic period, the Magdalenian period (White 1986: 138). For example, radiocarbon dating of the charcoal remains in the Lascaux lamps indicates that the site was used about 17,000 years ago (Arlette Leroi-Gourhan 1982: 107) during the Magdalenian period. A recent French discovery, however, has indicated that techniques of cave painting were well developed by the earliest phases of the Upper Paleolithic period in Europe. A series of radiocarbon dates from the Grotte Chauvet in France indicates that those images were painted approximately 30,000 years ago. These dates suggest that the traditions and techniques of parietal art were established early in the Upper Paleolithic period and then continued for approximately 20,000 years.

Interpretation of Paleolithic Art

One of the most challenging tasks facing Paleolithic archaeologists is attempting to understand the function and meaning of parietal and mobiliary art. Many scholars of the early twentieth century, including the Abbé Henri Breuil, assumed that the images represented a kind of hunting magic, designed to ensure the abundance of wild game animals. There is no question that many of the images depict large herd animals, such as horses, bison, wild cattle, deer, and reindeer, that we know were hunted by Upper Paleolithic people. In addition, the images display the detailed knowledge of animal anatomy and behavior that would be expected from a foraging population. For example, Sally Casey (1995) has recognized images of animals in both their summer and their winter coats (**Figure 11.8**). There are several problems, however, with the interpretation of all Paleolithic art as hunting magic. While many of the images are those of large game species, large predators such as felines and bears occasionally appear in the art. Would Paleolithic hunters have wanted to face increasing numbers of predatory species? In addition, there is a difference between the species of animals most commonly painted on the cave walls and the species that were actually hunted by Paleolithic hunters. Horses, wild cattle, and bison are the species that occur most frequently in parietal art, while Upper Paleolithic faunal assemblages in southern France are dominated by the remains of reindeer, and those in northern Spain are often dominated by red deer (Chapter 10). Since the hunting magic hypothesis does not explain the range of animals depicted in Paleolithic cave art, modern scholars have sought other explanations.

One of the most innovative approaches was pioneered by the French prehistorian, André Leroi-Gourhan (1968). Leroi-Gourhan began by examining the distribution of the images within the caves. He found that most of the images of horses, bison, and wild cattle were concentrated in the central areas of the caves, while images of rare animals such as bears and felines were concentrated in the more remote areas. He used these data to suggest that Upper Paleolithic painted caves had

Figure 11.8

Horse from Lascaux (Dordogne) showing its short, smooth summer coat. In winter the horses' coats are shaggier and darker.

a standardized layout, much like a modern church or temple. His interpretation of the meaning of these images is far more controversial. Leroi-Gourhan suggested that these images reflected a structural opposition between males and females. Not only did he interpret the horse images as male and the bovids (cattle and bison) as female, he also interpreted many of the nonfigurative signs as male and female symbols. Arrows, for example, were seen as male. One of the problems with this interpretation is that the images of horses, bison, and cattle include both male and female animals. Why should all the horses be male symbols and all the bovids be female?

Other scholars have emphasized the role of art as a means of symbolic communication. As noted in Chapter 10, some of the largest European Upper Paleolithic sites may have served as seasonal aggregation sites (Conkey 1980) where small hunter-gatherer bands congregated to form larger social units for a short period of time. Many of the large Upper Paleolithic sites, such as Laugerie-Basse in southwest France, have produced large numbers of art objects (White 1986: 85). The art may have played a role in the ritual activities that took place at these seasonal aggregation sites.

Some cave art may have helped communicate traditional stories or myths. The famous scene in the shaft at Lascaux **(Figure 11.9)** suggests this interpretation. Hidden deep in a recess in the cave, the painting juxtaposes the figures of a disemboweled bison, a strange bird-headed man, and an equally enigmatic "bird on a stick" object, as well as a painting of a rhinoceros. What this scene conveys (if indeed it is a single, unified scene) is, of course, a mystery to us.

While we can marvel at the artistry and technical skill manifest in Paleolithic art, much of its meaning remains elusive. Detailed studies of the contexts in which particular images are found may shed some light on the symbolic and religious systems of which these images were a part. However, as Ucko and Rosenfeld (1967: 239) noted more than 30 years ago, "perhaps many Palaeolithic representations were made for reasons which still totally escape the modern observer."

Rock Art from Other Regions of the World

While this chapter has focused on the parietal and mobiliary art of western Europe, rock art has been produced in a number of

Figure 11.9

Shaft scene from Lascaux (Dordogne) showing disemboweled bison, human, bird on a staff, and rhinoceros.

Figure 11.10

Rock painting showing naturalistic animals and human figures from Makwe, near Wedza, Zimbabwe.

other areas of the world, including the American southwest, southern Africa, and Australia. While the American rock art is relatively recent (Howard 1996), there is an increasing body of evidence to suggest that the African and Australian examples may have roots in the Pleistocene. African rock art, which includes naturalistic paintings and engravings of animals and people **(Figure 11.10)**, often appears on the walls of shallow caves and rock shelters and on rocky outcrops. It is therefore far more exposed to the elements than is European cave art, which is located deep within the recesses of caves. Many of the extant paintings are therefore likely to be recent. The engravings, however, are less susceptible to deterioration (Phillipson 1993: 74). In southern Namibia, slabs bearing naturalistic painted images of animals have been found at **Apollo 11 Cave;** these images may be 28,000 years old (Wendt 1976). These data suggest that the South African tradition of rock art may be as old as the European.

 ## Conclusion

It is important to emphasize that the rock and cave art of Ice Age Europe, prehistoric southern Africa, and Australia was produced by populations who made their living by hunting and gathering. While we may not be able to reconstruct the function and meaning of these prehistoric images, the mere survival of these artistic treasures gives us a glimpse into the rich symbolic and expressive world in which these ancient foragers lived.

 ## Glossary

Altamira. A cave site in northern Spain where some of the first examples of Paleolithic parietal art were discovered by a local nobleman, de Sautuola. The Altamira images date to the Magdalenian period, about 15,500 years ago.

Apollo 11 Cave. A site in southern Namibia that has produced painted images of animals dated to 28,000 years ago.

Batons (or *batons de commandement*). Enigmatic objects of mobiliary art, usually made of reindeer antler and pierced at one end. The function of these items remains unknown.

Grotte Chauvet. A painted cave site located in Vallon-Pont-d'Arc (Ardèche) in southern France and discovered in 1994 that has revealed an unusual range of Ice Age images. In addition to painted pictures of horses, bovids, and other common animals, the Grotte Chauvet included depictions of woolly rhinos and carnivores such as cave bears and felines. The images date to approximately 30,000 years ago.

Grotte Cosquer. A recently discovered painted cave near Marseilles whose entrance lies 37 meters (120 ft.) underwater. The images in the cave were painted between 19,000 and 27,000 years ago.

Lascaux Cave. A cave site located in the Dordogne region of southwest France, which was discovered in 1940. The extensive series of painted images, including horses, bison, deer, wild cattle, and an enigmatic human figure holding a bird-headed staff, have been the subject of detailed scientific investigations in recent years. Radiocarbon dating of the lamp wicks indicates that the cave was painted about 17,000 years ago.

Mobiliary art. Portable objects made of stone, bone, antler, and ivory, including such items as decorated spear throwers, incised plaques, and female figurines.

Parietal art. The art that appears on the walls and ceilings of caves, including both cave painting and low-relief carving. The images painted and carved in cave walls include naturalistic animal figures and enigmatic signs. Human figures are comparatively rare and stylized.

 ## Further Reading

Bahn, Paul G., and Jean Vertut
    1988. *Images of the Ice Age.* London: Windward.
    A thorough and readable introduction to Upper Paleolithic art, including excellent photographs by Vertut.

Leroi-Gourhan, Arlette
    1982. The Archaeology of Lascaux Cave. *Scientific American* 246 (6): 104–112.
    A noted French prehistorian describes the recent research that has been conducted at Lascaux.

Ucko, Peter J., and Andrée Rosenfeld
    1967. *Palaeolithic Cave Art.* New York: McGraw-Hill.
    An older, but still very useful, introduction to parietal art.

White, R.
    1986. *Dark Caves, Bright Visions: Life in Ice Age Europe.* New York: Norton.
    This volume was originally designed as a guide to the American Museum of Natural History's exhibit of the same name. It provides a well-illustrated introduction to life in Upper Paleolithic Europe.

◔ Other Bibliography

Breuil, Henri
1952. *Four Hundred Centuries of Cave Art.* Montignac, France: Centre d'Études et de Documentation Prehistoriques.

Casey, S.
1995. Examining Seasonality in Upper Paleolithic Art: Methodology and Research Implications. In *Before Farming,* edited by D. V. Campana, pp. 3–22. Philadelphia: MASCA Research Papers in Science and Archaeology, Vol. 12 Supplement.

Chase, P., and H. L. Dibble
1987. Middle Paleolithic Symbolism: A Review of Current Evidence and Interpretations. *Journal of Anthropological Archaeology* 6: 263–296.

Chauvet, Jean-Marie, E. B. Deschamps, and C. Hillaire
1996. *Dawn of Art: The Chauvet Cave: The Oldest Known Paintings in the World.* New York: Abrams.

Clottes, Jean
1996. Thematic Changes in Upper Paleolithic Art: A View from Grotte Chauvet. *Antiquity* 70: 276–288.

Clottes, Jean, and Jean Courtin
1996. *The Cave beneath the Seas: Paleolithic Images at Cosquer,* translated by Marilyn Garner. New York: Abrams.

Conkey, Margaret
1980. The Identification of Prehistoric Hunter-Gatherer Aggregation Sites: The Case of Altamira. *Current Anthropology* 21: 609–630.

De Beaune, A., and Randall White
1993. Ice Age Lamps. *Scientific American* 266 (3): 108–113.

Howard, Ken
1996. Artful Dating. *Scientific American* 274 (6): 24.

Leroi-Gourhan, André
1967. *Treasures of Prehistoric Art.* New York: Abrams.
1968. The Evolution of Paleolithic Art. *Scientific American* 218 (2): 58–70.

Marshack, Alexander
1972. *The Roots of Civilization.* London: Weidenfeld and Nicolson.

Martin, Yves
1993. Analyse des pigments. In *L'art Pariétal Paléolithique,* edited by the Groupe de Réflexion sur l'art Pariétal Paléolithique, pp. 261–264. Paris: Éditions du CTHS.

Pfeiffer, John
1983. *The Creative Explosion.* New York: Harper and Row.

Phillipson, David W.
1993. *African Archaeology,* 2d ed. Cambridge: Cambridge University Press.

Rice, P. C.
1981. Prehistoric Venuses: Symbols of Motherhood or Womanhood? *Journal of Anthropological Research* 37: 402–414.

Wendt, W. E.
1976. *Art Mobilier* from the Apollo 11 Cave, South West Africa: Africa's Oldest Dated Works of Art. *South African Archaeological Bulletin* 31: 5–11.

Yellen, J. E., A. S. Brooks, E. Cornelissen, M. J. Mehlman, and K. Stewart
1995. A Middle Stone Age Worked Bone Industry from Katanda, Upper Semliki Valley, Zaire. *Science* 268: 553–556.

Chapter 12

The Initial Human Colonization of Australia and the Americas

Introduction

The first 5 million years of human prehistory center on the evolution of early humans in Africa and the subsequent human settlement of Eurasia. During the late Pleistocene, humans first moved out of Aseurica (the landmass that includes Africa, Asia, and Europe) into other regions of the world. The questions of how, when, and why humans settled Australia and the New World have intrigued scholars for generations. In this chapter we will trace the movement of human populations out of Asia into both Greater Australia (Australia, New Guinea, and Tasmania) and the Americas. We will begin with the early settlement of Australia, which recent discoveries indicate may have taken place as early as 50,000 years ago.

Greater Australia: The Environmental Background

Today, Australia, New Guinea, and Tasmania are three large but separate islands in the South Pacific. In late Pleistocene times, this region was quite different in appearance. Sea levels were as much as 160 meters (525 ft.) lower during the height of the last glaciation. Sea levels dropped worldwide because much of the earth's water was trapped in the large ice masses that covered northern Eurasia and North America. **Eustatic sea level changes** are variations in world sea levels that result from the growth and melting of glacial ice (Van Andel 1989). A drop of only 30 meters (100 ft.) in sea level is necessary for New Guinea to be joined to the Australian continent, and sea levels were at least that low between 80,000 and 6,500 B.P. (before present). When sea levels dropped 65 meters (213 ft.) below the present level, the island of Tasmania was also joined to Australia. This occurred between 25,000 and 12,000 years ago and may have occurred three other times during the late Pleistocene (Cosgrove 1989). The large continent formed by the joining of Australia, New Guinea, and Tasmania is often termed Greater Australia, or **Sahul** (White and O'Connell 1982: 6). At the height of the last glaciation, the lowered sea levels would have increased the land area of the Sahul by about one-quarter, to about 10.6 million square kilometers (4 million sq. mi.) **(Figure 12.1)**.

Although world sea levels were considerably lower throughout the late Pleistocene, the Sahul region was never connected to the southeast Asian mainland by a land bridge. This means that the crossing to Australia must have involved some form of sea craft, such as rafts or boats. The initial colonists of Australia, however, would not have sailed off into an undifferentiated open sea. The open sea between mainland southeast Asia and New Guinea is dotted by chains of high islands, and no leg of the voyage is likely to have been longer than about 100 kilometers (62 mi.) in Pleistocene times. Birdsell (1977) identified a series of five possible routes between the southeast Asian mainland and Greater Australia (see Figure 12.1). The routes involved between 8 and 17 stages. The more northerly routes led to New Guinea, while the southerly routes led directly to the Australian mainland. One of these routes provides intervisibility between the islands all along the route to New Guinea, and two others are at the margins of intervisibility (Irwin 1992: 21). This intervisibility makes deliberate exploration, rather than simply accidental settlement, a real possibility. However, whether the initial colonists of Australia were purposeful settlers or simply early island-hoppers who were blown off course is a question that cannot be answered on the basis of archaeological data alone.

Figure 12.1

The Sahul region, showing the approximate coastline when sea levels were 150 meters (500 ft.) lower than today, and the possible sea routes to New Guinea and Australia.

The Archaeological Evidence for the Initial Colonization of the Sahul

When did early humans first settle Greater Australia? In the late nineteenth and early twentieth centuries, Australia was seen as having a short prehistory. It was believed to have been settled quite late, and the Australian archaeological record was seen as limited and unchanging. The arrival of humans in Australia was measured in centuries rather than millennia (Mulvaney 1964: 263). By the mid-1960s archaeologists recognized that Australia had been settled by late Pleistocene times (Mulvaney 1964). However, it was the discovery of artifacts and human remains at the site of **Lake Mungo** in New South Wales in 1968 that revolutionized the chronology of the human settlement of Australia.

Case Study
Lake Mungo

Lake Mungo is one of a series of extinct lakes, known as the Willandra Lakes, that are located in New South Wales, northwest of Melbourne, Australia. The lakes were a series of overflow basins, filled by the Lachlan River when it was in flood. Although these lakes have never been filled in **Recent,** or Holocene (post-Pleistocene), times, during the Pleistocene the lakes were permanently filled. The geology of these extinct lakes was being studied by geomorphologist Jim Bowler in 1968 when he discovered burnt bones in a deposit known to be more than 20,000 years old. Bowler (Bowler et al. 1970) assumed that these were food bones burnt by early humans and marked them for future excavation by archaeologists.

Excavation of the site the following year revealed that the burnt bones were, in fact, a human cremation. Subsequent survey revealed a highly fragmented cranium about 0.5 kilometer (0.3 mi.) from the original find. The initial skeleton, Mungo I, has been dated by radiocarbon to between 24,500 and 26,500 years ago (Bowler et al. 1972). It represents the charred and fragmented remains of a young woman. In 1974, the buried remains of an adult male, Mungo III, were discovered during additional geological surveys of the area (Bowler and Thorne 1976). The position of Mungo III, below that of the cremation within the Lake Mungo stratigraphic sequence, suggests that it dates to between 28,000 and 30,000 years ago. The Lake Mungo specimens therefore represent the earliest human remains known from the Sahul.

Additional archaeological evidence has been recovered from the Lake Mungo area, including stone tools and 16 circular patches of carbon that appear to be hearths. The hearths contained a range of faunal remains, including bird and mammal bones, freshwater shellfish, the bones of golden perch, and emu eggshells. The emu eggs would have been available in the region in late winter, while the fish and shellfish were probably caught in the late spring to summer. The excavators concluded that the site probably represents a seasonal, lakeside campsite (Bowler et al. 1970).

Most of the Lake Mungo stone tools were made of silcrete, a fine-grained stone that was available in the area. The tools include choppers that may have been used for heavy woodworking and scrapers made from flakes **(Figure 12.2)**.

Placing the Lake Mungo finds in a broader economic system presents a more difficult challenge (White and O'Connell 1982: 39). The differing dates for the Mungo I and Mungo III human remains suggest that the region may have been occupied, at least sporadically, over several thousand years. If the Lake Mungo hearths represent seasonal campsites, then those remains must be part of a broad range of seasonally occupied campsites in

Figure 12.2

Choppers and flakes from the Lake Mungo excavations.

the region. Stone tool workshops and kill-butchery sites are needed to reconstruct the full range of Pleistocene subsistence activities.

The Lake Mungo finds indicated that the Australian continent had been colonized by modern humans by about 30,000 years ago. Subsequent archaeological research has identified additional early sites in the Sahul. These include the site of **Kuk** in the New Guinea highlands, where charcoal and fire-cracked rocks transported by humans have been radiocarbon dated to about 30,000 years ago (Golson and Hughes 1977), and the site of **Devil's Lair** in western Australia, where possible stone and bone artifacts and chips of nonlocal stone were found in deposits that may date to as early as approximately 33,000 years ago (Dortch 1979). More recently, charcoal fragments associated with stone tools from the site of **Upper Swan** near Perth in southwestern Australia have been dated to 38,000 years ago (Pearce and Barbetti 1981). In addition, new radiocarbon dates indicate that a coastal midden site on the island of New Ireland was initially occupied by 32,000 B.P. New Ireland is near Greater Australia, but even at the height of the Pleistocene it would not have been attached to Greater Australia. The data indicate that New Ireland must have been colonized from the Australian mainland via the island of New Britain by 32,000 years ago (Allen et al. 1989).

The data from Upper Swan indicate that the areas of Greater Australia that were farthest from southeast Asia were settled nearly 40,000 years ago. In addition, radiocarbon dates from two sites in Tasmania indicate that the inland regions of Tasmania were colonized by about 30,000 years ago (Cosgrove 1989). More recently, thermoluminescence (TL) dates have been obtained for two previously excavated sites in northern Australia, Malakunanja II and Malangangerr (Roberts et al. 1990). The TL dates suggest that humans first arrived at Malakunanja II between 45,000 and 61,000 years ago. Malakunanja II, which is located along the base of the prominent Arnhem Land escarpment in northern Australia, is likely to have been brought into use shortly after the initial colonization of the area. These TL dates, therefore, may mark the time of the initial human settlement of greater Australia. Similar dates have been obtained for an archaeological site on the Huon terrace in Papua New Guinea. The site yielded a large number of waisted stone axes and appears to have been occupied at least 40,000 years ago (Groube et al. 1986). The early dates from these sites in northern Sahul led Flood (1990: 94) to suggest that the most likely time of human arrival in Australia is the period of low sea levels about 52,000 years ago.

While the recent radiocarbon and thermoluminescence dates suggest that the Australian continent may have been settled by modern humans from mainland southeast Asia about 50,000 years ago (Roberts et al. 1990), the ways human populations spread throughout this vast, environmentally diverse continent are not well understood. Today much of New Guinea is covered with tropical rain forest, while the vegetation of Australia ranges from tropical rain forests in the northernmost areas to deserts in the west. Changes in temperature, sea levels, rainfall patterns, and oceanic currents would all have affected the environment of Greater Australia during the Pleistocene. Long-term paleoenvironmental investigations have been carried out only in a few areas, such as the Willandra Lakes region. Clearly, more archaeological and environmental research is required to reconstruct the pattern of settlement of Greater Australia.

Three differing models for the peopling of Australia have been proposed. Birdsell (1977) favored a rapid, radiational settlement of the Australian continent from a point of entry in the north. Bowdler (1977), however, argued for an initial settlement of the coastal regions, followed by the use of the Murray River system to reach inland areas such as Lake Mungo. She maintained that the initial inhabitants of Australia were adapted to a coastal way of life, and that adaptations to the desert and montane regions of Australia took place considerably later (Bowdler 1977: 205). However, recent research at the **Puritjarrn rock shelter** near Alice Springs in the dry center of Australia has shown that at least some portions of the interior were settled by 22,000 B.P. (Flood 1990: 79). These data indicate that desert adaptations in Australia may have a much greater antiquity than was originally thought. Horton (1981), on the other hand, has emphasized that Greater Australia would have been a wetter continent at the time of the initial Pleistocene colonization. He argued that early settlement may have focused on the slopes and plains of eastern Australia, which are located between the east coast and the desert. With the addition of a number of large Pleistocene animals that have since become extinct, this intermediate zone would have been a highly productive environment for early hunter-gatherers. As Horton (1991: 350) notes, additional archaeological research in central Australia is needed to choose between these competing models of Australian settlement.

In general, it is likely that the Pleistocene inhabitants of Australia lived in small, geographically dispersed groups (Allen et al. 1989: 559). The accumulating evidence suggests that they may have adapted to a diverse range of environments as early as 30,000 to 35,000 years ago (Allen 1989: 153). The early inhabitants of New Britain relied on shellfish and marine fish (Allen et al. 1989) over 30,000 years ago, while the earliest inhabitants of Tasmania were hunting kangaroos and birds and collecting emu eggs at about the same time (Cosgrove 1989). The stone tools used by the early inhabitants of Greater Australia show little variability; most are simple choppers and flakes. However, the wide range of environments inhabited by these colonists provides evidence for great inventiveness and adaptability (Allen 1989).

The Peopling of the Americas

While an increasing body of archaeological evidence indicates that the Australian continent may have been colonized as early

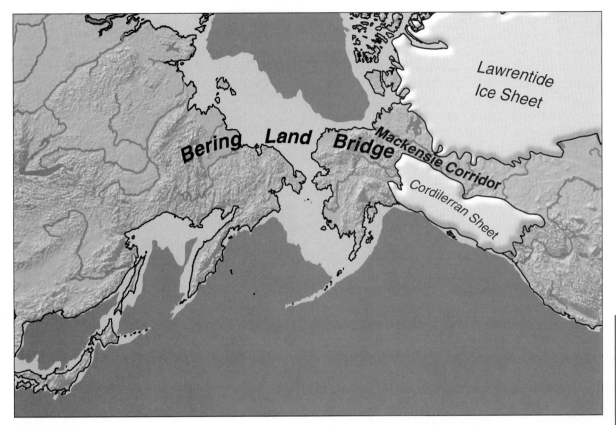

Figure 12.3

Beringia during the late Pleistocene.

as 50,000 years ago, there is considerably less evidence for the settlement of the Americas before the last few millennia of the Pleistocene. For nearly 150 years, questions regarding the peopling of the Americas have been the subject of intense and sometimes acrimonious archaeological debate. As early as 1856, Samuel Haven, the librarian of the American Antiquarian Society, argued that the Americas had been populated from Asia (Haven 1856). This view has never been seriously challenged. In fact, it has received additional support from biological studies of Native American teeth. Turner (1989, 1994) identified certain features of tooth crowns and roots, such as shovel-shaped incisors, that he termed the Sinodont pattern. The distribution of these distinctive features suggests that Native Americans are more closely related to northern Asians than they are to southeast Asians or Europeans. Moreover, Turner suggested that Native American and north Asian populations may have separated

about 15,000 years ago. Any discussion of the settlement of the Americas therefore must begin with the late Paleolithic archaeology of northeast Asia and Alaska.

During the height of the last glaciation, when sea levels were considerably lower than they are today, northeast Asia was connected to Alaska by the **Bering Land Bridge (Figure 12.3)**. A drop of approximately 50 meters (165 ft.) in sea level below today's levels was necessary for the creation of the land bridge. Recent geological studies indicate that the land bridge would have been open throughout the late Pleistocene from 60,000 until after 10,000 years ago.

The term **Beringia** has been used to describe the landmass that would have stretched between the Verkhoyansk Mountain Range in eastern Siberia and the maximum limit of the Laurentide (North American) ice sheet, west of the Mackenzie River in the Canadian Yukon (Hoffecker et al. 1993). The nature of the environment of this landmass has been subject to serious debate among both archaeologists and environmental scientists. Some scholars have argued, based primarily on pollen data (see Chapter 13), that Beringia was a "dry, bleak, windswept land bridge" (Colinvaux and West 1984: 11), which supported only sparse and scattered populations of horse, bison, and mammoth. Others have used faunal data to suggest that Beringia may have been more steppe-like than tundra-like and could have supported a rich and diverse community of large mammals (Guthrie 1990; Hopkins et al. 1982). While debate continues over the nature of the environment of Beringia at the height of the Pleistocene glaciation, it is likely that later glacial Beringia included a mosaic of different environments that could have supported human settlement (Hoffecker et al. 1993: 48).

The pollen data do provide evidence for climatic amelioration beginning about 14,000 years ago. These improvements are part of a series of worldwide climatic changes that took place between about 14,000 and 10,000 years ago, marking the end of the Pleistocene (see Chapter 13). Pollen evidence from Alaska and the Yukon indicates an increase in birch tree pollen at that time. The reappearance of trees in river valleys and elsewhere would have provided greater access to firewood, a necessity in cold, late glacial Beringia (Hoffecker et al. 1993: 51).

The Early Archaeological Record from Alaska

The climatic improvement that marks the last four millennia of the Pleistocene appears to coincide with the initial human settlement of Beringia. Recent radiocarbon dates from the Russian far east indicate that western Beringia, including the Indigirka River basin and the Kamchatka Peninsula, was initially occupied between 14,000 and 12,000 years ago (Kuzmin 1994: 375). The earliest archaeological sites in Alaska are found in the north-central foothills of the Alaska mountain range in the Tanana and Teklanika Valleys. The earliest occupants appear to have entered the region between 12,000 and 11,000 years ago during an interstadial, a warm period marked by the expansion of trees in the river valleys. The river valleys served as

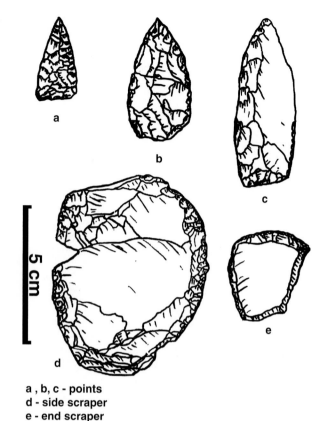

a , b, c - points
d - side scraper
e - end scraper

Figure 12.4

Typical tool kit of the Nenana Complex: bifacially retouched points, end scrapers, and side scrapers.

refugia for steppe-tundra animals during the late Pleistocene and would have been attractive to bison and mammoth at a time when central Alaska was becoming increasingly forested (Powers and Hoffecker 1989: 271). The hunters' tool kit, known as the **Nenana Complex,** was based on a flake and blade core technology, including small bifacially worked projectile points, retouched blades, scrapers, wedges, and planes **(Figure 12.4)**. The bearers of the Nenana Complex hunted sheep, bison, and elk in central Alaska and may also have taken small mammals, fish, and birds.

The Nenana Complex differs markedly from the Late Paleolithic stone tool industries that were common in many parts of northeast Asia between 10,000 and 15,000 years ago. Those industries are characterized by the presence of microblades (very small blades), which were removed from small, wedge-shaped cores **(Figure 12.5)**. The microblade industry first appears in Alaska, where

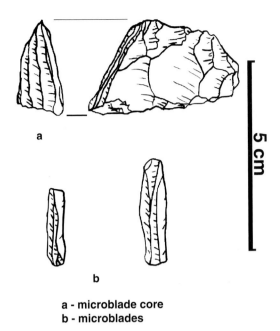

a - microblade core
b - microblades

Figure 12.5

Microblades and typical wedge-shaped core from sites of the Denali Complex in Alaska and late Pleistocene sites in northeast Asia.

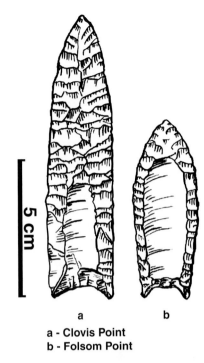

Figure 12.6

Fluted points from the Clovis and Folsom cultures.

a   b

a - Clovis Point
b - Folsom Point

it is known as the **Denali Complex,** at about 10,700 B.P. (Hoffecker et al. 1993: 52), and may represent the spread of a new population into Alaska. The earlier Nenana Complex appears to have more in common with pre-microblade Eurasian Upper Paleolithic stone tool industries.

The Nenana Complex is important not only because it appears to represent the earliest human settlement of Alaska, but also because of its relationship to the peopling of the rest of the Americas. By 14,000 B.P. the melting of the continental ice sheets in northern Canada would have provided an access route for humans from Beringia to the North American Great Plains (Hoffecker et al. 1993: 47). While an ice-free corridor may well have existed between the Laurentide ice sheets that covered much of northern North America and the Cordilleran ice sheets that covered the coastal mountain ranges throughout the height of the late glacial period (25,000 to 14,000 B.P.), it probably sustained few plants and animals. Pollen data indicate, however, that by shortly after 12,000 B.P., sage, willow, grass, and poplar would have invaded this corridor, thus creating an environment that was more favorable to human settlement (Haynes 1987: 83).

In North America the earliest well-dated archaeological sites south of Alaska are part of the **Clovis** culture. Clovis sites date to between 11,200 and 10,900 B.P. (Haynes 1992: 364). The sites are characterized by the presence of distinctive fluted points **(Figure 12.6)**. Flutes are long, narrow flakes that are removed from both sides of spear points. They make it easier to mount the spear point into a split shaft, and they also make the point more streamlined, improving both its stability in the haft and its penetration into game animals (Haynes 1987: 91). Clovis sites have traditionally been identified by the presence of these distinctive spear points. However, with the exception of the distinctive Clovis points, there are remarkable similarities between Clovis stone tool assemblages and those of the earlier Alaskan Nenana Complex. They share many artifact types in common, including bifacially flaked projectile points, convex side scrapers, end scrapers, gravers, and wedges. Since radiocarbon dates for the Nenana Complex fall between 11,800 and 11,000 B.P. (Haynes 1992: 368), it is reasonable to trace the origins of the Clovis culture to the Alaskan Nenana Complex.

◉ Clovis Hunters in North America

Clovis points were first discovered at the site of **Blackwater Draw** near Clovis, New Mexico **(Figure 12.7)**. At Blackwater Draw, a series of ancient springs formed a deep pond with a marshy drainage channel. The lowermost levels of the site yielded Clovis projectile points and other stone tools associated with mammoth bones. Clovis points have been associated with mammoth remains at a number of other early sites in the American southwest. For example, at the **Lehner** site in the extreme southeastern part of Arizona, Clovis points were found associated with the remains of mammoth, horse, bison, and tapir. The animals, including the mammoths, appear to have been killed and butchered on the spot. At the **Colby** site in Wyoming, limb bones, including the remains of three mammoths, were piled into stacks. These bone stacks may represent caches of meat for later use (Jennings 1989: 88).

The evidence from the American southwest suggests that the Clovis people were successful and efficient hunters of large game, including mammoth. Thirteen mammoths were killed at the Lehner site, and eleven were killed at the nearby Murray Springs site, also in southeastern Arizona. Often the mammoth carcasses were only partially disarticulated (Fagan 1995: 83).

How were mammoths and other large game hunted by the Clovis people of the American southwest? Studies of African elephants indicate that these animals return to the same water holes and vegetation patches on a regular basis (Fagan 1995: 82). In general, Clovis sites are located on low terraces along streams and rivers where mammoths and other large game may have obtained food and water. Several techniques may have been used to hunt mammoths. Clovis hunters may have used spear throwers; they may have stabbed mammoths directly with spears; or they may have used spears with detachable foreshafts (Fiedel 1992: 66). The stone spear point would be lashed to a bone foreshaft that would detach from the main shaft, allowing the spear shaft to be retrieved and reused. Mammoths, like all other members of the elephant family, were formidable beasts. Hunters may have waited until one animal became separated from the herd and then at-

Figure 12.7

Locations of North and South American sites discussed in this chapter. Murray Springs is located very close to the Lehner site.

tacked the straggler. If the other mammoths became aware of the attack, hunters may have had to kill the whole herd (Fiedel 1992: 69). A whole herd of mammoths appears to have been killed at the Lehner site. The question of whether early Native American hunters played a role in the extinction of the mammoths and other Pleistocene megafauna will be considered in Chapter 13.

Although attention is often focused on the spectacular mammoth kill sites in the American southwest, Clovis sites are widespread across North and Central America. It has been suggested that these sites were occupied by groups of related, highly mobile hunting bands. In addition to the well-known kill sites, hunters' camps, base camps, and quarry sites have also been identified. Base camps are generally identified by their large size and by the presence of hearths and a greater diversity of tool types, indicating that tasks in addition to hunting and butchery took place there. Quarries include the site of **Flint Run** in northern Virginia, about 80 kilometers (36 mi.) west of Washington, DC, which was exploited for high-quality jasper. In general, Clovis tools are made of high-quality raw materials such as flint, chalcedony, and jasper.

The subsistence practices of the Clovis hunters in the eastern parts of North America are less well known because bone is often poorly preserved at eastern sites. At the **Kimmswick** site, approximately 30 kilometers (18 mi.) south of St. Louis, Missouri, Clovis points were found associated with the bones of a mastodon (Graham 1981). At the time the Clovis hunters occupied the site, about 11,000 years ago, the environment would have been a deciduous woodland with open patches of grass. In the northeast, environmental studies indicate that the vegetation would have been a patchy, variable woodland offering a scattered diversity of food resources. It is likely that this varied environment was occupied by a low-density, highly mobile foraging population (Jennings 1989: 96).

Folsom Hunters

As noted above, Clovis sites in the west date to between 11,200 and 10,900 B.P. About 10,900 years ago the descendants of the Clovis hunters began to make a slightly different style of projectile point. **Folsom** points (see Figure 12.6) are characterized by longer flutes than the earlier Clovis points. Initial excavations in 1926 and 1927 at the Folsom type site in New Mexico revealed 19 Folsom points associated with 23 individuals of an extinct, long-horned species of bison, *Bison antiquus*. These excavations were the first to reveal that Native Americans occupied the North American continent at the same time as late Pleistocene fauna (Jennings 1989: 83). (The even earlier Clovis complex was not identified until 1932.)

Since mammoth became extinct in North America about 11,000 years ago, Folsom hunters in the Great Plains focused primarily on bison. Folsom sites date from between 10,900 and 10,200 years ago (Haynes 1992: 364). Reanalysis of the fauna from the Folsom type site indicates that all 23 bison were killed at the same time in early winter (Frison 1978). The animals appear to have been driven into an arroyo (dry creek) where they were then killed with spears. At other Folsom sites herds of bison were driven over cliffs or into box canyons, which served as natural traps. The successful hunting of large numbers of bison at one time provides indirect evidence for strategic planning, for cooperation between hunters, and for an intimate knowledge of animal behavior. Other Folsom kill sites include the remains of only a single bison, indicating that hunting strategies and techniques may have varied depending on the season, the numbers of hunters available, and other factors.

Pre-Clovis Occupation of the Americas: The Evidence from Monte Verde

For over a century archaeologists and other scholars have suggested that humans were present in North America before about 12,000 years ago. (For an up-to-date review of the evidence, see Nemecek [2000].) Various sites have been claimed as presenting evidence of a human presence in the Americas prior to the **Paleoindian** tradition. (The general term *Paleoindian* is applied to the Clovis, Folsom, and Nenana Complexes of late Pleistocene North America.) Some sites have yielded crude stone flakes, while others have included only bones that were allegedly modified by prehistoric humans. Over the years, the dating evidence, stratigraphic position, and the nature of the artifacts from many of these sites have been challenged. The following is just one example: Alleged bone "tools" from the Old Crow Flats site in the Canadian Yukon were claimed to provide evidence for human settlement of Beringia as early as 30,000 years ago. Since the claim was first advanced, the stratigraphic position of the bones has been questioned; taphonomic analyses have shown that the so-called worked bones were likely produced by non-human agencies; and radiocarbon dating has shown that some of the worked bones are only about 1,300 years old (Nelson et al. 1986). Moreover, the Old Crow Flats assemblage shows no similarity to any known Old World Paleolithic assemblage. Most other claims for a pre-Clovis presence in the Americas have met a similar fate (see Dincauze 1984; Lynch 1990).

The notable exception is the site of **Monte Verde** in south central Chile (Dillehay 1989, 1997). Excavations at the site have yielded artifacts and organic remains, including wood, bone, and skin, on an occupation surface that has been dated to approximately 12,500 B.P. The chipped stone artifacts include large bifaces made of basalt and quartize **(Figure 12.8)**. The site of Monte Verde is so important for archaeologists studying the peopling of the Americas that in January 1997 it was visited by a group of well-respected Paleoindian specialists (Meltzer et al. 1997). These scholars noted that the Monte Verde stone tools were unquestionably manufactured by humans, and that the radiocarbon dates from the site are internally consistent. They concluded that the Monte Verde site was occupied by early humans approximately 12,500 years ago.

The evidence from Monte Verde has important implications for our understanding of the peopling of the New World. Although Monte Verde is only about 1,300 years older than the oldest known Clovis sites in North America, Monte Verde is located approximately 16,000 kilometers (10,000 mi.) south of the Bering Strait. The results of the excavations at Monte Verde "imply a fundamentally different history of human colonization of the New World than envisioned by the Clovis-first model and raise intriguing issues of early

Figure 12.8

Bifacial tools made of exotic basalt from the site of Monte Verde in south central Chile.

5 cm

human adaptations in the Americas" (Meltzer et al. 1997: 662). The questions that these new finds raise include the following: How did early human populations reach South America from the Bering Land Bridge? How did these early hunter-gatherers in Chile make a living? What is the relationship between the Monte Verde settlers and the later Clovis hunter-gatherers in the Americas? Clearly, these questions can be answered only by further research and by the identification of other pre-Clovis sites in the Americas.

Two recently discovered sites in Peru may shed light on the route by which some early Americans reached South America. The sites of **Quebrada Jaguay** and **Quebrada Tacahuay** are located along the south coast of Peru and are contemporary with the Paleoindian sites in other parts of the Americas (ca. 11,000 to 10,000 years ago) (Keefer et al. 1998; Sandweiss et al. 1998). The occupants of these sites made ample use of marine resources, including seabirds, shellfish, and small, schooling fish such as anchovies and drums. The inhabitants of these coastal Peruvian sites probably used nets to catch these small fish. These coastal sites offer support for the idea that some early Americans used a coastal route to enter the New World.

Conclusion

Recent archaeological research in Greater Australia and in the Americas has shed new light on the expansion of modern human populations out of Europe, Asia, and Africa. An increasing number of archaeological sites from various parts of Australia indicate that the continent of Australia may have been colonized as early as 50,000 years ago. By 30,000 years ago, these early settlers had adapted to a diverse range of environments throughout the Sahul region. In the Americas, recent excavations at the site of Monte Verde in Chile have indicated that humans had reached South America by 12,500 B.P. This site is over 1,000 years older than the oldest known Clovis Complex site in North America. It raises important new questions about the initial human settlement of the Americas that can be answered only by additional research.

Glossary

Bering Land Bridge. A land bridge that connected northeast Asia and Alaska, across what today is the Bering Sea, during late Pleistocene times. Humans moved from Asia to the Americas by way of this land bridge.

Beringia. The term that is applied to the landmass that extended from the Verkhoyansk Mountain Range in eastern Siberia to the maximum limit of the Laurentide (North American) ice sheet, west of the Mackenzie River in the Canadian Yukon, during the late Pleistocene.

Blackwater Draw. The type site for the Clovis Complex, near Clovis, New Mexico. In 1932 Clovis points and other stone tools were found in association with the remains of mammoth.

Clovis. Sites identified by the presence of distinctive, fluted spear points, known as Clovis points. In the American southwest Clovis sites often produce the remains of mammoth and date between 11,200 and 10,900 years ago. Sites of the Clovis complex are widespread across North and Central America.

Colby. A Clovis Complex site in Wyoming where stacks of mammoth bones were recovered. It has been suggested that the bone stacks represent some form of meat storage.

Denali Complex. A stone tool tradition based on microblades produced from small, wedge-shaped cores that first appears in Alaska about 10,700 years ago. It appears to be closely related to the microblade industries that are seen in Japan, China, and eastern Siberia between 10,000 and 15,000 years ago and may indicate the movement of a second wave of colonists into Alaska.

Devil's Lair. A site in western Australia that may date to as early as 33,000 years ago.

Eustatic sea level changes. Variations in world sea levels that result from the growth and melting of glaciers. When large quantities of the earth's water are trapped in glacial ice, worldwide sea levels will fall, as they did many times during the Pleistocene.

Flint Run. A Clovis quarry site in northern Virginia that was exploited for high-quality jasper.

Folsom. A complex named after the type site in Folsom, New Mexico, where fluted points were found in association with the remains of an extinct form of bison. Folsom hunters used fluted points to hunt bison on the Great Plains between 10,900 and 10,200 years ago.

Kimmswick. A site near St. Louis, Missouri, where Clovis artifacts were found in association with the skeleton of a mastodon.

Kuk. A site in the highlands of New Guinea where charcoal associated with fire-cracked rocks has been dated to about 30,000 years ago.

Lake Mungo. An archaeological locality in the Willandra Lakes region of New South Wales, Australia, that yielded human burials, stone tools, and hearths that were approximately 25,000 to 30,000 years old.

Lehner. A Clovis kill site in extreme southeastern Arizona dated by radiocarbon to about 10,900 years ago. At the site numerous mammoths, as well as horses, bison, and tapirs, appear to have been killed and butchered on the spot.

Monte Verde. A site in south central Chile that provides evidence for human occupation of the region at about 12,500 B.P. The site has yielded evidence for stone tools and organic remains, including wood, bone, and skin.

Nenana Complex. A hunters' tool kit, found in the earliest Alaskan sites and dated to between 12,000 and 11,000 years ago. It included small bifacially worked projectile points, retouched blades, scrapers, wedges, and planes.

Paleoindian. A general term that is applied to the Late Pleistocene big-game hunting cultures of North America. It has recently been argued that the term, originally applied to only the Clovis and Folsom cultures, should also include the Nenana Complex.

Puritjarrn rock shelter. A rock shelter near Alice Springs in the dry central portion of Australia that appears to have been occupied about 22,000 years ago. The site provides evidence for the Pleistocene occupation of at least some of the arid regions of the Australian continent.

Quebrada Jaguay and **Quebrada Tacahuay.** Two late Pleistocene sites located along the south coast of Peru. The sites were occupied between about 11,000 and 10,000 years ago and provide evidence for extensive use of marine resources.

Recent. The epoch that begins with the end of the Pleistocene, about 10,300 years ago; also called the Holocene. The beginning of the Recent epoch is marked by a worldwide rise in temperatures, signaling the end of the Pleistocene glaciations.

Sahul. The geographical region that includes New Guinea, Australia, and Tasmania. At the height of the last glaciation, these three areas would have been joined to form a single large continent. This region is also referred to as Greater Australia.

Upper Swan. A site near Perth in southwestern Australia where charcoal associated with stone tools has been dated to 38,000 years ago.

Further Reading

Flood, J.
  1990. *The Archaeology of the Dreamtime: The Story of Prehistoric Australia and Its People,* rev. ed. New Haven, CT: Yale University Press.
  A well-illustrated and authoritative review of the prehistory of Australia.

Hoffecker, John F., W. Roger Powers, and Ted Goebel
  1993. The Colonization of Beringia and the Peopling of the New World. *Science* 259: 46–53.
  A comprehensive review of the recent archaeological evidence for the colonization of Beringia and its relationship to the initial settlement of the Americas. The article includes an extensive bibliography.

Horton, David
  1991. *Recovering the Tracks: The Story of Australian Archaeology.* Canberra, Australia: Aboriginal Studies Press.
  This recent book details the history of archaeology in Australia. It includes extensive excerpts from the original scientific papers describing the Lake Mungo finds.

Meltzer, D. J.
  1993. *Search for the First Americans.* Washington, DC: Smithsonian Books.
  A well-illustrated and easy-to-read account of the search for early humans in the New World.

White, J. Peter, and James F. O'Connell
  1982. *A Prehistory of Australia, New Guinea and Sahul.* New York: Academic Press.
  An authoritative account of the prehistory of Australia, New Guinea, and Tasmania for the serious student.

Other Bibliography

Allen, J.
  1989. When Did Humans First Colonize Australia? *Search* 20 (5): 149–154.

Allen, J., C. Gasden, and J. P. White
  1989. Human Pleistocene Adaptations in the Tropical Island Pacific: Recent Evidence from New Ireland, a Greater Australia Outlier. *Antiquity* 63: 548–561.

Birdsell, J. B.
  1977. The Recalibration of a Paradigm for the First Peopling of Australia. In *Sunda and Sahul: Prehistoric Studies in Southeast Asia, Melanesia and Australia,* edited by J. Allen, J. Golson, and R. Jones, pp. 113–167. London: Academic Press.

Bowdler, S.
  1977. The Coastal Colonisation of Australia. In *Sunda and Sahul: Prehistoric Studies in Southeast Asia, Melanesia and Australia,* edited by J. Allen, J. Golson, and R. Jones, pp. 205–246. London: Academic Press.

Bowler, J., R. Jones, H. Allen, and A. Thorne
1970. Pleistocene Human Remains from Australia: A Living Site and Human Cremation from Lake Mungo, Western New South Wales. *World Archaeology* 2: 39–60.

Bowler, J., and A. Thorne
1976. Human Remains from Lake Mungo: Discovery and Excavation of Lake Mungo III. In *The Origin of the Australians,* edited by R. L. Kirk and A. G. Thorne, pp. 127–138. Canberra, Australia: Australian Institute of Aboriginal Studies.

Bowler, J., A. Thorne, and N. Polach
1972. Pleistocene Man in Australia: Age and Significance of the Mungo Skeleton. *Nature* 240: 48–50.

Colinvaux, P. A., and F. H. West
1984. The Beringian Ecosystem. *Quarterly Review of Archaeology* 5 (3): 10–16.

Cosgrove, R.
1989. Thirty Thousand Years of Human Colonization in Tasmania: New Pleistocene Dates. *Science* 243: 1706–1708.

Dillehay, Tom D.
1989. *Monte Verde: A Late Pleistocene Settlement in Chile. Volume I: Palaeoenvironment and Site Context.* Washington and London: Smithsonian Institution Press.
1997. *Monte Verde: A Late Pleistocene Settlement in Chile. Volume II: The Archaeological Context.* Washington and London: Smithsonian Institution Press.

Dincauze, D.
1984. An Archaeo-Logical Evaluation of the Case for Pre-Clovis Occupations. In *Advances in World Archaeology,* vol. 3, edited by F. Wendorf and A. Close, pp. 275–323. New York: Academic Press.

Dortch, C.
1979. Devil's Lair: An Example of Prolonged Cave Use in Southwestern Australia. *World Archaeology* 10: 258–279.

Fagan, B. M.
1995. *Ancient North America: The Archaeology of a Continent,* 2d ed. London: Thames and Hudson.

Fiedel, S. J.
1992. *Prehistory of the Americas,* 2d ed. Cambridge: Cambridge University Press.

Frison, G. C.
1978. *Prehistoric Hunters of the High Plains.* New York: Academic Press.

Golson, J., and P. J. Hughes
1977. Ditches before Time. *Hemisphere* 21 (2): 13–21.

Graham, R. W., C. V. Haynes, D. L. Johnson, and M. Kay
1981. Kimmswick: A Clovis-Mastodon Association in Eastern Missouri. *Science* 213: 1115–1117.

Groube, L., J. Chappell, J. Muke, and D. Price
1986. A 40,000-Year-Old Human Occupation Site at Huon Peninsula, Papua New Guinea. *Nature* 324: 453–455.

Guthrie, R. Dale
1990. *Frozen Fauna of the Mammoth Steppe: The Story of Blue Babe.* Chicago: University of Chicago Press.

Haven, S.
1856. *Archaeology of the United States.* Washington, DC: Smithsonian Contributions to Knowledge, No. 8 (2).

Haynes, C. V.
1987. Clovis Origins Update. *The Kiva* 52 (2): 83–93.
1992. Contributions of Radiocarbon Dating to the Geochronology of the Peopling of the New World. In *Radiocarbon after Four Decades: An Interdisciplinary Perspective,* edited by R. E. Taylor, A. Long, and R. S. Kra, pp. 355–374. New York: Springer-Verlag.

Hopkins, D., J. Matthews, C. Schweger, and S. Young, eds.
1982. *Paleoecology of Beringia.* New York: Academic Press.

Horton, D. R.
1981. Water and Woodland: The Peopling of Australia. *Australian Institute of Aboriginal Studies Newsletter* 16: 21–27.

Irwin, Geoffrey
1992. *The Prehistoric Exploration and Colonisation of the Pacific.* Cambridge: Cambridge University Press.

Jennings, J. D.
1989. *Prehistory of North America,* 3d ed. Mountain View, CA: Mayfield.

Keefer, D. K., S. D. de France, M. E. Moseley, J. B. Richardson, D. R. Satterlee, and A. Day-Lewis
1998. Early Maritime Economy and El Niño Events at Quebrada Tacahuay, Peru. *Science* 281: 1833–1835.

Kuzmin, Y. V.

1994. Prehistoric Colonization of Northeastern Siberia and Migration to America: Radiocarbon Evidence. *Radiocarbon* 36: 367–376.

Lynch, T. F.

1990. Glacial-Age Man in South America? A Critical Review. *American Antiquity* 55 (1): 12–36.

Meltzer, D. J., D. K. Grayson, G. Ardila, A. W. Barker, D. F. Dincauze, C. V. Haynes, F. Mena, L. Nuñez, and D. J. Stanford

1997. On the Pleistocene Antiquity of Monte Verde, Southern Chile. *American Antiquity* 62 (4): 659–663.

Mulvaney, D. J.

1964. The Pleistocene Colonization of Australia. *Antiquity* 38: 263–267.

Nelson, D. E., R. E. Morlan, J. S. Vogel, J. R. Southon, and C. R. Harrington

1986. New Dates on Northern Yukon Artifacts: Holocene Not Upper Pleistocene. *Science* 232: 749–751.

Nemecek, S.

2000. Who Were the First Americans? *Scientific American* 283 (3): 80–87.

Pearce, R. H., and M. Barbetti

1981. A 38,000-Year-Old Site in Upper Swan, Western Australia. *Archaeology in Oceania* 16 (3): 173–178.

Powers, W. R., and J. F. Hoffecker

1989. Late Pleistocene Settlement in the Nenana Valley, Central Alaska. *American Antiquity* 54 (2): 263–297.

Roberts, Richard G., Rhys Jones, and M. A. Smith

1990. Thermoluminescense Dating of a 50,000-Year-Old Human Occupation Site in Northern Australia. *Nature* 345:153–156.

Sandweiss, D. H., H. McInnis, R. L. Burger, A. Cano, B. Ojeda, R. Paredes, M. Sandweiss, and M. D. Glasscock

1998. Quebrada Jaguay: Early South American Maritime Adaptations. *Science* 281: 1830–1832.

Turner, C. G., II

1989. Teeth and Prehistory in Asia. *Scientific American* 260: 88–96.

1994. Relating Eurasian and Native American Populations through Dental Morphology. In *Method and Theory for Investigating the Peopling of the Americas,* edited by R. Bonnichsen and D. G. Steele, pp. 131–140. Corvalis, OR: Center for the Study of the First Americans.

Van Andel, T. H.

1989. Late Quaternary Sea-Level Changes and Archaeology. *Antiquity* 63: 733–745.

Part V

How Did Human Societies Change at the End of the Ice Age?

Although the end of the Pleistocene Ice Age is traditionally dated to approximately 10,300 years ago, the late Pleistocene period from about 14,000 to 10,300 years ago was a period of worldwide climatic instability. The end of the Pleistocene saw the extinction of many large mammal species such as the mammoth and marked changes in vegetation in many areas of both the Old and New Worlds. In Europe and eastern North America, for example, dense forests replaced the more open Pleistocene landscape.

This section of the text examines the effects that climatic changes had on hunter-gatherer populations in the late Pleistocene and early Holocene. Case studies are drawn from Mesolithic sites in Europe, including Star Carr in northern England, and Archaic sites in North America. While early postglacial societies in Europe have traditionally been viewed as impoverished, we argue that the archaeological evidence shows that these postglacial hunters and gatherers were making use of the new forested environments in active and creative ways.

Chapter 13

The Changing World
at the End of the Ice Age

Introduction

It is hard for us today to imagine a world in which Magdalenian hunters killed reindeer in the Paris basin and Native Americans hunted mammoths in the American southwest; yet these conditions existed as recently as 11,000 years ago. The end of the Pleistocene Ice Age, conventionally dated to 10,300 years ago, was marked by profound climatic changes throughout the world. After a period of climatic instability that lasted from 14,000 to about 10,000 years ago, the world experienced rapidly rising temperatures that led to the retreat of the continental ice sheets and the onset of postglacial climatic conditions. Northern Europe and North America were the areas that were most directly affected by the process of deglaciation, which began approximately 18,000 years ago.

In this chapter we will examine the effects of those climatic changes on both the Old World and the Americas. We will also examine the ways human hunter-gatherer populations adapted to the changed environmental conditions and how they, in turn, may have altered their environment. In both the Old and New Worlds, hunting and gathering peoples had to find new ways to cope with the changing environment and to exploit the new range of resources that became available to them.

To study the relationships between changing human environments and past human populations, archaeologists need to be able to reconstruct prehistoric environments. This is especially true for late Pleistocene and early post-Pleistocene periods, because in many areas of the world the environments of 10,000 years ago have no modern analogs. Pollen analysis has played a crucial role in the reconstruction of prehistoric environments. In the Archaeology in Practice box, we examine the ways pollen analysis has been used in environmental reconstruction.

Causes of Climatic Change

The climatic changes that took place at the end of the Pleistocene were worldwide, although the nature of the changes varied in different parts of the world. In this chapter we will concentrate on the changes that took place in Europe and North America, since those regions experienced some of the most dramatic changes at the end of the Pleistocene. Why did the climate change dramatically about 10,000 years ago? The changes in the world climate appear to have been triggered by alterations in the earth's orbit that led to increased solar radiation during the summer in the northern hemisphere (where most of the earth's landmass lies). A combination of eccentricities in the earth's orbit, an increase in the earth's tilt on its axis, and changes in the season when the earth is closest to the sun may have triggered the climatic changes. The changes in earth-sun geometry (Figure 13.1) began about 18,000 years ago but reached their maximum about 9,000 years ago, when the solar radiation during the summer in the northern hemisphere was about 7 percent greater than it is today (Kutzbach and Webb 1991: 191).

The effects of increased summer insolation were tempered by the effects of the slowly melting ice sheets that covered parts of Eurasia and much of northern North America. These huge ice masses reflected sunlight away from the earth's surface and also affected patterns of global air circulation. The complex interaction of these factors altered storm tracks, which influenced precipitation patterns in different areas of the world. Changes in temperature and rainfall patterns, in turn, affected the distributions of the plant and animal resources on which humans depended. Those changes are reflected in the palynological and geological records for different parts of the world.

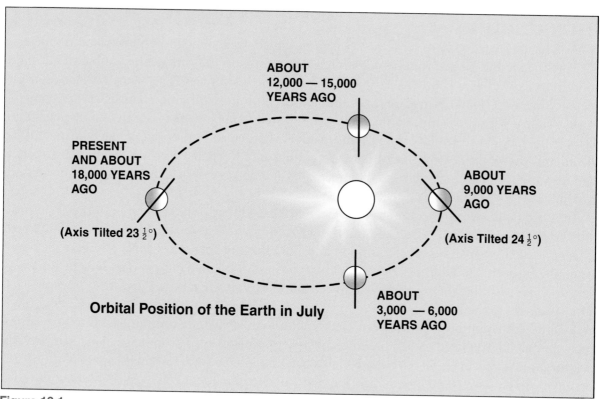

Figure 13.1

Schematic drawing showing changes in earth-sun geometry since 18,000 B.P.

Geological evidence indicates that sudden, major climatic changes occurred about 10,300 years ago, including, among others, changes in the proportion of carbon dioxide in the earth's atmosphere. The amount of CO_2 rose steadily from 17,000 to 10,000 years ago and has remained at that higher level until quite recently. (In recent years increasing industrialization and global population growth have caused the proportion of carbon dioxide in the atmosphere to begin rising once again.) It should be noted, however, that the rise in the percentage of atmospheric CO_2 (one of the so-called greenhouse gases) at the end of the Pleistocene is not nearly enough to account for the massive global climatic changes that took place at that time. Moreover, the rise in CO_2 may be a consequence, rather than a cause, of late Pleistocene global warming (Pielou 1992: 228). Other effects include changes in the kinds of small animals (called foraminifera) found on the ocean floor, which indicate sharply rising ocean temperatures and the extinction of a large

number of mammal species. The possible causes of these mammalian extinctions will be discussed in greater detail below, but first we will explore the ways the climate changed in Europe and North America.

Northern Europe at the End of the Ice Age

Evidence from pollen analyses (see the Archaeology in Practice box), fossil faunas, and permafrost features indicates that Europe had an extremely cold climate between 24,000 and 13,000 years ago. Although the northern European ice sheets began to decrease in size as early as 18,000 to 17,000 years ago as a result of rising summer temperatures, winter temperatures remained cold until about 14,000 B.P.

Pollen analyses, studies of fossil beetles, oxygen isotope records, and evidence of marine fauna in the North Atlantic indicate that temperatures rose rapidly in northwest Europe about 13,000 years ago. It is estimated

Pollen Analysis

Palynology, or pollen analysis, is the study of pollen grains. Archaeologists are particularly interested in using pollen recovered from fossil and subfossil contexts as a tool for reconstructing past human environments (Moore et al. 1991). Pollen, produced by seed plants, is part of the plant's reproductive system. Pollen grains are produced in the anthers, the male part of the flower. When pollen grains are released by plants, they are mixed in the atmosphere and ultimately fall onto land and water surfaces. This pollen rain is a reflection of the vegetation that produced it. Thus analyzing fossil and subfossil pollen helps archaeologists reconstruct past environments and climatic change.

Pollen analyses can be used in several ways by archaeologists. As noted above, pollen data can be used to trace the vegetational history of a particular area. Since a region's vegetation is a reflection of temperature, rainfall, and soil conditions, changes in vegetation over time may reflect changes in climatic variables such as temperature and precipitation. Pollen analysis can also be used to assess past human impact on vegetation. As we will see in Part VI, the beginnings of agriculture led to significant changes in vegetation history. In addition to the introduction of cultivated crops and the weeds of cultivation, the beginning of farming was sometimes accompanied by forest clearance in areas such as northern and central Europe and eastern North America (Delacourt et al. 1998). Finally, the analysis of pollen recovered from specific features, such as pits and burials,

Figure 13.2

Illustrations of pollen grains of pine, elm, and tree birch. Differences in size, shape, and external morphology can be used to distinguish the pollen of different plant taxa.

Pine

elm

tree birch

25 microns

within archaeological sites may produce information about past human behavior. As noted in Chapter 7, pollen samples recovered from one of the Shanidar Neanderthal burials suggested that the individual had been buried with flowers.

Pollen is preserved best under conditions that inhibit microbiological activity, such as waterlogging, extreme aridity, high acidity, and an excess of salt or metal ions in the soil (Dimbleby 1985: X). Most pollen samples used for environmental reconstruction come from stratified waterlogged deposits, such as peat or lake mud, where pollen accumulates progressively through time. The dating of pollen samples, especially those from non-archaeological deposits such as lake beds, has been a persistent

problem for environmental archaeologists. Radiocarbon dating (see Chapter 10) of the organic materials within a pollen core sample can provide independent dating for pollen records.

Once the pollen samples have been taken, recorded, and dried, the extraction and identification of pollen becomes a specialist task requiring laboratory facilities (Dimbleby 1985: 25). Pollen extraction (separating the pollen grains from the soil matrix) often requires the use of caustic and toxic chemicals such as hydrofluoric acid. Pollen samples are then mounted on slides so that the pollen grains may be identified and counted. Differences in the size and form of the pollen grain **(Figure 13.2)** are used to distinguish the pollen of different plants (Pearsall 1989: 251).

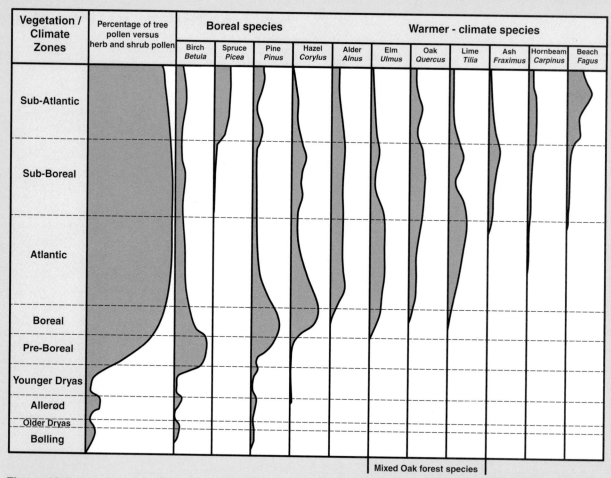

Vegetation / Climate Zones	Percentage of tree pollen versus herb and shrub pollen	Boreal species					Warmer - climate species					
		Birch *Betula*	Spruce *Picea*	Pine *Pinus*	Hazel *Corylus*	Alder *Alnus*	Elm *Ulmus*	Oak *Quercus*	Lime *Tilia*	Ash *Fraximus*	Hornbeam *Carpinus*	Beach *Fagus*
Sub-Atlantic												
Sub-Boreal												
Atlantic												
Boreal												
Pre-Boreal												
Younger Dryas												
Allerød												
Older Dryas												
Bølling												

Mixed Oak forest species

Figure 13.3

Generalized pollen diagram showing the vegetational changes that took place in southern Scandinavia in late glacial and early postglacial times. The column on the left shows the percentage of tree versus shrub and herb pollen. Note the rapid development of forests in Europe in the early postglacial period. The Alleröd, Older Dryas, and Bölling chronological zones have recently been combined into the Windermere interstadial.

Once the identifications have been completed, pollen data are usually presented in the form of a pollen diagram. In a typical pollen diagram, the vertical axis is used to depict the soil depth, while the horizontal axis shows the relative or absolute abundance of different types of pollen. The soil depth reflects the relative age of the pollen samples, while the pollen abundance reflects the general prevalence of plant species in the environment. Pollen diagrams may also show the relative abundance of different groups of plants. For example, one common measure is the proportion of arboreal (tree) pollen to nonarboreal pollen. The relative abundance of different groups of species, such as aquatic plants, shrubs, and herbs, may also be depicted (Moore et al. 1991).

A generalized pollen diagram showing the vegetational changes in late glacial and early postglacial southern Scandinavia is shown in **Figure 13.3**. The column to the left shows the percentage of tree pollen in relation to the proportion of herb and shrub pollen. This diagram shows a clear increase in tree pollen beginning about 10,000 years ago. The increase in trees is a reflection of the increasing temperatures that prevailed after about 10,000 years ago. The first trees to appear are pioneer species such as birch and pine. About 8,000 years ago, warm-loving mixed-oak forest species begin to replace those trees.

that summer temperatures in Britain may have risen as much as 8° to 10° Celsius (14° to 18°F.) at that time. This marked climatic warming caused a rapid retreat of the glaciers. The ice sheets covering much of the British Isles began to decrease in size, and broad regions of the North European Plain became deglaciated. This late glacial warm period is termed the **Windermere interstadial;** it lasted from about 13,000 to 11,000 years ago.[1] By 11,500 years ago, birch and pine forests had replaced steppe and tundra in many areas of central, southern, and eastern Europe, but a broad zone of steppe parkland still covered much of France, southern Britain, the Low Countries, and northern Germany. The retreat of the glaciers opened new areas to human settlement.

Subsequently, however, oxygen isotope records show that there was a considerable drop in temperatures about 11,000 years ago in Europe. The causes of this rapid climatic deterioration are unknown, but changes in atmospheric circulation patterns clearly played a role. In addition, the draining of the floodwaters of Lake Agassiz (an enormous North American lake formed by glacial meltwaters) into the North Atlantic at that time may also have played a role in global cooling (Dawson 1992: 108). The result was a return to almost full glacial conditions. The decrease in temperature was most dramatic in northwestern Europe, where it is estimated that summer temperatures dropped by 8° to 10° Celsius (14° to 18°F.). Glaciers increased in size in Scandinavia, the Alps, and Siberia, as well as other parts of the world. In northern Scotland, where the ice sheets had disappeared during the Windermere interstadial, new glaciers began to form. This cold period, termed the **Younger Dryas,** lasted for nearly a millennium, although the period from 11,000 to 10,500 years ago was coldest in Europe. (The

name Dryas comes from the mountain avens plant, *Dryas octopetala,* which commonly occurs in arctic plant communities and appears in many pollen cores in northern Europe at this time.) As a result of this cold spell, the forestation of Europe was halted; the forest belt moved southward, leading to an increase in tundra. For example, during the Younger Dryas, many areas of Scandinavia that had been ice-free were covered with an arctic tundra vegetation with low bushes and scattered birch trees **(Figure 13.4)**.

The Younger Dryas period was followed by a rapid change to postglacial conditions about 10,300 years ago, marking the beginning of the **Holocene,** or Recent, period. The rapidly rising temperatures led to the final melting of the European glaciers between 9,200 and 8,500 years ago. With rising sea levels, the island of Great Britain separated from the European continent between 8,500 and 8,000 years ago. Trees replaced tundra in southern Scandinavia—first birch, then pine, and finally a broad-leaved, mixed-oak forest between 8,000 and 3,000 years ago (see Figure 13.3). As we will see in Chapter 15, the rapidly changing environmental conditions of the early Holocene, or Recent, period (after 10,300 B.P.) provided both new challenges and new opportunities for hunting and gathering populations in Europe. Reindeer were replaced by forest animals such as wild cattle and wild pigs, and the appearance of plants such as hazel provided new opportunities for plant collection.

Late Pleistocene Hunters and Fishers in Northern Europe

As noted above, the glacial retreat that began in the late Pleistocene opened up new areas of north central Europe to human settlement. Between 14,000 and 10,000 years ago humans were able to resettle many parts of the Low Countries, northern Germany, and southern Scandinavia. These hunters, long dependent on reindeer, were not simply following the migrating herds northward; instead, they were finding new ways to make use of the resources becoming available in the northern environments. Recent research in northern Europe has shown that these foragers were adaptable pioneers who moved

---

[1]In Scandinavia the pattern of glacial warming is more complex. An initial warm period, the Bölling interstadial (13,000 to 12,000 B.P.), was followed by a brief return to colder conditions. This brief cold snap, known as the Older Dryas stadial, extended from 12,000 to 11,800 B.P. The Older Dryas was followed by a second warm period known as the Alleröd interstadial (11, 800 to 11,000 B.P.) (Dawson 1992: 79).

Figure 13.4

Europe during the Younger Dryas period showing the extent of the remaining glaciers and the vegetation zones at that time. The location of the late Paleolithic site of Stellmoor is also shown.

The map legend reads:

- Tundra or Steppe
- Birch forest
- Boreal Pine - Spruce forest
- Broad-leaved / Hazel forest
- Partly forested parkland

Stellmoor

into a previously uninhabitable landscape (Fischer 1991). These late Pleistocene hunters used a simple and expedient blade technology to manufacture stone tools, which included a number of points designed specifically for hunting. There is evidence for the hunting of moose, reindeer, bear, wolverine, swan, and possibly roe deer (Fischer 1991: 113). Pike bones also have been recovered from some sites, and the location of many sites along lakes and streams suggests that fishing played an important role in the economy.

Excavations at the site of **Stellmoor** in northern Germany have provided insights into the hunting techniques used by the late Pleistocene foragers. Faunal evidence suggests that the reindeer were hunted in the autumn, but that humans subsisted on dried meat and stored grease and marrow on a year-round basis (Bokelman 1991). At Stellmoor hunters appear to have driven a herd of reindeer into a lake where they then shot them with arrows. Over 100 pinewood arrows and arrow fragments were recovered from the site. The arrows were tipped with flint and had a detachable wooden foreshaft that facilitated repairs (Bokelman 1991: 79). The site provides early evidence for the use of the bow and arrow during the late Upper Paleolithic.

Two distinct types of late Pleistocene sites have been identified in northern Europe. Residential campsites, which are located near permanent sources of freshwater, contain a central hearth surrounded by domestic refuse. Hunting camps, on the other hand, are often located on elevated spots on the landscape where game movements could be observed. The deglaciation of Europe would have opened up a large land area that was rich in food and raw materials. Population densities appear to have been low, as most sites would have housed no more than a few families, but the conditions of life may have been quite favorable for these north European pioneers (Fischer 1991: 117).

Climatic Changes: Late Glacial and Early Postglacial North America

As was noted in Chapter 12, the initial settlement of the American continents must be seen against the backdrop of changing environmental conditions in late glacial Beringia. Pollen and geological data indicate that similar changes were happening throughout the North American continent in the late glacial and early postglacial periods. Although there are many similarities in the patterns of deglaciation in Europe and North America, the final melting of the large North American ice sheets took about 500 years longer. The larger landmass of Eurasia in comparison with that of North America allowed for more rapid postglacial warming and therefore more rapid glacial melting (Kutzbach and Webb 1991).

In North America the glaciers began to retreat between 18,000 and 14,000 years ago. By about 14,000 years ago the southern portions of the Great Lakes region were deglaciated, and ice-dammed lakes (eventually to become the Great Lakes) began to form between the southern ends of the lake basins and the retreating glaciers (Figure 13.5). Geological evidence indicates that significant climatic amelioration occurred in North America between 14,000 and 11,000 years ago. All sections of the North American ice sheets began to retreat. It is during that period that we see the earliest well-dated sites indicating human settlement in eastern Beringia and Alaska. By 11,000 years ago the coast of Maine had been deglaciated; the Cordilleran ice sheet covering the western mountains had retreated; and the Great Lakes region was largely free of ice. As in Europe, this period is also marked by the spread of deciduous forests, although some steppe and tundra conditions persisted in deglaciated regions in the east.

Although the evidence for the Younger Dryas event is not as marked in some regions of North America as it is in Europe, both geological and pollen evidence for this event is found in eastern North America. Glaciers advanced in both Newfoundland and Nova Scotia in the Canadian maritimes, and pollen records for the midwestern United States also show evidence for temperature decreases.

In North America there is clear evidence for increasing temperatures and a rapid melting of glacial ice after 10,000 years ago. Rising temperatures led to dramatic vegetational changes in North America. The open tundra and prairie zone south of the ice sheets disappeared and was replaced by birch forests in the east, mixed coniferous and deciduous forests in the midwest, and wide open prairie westward into the plains states. Deciduous forests expanded rapidly south and east of the Great Lakes in early Holocene times. While the eastern parts of North America became increasingly forested during the early postglacial period, the western parts, including both the Great Basin and the desert Southwest, became progressively more arid. By about 8,000 years ago present-day desert conditions had been established. In Chapter 16 we will examine the ways Native American foragers in the American West adapted to these arid postglacial conditions. Native American populations in the eastern United States, much like their counterparts in temperate Europe, adapted to the increasingly forested conditions of the postglacial period by making use of a wide range of plant and animal resources (see Chapters 15 and 16).

Late Pleistocene Extinctions

Changes in world climate and vegetational patterns were not the only characteristics of the end of the Ice Age. One of the most striking features of the period was the extinction of a wide range of large mammal species in a number of different areas of the world. In Eurasia, the mammoth and the woolly rhino had disappeared by the end of the Ice Age. In North America a much larger range of megafauna became extinct, including both large herbivorous mammals, such as mammoths, horses, tapirs, and camels, and the large carnivores that may have preyed on

14,000 B.P.

11,000 B.P.

9,000 B.P.

Figure 13.5

Views of the Laurentide (major North American) ice sheet between 14,000 and 9,000 B.P. showing the extent of the ice sheet and the formation of the glacial meltwater lakes that were the precursors of the Great Lakes.

them, including the sabre-toothed tiger and the dire wolf **(Figure 13.6)**. Australia saw the extinction of a substantial number of large marsupial mammals, although the Australian extinctions began over 10,000 years before the North American extinctions. While the cause or causes of these great mammal extinctions remains a mystery (Pielou 1992: 265), vertebrate paleontologists and archaeol-ogists have vigorously debated a number of theories. Most scientists would argue that the profound climatic changes that took place at the end of the Pleistocene played a critical role in the extinction of these large mammals. However, some archaeologists and paleontol-ogists have suggested that human hunting may have caused the extinction of at least some species of Pleistocene megafauna.

Figure 13.6

The dire wolf (Canis dirus) *is a larger and more heavily built relative of the extant timber wolf, with much larger teeth. The dire wolf became extinct about 10,000 years ago.*

The Pleistocene Overkill Hypothesis

The argument that human hunting played a role in the late Pleistocene extinctions is known as the **prehistoric overkill hypothesis** and has been put forward by the paleontologist P. S. Martin (1984). Simply put, the prehistoric overkill hypothesis states that human hunters may have caused the extinction of Pleistocene large mammals such as the mammoth. Martin notes that Pleistocene extinctions were more common in Australia and the Americas, continents that were not occupied by humans until late Pleistocene times, than they were in Eurasia and Africa. In Australia 19 genera and more than 50 species have disappeared in the past 40,000 years, while in the Americas more than 70 genera have disappeared. Martin (1984: 394) argues that most, if not all, of the American extinctions have taken place within the last 15,000 years. Moreover, Martin notes that the Australian extinction events took place somewhat earlier than the American extinctions did, mirroring the earlier human settlement of the continent of Australia. He concludes that the record of late Pleistocene extinctions more closely reflects the movements and activities of humans than the late glacial climatic changes that took place between 18,000 and 10,000 years ago (Martin 1984: 396). Martin suggested that intensive hunting would have maximized the speed and intensity of the human impact on indigenous fauna while minimizing the amount of time between the initial human settlement of an area and the disappearance of its native fauna.

Although the prehistoric overkill hypothesis seems quite plausible at first glance, there are a number of strong arguments against this theory (Pielou 1992: 257). First, it is important to note that the Clovis period population of North America appears to have been quite low, perhaps too low to have had an effect on the populations of other animal species.

An even more compelling argument against the overkill model focuses on the chronology of large mammal extinctions in North America. The archaeologist D. K. Grayson (1991) has recently reviewed the evidence for late Pleistocene mammalian extinctions in North America. He noted that the radiocarbon evidence shows that not all Pleistocene extinctions in North America took place between 12,000 and 10,000 years ago, the period of the widespread early human settlement of the North America continent. Large mammals such as the short-faced bear and the American cheetah became extinct well before the appearance of the Clovis hunters. Of those species that did become extinct between 12,000 and 10,000 years ago, only two, mammoth and mastodon, have been recovered from human kill sites.

Similar objections can be raised against the overkill hypothesis as it has been applied to Australia. As was shown in Chapter 12, Australia appears to have been settled by modern humans sometime between about 40,000 and 50,000 years ago. However, the wave of late Pleistocene extinctions in Australia began about 26,000 years ago and extended over a period of approximately 11,000 years (Pielou 1992: 255). The Australian data certainly do not support Martin's scenario, in which newly arrived human hunters rapidly exterminated a number of indigenous animal species.

Alternative Explanations for Late Pleistocene Megafaunal Extinctions

Most archaeologists and paleontologists reject Martin's prehistoric overkill hypothesis because it does not explain the vast majority of megafaunal extinctions that took place at the end of the Pleistocene. A variety of alternative explanations have been suggested that focus on the effect that late Pleistocene climatic changes would have had on large mammal populations. The massive climatic changes that took place at the end of the Pleistocene radically altered the range and composition of plant communities and may therefore have dramatically restricted the ranges of certain animal species. Late Pleistocene climates may have been more equable than those of today. While average yearly temperatures were relatively low during the late Pleistocene, equability means that the seasonal changes between summer and winter would have been less marked. Increasing summer temperatures in the early Holocene may have led to shifts in the vegetational communities, which in turn affected the animal populations that depended upon them (see Grayson 1991).

Dale Guthrie (1984) has developed an ecological theory to explain the megafaunal extinctions in North America based on the vegetational changes that took place at the end of the Pleistocene and the effects that those changes would have had on certain large mammal species. He argued that increasing seasonality (hotter summers and colder winters) at the end of the Pleistocene would have led to increasing zonation of plant communities. That is, some plant species that were found together during the Pleistocene were found in separate environmental zones during the early Holocene. The smaller variety of plant species in any given zone resulted in a shortened and less diverse growing season in that region, reducing the quantity and quality of plant foods available to many large mammal species. For animal species that relied on a "long growing season and a diverse vegetation to provide a balanced diet, the new Holocene buffet was ultimately a disaster" (Guthrie 1984: 290). For animals such as horses, mammoths, and mastodons, the result was extinction.

Case Study
The Murray Springs Clovis Site

The Murray Springs site in southern Arizona is important because it illustrates how difficult it can be to distinguish the effects of human predation on large mammal populations from the effects of environmental change. The site does provide clear evidence for human hunting of mammoth, a species that did become extinct at the end of the Pleistocene. At the same time, however, detailed environmental research at the site has revealed dramatic climatic changes that may have affected the viability of mammoth populations in the American southwest.

Most of the Clovis kill sites in the American southwest are associated with mammoths. If humans did play a role in the extinction of any of the large Pleistocene mammals in North America, then mammoths would certainly have been the most likely victims of human hunting practices. In analyzing the data from the **Murray Springs** Clovis site **(Figure 13.7)**, Haynes (1991) has recently suggested a model for the ways both climatic change and human hunting may have led to the extinction of the North American mammoths.

As noted in the last chapter, the Murray Springs Clovis site is one of a number of Clovis Complex mammoth kill sites in extreme southeastern Arizona. The site was discovered in 1966, and additional excavations took place there in 1974 to 1975. These excavations yielded evidence for a mammoth kill, a bison kill, and a hunters' camp (Haynes 1991). The presence of projectile (spear) points, other stone artifacts, and **debitage** (waste flakes from stone tool production) at the mammoth kill site indicate that the mammoths were killed by human hunters (Figure 13.7). Radiocarbon dates for the Murray Springs site average 10,900 B.P. (Haynes 1992: 363), indicating that it is a very early site, contemporary with the initial widespread settlement of the North american continent. This is the kind of evidence one might use to support Martin's prehistoric overkill hypothesis.

On the other hand, geological evidence from Murray Springs and other contemporary sites indicates that there was a major drought in the southwest at that time. The dry interval dates from between 11,300 and 10,900 years ago. This drought may coincide with the Younger Dryas climatic event in other parts of the world. It would have produced a significant reduction in the traditional watering places used by large mammals such as mammoths. The drought would have placed these large mammals under severe stress at the very time that the opportunistic Clovis hunters arrived in North America (Haynes 1991: 447). Animals under stress would have been easier prey for human hunters. The data from Murray Springs suggest that both climatic changes and human predation may have contributed to the extinction of the mammoths in North America. The extinction of at least one species of Pleistocene megafauna may have been a result of the combined effects of prolonged drought and the success of the Clovis hunters.

Figure 13.7

Excavations at the Murray Springs site, southeastern Arizona, showing the bones, tusks, and teeth of a mammoth.

 Conclusion

The sweeping climatic changes that took place at the end of the Pleistocene provided both challenges and opportunities for human hunting and gathering populations. In the early Holocene, the progressive reforestation of both Europe and eastern North America created environments that were very different from the late Pleistocene conditions in those regions. In the following three chapters we will examine the ways

human hunter-gatherers in Europe and North America adapted to these newly created environments.

Glossary

Debitage. Small waste flakes and chips produced during the manufacture of stone tools.

Holocene. The geological period (also known as the Recent period) that began 10,300 years ago with the end of the Pleistocene and continues to the present day.

Murray Springs. A Clovis Complex site located in extreme southeastern Arizona. It includes a mammoth kill, a bison kill, and a hunters' camp. The site has also produced environmental evidence for a Clovis period drought that ended about 10,900 years ago.

Palynology. The study of pollen grains. Archaeological pollen analysis focuses on the study of pollen recovered from both geological and archaeological contexts to reconstruct past vegetational history, climatic changes, human impact on the landscape, and human uses of plants.

Prehistoric overkill hypothesis. The hypothesis suggesting that humans may have played a major role in the extinction of many large mammal species during the late Pleistocene.

Stellmoor. A late Pleistocene (Younger Dryas period) site in northern Germany that provides evidence for the use of bows and arrows by late glacial hunters in northern Europe. The weapons were used to kill reindeer that had been driven into a lake.

Windermere interstadial. A late glacial warm period that lasted from about 13,000 to 11,000 B.P. in Europe.

Younger Dryas. A short stadial, or cold period, that began about 11,000 years ago and lasted for less than a millennium. During the Younger Dryas in Europe, temperatures dropped significantly and the glaciers began to advance again. Evidence of the Younger Dryas event has also been found in the Near East (Chapter 17) and in eastern North America.

Further Reading

Andersen, B. G. and H. W. Borns
   1994. *The Ice Age World.* Oslo, Norway: Scandinavian University Press.
   A well-illustrated and authoritative account of Pleistocene geology with an extensive glossary of terms.

Other Bibliography

Bokelman, Klaus
   1991. Some Thoughts on Humans and Reindeer in the Ahrensburgian Tunnel Valley in Schlesweg-Holstein, Germany. In *The Late Glacial in North-West Europe: Human Adaptation and Environmental Change at the End of the Pleistocene,* edited by N. Barton, J. Roberts, and D. A. Roe, pp. 72–81. London: Council for British Archaeology Research Report No. 77.

Dawson, Alastair G.
   1992. *Ice Age Earth: Late Quaternary Geology and Climate.* London and New York: Routledge.

Delacourt, P. A., H. R. Delacourt, C. R. Ison, W. E. Sharp, and K. J. Gremillion
   1998. Prehistoric Human Use of Fire, the Eastern Agricultural Complex, and Appalachian Oak-Chestnut Forests: Paleoecology of Cliff Palace Pond, Kentucky. *American Antiquity* 63 (2): 263–278.

Dimbleby, G. W.
   1985. *The Palynology of Archaeological Sites.* New York: Academic Press.

Fischer, A.
   1991. Pioneers in Deglaciated Landscapes: The Expansion and Adaptation of Late Paleolithic Societies in Southern Scandinavia. In *The Late Glacial in North-West Europe: Human Adaptation and Environmental Change at the End of the Pleistocene,* edited by N. Barton, J. Roberts, and D. A. Roe, pp. 100–121. London: Council for British Archaeology Research Report No. 77.

Grayson, D. K.
   1991. Late Pleistocene Mammalian Extinctions in North America: Taxonomy, Chronology, and Explanations. *Journal of World Prehistory* 5 (3): 193–231.

Guthrie, R. Dale
   1984. Mosaics, Allelochemics and Nutrients: An Ecological Theory of Late Pleistocene Megafaunal Extinctions. In *Quaternary Extinctions: A Prehistoric Revolution,* edited by P. S. Martin and R. G. Klein, pp. 259–298. Tucson: University of Arizona Press.

Haynes, C. V.
   1991. Geoarchaeological and Paleohydrological Evidence for a Clovis-Age Drought in North America and Its Bearing on Extinction. *Quaternary Research* 35: 435–450.
   1992. Contributions of Radiocarbon Dating to the Geochronology of the Peopling of the New World. In *Radiocarbon after Four Decades: An Interdisciplinary Perspective,* edited by R. E. Taylor, A. Long, and R. S. Kra, pp. 355–374. New York: Springer-Verlag.

Kutzbach, J. E., and Thompson Webb III
   1991. Late Quaternary Climatic and Vegetational Change in Eastern North America: Concepts, Models, and Data. In *Quaternary Landscapes,* edited by L. C. K. Shane and

E. J. Cushing, pp. 175–217. Minneapolis: University of Minnesota Press.

Martin, P. S.
    1984. Prehistoric Overkill: The Global Model. In *Quaternary Extinctions: A Prehistoric Revolution,* edited by P. S. Martin and R. G. Klein, pp. 354–403. Tucson: University of Arizona Press.

Moore, P. D., J. A. Webb, and M. E. Collinson
    1991. *Pollen Analysis,* 2d ed. Oxford: Blackwell Scientific Publications.

Pearsall, D. M.
    1989. *Paleoethnobotany: A Handbook of Procedures.* New York: Academic Press.

Pielou, E. C.
    1992. *After the Ice Age: The Return of Life to Glaciated North America.* Chicago and London: University of Chicago Press.

Chapter 14

Theories of Hunter-Gatherer Subsistence Strategies:
Hunter-Gatherers in Postglacial Europe and North America

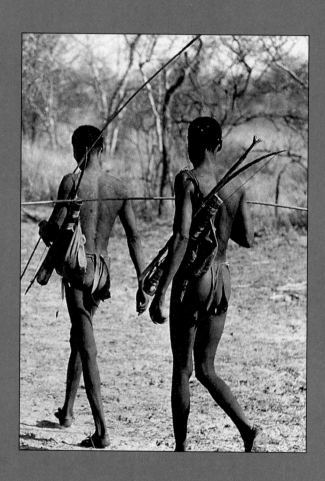

Introduction

The environmental studies described in Chapter 13 have provided archaeologists with a detailed picture of the climatic changes that affected Europe and North America at the end of the Pleistocene. Archaeological research in these two regions has provided important information on the ways hunting and gathering populations responded to the changing postglacial landscapes. The archaeological record for postglacial hunter-gatherers in Europe and North America will be presented in Chapters 15 and 16. Before we examine the archaeological evidence in detail, however, we plan to discuss some general theories of hunter-gatherer behavior and the ways they might be applied to the study of postglacial hunter-gatherers in Europe and North America.

Figure 14.1
!Kung San foragers.

Hunter-Gatherers: Ancient and Modern

Archaeological research has shown that humans and their ancestors have lived by some combination of plant collection, scavenging, hunting, and fishing for almost all of human history. Within the past 10,000 years, however, farming has replaced hunting and gathering as the primary way of obtaining food. Today, very few hunter-gatherers remain, and those few people who continue to provide for themselves by hunting and gathering live in areas such as the Arctic that are inhospitable to agriculture. Since the 1950s, both cultural anthropologists and archaeologists have sought to study the remaining hunting and gathering populations to understand how they make a living.

In the early 1960s, Richard B. Lee (1968, 1979) began a program of long-term ethnographic research among the !Kung San people (formerly known as Bushmen) of southern Africa (**Figure 14.1**). The !Kung San subsist by hunting and gathering in the Kalahari Desert. Lee found that approximately two-thirds of the !Kung San diet was made up of vegetable foods that were collected primarily by women. The mongongo nut, which was available year-round, formed a staple of the !Kung diet. Hunting provided only about one-third of the !Kung food supply. The !Kung moved approximately six times per year to make use of plant and animal resources that were available in different areas at different seasons of the year. Lee's research showed that, at least among the !Kung, gathering played a more important role in the diet than did hunting.

Lee's research was widely publicized, and many archaeologists used the !Kung hunting and gathering practices as models for ancient hunters and gatherers. Unfortunately, the !Kung, who live in a hot, dry environment, are not necessarily good ethnographic models for ancient hunters and gatherers who lived in temperate environments such as Europe and North America. The temperate regions are characterized by warm summers and cold winters. While wild plants may be abundant in the summer and early fall, fresh plant foods are generally not available during the winter months. In the cold season in temperate regions, hunter-gatherers must rely on hunting, fishing, and/or stored plant materials. The availability of different plant and animal foods in different seasons can affect the ways hunter-gatherers organize their annual round.

In the late 1960s and early 1970s the archaeologist Lewis Binford conducted research while living among the Nunamiut Inuit (Eskimo) in north central Alaska. He found that Nunamiut mobility patterns differed from those that had been described for the !Kung and other San foragers in the Kalahari. Binford (1980) developed two different models for the ways hunter-gatherers organize their settlement and subsistence systems. He termed these patterns foraging and collecting.

Hunter-Gatherer Mobility Strategies

Foragers, such as the !Kung San of the Kalahari, move their campsites on a periodic or seasonal basis to make use of separate patches of food resources. Foragers do not generally store food; they hunt and gather nearly every day. In the Kalahari, the San

move their camps to make use of melons during the dry season. During the wet season they move close to seasonal marshes that are attractive to game. **Collectors,** on the other hand, are logistically organized; rather than moving their camps on a periodic or seasonal basis, they obtain "specific resources through specially organized task groups" (Binford 1980: 10). These groups often seek large quantities of food that can serve as stores for considerable periods. An example is the Nunamiut hunting of caribou during their spring migration **(Figure 14.2)**. Binford's notions of foragers and collectors represent the end points of a continuum of hunter-gatherer mobility strategies. Most ancient and modern hunter-gatherers fall somewhere in between these end points.

Social Complexity among Hunter-Gatherers

When most people think of hunters and gatherers, they think of groups such as the !Kung San of the Kalahari, highly mobile people who live in small-scale, largely egalitarian societies. An increasing body of ethnographic, historical, and archaeological evidence (Price and Brown 1985) has shown, however, that not all hunter-gatherers are members of small mobile bands. For example, Native American people living along the northwest coast of North America traditionally lived in large, permanent villages and based their economy on fishing, supplemented by hunting. Northwest coast societies were stratified; chief and commoner differed in terms of wealth, power, and social status.

The Native Americans living on the northwest coast of North America are examples of **complex foragers.** Complex foragers are characterized by "large, sedentary, materially rich, and socially stratified communities" (Henry 1989: 11). These complex foragers exhibit many traits that are more typically associated with farmers and city dwellers, including sedentism, large community size, and social ranking. Archaeological researchers have identified complex foraging societies throughout the world (Price and Brown 1985), including some hunting and gathering societies in postglacial Europe and North America (Chapters 15 and 16).

Figure 14.2

Nunamiut hunter skinning a caribou killed during the spring migration.

One salient characteristic of complex hunter-gatherers is **sedentism,** the occupation of a single site on a year-round basis. Sedentism can be related to population growth, although the relationship is complex. It is important to emphasize that population growth is not inevitable. Human population levels were relatively low throughout the Pleistocene. Ethnographic studies of some modern hunter-gatherer populations indicate that they often act to limit their fertility through prolonged lactation, infanticide, and other cultural practices such as postpartum sex taboos. However, archaeological data suggest that hunter-gatherer populations in some parts of Europe and North America increased significantly during the Holocene. What factors can explain those increases? One possibility is that the economic role and contributions of children may have changed as items such as seeds, nuts, tubers, and shellfish came to play an increasingly important role in Holocene diets in Europe, North America, and elsewhere.

Children are often somewhat of a liability in mobile foraging societies that rely heavily on hunting. Since children are unable to walk long distances, they do not usually take part in the hunt, and small children need to be carried from place to place when a group moves. In such societies, births may be widely spaced and overall fertility is low because mothers are simply unable to carry more than one child at a time (Lee 1979). In forested environments, such as those that prevailed during the Holocene periods in Europe and eastern North America, children may not have been such a liability. Many forest resources, such as berries and tubers, are within the reach of children (Ford 1979: 236; Bogucki 1988: 44). Children can also take part in shellfish collection. As a result, children can be an economic asset for forest foragers who rely heavily on plant and shellfish resources. Just as many nineteenth-century American farmers wanted large families to help with the chores, so Holocene foragers in temperate regions may have benefited by the contributions that children made to subsistence. If children were valued increasingly for their economic contributions, this would clearly lead to population growth, resulting in increasing site densities, and possibly, increased sedentism, as group territories become increasingly circumscribed.

Sedentism itself may also lead directly to population growth. A minimum level of body fat is necessary for ovulation and therefore conception to take place in women. High mobility, when combined with long periods of nursing, may make it difficult for women to regain sufficient body fat to conceive again. Decreased mobility therefore may shorten the interval between births by reducing the time needed to replenish women's fat reserves. The availability of starchy weaning foods may also reduce the interval between births.

Hunter-gatherers can respond to population growth in a variety of different ways. Hunter-gatherers may expand into new environments, just as Eurasian foraging populations moved into northeast Siberia about 18,000 years ago (Chapter 10). As populations increase, foragers may also choose to diversify their subsistence base, making use of a wider range of plant and animal resources, including foods that require substantial processing times such as small seeds (Cohen 1977). Alternatively, foragers may choose to intensify the procurement of key resources through the use of different hunting and gathering technologies. The use of nets for hunting, for example, can provide a greater overall meat yield than bow hunting, but net hunting requires more labor than bow hunting (Abruzzi 1979). The beginning of farming—agriculture and animal husbandry—is one form of intensification, an issue we will return to in Chapter 17.

Conclusion

The relationship between resource availability, settlement mobility, and population is complex, and the Holocene archaeological record for Europe and North America reveals a great diversity in settlement patterns and subsistence systems. In the following two chapters, we will examine the archaeological record for Holocene hunters and gatherers in

Europe and North America. We will focus on the changing relationships between subsistence practices, technology, settlement, population, and social organization in a period of dramatic climatic change.

Glossary

Collectors.   Logistically organized hunter-gatherers. Rather than moving their camps on a periodic or seasonal basis, collectors obtain particular resources through specially organized task groups.

Complex foragers.   People who make a living by hunting, gathering, and/or fishing. Complex foragers live in large, sedentary, materially rich, and socially stratified communities.

Foragers.   Hunter-gatherers who move their campsites on a periodic or seasonal basis to make use of separate patches of food resources.

Sedentism.   The settling of a group of people in one location for all or much of the year.

Further Reading

Price, T. D., and J. A. Brown, eds.
   1985. *Prehistoric Hunter-Gatherers: The Emergence of Cultural Complexity*. New York: Academic Press.
   This volume, featuring archaeological and ethnographic studies of complex hunter-gatherers, is edited by a specialist in Mesolithic Europe and a specialist in eastern North American prehistory.

Other Bibliography

Abruzzi, William
   1979. Population Pressure and Subsistence Strategies among the Mbuti Pygmies. *Human Ecology* 7: 183–189.

Binford, L. R.
   1980. Willow Smoke and Dogs' Tails: Hunter-Gatherer Settlement Systems and Archaeological Site Formation. *American Antiquity* 45 (1): 4–20.

Bogucki, P. I.
   1988. *Forest Farmers and Stockherders: Early Agriculture and Its Consequences in North-Central Europe*. Cambridge: Cambridge University Press.

Cohen, M. N.
   1977. *The Food Crisis in Prehistory*. New Haven, CT: Yale University Press.

Ford, R. I.

1979. Gathering and Gardening: Trends and Consequences of Hopewell Subsistence Strategies. In *Hopewell Archaeology: The Chillicothe Conference,* edited by D. Brose and N. Greber, pp. 234–238. Kent, OH: Kent State University Press.

Henry, D. O.

1989. *From Foraging to Agriculture: The Levant at the End of the Ice Age.* Philadelphia: University of Pennsylvania Press.

Lee, R. B.

1968. What Hunters Do for a Living, or, How to Make Out on Scarce Resources. In *Man the Hunter,* edited by R. B. Lee and I. Devore, pp. 30–48. Chicago: Aldine.

1979. *The !Kung San: Men, Women and Work in a Foraging Society.* Cambridge: Cambridge University Press.

Chapter 15

The Mesolithic Period in Europe

Introduction

In Europe, the retreat of the glaciers opened up many areas of central and northern Europe for human settlement (Chapter 13). The gradual reforestation of Europe created environments that were unlike any known there during the late Pleistocene. In this chapter we will examine the ways hunting and gathering populations in Europe responded to those marked environmental changes.

Climatic Changes in Europe in the Early Postglacial Period

The end of the Pleistocene was marked by a rapid rise in the earth's temperatures, beginning about 8300 b.c. (10,300 years ago).[1] In Europe, the summers may have been as warm as those of today, although winter temperatures were still somewhat cooler. This rapid temperature rise caused significant changes in the European landscape. The melting ice caused sea levels to rise quickly between 8000 and 5000 b.c. By about 6500 to 6000 b.c. the island of Great Britain became separated from the European continent. (Ireland appears to have been separated from the European continent throughout the entire late Pleistocene, 35,000 to 10,300 years ago.)

While temperatures rose quite quickly at the end of the Ice Age, changes in vegetation took place somewhat more slowly. Gradually, the open steppe and tundra landscapes of the Pleistocene were replaced by parkland and forest vegetation. Initially, birch, a pioneer species, began to colonize areas that were previously dominated by periglacial and tundra vegetation. Later, pines and then a range of deciduous trees and shrubs, including oak, elm, linden, and hazel, came to dominate Europe's forests. These changes in vegetation led to significant alterations in Europe's animal populations. Animals such as reindeer and wild horse that prefer steppe and tundra environments were replaced by forest forms, including red deer (a large deer closely related to the North American elk), roe deer (a small deer about the size of a North American whitetail), wild pigs, and wild cattle. During the Holocene, reindeer populations were limited to the very northern reaches of Europe (primarily northern Scandinavia), while wild horses were restricted to the drier, steppic areas of eastern Europe and central Asia.

Mesolithic Societies in Europe

The term **Mesolithic** (from *meso*, meaning "middle," and *lithic*, meaning "stone") is used to describe the postglacial hunters and gatherers of Europe. The Mesolithic period begins with the end of the Pleistocene Ice Age about 10,300 years ago (8300 b.c.) and ends with the beginnings of farming, including agriculture and animal husbandry. The earliest European agriculture appeared in Greece, where it was introduced from the Near East about 6000 b.c., but agriculture and animal husbandry did not appear in parts of northern Europe until almost 3,000 years later. For example, agriculture and animal husbandry were not adopted in Denmark until about 3200 b.c. As we shall see in Chapter 20, the spread of agriculture throughout Europe was a gradual process involving both the movement of farmers into Europe and the adoption of agricultural practices by native hunting and gathering peoples.

Mesolithic people were the last indigenous hunters and gatherers in Europe. Their sites lack the spectacular cave paintings and art objects that are found in many Upper Paleolithic sites in western Europe (Chapter 11). It is not clear why art played a less important role in Mesolithic life, but archaeologists have

---

[1]With the transition from the Pleistocene to the Holocene, we will shift to the use of dates in years B.C. and A.D. We will use b.c. and a.d. (lowercase) for uncorrected radiocarbon dates, and B.C. and A.D. for historical dates and corrected radiocarbon age determinations (see Chapter 24).

Figure 15.1

Map of Europe showing the four main geographic zones (Mediterranean zone, Alpine zone, loess belt, and North European Plain) and the locations of the sites mentioned in this chapter.

formed some hypotheses based on the role that art played in Upper Paleolithic life in western Europe. Paintings and sculptures are often found at Upper Paleolithic aggregation sites, locations where large numbers of people came together on a seasonal basis (Conkey 1980). Wall paintings (parietal art) may have played a role in unifying this diverse community by communicating a shared ideology. As we will see in this chapter, most early Mesolithic sites are quite small and would have been occupied by no more than perhaps a dozen families. Parietal art may not have been needed to unify the smaller and more homogeneous Mesolithic communities. It is also possible that Mesolithic art was made of perishable materials such as hides and wood and simply has not survived in the archaeological record.

By comparison with Upper Paleolithic peoples, the European Mesolithic folk were traditionally seen as impoverished. Scholars of the first half of the twentieth century viewed Mesolithic hunters and gatherers as poor foragers who eked out a meager existence in a changed and changing environment. Their lives were supposed to have been nasty, brutish, and short (see Price 1987 for a brief review of the history of Mesolithic research). However, recent research on Mesolithic sites throughout Europe has radically changed our perception of these postglacial foragers. As a result of a series of important excavations that have been conducted since the end of World War II, including the sites of Star Carr and Mount Sandel (described in this chapter), archaeologists now recognize that the Mesolithic hunters and gatherers actively exploited the new postglacial environments in a variety of innovative ways **(Figure 15.1)**.

Mesolithic Stone Technology

The stone tools used by Mesolithic peoples provide clues as to the ways these

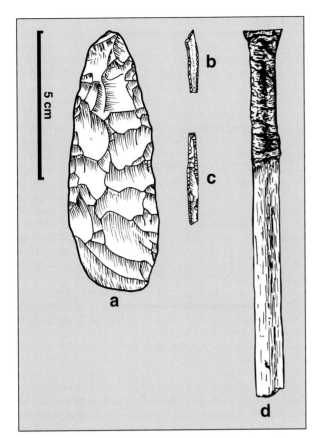

Figure 15.2

Typical examples of Mesolithic stone tool technology: (a) large, chipped stone axes that were used for felling trees and/or working wood; (b,c) small, geometric microliths that could be used as parts of composite tools; and (d) a microlith mounted as an arrow tip.

hunters and gatherers made use of the forested environments of early Holocene Europe. Two types of stone tools are commonly found in Mesolithic sites **(Figure 15.2)**. The first type is large, chipped stone axes made of flint. They were used to fell trees and, when mounted as adzes, to work wood. The second type is a group of small flint tools known as **microliths,** produced by snapping long flint blades into small geometric pieces 1 to 2 centimeters (0.4 to 0.8 in.) long. They were used as parts on composite tools, for example, as barbs for arrows. The advantage of the microlithic technology is that tools are easily repaired and versatile. It was "well suited to situations where the type and quantity of game are unpredictable" (Zvelebil 1986: 108).

How Did Mesolithic Peoples Make a Living?

For the most part, the Mesolithic hunters and gatherers who inhabited early postglacial Europe were broad-spectrum foragers who made use of a wide range of animal and plant resources, including large mammals such as deer, wild pigs, and wild cattle; birds; fish; shellfish; and plant foods such as nuts and tubers. The establishment of forested conditions in the early postglacial period (or early Holocene) created conditions favorable to forest animals such as roe deer, red deer, wild cattle, and wild pigs. Unlike reindeer, which were the primary game during the late Upper Paleolithic, these forest species do not migrate great distances. They are territorial and live within a relatively small geographical area. Moreover, deer and wild pigs reproduce rapidly; therefore, they can survive heavy annual harvesting.

As we shall see below, Mesolithic peoples developed a range of new hunting, fishing, and plant-collecting technology that allowed them to forage in the diverse, forested environments of postglacial Europe. In addition, Mesolithic foragers made increasing use of technologies such as the bow and arrow that were initially developed during the late Upper Paleolithic but that were particularly useful for hunting forest game animals. When tipped with a single microlith mounted transversely, bows and arrows could be used to hunt small game. Alternatively, a group of microliths could be used as barbs on arrows that were designed to bring down large animals such as deer and wild pigs.

The foragers of Mesolithic Europe supplemented hunted meat by fishing and fowling. As we saw in Chapter 10, fishing played an increasingly important role in the economies of late Upper Paleolithic Europe. This trend intensified during the Mesolithic. In addition to the migratory species such as salmon, the rivers and lakes of postglacial Europe would have been full of fish such as carp and perch. Fish traps constructed of reeds have been recovered from waterlogged sites in northern Germany and Denmark. Boats would have been useful both for fishing and for hunting wild birds. A dugout canoe has been recovered

Figure 15.3

Preserved leisters recovered from the site of Tybrind Vig, a submerged late Mesolithic settlement in Denmark.

from the site of Pesse in Holland. On the basis of the pollen associated with the find, the canoe from Pesse appears to date to approximately 7000 b.c. Parts of fish spears known as **leister prongs** provide additional evidence for fishing in lakes and streams. Two of these prongs, which are sometimes barbed on the inside edge, would have been attached to a wooden shaft and used to spear fish **(Figure 15.3)**. Arrows with blunt, wooden heads would have been used for fowling. The blunt darts would stun the birds, which could then be collected by hunters.

Shellfishing played an increasingly important role in the later Mesolithic cultures of Denmark and northern Germany. **Kitchen middens,** shell mounds found along the coasts of Denmark and northern Germany, contain the remains of oysters, mussels, and cockles, as well as the bones of mammals, birds, and fish. Unlike earlier Mesolithic hunters and gatherers, who moved on a seasonal basis to make use of various plant and animal resources, the inhabitants of coastal Germany and Denmark may have been sedentary foragers, who occupied these sites on a permanent basis. This increasing settlement permanence is certainly a reflection of the abundant food resources that would have

been available along the coastal regions of northern Europe during the later Mesolithic period. The coastal foragers did not have to move on a seasonal basis to make use of plants and animals that were available in different areas during different parts of the year. Adequate food resources, including shellfish, fish, game mammals, and wild birds, would have been available in the vicinity of these coastal sites on a year-round basis.

Archaeologists know less about the uses of plant foods by Mesolithic hunters and gatherers than they do about hunting, fowling, and fishing, because plant remains are often less well preserved than animal bones and marine shells. However, an increasing body of evidence, including the charred remains of seeds, tubers, and other plant parts, suggests that Mesolithic peoples made widespread and intensive use of a variety of plant foods (Zvelebil 1994). Many Mesolithic sites dated after 7000 b.c. have provided evidence for the use of hazelnuts, a storable, high-calorie food source that would have played an important role in the Mesolithic diet. Mesolithic sites in the east Baltic areas have provided evidence for the intensive harvesting, processing, and storage of water chestnuts (Zvelebil 1994). Other plant foods, such

Figure 15.4

Scanning electron micrograph of a tuber recovered from a Mesolithic archaeological site in the Netherlands (fragment of Beta vulgaris, *[NP3–11484: 369/30], tertiary vascular tissue).*

as tubers, were also harvested by Mesolithic foragers (Perry 1997). The presence of mattocks and hoes at many northern European Mesolithic sites suggests that these foragers regularly worked or interfered with the soil. There is a clear correspondence between the distribution of Mesolithic antler mattocks in the forest zone and the distribution of roots and tubers (Clarke 1976), and it has long been suggested these plant foods may have been part of the Mesolithic diet. Archaeologists are just now beginning to develop the techniques, such as scanning electron micrography of charred plant remains, to allow them to identify the charred remains of tubers and similar plant remains from archaeological sites **(Figure 15.4)** (see Perry 1997).

Mesolithic people appear to have taken an active role in modifying their environments by using fire to manipulate the natural vegetation. Mesolithic pollen diagrams from Britain (Mellars 1975, 1976) show the appearance of plants that favor an open habitat, suggesting that people used fire to clear the natural forest vegetation. Recent research on pollen diagrams from the Mesolithic period in both Britain (Simmons et al. 1989) and Scandinavia (Welinder 1989) has revealed episodes of vegetational change, known as disturbance phases, in which tree pollen decreases while pollen of more open vegetation, such as light-demanding herbs, increases. These disturbance episodes are often accompanied by the presence of charcoal and can reasonably be interpreted as evidence of forest clearance. This is the earliest evidence from Europe for the use of large-scale fires for land clearance.

What are the advantages of planned burning? Dense arboreal vegetation will shade out scrub vegetation such as hazel that was used both as a food source and as raw materials for basketry and mats. Planned burning can increase plant and animal food yields by between 500 and 900 percent (Mellars 1976: 22–26) by increasing plant resources such as hazel and by increasing the density of low-lying shrubs and berries that are attractive to deer and other wildlife. Burning would have provided additional benefits as well. Burned soil absorbs and retains heat, causing grasses and other plants to appear two to three weeks earlier in the spring in burned-out areas. This would have been particularly advantageous for Mesolithic Europeans who lived in a strongly seasonal environment with long winters (Bogucki 1995).

Mesolithic Settlement Patterns

Mesolithic foragers were not uniformly distributed across Europe. In the Alpine regions and along parts of the Mediterranean coast, Mesolithic foragers often occupied cave sites. Along the Atlantic coast and across the **North European Plain,** the low-lying areas that were covered by the Scandinavian ice sheet at the height of the Ice Age, Mesolithic sites are often located along the shores of lakes and rivers (see Figure 15.1). Mesolithic sites are much less common in the **loess belt,** the area of central Europe that lay between the Scandinavian and the Alpine ice sheets at the height of the last glaciation. During the late Pleistocene, this area was covered by fine, windblown sediments known as loess. The loess belt was less attractive to Mesolithic foragers because the environment was relatively dry between the river systems and because the area lacked biological diversity. The coastal regions, the Alpine areas, and the North European Plain were more diverse environments, with lakes, rivers, coastal areas, and a variety of soil types. The environmental diversity was especially attractive to Mesolithic foragers because it supported a wide variety of plant and animal species.

🏺 An Example of a Mesolithic Settlement: Mount Sandel in Northern Ireland

Most early Mesolithic settlements in northern Europe are small sites composed of between one and three round or oval huts, about 2 to 3 meters (6 to 10 ft.) in diameter and marked by postholes. An example of an early Mesolithic campsite is the site of **Mount Sandel,** located on the Bann River in Northern Ireland (Woodman 1981, 1985). Excavations at Mount Sandel revealed four hearth areas within a small hollow. Each hearth was associated with a circle of postholes (Woodman 1981: 120–121), which marked the outlines of huts that were about 6 meters (20 ft.) across. The postholes were set at an angle, suggesting that the huts were dome-shaped **(Figure 15.5)**. The postholes, which were about 20 centimeters (8 in.) deep, may have held sturdy saplings, which could have been bent inward and lashed together at the top (Woodman 1981: 121). Lighter branches could then have been woven into the framework, and the hut may have been covered with a lighter material, such as bark or hides.

The plant and animal remains from Mount Sandel reveal a diversified economy based on fishing, hunting, and plant collecting (Woodman 1981). Salmon run up the Bann River in summer and would have been available in June, July, and August. Eels, which were also procured by the Mount Sandel fishers, run down the Bann in the fall. Animal bones indicate that pigs were hunted in the late winter. Hazelnuts, which ripen in the fall, could have been stored for winter consumption. Thus, the plant and animal remains from Mount Sandel suggest that the site may have been occupied for a substantial portion of the year. In addition, the presence of the bones of sea bass indicates that the inhabitants of Mount Sandel traveled several miles to the coast to obtain marine fish.

Figure 15.5

Reconstruction of a small, circular hut from the early Mesolithic site of Mount Sandel in Northern Ireland.

The subsistence and settlement evidence from Mount Sandel indicates that these early Mesolithic hunter-fisher-gatherers were collectors (Binford 1980). The site of Mount Sandel overlooks the rapids of the Bann River, where Mesolithic peoples would have fished for salmon and eels. Other critical resources, including sea bass and flint for tool-making, were located some distance from the site and may have been obtained by a specially organized task group.

Case Study

Star Carr: Interpreting Mesolithic Seasonality

Ethnographic studies of modern hunter-gatherers have shown that many of these foraging peoples move their campsites on a seasonal or periodic basis to make use of different food resources that are available in different areas at different times of the year. This is a pattern that Binford (1980) has termed foraging (see Chapter 14). Most early Mesolithic peoples probably moved their base camps on a seasonal basis. Therefore, archaeologists who study the European Mesolithic have been interested in trying to determine the season or seasons in which these sites were occupied. The early Mesolithic site of **Star Carr** in northern England is a classic case study of the methods archaeologists have used to determine the season a site was occupied.

Star Carr (Clark 1954, 1972) is perhaps the best known of all the Mesolithic sites in Europe. The site, first excavated between 1949 and 1953 by the late Professor Graham Clark of Cambridge University, is

Figure 15.6

Early Mesolithic fragment of red deer antler from the site of No Name Hill, Vale of Pickering, near Scarborough, England. Each line results from one cutting action with a flint burin. This item has been directly dated to 9510 plus or minus 60 BP unrecalibrated (Beta-104484). Similar fragments of worked antler were recovered from the initial excavations at Star Carr.

located on a former lakeshore in the Vale of Pickering between the North York Moors and the Yorkshire Wolds. Additional excavations were conducted at the Star Carr site between 1985 and 1997 (Mellars and Dark 1998). Star Carr was occupied during the early Mesolithic and has been dated on the basis of radiocarbon to approximately 7500 b.c. The site was of particular interest because the deposits were waterlogged, which allowed for the preservation of organic materials such as bone and wood.

Analysis of the animal bones recovered from the Star Carr site indicated that the Mesolithic hunters killed a range of large game animals, including red deer, wild cattle, moose, roe deer, and wild pigs. Red deer provided about 60 percent of the meat supply. In the initial analysis of the Star Carr site (Clark 1954, 1972), the season of occupation was determined primarily on the basis of the deer antlers present. Red deer, roe deer, and moose shed and regrow their antlers each year. Red deer, in

particular, shed their antlers in April. Since the vast majority of the deer antlers recovered from the Star Carr site were still attached to their skulls, Clark and his colleagues argued that the site was occupied during the winter months. The few shed red deer antlers that were recovered indicated that the site may have been occupied until April. Moose shed their antlers in January, and since almost half the moose antlers recovered were unshed, the excavators argued that the site must have been initially occupied before January.

However, reanalyses of the mammal bones from Star Carr (Legge and Rowley-Conwy 1989) have cast doubt on Clark's interpretation. Two British archaeologists, Anthony Legge and Peter Rowley-Conwy, have argued that the deer antlers may not be a good indicator of seasonality because antler was an important raw material for toolmaking and was therefore kept for long periods. At Star Carr, antlers were used as raw material for the production of small, barbed bone points (Figure 15.6). Instead of examining antlers, Legge and Rowley-Conwy examined animal teeth, because teeth can be good indicators of age in juvenile animals. The teeth came from many jaws of young deer that must have been killed between April and August. A single moose mandible came from an animal killed in September or October. In addition, the animal bones included the remains of a very young moose that must have died shortly after its birth in May, June, or July. Legge and Rowley-Conwy concluded that Star Carr must have been occupied during the summer months rather than in winter. Nevertheless, their work confirms that Star Carr was occupied on a seasonal basis by a small, mobile hunter-gatherer population.

The new excavations conducted at Star Carr between 1985 and 1997 provided additional information on the seasonal use of this Mesolithic site that supplements Legge and Rowley-Conwy's analysis (Mellars 1998: 216). The charred reed remains recovered from the new excavations have tightly rolled leaf stems which indicate that these plants were burned in the early part of the growing season, most likely March or April. Carbonized fragments of aspen catkins are likely to have been burned shortly after they were shed, probably between April and June. New analyses of the birch bark resin from the original excavations show high sugar levels, suggesting that the bark was collected in late April or early May. Finally, radiographs of the roe deer lower jaws indicate that these animals were between 10 and 11 months old when they died. Since roe deer are generally born in May, it is most likely that these deer were killed in March or April. When these data are combined with Legge and Rowley-Conwy's evidence, it seems most likely that the Star Carr site was occupied by hunter-gatherers from late March or early April until June or early July.

Population Growth and Economic Transformations in the Later Mesolithic

Both Mount Sandel and Star Carr are early Mesolithic sites that were occupied by small bands of early postglacial foragers. The Star Carr site was clearly occupied on a seasonal basis, whereas Mount Sandel may have been occupied for a more extended portion of the year. Both sites are quite small, and were probably occupied by a small number of fam-

ilies. Early Mesolithic sites, those dating before 6000 b.c., are generally small. Population density was probably quite low, and the conditions of life were not very different from those of the late Paleolithic when hunter-gatherers resettled northern Europe after the glaciers retreated.

A wide range of archaeological data suggest that substantial social and economic changes took place in Europe within the Mesolithic period. Many of those changes may have been related, either directly or indirectly, to population growth. While population densities may have been low during the early Mesolithic, the reliability of Mesolithic hunting, the presence of a larger hoofed-mammal biomass, and the increasing availability of plant foods almost guaranteed a population increase during Mesolithic times (Rowley-Conwy 1986: 24). The shift to larger settlements in the western part of the North European Plain at about 5000 b.c. probably resulted from that population increase (Newell 1973).

Mesolithic social groups occupied territories in which they hunted and gathered throughout the year. Subtle stylistic variations in stone tool manufacture have been used to define the individual territories of Mesolithic social groups in northern Europe. These stone tool studies suggest that early Mesolithic groups occupied territories of about 200 kilometers (124 mi.) in diameter. During the later Mesolithic (ca. 6000–4000 b.c.), group territories were smaller, about 100 kilometers (62 mi.) in diameter (Price 1981). These shrinking territories probably reflect the increasingly intensive and localized use of the landscape by larger numbers of Mesolithc foragers.

Late Mesolithic sites in southern Scandinavia and northern Germany also provide evidence for increasing settlement permanence. Many of the Danish kitchen midden sites, associated with the late Mesolithic culture known as the **Ertebølle** culture, appear to have been occupied throughout the year. Ertebølle sites were located along the coast, allowing foragers to make use of rich beds of marine shellfish. Other resources, such as mammals, wild birds, and fish, were probably obtained by organized collecting parties.

Some western Baltic Ertebølle sites were clearly used for special purposes such as sealing and swan hunting (Whittle 1996: 196). The intensive use of shellfish, combined with hunting, fishing, and fowling, allowed these late Mesolithic foragers to occupy coastal sites on a year-round basis.

A Late Mesolithic Site: Tybrind Vig in Denmark

Tybrind Vig is a Danish Mesolithic settlement located on the island of Fyn that was occupied between 4500 and 3200 b.c. (Andersen 1987). The site is unique because it is located underwater. It was initially discovered by amateur divers and had to be excavated by divers using tanks. As a result of rising sea levels in the late glacial and early postglacial periods, many Mesolithic sites in southern and southwestern Denmark are now submerged; the Tybrind area has sunk 2 to 3 meters (6 to 10 ft.) since late Mesolithic times. The waterlogged conditions at Tybrind are ideal for the preservation of organic materials such as wood, and excavations there have expanded our knowledge of late Mesolithic technology and material culture.

In Mesolithic times, the Tybrind area formed a protected cove surrounded by reeds. Pollen analysis reveals that the surrounding area was covered by oak forest, with some lime, elder, and pine trees (Andersen 1987: 260). The main habitation area at Tybrind eroded away when the site was inundated, but excavations revealed the northwestern portion of the settlement, the beach, and the shallow area off the coast. Rows of pointed hazel stakes, probably the remains of fish traps, were found in this shallow area. In addition, the discovery of several leister prongs that were probably lost during fishing and of two dugout boats also points to the maritime orientation of the settlement. A burial of a young woman with an infant placed across her chest was also found; this burial is probably part of a larger Mesolithic cemetery. Chemical analyses of the young woman's bones indicate that her diet was composed primarily of marine foods such as fish, shellfish, and sea mammals. A large number of fish bones were also recovered

from the site, providing additional evidence for the important role of marine foods in the diet.

In addition to fish bones, the shells of oysters, clams, mussels, and periwinkles were also recovered. Red deer, wild pigs, and roe deer were commonly hunted, and seals and whales were hunted both at sea and along the coast. The remains of hazelnuts and acorns show that plant foods also played a role in the diet. Specialized and intensive fishing is reflected in the many bones of fish, including small cod, eel, and spurdog, and in the wealth of artifacts associated with fishing—nets, hooks, leisters, fish traps, and fish weirs (Andersen 1987: 266). Intensive fishing was supplemented by the more extensive and opportunistic use of a wide range of plant and animal resources. At Tybrind, and at many other late Mesolithic sites in northern Europe, the combination of specialization and diversification could have ensured an adequate and reliable food supply (Zvelebil 1986: 108).

The striking feature of the excavations at Tybrind Vig was the recovery of a wide range of artifacts made of organic materials, especially wood. These include the remains of two wooden dugout boats and a number of paddles (Figure 15.7).

Social Changes in the Later Mesolithic: The Emergence of Cultural Complexity

Population growth and the increasing intensity of land use may have led to social changes in the later Mesolithic period. Cemeteries, as opposed to individual burials, become increasingly common in the later Mesolithic. Mesolithic cemeteries have provided evidence for individual differences in status and social roles (Clark and Neely 1987). At the sixth-millennium b.c. Deer Island cemetery on Lake Onega in northern Russia, for example, some individuals were buried with necklaces of bear teeth, others with necklaces of moose teeth or deer incisors, and others with no grave goods at all. A group of male graves contained deposits of bone spear points, suggesting that those individuals may have had special responsibilities

Figure 15.7

Wooden boat paddles recovered from the late Mesolithic site of Tybrind Vig, Fyn, Denmark.

as hunters (Zvelebil 1986). In central Europe, the presence of Mediterranean shells at Mesolithic sites in Switzerland and southern Germany provides evidence for the existence of trade and exchange networks. These exchange networks may have mitigated the effects of occasional food shortages. In addition, some form of decision-making hierarchy may have emerged by the end of the Mesolithic (Bogucki 1988: 46–48). As population and settlement densities increased, more formalized leadership was necessary to coordinate both within-group activities and relationships between groups. The need for more formalized decision making may have led to some degree of social inequality.

Conclusion

The evidence for social differentiation, permanent or semipermanent settlements, and a combination of specialized and multipurpose technology has led some archaeologists to classify the late Mesolithic foragers of northern Europe as complex hunter-gatherers or affluent foragers (Price 1985). Complex hunter-gatherers exhibit many features that are commonly associated with agricultural societies: permanent residences, specialized tool

kits and storage facilities, the development of trade and exchange, and social elaboration (Zvelebil 1995). Thus, the Mesolithic was a period of significant social and economic change. Within a few thousand years the highly mobile, small-scale hunting and gathering societies seen at sites like Star Carr had developed into affluent foragers with elaborate technologies, trade networks, and decision-making hierarchies. The Mesolithic period can no longer be seen as a great hiatus between the reindeer-hunting artists of the Upper Paleolithic and the farmers and herders of the Neolithic (early farming) period; the Mesolithic was an era of innovative human response to the changed and changing environmental conditions of early postglacial Europe.

Glossary

Ertebølle. A late Mesolithic (ca. 4500 to 3000 b.c.) culture of Denmark characterized by a heavy reliance on shellfishing, plus hunting, fishing, and fowling. Ertebølle sites appear to have been occupied on a year-round or near year-round basis.

Kitchen middens. Late Mesolithic shell mounds found in Denmark and northern

Germany, which contain the remains of oysters, mussels, and cockles, as well as the bones of wild mammals, birds, and fish.

Leister prongs. Parts of spears that are used to catch fish. Mesolithic leister prongs were often made of bone or antler and barbed along the inside edges.

Loess belt. The area of central Europe that lay between the Scandinavian ice sheet and the Alpine ice sheet during the height of the last glaciation. This area was covered by fine, airborne sediments known as loess.

Mesolithic. The time in Europe (ca. 8000 to approximately 4000 b.c.) between the end of the Pleistocene Ice Age and the beginnings of farming. It is the period of postglacial foraging in Europe.

Microliths. Small, geometric stone tools, 1 to 2 centimeters (0.4 to 0.8 in.) in length, produced by snapping flint blades into a series of small pieces. They were generally used as parts of composite tools, for example, as barbs for arrows.

Mount Sandel. An early Mesolithic (ca. 7000 b.c.) site in Northern Ireland that has produced evidence for small, circular dwellings and a diversified economy based on hunting and fishing.

North European Plain. The plain stretching from northern France, across northern Germany, southern Scandinavia, Poland, and eastward into Russia. These areas were covered either by the Scandinavian ice sheet or by the outwash gravels and sands in front of it. This region is characterized by a great diversity of soil types.

Star Carr. An early Mesolithic hunters' camp located in North Yorkshire in England. Recent reanalysis of the fauna from this site indicates that it was occupied during the summer months.

Tybrind Vig. A submerged late Mesolithic (ca. 4500 to 3200 b.c.) site located on the island of Fyn in Denmark. Underwater excavations carried out at the site have produced well-preserved wooden artifacts, including boats and paddles, as well as evidence for intensive fishing.

Further Reading

Bogucki, P. I.
   1988. *Forest Farmers and Stockherders: Early Agriculture and Its Consequences in North-Central Europe.* Cambridge: Cambridge University Press.
   For the more advanced reader. Bogucki provides an ecologically oriented study of the beginnings of agriculture in central Europe. The volume includes an excellent overview of the central European Mesolithic.

Price, T. Douglas
   1987. The Mesolithic of Western Europe. *Journal of World Prehistory* 1 (3): 225–305.
   A detailed and comprehensive overview of the western European Mesolithic.

Woodman, P. C.
   1981. A Mesolithic Camp in Ireland. *Scientific American* 245: 120–128.
   A well-illustrated introduction to the archaeology of the early Mesolithic (ca. 7000 b.c.) site of Mount Sandel in Northern Ireland.

Zvelebil, Marek
   1986. Postglacial Foraging in the Forests of Europe. *Scientific American* 254 (5): 104–115.
   Rather than seeing Mesolithic hunting and gathering as simply a prelude to agriculture, Zvelebil argues that foraging was a parallel development that could be as productive as early agriculture in some areas of northern Europe.

Other Bibliography

Andersen, S. H.
   1987. Tybrind Vig: A Submerged Ertebølle Settlement in Denmark. In *European Wetlands in Prehistory,* edited by J. M. Coles and A. J. Lawson, pp. 253–280. Oxford: Clarendon Press.

Binford, Lewis R.
   1980. Willow Smoke and Dogs' Tails: Hunter-Gatherer Settlement Systems and Archaeological Site Formation. *American Antiquity* 45 (1): 4–20.

Bogucki, P. I.
   1995. Prelude to Agriculture in North-Central Europe. In *Before Farming: Hunter-Gatherer Society and Subsistence,* edited by D. V. Campana, pp. 105–116. Philadelphia: MASCA Research Papers in Science and Archaeology, Vol. 12 Supplement.

Clark, G. A., and M. Neely

1987. Social Differentiation in European Mesolithic Burial Data. In *Mesolithic Northwest Europe: Recent Trends,* edited by P. Rowley-Conwy, M. Zvelebil, and H. P. Blankholm, pp. 121–130. Sheffield, England: University of Sheffield.

Clark, J. G. D.

1954. *Excavations at Star Carr.* Cambridge: Cambridge University Press.

1972. *Star Carr: A Case Study in Bioarchaeology.* Reading, MA: Addison-Wesley Module in Anthropology 10.

Clarke, D.

1976. Mesolithic Europe: The Economic Basis. In *Problems in Economic and Social Archaeology,* edited by G. de G. Sieveking, I. H. Longworth, and K. E. Wilson, pp. 449–481. London: Duckworth.

Conkey, M. W.

1980. The Identification of Prehistoric Hunter-Gatherer Aggregation Sites: The Case of Altamira. *Current Anthropology* 21: 609–630.

Legge, A. J., and P. Rowley-Conwy

1989. *Star Carr Revisited.* London: Birbeck College.

Mellars, P.

1975. Ungulate Populations, Economic Patterns, and the Mesolithic Landscape. In *The Effect of Man on the Landscape, the Highland Zone,* edited by J. G. Evans, S. Limbrey, and M. Cleere, pp. 49–63. London: Council for British Archaeology, Research Report No. 11.

1976. Fire Ecology, Animal Populations and Man: A Study of Some Ecological Relationships in Prehistory. *Proceedings of the Prehistoric Society* 42: 15–45.

1998. Postscript: Major Issues in The Interpretation of Star Carr. In *Star Carr in Context: New Archaeological and Palaeoecological Investigations at The Early Mesolithic Site of Star Carr, North Yorkshire,* by Paul Mellars and Petra Dark, pp. 215–241. Cambridge: McDonald Institute for Archaeological Research Monographs.

Mellars, Paul, and Petra Dark

1998. *Star Carr in Context: New Archaeological and Palaeoecological Investigations at The Early Mesolithic Site of Star Carr, North Yorkshire.* Cambridge: McDonald Institute for Archaeological Research Monographs.

Newell, R. R.

1973. The Post-Glacial Adaptations of the Indigenous Population of the North-West European Plain. In *The Mesolithic in Europe,* edited by S. K. Koslowski, pp. 399–440. Warsaw, Poland: University of Warsaw Press.

Perry, David

1997. *The Paleoethnobotany of Hunter-Gatherers: Analysis of Botanical Remains from Mesolithic Sites in the Province of Groningen, the Netherlands.* Unpublished Ph.D. Dissertation, New York University.

Price, T. D.

1981. Regional Approaches to Human Adaptation in the Mesolithic of the North European Plain. In *Mesolithicum in Europa,* edited by B. Gramsch, pp. 217–234. Potsdam, Germany: Museum für Ur- und Frühgeschichte, Veröffentlichtungen 14–15.

1985. Affluent Foragers of Mesolithic Southern Scandinavia. In *Prehistoric Hunter-Gatherers: The Emergence of Cultural Complexity,* edited by T. D. Price and J. A. Brown, pp. 341–360. Orlando, FL: Academic Press.

Rowley-Conwy, P.

1986. Between Cave Painters and Crop Planters: Aspects of the Temperate European Mesolithic. In *Hunters in Transition,* edited by M. Zvelebil, pp. 17–32. Cambridge: Cambridge University Press.

Simmons, I. G., J. Turner, and J. B. Innes

1989. An Application of Fine-Resolution Pollen Analysis to Later Mesolithic Peats of an English Upland. In *The Mesolithic in Britain,* edited by C. Bonsall, pp. 206–217. Edinburgh: John Donald.

Welinder, S.

1989. Mesolithic Forest Clearance in Scandinavia. In *The Mesolithic in Europe,* edited by C. Bonsall, pp. 362–366. Edinburgh: John Donald.

Whittle, Alasdair

1996. *Europe in the Neolithic: The Creation of New Worlds.* Cambridge: Cambridge University Press.

Woodman, P. C.

1985. *Excavations at Mount Sandel 1973–77.* Northern Ireland Archaeological Monographs No. 2. Belfast: Her Majesty's Stationery Office.

Zvelebil, M.

1989. Economic Intensification and Postglacial Hunter-Gatherers in North Temperate Europe. In *The Mesolithic in Europe,* edited by C. Bonsall, pp. 80–88. Edinburgh: John Donald.

1994. Plant Use in the Mesolithic and the Implications for the Transition to Farming. *Proceedings of the Prehistoric Society* 60: 95–134.

1995. Hunting, Gathering or Husbandry? Management of Food Resources by the Late Mesolithic Communities of Temperate Europe. In *Before Farming,* edited by D. V. Campana, pp. 79–104. Philadelphia: MASCA Research Papers in Science and Archaeology, Vol. 12 Supplement.

Chapter 16

Post-Pleistocene Adaptations in the Americas
The Development of the Archaic

Introduction

The climatic changes associated with the end of the Pleistocene had profound effects on the North American environment. In addition to the disappearance of the Pleistocene megafauna, postglacial climatic changes led to increasing forestation in many parts of the eastern United States. In the west, increasing aridity led to the formation of deserts in areas such as the **Great Basin.** The Great Basin is the region of the American West that lies between the Sierra Nevada–Cascade Mountains and the Wasatch Range and includes nearly all of Nevada and parts of the surrounding states **(Figure 16.1)**. In this chapter, we will examine the ways native North Americans adapted to the changed environmental conditions in both the eastern woodlands and the Great Basin region of the American West. The effects of postglacial climatic changes in Mesoamerica will be considered in Chapter 19.

As noted in Chapter 12, the term *Paleoindian* has been used to describe the late Pleistocene inhabitants of the Americas, whose tool kits often included distinctive fluted points. The term **Archaic** has been applied to the hunting and gathering cultures of the post-Pleistocene period throughout the Americas (Willey and Phillips 1958: 107). Archaeologists of past generations saw the distinction between Paleoindian and Archaic as one that reflected both differences in chronology and differences in adaptation. Paleoindians were viewed as hunters who relied extensively on large mammals, while the later Archaic period Native Americans were seen as broad-spectrum foragers who made greater use of plants, fish, and small mammals. The

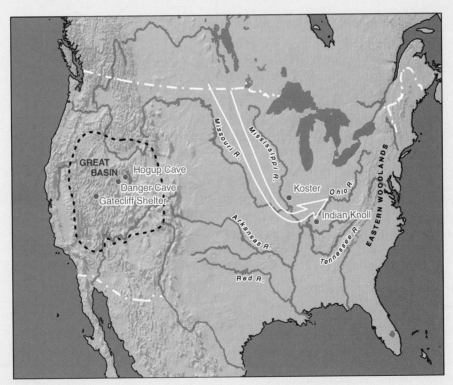

Figure 16.1

Locations of sites and geographical regions mentioned in this chapter. The arrow shows the well-defined river valley route to the east.

well-known late Pleistocene mammoth and bison kill sites from the southern Great Plains have undoubtedly contributed to the impression that hunting played a major role in Paleoindian subsistence. However, these kill sites are not typical of Paleoindian adaptations in either the Great Basin or the eastern United States. In those regions, one cannot draw a simple dichotomy between late Pleistocene hunters and Holocene foragers. The changes in subsistence that took place between the end of the Pleistocene and the early Holocene are far more complex and reflect human adaptations to local changes in resource availability.

The American Great Basin

In late Pleistocene times, the American Great Basin (see Figure 16.1) was a land filled with lakes. These shallow lakes and marshes and the flowing streams and springs that fed them would have been attractive habitats for human hunter-gatherers because they were rich in both plant and animal resources. In the drier areas, cool sagebrush steppe supported large herbivores, including animals now extinct in America, such as horses, camels, and mammoths. The late Pleistocene lakes began to shrink in size around 12,000 years ago, but they rose briefly around 11,000 years ago.[1] The lake levels started to drop again between 10,300 and 9,800 years ago as a result of increasing summer temperatures during the early Holocene. By 7,500 years ago, however, the continuing postglacial warmth and decreasing precipitation had produced environmental conditions that are similar to those of today. Many of the lakes, marshes, and streams had disappeared, and desert scrub vegetation replaced marshland and sagebrush steppe (Beck and Jones 1997).

The Paleoindian and Early Archaic Background

The archaeological record of human settlement in the Great Basin during the terminal Pleistocene and early Holocene is based primarily on stone tools that have been recov-

Figure 16.2

Examples of fluted and stemmed points from the terminal Pleistocene and early Holocene of the Great Basin: (a) Fluted; (b) Windust Square Stem/Cody; (c) Lind Coulee.
Source: After Beck and Jones 1997.

ered from surface sites. Few deeply stratified sites have been excavated, and plant and animal remains are rarely preserved. However, an increasing sample of radiocarbon dates from these early sites indicates that humans were present in the Great Basin by 11,200 years ago (Beck and Jones 1997: 196). The fluted and stemmed points **(Figure 16.2)** that have been recovered from these early sites are referred to as **Paleoarchaic,** a general term used for the human populations that lived in the Great Basin during the terminal

---

[1]This change correlates with the Younger Dryas event.

Pleistocene and early Holocene. Sites containing these fluted and stemmed points date between 11,200 and 7,500 years ago. The fluted points, which appear to be the earliest forms, are similar to Clovis points recovered from other parts of North America. All these tools could have been used as spear points or dart tips, although some of them may also have been used to cut and scrape animal carcasses (Beck and Jones 1997: 204). In short, the lithic evidence suggests that hunting played an important role in Great Basin subsistence during the terminal Pleistocene–early Holocene period.

Ground stone artifacts, including grinding stones and milling slabs, may have been used to process small seeds. While a small number of ground stone tools first appear in the Great Basin during the terminal Pleistocene period, the use of this technology increases dramatically after 7,500 years ago (5550 b.c.). Therefore, the use of ground stone tools increases at a time when marshlands were drying out and the sagebrush steppe was contracting. The increased aridity would have decreased the availability of both large game and marsh resources such as waterfowl and fish. The deteriorating environmental conditions after 5500 b.c. may have led to the increased use of small seeds and other plant resources.

Case Study
Great Basin Subsistence: Danger Cave and Hogup Cave

Pioneering excavations at a series of deeply stratified cave sites have provided information on human subsistence and settlement in the desert west (Aikens 1978). The arid conditions of the Holocene Great Basin have preserved organic materials such as basketry and plant remains in these caves. **Danger Cave** in western Utah (Jennings 1957) was one of the first caves to be excavated. This site revealed a deeply stratified sequence of occupations covering nearly the entire Holocene period. The cave appears to have been repeatedly occupied on a seasonal basis by small bands of mobile hunter-gatherers. Studies of **coprolites,** fossilized human excrement, and other plant and animal materials indicate that the inhabitants of Danger Cave collected small seeds and other plant materials, and hunted a wide range

Figure 16.3

Duck decoys from excavations at Lovelock Cave in west central Nevada. The excavations at Lovelock Cave showed the importance of lacustrine resources in prehistoric subsistence in the Great Basin.

of small- and medium-sized mammals. The material culture was generally light and portable, including such items as baskets, milling stones, and small tools made of chipped stone. The inhabitants of Danger Cave have been seen as highly mobile foragers who made use of a broad range of plant and animal resources and whose lifeways changed very little from the early Holocene to historic times. The excavator of the cave, Jesse Jennings, emphasized the continuities in lifeways between the hunter-gatherers known from the archaeological record of Danger Cave and the Native American foraging populations that continued to occupy the Great Basin in the twentieth century.

Similar information has been recovered from the excavation of **Hogup Cave** on the Great Salt Lake in northern Utah (Aikens 1970). Hogup Cave yielded over 4 meters (13 ft.) of archaeological deposits spanning the past 8,500 years. The earliest inhabitants (ca. 6500 b.c.) foraged along the edge of a lake, which became progressively shallower through time. A nearby salt marsh supported waterfowl and aquatic plants, which were collected by the Hogup inhabitants. A duck decoy recovered from Lovelock Cave (**Figure 16.3**) provides

Figure 16.4

Making a duck decoy—shredded cattails are stuffed into a duck's skin.

Figure 16.5

Making a duck decoy—a stick holds the neck upright.

information on the way waterfowl were hunted during the early Holocene. Similar duck decoys were made by the Paiute peoples of the Great Basin in the first half of the twentieth century **(Figures 16.4, 16.5, and 16.6)**. In addition, the early inhabitants hunted bison, pronghorn, mule deer, mountain sheep, hares, and small mammals in the marshlands and the nearby uplands. A rise in the level of the lake, which drowned the spring-fed marsh sometime between 3,500 and 2,200 years ago, led to a

Figure 16.6

Making a duck decoy—the skin is stretched over the reed frame.

decrease in the intensity of occupation of the site. The history of the site illustrates the important role that marshland resources could play in Great Basin subsistence practices in areas where the marshlands survived after 7,500 years ago.

Recent Research on Great Basin Adaptations

The variability and diversity that is seen in Great Basin subsistence practices throughout the Holocene continues to interest archaeologists working in the region today. In particular, models derived from ecological theory have been used to explain the increased use of small seeds and other plant foods in the Great Basin after 5550 b.c. (see, for example, O'Connell et al. 1982). Experimental research on the collection and processing of small seeds has shown that these plant resources yield far fewer calories per hour than does hunting large and small mammals (Simms 1987). If hunting large and small mammals produces higher food yields per hour, why and under what circumstances would hunter-gatherers bother to collect plant foods?

The problem that these hunter-gatherers faced is that the abundance of large and small game varied widely through both space and time in the Great Basin. When game animals were rare, hunter-gatherers were forced to rely on less productive plant resources. In addition, seeds may have been collected and stored for winter use (Simms 1987: 79). What the ecological perspective reveals is that diet breadth is likely to have been variable throughout the Holocene in the Great Basin. Instead of focusing on long-term continuities in Great Basin subsistence practices, ecological models and recent archaeological research emphasize the "general level of subsistence variability" in Great Basin prehistory (Simms 1987: 90).

This variability is reflected in some recent Great Basin archaeological projects. For example, excavations at the **Gatecliff Shelter** in the Monitor Valley in Nevada revealed 10 meters (33 ft.) of sediments and 16 cultural horizons. The Gatecliff rock shelter was initially occupied by human foragers about 3400 b.c. Throughout its history Gatecliff appears to have served as a short-term field camp, "a place where small groups of people stayed no more than a few days" (Thomas et al. 1983: 527). While Gatecliff functioned as a short-term field camp throughout its long history, the ways it was used changed through time. During the Middle Holocene (approximately 3400 to 3000 b.c.), the site was visited by small groups of hunters who made tools from cobbles of green chert that could be collected near the shelter. After 1500 b.c. the rock shelter was more intensively occupied; it appears to have been visited both by hunters and by gatherers who used large limestone slabs to process seeds. One of the final occupations of the site reveals a different pattern of activities. About a.d. 1300, the site was occupied briefly by a group of hunters who had killed approximately two dozen bighorn sheep nearby. At that time the Gatecliff shelter was used for the rapid field butchering of these animals so that the meat could be transported elsewhere for consumption. It is estimated that the hunters carried at least a ton of bighorn carcasses into the shelter and that they left bearing about 700 kilograms (1,500 lb.) of meat (Thomas et al. 1983: 529).

Eastern North America: The Paleoindian Background

Studies of Paleoindian lifeways most often focus on the Clovis and Folsom hunters of the American Great Plains (see Chapter 12). However, Clovis-type projectile points are commonly found east of the Mississippi, indicating that the eastern United States was also settled by Clovis foragers in the late Pleistocene. Mobile hunter-gatherer populations who traveled down the ice-free corridor from Alaska would have encountered the Missouri, Arkansas, Platte, and Red Rivers, all of which led to the Mississippi. From the Mississippi Valley, the Ohio, Cumberland, and Tennessee Rivers would have provided well-defined routes to the east (see Figure 16.1) (Anderson 1996: 36). These river valleys would have been particularly attractive areas for early human settlement because they supported a wide variety of game animals and supplied raw materials for stone tool manufacture.

Two different environmental zones have been identified in eastern North America in late Pleistocene and early Holocene times. The periglacial regions in the north were dominated by a tundra vegetation, while a complex boreal forest extended across a broad region south of the tundra, covering much of the eastern and southeastern United States. The boreal forest was dominated by spruce but included such deciduous trees as black ash, oak, and elm (Meltzer and Smith 1986).

Subsistence practices are likely to have differed greatly between the two regions. Although plant and animal remains are generally poorly preserved at eastern Paleoindian sites, the available archaeological data suggest that the inhabitants of the tundra zone may have been specialized caribou hunters. Tool kits from sites in the tundra zone are dominated by projectile points, scrapers, bifacial knives, and drills, and most tools are heavily worn. In contrast, sites in the boreal forest zone appear to have been occupied by generalized foragers who used a wide range of plant and animal species. Forest zone tool kits are far less specialized and are dominated by simple flake tools. The more generalized adaptive strategy that was adopted by the inhabitants of the boreal forest zone continued into early Archaic times (Meltzer and Smith 1986: 13), while the specialized tundra zone adaptations appear to have disappeared at the end of the Pleistocene.

Early Archaic Subsistence in the Eastern Woodlands

Early Archaic sites in the forest zone have produced the remains of a range of small and large mammals, birds, fish, reptiles, invertebrates, and plants, including acorns, hickory nuts, and walnuts (Meltzer and Smith 1986: Table 1-3). The variety of plants and animals present at early Archaic sites suggests that these foragers were using resources of the forest, forest edge, and more open or disturbed habitats. These data suggest that the generalized use of a broad range of plant and animal resources has a great antiquity in the eastern United States.

While it has generally been assumed that the population of the northeastern United States was highly mobile and quite low in density in early Archaic times, it is important to bear in mind that the early postglacial environment of New England was considerably different from the environment of more recent times. In Early Holocene times (ca. 8000 to 5000 b.c.) former glacial lake basins may have provided wetland-dominated environments that were rich in both resource diversity and overall biomass (Nicholas 1988). These basins appear to have provided focal points for early human settlement; in the northeast, human settlements are most often found near glacial lake basins. These areas would have been characterized by lowered or fluctuating lakes, ponds, extensive wetlands, and streams, and would have provided prehistoric hunter-gatherers with a diverse range of plant and animal resources. Glacial lake basins did not continue as focal points for human settlement in later prehistoric times, however. The warmer, drier conditions of the postglacial climatic optimum (6000 to 3000 b.c.) led to wetland shrinkage and shifts in vegetation.

Archaic hunters and gatherers may have burned some wooded areas, encouraging new plant growth, which in turn would have attracted game and maintained resource diversity (Nicholas 1988: 277). As Nicholas notes:

> Controlled burning can be utilized in land clearing; in this it also provides an influx of nutrients into the soil. In hunting it can be used as part of an immediate return strategy to drive or concentrate game, or with longer-term goals of encouraging new browse that will attract deer that can later be exploited. Burning can also stimulate the growth of many different plants (e.g., berries) and improve the yield of the harvest. Finally, it creates and maintains ecologically heterogeneous mosaics. (1999: 35)

The use of fire in the northeastern United States during the Archaic is clearly similar to its use in the European Mesolithic.

Middle Holocene Changes in Subsistence and Settlement

As noted above, a broad range of evidence suggests that the Paleoindian and early Archaic inhabitants of the forest zone in eastern North America had a generalized subsistence base. However, the range of species exploited by eastern hunter-gatherers appears to have increased during Archaic times. In particular, the use of shallow water mollusks appears to have increased dramatically in many parts of the southeast and midwest (Smith 1986: 22). Climatic changes that took place during the Middle Holocene (5000 to 3000 b.c.) led to the expansion of shallow-water and shoal-area aquatic habitats along some midlatitude river

systems. These areas would have provided an easily accessible variety of aquatic plant and animal resources (Smith 1992: 102), especially freshwater mollusks. The increased use of shellfish in the diet has been described as "an opportunistic response to a localized, seasonally abundant, dependable and easily collected resource" (Smith 1986: 24).

The increasingly intensive use of these riverine resources was accompanied by a shift in human settlement patterns. Floodplain settlements were more intensively occupied over a wide area from southern Illinois to northern Mississippi. Specific floodplain locations were occupied throughout the late spring to early winter growing season and were reoccupied on an annual basis. Deep shell mounds and midden mounds point to the repeated reoccupation of a limited range of locations after about 4500 b.c. The shell mounds were formed from large quantities of freshwater mollusk shells, while the midden mounds included a broader range of domestic rubbish, such as animal bones and plant remains. The increasing use of freshwater mollusks led to increasing sedentism and decreasing residential mobility. The Archaic subsistence and settlement system of the eastern woodlands provides some striking parallels with the late Mesolithic settlement patterns and subsistence practices in northern Europe.

Case Study
Excavations at the Koster Site and the Emergence of Complex Hunter-Gatherers

Few sites have had a greater impact on archaeological understanding of Archaic settlement patterns and subsistence practices than the **Koster** site in southwestern Illinois. Excavations began at the Koster site in 1969 as the Northwestern University archaeological field school. The site was chosen because it possessed a large and well-preserved Late Woodland (a.d. 450 to 1100) component and because it also might include an undisturbed record of the then poorly known Archaic. During the first season of excavation, it became clear that the site possessed a deeply stratified archaeological sequence extending as far back as the Early Archaic period (ca. 7500 to 5000

Figure 16.7

Excavations at the Koster site showing the deeply stratified nature of the excavation.

b.c.). As a result of the discovery of the well-preserved Archaic levels at the site, the study of Archaic settlement patterns and subsistence practices became the focus of the excavations. By 1977 the research, which centered on the study of increasingly complex hunter-gatherer subsistence and settlement systems, had taken on a distinctly ecological orientation.

The Koster site (Figure 16.7) is made up of at least 23 stratigraphically distinct cultural layers situated on an alluvial fan (Hajic 1990: 68). This deeply stratified site provided evidence for increasing settlement permanence and for increasingly intensive use of a wide range of plant and animal resources. When the Koster site was initially occupied, around 6500 b.c., it served as a temporary campsite for seasonally mobile hunters and gatherers. Hearths, pits, and dense middens are present, but there is no evidence for substantial houses (Brown 1985: 215). These early Koster foragers hunted and collected a wide range of plant and animal foods, including deer, small mammals, fish, freshwater mussels, hickory nuts, and pecans. The early Archaic levels at the Koster site have also produced burials of domestic dogs. Dogs are the only animals that were domesticated in both the Old World and the Americas; domestic dogs are also commonly found in Mesolithic sites in Europe, including Star Carr and Mount Sandel (see Chapter 15).

The nature of the Koster settlement changed dramatically between 5600 and 5000 b.c. Substantial buildings appear for the first time, covering an area of 0.7 hectares (1.7 acres). The buildings were approximately 7 by 4 meters (23 by 13 ft.) in area, and their long walls were built of wooden posts set in trenches. The gaps between the posts were filled with clay and branches. The houses appear to have been occupied for a sizable portion of the year, at least from early spring through the fall. Environmental changes that took place between 6000 and 4000 b.c. in the Illinois River Valley would have increased the proportions of backswamps, which are home to waterfowl, fish, shellfish, wild seeds, and marshland roots and tubers. The changes would have greatly increased the natural productivity of this habitat (Brown 1985). Human foragers responded by shifting away from the wide-ranging and opportunistic foraging seen in the early Archaic. Instead, they concentrated on a smaller number of highly productive resources, including freshwater mussels, deer, and hickory nuts (Winters 1974).

Further changes in settlement and subsistence are seen during the late Archaic period at the Koster site. Between 3900 and 2800 b.c. the site appears to have been occupied on a year-round basis. The late Archaic houses were built of large wooden posts and had sunken earthen floors. Each dwelling had a floor area of approximately 12 to 15 square meters (130 to 160 sq. ft.). The village, which covered an area of 2 hectares (5 acres), may have housed up to 100 to 150 people (Fagan 1995: 387). This relatively large population needed substantial and reliable sources of food. The late Archaic inhabitants of the Koster site intensively fished the backwater lakes and swamps surrounding the site for shallow-water species, such as catfish, buffalo fish, and bass. They also hunted waterfowl during the spring and fall migrations, collected nuts, hunted deer and small game, and collected and processed many small seeds, including marsh elder. The site was abandoned about 2800 b.c. and was not reoccupied until about 800 years later.

Later Archaic Settlement and Subsistence in the Eastern Woodlands

The Koster case study illustrates a number of important changes in settlement patterns and subsistence practices that are also seen at many other Archaic period sites in the eastern woodlands. There is evidence for population growth, increasing settlement permanence, and the exploitation of new plant and animal resources, such as fish, shellfish, and small seeds. Plant and aquatic foods clearly played more important roles in Archaic subsistence than they did during the Paleoindian period, and their increasing importance can be seen in Archaic tool kits; these include new tools, such as grinding stones and plant processing equipment (Custer 1985: 65).

In eastern North America, the seeds of such plants as goosefoot, sumpweed, and sunflower **(Figure 16.8a, b, and c)** were collected by humans and thereby introduced to the disturbed midden areas surrounding human settlements. The plants would have quickly established themselves in the disturbed habitats. Once humans recognized the value of those stands, they may have begun to eradicate competing weeds and even to plant the seeds of those species. The beginnings of deliberate planting, if continued over the long term, would have led to the establishment of domesticated species of goosefoot, sumpweed, and sunflowers that were different in appearance from their wild relatives. In eastern North America domesticated varieties of these plants have been recovered from a number of archaeological sites dating to be-

Figure 16.8

Early North American cultigens—(a) goosefoot, (b) sumpweed, and (c) sunflower.

tween 2050 and 1050 b.c. (Smith 1992), indicating that they had been domesticated by late Archaic times.

In addition to incipient domestication, later Archaic foragers may have intensified the collection of highly productive animals and plants. The late American prehistorian Howard Winters (1974) has argued that later Archaic sites such as **Indian Knoll** in southwestern Kentucky had a narrow-spectrum, or harvesting, economy that focused on a small number of highly productive resources. At Indian Knoll those resources included deer, freshwater mussels, and nuts such as acorns and hickory. In Winters's view, the Indian Knoll economy was characterized by the "intensive exploitation of a small number of plant and animal species" (Winters 1974: X).

These well-documented changes in subsistence and technology during the Archaic period were accompanied by changes in social organization. Beginning between 5000 and 4000 b.c., there is evidence for long-distance trade in exotic items, such as marine seashells, galena, copper, and exotic flints. These prized materials may have formed part of a system of intergroup cooperation and exchange that included reciprocal social obligations (Brown 1985: 223). Cemeteries also appeared for the first time in eastern North America during the middle Archaic period. The presence of formal cemeteries and fixed burial places may reflect the increased identification of particular families or kin groups with particular places in the landscape. They may be a visible reflection of a social group's claim to the use of a particular territory. In addition, late Archaic graves in the midwest and southeast often include exotic and utilitarian grave goods, including copper, shells, beads, projectile points, and axe heads. For example, at the Indian Knoll site in southwestern Kentucky (Webb 1974), about 4 percent of the roughly 1,000 graves excavated during the Great Depression contained exotic objects, such as copper from the Great Lakes and marine shells. These elaborate burials may reflect emerging differences in wealth and social status. In addition, the challenge of organizing the more intensive and highly scheduled subsistence systems needed to support higher population densities may have led to the emergence of some degree of hierarchy in decision making (Bogucki 1988; Green and Sassaman 1983).

Conclusion

Human populations adapted to the changing environments of postglacial North America in very different ways. In the Great Basin, variability in subsistence practices reflected the environmental variability that existed in that region, both spatially and temporally. Highly ranked resources such as large and small game were not always available, and foragers often had to make use of small seeds and other plant resources that required significant processing time. Seeds may also have provided storable resources for the winter months. This variability continued until the twentieth century. As Simms (1987: 89) notes, "Subsistence strategies in the Great Basin, characterized by a generalized technology used by mobile hunter-gatherers, could be changing by the week, month, season, or year."

In the eastern United States, on the other hand, mid-Holocene climatic changes led to the creation of rich floodplain environments that included large quantities of freshwater mollusks. The abundance and dependability of those resources led to a decreasing diet breadth in the mid-Archaic as foragers chose to focus on highly productive resources, such as mollusks, deer, nuts, and seeds. The changes led to increasing sedentism and increasing cultural complexity.

Glossary

Archaic. The term used to describe the post-Pleistocene hunting and gathering cultures of the Americas.

Coprolites. Remains of fossilized human excrement. The study of these remains can shed light on prehistoric diet, because many coprolites include small seeds, small bones, and other food remains.

Danger Cave. A deeply stratified cave site in western Utah that appears to have been occupied by small, highly mobile bands of hunter-gatherers who subsisted on a broad range of plant and animal resources.

Gatecliff Shelter. A site located in the Monitor Valley in Nevada. Excavations at the site revealed 10 meters (33 ft.) of sediments and 16 cultural horizons. From 3400 b.c. onward, the shelter appears to have been occupied periodically as a short-term camp by small groups of hunter-gatherers.

Great Basin. The region of the American West that lies between the Sierra Nevada–

Cascade Mountains and the Wasatch Range and includes nearly all of Nevada and parts of the surrounding states.

Hogup Cave. A cave site located on the Great Salt Lake in northern Utah. The site yielded over 4 meters (13 ft.) of archaeological deposits spanning the past 8,500 years.

Indian Knoll. A late Archaic (ca. 2500 b.c.) site in southwestern Kentucky that yielded the remains of more than 1,000 burials. Many of the grave goods were utilitarian items such as axes, woodworking tools, and nutcracking stones, but some burials also included exotic materials such as copper and marine shells.

Koster. A deeply stratified site in southwestern Illinois that has provided a wealth of information on Archaic subsistence practices and settlement patterns in the American midwest. The data reflect a shift toward increasing settlement permanence and increasingly intensive use of aquatic resources.

Paleoarchaic. The term used to describe the terminal Pleistocene and early Holocene hunter-gatherers of the Great Basin (ca. 11,200 to 7,500 years ago) whose tools kits include fluted and stemmed points. These points appear to have been used to hunt and process large game animals.

Further Reading

Beck, Charlotte, and George T. Jones
1997. The Terminal Pleistocene/Early Holocene Archaeology of the Great Basin. *Journal of World Prehistory* 11 (2): 161–236.
A recent and comprehensive overview of early Great Basin prehistory with an extensive bibliography. Highly recommended for the advanced student.

Fagan, Brian M.
1995. *Ancient North America,* 2d ed. New York: Thames and Hudson.
An authoritative and comprehensive overview of North American prehistory.

Struever, S., and F. A. Holton
1979. *Koster: Americans in Search of Their Prehistoric Past.* Garden City, NY: Anchor/Doubleday.
A popular and readable account of the research program at the Koster site.

Other Bibliography

Aikens, C. Melvin
1970. *Hogup Cave.* Salt Lake City: University of Utah, Anthropological Paper 93.
1978. Archaeology of the Great Basin. *Annual Review of Anthropology* 7: 71–87.

Anderson, D. G.
1996. Models of Paleoindian and Early Archaic Settlement in the Lower Southeast. In *The Paleoindian and Early Archaic Southeast,* edited by D. G. Anderson and K. E. Sassaman, pp. 29–45. Tuscaloosa: University of Alabama Press.

Bogucki, P. I.
1988. *Forest Farmers and Stockherders: Early Agriculture and Its Consequences in North-Central Europe.* Cambridge: Cambridge University Press.

Brown, James A.
1985. Long-Term Trends to Sedentism and the Emergence of Complexity in the American Midwest. In *Prehistoric Hunter-Gatherers: The Emergence of Cultural Complexity,* edited by J. A. Brown and T. D. Price, pp. 201–231. Orlando, FL: Academic Press.

Custer, J. F.
1985. *Delaware Prehistoric Archaeology: An Ecological Approach.* Newark: University of Delaware Press.

Green, S. W., and K. E. Sassaman
1983. The Political Economy of Resource Management: A General Model and Application to Foraging Societies in the Carolina Piedmont. In *Ecological Models in Economic Prehistory,* edited by G. Bronitsky, pp. 261–290. Tempe: Arizona State University, Anthropological Research Paper 29.

Hajic, E. R.
1990. *Koster Site Archeology I: Stratigraphy and Landscape Evaluation.* Kampsville, IL: Center for American Archeology, Research Series Vol. 8.

Jennings, J. D.
1957. *Danger Cave.* Salt Lake City: University of Utah, Anthropological Paper 27.

Meltzer, D. J., and B. D. Smith
1986. Paleoindian and Early Archaic Subsistence Strategies in Eastern North America. In *Foraging, Collecting, and Harvesting: Archaic Period Subsistence and Settlement in the Eastern Woodlands,* edited by S. W. Neusius, pp. 3–31. Carbondale: Southern Illinois University Center for Archaeological Investigations, Occasional Paper No. 6.

Nicholas, G. P.

1988. Ecological Leveling: The Archaeology and Environmental Dynamics of Early Postglacial Land Use. In *Holocene Human Ecology in Eastern North America*, edited by G. P. Nicholas, pp. 257–296. New York: Plenum.

1999. A Light but Lasting Footprint: Human Influences on the Northeastern Landscape. In *The Archaeological Northeast*, edited by M. A. Levine, K. E. Sassaman, and M. S. Nassaney, pp. 25–38. Westport, CT: Bergin and Garvey.

O'Connell, J. F., K. T. Jones, and S. R. Simms

1982. Some Thoughts on Prehistoric Archaeology in the Great Basin. In *Man and Environment in the Great Basin*, edited by D. B. Madsen and J. F. O'Connell, pp. 227–240. Washington, DC: Society for American Archaeology, SAA Papers No. 2.

Simms, Steven R.

1987. *Behavioral Ecology and Hunter-Gatherer Foraging: An Example from the Great Basin.* Oxford: British Archaeological Reports, International Series 381.

Smith, B. D.

1986. The Archaeology of the Southeastern United States: From Dalton to de Soto, 10,500–500 B.P. In *Advances in World Archaeology*, vol. 5, edited by F. Wendorf and A. E. Close, pp. 1–92. Orlando, FL: Academic Press.

1992. Prehistoric Plant Husbandry in Eastern North America. In *The Origins of Agriculture: An International Perspective*, edited by C. W. Cowan and P. J. Watson, pp. 101–119. Washington, DC: Smithsonian Institution Press.

Thomas, D. H., J. O. Davis, D. K. Grayson, W. N. Melhorn, Trudy Thomas, and D. T. Trexler

1983. *The Archaeology of Monitor Valley 2. Gatecliff Shelter.* New York: Anthropological Papers of the American Museum of Natural History 59 (1).

Webb, W. S.

1974. *Indian Knoll.* Knoxville: University of Tennessee Press.

Wheat, Margaret M.

1967. *Survival Arts of the Primitive Paiutes,* Reno: University of Nevada Press.

Willey, G. R., and P. Phillips

1958. *Method and Theory in American Archaeology.* Chicago: University of Chicago Press.

Winters, Howard D.

1974. Introduction to the new edition. In *Indian Knoll,* by William S. Webb, pp. v–xxvii. Knoxville: University of Tennessee Press.

Part VI

Why Did Certain Peoples Abandon a Life of Hunting and Gathering to Take Up Farming?

Part VI explores the complex issue of agricultural origins in both the Old and New Worlds. It begins with a brief review of the history of research on domestication, raising questions about where, when, and why farming originated. Chapters 18 and 19 detail the archaeological record of plant and animal domestication in the Near East and Mesoamerica. These chapters address the archaeological evidence for early agriculture as well as recent theories seeking to explain agricultural origins. Case studies include the Téhuacan Valley project in Mexico and a variety of Levantine and Zagros sites in the Middle East. Archaeology in Practice boxes focus on the archaeological recovery of plant remains and the identification of plant and animal domestication in the archaeological record. We conclude by considering the question of why domestication arose independently in various parts of the world.

Chapter 20 examines the consequences of the agricultural revolution, including the spread of farming out of nuclear areas, such as the Jordan Valley, into adjacent areas, such as Mediterranean and temperate Europe. We also consider the effects that the beginnings of farming had on settlement patterns, population growth, technology, and human health and disease.

Chapter 17

The Origins of Agriculture
A Crucial Step

Introduction

For more than 4 million years, more than 99 percent of human existence, our ancestors subsisted by hunting, scavenging, fishing, and gathering wild plants. These ancient adaptations were eminently successful. As we have seen in the past few chapters, hunter-gatherer populations were able to expand beyond their African homeland, spread across Europe and Asia, colonize Australia, and ultimately, people both continents of the New World. In biological terms, these foragers were most successful indeed; they created niches for themselves from the Tropics to the Arctic.

There were real advantages to a foraging economy. Ethnographic data suggest that if wild game and plant resources were plentiful, the time and effort needed to obtain a livelihood would not have been excessive. Among the present-day !Kung San hunter-gatherers of the Kalihari Desert in southern Africa, for instance, about 25 hours of effort a week per adult are needed to obtain an adequate diet for the community (Lee 1968). Presumably, in the rich environments of the Pleistocene, plenty of extra time would have been available for leisure and social activities. The food supply was very likely adequate to ensure a substantial measure of security. The population in a region, however, could not exceed its natural **carrying capacity,** the maximum population size that an environment can support using a particular technology. Although foragers sometimes practiced activities such as burning to encourage wild plant growth and to provide browse for game, they did not directly control the populations of wild resources on which they depended. So long as those resources met their needs, there was no reason to do so.

Changing Relationships between Humans and the Environment: Climatic Change and Population Growth

What, then, was the reason for the broad economic changes that occurred at the close of the Paleolithic? Fundamentally, the stimulus for technological and social change must have derived from an alteration of the relationship of those foraging societies to their natural resource base. The root cause for this new relationship may have been a change in the environment; alternatively, human populations may have gradually grown to exceed the carrying capacity of the environment.

Climatic change has frequently been cited as a prime mover behind cultural change. Clearly, humans must live within the framework of their natural environment. As other animals replace traditional game species, hunting societies must also change if they are to continue to exist. Changing plant communities may make traditional diets difficult but may also provide new opportunities for foragers.

Climatic change is not necessary, however, for an alteration in the relationship between a human society and the natural environment to occur. Population growth, for instance, either through natural increase or through the movement of new groups into an area, can eventually cause populations to approach or exceed the carrying capacity of the region (Binford 1968). People must respond to these difficult conditions either by limiting population growth; by changing their technology to utilize their traditional resource base more intensively; by finding new, previously unutilized resources in the region; by seeking new territory; or finally, by modifying their environment to increase its carrying capacity.

Chapters 15 and 16 discussed how European Mesolithic peoples and the Archaic peoples of eastern North America responded to the changing flora and fauna at the close of the Pleistocene. On both sides of the Atlantic the postglacial era brought widespread forestation and, with the forest, a wealth of new game animals. Hunting and gathering populations modified their subsistence strategies and diversified their diets to take advantage of the changes in plant and animal species. At the same time, the richness and diversity of the forest resources permitted them to remain foragers.

Some peoples of the Near East, however, followed a different trajectory. Whatever the basic cause, the path followed by those peoples would ultimately lead them to replace wild plant gathering with cereal agriculture, and hunting with animal husbandry. A similar process occurred in the New World at a somewhat later date. The primacy of the Near East in the development of wheat and barley agriculture has long been accepted; why it developed has been a topic of intense debate among archaeologists for more than 60 years. The theoretical debate over the origins of agriculture will be discussed in this chapter; the following chapter will provide a fuller description of the evidence for early Near Eastern agriculture. Agricultural origins in the New World will be discussed in Chapter 19, as will other early centers of plant and animal domestication.

The Differences between Farming and Foraging Societies

Farming societies differ from foraging societies in many ways, and the social consequences of the introduction of agriculture will be discussed subsequently. The primary difference, however, is that while foragers depended on wild resources, farmers made use of plants and animals that had been domesticated. Foraging peoples may have manipulated their environment to provide improved conditions for plants or to attract game, but they did not directly control the plant and animal populations. When the early farmers domesticated plants and animals, they took control over the reproduction of these species. In doing so, they modified plant and animal populations to make them more suitable for human exploitation. Crops were planted in locations convenient for the farmer, and animal herds were confined or their movements were restricted. Under these conditions the plants and animals began to change, as a result of the selective pressures exerted by humans. In effect, the plants and animals were on their way to becoming new **species.** (A species is

defined as an interbreeding population of plants or animals.) Domestication can be considered partial speciation under human control (Crabtree 1993). Some of the changes may have been selected consciously or unconsciously because they were advantageous for humans; other changes may have been more subtle adaptations to environments that had been heavily modified by human activities. Farmers and their domesticates became dependent on each other for their existence.

Anyone who has ever worked on a farm or known a farmer realizes that farming is hard work. Farmers generally spend more hours per week earning a living than do hunters and gatherers. In times of stress, such as severe drought or extreme flooding, farming may be more risky than foraging. When farmers experience a crop failure or loss of livestock, they may lose their livelihood. If a wild plant or animal is unavailable, foragers may be able to make use of other wild plant and animal resources. The one major advantage that farming provides over hunting and gathering is that farming can produce a higher yield per hectare. In examining the theories that have been put forward to explain the origins of agriculture, we must ask why past human populations needed to increase food yields. Changes in either the environment or human population numbers or both could force humans to take steps to increase yields.

Theories of Agricultural Origins: The Pioneering Work of V. Gordon Childe

The eminent prehistorian Vere Gordon Childe (1893–1957) was among the first to emphasize the pivotal role of the origin of agriculture in human history. Childe's primary interest had always been the rise of complex, urban societies in the Old World. He recognized, however, that ancient urban societies, such as Egypt and Sumer, depended on an economy based on agriculture and stock rearing. Childe knew that to understand the development of ancient civilizations, he must first approach the problem of their economic underpinning. Childe (1936) termed the initial appearance of farming and stock raising the Neolithic revolution. Childe saw a clear analogy between the prehistoric Neolithic revolu-

Figure 17.1

The primary Near Eastern domesticates: (a) emmer wheat, Triticum dicoccum *(wild form* T. dicoccoides*); (b) einkorn wheat,* Triticum monococcum *(wild form* T. boeoticum*); (c) barley,* Hordeum vulgaris *(wild form* H. spontaneum*); (d) goats,* Capra hircus *(wild form* C. aegagrus, *the Bezoar goat); and (e) sheep,* Ovis aries *(wild form* O. orientalis, *the Asiatic mouflon).*

tion and the nineteenth-century industrial revolution. In both instances, changes in technology led to alterations in many other aspects of people's lives. In the case of the Neolithic revolution, the adoption of farming technologies led to changes in village size, settlement permanence, land ownership and use, and many other aspects of social life.

To Childe, writing on the topic in 1929, the answer to where agriculture first developed seemed quite clear. Only in the Near East were the wild ancestors of the ancient domesticates to be found. These included the wild ancestors of **emmer** and **einkorn wheat, barley,** and goats and sheep (**Figure 17.1**). The reasons farming appeared when it did also seemed fairly straightforward. The prevailing view among geologists at that time was that the Pleistocene glaciations in Europe were accompanied by a southward shifting of the moisture-carrying winds, resulting in periods of markedly increased rainfall, termed **pluvials,** over the southern Mediterranean. As the Pleistocene drew to a close, the rain track moved northward to its present location, and the Near East became increasingly desiccated. Childe argued that the climatic changes at the end of the Pleistocene

Figure 17.2

Map of the Near East showing the approximate location of the Mediterranean vegetation zone in the southern Levant. The shaded area marks the hilly flanks, where rainfall agriculture was possible. The locations of Jarmo and the Lake Zeribar and Lake Hula pollen cores are also shown.
Source: After Braidwood 1975.

would have forced humans, animals, and plants together near the remaining sources of water. Childe's concept is known as the **oasis** or **propinquity theory** of domestication:

> Animals and men would be herded together round pools and wadis that were growing increasingly isolated by desert tracts, and such enforced juxtaposition might almost of itself promote that sort of symbiosis between man and beast that is expressed in the word "domestication." (Childe 1929: 42)

In this view, climatic change was the underlying cause of the Neolithic revolution.

A Modern View of Post-Pleistocene Climatic Changes in Southwest Asia

Although the Near East was never covered with massive ice sheets during the height of the last glaciation, the climate of the Near East in the late Pleistocene was very different from the climate of the region today. Pollen cores, such as the core taken from former Lake Huleh in northern Israel, have allowed archaeologists to trace the vegetational changes that occurred in the Near East at the end of the Ice Age. During the height of the last glaciation, about 18,000 years ago, the climate of the Near East was relatively cold and dry. Woodland was very limited, and **Mediterranean vegetation,** a mixed-oak–pistachio woodland, was probably restricted to a small number of refuge areas in northern Africa. About 13,000 to 14,000 years ago, the climate in the Near East became warmer and wetter, and the areas of Mediterranean vegetation expanded, especially in the southern Levant (modern Israel, the West Bank, Jordan, southern Lebanon, and southern Syria). **Figure 17.2** shows the extent of the Mediterranean parkland in the Near East today in

How Do We Reconstruct the Near Eastern Climate at the Close of the Pleistocene?

Climate—temperature, rainfall, and seasonal variability—clearly was of great importance in shaping prehistoric societies. Childe hypothesized that climatic change was crucial in stimulating the Neolithic revolution. In previous chapters we have discussed how deep-sea cores and palynology have contributed to our understanding of ancient climates. Can we apply these methods to the Near East?

Numerous disciplines have had input into our understanding of ancient climates. Until recently, the most important evidence has come from geology. Fossil beaches, ancient beaches above the present shoreline, indicate periods of higher sea levels. Glacial **moraines**—deposits of soil and stone pushed along by a glacier and deposited at its margins—can indicate the greatest extent reached by mountain glaciers in the past. There is clear evidence of mountain glaciers in Anatolia and Iraqi Kurdistan during the late Pleistocene. Mountain glaciers imply extended periods of cold. On the other hand, **fluvial deposits**—sediments laid down by rivers—dating to the last glacial are common within the Mediterranean lowlands. Such deposits in the lower reaches of streams can indicate periods of greater runoff, which may imply higher rainfall.

Plants and Animals as Environmental Indicators

Plant and animal remains provide another line of evidence for Near Eastern climate. The abundance of large woodland animals, most notably the fallow deer, *Dama mesopotamica*,

Figure 17.3

Diagrams showing the proportions of arboreal (tree) pollen from Zeribar, Iran, and the Hula Valley, Israel. A high arboreal pollen proportion suggests widespread forests and relatively high rainfall. Note the marked contrast between the two cores at about 12,000 years ago and the dip in the Hula pollen at 11,000 years ago.
Source: Data derived from van Zeist 1969 and Baruch and Bottema 1991.

at a number of late Pleistocene archaeological sites suggests that forests were extensive at that time. Small mammals such as rodents, however, are much more sensitive indicators of fine-scale environmental differences. In the Levant—the lands bordering the eastern Mediterranean—during the Kebaran period, there was a decrease in arboreal rodents and an increase in species favoring an open environment (Tchernov 1981). Although a few arid zone species appear, the large temperate zone mammals persist; there is no evidence

of the extreme desiccation Childe's hypothesis requires.

The Pollen Evidence

By far the most important evidence, however, comes from a number of pollen cores scattered over the Near East, most notably from Lake Zeribar in the Zagros Mountains of western Iran (van Zeist 1969) and from the Hula Valley in northern Israel (Baruch and Bottema 1991). As might be expected, these two widely separated samples show a number of differences (Figure 17.3). In the Zeribar core there is very little arboreal (tree) pollen during the last glacial at 30,000 years ago. By about 10,000 years ago, however, arboreal pollen starts to increase gradually until about 6,000 years ago, indicating an open woodland environment dominated by oaks and pistachios. By 6,000 years ago the present oak forest became established.

The Hula pollen shows a somewhat different picture. Prior to 15,000 years ago trees must have been quite limited, but after that date, forests began gradually to expand, suggesting a considerable increase in rainfall. At 11,500 years ago, however, and for about 1,000 years, the forest contracted markedly, indicating a rapid drop in precipitation; following that period, the forest slowly began to expand once more.

These climatic changes do not approach the severe desiccation envisioned by Childe. Wild wheat and barley grew within the oak-pistachio woodlands. During relatively dry periods, however, such as that beginning at 11,000 years ago, these cereal resources would have been more limited, possibly providing an incentive for cereal collectors to experiment with agriculture.

relationship to the sites mentioned in this chapter. The wild ancestors of wheat and barley were found within this Mediterranean forest zone, and these areas would have been attractive to human hunter-gatherers.

We now know that Childe's explanation for the origins of agriculture was too simple; the Near Eastern terminal Pleistocene desiccation was not nearly as marked as he supposed. In fact, the most recent evidence suggests that although there was a marked cold, dry period about 11,000 years ago in the Jordan Valley, corresponding to the Younger Dryas event, after 8,000 b.c. when cereal agriculture first appears in the Near East, the climate was becoming gradually more moist (Baruch and Bottema 1991).

Where Did Near Eastern Agriculture Originate? Robert Braidwood's Hilly Flanks Hypothesis

Childe had pointed out that the earliest farming must have appeared in an area where the natural progenitors of the ancient domesticates could all be found together. His assumption was that the Neolithic revolution was a single, unified phenomenon during which both **plant domestication** and **animal domestication** were undertaken simultaneously. As did most scholars, Robert J. Braidwood, of the Oriental Institute in Chicago, accepted this assumption. Consequently, when he set out to discover the archaeological evidence for the first farmers, he decided to concentrate his efforts on that area of the Near East where wild wheat and barley and the

wild progenitors of both sheep and goats were known (Braidwood, and Howe 1960).

Modern representatives of these species were spread over broad areas of Anatolia, the Levant, and mountainous areas of Iraq and Iran **(Figure 17.4)**. The species overlapped, however, in only a limited area: the low foothills of the Zagros-Taurus mountain arc that surrounds the Mesopotamian floodplain.

Braidwood termed this area the **hilly flanks** of the **fertile crescent.** The fertile crescent is the arc-shaped region including the Jordan Valley and the Tigris-Euphrates floodplain of Mesopotamia where the earliest civilizations flourished (see Figure 17.2). The hilly flanks are the low grass-covered foothills of the Zagros, Taurus, and Lebanon-Amanus mountains that surround the fertile crescent. Today this region receives sufficient winter rainfall—25 to 50 centimeters (10 to 20 in.) per year—to support agriculture without irrigation. The high mountains above would not be suitable for agriculture; the Mesopotamian floodplain, although very fertile, receives very little rainfall and required irrigation before it could support cereal crops. The foothills, reasoned Braidwood, had to be the area of the first farming villages, and in the 1940s and 1950s he organized an expedition to search for them.

Braidwood recognized that to understand how farming originated, he must reach beyond the usual confines of an archaeological expedition. Farming was closely tied to the environment; many new data were needed so that the landscapes, climate, flora, and fauna of the region, both today and in earlier times,

Figure 17.4

The distribution of wild wheats, barley, sheep, and goats in the modern Near East.

Source: Plant distributions after D. Zohary 1969.

could be understood. Braidwood, therefore, included a range of natural scientists—geologists, geographers, botanists, and zoologists—in his expedition staff. These specialists gathered a wealth of new information. In addition to identifying and interpreting what was found in the archaeological sites, they gathered information on the local geology, soils, plants, and animals. Working in a frame of reference quite outside that of archaeology, they also had a great deal to offer in terms of new ideas about the possibilities of early farming.

Braidwood's investigations in Iraqi Kurdistan did produce some sites that seemed to qualify as among the earliest farming communities. Particularly noteworthy is **Jarmo,** with a radiocarbon age of about 6750 ± 200 b.c. Preserved cereal grains included domesticated emmer and einkorn wheat and barley, and the animal bones indicated domesticated dogs, sheep, and goats—the full suite of Near Eastern domesticates. At the time of its discovery, Jarmo was the earliest known farming village. As will be seen in Chapter 18, we know now that cereal agriculture began far earlier, about 10,000 years ago.

Braidwood's research failed to find evidence for the widespread desiccation that Childe's oasis model required. It had become clear that the climate of the Zagros foothills 10,000 years ago was not radically different from that of today. If the relatively well-watered hilly flanks were indeed the earliest agricultural hearth, models for the origin of agriculture based on environmental stress appeared to be untenable. The root cause for the Neolithic revolution had to be sought elsewhere. Numerous researchers, therefore, turned from models based on environmental change to models based on population growth.

Demographic Changes and Agricultural Origins

Questions of population growth and its consequences interested social scientists from a variety of disciplines, including anthropology and archaeology, in the 1960s. Ethnographic studies of modern hunting and gathering peoples suggested that foraging peoples generally maintained population levels well below the carrying capacity of the land. However, specific historical circumstances, such as rising sea levels and decreasing seasonal mobility, might cause an imbalance between human population levels and the available wild plant and animal foods (see Binford 1968). Under those circumstances, human populations might be forced to adopt agriculture as a way of increasing food yields. The American archaeologist Nathan Cohen (1977) argued that this phenomenon was occurring on a worldwide basis during late Pleistocene and early Holocene times. He argued that human population levels had been rising slowly throughout the Pleistocene, and the late Pleistocene human populations had settled all the available regions of the globe. As populations continued to grow, humans faced a food crisis. People around the world began to make use of foods such as fish, shellfish, and wild seeds, and ultimately, people began to domesticate plants and animals as a way of providing more food for a growing population. Contrary to Cohen's hypothesis, however, the archaeological record indicates that population growth is a primary *consequence* of the adoption of farming (Chapter 20); there is far less evidence for sustained worldwide population growth before the beginnings of agriculture.

Current Approaches

During the past 30 years, while the theorists debated the merits of their alternative explanations, the interpretation of some older data has been reevaluated. New data have also continued to accrue. Many new sites have been excavated, and what has been found in them has led us to reevaluate some of our basic assumptions. The archaeological evidence now indicates that plant domestication took place before the domestication of animals, and very likely in different areas as well.

Current evidence suggests that cereal domestication first took place in the region stretching from the Jordan River Valley northward into Syria during the late ninth and early eighth millennia b.c. Only a few sites from this period have been excavated; these will be discussed in greater detail in Chapter 18. Domesticated animals do not appear until somewhat later, after 7500 b.c. We are left, therefore, with two questions where there had been one: (1) Why did the gatherers of wild cereals begin to cultivate these crops? and (2) Why did early cereal farmers take up animal husbandry?

Conclusion

To some degree, thinking about the origin of cereal domestication has come full circle. Braidwood, like most other scholars, was misled in assuming that plant and animal domestication was a unified phenomenon. Instead, these processes seem to have occurred independently. Plant domestication came first, and it occurred in an area where, unlike the hilly flanks in Iran and Iraq, there had been significant climatic fluctuations during the late Pleistocene and early Holocene. The cold, dry snap 11,000 years ago (corresponding to the Younger Dryas) could well have led to the contraction of the wild cereals on which people were dependent, leading them to experiment with agriculture in order to maintain their way of life. The returning moisture in the subsequent Neolithic then provided the conditions under which the new agriculturalists could flourish.

Glossary

Animal domestication. The process through which animal reproduction comes under human control. Humans isolate a portion of a wild animal population by restricting its movement or breeding practices. Over time, the portion of the population under human control begins to differ morphologically from the wild population.

Barley. *Hordeum vulgaris* emmer wheat, the most important of the ancient grain crops in the Near East.

Carrying capacity. The maximum population size that an environment can support using a particular technology.

Einkorn wheat. *Triticum monococcum*—an ancient cereal of somewhat lesser importance than emmer and barley. Einkorn was widespread in Anatolia.

Emmer wheat. *Triticum dicoccum*—one of the principal ancient cereal crops.

Fertile crescent. The arc-shaped region including the Jordan Valley and the Tigris-Euphrates floodplain of Mesopotamia where the earliest civilizations flourished.

Fluvial deposits. Sediments laid down by rivers.

Hilly flanks. The low grass-covered foothills of the Zagros, Taurus, and Lebanon-Amanus mountains that surround the fertile crescent, an area that today receives sufficient winter rainfall to support agriculture without irrigation.

Jarmo. A prehistoric site, dated to circa 6750 b.c. and located in Iraqi Kurdistan, that provided evidence for early domesticated wheat, barley, sheep, and goats, as well as domesticated dogs.

Mediterranean vegetation. The mixed-oak–pistachio parkland that historically covered many of the less arid parts of the Middle East. The Mediterranean vegetation zone expanded around 13,000 B.P. as a result of the warmer, wetter climatic conditions that prevailed during the late glacial period.

Moraines. Deposits of soil and stone pushed along by a glacier and deposited at its margins.

Oasis or **propinquity theory.** The theory arguing that a widespread desiccation at the end of the Pleistocene led to the concentration of humans, plants, and animals in well-watered oases where humans learned to domesticate plants and animals. This theory was first proposed by V. Gordon Childe.

Plant domestication. The process through which plant reproduction comes under human control. Plant domestication involves more than simply creating optimal conditions for the growth of plants through watering and weeding. It entails the planting and harvesting of crops, and often the storage of seeds for use in future years. The process of plant domestication can lead to changes in plant morphology, including changes in seed size.

Pluvials. Periods marked by abundant rainfall.

Species. An interbreeding population of plants or animals.

Further Reading

Henry, Donald O.
 1989. *From Foraging to Agriculture: The Levant at the End of the Ice Age.* Philadelphia: University of Pennsylvania Press.
 A comprehensive study of the Levant during the transition to agriculture, this work is especially strong on material culture.

McCorriston, Joy, and Frank Hole
 1991. The Ecology of Seasonal Stress and the Origins of Agriculture in the Near East. *American Anthropologist* 93 (1): 46–69.
 An up-to-date summary of the botanical evidence for plant domestication.

Other Bibliography

Baruch, U., and S. Bottema
 1991. Palynological Evidence for Climatic Changes in the Levant ca. 17,000–9,000 B.P. In *The Natufian Culture in the Levant,* edited by O. Bar-Yosef and F. R. Valla, pp. 11–20. Ann Arbor, MI: International Monographs in Prehistory.

Binford, L. R.
 1968. Post-Pleistocene Adaptations. In *New Perspectives in Archaeology,* edited by S. R. Binford and L. R. Binford, pp. 313–341. Chicago: Aldine.

Braidwood, R. J.
 1975. *Prehistoric Men,* 8th ed. Glenview, IL: Scott, Foresman.

Braidwood, R. J., and B. Howe
 1960. *Prehistoric Investigations in Iraqi Kurdistan.* Chicago: University of Chicago Press.

Childe, V. G.
 1929. *The Most Ancient East: The Oriental Prelude to European Prehistory.* New York: Knopf.
 1936. *Man Makes Himself.* London: Watts.

Cohen, M.
 1977. *The Food Crisis in Prehistory.* New Haven, CT: Yale University Press.

Crabtree, Pam J.
 1993. Early Animal Domestication in the Near East and Europe. In *Archaeological Method and Theory,* vol. 5, edited by M. B. Schiffer, pp. 201–245. Tucson: University of Arizona Press.

Lee, R. B.
 1968. What Hunters Do for a Living, or, How to Make Out on Scarce Resources. In *Man the Hunter,* edited by R. B. Lee and I. DeVore, pp. 30–48. Chicago: Aldine.

Tchernov, E.
 1981. The Biostratigraphy of the Middle East. In *Colloques Internationaux du C.N.R.S. No. 598—Préhistoire du Levant,* pp. 67–97. Paris: Éditions du CNRS.

van Zeist, W.
 1969. Reflections on Prehistoric Environments in the Near East. In *The Domestication and Exploitation of Plants and Animals,* edited by P. J. Ucko and G. W. Dimbleby, pp. 35–46. London: Duckworth.

Zohary, D.
 1969. The Progenitors of Wheat and Barley in Relation to Domestication and Agricultural Dispersal in the Old World. In *The Domestication and Exploitation of Plants and Animals,* edited by P. J. Ucko and G. W. Dimbleby, pp. 47–66. London: Duckworth.

Chapter 18

Last Foragers and First Farmers
The Origins of Agriculture in the Old World

Introduction

As Childe recognized over 50 years ago, the beginnings of agriculture and animal husbandry led to profound changes in many aspects of human society. Sedentary villages replaced mobile campsites, concepts of property and land ownership changed, and populations grew. In this chapter we will examine the archaeological record of the earliest villages and the beginning of farming in the ancient Near East.

Late Pleistocene Hunter-Gatherers in Southwest Asia

Before about 14,000 years ago, the population of the Near East appears to have been quite low. The southern Levant was populated by small, mobile hunter-gatherer bands who moved on a seasonal basis. Small campsites such as Ein Gev I near the Sea of Galilee (see Chapter 9) were used by hunter-gatherers as part of their annual rounds. The climatic amelioration that began between 13,000 and 14,000 years ago led to profound changes in human settlement and subsistence in the Near East. These changes are seen most clearly in the southern Levant, where sites of the **Natufian culture** first appeared about 12,800 years ago.

The first Natufian site to be excavated was **Shukbah** in northern Israel (Figure 18.1). Shukbah is located on the Wadi Natuf, a seasonal stream that gave its name to the culture. Shukbah was excavated by the British archaeologist Dorothy Garrod in the 1920s, and it was Garrod who provided the first systematic description of the Natufian culture in the 1950s. Natufian sites have produced a wide variety of artifacts, including small lunate (half-moon-shaped) microliths; flint sickle blades, including some with a characteristic **sickle gloss** (polish left on flint from cutting grain stalks); bone sickle hafts; and stone mortars and pestles (Figure 18.2). Garrod saw the Natufians as a kind of Mesolithic with agriculture (Garrod 1957). She described the Natufians as Mesolithic because the many small microliths reminded her of the microlithic assemblages of Mesolithic Europe. However, the presence of sickle blades, sickle hafts, and grinding equipment at Natufian sites led Garrod to suggest that the Natufians may have been the first farmers in the Near East.

Garrod's pioneering work on the Natufians ushered in several decades of intensive research on the late Pleistocene cultures of the Levant. One of the most important excavations was the site of **Mallaha/Eynan,** located in the northern Jordan Valley in Israel (Perrot 1966, 1968). Extensive excavations at the site during the 1950s and 1960s revealed a series of small, circular dwellings with stone foundations and a number of human burials (Figure 18.3). The stone foundations and burials suggested a degree of settlement permanence that is not typically associated with hunter-gatherers. The excavator of the site concluded that Mallaha was occupied by a sedentary population, but one that made its living by hunting and gathering rather than by agriculture. The Natufians, like the late Mesolithic Ertebølle peoples of northern Europe, were complex foragers whose use of storable resources such as wild cereals allowed them to occupy sites on a year-round or nearly year-round basis (Henry 1985).

Mallaha is one of a number of Natufian sites that have provided evidence for small, circular huts with stone foundations. Other sites with similar architectural features are **Hayonim Terrace** in northern Israel and **Wadi Hammeh 27** in northern Jordan. In fact, most of the Natufian sites with stone architecture are found in northern Israel and Jordan. Many of these sites are located on ecotones, the borders between different ecological zones, allowing the inhabitants to make use of the wild cereals and nuts from

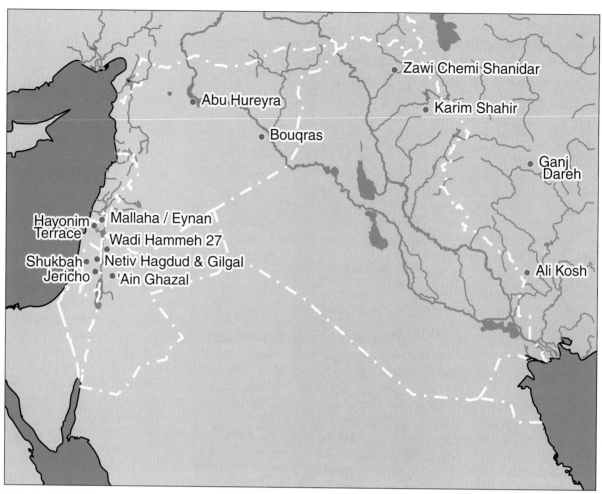

Figure 18.1

Map of the Near East showing the locations of the sites mentioned in this chapter.

the Mediterranean zone as well as the resources of the drier steppe zone. Not all Natufian sites, however, include stone architecture. Smaller sites in southern and eastern Jordan and in the Jordan Valley appear to lack the architecture and human burials that are found at the larger sites such as Mallaha.

Several lines of zooarchaeological evidence suggest that the larger Natufian sites were occupied on a year-round, or nearly year-round, basis. The first is the high frequency of house mice and other commensal species found at Natufian sites such as Mallaha (Tchernov 1984). Commensalism is a one-sided relationship in which the active partners, the mice in the Natufian case, are benefited, while the human hosts are neither

benefited nor harmed (Tchernov 1984: 91). Permanent human settlements would have provided food and shelter for these commensal species; therefore, high numbers of house mice may indicate that human habitations were occupied on a year-round basis. In addition, studies of seasonal increments on gazelle teeth indicate gazelles were being hunted at a number of different seasons at many, but not all, Natufian sites (Lieberman 1993). These data strongly suggest that these sites were occupied on a multiseasonal basis. The Natufian settlement pattern has been described as a radiating one. Large base camps such as Mallaha were occupied throughout most of the year, and smaller sites were occupied on a temporary basis for specific pur-

Figure 18.2

Typical artifacts recovered from Natufian sites include (a) small lunate microliths, (b) flint sickle blades, (c, d) basalt mortars and pestles, and (e) bone sickle hafts.

Source: (a) through (d) after Perrot 1968. (e) courtesy Israel Antiquities Authority.

poses, such as hunting or plant collecting. The smaller sites in the Jordan Valley that lack permanent architecture may well represent sites used for logistical purposes. Faunal evidence indicates that these sites were occupied on a seasonal basis (Lieberman 1993).

The economic basis of the Natufian settlements has been subject to intensive research and debate. Over 30 years ago the American archaeologist Kent Flannery (1969) argued that late Pleistocene hunters in the Near East began a broad-spectrum revolution in their subsistence practices and diet. This broad-spectrum revolution was seen as a shift away from intensive large mammal hunting and to-

ward the use of a wider range of food resources, including small mammals, birds, amphibians, reptiles, fish, invertebrates, and possibly, wild cereals. However, recent archaeological research does not support Flannery's original notion of a broad-spectrum revolution (Edwards 1989; Henry 1989). Most Natufian faunal assemblages are dominated by the remains of gazelles (Byrd 1989), and some sites have provided evidence for communal hunting of entire gazelle herds, probably through the use of game drives or surrounds (Henry 1975; Legge and Rowley-Conwy 1987; Campana and Crabtree 1990). While many species of smaller vertebrates

Figure 18.3

Plan of Mallaha/Eynan showing small, circular dwellings with stone foundations.

have been recovered from Natufian sites, gazelles clearly would have provided the bulk of meat in the diet. The faunal evidence suggests that the Natufians were specialized, intensive gazelle hunters, not broad-spectrum foragers.

It has been more difficult to determine the role of different plant foods in the Natufian diet; however, the presence of flint sickle blades, sickle hafts, and mortars and pestles at many Natufian sites certainly suggests that plant foods such as wild cereals may have played an important role in the Natufian economy. In the Near East, wild cereal grains could have been harvested in the spring and stored for use throughout the year. Unfortunately, soil conditions in many parts of the southern Levant are not favorable to the preservation of plant remains. At sites such as Wadi Hammeh 27 in Jordan (Edwards 1991), where plant remains have been preserved, Natufian foragers appear to have col-

lected many different plants from a wide range of habitats. At present there is no clear evidence to suggest that the Natufians experimented with plant cultivation. However, that possibility cannot be ruled out on the basis of the meager botanical evidence available. In summary, the archaeological data suggest that the Natufians were intensive gazelle hunters who also made use of a wide range of other plant and animal foods, including wild cereals.

The Natufians of the southern Levant are the best known of a number of late Pleistocene hunter-gatherer populations who inhabited the Near East immediately before the beginnings of agriculture. The inhabitants of the earlier levels at **Abu Hureyra** in northern Syria seem to have had a similar way of life, relying on a combination of wild plant collection and seasonal hunting of goitered gazelles (Moore 1979, 1991; Legge and Rowley-Conwy 1987). Recently, Gordon Hillman and Sarah

Colledge of the University of London have identified cultivated rye from Abu Hureyra, dated to approximately 13,000 years ago. If these dates are correct, the Abu Hureyra rye may be the earliest cultivated cereal grain in the Near East (Pringle 1999). This process, however, appears to be independent of the somewhat later domestication of emmer wheat and barley in the southern Levant.

Case Study
Karim Shahir and the Background to Agriculture in the Zagros

In the Zagros regions of northern Iraq, excavations at the site of Karim Shahir revealed the lifeways of the preagricultural inhabitants of that region. An archaeological site need not be large, deeply stratified, or complex to be of major importance. **Karim Shahir,** a small site excavated in 1951 by Dr. Bruce Howe of the Braidwood team (Braidwood and Howe 1960: 52; Braidwood 1967: 104–108), lies on the top of a hill about a mile from Jarmo. The area of the settlement was about 60 by 70 meters (200 by 230 ft.) but the actual archaeological deposit was very thin, nowhere deeper than 40 centimeters (16 in.) below the surface. About 500 square meters (600 sq. yds.) of the site were excavated. There was no architecture, but the surface was covered with a sort of irregular pavement of stream pebbles. These stones were not found in their natural context and were clearly carried into the site. There were some rock-filled pits and traces of fire in the form of charcoal and many fire-cracked rocks. Karim Shahir appeared to the excavators to represent a brief or seasonal encampment.

Mingled with the stones were some 30,000 artifacts and many animal bones. The chipped stone tool kit included, in addition to chipping debris and cores, many notched blades and flakes plus some microlithic bladelets. With the chipped tools, however, appeared representatives of a new technology: stone that had been pecked, or shaped by battering with a hammerstone to remove small fragments, and then ground and polished **(Figure 18.4).** The inventory included querns, pestles, and rubbing stones. Such pecked and ground stone artifacts are hallmarks of early farming villages in the Near East and elsewhere. In fact, the term *Neolithic* (*neo,* meaning "new," and *lithic,* meaning "stone"), or *New Stone Age,* originally referred to the

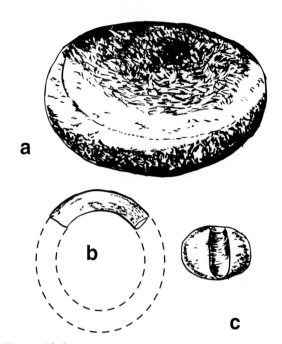

Figure 18.4

Ground stone artifacts from Karim Shahir: (a) quern, (b) stone ring, (c) possible shaft smoother.

Source: Redrawn from Braidwood, Robert, 1967: *Prehistoric Men,* 7th ed. Glenview, IL: Scott, Foresman. Reproduced with the permission of the McGraw-Hill Companies.

appearance of these new pecked and ground stone implements. Now, however, the term is used to refer to early farming societies in the Old World (as in Childe's Neolithic revolution).

Decorative items at Karim Shahir included stone beads and pendants as well as marble bracelets and rings. These items seemed to be antecedent to similar artifacts found at Jarmo. There was no pottery, but of particular interest were two crudely shaped, little animal figurines of baked clay. Similar, better-made animal figurines were also found at Jarmo.

The animal species represented in the bone assemblage included many that were potential domesticates—sheep, goats, pigs, and cattle—although there is no indication that any of them actually were domesticated, nor were there any remains to indicate domesticated cereals. The combination of traits found at Karim Shahir, however, suggested to Braidwood and Howe that the site represented a critical juncture in the development of the region that would lead to the appearance of the Neolithic. "This combination of the old with at least some of the new hints, we believe, at a position for Karim Shahir on the threshold of the transition" (Braidwood and Howe 1960: 54).

Archaeology in Practice

Archaeological Evidence for Plant Domestication

By examining the remains of plants recovered from archaeological sites, **archaeobotanists** can distinguish wild cereals from domestic grains. However, the study of early cereal husbandry depends on the recovery of very small and often fragile plant remains.

Plant remains are preserved by waterlogging and extreme aridity; they can also be preserved by charring. The technique of **flotation,** or water separation, is often used to recover organic remains from archaeological deposits. Flotation uses moving water to separate light organic materials, such as seeds and wood charcoal, from heavier archaeological soils, for example, the fill of a pit. The moving water holds the light materials in suspension so that they can be removed from the water with a fine-mesh sieve. A number of flotation machines have been designed to process large quantities of archaeological soils quickly (Figure 18.5). Where flotation machines and running water are not available, plant remains, along with other small archaeological finds, can be recovered using wet sieving and very fine mesh screening (often 1-millimeter mesh).

How do domesticated cereals differ from wild grains, and how can

Figure 18.5
Flotation machine in operation.

archaeologists identify domesticated cereals in the archaeological record? Wild cereals such as wheat and barley have a brittle **rachis,** the axis

Archaeological Evidence for Early Plant Domestication in the Near East

Sites that have provided archaeological evidence for early agriculture extend in a band northward from the southern Jordan Valley into northern Syria (Bar-Yosef and Belfer-Cohen 1989). In general, these sites are located on alluvial fans near permanent sources of fresh water. Radiocarbon dates for these early farming villages range between 8300 and 7500 b.c. A cluster of early farming sites has been identified in the lower Jordan Valley near Jericho. Sites that have produced evidence of domesticated plants include **Jericho** itself, **Gilgal** (Noy et al. 1980; Noy 1989), and **Netiv Hagdud** (Bar-Yosef et al. 1991).

Ripe spikelets
disarticulating (and
falling to ground) as
the ripening rachis
breaks into its segments

1 cm

Ripe spikelets
remaining in ear

Ear shatters
Only when threshed

Near-ripe spikelets
still attached in ear

Dense ear due to
shorter rachis
segments

The basal few spikelets
which generally fail to
disarticulate

Wild Einkorn Wheat   **Domesticated Einkorn Wheat**

Figure 18.6
Changes in the structure of wild wheat as a result of domestication.

of the plant to which the grains are attached (Figure 18.6). When the cereal grains ripen, the rachis shatters, allowing the wild plant to reseed itself. Domestic cereals, unlike their wild relatives, have a nonbrittle rachis. When the grains ripen, the axis of the plant does not shatter. These cereals are unable to reseed themselves and must be planted by humans.

How could the change from a brittle to a nonbrittle rachis take place? The genetic mutation that causes a nonbrittle rachis can occur naturally. In most circumstances, natural selection would work against this mutation, since these plants would be unable to reseed themselves. However, if humans are harvesting cereals using sickles, the cereals with the nonbrittle rachises are less likely to shatter when harvested. They would be more likely to be carried home in harvest baskets and therefore more likely to form part of the seed grain for next year's planting. Under early farming conditions, the shift from a brittle to a nonbrittle rachis could have taken place rapidly if early cultivators were using sickles to harvest the grains (see Hillman and Davies 1990). Since both sickle blades and sickle hafts have been found at many Natufian sites, the assumption that early farmers were harvesting with sickles seems a reasonable one.

Small quantities of domesticated emmer wheat and barley were found at Jericho (Hopf 1969); Netiv Hagdud and Gilgal both yielded large quantities of seeds and nuts, particularly barley (Bar-Yosef and Kisler 1989; Noy 1989). The ancient city of Jericho is a huge city mound, including extensive archaeological remains from many prehistoric and early historic periods (Kenyon 1957, 1981; Kenyon and Holland 1983). In addition to providing evidence for early cereal agriculture, the early Neolithic levels at Jericho have revealed an enigmatic stone tower. It is impossible to determine whether this tower was part of a larger structure, because only a small area of the early Neolithic settlement was excavated. The architectural remains recovered from the nearby early Neolithic site

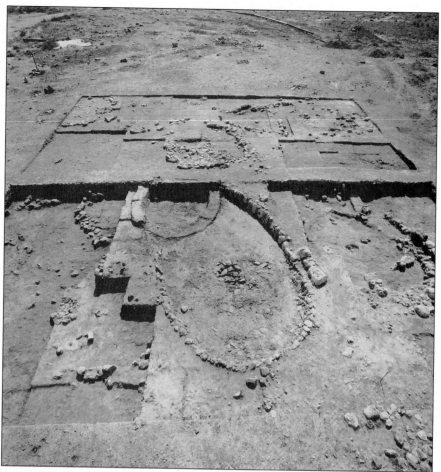

Figure 18.7

*Foundations of the small, oval dwelling structures at the early Neolithic site of
Netiv Hagdud in the West Bank.*

of Netiv Hagdud are probably more typical of
early Neolithic settlements in the Middle
East. Excavations at Netiv Hagdud revealed a
series of small oval dwellings with stone
foundations **(Figure 18.7)**. The structures recovered from Netiv Hagdud are not very different from those recovered from earlier
Natufian hamlets in the Levant. The inhabitants of Netiv Hagdud grew barley and supplemented their diet by hunting gazelles, wild
pigs, wild birds, and other wild mammals
(Tchernov 1994).

The archaeological evidence clearly indicates that cereal agriculture was established
at a number of sites in the West Bank, Israel,
and Syria by 7500 b.c. The question of why
people shifted from plant collection in the
Natufian to cereal cultivation in the early Neolithic is difficult to answer. It is important to

emphasize that while agriculture is more
labor-intensive than hunting and gathering, it
can provide a higher yield per hectare. Most
explanations for the origins of agriculture in
the Near East have focused on some combination of sedentism (Bar-Yosef and Belfer-
Cohen 1989), population growth (Cohen
1977), climatic changes (Henry 1989), and social change (Bender 1978).

Clearly, one of the hallmarks of the Natufian culture in the Levant is the shift to
sedentism. As noted above, the presence of
substantial stone architecture, cemeteries,
high frequencies of commensal species, and
multiseasonal hunting at the larger Natufian
sites suggests that those sites were occupied
on a year-round or nearly year-round basis.
This sedentism represents a fundamental
change in the archaeological record of the

Near East, because earlier Upper Paleolithic sites in the region provide clear evidence for seasonal mobility (Chapter 9). While the availability of a wide range of plant and animal resources in the immediate vicinity of these Natufian sites may have made sedentism possible, sedentism can have long-term consequences for human populations. Sedentary human populations may deplete the wild plant and animal resources in the immediate vicinity of the site, leading to experiments with cultivation. Sedentism can lead to population growth if decreased mobility leads to a decrease in human birth spacing. Moreover, the availability of starchy foods made from cereals may have allowed for earlier weaning of infants, thereby reducing birth spacing and encouraging population growth. Population growth may have encouraged human attempts to extend the natural ranges of wild cereals through cultivation (Flannery 1969).

Sedentism was accompanied by a wide range of social and cultural changes during Natufian times. Differences in the nature and quantity of grave goods that accompany Natufian burials may reflect some degree of social inequality (Wright 1978; Byrd and Monahan 1995). For example, some Natufian burials include elaborate headdresses and belts made of *Dentalium* shells. *Dentalium* shells from the Mediterranean and the Red Sea have been recovered from many inland Natufian sites, providing evidence for extensive trade networks. The need to increase production for trade and exchange may well have encouraged experiments with plant domestication (Bender 1978).

Finally, climatic change may have played a role in the transition to agriculture in the Near East. The later part of the Natufian period coincides with the Younger Dryas climatic event. As noted in Chapter 13, environmental evidence from both northern Europe and eastern North America indicates a return to nearly full glacial conditions about 11,000 years ago. In the Near East the climate became both colder and drier about 11,000 years ago. These climatic changes would have reduced the range of Mediterranean vegetation, including wild cereals. Human populations may have attempted to increase the range of those cereals through cultivation. The return to warmer, wetter conditions at the beginning of the Holocene may have contributed to the success of those early farming ventures.

To answer the question of why human populations began to cultivate cereals in the Near East, we need more archaeological, and especially floral, data from late Natufian sites. The vast majority of the extensively excavated Natufian sites date to the earlier Natufian period, before the Younger Dryas climatic deterioration. While early experiments in plant cultivation may be difficult to detect in the archaeological record, excavations at late Natufian sites may allow us to determine the long-range effects of sedentism and social elaboration on human subsistence practices.

The Archaeology of Animal Domestication

As a result of the pioneering work of Robert Braidwood and his colleagues, research into early animal domestication in the Near East intensified in the 1960s and 1970s. Many archaeologists claimed to have found evidence for early domesticated animals, but not all the claims have withstood the test of time. Today archaeologists are more interested in studying the pattern and process of animal domestication that in simply identifying the earliest domestic sheep or goats.

The study of the domestication of sheep in the Near East shows how archaeological thinking about animal domestication has changed over the past 30 years. **Zawi Chemi Shanidar** (Solecki 1981), a small village site located in the Zagros region of northern Iraq, has been radiocarbon dated to 8900 b.c. and is therefore contemporary with the late Natufian or very early Neolithic sites in the Levant. While Zawi Chemi may have been a sedentary village, there is no evidence that agriculture was practiced at the site. In 1964 the zooarchaeologist Dexter Perkins (1964) claimed that sheep bones recovered from Zawi Chemi were the remains of domesticated sheep. Although the Zawi Chemi sheep were morphologically indistinguishable from wild sheep, Perkins argued that the high numbers of juvenile sheep in the faunal assemblage meant that the bones must have come from domesticated

Archaeology in Practice

What Is a Domestic Animal?

As noted in Chapter 17, modern archaeological research has shown that plant domestication preceded animal domestication in the Near East. While the earliest evidence for plant domestication in the Near East appears in the late ninth millennium b.c., the earliest evidence of animal domestication, with the notable exception of the domestic dog, does not appear until almost a millennium later. Archaeologists want to determine why early agriculturalists in the Near East began to experiment with the domestication of animals. What is a domesticated animal, and how do we recognize animal domestication in the archaeological record?

Animal domestication is both a biological and a cultural process (Clutton-Brock 1981: 21). Domesticated animals reproduce under human cultural control, and the process of animal domestication leads to significant changes in an animal's biology. A number of morphological changes can be recognized in early domestic animals; the most obvious is a decrease in body size. Domestic animals are smaller than their wild counterparts **(Figure 18.8)**. In addition, domestication can produce changes

Figure 18.8

Morphological changes that result from animal domestication include (A) size diminution and (B) changes in horn core form.

in the shape and size of horn cores, the bone that lies under the horn, in sheep and goats. Domestication will generally lead to an increase in the numbers of the newly domesticated species because domestication makes animals more accessible to humans (Hecker 1982: 219). It can often produce changes in the age and sex structure of an animal population, in part because only a small number of adult males may be needed for reproductive purposes. Finally, animal domestication may lead to the

appearance of an animal outside its natural range. Unfortunately, this criterion is often difficult to use because the late Pleistocene and early Holocene distributions of many wild species are still poorly known. Size decrease and changes in animal population structure can also result from causes other than animal domestication. Therefore, archaeologists often use several criteria when trying to identify animal domestication in the archaeological record.

---

livestock. Unfortunately, the sample of animal bones on which Perkins based his conclusions was relatively small.

Since the early 1960s, a number of sites in Syria and Anatolia have produced more convincing evidence for domesticated sheep at a considerably later date. Sheep bones from the late seventh-millennium b.c. levels at the early Neolithic village of **Bouqras** in Syria are smaller than earlier sheep from that region. The high percentage of sheep in the

Bouqras assemblage and the evidence for size decrease led the excavators to argue that the Bouqras sheep were domesticated (Akkermans et al. 1983). Unlike Zawi Chemi, Bouqras is one of a number of sites producing evidence for early domesticated sheep in the northern Levant during the late seventh and early sixth millennia b.c. By the later seventh millennium there is a clear pattern of sheep domestication in the eastern Mediterranean (Crabtree 1993: 220–221).

The evidence for goat domestication reveals a similar patterning. Some of the earliest evidence for goat domestication comes from the mid-eighth-millennium levels at the site of **Ganj Dareh** in western Iran (Hesse 1984; see also Zeder and Hesse 2000). At that time there is evidence for an increased slaughter of 1- to 2-year-old male goats, animals that were most likely slaughtered for meat. There is also some evidence for changes in the form of the goat horn cores at that time. In addition, the excavators found footprints in some of the mud bricks at the site, suggesting that tamed goats were being kept near the brickyard. The nearest wild goat populations would have been located in the mountains well away from the site.

The evidence for goat domestication at Ganj Dareh does not stand in isolation. At the site of **Ali Kosh** in southwestern Iran, goats are the predominant species as early as the mid-eighth millennium b.c. By the seventh millennium b.c., there is clear evidence of goats with medially flatted horn cores (see Figure 18.8). Age profiles also indicate that a high proportion of young animals were slaughtered before they reached maturity.

There is also evidence to suggest that domestic goats first appeared in the southern Levant in the late eighth and seventh millennia b.c. At that time, there is a clear increase in the proportion of goats and a corresponding decrease in the numbers of gazelles in many faunal assemblages (Davis 1982). At Jericho changes in the shape of goat horn cores appear at that time (Clutton-Brock 1979), and at the Neolithic site of **'Ain Ghazal** in Jordan, a majority of the goats appear to have been killed before reaching maturity. The 'Ain Ghazal goats also show evidence for arthritis, which may have resulted from unsuitable husbandry conditions (Köhler-Rollefson et al. 1988). What is not yet clear is whether goats were independently domesticated in the southern Levant or whether they were introduced to the Levant from the Zagros region.

Goats and sheep appear to have been domesticated by early farmers after the appearance of cereal cultivation in the Near East. It is possible that game depletion around early farming villages may have encouraged experiments with the domestication of sheep and goats. Domestic animals may also have served as "walking larders" (Clutton-Brock 1989) that could absorb agricultural surpluses and be slaughtered in times of food shortage. One animal, however, was domesticated considerably earlier, and that is the dog. Early domestic dogs appear at Natufian sites (Davis and Valla 1978) in the Near East; they also appear at both Mesolithic and late Upper Paleolithic sites in Europe. The reasons wolves were domesticated by hunting and gathering populations in both the Near East and Europe are unclear. They may have been used primarily as hunting and guard dogs, or they may have served as walking larders for hunting populations.

Pigs and cattle appear to have been domesticated somewhat later than goats and sheep. The ancestors of domestic cattle and pigs were widely distributed across Europe, Asia, and North Africa during the early Holocene, and it is possible that these animals may have been domesticated more than once. Domestic cattle and pig bones have been recovered from a number of sites in the Near East and the eastern Mediterranean dating to about 6000 b.c. At present there is not enough evidence to determine whether cattle and pigs were domesticated only once or whether they were domesticated independently in several different parts of the eastern Mediterranean.

Other Centers of Plant and Animal Domestication in the Old World

Much of the archaeological research on early farming societies in the Old World has focused on the beginnings of cereal agriculture in the Near East. However, archaeological and biological researchers have identified a number of other important centers of early plant and animal domestication in the Old World. Although "studies of indigenous African agriculture have been much neglected" (Harlan 1992: 59), a wide variety of plants were domesticated throughout sub-Saharan Africa. Important indigenous African domesticates include sorghum, pearl millet, African rice (*Oryza glaberrima*), yams, and watermelon. While archaeological evidence for these early African domesticates remains limited, the distribution of these African crops and their wild ancestors does not reveal a single center of African plant domestication. Instead, "plants were domesticated throughout sub-Saharan Africa, from one side of the continent to the other" (Harlan 1992: 69).

At least two separate centers of plant domestication have been identified in east Asia. Traditionally, archaeologists thought that Asian rice (*Oryza sativa*) was domesticated in tropical or subtropical southeast Asia (Crawford 1992: 24). However, recent archaeological research suggests that Asian rice was domesticated farther north along the banks of the Yangtze River in Southern China. The earliest domestic rice grains known from this region date to about 8,000 years ago. Recent research on rice phytoliths (silica bodies in plant tissues) from Diaotonghuan Cave along the Middle Yangtze River suggests that rice cultivation may have an even longer history in this part of China (Pringle 1999: 1449; Zhao 1998). However, domestic rice did not become a staple until about 7,000 years ago. Today domesticated Asian rice is a staple of diets throughout the world.

Common, or broomcorn, millet (*Panicum miliaceum*), a cereal grain that was widely used for food during prehistory, appears to have been domesticated in China. Remains of domesticated broomcorn millet have been identified from a number of Neolithic sites in the loess plateau region of North China. Loess is a fine-grained soil that was deposited by wind during the late Pleistocene. Light, fertile loess soils were attractive to early farmers in both northern Asia and central Europe (Chapter 20). Broomcorn millet requires less water that many other cereals, making it particularly suitable for the relatively dry loess plateau regions of North China. The earliest domesticated broomcorn millets date to 6500 b.c. (Crawford 1992: 23). Thus plant domestication appears to have taken place at roughly the same time in Eastern Asia and the Near East.

Conclusion

The archaeological evidence from early Neolithic sites in the Near East indicates that farming villages based on a mixture of cereal agriculture and animal husbandry were wide-

spread through the region by 6000 b.c. Although the Near East has been an important center for archaeological research on the origins of agriculture, archaeological and botanical studies indicate that the Near East was but one of a number of independent centers of plant domestication in the Old World. Additional research on early plant domestication in Africa and East Asia will shed light on the transition from foraging to farming in the Old World.

While the role of population growth in the origins of agriculture remains unclear, there is no question that one of the *consequences* of the establishment of farming villages was population increase. After examining the origins of farming villages in the New World (Chapter 19), we will examine the consequences of the agricultural revolution for human societies in both the Old World and the Americas (Chapter 20).

Glossary

Abu Hureyra. A large early Neolithic site near the Euphrates River in Syria. The lowest levels resemble the roughly contemporary Natufian culture. Like the Natufian people, the early preagricultural inhabitants of Abu Hureyra hunted gazelle and gathered wild barley and other plants for sustenance.

'Ain Ghazal. An early Neolithic site near Amman in Jordan that has provided archaeological evidence for early domestic goats.

Ali Kosh. An early Neolithic site located in the Deh Luran plain in western Iran that has provided evidence for early goat domestication.

Archaeobotanists. Scientists who study plant remains recovered from archaeological sites.

Bouqras. An early Neolithic site in Syria that has provided evidence for early domesticated sheep dated to the late seventh and early sixth millennia b.c.

Flotation. A technique (also known as water separation) that uses rapidly moving water to hold light organic remains in suspension so that they can be separated from archaeological soils.

Ganj Dareh. An early Neolithic site in western Iran that has provided evidence for the world's earliest domesticated goats.

Gilgal. An early Neolithic site located in the Jordan Valley north of Jericho that has provided evidence for very early domesticated barley.

Hayonim Terrace. A Natufian site in northern Israel that has provided evidence for small, circular structures with stone foundations.

Jericho. A deeply stratified site located in the West Bank. The earliest Neolithic levels at Jericho have revealed an enigmatic stone tower and evidence for early domesticated wheat and barley.

Karim Shahir. A late Pleistocene site in northern Iraq that appears to have been occupied by mobile hunter-gatherers, but that shares some features, such as pecked and ground stone tools, with early Neolithic sites in the region.

Mallaha/Eynan. A site, known as Mallaha (Arabic) and Eynan (Hebrew), located in the northern Jordan Valley in Israel. Excavations during the 1950s and 1960s revealed the stone foundations of small, circular huts that appear to have been occupied by hunter-gatherer populations on a permanent basis.

Natufian culture. A culture that extended over much of the southern Levant between 12,800 and 10,500 years ago. The Natufians were complex foragers who relied on a combination of intensive gazelle hunting and plant collection. Typical Natufian artifacts include small lunate microliths, flint sickle blades, sickle hafts, and stone mortars and pestles.

Netiv Hagdud. An early Neolithic site located in the lower Jordan Valley north of Jericho that has provided evidence for small, oval houses and early domesticated barley.

Rachis. The axis of a cereal plant to which the individual grains are attached.

Shukbah. A Natufian site located in the Wadi Natuf that was excavated by Dorothy Garrod in the 1920s. The site location gave its name to the Natufian culture.

Sickle gloss. The sheen that appears on flint sickles when they are used to harvest plants such as grains and reeds. The gloss results from the contact between the flint sickle and tiny silica bodies within the stems of plants.

Wadi Hammeh 27. A Natufian site located in northern Jordan that has provided evidence for substantial architecture, ground stone artifacts, and human burials. The site and its artifact assemblage show many similarities to the well-known site of Mallaha/Eynan.

Zawi Chemi Shanidar. An early village site in northern Iraq, dated to 8,900 b.c., that was claimed to have evidence for the world's earliest domesticated sheep. Subsequent research has indicated that the sheep were probably not domesticated.

 ## Further Reading

Bar-Yosef, O., and F. R. Valla, eds.
    1991. *The Natufian Culture in the Levant.* Ann Arbor, MI: International Monographs in Prehistory.
    This volume provides an overview of current research on the Natufian, including reports on many of the recently excavated sites.

Crabtree, P. J.
    1993. Early Animal Domestication in the Middle East and Europe. In *Archaeological Method and Theory*, vol. 5, edited by M. B. Schiffer, pp. 201–245. Tucson: University of Arizona Press.
    This article provides a comprehensive review of animal domestication in both the Near East and Europe, and includes an extensive bibliography.

Henry, D. O.
    1989. *From Foraging to Agriculture: The Levant at the End of the Ice Age.* Philadelphia: University of Pennsylvania Press.
    Recommended for the advanced student. This text provides a detailed overview of the late Pleistocene cultures of the southern Levant. The text includes detailed descriptions of late Pleistocene stone tool technology, but it is written from an ecological perspective.

Legge, A. J., and P. Rowley-Conwy
    1987. Gazelle Killing in Stone Age Syria. *Scientific American* 238 (8): 88–95.
    The authors present evidence for communal hunting of gazelles at the Natufian period site of Abu Hureyra in northern Syria.

 ## Other Bibliography

Akkermans, P. A., J. A. K. Boerma, A. T. Clason, S. G. Hill, E. Lohof, C. Meiklejohn, M. le Mière, G. M. F. Molgat, J. J. Roodenberg, W. Waterbolk-van Rooyen, and W. van Zeist
    1983. Bouqras Revisited: Preliminary Report on a Project in Eastern Syria. *Proceedings of the Prehistoric Society* 49: 335–372.

Bar-Yosef, O., and A. Belfer-Cohen

1989. The Origins of Sedentism and Farming Communities in the Levant. *Journal of World Prehistory* 3: 447–498.

Bar-Yosef, O., A. Gopher, E. Tchernov, and M. E. Kislev

1991. Netiv Hagdud: An Early Neolithic Village Site in the Jordan Valley. *Journal of Field Archaeology* 18: 405–424.

Bar-Yosef, O., and M. E. Kislev

1989. Early Farming Communities in the Jordan Valley. In *Foraging and Farming: The Evolution of Plant Exploitation*, edited by D. R. Harris and G. C. Hillman, pp. 632–642. London: Unwin and Hyman.

Bender, B.

1978. Gatherer-Hunter to Farmer: A Social Perspective. *World Archaeology* 10: 204–222.

Braidwood, R. J.

1967. *Prehistoric Men*, 7th ed. Glenview, IL: Scott, Foresman.

Braidwood, R. J., and B. Howe

1960. *Prehistoric Investigations in Iraqi Kurdistan.* Chicago: University of Chicago Press.

Byrd, B. F.

1989. The Natufian: Settlement Variability and Economic Adaptations in the Levant at the End of the Pleistocene. *Journal of World Prehistory* 3 (2): 159–197.

Byrd, B. F., and C. M. Monahan

1995. Death, Mortuary Ritual, and Natufian Social Structure. *Journal of Anthropological Archaeology* 14: 251–287.

Campana, D. V., and P. J. Crabtree

1990. Communal Hunting in the Natufian of the Southern Levant: Social and Economic Implications. *Journal of Mediterranean Archaeology* 3: 223–243.

Clutton-Brock, J.

1979. The Mammalian Remains from Jericho Tell. *Proceedings of the Prehistoric Society* 45: 135–157.

1981. *Domesticated Animals from Early Times.* Austin: University of Texas Press.

Clutton-Brock, J., ed.

1989. *The Walking Larder: Patterns of Domestication, Pastoralism, and Predation.* London: Unwin Hyman.

Cohen, M.

1977. *The Food Crisis in Prehistory.* New Haven, CT: Yale University Press.

Crawford, G. W.

1992. Prehistoric Plant Domestication in East Asia. In *The Origins of Agriculture: An International Perspective*, edited by C. W. Cowan and P. J. Watson, pp. 7–38. Washington, DC: Smithsonian Institution Press.

Davis, S. J. M.

1982. Climatic Change and the Advent of Domestication: The Succession of Ruminant Artiodactyls in the Late Pleistocene-Holocene in the Israel Region. *Paléorient* 8: 5–15.

Davis, S. J. M., and F. Valla

1978. Evidence for Domestication of the Dog 12,000 Years Ago in the Natufian of Israel. *Nature* 276: 608–610.

Edwards, P. C.

1989. Revising the Broad Spectrum Revolution and Its Role in Southeast Asian Food Production. *Antiquity* 63: 225–246.

1991. Wadi Hammeh 27: An Early Natufian Site at Pella, Jordan. In *The Natufian Culture in the Levant*, edited by O. Bar-Yosef and F. R. Valla, pp. 123–148. Ann Arbor, MI: International Monographs in Prehistory.

Flannery, K. V.

1969. Origins and Ecological Effects of Early Domestication in Iran and the Near East. In *The Domestication and Exploitation of Plants and Animals*, edited by P. J. Ucko and G. W. Dimbleby, pp. 73–100. London: Duckworth.

Garrod, D.

1957. The Natufian Culture: The Life and Economy of a Mesolithic people in the Near East. *Proceedings of the British Academy* 43: 211–227.

Harlan, J. R.

1992. Indigenous African Agriculture. In *The Origins of Agriculture: An International Perspective*, edited by C. W. Cowan and P. J. Watson, pp. 59–70. Washington, DC: Smithsonian Institution Press.

Hecker, H. M.

1982. Domestication Revisited: Its Implications for Faunal Analysis. *Journal of Field Archaeology* 9: 217–236.

Henry, D.

1975. Fauna in Near Eastern Archaeological Deposits. In *Problems in Prehistory: North Africa and the Levant*, edited by F. Wendorf, pp. 379–385. Dallas: Southern Methodist University Press.

1985. Preagricultural Sedentism: The Natufian Example. In *Prehistoric Hunter-Gatherers: The Emergence of Cultural Complexity*, edited by T. D. Price and J. A. Brown, pp. 365–383. Orlando, FL: Academic Press.

Hesse, B.
1984. These Are Our Goats: The Origins of Herding in West Central Iran. In *Animals and Archaeology: 3. Early Herders and Their Flocks,* edited by J. Clutton-Brock and C. Grigson, pp. 243–264. Oxford: British Archaeological Reports, International Series 202.

Hillman, G. C., and M. S. Davies
1990. Measured Domestication Rates in Wild Wheats and Barley under Primitive Conditions, and Their Archaeological Implications. *Journal of World Prehistory* 4: 157–222.

Hopf, M.
1969. Plant Remains and Early Farming in Jericho. In *The Domestication and Exploitation of Plants and Animals,* edited by P. J. Ucko and G. W. Dimbleby, pp. 355–359. London: Duckworth.
1983. Jericho Plant Remains. In *Excavations at Jericho,* vol. 5, edited by K. M. Kenyon and T. A. Holland, pp. 576–621. London: British School of Archaeology in Jerusalem.

Kenyon, K. M.
1957. *Digging Up Jericho.* London: Ernest Benn.
1981. *Excavations at Jericho,* vol. 3. London: British School of Archaeology in Jerusalem.

Kenyon, K. M., and T. A. Holland
1983. *Excavations at Jericho,* vol. 5. London: British School of Archaeology in Jerusalem.

Köhler-Rollefson, I., W. Gillespie, and M. Metzger
1988. The Fauna from Neolithic 'Ain Ghazal. In *The Prehistory of Jordan: The State of Research in 1986,* edited by A. N. Garrard and N. H. Gebel, pp. 423–430. Oxford: British Archaeological Reports, International Series 396 (i).

Legge, A. J., and P. Rowley-Conwy
1987. Gazelle Killing in Stone Age Syria. *Scientific American* 238 (8): 88–95.

Lieberman, D. E.
1993. The Rise and Fall of Seasonal Mobility among Hunter-Gatherers: The Case of the Southern Levant. *Current Anthropology* 34 (5): 599–631.

Moore, A. M. T.
1979. A Pre-Neolithic Farming Village on the Euphrates. *Scientific American* 241 (2): 62–70.
1991. Abu Hureyra 1 and the Antecedents of Agriculture on the Middle Euphrates. In *The Natufian Culture in the Levant,* edited by O. Bar-Yosef and F. R. Valla, pp. 277–294. Ann Arbor, MI: International Monographs in Prehistory.

Noy, T.
1989. Gilgal I. A Pre-Pottery Neolithic Site, Israel. The 1985–1987 Seasons. *Paléorient* 15 (1): 15–22.

Noy, T., J. Schuldenrein, and E. Tchernov
1980. Gilgal, A Pre-Pottery Neolithic A Site in the Lower Jordan Valley. *Israel Exploration Journal* 30: 63–82.

Perkins, D., Jr.
1964. Prehistoric Fauna from Shanidar, Iraq. *Science* 144: 1565–1566.

Perrot, J.
1966. Le gisement Natoufien de Mallaha (Eynan), Israël. *L'Anthropologie* 70: 437–483.
1968. La Préhistoire Palestinienne. In *Supplément au Dictionnaire de la Bible* Vol. 3 (#43) pp. 286–446. Paris: Letouzey et Ané.

Pringle, H.
1999. The Slow Birth of Agriculture. *Science* 282: 1446–1450.

Solecki, R. L.
1981. *An Early Village Site at Zawi Chemi Shanidar.* Biblioteca Mesopotamica 13. Malibu, CA: Undena Publications.

Tchernov, E.
1984. Commensal Animals and Human Sedentism in the Middle East. In *Animals and Archaeology: 3. Early Herders and Their Flocks,* edited by J. Clutton-Brock and C. Grigson, pp. 91–115. Oxford: British Archaeological Reports, International Series 202.
1994. *An Early Neolithic Village in the Jordan Valley. Part II: The Fauna of Netiv Hagdud.* American School of Prehistoric Research, Bulletin 44. Cambridge, MA: Peabody Museum of Archaeology and Ethnology, Harvard University.

Wright, G. A.
1978. Social Differentiation in the Early Natufian. In *Social Archaeology: Beyond Subsistence and Dating,* edited by C. L. Redman, M. J. Berman, E. V. Curtin, W. J. Langhorne, N. M. Versaggi, and J. C. Wanser, pp. 201–233. New York: Academic Press.

Zeder, Melinda A., and Brian Hesse
2000. The Initial Domestication of Goats (*Capra hircus*) in the Zagros Mountains 10,000 Years Ago. *Science* 287: 2254–2257.

Zhao, Zhijun
1998. The Middle Yangtze Region in China Is One Place Where Rice Was Domesticated: Phytolith Evidence from the Diatonghuan Cave, Northern Jiangxi. *Antiquity* 72 (278): 885–897.

Agricultural Origins in the New World

Introduction

Every American schoolchild learns that in 1492 Columbus discovered America. Both archaeology and history have shown that Christopher Columbus did not really "discover" America. After all, Native American peoples have inhabited both North and South America since at least late Pleistocene times. Moreover, the Norse (Vikings) from Greenland established a settlement in Newfoundland (eastern Canada) about 500 years before Columbus set sail for the New World. Columbus's voyages, however, and the voyages of discovery that followed them ushered in a period of intensified contact between the Old World and the Americas. Nowhere can this be seen more clearly than in the study of food.

It is almost impossible for Americans today to imagine a diet without potatoes, tomatoes, and corn (maize), but the medieval European diet was, in many respects, quite limited. While a variety of meats, including beef, pork, mutton, and poultry, would have been available, there was little variety in the plant portion of the diet. Cereals, such as wheat, barley, oats, and rye, would have been used for breads and gruel, but only a small number of vegetables—beans and peas, carrots, onions, and cabbages—would have been included in the medieval diet.

Potatoes, tomatoes, and corn were all domesticated in the New World by Native American peoples. Other plants that were domesticated in the Americas include chili peppers, squashes, gourds, pumpkins, avocados, and several kinds of beans (different kinds of beans were domesticated in the New World and the Old World).

In this chapter we will examine the archaeological evidence for the domestication of plants and animals in the New World. Particular emphasis will be placed on the domestication of maize, beans, and squash. These three plants, known as the New World triad, or "three sisters," played a central role in the farming economies throughout the Americas before the arrival of Columbus. The study of plant domestication in the Americas is important for several reasons. First, just as wheat and barley agriculture served as an economic foundation for the development of complex urban societies in the Near East, so maize agriculture was equally important for the development of the pre-Columbian civilizations of the Americas (see Part VIII). Second, New World agriculture developed completely independently of Old World agriculture. Comparisons between the regions allow us to study similarities and differences in the transition to agriculture in different parts of the world. Finally, New World domesticates form an important part of modern diets throughout the world. Maize meal is a staple of West African cuisine; the tomato is basic to southern Italian cooking; and the potato forever changed Irish history. In studying the origin of these New World domesticates, the descendants of both New and Old World peoples learn more about their cultural heritage.

The Domestication of Maize

At the time Columbus arrived in the New World, domesticated maize (*Zea mays*), or what Americans call corn, was grown from eastern Canada to South America. The origin of maize is one of the most controversial is-sues in all of botany, one that has been debated for over a century. Some scholars argued that the wild ancestor of maize is a now extinct wild popcorn (Mangelsdorf 1974; see also Mangelsdorf 1986). Today, however, most scholars think that domesticated maize is descended from a wild grass known as **teosinte**

Figure 19.1

Map of the Americas showing the locations of sites mentioned in the text and the major early New World domesticates.

(*Zea mexicana*), which is closely related to domestic maize. Some varieties of teosinte are found in the arid, highland regions of **Mesoamerica,** the geographical region that includes southern Mexico and the adjacent regions of Central America—Guatemala, El Salvador, Belize, and the western parts of Honduras, Nicaragua, and Costa Rica **(Figure 19.1)**; see Chapter 25). It is in the highland regions of southern Mexico that the search for the early ancestors of modern maize has taken place.

Case Study
The Tehuacán Valley Project

The **Tehuacán Valley project** was designed to study the origins of agriculture in Mesoamerica. The project was directed by Richard MacNeish who, like Childe and Braidwood in the Old World, was interested in studying the origins of plant cultivation because maize agriculture formed the economic basis of later complex societies such as the Maya and the Aztec (Chapter 25). The Tehuacán Valley is located in the state of Puebla, Mexico (see Figure 19.1). During the course of the project, which was conducted between 1961 and 1965, 9 stratified sites were excavated and an additional 18 were tested archaeologically (MacNeish 1991: xvii).

The Tehuacán Valley project was important both methodologically and theoretically. It was one of the first archaeological projects in Mesoamerica that was designed specifically to collect data on plant domestication. One reason the Tehuacán Valley was chosen as a site for this project was that the dry caves of the Mexican highlands preserve organic materials such as seeds and bones quite well. During the excavation project over 40,000 plant remains and human feces containing plant remains were collected.

The Tehuacán Valley is located in an area of great ecological diversity within the Mexican highlands. The region includes humid river bottom areas, valley steppes, slopes, and an oak-pine forest in the higher elevations (MacNeish 1991: 112–113). A range of potentially domesticable plant species would have been available in the area. The region is subject to marked seasonal variations in rainfall. Most of the rain falls between May and November, and the winter dry season is harsh. However, at one oasis in the valley, the vegetation remains lush throughout the year, and animals are available even in the dry months.

MacNeish (1967) and his collaborators defined four major prepottery phases as a result of the excavations in the Tehuacán Valley (see Hardy 1996 for an alternative viewpoint). MacNeish based the dates for the phases on 120 radiocarbon age determinations. These original dates were based on wood charcoal recovered from individual archaeological layers within the excavated sites.

Recently, some of the actual plant remains recovered from the Tehuacán Valley project have been dated using the AMS radiocarbon method (see the Archaeology in Practice box, Chapter 10). The new AMS dates have led to new interpretations of the process of plant domestication in Mesoamerica. Although MacNeish's interpretation of the sequence of events that occurred in the Tehuacán Valley still appears valid, the new AMS dates indicate that the domestication of maize took place later than MacNeish believed.

The Ajuereado phase (12,000 to 7600 b.c.) as defined by MacNeish (1967) and his colleagues reflects the earliest occupation of the Tehuacán Valley. During the early Ajuereado phase, Pleistocene animals such as horses, giant jackrabbits, antelopes, giant wolves, and giant tortoises still existed in the valley. Meat made up a major portion of the diet, and animals were obtained through rabbit drives, ambush hunting, and stalking with spear throwers. When the large Pleistocene animals became extinct, trapping and collecting of small mammals became more important, as did the collection of fruits, pods, leaves, and grass seeds (MacNeish 1991: 107).

During the following El Riego phase (7600 to 5000 b.c.), there is archaeological evidence for a scheduled use of plant and animal resources on a seasonal basis **(Figure 19.2)**. El Riego hunters and gatherers relied on a wide range of plant and animal resources. Hunting, trapping, and leaf cutting took place during the winter months; seed collecting began in the spring and continued into the summer; and fruit picking became more important during the fall. Excavations revealed a series of small camps that might have housed single families and large camps that would have been home to several families. All the camps appear to have been occupied on a seasonal basis. El Riego foragers moved their campsites seasonally to take advantage of different plant and animal resources that would have been available in different parts of the Tehuacán Valley at different times of the year. By the later part of the El Riego period, the Tehuacán Valley foragers appear to have experimented with planting seeds and fruit pits; however, cultivated plants played only a very minor role in the diet.

MacNeish and his collaborators argued that subsistence practices continued to change during the subsequent Coxcatlán phase, originally radiocarbon dated to between 5000 and 3400 b.c.

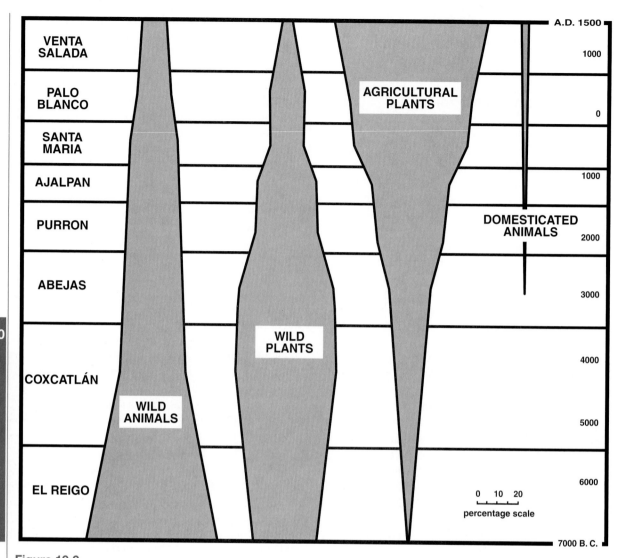

Figure 19.2

The relative importance of wild animals, wild plants, and agricultural plants in the Tehuacán Valley diet through time. Note that domesticated animals play only a very minor role in the diet.

While hunting, leaf cutting, and trapping continued to be the dominant winter activities, a range of domestic plant species were planted during the spring and summer, including maize, beans, squash, gourds, avocados, chilies, and amaranth. By this phase the corncobs had begun to increase in size, indicating increased biological divergence from the wild ancestors of corn **(Figure 19.3)**.

The new AMS dates (Long et al. 1989) indicate that the earliest maize cobs from the Tehuacán Valley are only 4,700 to 4,600 years old. In other words, maize first appeared in the Tehuacán Valley about 2650 b.c., not between 5000 and 3500 b.c. as MacNeish and his colleagues originally suggested. The AMS dates for beans are even more surprising. The earliest bean pod fragment from the Tehuacán Valley is only 2,285 years old (Smith 1994: 163). While the Tehuacán specimens remain the oldest known maize and beans from Mexico, the new dates indicate that early farming began much later in the Tehuacán Valley than the original researchers thought (Fritz 1994).

TEOSINTE   MAIZE

Figure 19.3

Domesticated maize compared with its wild ancestor, teosinte.

The new dates have some interesting implications for our understanding of plant domestication in Mesoamerica. One possibility is that the Tehuacán Valley may not be an area in which the initial domestication of maize took place. It is important to note that the early maize from the Tehuacán Valley was fully domesticated; it had lost its ability to reproduce without human intervention. The beginnings of maize domestication certainly took place in areas where teosinte, the wild progenitor of maize, was available. The variety of teosinte that is most similar to maize grows along the central Balsas River drainage about 250 kilometers (160 mi.) west of the Tehuacán Valley (Doebley 1990). The initial domestication of maize may have taken place in western Mexico, and the already domesticated maize may then have been adopted by hunter-gatherer populations in the Tehuacán Valley.

During the subsequent Abejas period, originally dated to between 3400 and 2300 b.c., there is evidence for increasing settlement permanence in the Tehuacán Valley. The camps appear to have been occupied for longer periods, and three large sites yielded evidence for dwellings. These pit houses were about 5 to 6 meters (16 to 20 ft.) long by 3 meters (10 ft.) wide and about 1 meter (3 ft.) deep. Poles were used to construct a tentlike roof frame, which was probably covered with a brush roof. These houses, which were located in the fertile river bottom areas, appear to have been occupied on a year-round basis. The Abejas phase inhabitants of the Tehuacán Valley continued the subsistence practices that were established in the earlier Coxcatlán period, but the Abejas farmers planted new, more productive types of maize. Annual schedules were adjusted to accommodate the planting of maize and other domesticated crops during the spring and summer. Other subsistence activities, such as hunting and trapping, were concentrated in the nonagricultural seasons of the year (Flannery 1968).

If we assume that the Tehuacán Valley archaeological sequence reflects the initial domestication of maize and beans, then it appears that sedentism follows plant domestication in Mesoamerica. This pattern is in marked contrast to the Near Eastern pattern where sedentary populations clearly precede the beginnings of agriculture by over 2,000 years. The Near Eastern pattern appears to be more typical of the beginnings of farming in other parts of the world. In other areas of the world, such as eastern North America, where plants were domesticated independently, agriculture appears initially among increasingly sedentary hunters and gatherers who have access to an abundance of plant and animal resources (Gebauer and Price 1992a; Price and Gebauer 1995). If, on the other hand, maize was domesticated somewhere other than the Tehuacán Valley, then the initial farming populations may well have been semisedentary, affluent foragers (Gebauer and Price 1992b: 8). The central Balsas River drainage, where teosinte is found today, is a region that may well have supported semisedentary foragers. Only additional research on plant domestication in other areas of Mesoamerica, including the Balsas River drainage, can answer this question definitively.

Guilá Naquitz

While no studies of the size and scope of the Tehuacán Valley project have been undertaken in recent years, smaller archaeological projects have shed light on the beginnings of farming in Mesoamerica. Of particular importance is the site of **Guilá Naquitz,** located in the Valley of Oaxaca in highland southern Mexico. The site itself is located about 6 kilometers (4 mi.) northeast of the town of Mitla. It appears to be a small encampment, housing perhaps only 3 to 5 people. An interdisciplinary team, under the direction of Kent Flannery (1986), excavated the entire site to study the transition from foraging to farming in Oaxaca.

The site was occupied between 8700 and 6700 b.c. It is therefore broadly contemporary with the late Ajuereado and earlier El Riego phases in the Tehuacán Valley. The earliest levels at the site produced no domesticated plants. However, evidence for rinds of bottle gourds were found in archaeological layers dating between 7400 and 6700 b.c. Remains of domesticated squash also date to that period.

In the light of the newer, younger dates for domesticated maize and beans in the Tehuacán Valley, a program has been initiated to restudy and redate the squash remains from Guilá Naquitz. The seeds of these early domesticates will be dated directly using the AMS method of radiocarbon dating. While the evidence for early domesticated squash and gourds at Guilá Naquitz remains in limbo, pending further biological analyses and new dating methods, Flannery's work at Guilá Naquitz has led to new models for the transition from foraging to farming in Mesoamerica. Flannery (1986: 515) suggests that early experimentation with agriculture would have been a logical extension of the preagricultural pattern of subsistence, which was based on the collection of a broad range of plant and animal resources. He notes that there is long-term stability in the plant and animal species used by the Guilá Naquitz foragers, but that this is coupled with a gradually increasing commitment to agriculture.

Flannery suggests that foragers might try out new subsistence strategies, such as planting, during periods of abundance (wet years). Those strategies might be expanded if they proved successful. A goal of the early agricultural strategies was risk reduction, evening out the variations between the good years and the bad years. Thus agriculture developed gradually as hunter-gatherers attempted to adapt to "the unpredictable availability of subsistence resources" (McClung de Tapia 1992: 161).

The Guilá Naquitz data are even more important for what they do not show. In 1977, M. N. Cohen wrote *The Food Crisis in Prehistory,* in which he argued that

> the nearly simultaneous adoption of agricultural economies throughout the world could only be accounted for by assuming that hunting and gathering populations had saturated the world approximately 10,000 years ago and had exhausted all possible (or palatable) strategies for increasing their food supply within the constraints of the hunting-gathering life-style. The only possible reaction to further growth in population, worldwide, was to begin artificial augmentation of the food supply [i.e., agriculture]. (Cohen 1977: 279)

In short, Cohen argued the origin of agriculture was the result of worldwide population growth that had reached a crisis level during the late Pleistocene or early Holocene. The Guilá Naquitz project, however, provides no evidence to support the notion that population growth or population pressure forced Mesoamerican foragers to adopt agriculture as a way of feeding a population that had exceeded the limits of the available food resources. Population levels appear to have been quite low throughout the occupation of the Guilá Naquitz site. Similarly, the Tehuacán Valley project provides no evidence to suggest that overpopulation forced people in the Mexican highlands to begin to practice agriculture.

Plant Domestication in Highland South America

The South American highlands were another major center for the domestication of plants in the New World. A number of different early domesticates form part of the high-elevation agricultural complex. The best known of these plants, and the only one that spread widely outside this highland region, is the potato. The other plants that make up the highland complex are grown primarily at altitudes between 3,000 and 3,500 meters (10,000 to 11,500 ft.) above sea level. They include quinoa and several tubers. Quinoa is a small-seeded, cereal-like plant that can be used to make bread and similar foods.

Few highland archaeological sites have produced evidence for early cultivated plants. Most of the evidence for the initial domestication of this highland complex of plants comes from sites at middle elevations (between 1,500 and 3,000 meters [5,000 to 10,000 ft.] above sea level). Plant remains from these mid-elevation sites indicate that both potatoes, quinoa, and possibly other high-altitude crops were domesticated by the fifth millennium b.c. (Pearsall 1992: 188).

Animal Domestication in the Americas

Domestic animals played a much smaller role in the economies of early farming villages in Mesoamerica than they did in the Old World. Domestic animals played an important role in the early farming economies of the Near East and other parts of the Old World. While the archaeological evidence from the Near East indicates that plant domestication preceded animal domestication in the eastern Mediterranean regions, by about 6000 b.c. farming communities from Greece to Pakistan were keeping domestic animals, including cattle, sheep, goats, and pigs. The situation is different in the Americas. Only two domestic animals have been recovered from pre-Columbian archaeological sites in Mesoamerica: the dog and the turkey. The dog is the only animal that was domesticated in both the Old World and the Americas. Domestic dogs first appear in the Tehuacán Valley during the Abejas period. They appear to have been used as a source of food and were probably not locally domesticated. As noted in Chapter 16, domestic dogs appear at a much earlier date in prehistoric North America. Domestic turkeys appear in Mesoamerica at approximately a.d. 180.

One reason domestic animals played a less important role in the pre-Columbian societies of Mesoamerica than they did in Eurasia is that there were simply fewer animal species in Mesoamerica that could be easily and successfully domesticated. Animals such as deer, which was one of the commonest large mammals in pre-Columbian Mesoamerica, are not easily domesticated. If deer are constrained in a pen or herded too closely together, they will not feed or breed readily (Clutton-Brock 1981: 15).

The situation is very different in highland South America. The indigenous population of South America had a number of small domesticated animals, including guinea pigs, muscovy ducks, and dogs. While we are familiar with guinea pigs as popular pets and laboratory animals, in pre-Columbian times Peruvians raised guinea pigs for meat and also used them in religions ceremonies (Clutton-Brock 1981: 152). In addition to these small domestic animals, two large mammals—the llama and the alpaca—were domesticated in the South American highlands. The llama (*Lama glama*) and the alpaca (*Lama pacos*) are members of the camel family **(Figure 19.4)**. The larger llama was a multipurpose animal used for meat and for bearing burdens, while the smaller alpaca was raised primarily for its fine wool. Both animals may have been domesticated from the guanaco (*Lama guanacoe*), a wild member of the camel family that today is distributed from the Andes highlands to the Patagonian plains. A smaller wild camelid, the vicuña (*Vicugna vicugna*), was widely hunted in prehistory.

Archaeological sites from the Peruvian Andes document the transition from the intensive hunting of wild camelids (members of

Figure 19.4

The alpaca and the llama, two members of the camel family that were domesticated in highland South America in prehistoric times. The smaller alpaca was kept primarily for its wool. The larger llama was a multipurpose animal that was raised for both meat and transport.

the camel family) through the appearance of domesticated forms of those animals (Wheeler 1984). The domestication of these animals appears to have taken place in the **puna** zone, the highest area in the Andes that is fit for human habitation. The puna lies at an elevation between 3,900 and 5,000 meters (13,000 to 16,000 ft.) above sea level. Although the environment is somewhat of a mosaic, the abundant grasslands would have supported sizable wild camelid populations in prehistory. The evidence from the **Telarmarchay** rock shelter, a deeply stratified site located 170 kilometers (105 mi.) northeast of Lima, Peru, at an elevation of 4,420 meters (14,500 ft.) above sea level, can be used to trace the development from hunting to camelid herding. The Telarmarchay evidence indicates that between 7000 and 5200 b.c., hunters in the puna hunted both wild camelids and deer. Between 5,200 and 4,000 b.c., hunters began to specialize in the hunting of guanacoes and vicuña, and early domestic camelids first appear by 4000 to 3500 b.c. Fully domestic animals appear after 3500 b.c. The evidence indicates that camelid herding has a great antiquity in the Peruvian Andes. The cold, dry puna region is near the absolute limits for crop growth; the area experiences 330 nights of frost per year, and rainfall can be irregular. Grazing animals are the most reliable food resources in the region because they can convert the dry grasses of the puna into stored protein, which can be used for human consumption (Wheeler 1984: 397). In general, domesticated animals played a greater role in early farming economies in the Old World, while a rich variety of domestic plants formed the basis of early agricultural economies in the Americas. However, in areas such as the highland South American puna, where domestic and wild plant resources were limited, domestic animals came to play a central role in early food-producing economies.

Other Centers of Plant Domestication in the Americas

As noted in Chapter 16, Archaic hunter-gatherers in eastern North America domesticated a number of plants, including sumpweed (*Iva annua*), sunflowers (*Helianthus*

annus), and goosefoot (*Chenopodium berlandieri*), beginning as early as 2050 to 1050 b.c. (Smith 1992). The lowland tropical forest region of eastern South America is another center of early plant domestication in the New World. One of the most important early domesticates from the tropical forest regions is manioc (*Manihot escuelenta*), a root crop whose edible, fleshy rootstocks yield a nutritious starch. Unfortunately, plant remains are often poorly preserved in the tropical lowland regions in South America. While the initial domestication of manioc and other tropical root crops may have taken place by the late third millennium b.c. (Pearsall 1992: 194), archaeological remains of domesticated manioc from the tropical lowlands have been recovered only from much more recent contexts.

Agricultural Hearths: Similarities and Differences

The archaeological evidence from both the New World and the Old World indicates that plant and animal domestication took place in a number of different localities throughout the world during the early to middle Holocene period. What can the similarities and differences between the various centers of plant and animal domestication tell us about the process or processes by which foragers became farmers?

An important similarity is that many of the early plant domesticates were starchy cereals and root crops: maize in Mesoamerica, wheat and barley in the Near East, rice in Southeast Asia, potatoes in highland South America, manioc in tropical South America, and sorghum in sub-Saharan Africa. Many hunter-gatherer populations may have had only limited access to starchy foods. Studies of exchanges between foraging and farming populations have shown that "a recurring theme is the exchange of wild protein obtained by hunting populations for domestic carbohydrates produced by farmers" (Bogucki 1988: 107). Early domesticated root and cereal crops would have provided easily storable sources of high-quality carbohydrates.

An important difference is seen in the timing of the beginnings of plant and animal domestication. While the initial domestication of wheat and barley in the Near East began at least 10,000 years ago, the earliest domesticated plants in North America do not appear until about 4,000 years ago. Plant domestication appears to have begun in different places at various times throughout the early and middle Holocene. It is therefore very difficult to view the beginnings of farming as an adaptive response to the worldwide climatic changes that took place at the end of the Pleistocene. While the beginning of farming in the Near East does coincide with marked vegetational changes that occurred in that region during the final Pleistocene, this pattern is not seen in Mesoamerica. The Tehuacán Valley sequence indicates that foragers in Mesoamerica responded to the disappearance of large game animals at the end of the Pleistocene by shifting to the hunting of smaller game and the collection of a range of wild plant resources. Only later, during the El Riego phase, did Mesoamerican foragers begin to experiment with plant cultivation.

Similarly, the Mesoamerican data suggest that agriculture was not simply an adaptive response to worldwide population growth. While sedentism (and possibly population growth) clearly preceded the beginnings of farming in the Near East, the same cannot be said for Mesoamerica. In highland southern Mexico the beginnings of plant domestication clearly preceded sedentary villages. Permanent villages do not appear until well after the beginnings of farming. Moreover, population levels in highland Mesoamerica were low throughout the period of initial plant cultivation.

 ## Conclusion

With the exception of the domestication of the llama and alpaca in South America, domesticated animals were far less important than plant crops in the economies of the Americas. Maize, along with beans and squash, formed the basis of the Native American diet, and maize cultivation was crucial for the development of the New World complex societies.

Cereal agriculture, centered on maize, appears in Mesoamerica about 4,000 years ago, 6,000 years after the beginning of agriculture in the Near East. The beginnings of agriculture in areas as diverse as tropical lowland South America, southeast Asia, the ancient Near East, and highland southern Mexico cannot be explained by a single prime mover, such as climatic change or population growth. The environmental and cultural circumstances that led foragers to experiment with farming are probably unique to each region. Detailed archaeological records of early plant cultivation are available only from the Near East and Mesoamerica. Unfortunately, we cannot answer the question of why farming began until more archaeological data are recovered from areas of the world such as sub-Saharan Africa, southeast Asia, and tropical lowland South America. It is only through the comparative study of agricultural origins in different areas of the world that archaeologists can understand the processes of plant and animal domestication.

Glossary

Guilá Naquitz. A small campsite located in the Valley of Oaxaca in southern Mexico. The site yielded the remains of early domesticated squash and gourds, as well as evidence for a pattern of seasonal use of a range of wild plant and animal resources.

Mesoamerica. The geographic region that includes southern Mexico and the adjacent regions of central America, including Guatemala, El Salvador, Belize, and the western portions of Honduras, Nicaragua, and Costa Rica. The area lies between 10° and 22° north latitude and includes both cool tropical highlands and warm tropical lowlands (along the Yucatán and the Gulf of Mexico).

Puna. The highest environmental zone in the Andes that is suitable for human habitation. The puna lies between 3,900 and 5,000 meters (13,000 to 16,000 ft.) above sea level, and its rich grasslands would have supported abundant wild camelid populations in prehistory.

Tehuacán Valley project. An archaeological project, conducted between 1961 and 1965 in Puebla, Mexico, designed to study the domestication of maize and other plants in the highlands of southern Mexico. Over 40,000 plant remains were recovered from sites that range in date from the late Pleistocene to the era of the Spanish conquest of Mexico.

Telarmarchay. A deeply stratified site located 170 kilometers (105 mi.) northeast of Lima that provided evidence for the transition from the intensive hunting of wild camelids to their domestication at about 3500 b.c.

Teosinte. A wild grass (*Zea mexicana*) that is closely related to maize and appears to have been its wild ancestor.

Further Reading

Cowan, C. W., and P. J. Watson, eds.
    1992. *The Origins of Agriculture: An International Perspective.* Washington, DC: Smithsonian Institution Press.
    This volume presents a series of essays on the origins of agriculture in various parts of the Old World and the Americas. The coverage of agricultural origins in the Americas is particularly strong. Several essays on agricultural origins in different regions of the Americas (including North America, Mesoamerica, and South America) are included.

Other Bibliography

Bogucki, P. I.
    1988. *Forest Farmers and Stockherders: Early Agriculture and Its Consequences in North-Central Europe.* Cambridge: Cambridge University Press.

Clutton-Brock, J.
    1981. *Domesticated Animals from Early Times.* Austin: University of Texas Press.

Cohen, M. N.
    1977. *The Food Crisis in Prehistory: Overpopulation and the Origins of Agriculture.* New Haven, CT: Yale University Press.

Doebley, John
    1990. Molecular Evidence and the Evolution of Maize. In *New Perspectives on the Origin and Evolution of New World Domesticated Plants,* edited by P. K. Bretting, pp. 6–28. *Economic Botany* 44 (supplement).

Flannery, K. V.
    1968. Archaeological Systems Theory and Early Mesoamerica. In *Anthropological Archaeology in the Americas,* edited by B. Meggers, pp. 67–87. Washington, DC: Anthropological Society of Washington.
    1986. *Guilá Naquitz: Archaic Foraging and Early Agriculture in Oaxaca, Mexico.* Orlando, FL: Academic Press.

Fritz, G. J.
    1994. Are the First American Farmers Getting Younger? *Current Anthropology* 35 (3): 305–309.

Gebauer, A. B., and T. D. Price, eds.
    1992a. *Transitions to Agriculture in Prehistory.* Madison, WI: Prehistory Press, Monographs in World Prehistory No. 4.
    1992b. Foragers to Farmers: An Introduction. In *Transitions to Agriculture in Prehistory,* edited by A. B. Gebauer and T. D. Price, pp. 1–10. Madison, WI: Prehistory Press, Monographs in World Prehistory No. 4.

Hardy, Karen
    1996. The Preceramic Sequence from the Tehuacán Valley: A Reevaluation. *Current Anthropology* 37 (4): 700–716.

Long, Austin, Bruce F. Benz, J. Donahue, A. Jull, and L. Toolin
    1989. First Direct AMS Dates on Early Maize from Tehuacan, Mexico. *Radiocarbon* 31: 1035–1040.

MacNeish, R. S.
    1967. A Summary of the Subsistence. In *The Prehistory of the Tehuacán Valley, vol. 1: Environment and Subsistence,* edited by D. Byers, pp. 290–309. Austin: University of Texas Press.
    1991. *The Origin of Agriculture and Settled Life.* Norman: University of Oklahoma Press.

Mangelsdorf, P. C.
    1974. *Corn: Its Origin, Evolution and Improvement.* Cambridge, MA: Harvard University Press
    1986. The Origin of Corn. *Scientific American* 254 (2): 72–79.

McClung de Tapia, Emily
    1992. The Origins of Agriculture in Mesoamerica and Central America. In *The Origins of Agriculture: An International Perspective,* edited by C. W. Cowan and P. J. Watson, pp. 143–171. Washington, DC: Smithsonian Institution Press.

Pearsall, D. M.
    1992. The Origins of Plant Cultivation in South America. In *The Origins of Agriculture: An International Perspective,* edited by C. W. Cowan and P. J. Watson, pp. 173–205. Washington, DC: Smithsonian Institution Press.

Price, T. D., and A. B. Gebauer
    1995. *Last Hunters—First Farmers: New Perspectives on the Prehistoric Transition to Agriculture.* Santa Fe, NM: School of American Research.

Smith, B. D.

1992. Prehistoric Plant Husbandry in Eastern North America. In *The Origins of Agriculture: An International Perspective*, edited by C. W. Cowan and P. J. Watson, pp. 101–119. Washington, DC: Smithsonian Institution Press.

1994. *The Emergence of Agriculture.* New York: Scientific American Library.

Wheeler, Jane C.

1984. On the Origin and Early Development of Camelid Pastoralism in the Andes. In *Animals and Archaeology 3: Early Herders and Their Flocks*, edited by J. Clutton-Brock and C. Grigson, pp. 395–410. Oxford: British Archaeological Reports, International Series 202.

Chapter 20

The Consequences of the Agricultural Revolution

Introduction

Archaeologists have always been interested in origins—the origins of stone tools, the origins of modern humans, and the origins of agriculture. However, the consequences of a biological or technological change are just as important as its origins. In the past 10,000 years, our world has changed from a planet inhabited by small populations of human hunters and gatherers to one peopled by agriculturalists and city dwellers. We live with the consequences of the agricultural revolution—including overpopulation and epidemic diseases—every day of our lives. In this chapter we will examine the consequences of the agricultural revolution for early farming populations in the Old World.

Sedentism and Population Growth

While archaeologists have debated the role that population growth played in encouraging the initial adoption of agriculture in the Near East and elsewhere, there is no question that adoption of agriculture led to significant population increases. Several factors underlie such population growth. First, farmers are generally less mobile than hunter-gatherers. Highly mobile hunter-gatherer populations often space the birth of their children as much as five years apart so that women do not have to carry more than one child at a time from place to place. Although farmers need not live in the same location all year around, they must stay in one location during the growing season to plant, tend, and harvest their crops. Activities that require greater mobility, such as hunting, are scheduled around the growing season. Since agriculture generally leads to decreased mobility, birth spacing may also decrease.

In addition, the economic role of children changes when foragers adopt agriculture. Small children are unable to participate in lengthy hunting or gathering expeditions because they do not have the stamina to walk great distances. Children may be economic assets, however, for early farmers. Children can help in planting, weeding, and harvesting, and can also help tend domestic animals—tasks that do not require great physical strength or stamina. Larger families may be advantageous to early farmers, since additional children can mean more available labor at planting and harvesting time.

Finally, the availability of carbohydrates may encourage early weaning. Mobile hunter-gatherers may nurse children for as long as four to five years. One reason for this long period of nursing may be that many hunter-gatherer populations lack the starchy carbohydrates that often serve as early foods for babies. The cultivation of cereals and other starchy food would have allowed for earlier weaning. Since lactation can suppress ovulation, and thereby limit a woman's fertility, earlier weaning may lead to closer birth spacing and population growth.

Studies of human skeletal populations (see Chapter 27) in the lower Illinois River region of the American Midwest have shown that the birthrate rose significantly during the period when maize agriculture was adopted and intensified. While a number of factors may have played a role in this increase, "the shift to a high starch diet . . . would have facilitated earlier weaning and decreased birth interval because of the availability of soft, easily digestible foods" (Larsen 1995: 198).

The archaeological record for early farming villages in the Near East also points to population growth and increased residential stability. While many of the earliest Neolithic sites in the southern Levant are small villages like Netiv Hagdud (Chapter 18) in the West Bank, the site of **Jericho** seems to represent a far more substantial settlement. Jericho, a

Figure 20.1

Map of Europe and the eastern Mediterranean showing the location of the sites mentioned in this chapter.

deeply stratified tell (city-mound) site, is also located in the West Bank **(Figure 20.1)**. The ancient city of Jericho rises to a height of 21 meters (70 ft.) and covers an area of 4 hectares (10 acres). The tell is located at a permanent spring, Ain es Sultan, which has made it a focal point for human settlement since late Pleistocene times. The early Neolithic levels of the site are deeply buried under many meters of occupation debris because the ancient city of Jericho was intensively occupied during biblical times. Therefore only a small portion of the early Neolithic settlement of Jeri-

cho was excavated when Kathleen Kenyon (1957) carried out a major program of excavation at the site in the 1950s. Kenyon's excavations revealed an early Neolithic settlement surrounded by a city wall that was 2 meters (6 ft.) thick and survived to a height of 4 meters (13 ft.). A large stone tower **(Figure 20.2)** was built against the inside of the wall, surviving to a height of 10 meters (33 ft.). The wall and tower date to the earliest part of the Neolithic of Palestine, often termed the **Pre-Pottery Neolithic A (PPNA);** they appear to have been constructed about 10,000 years ago.

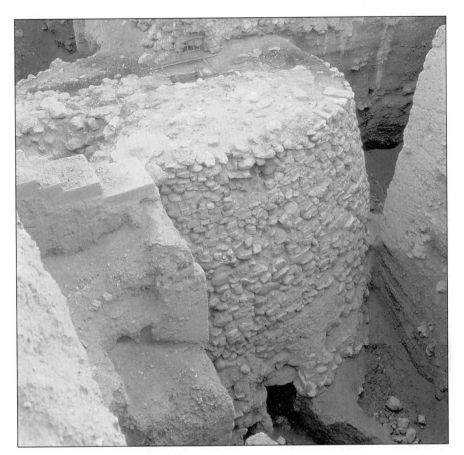

Figure 20.2
Early Neolithic (PPNA) tower from the site of Jericho, West Bank.

The tower and town wall were probably part of a much more extensive system of fortifications. Why would an early farming village need such sizable defenses? An obvious possibility is that they were designed to protect and control access to the Ain es Sultan spring. As Kenyon (1970: 39) notes, "Only in areas within reach of the waters of some permanent source such as that of the spring of Ain es Sultan at Jericho can the rich soil of the [Jordan] valley be made truly productive." In a broader sense, the fortifications may reflect changing relationships between people and the landscape. Mobile hunter-gatherers may exercise the rights to use a particular land area in a particular season, but they generally do not own land. When farmers establish permanent, year-round settlements, they may also claim ownership of the territory surrounding their settlement, including its natural resources. The Jericho walls may reflect this changing concept of land ownership.

The PPNA settlement at Jericho was replaced by a slightly later farming community that built rectangular mud-brick houses. This second phase of the aceramic Neolithic in the southern Levant is often referred to as the **Pre-Pottery Neolithic B,** or **PPNB.** One of the most striking features of the PPNB settlement at Jericho is the presence of a series of plastered human skulls whose eyes had been replaced by shells **(Figure 20.3)**. The plastered features give the skulls a very naturalistic appearance, almost suggesting portraits. The special treatment of the human skull appears to be a feature of PPNB burial rites. Similar plastered skulls were recovered from the important PPNB site of 'Ain Ghazal in Jordan.

Figure 20.3

Plastered human skull from the PPNB levels at Jericho, West Bank.

Case Study
'Ain Ghazal, Jordan

'Ain Ghazal, located on the outskirts of the Jordanian capital of Amman, is one of the largest early farming settlements in the southern Levant. This early farming village was excavated over six seasons between 1982 and 1989 (Rollefson et al. 1992) and again in the early 1990s. The site covers 12 to 13 hectares (30 to 32.5 acres) and has yielded an unbroken sequence of early Neolithic occupation from 7250 to 5000 b.c. Only about 700 square meters (840 sq. yd. or 0.5 percent) of the site could be excavated. While most of the excavated remains from 'Ain Ghazal date to the PPNB (7250 to 6000 b.c.), the site continued to be occupied throughout the sixth millennium.

The inhabitants of 'Ain Ghazal made their living by farming. Plant remains indicate that they grew wheat, barley, peas, lentils, and chickpeas. Goats were domesticated by 6500 b.c., and by the beginning of the sixth millennium the inhabitants of 'Ain Ghazal raised goats, pigs, cattle, and possibly sheep.

The houses at 'Ain Ghazal were built with stone walls and lime plaster floors. During the Middle PPNB (7200 to 6500 b.c.), the rooms were generally 5 meters by 5 meters (16 by 16 ft.) in floor area, with circular hearths built into the centers of the floors. Over 100 human burials were recovered during the 'Ain Ghazal excavations. During the PPNB period, most of the adolescents and adults were buried underneath the floors of the houses or under the courtyards. The heads were removed from the bodies some time after the initial burial. Burial underneath the floors of buildings is a continuation of a tradition that was originally established during the Natufian period at sites such as Mallaha/Eynan. In 1983 a cache of four skulls was found at 'Ain Ghazal, two of which had been plastered. The parallel to the plastered skulls from Jericho is striking and suggests that PPNB burial practices may have been quite standardized, at least throughout parts of the southern Levant. The meaning of these plastered skulls is far more difficult to reconstruct. Clearly, they reflect elaborate rituals surrounding death, but whether they reflect ancestor cults, clan rituals, or something entirely different is difficult to determine on the basis of the archaeological evidence alone.

While the majority of the adults and adolescents were buried under floors and courtyards, about one-third of the adolescent and adult burials were found in trash deposits with their skulls attached. The differences in burial practice may reflect some broader social differences, perhaps indicating the beginnings of real social inequality. Infants were also discarded in the trash. Infant mortality appears to have been high; about one-third of children died during infancy. In addition, many adolescent and adult teeth showed defects in the enamel, which can result from poor childhood health, inadequate nutrition, congenital or developmental abnormalities, or sustained stress (Rollefson et al. 1992: 463). This evidence indicates that life in an early farming village in the Near East may have been rather hard. One of the consequences of agriculture may well have been an increased disease load. With the establishment of permanent villages, early farmers could no longer simply pack up and walk away from their disease-ridden refuse. Moreover, the larger and denser populations in these villages may have facilitated the spread of infectious diseases.

Increased Disease Load and Early Farming Communities

The evidence that the beginning of farming may have been associated with poorer health and an increased disease load is not limited to 'Ain Ghazal. Studies of human skeletons from early farming communities in North America, South America, and Europe reveal similar patterns. As Clark Larsen, an anthropologist who has studied biological changes associated with the beginnings of agriculture, notes:

> Reduced population mobility and increased aggregation provide conditions that promote the spread and maintenance of infections and parasitic diseases and the increase in pathogen load in humans. That is, closer, more crowded living conditions facilitate greater physical contact between members of a settlement, and permanent occupation can result in decreased sanitation and hygiene. (1995: 198)

In short, the establishment of sedentary farming communities may have produced larger but less healthy human communities.

Population Growth and the Expansion of Agricultural Settlements

As noted, one of the consequences of the establishment of permanent agricultural villages was population growth. Early farming villages such as 'Ain Ghazal and Jericho were clearly larger than the hunter-gatherer settlements that preceded them in the Near East. One of the consequences of this population growth was the spread of agricultural settlements outside the southern Levant, where the transition to wheat and barley agriculture first took place. Agricultural settlements initially expanded into areas that were similar to the southern Levant in both climate and topography, such as Anatolia and Greece. The regions surrounding the Mediterranean all share a Mediterranean climate characterized by hot, dry summers and cooler, wetter winters. From the eastern Mediterranean, agricultural settlements then expanded into the Balkans and eventually into central Europe. These areas differ in both climate and vegetation from the southern Levant, and agricultural practices had to be adjusted accordingly. In this chapter we will trace the spread of agricultural technology from the southern Levant to Anatolia and Greece, and then to southeastern and central Europe.

Early Farming Villages in Turkey

As noted in Chapter 18, the earliest farming villages in the eastern Mediterranean are located in an arc that extends from the southern Jordan Valley northward into Syria. Early farming villages are also known from eastern Turkey, and the question of whether these villages represent a movement of early farming populations northward from the Levant or the adoption of agricultural technologies by indigenous foraging populations remains an open one. Until recently, little was known about the late Pleistocene settlement of eastern Anatolia. However, new research in the region has revealed a number of late Paleolithic sites that are broadly contemporary with the Natufian settlements in the southern Levant. In particular, the recently excavated site of Hallan Çemi in eastern Turkey (Rosenberg et al. 1998) revealed a small village that relied on the gathering of nuts and pulses, hunting, and possibly pig husbandry during the ninth millennium b.c. (see Chapter 18).

Some early farming villages in eastern Turkey appear to have close ties with PPNB populations of the southern Levant. The site of **Gritille** (Voigt 1985), located on the Euphrates River in southeastern Anatolia, is an early Neolithic settlement dated between 7000 and 5500 b.c. Gritille produced a chipped stone industry that shows broad similarities to the Levantine PPNB. The site also yielded a number of small clay figurines of humans and animals that are quite similar to figurines recovered from 'Ain Ghazal in Jordan. The Gritille economy, which was based on emmer wheat, barley, legumes, and domesticated animals, including sheep and goats, also shows broad similarities to PPNB sites farther south. Gritille may be an example of the gradual movement of farming communities northward along the Euphrates (Voigt 1985: 21).

The data from **Çayönü,** an early farming village located northeast of Gritille in Turkey, present a somewhat different picture. The site, which was occupied between about 7500 and 6500 b.c., yielded the remains of early domesticated einkorn wheat. This cereal, whose wild ancestor is widely distributed in Anatolia, was originally thought to have been introduced to Çayönü from western Turkey (Van Zeist 1972). Recent microbiological studies, however, have shown the domesticated einkorn is most closely related to the wild einkorn found in southeastern Turkey (Heun et al. 1997). The domestication of einkorn appears to be completely independent of the domestication of emmer wheat and barley in the southern Levant. These data suggest that Anatolia may have been an independent center of plant domestication. Thus, the beginnings of farming in Turkey involved at least two processes. Indigenous hunting and gathering populations may have independently domesticated einkorn and pigs, while early farming populations may also have moved into Turkey from the south bringing Levantine domesticates, including emmer and barley, with them.

Early Farmers in Greece and Southeast Europe

Greece is the region of Europe that is geographically closest to the Near East, and it is not surprising to find that Greece was home to the earliest farming communities in Europe. The Mediterranean climate of Greece, with its hot, dry summers and cooler, moister winters, also resembles the climate of the Levantine regions of the Near East. The earliest farming villages in Greece date to about 6000 b.c. At sites such as **Nea Nikomedeia** in Greek Macedonia (Rodden 1962, 1965) farmers inhabited small, single-roomed, square houses and raised wheat, barley, sheep, goats, cattle, and pigs.

The question of how farming was introduced to Europe has been a subject of intensive debate for at least 50 years (see Dennell 1992 for a recent review of the issue). Most archaeologists would argue that agriculture was introduced to Europe by immigrant farmers who brought domesticated emmer wheat, barley, sheep, and goats with them (but see Whittle 1996 for an alternative model). Several lines of evidence support this view. First, the wild ancestors of sheep, goats, emmer wheat, and barley were not generally available in southeast Europe, making local domestication impossible. Second, the earliest farming villages in Turkey, Syria, and the southern Levant are considerably earlier than the earliest agricultural settlements in southeast Europe (Whittle 1985: 54). Finally, the pre-Neolithic population of Greece appears to have been very low; the number of early Neolithic sites is much higher, suggesting significant population increase during the early Neolithic period.

Similar early Neolithic sites are known from southern and central Bulgaria dating to the early sixth millennium b.c. At the site of **Karanovo (Figure 20.4)** small, square houses—about 7 by 7 meters (23 by 23 ft.) in floor area—were framed with poles and plastered with mud. The earliest farming village at Karanovo would have contained about 60 of these small houses, sheltering about 300 people. By the end of the sixth millennium b.c., successful farming settlements had been established throughout Greece and the Balkans. However, farming settlements were not established in temperate Europe until considerably later.

Figure 20.4

Plans of Neolithic mud-walled and wattled houses from Karanovo, Bulgaria.

Early Farmers in Temperate Europe

The climate of temperate Europe, the area of Europe north of the Mediterranean zone, is characterized by cool, wet summers and cold winters. Systems of agriculture and animal husbandry that were developed in the Mediterranean regions of the Near East and Europe had to be adapted to the more rigorous climate of central and northern Europe. For example, Near Eastern cereals are planted in the fall and harvested in the late spring and early summer. In temperate Europe, cereals are planted in either the fall or

spring. Cereal crops grow throughout the spring and summer, and the harvest takes place in the late summer to early fall.

It was not until about 4500 b.c. that farming villages first appeared in central Europe. These early farming settlements are found in the valleys and tributaries of the Danube and Rhine Rivers in a region known as the **loess belt.** This region lay between the Scandinavian and Alpine ice sheets during the height of the last glaciation. The fine soils of this region were deposited by wind during the late Pleistocene. Since the loess belt is relatively dry and uniform in vegetation, it was not a particularly attractive area for settlement by Mesolithic hunter-gatherers (see Chapter 15). However, these light and easily tilled soils would have been ideal for early cultivators.

The earliest farming settlements in central Europe are part of the **Linear Pottery culture,** named for its distinctive pottery, which was decorated with curvilinear designs **(Figure 20.5)**. Linear pottery settlements spread rapidly across the loess belt of central and western Europe between 4500 and 4000 b.c. The Linear Pottery houses are long, rectangular structures built of large posts **(Figure 20.6)**. The walls would have been filled in with wickerwork and plastered with mud. The farming economy of the Linear Pottery culture was based on the cultivation of cereals, particularly emmer wheat, and on stock rearing. Agricultural plots were located in fertile riverine environments that could have produced sustained crop yields for many decades (Bogucki 1988: 82).

At a somewhat later date, farming settlements expanded into the North European Plain, a far more diverse environment, with a variety of soil types, as well as lakes, bogs, and streams. Pioneering agricultural villages were established in this area between 3900 and 3300 b.c. A well-documented example of an early farming village in the North European Plain is the site of **Brześć Kujawski** (Bogucki and Grygiel 1983, 1993), located northwest of Warsaw in Poland **(Figure 20.7)**. The settlement is composed of a series of trapezoidal longhouses whose narrow ends faced into the prevailing winds. The farmers

Figure 20.5

A Linear Pottery vessel from the site of Eitzum in Germany.

Figure 20.6

Idealized plan of a Linear Pottery house. Such a house can be up to 50 meters (165 ft.) in length.

 Postholes

 Pit from which clay for walls was dug

at Brześć Kujawski raised emmer wheat and may have supplemented their diets through plant collection. They also herded cattle, sheep, goats, and pigs, but domestic animals were supplemented by fishing, hunting, fowling, and shellfish collecting. Hunting was generally carried out in the winter when agricultural activities were less demanding. The Brześć Kujawski economy was highly diversified, especially when compared with the Linear Pottery economies, which were based primarily on cattle rearing and cereal cultivation. This difference reflects the greater environmental diversity of the North European Plain and, possibly, interaction with native Mesolithic populations.

The initial farming settlements in both the loess belt and North European Plain were most likely established by colonists who were not native to the area. The case for colonization is based on the marked differences in settlement patterns, subsistence systems, and material culture (e.g., pottery) between the indigenous Mesolithic populations of central Europe (Chapter 15) and these early agriculturalists (Bogucki 1988: 50). While the homogeneous loess belt supported very limited Mesolithic settlement, the North European Plain supported a much larger indigenous hunter-gatherer population. Early farming populations must have come in regular con-

Figure 20.7

Plan of the early Neolithic settlement of Brześć Kujawski, Poland.

tact with native hunter-gatherers in central Europe, although the nature of those contacts is not well understood. Did the Mesolithic hunter-gatherers provide the farmers with meat and labor in exchange for cereals (Bogucki 1988: 108), or were the contacts of a more hostile nature? Eventually, these foragers adopted agricultural technology, although the process was by no means a simple and straightforward one. Initially, foragers may have incorporated some domestic animals or crops into a hunting and gathering way of life. The increasing sedentism of many late Mesolithic populations in Europe may have facilitated the adoption of domestic plants and animals. By the mid-third millennium b.c., agriculture and stock raising had replaced hunting and gathering throughout most of temperate Europe.

The important lesson to be learned from the study of early farming communities in Europe is that the spread of agriculture was a complex process; it was not simply the result of population growth. The spread of agriculture outside the southern Levant involved several changes, including population growth and colonization, the adoption of agricultural practices by indigenous foraging communities, technological changes, and indigenous domestication of crops such as einkorn.

The Development of New Technologies and Crafts

The adoption of agriculture led to several important changes in technology and craft production. Among the most important were changes in the technology of stone tool manufacture. Before the beginnings of farming, stone tools were manufactured primarily by flaking. Although today archaeologists recognize that ground stone objects actually were first made much earlier, with the beginnings of the Neolithic we see the widespread use of stone tools that are shaped by grinding and polishing. The most important of these new

Figure 20.8
Neolithic polished stone axes.

tools were ground and polished stone axes **(Figure 20.8)**. The manufacture of these stone tools was a multistage process. A stone nodule was initially flaked into the approximate shape of an axe. The blank was then ground to shape by rubbing it against a gritty rock such as sandstone. The final polish was provided by rubbing the axe with a more finely grained stone, using sand as an abrasive (Bordaz 1970: 99). These tools were particularly useful for woodworking and for forest clearance because they were able to penetrate wood more deeply than a flaked stone axe. They were also more durable, and the edges of these ground and polished stone tools were also less likely to chip or break.

An equally important technological innovation was the development of pottery. While the world's earliest pottery was manufactured by late Pleistocene hunter-gatherers in Japan, the widespread use of pottery containers is associated with early agricultural societies in both the Old World and the Americas. The earliest farmers in the Near East did not manufacture pottery, and the period between roughly 8000 and 6000 b.c. is often referred to as the aceramic or prepottery Neolithic. However, after 6000 b.c. pottery was widely manufactured throughout the Near East. Its spread through Europe coincides with the introduction and spread of agriculture throughout the continent. The Archaeology in Practice box describes how pottery is manufactured, how it is used, and why it is of particular interest to archaeologists studying ancient societies.

The Development of Pottery Technology

Pottery is made of clay, a fine-grained material that is plastic when wet but becomes hard and brittle when heated. Clay's plasticity when wet means that it can be pressed into almost any shape, from bowls and jugs to figurines and statues. As the clay dries, it loses its plasticity. When the clay is heated to a high temperature in either a bonfire or a kiln, it undergoes an irreversible chemical change, producing a hard and durable material. The physical properties of clay make it an ideal material for the construction of storage jars and other containers. The temperature at which pottery is fired greatly influences the nature of the finished product. Low-fired ceramics are generally soft and porous; highly fired ceramics tend to be very hard and impermeable.

Storage vessels would have been especially useful to early farmers. Farmers rely on a small number of staple crops, such as barley or maize, which are harvested once a year. The crops must be stored so that they can be used throughout the year as food. Additionally, a portion of the harvest must be stored to serve as seed for the following year's crop. Large pottery storage jars can protect stored crops from rodents and other pests. Pottery also served a variety of other purposes in past societies, as cooking pots and serving bowls and, of course, as dinnerware.

Even before the appearance of the first pottery vessels, there is evidence that early farmers were beginning to work with clay and to investigate its unique properties. For example, the pre-pottery levels at the site of 'Ain Ghazal in Jordan have produced a variety of human and animal figures made of both fired and unfired clay (Figure 20.9).

Pottery's hardness and durability mean that it can survive for millennia. It is therefore one of the most common classes of artifacts recovered from archaeological sites. Archaeologists examine several different criteria in order to analyze and classify pottery (Figure 20.10). The first criterion is the nature of the clay that is used to manufacture the pottery vessel. The clays used to make pottery can differ in structure, chemical composition, and impurities. In the manufacture of a pottery vessel, clays are usually combined with nonplastic materials known as **temper.** Temper counteracts shrinkage and reduces the risk of cracking as a clay vessel dries. A wide variety of nonclay materials can be used for temper, including sand, shell, and straw.

Pottery can be manufactured in a number of different ways. Pottery can be thrown on a potter's wheel, or a variety of different hand-building techniques can be used. The simplest technique is to form the vessel by hand from a lump of clay, much the way a first-grader makes a clay bowl. Vessels can also be hand-built from coils of clay that are

Figure 20.9

Animal figurines made of clay from the pre-pottery Neolithic levels at 'Ain Ghazal, near Amman, Jordan.

The fabric of a vessel may be described in terms of type of clay, inclusions or temper, method of manufacture, firing method, hardness, and color

RIM

NECK

HANDLE

BODY

BASE

Vessel terminology. The shape of a ceramic vessel may be described in terms of many different forms of rim, neck, body, and base, plus attachments such as handles

INCISING AND CORD-MARKING

APPLIED SLIP

MOLDED DECORATION

POLYCHROME UNDERGLAZE PAINTING

A few of the vast variety of ceramic surface treatments

pressed together or from large, flat slabs. In addition, pottery can be shaped in a mold.

Pottery vessels can be produced in an almost endless variety of forms—including bowls, cups, jars, plates, and pitchers. The base of the pot can be flat or rounded; the rim can be shaped in a number of different ways; and various handles or decorations can be attached. The outer and inner surfaces of the vessel may be either left plain or decorated. The possibilities for decoration are almost limitless. Early pottery was frequently decorated with surface incisions; or fingertips, a shell, or a cord-wrapped paddle might have been used to press patterns into the wet clay surface. The clay surface may be **burnished,** rubbed with a small stone or other hard object after firing to make the surface shinier. Burnishing also closes the pores in the clay vessel, thus decreasing its porosity. Before firing, the vessel may be covered with a **slip,** a thin wash of clay and water, or painted with various earth pigments. Sometimes a combination of decorative techniques was used. Later pottery is frequently covered with a **glaze,** a material that melts during firing to produce a glasslike surface.

The multitude of combinations of pottery fabric, temper, firing methods, surface decorations, and glazes make the pottery produced by any culture or period unique. Archaeologists use these characteristics to classify pottery, permitting them to trace the changes in pottery technology and style within an archaeological culture. Studies have shown that the shapes of pottery vessels, their forms of decoration, and even the ways they are manufactured change through time. Pottery, therefore, is a particularly useful indicator of relative chronology. The distribution of certain distinctive pottery types over wide geographical areas provides archaeologists with a clear indication that the sites containing the pottery were contemporaneous and that cultural contact existed among them.

Trade and Exchange in Early Farming Communities

Many early archaeologists viewed Neolithic villages as isolated and self-sufficient, producing everything they needed to sustain life. Subsequent research, however, has shown that Neolithic communities almost always engaged in trade and exchange, including the long-distance distribution of a variety of functional and decorative items. For example, Mediterranean seashells are sometimes found as grave goods in early Neolithic cemeteries in central Europe (Bogucki 1988: 126). High-quality stone for the manufacture of stone tools was also exchanged throughout both Europe and the Near East. In particular, small quantities of obsidian (a volcanic glass that can be obtained from a limited number of sources in the eastern Mediterranean) are often recovered from early Neolithic sites in the Near East. One source of this obsidian is located in south central Turkey, near the important early Neolithic site of **Çatal Höyük.** As we shall see below, the excavation of this important Neolithic site has also shed new light on the importance of ritual and religion in early farming societies.

Case Study
Çatal Höyük and the Study of Neolithic Ritual Life

The site of Çatal Höyük is located in the Konya lowlands in the southern part of Central Anatolia. The Neolithic remains at the site cover an area of about 13 hectares (32 acres) (Mellaart 1975: 98), making Çatal Höyük one of the largest Neolithic sites in the ancient Near East. The initial excavations at Çatal Höyük took place between 1961 and 1963 under the direction of the British archaeologist James Mellaart (1967; 1975). Mellaart's excavations revealed a Neolithic settlement constructed of small (25 square meters [270 sq. ft.]), square dwellings with flat roofs. The houses were built of sun-dried

mud bricks and were entered through the roof by means of a ladder **(Figure 20.11)**. Each house had its own walls, but the houses were built up against one another **(Figure 20.12)**. The size of the site and the density of the housing indicate that Çatal Höyük

Figure 20.11

Reconstruction of a small, square dwelling from Çatal Höyük.

S - Shrine

Figure 20.12

Plan of Çatal Höyük (southeast quarter, Level VIB) showing houses built up against one another.

Figure 20.13

Two leopards depicted in clay and plaster relief from the north wall of shrine VII.44 at Çatal Höyük.

was home to several thousand people. Mellaart excavated only about one-thirtieth of the mound at Çatal Höyük. A series of radiocarbon dates indicates that the site was occupied from about 6250 to 5400 b.c.

The most striking feature of Mellaart's excavation was the evidence for ritual and religious life that he uncovered. The burial rituals at Çatal Höyük were unique. After death, the bodies were exposed to vultures and the elements. The defleshed bones were then wrapped in cloth, mats, or baskets and buried beneath the sleeping platforms in the houses. Nearly all the houses produced evidence for wall paintings, statues, plaster reliefs, or cattle crania and horns set into the walls. Many of the wall paintings seem to depict textile-like patterns, while others show hunting and burial scenes. The reliefs and carvings include images of animals **(Figure 20.13)**, female figures, and even women giving birth to bulls. The elaborate imagery certainly reflects a well-developed set of religious beliefs and practices. Because many statues of women have been identified from Mellaart's excavations, the role of women in the ritual life of Çatal Höyük is particularly intriguing.

The role of women in Neolithic ritual is one of the questions that is being explored by a new program of excavations that began at Çatal Höyük in 1995. The new excavations are being conducted under the direction of Dr. Ian Hodder from Cambridge University and will continue for approximately 25 years. Dr. Hodder's team is using up-to-date methods of excavation, conservation, and interpretation to explore the site and its environment, to conserve the wall paintings and other artifacts, and to develop Çatal Höyük as a well-planned heritage site that will attract visitors from all over the world. The research team plans to study the environmental, economic, and social contexts of the wall paintings as well as their religious symbolism.

The archaeological evidence from Çatal Höyük demonstrates that this Neolithic settlement was home to perhaps 10,000 people who were engaged in agriculture, animal keeping, hunting and gathering, trade, religious ritual, and a variety of craft activities. The site, however, is more of an overgrown village than a true town or city. The basic social units appear to be extended families grouped into clusters of four to five houses. There is no clear evidence for full-time craft specialists at Çatal Höyük. Craft activities, such as obsidian working, were carried out by individual households (Balter 1998).

As we shall see in Part VII, craft production, trade, and religion came to play increasingly important roles in later urban societies in Mesopotamia, Egypt, the Indus Valley, and temperate Europe. The appearance of full-time craft specialists, who are not engaged in agriculture and other subsistence pursuits, is one of the hallmarks of truly urban societies.

 Conclusion

While archaeologists have often focused on the origins of farming communities, the results of the adoption of agriculture are equally important. The consequences of the adoption of agriculture included increased disease load and poorer health, population growth, and the resulting expansion of agricultural communities outside the initial centers of plant and animal domestication. This expansion took place relatively rapidly. In approximately three millennia, Europe was transformed from a land of hunters and gatherers to a continent populated by farmers and stockkeepers.

 Glossary

'Ain Ghazal. One of the largest early farming settlements in the southern Levant, located near Amman, Jordan. The site covers 12 to 13 hectares (30 to 32.5 acres) and has yielded an unbroken sequence of early Neolithic occupations from 7250 to 5000 b.c.

Brześć Kujawski. A well-documented example of an early farming village in the North European Plain. The settlement, dated to 3900 to 3300 b.c., is located northwest of Warsaw in Poland and is composed a series of trapezoidal longhouses.

Burnished. The term used to describe a clay surface that has been rubbed with a small stone or other hard object after firing in order to make the surface shinier and less porous.

Çatal Höyük. A large Neolithic site located in the southern part of Central Anatolia. The site was occupied between 6520 and 5400 b.c. and may have been home to several thousand people.

Çayönü. An early farming village located in eastern Turkey. The site, which was occupied between about 7500 and 6500 b.c., yielded the remains of early domesticated einkorn

wheat, a cereal that appears to have been domesticated independently in Anatolia.

Glaze. A material that melts during firing to produce a glasslike surface on pottery.

Gritille. An early Neolithic settlement dated between 7000 and 5500 b.c., located on the Euphrates River in southeastern Anatolia. The artifacts from the site show many similarities to the Levantine PPNB.

Jericho. A deeply stratified tell (city-mound) site located in the West Bank territory. The early Neolithic (PPNA) levels include a tower and wall that appear to have been part of a larger system of fortifications.

Karanovo. An early sixth-millennium b.c. farming village in central Bulgaria. At Karanovo, small, square houses were framed with poles and plastered with mud.

Linear Pottery culture. The culture named for its distinctive ceramics, which were decorated with curvilinear designs. Linear Pottery settlements spread rapidly across the loess belt of central and western Europe between 4500 and 4000 b.c. The Linear Pottery houses are long, rectangular structures built of large posts.

Loess belt. A region of light, fertile, glacially deposited soils along the Rhine and the Danube Valleys that was home to the earliest farming villages in central and western Europe.

Nea Nikomedeia. Site in Greek Macedonia dating to about 6000 b.c. and one of the earliest farming villages in all of Europe. At Nea Nikomedeia farmers inhabited small, single-roomed, square houses and raised wheat, barley, sheep, goats, cattle, and pigs.

Pre-Pottery Neolithic A (PPNA). The earliest part of the Neolithic in the southern Levant. Dated to between about 8300 and 7200 b.c., the PPNA is characterized by the presence of early domestic cereals (wheat and barley). PPNA houses generally have circular stone foundations.

Pre-Pottery Neolithic B (PPNB). The later part (ca. 7200 to 6000 b.c.) of the aceramic Neolithic in the southern Levant. PPNB sites are generally characterized by rectangular houses, and many PPNB sites have economies based on cereal agriculture and animal husbandry.

Slip. A thin wash of clay and water that is applied to a pottery vessel before it is fired.

Temper. A nonplastic material that is combined with clay before it is fired. Temper counteracts shrinkage and reduces the risk of cracking as a clay vessel dries.

 Further Reading

Whittle, Alasdair
　1985. *Neolithic Europe: A Survey.* Cambridge: Cambridge University Press.
　This volume provides a comprehensive and authoritative survey of the archaeology of Neolithic Europe. It is a high-level text that is designed for advanced students. An updated version (Whittle 1996) reflects new theoretical trends in archaeology.

Çatal Höyük website
　Currently located at http://catal.arch.cam.ac.uk
　This Internet website provides news about the ongoing excavation at Çatal Höyük, background information, and reports concerning recent work at the site.

 Other Bibliography

Balter, M.
　1998. Why Settle Down? The Mystery of Communities. *Science* 282: 1442–1445.

Bogucki, P. I.
　1988. *Forest Farmers and Stockherders: Early Agriculture and Its Consequences in North-Central Europe.* Cambridge: Cambridge University Press.

Bogucki, P. I., and R. Grygiel
　1983. Early Farmers on the North European Plain. *Scientific American* 248 (4): 104–112.
　1993. Neolithic Sites in the Polish Lowlands: Research at Brześć Kujawski, 1933 to 1984. In *Case Studies in European Prehistory,* edited by P. I. Bogucki, pp. 147–180. Boca Raton, FL: CRC Press.

Bordaz, J.
　1970. *Tools of the Old and New Stone Age.* Garden City, NY: Natural History Press.

Dennell, R. W.
　1992. The Origins of Crop Agriculture in Europe. In *The Origins of Agriculture: An International Perspective,* edited by C. W. Cowan and P. J. Watson, pp. 71–100. Washington, DC: Smithsonian Institution Press.

Heun, M., R. Schäfer-Pregl, D. Klawan, R. Castagna, M. Accerbi, B. Borghi, and F. Salamini
　1997. Site of Einkorn Wheat Identified by DNA Fingerprinting. *Science* 278: 1312–1314.

Kenyon, Kathleen
　1957. *Digging Up Jericho.* London: E. Benn.
　1970. *Archaeology in the Holy Land,* 3d ed. New York: Praeger.

Larsen, C. S.
　1995. Biological Changes in Human Populations with Agriculture. *Annual Review of Anthropology* 24: 185–213.

Mellaart, James
　1967. *Çatal Hüyük: A Neolithic Town in Anatolia.* London: Thames and Hudson.
　1975. *The Neolithic of the Near East.* New York: Scribner's.

Rodden, R. J.
　1962. Excavations at the Early Neolithic Site of Nea Nikomedeia, Greek Macedonia. *Proceedings of the Prehistoric Society* 28: 267–288.
　1965. An Early Neolithic Village in Greece. *Scientific American* 212 (4): 82–92.

Rollefson, G. O., A. H. Simmons, and Z. Kafafi
　1992. Neolithic Cultures at 'Ain Ghazal, Jordan. *Journal of Field Archaeology* 19 (4): 443–470.

Rosenberg, M., R. Nesbitt, R. W. Redding, and B. L. Peasnall
　1998. Hallan Çemi, Pig Husbandry, and Post-Pleistocene Adaptations along the Taurus-Zagros Arc (Turkey). *Paléorient* 24 (1): 25–41.

Van Zeist, W.
　1972. Paleobotanical Results of the 1970 Season at Çayönü, Turkey. *Helinium* 12: 3–19.

Voigt, M. M.
　1985. Village on the Euphrates: Excavations at Neolithic Gritille in Turkey. *Expedition* 27 (1): 10–24.

Whittle, A.
　1996. *Europe in the Neolithic: The Creation of New Worlds.* Cambridge: Cambridge University Press.

Part VII

How and Why Did Cities and States Develop in the Old World?

Part VII focuses on the development of complex societies in the Old World. Complex societies are characterized by marked inequality and by social and economic differentiation. Chapter 21 examines a number of models for the evolution of complex societies in the Old World, focusing on such factors as trade, irrigation, religion, and social change. Particular emphasis is placed on the origins and growth of cities and the formation of states. The chapter focuses on the emergence of complex societies in Mesopotamia, a region that has been studied by archaeologists for most of the twentieth century. Subsequent chapters outline the development of cities and states in the Indus Valley and Egypt. The final chapter focuses on prehistoric Europe, a region characterized by a very different pattern of social evolution.

Archaeologists sometimes use the term *civilization* to describe complex, urban societies; they often speak of ancient Egyptian civilization or of the Inca and Aztec civilizations of the Americas. The implication is that we are speaking of societies that have complex political organizations, sophisticated technologies, advanced art and architecture, and often, writing. Unfortunately, civilization has been, and remains, a rather loosely defined term in archaeology and anthropology. Moreover, the term is certainly value-laden. After all, ancient societies that were not civilizations were certainly not uncivilized. In this text, whenever possible we will avoid the use of the term *civilization*. Instead, we will focus on the development of complex societies, the beginnings of urbanism, and the formation of the state. These terms are well defined and are value-neutral.

Chapter 21

The Development of Cities and States
Mesopotamia and the Urban Revolution

Introduction

In Chapter 20 we examined the effects of the beginnings of agriculture on population growth, health and disease, trade, technology, and the development of ritual life. One of the most important consequences of the beginnings of farming in both the Old World and the Americas was that it laid the foundation for the development of **complex societies** (McGuire 1983). Complex societies are characterized by marked social inequality. In the preceding chapters we have studied societies that were relatively egalitarian. Most hunter-gatherer and simple agricultural societies are characterized by relatively small differences in social status, political power, and material wealth. It is important to emphasize, however, that no society is completely egalitarian. Differences exist, for example, between the roles of men and women and between the roles of children and adults. In complex societies certain individuals and groups of individuals have differential access to both material and social resources, and the differences in status and wealth between individuals are much greater in complex societies than they are in noncomplex societies. Complex societies, by definition, include both the haves and the have-nots. In addition, complex societies are heterogeneous. Many more social roles exist in complex societies. In simple societies, most of the population is engaged in subsistence activities. A small number of other social roles may exist—priest, part-time flint knapper, expert hunter, and the like—but the variations are strictly limited. In more complex societies, substantial portions of the population are engaged in activities other than farming, fishing, and foraging. Complex societies often include specialist potters and metalworkers, full-time priests and priestesses, scribes, tax collectors, and merchants.

The Origin of Complex Societies: The Contribution of V. Gordon Childe

The Australian prehistorian V. Gordon Childe was one of the first archaeologists to recognize the connection between the beginnings of farming and the development of complex societies. Childe recognized that the beginnings of farming, which he termed the Neolithic Revolution, were a necessary precondition for what he termed the Urban Revolution, the sweeping set of social, political, and economic changes that are often associated with the beginning of complex societies. The critical link is that agriculture, which produces a higher yield per hectare than hunting and gathering, can be used to produce a storable surplus of food. This food surplus can then be utilized to support a wide range of nonagricultural activities, including the production of crafts, religious activities, and trade. Increasingly intensified agricultural techniques, such as terracing or irrigation, may be required to support larger numbers of nonagricultural workers. Moreover, individuals or groups who are able to gain control of this agricultural surplus can clearly develop greater access to both material and social resources.

For V. Gordon Childe, the rise of **urbanism,** or the origin and growth of cities, was a critical feature of his Urban Revolution. Cities are more than mere dense concentrations of population. While cities are usually defined as concentrations of more than 5,000 persons, the critical feature of cities is that they are home to large numbers of non-subsistence workers. Farmers in the countryside must somehow supply these nonfarmers with food. Some administrative mechanism or other means must be developed to ensure that the nonfarmers in the city are fed (see, for example, Zeder 1991).

Archaeologists studying the emergence of complex societies have focused on the processes of urban growth. Most early archaeologists chose to excavate cities that yielded the remains of temples, palaces, and elaborate specialized crafts. Until relatively recently, less attention was paid to the transformation of the countryside. It is clear, however, that "in the process of city-state formation, the countryside was created as a hinterland of city-states and as a fertile no-man's land to be contested by rival city-states" (Yoffee 1995: 284). The character of the countryside changed with the beginnings of urbanism. Village farmers became producers and consumers in a more complex urban economy.

The Characteristics of Urban Societies

In 1950, Childe published a set of 10 characteristics of the Urban Revolution that could be recognized in the archaeological record. More recently, Charles Redman (1978), an archaeologist who has studied the rise of complex societies in the Near East, reorganized the criteria into five primary and five secondary characteristics. The five primary characteristics are the basic changes to society that resulted from the Urban Revolution; the secondary characteristics are the effects of those social changes that can be seen in the archaeological record (Table 21.1).

When we examine the five primary characteristics in detail, we can see important links between them. For example, cities are usually the home of large numbers of full-time craft specialists. The surplus food that is produced in the countryside must be mobilized and concentrated to support these non-agricultural workers. If certain groups of individuals regularly have greater access to social and material resources, such as surplus food and craft products, this difference in access may lead over time to the formation of a class-stratified society.

The fifth characteristic identified by Childe and Redman is the appearance of a form of political organization known as the **state.** State societies have been defined in several different ways. State societies have permanent government institutions that out-

Table 21.1

Childe's 10 Characteristics of Urban Civilization, as Reorganized by Redman 1978

Primary Characteristics	
1. Increased size and density of cities	Larger population requiring broader social integration
2. Full-time specialization of labor	Institutionalized labor specialization, distribution, and exchange
3. Concentration of surplus, termed the *social surplus*	Institutional control of surplus food and craft products
4. Class-structured society	Privileged religious, military, and political leaders
5. State organization	Political membership based on place of residence rather than kinship affiliations; permanent government institutions
Secondary Characteristics	
1. Monumental public works	Temples, palaces, storehouses, and irrigation systems
2. Long-distance trade	Organized exchange beyond the confines of the city or region
3. Standardized, monumental artwork	Art for enjoyment and social identification
4. Writing	Facilitates organization and management
5. Arithmetic, geometry, and astronomy	Beginnings of exact science and engineering

Source: Based on Redman 1978: 218.

last individual rulers or leaders. In American society, the institution of the presidency outlasts the term of office of any particular president. The institutions and machinery of the U.S. government—the IRS, the Bureau of the Census, the National Park Service, and the Department of State—remain in place regardless of who occupies the White House. In addition, states control particular territories and have the ability to defend those territories, if necessary, by military force. As complex societies develop, state institutions may take over many of the functions that kinship ties play in simpler societies. One of these important functions is defense and security; as a result, states usually monopolize military force, controlling the army and the police.

State institutions are clearly linked to other aspects of early urban societies. Government officials, such as soldiers, scribes, and bureaucrats, are often full-time specialists who must be supported by the surplus food produced in the countryside. Rulers and administrators clearly have increased access to social and material resources; they may develop into a distinct ruling class.

It is important to note that Childe saw the political, social, and economic changes associated with the Urban Revolution as truly revolutionary. He modeled his urban revolution on the Industrial Revolution of the nineteenth century, when changes in technology, such as the development of the steam engine, led to profound and rapid changes in almost every other aspect of nineteenth-century life. Today we recognize that social change can be evolutionary as well as revolutionary. Childe's Urban Revolution may well have taken centuries or even millennia. Moreover, modern and ancient human societies are highly varied. While urban, state-level societies are certainly complex societies, some societies that exhibit social and economic inequality and some degree of heterogeneity lack cities and state institutions. An example of a nonstate, nonurban complex society would be Ireland at the time of St. Patrick, approximately 1,500 years ago. Early Christian Ireland was certainly a class-stratified society. Wealthy chiefs, nobles, and landowners constituted the highest levels of society; at the bottom were poor farmers and even slaves. In between the social extremes were poets and men and women of arts, craftworkers in metal, and, of course, priests. The Ireland of St. Patrick's day, however, lacked cities (or even towns) and permanent governmental institutions. Irish chiefs governed more by their personal charisma and leadership abilities than by the machinery of government. Archaeologists have often used the term **chiefdom** to describe complex societies that lack urbanism and the institutions of the state.

The Evolution of Complex Societies in Mesopotamia

We have chosen to begin our story in **Mesopotamia,** the alluvial lowland lying between the Tigris and Euphrates Rivers in what today is Iraq **(Figure 21.1)**. Childe was particularly interested in Mesopotamia because that region is home to the world's oldest urban societies, beginning with the Sumerians some 5,000 years ago. In Chapter 18 we saw that early farming villages such as Jarmo had been established in northern Iraq by the early part of the seventh millennium b.c.

What led the descendants of modest farming communities such as Jarmo to the radical changes in social organization that in a few thousand years would create the great urban societies of the ancient world? Scholars have advanced a number of hypotheses to account for the rise of complex societies, each of which may tell some portion of the story. It is clear, however, that the beginning of complex or urban society in Mesopotamia followed the movement of farmers from the rain-watered hilly flanks down onto the dry Tigris-Euphrates floodplain.

To the north and east of the Tigris River the land rises up to form the foothills of the Zagros Mountains. This zone, the hilly flanks of the fertile crescent, was discussed in Chapters 17 and 18. At elevations of more than 350 meters (1,100 ft.), sufficient rain falls to permit crops to be grown without irrigation, and it was here that the earliest farming communities in the region were established. The eastern side of the fertile crescent, Mesopotamia, is, for the most part, a hot, dry, and barren plain; it could be made fertile only by long, concerted, and organized effort.

Mesopotamia (between rivers) is an ancient name. It refers, literally, to the alluvial

Figure 21.1

Map of Mesopotamia showing the sites discussed in this chapter.

lowland lying between the Tigris and Euphrates Rivers. These great rivers arise in the mountains of eastern Turkey and flow roughly parallel southeastward across the entirety of modern Iraq to join finally and empty into the Persian Gulf. In time, the name Mesopotamia came to refer to the whole of the Tigris-Euphrates lowland, the setting of the earliest urban societies of the ancient world. The land between the rivers 150 kilometers (93 mi.) or so north of Baghdad is a barren limestone plateau. To the south, however, the rivers have continuously deposited an annual load of silt, creating a vast, flat, potentially fertile plain, ideal for agriculture. Ideal, that is, provided the crops can be supplied with water. No rain falls in southern Mesopotamia during the summer, and temperatures frequently top 40° Celsius (104° F). When the mountain snows melt in the spring, the rivers flood, sometimes dangerously. The floods arrive in May or June, however, too late to water the crops planted in the fall and already harvested in April. Control of the river waters was essential for agriculture to succeed in Mesopotamia.

The Settling of the Mesopotamian Lowlands

By about 6000 b.c. village farmers had begun to move into the Mesopotamian lowlands. These early settlers are known as the **Hassuna culture,** after the type site of **Hassuna,** near Mosul in northwestern Iraq; the culture is better known, however, from the nearby site of **Yarim Tepe.** The Hassuna region, in the foothills of the Zagros Mountains, receives 300 to 400 millimeters (12 to 16 in.) of rain annually, so agriculture without irrigation was possible (Maisels 1993: 113). At Yarim Tepe the farmers raised einkorn, emmer, and bread wheats; spelt wheat; barley; lentils; and peas. They obtained most of their meat from domesticated animals, primarily cattle, but also sheep, goats, and pigs.

Figure 21.2

A typical Hassuna house.

Wild onager (a wild ass), deer, and gazelle were hunted (Maisels 1993: 124).

The Hassuna villages were small settlements with a few hundred inhabitants, differing little from earlier Neolithic farming communities. Still, the Hassuna settlements display, in rudimentary form, many of the features that would typify the archaeology of later Mesopotamian societies. The villagers lived in rectangular houses of several rooms, some with wooden doors, as shown by the pivot sockets in the stone doorsills. Several of the houses were grouped around a courtyard **(Figure 21.2)**. A few circular structures of uncertain function also occur. Coarse pottery bins, probably for grain storage, were sunk into the floor, and some of the rooms contained bread ovens. The walls were built of clay slabs, plastered on both sides, with floors of tamped earth. On the exterior the walls were buttressed. Perhaps originally used to strengthen clay walls, increasingly complex buttressing and niche patterns would continue to become dominant architectural features of the Sumerian temple.

By 6000 b.c., pottery had come into common use in Mesopotamia. From Hassuna times onward, pottery styles became increasingly standardized and geographically widespread. Pottery typology, therefore, has become one of the principal tools of the Mesopotamian archaeologist. Pottery styles are used to identify specific archaeological cultures and phases and to establish cultural and temporal relationships between archaeological sites and regions. Hassuna pottery includes well-made, well-fired bowls and straight-necked globular jugs decorated with incised herring bone designs, and/or chevrons and triangles in black paint. At the site of Hassuna itself these wares are later joined by other pots, evidently imports, known as Samarra pottery—finely made jars and bowls, covered with a fine slip (a thin clay coating) and painted with basketry-like patterns and sometimes stylized animal figures **(Figure 21.3)**.

It was the people of the **Samarran culture** who first became established in the Mesopotamian lowlands proper. The Samarran is best known from the site of **Tell-es-Sawwan,** on the banks of the Tigris about 100 kilometers (62 mi.) northwest of Baghdad, near the type site of **Samarra.** The two earliest levels of Tell-es-Sawwan, first settled about 5500 b.c., resemble Hassuna, both in

Figure 21.3

(a) Hassuna and (b) Samarra pottery.
Source: After Childe (1957, Plates XIV and XVIa).

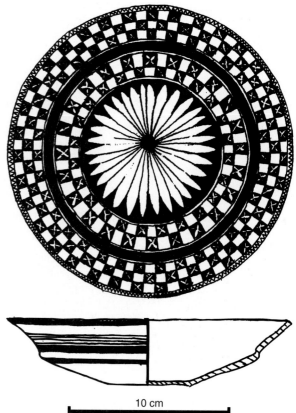

Figure 21.4

Halafian pottery.
Source: After Childe (1957, Plate XVIa).

the pottery types found and in the form of the externally buttressed, multiroomed rectangular dwellings. The houses are much larger, however, with up to 15 rooms. The next level, however, Level III (ca. 5350 b.c.), is markedly different. Hassuna pottery is joined by typical Samarran wares. (Hassuna wares are eventually completely displaced by Samarra pottery in the upper levels of the site). The architecture changed considerably, to become a group of separate, multiroomed dwellings, most having a T-shaped layout, which reappears at many later Mesopotamian sites. The settlement faces the Tigris on one side and is enclosed on the other three sides by a mudbrick wall. Outside the wall a ditch 3 meters (10 ft.) deep was cut into the rock. The presence of these clearly defensive structures implies that the people of Tell-es-Sawwan were threatened by outsiders, possibly raiders attracted to the village's growing wealth in grain and livestock.

The people of Tell-es-Sawwan grew wheats and barley, and raised sheep, goats, and cattle. They hunted deer, gazelle, boar, and onager, and took large fish from the river. The precipitation in the region would have been too low to permit agriculture based on rainfall, but the proximity of the river made farming possible.

> Most probably agriculture was conducted on the basis of the seasonal flood of the river, spill pools were exploited, run-off checked in favourable spots by primitive damming—and generally the activities which we may visualize as the forerunners of full-fledged canal irrigation. (Helbaek 1965: 47)

In the northern uplands the Hassuna and Samarra cultures are succeeded by another group of people, the **Halafians,** noted for their exceptionally attractive, finely made pottery, with complex red and black painted geometric patterns, sometimes combined with stylized animals **(Figure 21.4)**. Halafian ceramics are found over a wide area, suggesting an extensive trade network. In the south-

Figure 21.5

Figurine of woman with "coffee-bean eyes" from Choga Mami, similar to those found in the Ubaid period.

ern lowlands, though, the Samarran culture seems to lead directly to the culture generally recognized as the earliest manifestation of the later Mesopotamian urban societies: the **Ubaid.** Evidence for this continuity can be seen in the mound of **Choga Mami,** where several transitional levels, with pottery forms of intermediate style, separate the lower Samarran and the upper Ubaid levels at the site. Equally important, the Samarran levels at Choga Mami have produced a series of terracotta figures, mostly of women, that stylistically resemble the cult figurines of the Ubaid period (particularly in the feature of "coffee-bean eyes") **(Figure 21.5)**. These figurines may represent the predecessors of the classic Mesopotamian goddesses (Maisels 1993: 149).

The Ubaid Period

By about 5000 b.c., the southernmost extent of the Tigris-Euphrates floodplain had been settled by farmers. This early cultural phase is named after the small village site of

Al Ubaid, where it was first described, but settlements belonging to the Ubaid phase have been found in the lowest levels of the tell sites of many Sumerian cities, notably Ur, Uruk, and Eridu (see Figure 21.1). Earlier generations of Mesopotamian archaeologists tended to concentrate on the monumental structures (primarily temples) in these city-mounds, but some newer excavations have provided more insight into the broader society.

An exceptionally well-preserved example of a late Ubaid dwelling has recently been excavated at **Tell Madhhur,** near the Diyala River north of Baghdad **(Figure 21.6)**. The 14-meter by 14-meter (46-ft. by 46-ft.), mud-brick structure was built around a T-shaped central hall, with rows of flanking rooms on either side. The structure had been burned, leaving many of its contents inside. These objects—including many pots, quantities of carbonized barley, mullers and grindstones for grinding flour, and clay spindle whorls for making thread—attest to the domestic life of the period. Animal figurines were also found, along with thousands of clay sling bullets (Maisels 1993: 158). Maisels (1993) has argued that such a large, complex structure was not the dwelling of a single nuclear family, but rather, housed an extended family group, including servants.

Eridu, near Al Ubaid, far to the south in Mesopotamia, was believed by the Sumerians to be the first city in the world, a belief that, for Mesopotamia at least, archaeology has not refuted. Eridu lies in an area of environmental extremes, "a quagmire during the winter and a furnace during the summer" (Mallowan 1967: Part I, 7). Still, in ancient times nearby lakes would have provided the inhabitants with abundant fresh water (and plentiful fish for their diet). This mixed environment is reflected in the earliest houses, some of which are mud-brick structures while others seem to have been huts made from reeds plastered with clay. Even in modern times the Arab inhabitants of the marshlands near the Persian Gulf built dwellings made from reeds.

Unfired mud brick, on the other hand, soon became the prevalent Mesopotamian building material. Stable enough in the dry Mesopotamian climate and an effective insulator against the searing heat, mud brick is

Figure 21.6
Reconstruction of a house at Tell Madhhur.

still in use today in the remote villages of the region. In ancient times very little else was available. Other than potentially rich soil, the Mesopotamian plain offered practically nothing in the way of resources. Wood, for building or for firing brick, was nonexistent, and what was used had to be imported from far away. The same was true for building stone and metal ores. Still, by the end of the Ubaid period, Eridu had grown to more than 8 hectares (20 acres) and may have had a population of 4,000 to 5,000. The inhabitants were buried in an adjacent cemetery, each interred

with a cup and a plate (surely a food offering) within mud-brick coffins. Two individuals were buried with their pets—Saluki-like dogs (Mallowan 1967: Part I, 23).

During this transitional time Eridu grew from a village to a sizable town. Although the growth of the residential and craft areas of Eridu has received relatively little attention, they must have expanded greatly to support the construction of the increasingly impressive temples. Within the mound of Eridu the excavators uncovered a long series of superimposed temples from the Ubaid phase, be-

Figure 21.7
Plan of Eridu Temple VII.

ginning with a simple chapel at the base. By 3500 B.C. the temple had become a monumental mud-brick structure, marked by altars and offering tables and characterized by externally buttressed walls and a tripartite layout—a large central hall flanked by two rows of smaller chambers **(Figure 21.7)**. The tripartite plan of the temples appears to have its antecedents in the large domestic dwellings of the Ubaid period, such as the buildings discovered at Tell Madhhur.

Similar temple sequences, along with settlement growth, occurred at **Uruk** (biblical Erech), Ur, and other sites. The Ubaid culture spread throughout Mesopotamia, displacing the Halafian culture in the north. During the Ubaid phase, however, settlements remained near the rivers and natural water sources; irrigation systems were still relatively simple. Further expansion of settlements would depend on the development of far-reaching and elaborate systems for the distribution and control of the rivers' waters.

The Emergence of Cities

The changes that brought about the rise of **Sumer,** Mesopotamia's earliest urban society, took place in a span of 600 years, beginning with the end of the Ubaid phase at 3500 B.C. This period is known as the **proto-literate period.** The first Sumerian dynasties would appear in 2900 B.C. The earlier portion of this timespan is known as the **Uruk phase** (3500 to 3100 B.C.); the succeeding **Jemdat Nasr period** (3100 to 2900 B.C.) was essentially similar, showing continued development from the Uruk phase.

During this time many of the technologies that were to make complex, urban societies possible first appeared. A light, ox-drawn plow seems to have been invented during the fourth millennium B.C., enabling the farmers to till the Mesopotamian silts on a much larger scale. The wheel came into use. Wheeled carts pulled by draft animals would have facilitated the long-distance transport of materials and commodities. The invention of the potter's wheel led to the mass production of pottery. The working of metals became increasingly important. Metals were used not only for utilitarian objects and weapons but also for the manufacture of luxury goods and jewelry, symbols of status and wealth. Metal objects (copper ore frag-

ments, a copper ring and bead, and a lead bracelet) appear in Yarim Tepe as early as the Hassuna period (ca. 5500 b.c.), but metallurgy and metalworking, including the working of silver and gold, advanced greatly during the Uruk and Jemdat Nasr periods. Metal ores (along with precious and semi-precious stones, building stone, and wood) had to be imported from far away, implying the development of organized prospecting expeditions and trade networks.

The earliest written records appeared toward the end of the Uruk period. These consisted at first of pictorial representations impressed into clay with a stylus. The clay tablet was then dried to create a permanent record. Gradually, these pictures, or **pictographs,** evolved into **cuneiform** writing, made up of wedge-shaped symbols pressed into clay, each symbol representing a spoken syllable **(Figure 21.8)**. The earliest tablets were accounting documents—records of transactions and lists of commodities, including land, grain, and livestock. Literature and poetry would come later. Another characteristic Mesopotamian artifact, the **cylinder seal**—a smooth stone cylinder carved with intricate scenes, often including humans and animals—became widespread in the Uruk period **(Figure 21.9)**. These seals produced a unique mark of authorship or ownership when rolled over the wet clay of a tablet or the clay seal of a vessel.

Figure 21.8
Typical cuneiform tablet.

Figure 21.9
Clay impression produced from a typical cylinder seal.

Figure 21.10
City plan of Uruk.

Thousands of such sealings have been found, attesting to a well-developed concept of property rights.

During the Uruk phase, Eridu, Ur, and Uruk, along with Nippur and Kish (see Figure 21.1), expanded in size to become cities. Uruk was by far the largest settlement **(Figure 21.10)**. By the end of the period, Uruk had grown to an area of about 100 hectares (250 acres); such a large settlement must have been supported by the produce of an extensive region of surrounding countryside, watered by an effective system of irrigation canals. To the east, in what is modern Iran, other cities also developed to become Elam, an ancient complex society about which much less is known, because their early writing has not yet been deciphered. Alongside the cities, many other much smaller sites of the period have been found in southern Mesopotamia. They lay, for the most part, along the banks of now dry channels of the Euphrates that in Uruk times meandered

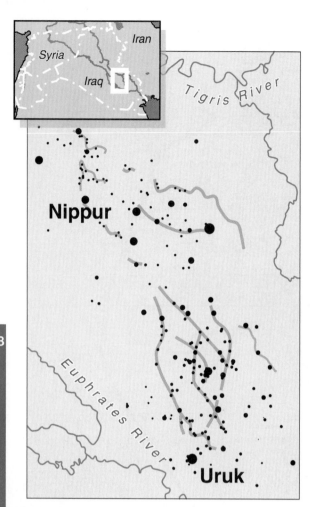

Figure 21.11

Early and Middle Uruk settlement patterns.
Settlements cluster along water channels, shown
as shaded lines.
Source: Adapted from Adams 1981, Fig. 12.

through much of the Mesopotamian plain **(Fig-ure 21.11)**. How the cities, towns, and villages of Uruk times were related to one another is still a matter of speculation. The larger cities may have been able to call upon the surrounding towns and villages for labor or agricultural produce, but the cities' political control does not seem to have extended beyond their immediate surroundings.

Each of the large cities was dominated by a temple of monumental proportions. A striking example is the so-called Eanna Precinct at Uruk, dating to 3100 B.C. Temple D at Uruk, with a great T-shaped central hall surrounded on all sides by many smaller chambers, measures 80 by 55 meters (262 by 180 ft.) **(Fig-**ure 21.12)**. Such a large structure implies that the temple priesthood could exercise control over a sizable force of laborers and craftspeople and that a sufficient agricultural surplus was available to support a nonfarming segment of the population. At a somewhat later time, when textual accounts became available, it is evident that the temples were receiving grain, livestock, and other agricultural commodities, as well as labor, from farmers who were essentially tenants of the temple. These goods were then used to provision workers and craftspeople and to reward favored individuals.

The early Sumerian cities were clearly religious centers, focused on a temple precinct. Surrounding the temples, however, was an increasing population of workers and craft specialists who had their homes and shops within the city. No longer full-time farmers, these people exchanged their wares and services to the temples and secular elites for their livelihood. The cities became production centers where the farmers from the surrounding countryside could obtain everyday items such as pottery, and for those who could afford them, luxury goods brought by traders from far away. The typical Sumerian city is surrounded by a massive defensive wall; in times of stress (perhaps occasioned by a bad agricultural season) the nearby farmers may have moved into the cities for protection from the raids of marauding nomads or the military adventures of other neighboring cities. It remains an open question whether the early cities grew because the inhabitants were drawn there by the opportunities the cities offered or because they were forced into the cities by the dangers of the countryside.

The Beginning of History

Uruk and Jemdat Nasr times are sometimes referred to as the proto-literate period. Later, the Sumerians would populate these times with a series of heroes and rulers they would call the kings before the flood. Indeed, the Sumerian cities of Shuruppak and Kish both contain deposits of flood silts overlying the Jemdat Nasr deposits. The Sumerian myth of the deluge (from which the biblical story of the Great Flood was derived) clearly recalls an actual event, a localized natural catastrophe, but one that encompassed much of the Sumerian world.

Figure 21.12

Temple D at Uruk (Warka).

The succeeding period, the **Early Dynastic** (beginning ca. 2900 B.C.), brings the beginning of the historical record. A crucial historical document, the King List, records the names of the rulers of the cities of Sumer **(Figure 21.13)**. The names of some of these kings also appear on inscriptions found in Early Dynastic sites; at Al Ubaid, for instance, a foundation stone of a temple was inscribed with the name of Mesannipadda, first king of the first dynasty of Ur. Gilgamish, the Sumerian epic hero, is based on an actual king of Uruk, where his name has been found in the Early Dynastic deposits.

The social world of Early Dynastic times was radically different from the simple, largely egalitarian society of the Neolithic. Full-time craft specialists, such as potters and metalworkers, depended on farmers for their sustenance. Specialist traders profited from the export of Mesopotamian produce and the import of raw materials and luxury goods. Elite groups developed, first among the priesthood and later as secular leaders, who could monopolize an increasing proportion of the wealth and power in the community. Many of the population were servants or tenants of the elites. Some less fortunate individuals were reduced to slavery.

Figure 21.13

The King List, copied by the Assyrians from an earlier document.

Case Study
The Royal Cemetery of Ur

The excavations of the British archeologist Sir Leonard Woolley at **Ur** during the 1920s have provided us with some spectacular insights into early Sumerian society. By the end of the Early Dynastic period, individual differences in wealth and power had grown enormously. Woolley excavated in a portion of the mound of Ur adjacent to the temples that had served the city first as a rubbish heap, but later became a major burial area. Thousands of overlapping graves were dug into the rubbish, mostly the simple burials of common people but also the tombs and funeral pits of the elite and powerful.

The common people of Early Dynastic Ur were buried in simple coffins, generally with only a cup of liquid pressed to their lips to take them into the next world. Some graves, however, were much richer in offerings than those of the common folk. One in particular stands out. The burial itself was that of a common person—a simple shaft dug into the ground, holding a wooden coffin. Surrounding the coffin, however, was a most remarkable array of offerings. At the head and foot of the coffin were copper-headed spears with golden hafts, stuck blade-down into the ground. Alongside the coffin were copper daggers, some mounted in gold; clay and alabaster vessels; and many copper and silver bowls. Within the coffin were even greater riches:

> The body lay in normal fashion on its right side; round the waist was a broad belt of silver, now decayed, from which hung a gold dagger . . . ; between the hands was placed a bowl of heavy gold, a larger oval gold bowl lay close by, and near the elbow a gold lamp in the form of a shell, while yet another gold bowl stood behind the head. (Woolley 1965: 58)

Axes of electrum (an alloy of gold and silver) were placed at either shoulder. A mass of golden jewelry—beads, bracelets, and earrings—also lay in the grave. Most striking, though, was the superbly worked golden helmet, still upon the head **(Figure 21.14)**. We

Figure 21.14
The golden helmet of Mes-kalam-dug.

know the name of this individual, because three of the golden objects bear the same inscription: "Mes-kalam-dug. Hero of the Good Land" (Woolley 1965: 59).

Yet, for all its splendor, this burial was modest in comparison with the 16 interments Woolley describes as the royal graves. Unlike the simple coffin of Mes-kalam-dug, these personages were buried in stone tombs, sunk deep into the ground, and they did not go alone to their graves. In an elaborate burial ceremony, not only were great material riches interred with the dead but also an entire cadre of servants and soldiers who were sacrificed beside the tomb.

Of these burials the best known is that of Queen Pu-abi. She was buried in a stone tomb at the base of a great ramped pit dug into the earth. An entire funeral procession followed her down the ramp into the pit. A chariot, inlaid with blue and white and decorated with gold, drawn by two

asses, was driven into the pit (Figure 21.15). Following the chariot were 10 women, in two rows, elaborately dressed with gold headdresses and beads. A harpist accompanied them (Figure 21.16). A group of soldiers followed behind. All who went into the pit were sacrificed, animals and humans. The bodies of the asses lay beside those of their grooms; the driver of the chariot died within it. The corpse of the harpist lay atop the harp. The bodies of the 10 women were found neatly arranged in rows. There is no sign of violence; the excavator concluded that they probably took poison. Although masses of stone, gold, and silver vessels and jewelry and many other wonderful objects accompanied the dead (Figure 21.17), it is the human cost that sets these graves apart. Clearly Queen Pu-Abi, or the elite group to which she belonged, commanded enormous power within the society of Ur, including the absolute power of life or death.

Figure 21.15
Plan of the royal graves.

Figure 21.16
Harp from the royal graves.

Figure 21.17
Gold and silver vessels from the royal graves.

What Led to the Rise of Early State Societies?

What forces led to the progressive concentration of power into the hands of certain individuals and groups and eventually to the political unification of much of Mesopotamia? Karl Wittfogel (1957) suggested that the most important factor was the power gained by those individuals and groups who could control the flow of water for irrigation and/or flood control. This idea has been called the hydraulic hypothesis. Survival on the Mesopotamian plain depended on access to water to irrigate the crops; settlements near the head of an irrigation canal could cut off or ration the water flowing to other settlements farther down the canal. Wittfogel argued that the more distant settlements, therefore, could be coerced into a subservient relationship. This, he believed, laid the foundation for the hierarchical associa-

tions among communities that would eventually develop into state society.

This model is surely overly simplistic. Other factors could also have given some individuals or groups of individuals advantages over their neighbors. Because Mesopotamia was dependent on long-distance trade for many basic resources such as wood, stone, and metals, and for luxury goods such as precious stones, traders were in a position to become increasingly wealthy and powerful. Cities that were located where they could control the trade routes had an advantage over others down the road. When certain individuals or groups, such as a temple priesthood or a local ruler, had amassed significantly greater wealth than their neighbors, they could afford to finance trading expeditions that would further enhance their status and wealth, extending their influence and control over increasingly larger territories.

The extension of the city-states' control over the surrounding countryside, as well as rivalries in pursuit of trade, led to competition, bickering, and eventually, warfare among the city-states, as evidenced by the thick defensive wall surrounding the cities. They came into conflict with other early urban societies, such as the neighboring Elamites to the east. The nomadic peoples of the deserts also found the wealth of the cities a tempting target for raiding. The need for defense led to the rise of military leaders. Mes-kalam-dug, whose burial is described in the Case Study, was probably such a leader. Powerful and effective military leaders could bring increasingly larger territories under their control by force of arms. The unification of a broad area of Mesopotamia would ultimately come with the conquests of Sargon of Akkad about 2350 B.C. Sargon was the ruler of the Semitic-speaking Akkadians to the north of Sumer. He was the first, by force of arms, to unite all of Mesopotamia politically, including the Sumerians and Elamites, under a single ruler.

Archaeological research conducted during the past 30 years has shown that single factors, such as irrigation or warfare, are not sufficient to explain the rise of the state. Instead, a number of conditions are necessary for state formation to occur. Johnson and Earle (1987: 270) have argued that two preconditions are necessary for state formation. The first is a high population with a need for a system of administrative integration. The second is the ability to mobilize sufficient economic resources, through control of trade and/or agricultural surpluses, to support a ruling class and administrative institutions. The second condition is similar to Childe's social surplus.

One of the ways states differ from complex chiefdoms is that states possess complex systems of administrative integration and decision making. Decision-making organizations in state societies are internally specialized and hierarchically structured. Johnson (1973) has suggested that states typically have three-tiered decision-making hierarchies. These complex bureaucracies allow state governments to control populations that may number in the hundreds of thousands or millions, often including significant economic and ethnic diversity.

The growth of state society in Mesopotamia was surely not the result of a single cause. Once certain individuals and groups, however, had gained an advantage in power and wealth, they could invest those resources to further enhance their position. They could finance improvements in architecture, crafts, and technology, and they could promote trade expeditions and military forays. Once initiated, the process of state formation and expansion was a self-sustaining cycle. Like a boulder rolling down a mountainside, the process of urbanization and state formation rapidly gained momentum, changing the nature of human society forever.

Conclusion

At about 6000 b.c. small farming communities were established in northern Mesopotamia, and within 1,000 years farmers had settled the southernmost regions of the Mesopotamian lowlands. During the Ubaid period, some of these small farming communities developed into sizable villages with increasingly elaborate temples. In the following proto-literate period, true cities developed in Mesopotamia along with cuneiform writing and increasingly elaborate systems of long-distance trade. No single factor can explain the rise of cities in Mesopotamia. However, it is clear that the development of simple systems of irrigation for agriculture was a prerequisite for the rise of cities, since the surplus agricultural production was necessary to support craft specialization, long-distance trade, and the construction of monumental architecture such as temples. Ultimately, factors such as the need for defense and the organization of long-distance trade would lead to the concentration of power and wealth in the hands of an elite and the development of a multitiered administrative hierarchy, characteristics of the nascent Mesopotamian states.

Glossary

Chiefdom. A complex society that lacks urbanism and the institutions of the state.

Choga Mami. Site exhibiting several transitional levels between the Samarran culture and the beginnings of the Ubaid period.

Complex societies. Societies characterized by inequality in access to resources and a wide variety of social roles.

Cuneiform. Writing made up of wedge-shaped symbols pressed into clay, each symbol representing a spoken syllable.

Cylinder seal. A smooth stone cylinder carved with intricate scenes, often including humans and animals, that produced a unique mark of authorship or ownership when rolled over the wet clay of a tablet or the clay seal of a vessel.

Early Dynastic period. The beginning (ca. 2900 B.C.) of the historical record in Mesopotamia. This period includes the reigns of the first kings, whose names are known from documentary evidence, the King List.

Eridu. City near Al Ubaid in southern Mesopotamia, believed by the Sumerians to be the first city in the world. Eridu is, in fact, one of the earliest urban centers of the region. It includes some of the earliest known temples of the Sumerian religion.

Halafians. Members of a culture that succeeded the Hassuna and Samarra cultures in the northern uplands, noted for their finely made pottery, with complex red and black painted geometric patterns, sometimes combined with stylized animals.

Hassuna. Type site, near Mosul in northwestern Iraq, of the Hassuna culture.

Hassuna culture. Village farmers of about 6000 b.c. who grew their crops at a sufficient altitude that rainfall agriculture was possible.

Jemdat Nasr period. Period (3100 to 2900 B.C.) just preceding the early Dynastic period, showing continued development from the Uruk phase.

Mesopotamia. The alluvial lowland lying between the Tigris and Euphrates Rivers where the ancient urban societies, beginning with Sumer, arose.

Pictographs. Pictorial representations impressed into clay with a stylus, preceding the development of cuneiform writing.

Proto-literate period. Period including Uruk and Jemdat Nasr times during which the earliest writing appears.

Samarra. Type site of the Samarran culture, about 100 kilometers (62 mi.) northwest of Baghdad.

Samarran culture. First people to become established in the Mesopotamian lowlands proper. The distinctive Samarran pottery is painted with basketry-like patterns and sometimes stylized animal figures.

State. A territorially based political unit with an institutionalized government.

Sumer. The first of the ancient urban societies of Mesopotamia.

Tell-es-Sawwan. Well-known site of the Samarra culture, located near the type site of Samarra.

Tell Madhhur. An exceptionally well-preserved example of a late Ubaid dwelling, near the Diyala River north of Baghdad.

Ubaid. The period of the earliest manifestation of classic Mesopotamian civilization (ca. 5300 to 3500 B.C.), named after the small village site of Al Ubaid, but found in the lowest levels of the tell sites of many Sumerian cities, notably Ur, Uruk, and Eridu.

Ur. One of the major early cities of Sumer, where Sir Leonard Woolley excavated the remarkable early Dynastic royal cemetery of Ur.

Urbanism. The origin and growth of cities—dense concentrations of at least 5,000 persons including a substantial number of nonagricultural workers.

Uruk. One of the major early cities of Sumer.

Uruk phase. The earlier period, 3500 to 3100 B.C., of proto-literate times, during which the earliest writing appears.

Yarim Tepe. Well-known settlement of Hassuna culture farmers, near the type site of Hassuna.

Further Reading

Lloyd, Seton
    1984. *The Archaeology of Mesopotamia, from the Old Stone Age to the Persian Conquest.* London: Thames and Hudson.
    A useful, well-illustrated, general introduction to this area.

Redman, Charles L.

1978. *The Rise of Civilization from Early Farmers to Urban Society in the Ancient Near East.* San Francisco: Freeman.

This volume remains one of the best discussions of the forces leading to the rise of urban society and states in the Near East.

Woolley, Sir Leonard

1965. *Excavations at Ur.* New York: Crowell.

Although some of his conclusions have since been superseded, Woolley provides a lively, detailed account of the excavations at Ur conducted during the 1920s and 1930s, including his work at the royal cemetery.

 ## Other Bibliography

Adams, Robert M.

1981. *Heartland of Cities: Surveys of Ancient Settlement and Land Use on the Central Floodplain of the Euphrates.* Chicago: University of Chicago Press.

Childe, V. Gordon

1957. *New Light on the Most Ancient East.* New York: Grove Press.

Helbaek, Hans

1965. Early Hassunan Vegetable Food at Tell as-Sawwan near Samarra. *Sumer* 20: 45–48.

Johnson, Allen W., and Timothy Earle

1987. *The Evolution of Human Societies: From Foraging Group to Agrarian State.* Stanford, CA: Stanford University Press.

Johnson, Gregory A.

1973. *Local Exchange and Early State Development in Southwestern Iran.* Ann Arbor: Museum of Anthropology, University of Michigan, Anthropological Papers No. 51.

Maisels, Charles Keith

1993. *The Near East: Archaeology in the "Cradle of Civilization."* London and New York: Routledge.

Mallowan, M. E. L.

1967. The Development of Cities from Al-'Ubaid to the End of Uruk 5, Parts I and II. In *The Cambridge Ancient History,* vol. 1, edited by I. E. S. Edwards, C. J. Gadd, and N. G. L. Hammond, chapter 8. Cambridge: Cambridge University Press.

McGuire, R. H.

1983. Breaking Down Cultural Complexity: Inequality and Heterogeneity. In *Advances in Archaeological Method and Theory,* vol. 6, edited by M. B. Schiffer, pp. 91–142. New York: Academic Press.

Wittfogel, Karl A.

1957. *Oriental Despotism: A Comparative Study of Total Power.* New Haven, CT: Yale University Press.

Yoffee, Norman

1995. Political Economy of Early Mesopotamian States. *Annual Review of Anthropology* 24: 281–311.

Zeder, M. A.

1991. *Feeding Cities: Specialized Animal Economy in the Ancient Near East.* Washington DC: Smithsonian Institution Press.

Chapter 22

Complex Societies in the Indus Valley

Introduction

The Indian subcontinent has a long literary and religious tradition. The oldest literature, the Rigveda, appears to have been compiled about 1500 to 1300 B.C. and was passed on orally for many generations. The Rigveda is made up of a series of hymns to gods such as Agni, the fire god, and Indra, the warrior charioteer. Later Vedic texts, probably composed between 1200 and 500 B.C., speak of ancient ruined mounds, of people who have gone away, and of finding pottery sherds in the wilderness along the banks of the Indus River. A scout who was sent on an excursion to the east by Alexander the Great in 326 B.C. described finding an area that included over 1,000 abandoned towns and villages that were deserted after the Indus River changed its course (Parpola 1994: 5).

Archaeological research since the 1920s has begun to shed light on the early urban society on the Indian subcontinent that existed long before the time of the Rigveda. The **Indus Valley, or Harappan, civilization** flourished in northwest India and Pakistan **(Figure 22.1)** during the third millennium B.C. The great cities of **Mohenjo-daro** and **Harappa** (which gave its name to the Harappan culture) were first investigated in the early 1920s, at a time when the whole Indian subcontinent was part of the British Empire. The excavation of these spectacular sites brought to light another great ancient society, to take its place alongside those in Mesopotamia and Egypt.

This chapter will begin with a brief overview of the environmental background of the Indus Valley region of Pakistan and India. This discussion will be followed by a consideration of the beginnings of farming in the Indus Valley area. The chapter will conclude with an extended discussion of the archaeology of the Indus Valley society, including the attempts to decipher its script, and the many elements of the Harappan culture reflected in later cultures and religions of the Indian peninsula.

The Geography and Ecology of the Indus Valley Region

The Indian subcontinent includes the modern countries of India, Pakistan, and Bangladesh. This region is separated from the rest of Asia by a series of mountain chains: the Suleiman-Kirthar Hills in the west, the Hindu Kush in the northwest, and the Himalayas to the northeast. The Indus River and its four main tributaries are critical to our understanding of the ecology of the Indus Valley region. These five rivers arise in the Punjab, meaning "five waters," region of northern India. The Indus has twice the flow of the Nile because it receives waters from both the eastern Afghan mountains and the Himalayas (Fairservis 1971: 228). It carries a vast quantity of alluvial soil and inundates a very wide floodplain. As a result, the Indus region is a very rich environment, but one that faces constant dangers of flooding.

Cereal agriculture in the Indus Valley region depends on the flooding of the river, and many Indus Valley archaeological sites are located along the active floodplain of the river and near the inundation lakes that form as a result of the flooding. The Indus Valley is flooded twice a year. Floods in April result from the melting of the snows in the Himalayas, while those in November and December result from summer monsoonal rains in the Punjab region. Cereals were grown in the Indus regions during the winter months; they were planted after the November-December floods and harvested before the spring flooding in April (Fairservis 1971: 229). The alluvial soils retain moisture quite well, even in the driest areas of Pakistan, facilitating wheat and barley cultivation.

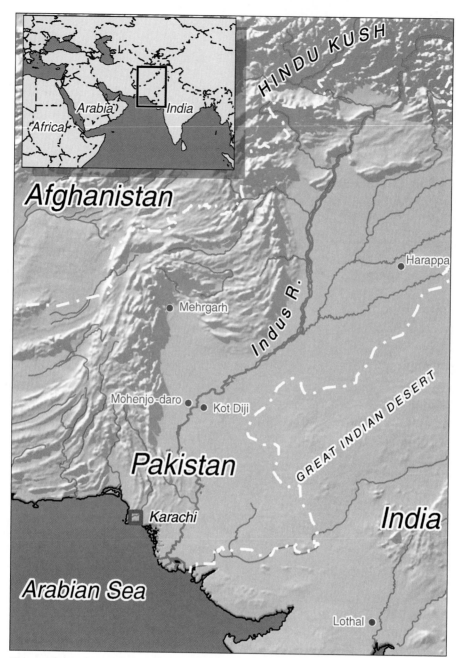

Figure 22.1

Map of the Indus Valley region showing the sites discussed in this chapter and the relation of the region to the larger Indian subcontinent.

The Beginnings of Farming in the Indus Region

At the end of the Ice Age, about 10,000 years ago, the Indian subcontinent, like much of the rest of Eurasia, was occupied by small bands of mobile hunter-gatherers. Until re-cently, it had been assumed that farming had spread gradually from the hilly flanks regions of the Middle East into the Indian subconti-nent. The earliest known farming villages dated only to the mid-fifth millennium b.c. (Meadow 1993: 295). However, recent archae-ological research at the site of **Mehrgarh** in

Pakistan (Jarrige and Meadow 1980) has shed new light on the origins of farming in the region.

Mehrgarh is located in the Kachi District of Baluchistan in Pakistan (see Figure 22.1). Although the site is bordered by high mountains to both the east and the west, it is located in an alluvial plain less than 200 meters (660 ft.) above sea level. The rich alluvial soils and the perennial Bolan and Nari Rivers would have made this site an attractive area for early farmers. A series of radiocarbon dates indicates that the site was initially occupied in the seventh millennium b.c., and was not finally abandoned until the middle of the third millennium b.c. Conservative dates for the aceramic Neolithic occupation range from 6300 to 5300 b.c. (Meadow 1993: 301).

The Bolan river cut a 12-meter (39 ft.) deep section through the cultural deposits and alluvium, revealing the presence of 7 to 8 meters (23 to 26 ft.) of aceramic Neolithic deposits. The earliest dwellings are simple, multiroomed buildings of mud brick. The spaces between these buildings were used for domestic purposes and for burials. The earliest inhabitants of Mehrgarh were cereal farmers who grew wheat and barley. There is no evidence to suggest that wheat was initially domesticated at Mehrgarh; wild wheat is not native to the Baluchistan region. It was probably introduced to the Mehrgarh region from the west. The evidence for barley is more problematic. Although wild barley is not native to the Mehrgarh region today, both wild and domesticated barley were recovered from the earliest levels of the Mehrgarh site. Whether this cereal was independently domesticated or introduced from farther west remains an open question. The faunal evidence, however, does suggest that this area may represent an independent center for animal domestication. In the earliest aceramic Neolithic levels, the faunal assemblages are dominated by the remains of wild game, such as gazelle, deer, and blackbuck. However, domestic goats also appear to have been kept by at least some of the early aceramic Neolithic inhabitants of the site. The numbers of domestic cattle, sheep, and goats increase throughout the aceramic Neolithic, and it is likely that cattle and sheep were domesticated from local wild stock at that time

(Meadow 1993). The Mehrgarh cattle appear to be zebu, or humped, cattle, animals that are well adapted to the hot, dry climate of South Asia. These animals continued to play an important role in the Indus Valley economy throughout prehistory and into historic and recent times. The data from Mehrgarh can be used to make "a very strong case for the indigenous process of domestication within the Indian subcontinent" (Possehl 1990: 265).

The Early Indus Period

The archaeological data from Mehrgarh indicate that village farming communities were established in the Indus Valley region by the mid-seventh millennium b.c. Archaeologists working in the Indus Valley, as in Mesopotamia, have been interested in how these small agricultural villages developed into a complex urban society. Recent archaeological research, beginning with the work at Mehrgarh, has shown that the complex Indus Valley urban society represents an essentially indigenous development (Parpola 1994). "There is continuity in the prehistoric sequence of northwestern India and Pakistan from the beginnings of the village farming community to the eclipse of the ancient cities of the Indus" (Possehl 1990: 267–268).

The evidence from the later phases of Mehrgarh and elsewhere in South Asia points both to agricultural intensification and to population growth during the ceramic Neolithic periods. During the fourth millennium b.c. at Mehrgarh, irrigation canals replaced simpler irrigation systems based on stone or earthen dams. In addition, settlements expanded from the Baluchistan area into the marshes and jungles of the Indus Valley proper at that time. The areas around the riverbanks were probably originally heavily wooded, providing habitats for jungle animals such as tigers. Agricultural settlements based on cereal growing and stock rearing appear throughout the Indus plain during the later fourth and early third millennia B.C.

The period between 3200 and 2600 B.C. has been termed the **Early Indus, or Pre-Urban, period.** Settlements from this period show many continuities with early Neolithic communities; however, some changes begin

Figure 22.2
Kot Dijian pottery.

concludes with two huge conflagrations (Allchin and Allchin 1982: 145–146). Similar events have been recorded at the end of the Early Indus period at other Indus Valley sites.

The Emergence of Complex Societies in the Indus Valley

Around 2600 B.C. the Indus Valley region underwent rapid social and cultural changes leading to the appearance of true urbanism in the Indus Valley. One of the most important changes was in the nature and intensity of trade. The focus of long-distance trade shifted from the overland caravan trade with central Asia and Iran to a more maritime orientation centering on the Persian Gulf, probably as a result of the adoption of water transport (Parpola 1994: 21–22). In recent years, a number of sites with clear links to the Indus Valley have been discovered on the Arabian peninsula.

In addition to the growth in the volume of trade, significant changes are evident in settlement patterns at that time. While Early Indus sites are generally small and show little differentiation in size, the beginning of the **Mature Harappan, or Urban, phase** (2550 to 1900 B.C.) is marked by the appearance of a small number of very large settlements (Possehl 1990: 271). The larger Indus sites include an acropolis, a high platform of mud brick surrounded by walls, that may have served as an administrative center, and a lower town that included workshops, markets, and living quarters. The large Indus sites also include extensive public sewage and drainage systems, designed to carry wastewater away from the settlements **(Figure 22.3)**. These public sanitary systems would have required complex engineering and maintenance (Possehl 1990: 271). Evidence for intentional town planning can be seen at both the larger Indus cities and at the smaller towns. For example, at the Mature Harappan town of **Lothal,** located on the coastal flats at the head of the Gulf of Cambay in northwest India, residential quarters are clearly separated from areas of craft production. The archaeological evidence from Lothal and elsewhere points to significant craft specialization in metallurgy, pottery manufacture, stoneworking, and other crafts, implying a degree of occupational differentiation that is

to foreshadow the cultural transformations that mark the appearance of the mature urban Harappan period. During the Early Indus period, most settlement sites remain small, averaging only 5.4 hectares (13.3 acres) (Possehl 1990: 270). There is evidence for increasing trade during this period. An intensive caravan trade that linked the Indus Valley, the Iranian Plateau, and Central Asia peaked around 3000 B.C. (Parpola 1994: 17).

During the Early Indus period, distinctive local and regional styles of pottery were replaced by a widespread type of ceramics known as Kot Dijian ware. Kot Dijian wares include globular vessels with a wide black band painted around the neck **(Figure 22.2)**. The uniformity of this ceramic style over a wide area points to increased communications and trade between villages. Standardized brick sizes also appear at this time.

Kot Dijian pottery takes its name from the Early Indus site of **Kot Diji,** located near productive agricultural land along one of the ancient flood channels of the Indus near the Harappan city of Mohenjo-daro (see Case Study). The site of Kot Diji was excavated in the 1950s by the Pakistan Archaeological Service. Excavations revealed houses of stone and mud brick surrounded by a wall of limestone and mud brick. The function of this wall is unclear; it may have served to contain the floodwaters of the Indus. Alternatively, it may have served to keep people or livestock out. The Early Indus occupation at Kot Diji

Figure 22.3
Street with drains, from Mohenjo-daro.

Figure 22.4
The Harappan port site of Lothal in northwest India showing the possible loading dock.

not seen in the Early Indus period (Possehl 1990: 272). In addition, Lothal appears to have served as a gateway settlement **(Figure 22.4)** through which the Harappans gained access to raw materials from the Indian peninsula, including semiprecious stones, ivory, steatite, seashells, and possibly metals (Possehl and Raval 1989: 16).

Other important changes in material culture are apparent at this time. Perhaps the most important is the appearance of a system of writing (see the Archaeology in Practice box). Unlike the Sumerian writing system in Mesopotamia, whose gradual evolution has been traced by archaeologists, the Indus system appears at the beginning of the urban

Archaeology in Practice

Deciphering the Indus Valley Script

One of the most enigmatic features of the Indus Valley civilization is its written language. As was noted above, writing first appears in the twenty-sixth century B.C. at the beginning of the mature urban Harappan phase. The Harappan writing system cannot be derived directly from any other known script (Parpola 1994: 53). Moreover, no bilingual texts including inscriptions in Harappan and a second language are known.

The archaeologists and linguists who have attempted to decipher the Harappan writing system have faced a number of additional challenges and obstacles. Only about 4,000 examples of Harappan writing are known, and most are found on stone stamp seals (Figure 22.5), on amulets, and on fragments of pottery. The stamp seals are made on square fragments of soapstone and usually include both an inscription and a picture. Most of the Harappan inscriptions are quite short, averaging only about five or six characters (Fairservis 1983: 58). The longest known inscription includes only 26 signs.

The first challenge faced by scholars attempting to decipher this

Figure 22.5

A Harappan stone stamp seal showing an inscription. The character to the right of the animal's horns may indicate the number 3.

Figure 22.6

Impression of a stamp seal from Mohenjo-daro (M735) showing cramping of the final incised sign.

script is the question of whether the characters are read from left to right (as English is) or from right to left (as Hebrew is). One way to determine this is to look for cramping at the end of inscriptions when inscriptions are squeezed to fit into limited spaces (Figure 22.6). A few Harappan inscriptions show cramping along the left margin, suggesting that the script was read from right to left.

A second question facing linguists is the nature of the writing system itself. Does each character represent a single sound (an

alphabetic system like our own), a syllable (a syllabic system), or a word (a logographic system)? The Indus script includes between 400 and 450 signs (Parpola 1994: 85). True logographic systems, such as modern Chinese, include thousands of characters. On the other hand, the Indus script includes far too many characters to represent a purely syllabic language. The Indus script appears to use some signs to represent words and others to represent syllables. Such systems are termed logosyllabic. Egyptian

Harappan period without any obvious antecedents. The Harappan script appears to have been an indigenous development, although it may have some relationship with the proto-Elamite script that was used in Iran during the fourth and early third millennia B.C. The use of a standardized system of weights and measures, also adopted at the beginning of the Mature Harappan period, clearly reflects the increasing importance of trade and exchange in Harappan society.

Mature Indus Valley sites are found in a region that covers 1.25 million square kilometers (483,000 sq. mi.), about four times the size of southern Mesopotamia. The use of a common script, a uniform system of weights and measures, and a common system of urban planning, as well as the similarities in a broad range of artifact types over such a vast area, are remarkable. These commonalities certainly indicate intensive communication and trade between the Indus Valley hieroglyphics and early Sumerian writing are other examples of ancient logosyllabic languages.

A more difficult and fundamental question is the problem of what language is represented by these characters. Is it a member of any known language family? Many scholars have hypothesized that the Harappan language is likely to have belonged to the Dravidian language family (Allchin and Allchin 1982: 213). Twenty-five Dravidian languages are spoken in South Asia today, primarily in southern and southeastern India. The most widespread of these, Tamil, is spoken by 37.7 million individuals. One argument favoring a Dravidian reading for the Harappan script is based on the number system. The Harappan numbers from 1 to 7 are indicated by a series of strokes; a different character is used to represent the number 8 (Figure 22.7). This appears to represent a system with a base of 8 (our numerical system has a base of 10). Linguistic research indicates that the original Dravidian number system probably also had a base of 8. Recently, some scholars have suggested that the Harappan script may be a written form of a language in the proto-Elamo-Dravidian family (Possehl 1996: 165). This family would include both the proto-Elamite languages of Iran and the antecedents to the Dravidian languages of South Asia.

Figure 22.7

Characters representing the numbers from 1 to 8 in the Harappan script.

Once these basic questions have been answered, the process of decipherment of the language is almost like solving a crossword puzzle (Parpola 1994: 273). One clue is that many Indus Valley signs appear to be pictures of common objects. For example, one sign seems to resemble a fish. However, this sign appears too frequently in Harappan inscriptions to always mean "fish." Therefore, many hypothetical interpretations are based on the homophone principle: that words that sound alike but have different meanings are likely to be represented by the same character or characters. For example, in many Dravidian languages, the word for "fish," *min,* also means "star" (Parpola 1994: 181). Similar interpretations have been made of other signs (see, for example, Fairservis 1983).

Clearly, much work remains to be done before the Indus script can be deciphered. However, the results of this labor are likely to shed invaluable light on "Harappan polity, social organization and ideology" (Fairservis 1983: 66). These aspects of ancient societies are often difficult to reconstruct on the basis of archaeological evidence alone.

cities, towns, and villages, and they may also indicate some form of administrative or political integration within the Indus Valley region. However, the question of whether the whole Indus region was ever politically united is one that cannot be answered on the basis of present archaeological evidence.

Archaeological data do suggest that the beginnings of the Mature, or Urban, phase saw increasing social stratification. The larger Harappan urban sites have provided evidence for houses of varying sizes, ranging from one-room tenements to great houses with several courtyards and several dozen rooms (Allchin and Allchin 1982: 177). The Urban period also is marked by the increased use of luxury goods, including metals, beads, and other items of personal adornment (Possehl 1990: 272). As noted above, there is clear evidence for craft specialization and occupational differentiation, indicating that an increasing portion of the population was engaged in activities other than agriculture and animal husbandry. The ability to support a large number of nonfarm workers is a testament to the agricultural productivity of the Indus region.

A striking feature of the Indus Valley cities is the absence of temples or other monumental architecture of a religious nature. In addition, Harappan cities have provided no clear evidence for palaces. These data suggest that Harappan society may have been organized in a way very different from that of Sumer or Egypt. It is even possible that the Harappans had no kings (Possehl 1996: 14). The nature of Indus Valley political organization remains largely unknown.

Case Study
Indus Valley Urbanism: Mohenjo-daro and Harappa

Much of our knowledge of the urban period in the Indus region has come as a result of intensive archaeological excavations at two of the largest Indus Valley cities: Mohenjo-daro and Harappa. A large number of archaeological excavations have been carried out at both sites, including extensive excavations by the British archaeologist Sir Mortimer Wheeler in the 1940s (Wheeler 1968). Excavation was resumed at Harappa in 1986 under the direction of the late George Dales, and the project continues under the direction of Richard Meadow of Harvard University. Excavations at Mohenjo-daro and Harappa have shed light on the nature of urban development in the Indus Valley and on the relationship between the cities and the Indus Valley civilization as a whole (Dales 1992: 1).

Harappa is located in the Punjab region of northern Pakistan, adjacent to a dry bed of the Ravi River (one of the five rivers of the Punjab). Stamp seals were discovered at Harappa in the late nineteenth and early twentieth centuries, and archaeological excavations began there in 1920 to 1921 under the direction of the Archaeological Service of India. The site covers an area of at least 150 hectares (370 acres) (Kenoyer 1992: 33) and may have housed 40,000 people at its height (Parpola 1994: 6). The town included both a citadel (Mound AB) and a lower town (**Figure 22.8**). Recent excavations have revealed the presence of an Early Indus period settlement and continued occupation into the Mature, or Urban, Indus period with no

Figure 22.8

Plan of Harappa and Mohenjo-daro.

evidence of a break, or hiatus (Kenoyer 1992: 38). Excavations in the Mound E area indicate that the settlement was expanding in the late pre-urban period (Figure 22.9). During that period there is evidence for the laying out of large north-south streets and for the segregation of craft activities and residential areas (Kenoyer 1992: 57).

The beginning of the Urban Period occupation is marked by the use of baked brick, in addition to mud brick, for the construction of houses and other structures. There is evidence for extensive construction in the citadel area (Mound AB) at this time; this is followed by significant efforts at urban renewal in the Mound E area. By the latest part of the Harappan period, there is evidence of urban congestion in many areas of the site, possibly resulting from overpopulation. For example, brick

pavings and drains encroach on through streets, narrowing those thoroughfares. The final phases of occupation at Harappa have been heavily disturbed by brick robbing, and those periods have not been dated by radiocarbon. The available data, however, do not indicate urban decay, military invasions, or the abandonment of the site at the end of the Mature Harappan period (Kenoyer 1992: 56).

The other major Harappan urban center, Mohenjo-daro, is located approximately 670 kilometers (416 mi.) southwest of Harappa in the Indus Valley. Excavations at Mohenjo-daro have revealed a quite similar urban layout (see Figure 22.8). The citadel, or upper town, includes a number of public buildings, the most impressive of which is the Great Bath (Figure 22.10). The bath measures 12 by 7 by 3 meters (39 by 23 by 10 ft.) deep and was

Figure 22.9

Map showing the extent of occupation at Harappa during different periods. Periods 1 and 2 are Early Indus, while period 3A corresponds to the early part of the Mature Harappan period.

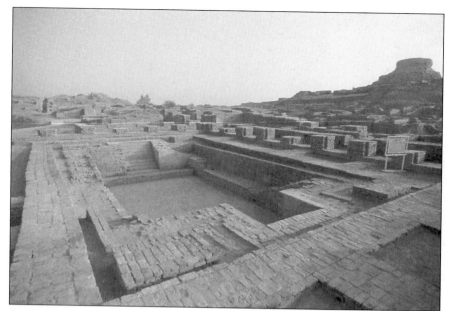

Figure 22.10

The Great Bath at Mohenjo-daro.

supplied with water from a well in an adjacent room. Ritual bathing has played an important role in Indian religion throughout history, and it is likely that it also played a role in the rituals of the Indus cities. Evidence for other public buildings on the citadel includes the foundations of a building that Wheeler (1968: 43) interpreted as a granary and a large block of buildings that may be associated with administrators or priests (Allchin and Allchin 1982: 181–182).

The lower town at Mohenjo-daro included a variety of dwellings, ranging from single-roomed tenements to houses with many rooms and courtyards. The lower town also included shops, dyers' vats, and workshops for pottery manufacture, metalworking, and shell bead making. Several buildings in the lower town have also been identified as temples, based on their large size or unusual plan (Allchin and Allchin 1982: 180).

The Post-Urban Phase and the Harappan Eclipse

Beginning around 1900 B.C., the Indus Valley region underwent significant cultural and economic changes. Those changes mark the beginning of the **Late Harappan, or Post-Urban, phase** of the Harappan civilization (1900 to 1500 B.C.). The most striking of the changes was the abandonment of many of the larger cities, including Mohenjo-daro. At that time, a number of items of material culture disappeared, including stamp seals, certain types of pottery, and the Indus Valley script. Long-distance trade declined, except for trade in metals, and a reduced range of specialized crafts was produced. The uniformity of the Mature Indus material culture was replaced by a cultural mosaic (Possehl and Raval 1989: 25). This transformation can be seen clearly in the changes in settlement and subsistence that mark the end of the Urban phase and the beginnings of the Post-Urban period. The number of sites in the Sind region of Pakistan (the area around Mohenjo-daro) was dramatically reduced, and many of the large urban sites disappeared forever. In the Punjab and northern India, however, archaeology has revealed a rich and varied post-urban settlement with many permanent agricultural communities. The Harappan town of **Rojdi** on the Saurashtra peninsula in northwest India reveals continuity from the Mature Harappan to the Late Harappan period (Figure 22.11). Around 2500 B.C. Harappans from the Sind region of Pakistan moved into Saurashtra, probably to obtain access to raw materials. Towns such as Rojdi were supported by a rich and diverse agricultural economy, including both summer and winter crops.

Figure 22.11

Rojdi, a town in northwest India that shows continuity from the Mature Harappan to the Late Harappan period.

While sites such as Rojdi provide clear evidence for continuity between the Mature Harappan and the Late Harappan periods, the evidence from Mohenjo-daro points to significant cultural changes at the end of the Mature Harappan phase. At Mohenjo-daro there is no evidence for a Late Harappan occupation. In addition, excavations of the final Late Harappan layers at the site have revealed groups of hastily buried corpses or unburied corpses left in the streets, as well as buried hoards of jewelry and copper items. Mortimer Wheeler interpreted these hastily buried bodies and hoards as evidence for an invasion of the Indus Valley by Aryan speakers, people speaking Indo-European languages. His interpretation relied heavily on literary records. The earliest Indian literature, the Rigveda, which is written in Sanskrit, an ancient Indo-European language, describes victorious invaders attacking the walled cities of the aboriginal Indian peoples. Wheeler argued that decadent Harappan urbanism was replaced by the heroic barbarism of the early Aryans (Wheeler 1968: 136).

Today few archaeologists would accept Wheeler's interpretation. The so-called massacre victims from Mohenjo-daro do not appear to have died of traumatic injuries (Kennedy 1982). Moreover, the uppermost levels of Mohenjo-daro provide no evidence for the kind of widespread destruction that could reasonably be associated with a major invasion or military defeat. In fact, by the end of the Mature Harappan period, parts of Mohenjo-daro may have become urban slums. The archaeological evidence points to economic and administrative decline, rather than military invasion.

In general, it has been difficult to identify Indo-European speakers on the basis of archaeological evidence such as pottery and metalwork. It has also been impossible to determine whether the introduction of Indo-European languages into the Indian subcontinent took place at the end of the Mature Harappan period when sites such as Mohenjo-daro were abandoned. As noted previously, Harappan eclipse was not a uniform phenomenon across the Indus Valley region. Sites such as Harappa in the Punjab and Rojdi in Saurashtra continued to be occupied into the Late Harappan period. A variety of causes have been suggested for the abandonment of sites in the Sind region of southern Pakistan at the end of the Mature Harappan period. Natural causes for the abandonment of Indus Valley sites may have included flooding and changes in river courses. Overirrigation (which can lead to a buildup of salt in

Figure 22.12

Stamp seal from Mohenjo-daro showing a male figure wearing a buffalo-horn headdress.

Figure 22.13

Female figurine from Mohenjo-daro.

the soil), administrative failure, and the decline in long-distance trade may also have played a role in the abandonment of these sites.

The Legacy of the Harappan Civilization

Although the Indus Valley civilization ended more that 3,500 years ago, elements in Indus Valley culture may have influenced later societies of the Indian subcontinent. Early archaeologists working in South Asia noticed some remarkable similarities between Indus Valley images and later Hindu gods. For example, a number of stamp seals (Figure 22.12) show a male figure sitting cross-legged in a low throne, often flanked by wild goats, and surrounded by other jungle creatures. The male figure wears a buffalo-horn headdress, and in some cases a plant sprouts in between the horns. All these features can be found in later descriptions of the Hindu god Siva. Similarly, many Indus Valley sites have produced numerous female figurines (Figure 22.13). These figures, which some scholars have interpreted as mother goddesses, may parallel the cult of Parvati, the spouse of Siva.

The Parvati cult described in Indian literature continues to be practiced in India today (Allchin and Allchin 1982: 213–214). In addition to possible continuities in religious practice, the Indus valley legacy can also be seen in areas of technology, craft production, and agricultural practice. For example, the terracotta model carts that have been recovered from Mohenjo-daro (Figure 22.14) are virtually identical to carts still in use in the upper Sind region of Pakistan today (Allchin 1982: 326).

Conclusion

At about 2600 B.C., the first true cities appear in the Indus Valley along with the Indus Valley script, increasing craft specialization, and significant social stratification. The factors that led to the development of Harappan urbanism are unclear, but the shift from overland to sea trade may have played a critical role.

Clearly, much remains to be learned about the ancient Harappans. The decipherment of the Indus Valley script will undoubtedly shed new light on Harappan trade practices, administrative patterns, and even

Figure 22.14

Terracotta model of a cart drawn by oxen, recovered from Mohenjo-daro.

religious ideology. However, even if the Indus script is never fully deciphered, ongoing excavations at Indus Valley sites such as Harappa will provide new insights into the nature of Indus Valley urbanism and the growth and development of Harappan society.

 Glossary

Early Indus, or Pre-Urban, period. The period in South Asia dated between 3200 and 2600 B.C. The period is marked by an increasing intensity of trade, especially the long-distance caravan trade that linked the Indus Valley with central Asia and Iran; by population growth; and by an increasing concentration of settlements in the Indus Valley itself.

Harappa. One of the largest urban centers of the Indus Valley civilization, located in the Punjab region of northern Pakistan. The site includes both a citadel and a lower town, and the city may have housed 40,000 inhabitants at its height.

Indus Valley, or Harappan, civilization. The earliest urban, literate society in the Indian subcontinent. Throughout the third millennium B.C. Indus Valley cities, towns, and villages were spread across Pakistan and

northern India. These sites shared a common written language and material culture, but it is not clear whether they were politically unified.

Kot Diji. An Indus Valley site that was occupied during the Early and Mature Harappan periods. The site is located near the major urban center of Mohenjo-daro. Kot Diji gave its name to a style of early Harappan pottery that was widely distributed throughout the Indus Valley.

Late Harappan, or Post-Urban, phase. A period (ca. 1900 to 1500 B.C.) of major cultural change in northern India and Pakistan. The beginning of the Late Harappan period is marked by the abandonment of a number of towns and cities (e.g., Mohenjo-daro), the disappearance of the Indus Valley script, a reduction in long-distance trade, and the development of regional styles of pottery and metalwork.

Lothal. A Mature Harappan town in northwestern India that has provided evidence for intentional urban planning, craft specialization, and trade in semiprecious stones, steatite, ivory, and seashells.

Mature Harappan, or Urban, phase. The period (2550 to 1900 B.C.) in the Indian subcontinent characterized by the appearance of large urban sites, the intensification of trade and craft specialization, increasing social stratification, and the appearance of the Indus Valley script.

Mehrgarh. A site in the Baluchistan region of Pakistan that was occupied from the mid-seventh millennium b.c. through the end of the Early Indus period (mid-third millennium B.C.). During the aceramic Neolithic (6300 to 5300 b.c.) occupation of the site, the farmers at Mehrgarh appear to have domesticated zebu cattle and probably also sheep from local wild animals.

Mohenjo-daro. One of the large Indus Valley urban centers. The site is located in the Indus Valley in southern Pakistan. It included both a citadel, or upper town, with a ritual bath and other administrative buildings and a lower town with residences, shops, and craft activities.

Rojdi. A Harappan town located on the Saurashtra peninsula in northwest India. The site was occupied continuously from the Mature Harappan to the Late Harappan period.

Further Reading

Jarrige, J. F., and R. H. Meadow

1980. The Antecedents of Civilization in the Indus Valley. *Scientific American* 243 (2): 122–133.

The article presents the results of the recent excavations at the site of Mehrgarh in Pakistan and their relationship to the development of the Harappan civilization.

Possehl, G. L.

1990. Revolution in the Urban Revolution: The Emergence of Indus Urbanization. *Annual Review of Anthropology* 19: 261–282.

This very readable review article focuses on the beginnings of village farming in the Indus region and the process of urban development during the third millennium B.C. The article includes a comprehensive bibliography.

Other Bibliography

Allchin, F. R.

1982. The Legacy of the Indus Civilization. In *Harappan Civilization: A Contemporary Perspective,* edited by G. L. Possehl, pp. 325–333. Warminster, U.K.: Aris and Phillips.

Allchin, B., and R. Allchin

1982. *The Rise of Civilization in India and Pakistan.* Cambridge: Cambridge University Press.

Dales, George F.

1992. Project Director's Introduction. In *Harappa Excavations 1986–1990: A Multidisciplinary Approach to Third Millennium Urbanism,* edited by R. H. Meadow, pp. 1–4. Madison, WI: Prehistory Press, Monographs in World Archaeology No. 3.

Fairservis, Walter A.

1971. *The Roots of Ancient India: The Archaeology of Early Indian Civilization.* New York: Macmillan.

1983. The Script of the Indus Valley Civilization. *Scientific American* 248 (3): 58–66.

Kennedy, Kenneth A. R.

1982. Skulls, Aryans and Flowing Drains: The Interface of Archaeology and Skeletal Biology in the Study of the Harappan Civilization. In *Harappan Civilization: A Contemporary Perspective,* edited by G. L. Possehl, pp. 289–295. Warminster, U.K.: Aris and Phillips.

Kenoyer, J. M.

1992. Urban Process in the Indus Tradition: A Preliminary Model from Harappa. In *Harappa Excavations 1986–1990: A Multidisciplinary Approach to Third Millennium Urbanism,* edited by R. H. Meadow, pp. 29–60. Madison, WI: Prehistory Press, Monographs in World Archaeology No. 3.

Meadow, R. H.

1993. Animal Domestication in the Middle East: A Revised View from the Eastern Margin. In *Harappan Civilization: A Recent Perspective,* 2d ed., edited by G. L. Possehl, pp. 295–320. New Delhi: American Institute of Indian Studies.

Parpola, Asko

1994. *Deciphering the Indus Script.* Cambridge: Cambridge University Press.

Possehl, G. L.

1996. *Indus Age: The Writing System.* Philadelphia: University of Pennsylvania Press.

Possehl, G. L., and M. H. Raval

1989. *The Harappan Civilization and Rojdi.* Leiden, The Netherlands, and New York: Brill.

Wheeler, R. E. M.

1968. *The Indus Civilization,* 3d. ed. Cambridge: Cambridge University Press.

Chapter 23

The Origin of the Ancient Egyptian Society

Introduction

To the average person, the cities and states of ancient Mesopotamia are obscure at best, and those of the Indus Valley are practically unknown. Ancient Egypt, by contrast, is a familiar image in our common culture. We think immediately of the Egypt of the pharaohs, illustrated, perhaps, by the pyramids and sphinx floodlit against the night sky in Cairo's nightly sound-and-light show **(Figure 23.1)**. We might recall the famous image of the British archaeologist Howard Carter crouched before the newly opened entrance to the tomb of the boy-king Tutankhamen, peering at the magnificent golden treasures within **(Figure 23.2)**. The Egyptian world has been a familiar subject of literature and the arts from Shakespeare's *Antony and Cleopatra* through the adventure movies of today.

The Egyptians left behind in the pyramids monumental structures that were among the wonders of the ancient world and that have been the subject of fascination ever since. Scholars, too, were fortunate that with the discovery of the **Rosetta stone** in 1799, they soon found the key to the Egyptian hieroglyphic writing **(Figure 23.3)**. The Rosetta stone is inscribed with the same text in Greek and two forms of Egyptian writing, a script and hieroglyphics. Starting with the premise that the language of the ancient Egyptians was related to Coptic, a language still spoken by their descendants, Jean François Champollion, in 1822, was able to decipher the meaning of the hieroglyphic writing. An enormous body of Egyptian writing has come down to us, engraved on tombs and monuments, and penned onto a multitude of papyrus (reed-paper) scrolls. Once this writing could be read, the politics, religious and moral beliefs, and daily life of the ancient Egyptians became a part of history.

This chapter, however, will deal with the archaeology of Egypt before the earliest hieroglyphics began the recording of history and before the rise of the pharaohs. We will discuss what is known of the inhabitants of the Nile Valley, who would become the Egyptian people, and we will conclude with the formation and development of the earliest Egyptian kingdom.

Figure 23.1

The popular image of Egypt: the floodlit pyramids and sphinx at Giza.

Figure 23.2

Howard Carter peering into the newly opened tomb of the boy-king Tutankhamen.

Figure 23.3

The Rosetta stone, the key to the decipherment of Egyptian hieroglyphics.

Ancient Egypt: The Gift of the Nile

The fifth-century B.C. Greek historian Herodotus wrote of Egypt as the gift of the Nile. Unlike the difficult-to-manage, unpredictable, and sometimes dangerous flooding of the Tigris-Euphrates plain or the Indus Valley, the flooding of the Nile was usually predictable, gentle, and well timed for the purposes of agriculture, arriving once each year around October. Unlike the irrigation waters from the Tigris and Euphrates, which each season brought with them a further deposit of salt to degrade the fertility of the soil, the annual layer of Nile silts continuously enriched the farmers' lands. Complex irrigation and drainage systems were unnecessary; the Nile's water needed only to be allowed to pool in the fields.

The early Egyptian farmers grew barley and emmer wheat, and raised sheep, goats, cattle, and pigs, along with greyhound-like dogs and donkeys. All these domesticates seem to have been introduced into Egypt from southwest Asia, with the possible exception of the pig and the donkey. Claims for early domestication of cattle in Egypt have not been well substantiated. The archaeological evidence is sparse, but agriculture appears to have arrived late in Egypt as compared with southwest Asia. The earliest agricultural settlements known in the Nile Valley date to about 5500 b.c., about 2,500 years later than the earliest agricultural villages in southwest Asia. In the past it was suggested that these domesticated plants and animals were introduced into the Nile Valley by an influx of migrant peoples from Asia. Today that scenario is regarded as unlikely; the material cultures of the early farmers generally resemble those of the late Paleolithic inhabitants of the Nile Valley. Most likely, the indigenous hunter-foragers of the Nile Valley adopted farming and stock rearing, as did some of the Mesolithic peoples of northern Europe (Chapter 20). Why they chose to adopt agriculture is still unclear.

The Egyptian Environment

The Nile Valley today is a place of remarkable contrasts. Virtually no rain falls south of Cairo, but in all those areas of bottomland that are flooded by the Nile, the land is lush and green, covered with farmers' fields, orchards, and palm groves. Beyond the Nile's silts the desert begins. The transition is so abrupt that in places one can literally stand with one foot in farmland and the other on the barren desert sands (Figure 23.4). In the north (Lower Egypt) the Nile floodplain is flat and broad, spreading out to form the Nile delta. As one travels south (into Upper Egypt), the strip of fertile floodplain becomes more and more constricted, enclosed between high cliffs, above which lie the Sahara desert to the west and the Arabian Desert to the east (Figure 23.5). The eastern cliffs are broken by a number of now dry tributary valleys that permit access to and from the world beyond the Nile. The unique semi-isolated and protected character of the Egyptian

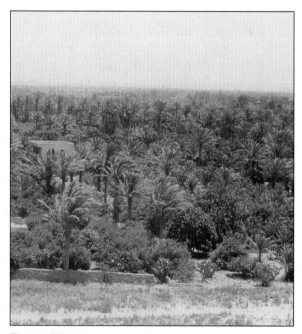

Figure 23.4

Desert and agricultural fields meet at Saqqara.

homeland has had profound effects on the nature of ancient Egyptian society.

The Egyptian environment in late Paleolithic times was quite different from today's. After the end of the Pleistocene, from about 9000 to 4000 b.c., north Africa received considerably more rainfall than it does today. In Upper Egypt the now dry streambeds flowed with water. Trees grew on the hillsides and grasses grew in the valleys. The wildlife of the area resembled that of sub-Saharan Africa, including elephants, rhinoceroses, giraffes, wild cattle, and antelopes. The streams, ponds, and rivers were

Figure 23.5

Map of the Nile Valley, showing the sites discussed in this chapter. The shaded area in the valley and across the delta indicates the region made fertile and green by the annual flooding of the Nile.

filled with fish, along with crocodiles and hippopotamuses. This rich environment provided a land of plenty for the hunter-foragers living there, which explains why farming was relatively late in reaching the Nile Valley. It is more difficult to explain why agriculture was adopted when it was. Perhaps expanding populations, combined with a gradually drying climate, drove away the game, making stock raising and planting more attractive. By the time of the first Egyptian dynasties (about 3000 B.C.) the largest animals, such as elephants and giraffes, had disappeared. By 2000 B.C., the smaller game such as ibex, antelope, and gazelle were gone as well, survived only by the crocodiles and hippos in the river (Butzer 1958, cited in Trigger et al. 1983).

The Earliest Egyptians

Perhaps surprisingly, Egypt before the first pharaohs is not very well known to archaeologists. A number of factors have contributed to this state of affairs. First, the very richness of later Egyptian architecture and material culture, as opposed to the simple remains of the most ancient sites, attracted most of the attention of earlier generations of scholars. Second, unlike the floodplains of Mesopotamia and the Indus Valley, the Nile floodplain has remained rich and productive and today sustains one of the highest population densities in the world. Thus the most ancient sites may lie buried beneath settlements still occupied, and many others may have been destroyed by millennia of continuous plowing. Third, the Nile itself has conspired either to destroy or to hide the earliest archaeological sites, either scouring them away or burying them ever deeper under the river's annual deposit of silt.

Despite these problems, archaeologists have gathered some information about the earliest settlers on the Nile. Before the unification of Egypt under the earliest pharaohs, the settlers in the Nile delta (Lower Egypt) seem to have been culturally distinct from those living in the south (Upper Egypt). The evidence for these early settlements is better preserved and studied in the delta than in the Nile Valley to the south.

A few sites represent the Neolithic period in the north of Egypt. The earliest known farmers in Egypt were found during excavations conducted in the 1930s in the **Fayum Depression,** an ancient lake bed west of the Nile in central Egypt (Caton-Thompson and Gardner 1934). The Fayum farmers, probably dating to about 5200 b.c., dug large numbers of straw-lined storage pits, in which were found quantities of well-preserved emmer wheat and barley. The Fayum Neolithic people harvested their crops with flint-edged sickles and hunted game with flint-tipped weapons. It is not certain whether they raised any domestic animals. They made pottery from clay tempered with straw, fine basketry **(Figure 23.6)**, and linen cloth woven from flax.

Early Settlements in the Delta

The best evidence for an early settlement comes from **Merimbda,** in the western delta (see Baumgartel 1965). The artifacts at Merimbda, especially the pottery, resemble those found in the Fayum, and the grains cultivated at Merimbda were much like those of the Fayum, including barley and emmer wheat. Dating to between 4800 and 4400 b.c., Merimbda was a large site, covering an area of 600 by 400 meters (2000 by 1300 ft.). Merimbda began as a scatter of temporary reed or matting shelters and eventually grew into a small village of oval or round mud-walled houses up to 6 meters (20 ft.) in diameter, arranged along either side of a path or street. The Merimbda people were buried lying on their sides in simple graves without grave offerings, interspersed among the houses.

The settlement at **Maadi,** near Cairo, dates to around 3650 B.C. (Caneva et al. 1987: 106). The site stretches over an area 1,300 meters (4300 ft.) long by over 100 meters wide (330 ft.), but different areas seem to have been occupied at different times. Like the people of Merimbda, the inhabitants of Maadi grew barley and emmer wheat, and they lived in houses made from mud and reed matting. They raised cattle, goats, sheep, and pigs, and kept dogs as well.

Figure 23.6

Basket found in the Neolithic settlement in the Fayum.

The dead were buried in a cemetery adjoining the settlement, in small, simple pits without any grave goods. Despite the general resemblance to the earlier Neolithic sites, Maadi is quite distinctive. This is especially apparent in the pottery, which, tempered with sand, resembles neither that from Merimbda nor that from the Upper Egyptian sites.

The distinctive artifacts in these sites, especially the pottery, and the simple burials without grave offerings set the delta sites apart from those in Upper Egypt. The late Neolithic sites in the delta are now often distinguished as the **Maadi culture.** Influences from western Asia are apparent in all these sites. The plants cultivated and the animals herded were all initially domesticated in western Asia and presumably entered the Nile delta from the Levant. Some of the pottery forms from the Fayum and from Merimbda resemble Levantine types. A small portion of the pottery at Maadi seems to have been imported directly from the Levant. Some other pottery at Maadi was imported from Upper Egypt, clearly demonstrating that while the people of Maadi were distinctive, they did not live in isolation.

Settlements and Cemeteries in Upper Egypt

In Upper Egypt, burials of the earliest farmers, dating to about 4800 to 4200 B.C.,[1] have been found along the middle portion of the Nile Valley, near the site of **Badari,** which gives its name to the **Badarian culture.** The limited settlement evidence suggests these people were probably mobile, perhaps living in simple tents or huts. They appear to have raised cattle, goats, and sheep; hunted; and fished. (Domesticated animals were buried in the cemeteries, in a manner similar to that of humans.) The Badarian settlement sites included storage pits, lined with basketry, containing emmer wheat and barley. Grinding stones and cooking pots show that the grain was prepared and eaten at the site (Baumgartel 1965: 8). Most of our knowledge of the Badarian, however, comes from the graves. Unlike those found in the delta, Badarian

---

[1]Most of the archaeology of predynastic Egypt was conducted before the advent of radiocarbon age determinations. Date ranges for the predynastic periods given in this chapter are estimates based on a variety of methods.

Figure 23.7

Badarian burials as excavated by Sir Flinders Petrie in the 1890s.

graves, well preserved by the extreme desert dryness, contain a wealth of grave goods. The dead were usually buried in oval pits covered with matting, lying on their sides with their knees drawn close to the body **(Figure 23.7)**. Fragments of their clothing have been preserved, which included robes and skirts of skin and linen fabric. Belts, necklaces, bracelets, and anklets of beads were worn, made from shell, coral, copper, and turquoise, but mostly of steatite that had been glazed blue to look like turquoise. Many graves held bone and ivory combs, spoons, and ladles, often decorated with carvings of birds and animals. Graves also held slate palettes, used to grind green malachite, which was kept in ivory vases and used as a cosmetic **(Figure 23.8)**. Pottery was the most common object in the graves; the most characteristic were hemispherical bowls, covered with a red slip, stroked with a comb to produce a rippled surface, and then polished smooth. These pots were fired in such a way as to produce a black band at the top, around the rim. Many of the burial practices and artifacts of the Badarians are clearly predecessors of the later dynastic Egyptians **(Figure 23.9)**.

In the 1890s the British archaeologist Sir Flinders Petrie excavated two settlements and several large cemeteries at **Naqada** (also spelled Nagada), in Upper Egypt. Among them, the cemeteries contain about 3,000 predynastic burials. Most of the graves belong to the time span following the Badarian and before the earliest Egyptian dynasty. Flinders Petrie was the first scientific archaeologist to excavate in Egypt. He was faced with the need to place these many burials (and the settlements associated with them) in some form of chronological sequence. To do this, Petrie devised a technique known as sequence dating, based on the sequential occurrence of pottery types in the grave assemblages (see the Archaeology in Practice box). He broke up the sequence into three succeeding phases, which he called Amratian, Gerzean, and Semainian, and which are now termed **Naqada I, Naqada II,** and **Naqada III.** The Naqada sequence dates to circa 4200 to 3100 B.C. Since Petrie's time, a few absolute dates have been obtained to anchor the sequence, and modern computer methods have refined Petrie's conclusions, but the Naqada sequence has largely stood the test of time.

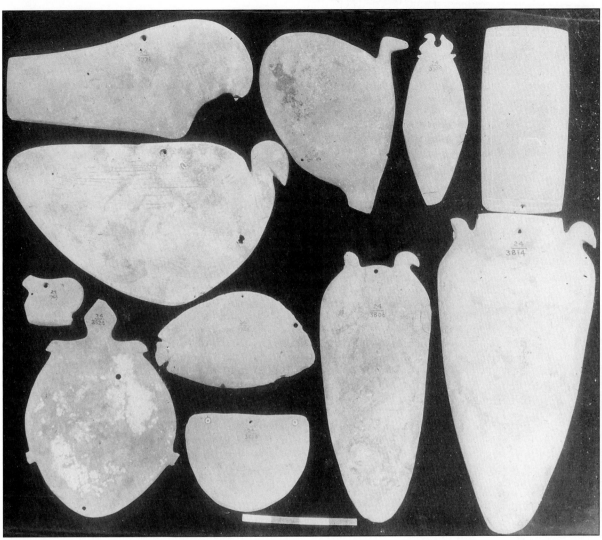

Figure 23.8

Typical slate pallets from the Badarian period.

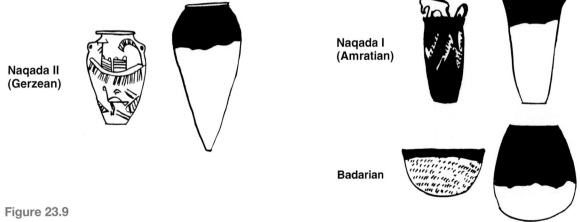

**Naqada II
(Gerzean)**

**Naqada I
(Amratian)**

Badarian

Figure 23.9

Typical pottery of the Badarian and Naqada phases.

Archaeology in Practice

Sequence Dating and Archaeological Seriation

When Sir Flinders Petrie excavated the thousands of artifact-laden burials at Naqada in the late nineteenth century, he was faced with a crucial analytical problem: How could this wide range of archaeological assemblages be ordered in time? No calendrical dates could be given to these prehistoric remains, and the absolute dating methods on which modern archaeologists rely would not be developed for many decades to come. Still, Petrie observed, "the main value of dates is to show the sequence of events . . . The order of events and the relation of one country to another is the main essential of history" (Petrie 1899: 295). Although Petrie was unable to assign actual dates to the Upper Egyptian prehistoric graves, he found he could logically order the various grave assemblages according to the types and forms of artifacts they contained. Petrie inferred that this order represented a temporal sequence.

Petrie termed his method **sequence dating.** An early version of Petrie's sequence dating procedure is illustrated in **Figure 23.10**. Each horizontal row represents some of the pottery types typical of the assemblages for seven successive chronological periods. With each successive period some pottery types disappear while other new types make their appearance. The vertical lines in the illustration indicate pottery types that persist from one period into the next. These links permitted Petrie to chain together the assemblages into a consistent temporal sequence. The pottery vessels on the far left, so-called wavy-handled jars, provide a second line of evidence. The style of the vessels changes gradually through time, shifting from rounded forms in the early periods to straight-sided forms in the later periods, accompanied by the evolution of the functional wavy handles in the early forms into purely decorative elements in the latest forms. This degeneration of a functional element into a decorative element allowed Petrie to determine which way was up, that is, which end of the connected chain of periods was the most recent.

During subsequent research, Petrie continued to alter and revise his criteria for the sequence dates assigned to the Egyptian prehistoric assemblages. Since his time, as more evidence has accumulated and has been analyzed, the specifics of the sequence dates have been found to be incorrect in various details. It has become clear that the actual time span represented by the sequence dates is not uniform; the more recent sequence dates represent progressively shorter periods of time.

Overall, however, the method remains valid. A modern statistical seriation study of a group of 60 Egyptian grave assemblages (Kendall 1969) reached conclusions very similar to those assigned according to the sequence dating method.

Since sequence dating relies on the appearance and disappearance of artifact types from one period to the next, it is sometimes referred to as occurrence seriation. Another form of seriation, frequency seriation, relies on changing *proportions* of various artifact types though successive time periods (see Trigger 1989: 200; Deetz 1967: 26–33). This method was first introduced in the early twentieth century as a means

Figure 23.10

Sir Flinders Petrie's original presentation of his method of sequence dating. The horizontal rows represent successive time periods. The vertical bars link pottery types that persist from one period to the next. The sequence of wavy-handled jars is shown on the left.

for chronologically ordering Native American pottery assemblages. It has since come into use worldwide.

Frequency seriations are often presented as a type of chart known as a battleship diagram. An example of such a diagram is shown in **Figure 23.11**. The horizontal rows in the chart represent the successive time periods. The width of the vertical bars represents the proportions of several artifact types (in this case, gravestones). When the rows representing the time periods are correctly ordered, the vertical bars indicate the gradual appearance of an artifact type, followed by its disappearance. This pattern looks like a battleship viewed from above.

The Naqada sequence appears to represent a continued development of the preceding Badarian. Sites from the earlier Naqada I period are found only in Upper Egypt. There is little settlement evidence. Only a few simple circular hut foundations, made from stone fragments and mud, have been properly excavated. The huts themselves were probably made from wattle and daub, interwoven sticks packed with mud. Graves continue to be the major source of evidence for Naqada I material culture. They are much like those of the Badarian and contain similar objects. The black-topped pottery gradually gives way to a red pottery painted with white lines, sometimes with images of animals. A tradition of fine flint working appears, to be developed further in the Naqada II period. The Naqada I people also ground hard stone into a variety of objects, including basalt vases and circular mace heads. Their burial costume included beads, bone and ivory rings, armlets, hairpins and combs, as well as slate cosmetic palettes. One hair comb shows a figure of what appears to be the earliest known representation of the Egyptian god Seth (Baumgartel 1965: 17). In historic times Naqada would become the cult center for the god Seth (Trigger et al. 1983: 35).

Greater changes appear during the succeeding Naqada II-Gerzean period. Naqada II

Figure 23.12

Reconstruction of burned Naqada II period house at Hierakonpolis.

sites are much more widely distributed, from the southern border of the delta in the north to the border with Nubia in the south. Major population centers are found at Naqada and, farther south, at **Hierakonpolis.** At Naqada, Petrie found the remains of a rectangular dwelling made from mud brick and what appeared to be a defensive wall. A Naqada II period grave also contained a pottery model of a rectangular house. Recent excavations at Hierakonpolis have uncovered much more extensive settlement evidence (Hoffman 1982), including the mud-brick footing of a rectangular house that was unusually well-preserved because it had been burned. Its walls were likely made of wattle and daub. Adjacent to the house was a pottery kiln, probably the source of the fire that destroyed it **(Figure 23.12)**. Surveys of the Hierakonpolis area indicate that the local population grew explosively around 3800 B.C., during the end of the Naqada I and beginning of the Naqada II

periods. Settlements consisted of groups of rectangular houses enclosed within walled compounds. The region was gradually taking on an urban character (Hoffman et al. 1986: 181). Late in the period the settlements become more concentrated. In addition to the more intensive residential development, an oval courtyard surrounded by wooden structures represents a possible temple complex.

Changes were occurring in the burial practices as well. In the Naqada II period some graves were much larger and more elaborate than others, indicating that differences in wealth and social status were appearing. A separate cemetery at Naqada included several very large rectangular tombs, lined with mud brick, with the body laid in a semiseparate niche at one side. One tomb of this type, now known to date to Naqada II times, was excavated at Hierakonpolis in 1898. This tomb (known as the Decorated Tomb) had a plastered wall on which were painted scenes, including

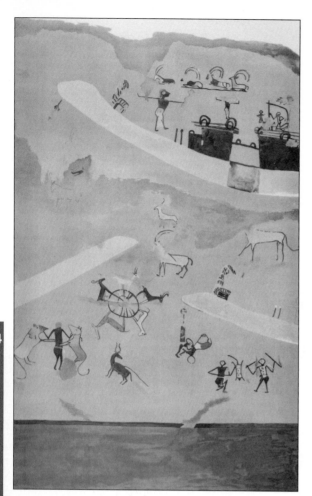

Figure 23.13
Wall paintings from the Decorated Tomb.

ited number of centers and distributed throughout all of Egypt. While a few copper artifacts have been found in Badarian and Naqada I sites, copper becomes much more common in the Naqada II period. Ornaments and weapons were made from both hammered copper and copper cast in molds. Objects were made from silver and gold as well.

The wider trade networks within Egypt were complemented by increasing contacts with Mesopotamia. Mesopotamian traders may have been attracted by Egyptian gold, to be found in the desert east of the Nile. Suggestively, the ancient name for Naqada is *Nubt,* which means "gold." Imports of Mesopotamian pottery vessels and cylinder seals have been found in Naqada II burials. Some Mesopotamian art motifs appear briefly as well. In the Decorated Tomb mentioned above, for instance, one of the paintings features a person holding apart two lions (see Figure 23.13), a distinctly Mesopotamian theme associated with the Sumerian *Epic of Gilgamesh.* This tomb is usually considered that of a local king or chieftain. Just what role contact with Mesopotamia may have played in instigating the development of the Egyptian state is an open question. It is interesting to observe, however, that the earliest palace architecture known, dating to the First Dynasty (ca. 3000 B.C.), displays elaborately niched and buttressed brick walls that are clearly derived from Mesopotamian palace prototypes.

Egyptian Kingdoms and the Unification of Egypt

The following Naqada III period is sometimes called the **Proto-dynastic period.** During this time the populations of the Naqada and Hierakonpolis regions gradually moved into the towns, which ultimately acquired walls. The earliest hieroglyphic writing appears around 3100 B.C., near the end of Proto-dynastic times. Very little is known of Proto-dynastic social structure and of the political events leading up to the unification of Egypt. Small kingdoms probably grew up with their capitals at Naqada and Hierakonpolis. Those centers

humans, animals, and boats, in the same style found on Naqada II pottery **(Figure 23.13)**.

These larger graves came to include more and more offerings of luxury goods, a practice that would remain a prominent feature of Egyptian culture. Specialized craft industries, including the manufacture of fine stone vessels, elaborate and ornate objects flaked from flint, and particularly pottery, grew up largely to furnish the tombs. Much of the economy, it seems, was fueled by the demand for luxury goods that were continually removed from circulation by the wealthy and prominent members of society who took those goods with them when they died.

Some types of pottery, notably red wares, began to be mass-produced in a limsurely competed with one another, perhaps for access to trade networks or mineral resources. Hierakonpolis eventually grew more powerful and became dominant. The ancient conflict between those kingdoms appears to be reflected in Egyptian mythology. Just as Seth was the patron god of Naqada, the falcon-headed god Horus was the patron deity of Hierakonpolis. According to the legend, Horus avenges the murder of his father Osiris by Osiris's brother Seth. Horus kills Seth, after which he becomes the ruler of all Egypt.

The unification of all Egypt under a single king is symbolized by the elaborate carving on a large slate palette found at Hierakonpolis **(Figure 23.14)**. The palette is a descendant of the functional cosmetic palettes found in graves since Badarian times, but elaborated into a ritual object. On one side of the palette is a representation of the king smiting an enemy with a mace while wearing the conical crown symbolic of Upper Egypt. On the other side the king (this time wearing the red crown of Lower Egypt) and his retinue view a group of decapitated enemies. Early hieroglyphic symbols identified with his name, **Narmer,** appear at the top of the palette. Narmer, whose reign precedes the earliest dynasties in the historic Egyptian lists of kings, is often regarded as the unifier of Egypt. Other earlier kings, however, may have held widespread domination. The symbol for a slightly earlier king known only as Scorpion has been found carved on a mace head at Hierakonpolis, wearing the crown of Lower Egypt, suggesting his control over Lower as well as Upper Egypt. Practically nothing is known of how the kingdoms of Upper and Lower Egypt came to be unified, but the carvings on the Narmer palette surely point to violence.

With Narmer, the seat of power moved northward to **Abydos,** north of Naqada. Narmer and his successors of the First Dynasty were buried at Abydos, which was probably their homeland. Abydos was located within a probable third predynastic kingdom with its center at This, just north of Abydos, but archaeologists know little of that region's early history.

Figure 23.14
The Narmer palette.

The Rise of the Pharaohs

At Abydos we see the beginning of the elaboration of royal burials, which would reach its peak with the pyramids of the Old Kingdom. The increasing size and complexity of the royal tombs reflect the steadily growing power of the pharaohs. The Abydos tombs consist of underground, rectangular brick chambers, roofed over and covered with a mound of sand. These large tombs were surrounded by multiple rows of small graves, joined into a common structure (Figure 23.15). Accompanying inscriptions indicate that these were the graves of the royal harem, servants, and various artisans. Very probably these people were sacrificed to serve their king in the afterlife (Trigger et al. 1983: 52).

Traditionally, the founder of the First Dynasty was **Menes,** who may have been Narmer or an immediate successor. Menes was said to have founded the city of **Memphis,** near modern Cairo, which was to become ancient Egypt's first capital. Nearby, at **Saqqara,** a new cemetery was founded. Im-

portant officials were buried there, in large tombs with an aboveground superstructure known as **mastabas** (Figure 23.16). These flat-topped, rectangular tombs, sometimes including internal rooms, were the predecessors of the pyramids. The earliest pyramid, the step-pyramid built by Djoser at Saqqara in the Third Dynasty, is essentially several successively smaller mastabas stacked one upon the other (Figure 23.17).

Pyramid building reached its peak during the Old Kingdom with the construction of the Great Pyramid of Cheops at Giza, near Cairo. (The Old Kingdom, ca. 2980 to 2475 B.C., includes the fourth through the sixth dynasties of pharaohs.) The immense size of the pyra-

Figure 23.15

Plan of the tombs of rulers and their attendants at Abydos.

mids and the enormous expenditure of labor commanded to construct them demonstrate the monopoly of power held by the pharaohs, who early on took on the role of god-king. The tombs also reflect the increasing centralization of Egyptian government, with the growth of a powerful nobility and the establishment of an extensive bureaucracy to serve their administrative needs. Hieroglyphic writing developed during the Early Dynastic period to provide the necessary record-keeping, just as cuneiform writing had evolved in Mesopotamia.

These powerful, wealthy elites provided the impetus for thriving arts and craft industries, including the highest levels of artistry in woodwork, metalwork, stone carving, and painting. Egypt would remain primarily a society of small agricultural villages throughout its history. Nevertheless, the Egyptians, protected from the outside world within the Nile Valley, formed a strongly unified society. Egyptian religious beliefs and legends legitimated the power of the pharaohs. The pharaohs and Egyptian nobility extracted much from the common people in taxes and labor. In turn Egypt grew into a self-contained, self-conscious, and unified state that remained remarkably stable for millennia.

The Formation of the Egyptian State

How can the growth and unification of the Egyptian state be explained? As we saw in Chapter 21, a number of causes may have led society to urbanization and state formation in Mesopotamia. Mesopotamian society was characterized by an economy based on an

Figure 23.16

A mastaba tomb, with a pyramid in the background.

Figure 23.17

The step-pyramid of Djoser at Saqqara, essentially a series of mastaba tombs piled one upon the other.

elaborate system of irrigation agriculture and dependent on raw materials obtained through long-distance trade. Certain favored groups may have gained an advantage because they could monopolize control over those vital resources. The need for protection from hostile neighbors may also have driven villagers into fortified cities, where they could seek the protection of increasingly powerful military leaders.

It is difficult to see similar forces at work in Egypt. The dependable, widespread flooding of the Nile required little in the way of engineering to ensure that the crops were watered. There was little opportunity for any particular group of people to monopolize or control the river's flow. Long-distance trade did bring in some luxury goods, as well as lumber from the Levant, but Egypt was relatively rich in stone and metals and was far less dependent on the outside world for raw materials than was Mesopotamia. Much of the unique character of ancient Egyptian society, in fact, derives from its isolation from its neighbors. The influence of Mesopotamia during the Predynastic period did not last long; trade with Mesopotamia had practically disappeared before the start of the Old Kingdom. Secure within the Nile Valley, the Egyptian people had no powerful, warlike neighbors to threaten them.

In this relatively benign environment it is very difficult to perceive any single driving force behind the rise of the Egyptian state. There were surely local rivalries and strife, and individuals or groups may have seized the advantage when the opportunity arose. Barry Kemp (1989: 32) has envisioned the growth of the Egyptian state as analogous to playing a game of Monopoly. In the inevitable competition among more or less equal individuals or groups, the luck of the draw will permit some groups to gain an advantage. Once they are ahead, they can use their added resources to consolidate more and more power and wealth.

> Thus the game inexorably follows a trajectory towards a critical point where one player has accumulated sufficient assets to outweigh the threats posed by the other players and so becomes unstoppable. It becomes only a matter of time before he wins by monopolizing the assets of all. (Kemp 1989: 32)

In this way the leaders of small agricultural communities may have ultimately extended their influence to become kings of a unified Egypt.

 ## Conclusion

Throughout its long history Egyptian culture has been shaped by the Nile. The Nile's reliable annual floods and deposits of rich silts provided early Egyptian farmers with a secure and highly productive environment for growing their crops. Along its length the Nile provided a ready route for communication and trade. In Upper Egypt, the steep sides of the Nile Valley provided a protective barrier from the outside world, except along certain well-defined routes. Limited trade contacts with Mesopotamia may have provided some impetus, but from the earliest times the peoples of the Nile Valley developed a culture that was uniquely Egyptian.

While hieroglyphic writing has provided us with a rich record of dynastic Egypt, the Egypt of predynastic times is far less well known. The erosion and silt deposition of the Nile has either destroyed or hidden from view many of the earliest sites. Despite a century of archaeology, the social structure and political character of the presumed predynastic kingdoms remain obscure. It seems clear, from evidence such as the Narmer palette, that the political unification of Egypt was achieved through warfare and conquest. In the absence of written documents, and with the archaeological evidence still limited, it is very difficult to discern what factors (such as access to needed resources or trade routes) may have led to conflicts among the early kingdoms or provided certain polities with the wherewithal to dominate the others.

 ## Glossary

Abydos. City about 500 kilometers (300 mi.) south of Cairo, occupied from Predynastic times throughout Egyptian history. Its cemetery is especially noteworthy as the burial place of Narmer and the kings of the First Dynasty.

Badari. A site in the middle portion of the Nile Valley, dating to about 4800 to 4200 B.C.

Numerous burials with elaborate grave goods were found there.

Badarian culture. The culture, belonging to the earliest farmers in Upper Egypt, associated with the burials found at Badari.

Fayum Depression. An ancient lake bed west of the Nile in central Egypt where the earliest known farmers in Egypt were found.

Hierakonpolis. The site in Upper Egypt of one of the most ancient cities in Egypt. Hierakonpolis was probably the capital of one of the kingdoms that preceded the unification of Egypt. The famous Narmer palette was found there. Hierakonpolis continued as an important center throughout Egyptian history.

Maadi. A site near Cairo, dating to around 3650 B.C. The people of Maadi lived in houses made from mud and reed matting. The dead were buried in a cemetery adjoining the settlement in simple pits without any grave goods.

Maadi culture. The term frequently used for the late Neolithic sites of the Egyptian delta.

Mastabas. Flat-topped, rectangular tombs, sometimes including internal rooms, that were the predecessors of the pyramids.

Memphis. Ancient Egypt's first capital, said to have been founded by Menes. It was located near modern Cairo.

Menes. The traditional founder of the Egyptian First Dynasty, who may have been Narmer or an immediate successor.

Merimbda. An early settlement site in the western delta, dating to between 4800 and 4400 b.c. Originally a few temporary reed or matting shelters, it grew into a small village of oval or round mud-walled houses. The dead were buried among the houses, without grave offerings.

Naqada. A settlement with several adjacent, large cemeteries (containing about 3,000 predynastic graves) excavated by the British archaeologist Sir Flinders Petrie in the 1890s. Most of the graves belong to the time span following the Badarian and before the earliest Egyptian dynasty.

Naqada I (Amratian). The period, found only in Upper Egypt, dating from approximately 4200 to 3800 B.C. The Naqada I period is much like the preceding Badarian. Most of the evidence comes from cemeteries; few settlements have been found.

Naqada II (Gerzean). The period dating to approximately 3800 to 3250 B.C. Naqada II is more widespread than Naqada I, appearing as far north as the delta and as far south as Nubia. Substantial settlements appear, and some of the burials become much more elaborate, indicating the beginning of a hierarchical society.

Naqada III (Semainian). The period, sometimes called the Proto-dynastic period, dating to approximately 3250 to 3100 B.C., just preceding the unification of Egypt. Small kingdoms probably grew up with their capitals at Naqada and Hierakonpolis. These towns gradually became increasingly populated. A ruling elite developed, and hieroglyphic writing appeared toward the end of the period.

Narmer. A ruler whose reign precedes the earliest dynasties in the historic Egyptian lists of kings, who is often regarded as the unifier of Egypt. Narmer is often identified with Menes. Narmer's name appears on the palette found at Hierakonpolis, showing a ruler wearing the double crowns of Upper and Lower Egypt, the first to do so.

Proto-dynastic period. The term sometimes used to describe the Naqada III period.

Rosetta stone. The key to the Egyptian hieroglyphic writing, discovered in 1799. The Rosetta stone is inscribed with the same text in Greek and two forms of Egyptian writing, a script and hieroglyphics.

Saqqara. Cemetery near Memphis where important officials were buried in mastaba tombs, the predecessors of the pyramids. The earliest pyramid, the Third Dynasty step-pyramid of Djoser, essentially several successively smaller mastabas stacked one upon the other, is at Saqqara.

Sequence dating. The relative dating technique devised by Sir Flinders Petrie to order the artifact assemblages from prehistoric Egyptian graves into a chronological sequence. The technique is based on the observation of gradual changes through time of stylistic traits on artifacts, as well as the appearance and disappearance of artifact types from one assemblage to the next.

Further Reading

Adams, Barbara
1988. *Predynastic Egypt.* Aylesbury, England: Shire Egyptology.
A brief but clearly written and well-illustrated description of the archaeology of predynastic Egypt.

Bard, Kathryn A.
1994. The Egyptian Predynastic: A Review of the Evidence. *Journal of Field Archaeology* 21: 265–288.
A review and synthesis of both early and recent excavations, including a full bibliography.

Kemp, Barry J.
1989. *Ancient Egypt: Anatomy of a Civilization.* London: Routledge.
An analysis, for the more advanced student, of the forces that shaped ancient Egyptian society.

Trigger, B. G., B. J. Kemp, D. O'Connor, and A. B. Lloyd
1983. *Ancient Egypt: A Social History.* Cambridge: Cambridge University Press.
A detailed discussion of the development of Egyptian society from earliest times through the New Kingdom.

Other Bibliography

Baumgartel, E. J.
1965. Predynastic Egypt. In *The Cambridge Ancient History*, vol. I, edited by I. E. S. Edwards, C. J. Gadd, and N. G. L. Hammond, chap. IX. Cambridge: Cambridge University Press.

Butzer, K. W.
1958. *Quaternary Stratigraphy and Climate in the Near East.* Bonn, Germany: F. Dummlers Verlag.

Caneva, I., M. Frangipane, and A. Palmieri
1987. Predynastic Egypt: New Data from Maadi. *African Archaeological Review* 5: 105–114.

Caton-Thompson, G., and E. W. Gardner
1934. *The Desert Fayum.* London: Royal Anthropological Institute of Great Britain and Ireland.

Deetz, James
1967. *Invitation to Archaeology.* Garden City, NY: Natural History Press.

Hoffman, M. A.
1982. *The Predynastic of Hierakonpolis. An Interim Report.* Cairo: Egyptian Studies Association, Publication No. 1.

Hoffman, M. A., H. A. Hamroush, and R. A. Allen
1986. A Model of Urban Development for the Hierakonpolis Region from Predynastic through Old Kingdom Times. *Journal of the American Research Center in Egypt* 23: 175–187.

Kendall, David G.
1969. Some Problems and Methods in Statistical Archaeology. *World Archaeology* 1: 68–76.

Petrie, W. M. Flinders
1899. Sequences in Prehistoric Remains. *Journal of the Anthropological Institute of Great Britain and Ireland,* vol. XXIX (New series vol. II): 295–301.

Trigger, Bruce G.
1989. *A History of Archaeological Thought.* Cambridge: Cambridge University Press.

Chapter 24

Later Prehistoric Europe
A Different Pattern
of Cultural Complexity

Introduction

Stonehenge, perhaps the world's most famous prehistoric monument, has fascinated scholars for centuries **(Figure 24.1)**. In 1620 Inigo Jones, King James I's architect, interpreted Stonehenge as a provincial Roman temple, while eighteenth-century antiquaries saw it as a sanctuary of the Druids, or Celtic priests. Even today, neo-Druids gather at Stonehenge on June 21 to observe the summer solstice. Archaeological research in and around Stonehenge has shown that this impressive monument is far older than the Romans or even the Druidic priests. Stonehenge was built by the prehistoric inhabitants of Britain nearly 4,000 years ago, a full 2,000 years before the Roman conquest of Britain. What kind of society could have organized the building of such a large and impressive stone structure?

Stonehenge was not built by people who lived in cities. Until the middle of the first millennium B.C. all the inhabitants of temperate Europe (Europe north of the Alps) lived in small agricultural villages, hamlets, and isolated farmsteads. Beginning about 3000 B.C., however, the inhabitants of temperate Europe began to develop many characteristics of complex societies, including widespread trade networks, craft specialization (especially in the production of metal artifacts), agricultural intensification, and elaborate social hierarchies. This chapter will trace the development of complex societies in later prehistoric Europe, beginning about 5,000 years ago.

Figure 24.1
Stonehenge today.

Changes in Settlement and Subsistence in the Later Neolithic of Temperate Europe

As we saw in Chapter 20, by about 3000 B.C. farmers had replaced hunter-gatherers throughout temperate Europe. Mixed farming villages, whose economy was based on cultivating cereals and herding domestic animals, extended from the Balkans to Scandinavia and from Ireland to the Ukraine. At that time several important changes took place in subsistence technology and settlement that set the stage for the development of more complex societies in temperate Europe.

One of the most important was the introduction of wheeled carts and the consequent use of oxen as draft animals. The introduction of wheeled carts allowed farmers to spread out across the landscape. In central Europe, villages and farms were no longer concentrated in the river valleys. Farming settlements spread into the upland areas between the watersheds; as a consequence, settlements became more dispersed, and the landscape filled up with small farming villages.

A second important technological innovation was the introduction of the scratch plow, or ard, which allowed farmers to till larger plots of land than could be planted using a simple digging stick or hoe. In addition, plowing would have maintained soil fertility by aerating and incorporating new organic mate-

rials into the soil (Bogucki 1988: 176). Traces of plow marks can be seen when old land surfaces are preserved, for example, under mounds of earth. The ard, like carts, would have been pulled by oxen. The use of animal power is one of the most important technological innovations in later Neolithic Europe.

During the early Neolithic period in Europe, farming settlements were uniformly small villages and hamlets. By the fourth millennium B.C., larger sites appear for the first time in central and western Europe. (All dates in this chapter are given in recalibrated radiocarbon years. See the Archaeology in Practice box.) Well-excavated examples from central Europe include the hilltop sites of **Bronocice** in Poland and **Dölauer-Heide** in Germany **(Figure 24.2)**. At Dölauer-Heide a

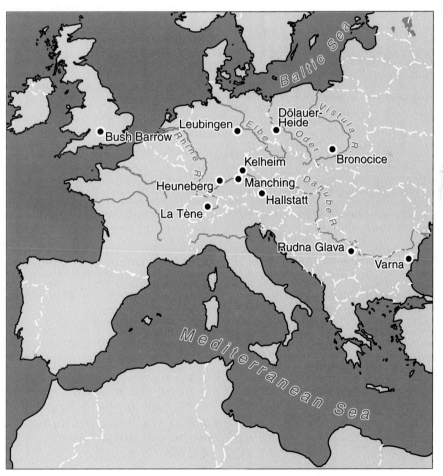

Figure 24.2
Map of temperate Europe showing locations of sites mentioned in this chapter.

Figure 24.3

Complex earthworks surrounding the Neolithic site of Dölauer-Heide in central Germany.

complex series of ditches and earthen banks encloses an area of 25 hectares (about 62 acres) **(Figure 24.3)**. The site of Bronocice (Milisauskas and Kruk 1993) is even larger, covering an area of over 50 hectares (125 acres). The site is located on high ground overlooking the floodplain of the Nidzica River, a tributary of the Vistula. At Bronocice a series of smaller earthworks was constructed over a long period of time. A number of functions have been suggested for these large fortified sites. Milisauskas and Kruk (1993: 86), the excavators of Bronocice, hypothesize that the site was the seat of authority for a small polity, a sort of regional capital. Alternatively, these sites may have served as periodical

gathering places for large groups of people for feasting or other ritual purposes (Whittle 1996: 223).

The fortified nature of these larger sites raises the possibility that they may have played some role in warfare or raiding. Neolithic warfare most likely served to resolve conflicts, maintain buffer zones between neighboring groups, and capture resources, for example, through cattle raiding (Bogucki 1988: 207). In those situations the larger fortified sites may well have served as refuge places for both people and livestock.

Whether the larger sites such as Bronocice served as refuge places during raiding or whether they served as seats of authority and ritual gathering places, their presence indicates that the later Neolithic inhabitants of central Europe had some form of political organization that was larger than the individual family or village. The nature of this political leadership, however, is very difficult to determine; later Neolithic burials provide little evidence for sizable differences in status and wealth. Did this leadership take the form of clan elders, community leaders, or even war leaders? Whatever form this incipient leadership took, the emergence of political organization beyond the level of the family clearly represents one of the first steps toward the development of more complex societies in later prehistoric temperate Europe.

A second, related change is seen in the patterns of trade and exchange during the later Neolithic. Long-distance trade in exotic items such as Mediterranean shells existed throughout the Neolithic in Europe. However, during the late Neolithic, regional trade networks developed for commodities such as flint and salt. A large number of later Neolithic flint mines are known from both the British Isles and continental Europe, and the miners appear to have used antler picks to extract the flint from the earth. Commodities such as flint and salt may have been exchanged as part of a process of alliance formation in the later Neolithic.

The Recalibration of Radiocarbon Dating

As we saw in Chapter 10, most archaeological sites that are younger than about 40,000 years are dated using the radiocarbon method. Radiocarbon dating is based on the assumption that the proportion of radioactive carbon-14 in the atmosphere is constant through time. In fact, scientific research carried out within the past 30 years has shown that this assumption is not entirely true. The first inkling of the problem came from the study of Egyptian wooden artifacts. Many of these artifacts can be closely dated on the basis of historical records. However, when radiocarbon dates were run for Egyptian artifacts that were known to be between 4,000 and 5,000 years old, the carbon-14 dates were consistently about 500 years too young.

Beginning in the 1960s, a program of research using tree rings was developed to calibrate or correct radiocarbon dates. The correction was based on the use of tree rings from the bristlecone pine, a long-lived species of tree that is found in the White Mountains of southern California and Arizona. Individual tree rings are formed each spring as the tree grows. The oldest standing bristlecone pine is about 4,900 years old, but the wood of older, dead trees was found lying in the forest. Unique patterns of narrow and wide tree rings allowed this older wood to be placed in the sequence (**Figure 24.4**, tree ring samples), and the tree ring sequence has been extended backward about 10,000 years. The deviations between radiocarbon years and calendrical years can be assessed by systematically radiocarbon dating tree rings of known age. The tree ring data have been used to create a calibration curve that allows radiocarbon dates to be converted into calendar years (see Klein et al. 1982). In general, uncorrected radiocarbon dates are written in lowercase as years b.c., a.d., or b.p. (before present), while corrected radiocarbon dates are listed in uppercase as years B.C., A.D., or B.P.

The dates used in this chapter are corrected radiocarbon dates, expressed as years B.C. Recalibration of radiocarbon dates from later prehistoric sites in Europe has had important consequences for archaeologists' understanding of the development of European societies and their relationship to the complex societies of the ancient Near East (see Renfrew 1972 for a comprehensive review of this issue). European sites were dated on the basis of radiocarbon, while Egyptian, Sumerian, and other eastern Mediterranean sites were dated using ancient calendars and historical documents. Unless the European dates are recalibrated, archaeologists are not comparing contemporary phenomena in different parts of the Old World. The recalibration curve is depicted in the line graph in Figure 24.4.

Figure 24.4

The drawing at the top shows how fragments of ancient wood are placed in a chronological sequence. The pieces of wood are sequenced by matching signatures, distinctive patterns of wide and narrow rings that represent particular periods of time. The line graph shows the radiocarbon recalibration curve. Redrawn with permission of Radiocarbon.

The Beginnings of Metallurgy in Europe

Small numbers of copper objects are found at Neolithic sites throughout the Near East and Europe. At some early Neolithic sites in Turkey, native copper (naturally occurring metallic copper) was hammered to shape as early as the seventh millennium B.C. However, the smelting of copper (the removal of impurities from copper ore) and the casting of copper objects require more sophisticated technologies. Copper can be separated from oxide and carbonate ores at temperatures of 700° to 800° Celsius (1300° to 1500° F), while sulphide ores are more difficult to reduce and require higher temperatures. Melting and casting copper requires temperatures of approximately 1100° Celsius (2000° F). It is important to note, however, that the development of metallurgy did not take place in isolation. Some forms of pottery from southeast Europe were regularly heated to temperatures of 700° Celsius (1300° F). In technological terms, pottery technology seems to have paved the way for early metallurgy in Europe (Renfrew 1972: 175). By the later fifth millennium B.C. the smelting and casting of copper had developed in southeast Europe. Molds, crucibles, and copper slag provide evidence for the development of a copper technology. In addition, sites such as **Rudna Glava** (Jovanovic 1980) provide evidence for the mining of copper ores. Rudna Glava is located in northeast Serbia, far from contemporary settlement sites. At Rudna Glava miners followed veins of copper ores up to 20 meters (65 ft.) into the ground. Alternating heating and cooling were used to break up the ore and to facilitate quarrying.

Copper is an attractive, but relatively soft, metal. Copper tools do not provide a technological advantage over stone implements. Therefore early copper items are more likely to have served as objects of prestige and display than as functional tools. Copper and gold ornaments are often found in burials from the later Neolithic in southeast Europe. One of the best-known sites is the fifth-millennium B.C. **Varna** cemetery on the Black Sea coast in Bulgaria. Of the 281 graves known from the Varna cemetery, 82 included copper objects and 61 included items of gold. The copper items recovered from the Varna graves included earrings, needles, and axes. Some of the graves at Varna were very richly furnished, while others contained only small numbers of grave goods. Grave 43, for example, included over 990 gold objects weighing over 1.5 kilograms (3.3 lb.) (Whittle 1996: 97). The striking variations in grave wealth are uncommon in the late Neolithic, but they become much more common in the subsequent Bronze Age.

The Beginnings of the Bronze Age in Temperate Europe

Metal technology was revolutionized in the third millennium B.C. with the development of bronze. Bronze was most commonly made by alloying copper with tin (about 10 percent tin was used), although copper-arsenic alloys were also produced. When compared with pure copper, bronze is a harder metal, and it is easier to cast. Bronze could be used to make tools that were technologically superior to stone tools. It was during the **Bronze Age,** beginning in the later third millennium B.C., that metal replaced stone for most tools and weapons. In addition, the evidence for the extraction and working of metals becomes far more widespread in temperate Europe. The technology of bronze metalworking developed rapidly and distinctively in Europe, and it is likely bronze was manufactured by individuals who were at least part-time specialists.

The widespread use of metals had two important social consequences. First, it provided new opportunities for the accumulation of wealth. Unlike earlier stone tools, metal objects could be melted down and reused. Second, the widespread use of metals required the development of trade networks to guarantee regular supplies of raw materials. Unlike flint, which is widely distributed throughout Europe, deposits of copper and tin are highly localized. Areas such as southern Scandinavia and northern Germany were entirely lacking in raw materials **(Figure 24.5)**; however, traces of molds and crucibles indicate that bronze was being cast in those regions. Scandinavian and northern German metalworking was dependent on the regular,

Figure 24.5

Map showing copper, tin, and gold sources in Europe.

long-distance trade networks in metals. The foundations for that trade may have been established through the development of regional trade networks in the later Neolithic.

The control of the trade in metals may have provided new opportunities for the accumulation of wealth. It is in the early Bronze Age, beginning about 2300 B.C., that we see real evidence for increasing differences in social status and material wealth in temperate Europe. They are reflected in variations in the wealth placed in burials and in the amounts of energy that are devoted to burial rituals. The differences are seen most clearly in areas that are near major ore sources or along important trade routes. One such area is in east central Europe, including parts of Austria, eastern Germany, and the Czech and Slovak Republics. Tin was available in the Bohemian Ore Mountains, along the border between the Czech Republic and eastern Germany, while copper could be obtained from the Hartz Mountains, the Alps, and the central part of the Slovak Republic.

This region has produced a small number of very rich graves that contrast sharply with typical burial practices. Most individuals were buried in pits with pottery vessels as the only grave goods. However, the **Leubingen burial** in eastern Germany included a far richer assemblage of grave goods **(Figure 24.6)**. The body of an elderly man was placed in an oak chamber and covered with a mound of stones, which, in turn, was covered with an earthen mound. A second body, possibly female and probably immature, was placed across his hips. Included among the grave goods were gold jewelry, pottery, a whetstone, a pick, a halberd, three daggers, two flanged axes, three chisels, and additional gold objects. The contrast between this rich burial and the typical Early Bronze Age burial is far greater than the contrast between the richest and the poorest Neolithic burials, suggesting increasing social and economic inequality.

Rich Early Bronze Age burials are not limited to east central Europe. In the area around Stonehenge in southern Britain, a

Figure 24.6

Diagram of the Leubingen burial showing the burial chamber and the location of grave goods.

group of very rich burials is contemporary with the final phase of construction of the monument around 2000 B.C. The Stonehenge region not only is rich in agricultural and pasture land, but also is near an important source of tin located in Cornwall, southwestern Britain. The elaborate Early Bronze Age burials in the Stonehenge area were placed under tumuli, or earthen mounds. One of the most spectacular is **Bush Barrow,** which yielded a diverse assemblage of metal objects **(Figure 24.7)**, including copper and bronze daggers, bronze rivets that may have formed part of a helmet, a gold clothing plate and belt hook, and a bronze axe. In addition, the grave goods included bone zigzag mountings that originally decorated the wooden shaft of a stone mace head. These items may well symbolize authority, suggesting that the person who was interred in Bush Barrow wielded some degree of political power. Traditionally, Early Bronze Age societies in temperate Europe have been viewed as **chiefdoms,** or societies that are ruled by a chief or leader but that lack a permanent government or bureaucracy (see Chapter 21). Political authority lies in the power and person of the chief.

By the end of the Early Bronze Age, temperate Europe had developed many of the characteristics seen in complex societies of the ancient Near and Middle East: craft specialization, regular patterns of long-distance trade and exchange, social differentiation, and the development of political organizations that were larger than the individual family or village. Bronze Age Europe differed, however, in one important respect from the ancient societies of Egypt, Mesopotamia, and the Indus Valley. Bronze Age Europe lacked towns and cities. It was not until the middle of the first millennium B.C., over 1,000 years later, that towns and cities began to develop in Europe north of the Alps.

Figure 24.7

Gold plate and belt buckle recovered from the Early Bronze Age Bush Barrow in southern Britain.

Europe's First Towns: Late Hallstatt Towns and Trade

Europe's towns first develop during the **Iron Age** (ca. 800 to 0 B.C.), a period in which iron gradually replaced bronze in the manufacture of tools and weapons. The European Iron Age is generally divided into two phases, an earlier period known as the **Hallstatt** (800 to 450 B.C.) and a later period known as the **La Tène** (ca. 450 to 0 B.C.). In prehistoric Europe, iron tools were wrought or forged, unlike bronze, which was cast. The production of wrought iron was a complex process, and early iron tools were often either too brittle or too soft. Iron, however, had one major advantage over bronze. Iron ores were ubiquitous across temperate Europe, while copper and tin sources were relatively rare. As we shall see, iron production increased through-

out the Iron Age in Europe, and by the late first millennium B.C. some temperate European communities were exporting iron, including finished iron objects, to the Romans.

Trade seems to have played a major role in the formation of Europe's first towns, which appear in west central Europe between about 600 and 480 B.C., during the later part of the Hallstatt period (Wells 1980). In the seventh and sixth centuries B.C. Greek merchants from the eastern Mediterranean established a number of trading colonies in the western Mediterranean (Boardman 1980). The Greek merchants needed to obtain raw materials and agricultural products for the rapidly increasing Greek populations. One of those colonies was Massilia (modern Marseille), located at the mouth of the Rhône River on a hill north of the old harbor.

At about 600 B.C. towns appear for the first time in eastern France and southern Germany. The best known of these early towns is the **Heuneberg** (Kimmig 1975), a site that overlooks the Danube in southern Germany and is surrounded by rich burials. Archaeological evidence indicates that pottery manufacturing, bronze working, and ironworking took place at the Heuneberg. In addition, a number of artifacts and features point to close contacts with the Mediterranean world. These include amphorae, which were used to transport wine, and Greek pottery, as well as part of the town wall itself. The wall was built of sun-dried bricks set on a limestone foundation, a technique that was common in the Mediterranean areas but previously unknown in temperate Europe.

The burial mounds that surround the Heuneberg also include Mediterranean imports. These Iron Age burials were often placed in wagons within wooden chambers and included imported objects such as bronze and pottery vessels, which reflected close ties with the Mediterranean world. The character of the individuals who are buried in these so-called princes' graves has been a subject of debate. Are they members of the traditional elite classes who were able to gain control over long-distance trade (Champion et al, 1984: 287), or do they represent a new class of wealthy entrepreneurs who were able to organize and profit from trade with the

Figure 24.8
Early La Tène art: a fifth-century B.C. *gold necklace from Rodenbach.*

Mediterranean (Wells 1984)? Regardless of who controlled the trade with the Mediterranean, it is clear that the initial development of towns in central Europe is closely related to the establishment of trade relationships with the Mediterranean world. Although we have no record of the types of goods that were exported from central Europe, it is likely that agricultural produce, animal products, and forest products such as timber and furs were exported from the Heuneberg region.

The reliance of the late Hallstatt towns such as the Heuneberg on trade with the Mediterranean is underscored by their rapid collapse in the early fifth century B.C. In the late sixth century B.C. the Greek colonists at Massilia developed trade relationships with the inhabitants of the Po Valley in northern Italy; trade with central Europe decreased dramatically; and by about 480 B.C., sites such as the Heuneberg were abandoned.

The Oppida and the Origins of Urbanism in Temperate Europe

Shortly after the abandonment of the late Hallstatt commercial towns, a new style of decorated metalwork appeared in temperate Europe. The style is known as La Tène, after the type site in Switzerland. The art included anthropomorphic and zoomorphic figures as well as stylized floral motifs borrowed from Greek and Etruscan art **(Figure 24.8)**. This style of decoration was associated with people whom the Greek and Roman authors called Celts. The Celts occupied a large part of central Europe, from the Atlantic to the Black Sea, in the last few centuries B.C. Greek and Roman accounts of the Celts can be used in conjunction with archaeology to provide information about the ways of life of these late Iron Age peoples.

Figure 24.9

Map of temperate Europe showing the distribution of the oppida (after Cunliffe 1979:64).

During the early La Tène period there is no archaeological evidence for towns and cities in Europe north of the Mediterranean. However, both archaeological and historical records indicate that Celtic populations were expanding rapidly throughout the fourth and third centuries B.C. Historical sources indicate that Celtic societies were chiefdoms. La Tène societies lacked a permanent bureaucracy and many formal institutions of government; instead, these societies were held together by bonds of **clientship.** Patron-client relationships are long-term relationships established between unequals. The patron, who is usually a wealthy, high-status individual, may provide the client with seed grain, livestock, or other necessities. In return the client may be required to labor on the patron's farm or to pay the patron in food as a form of rent. The client owes allegiance and loyalty to the patron, especially in times of war. Historical sources, such as Julius Caesar's account of the Gallic wars, indicate that clientship was a central organizing principal of late La Tène society.

About 200 B.C. large, fortified sites appear across much of central and western Europe. These sites, which are termed **oppida,** are permanently occupied, urban sites that appear to have served a variety of different functions. The oppida, like the earlier commercial towns of the late Hallstatt period, served as centers of craft production and trade. However, unlike their late Hallstatt predecessors, the oppida appear to have served a number of other political functions. They served as refuge places for people and livestock in times of war, and they may have served as residences of the landed nobility or patron classes (Bintliff 1984: note 67). As can be seen in **Figure 24.9**, the oppida are quite regularly distributed across the European landscape, suggesting that they may also have served as regional political capitals.

Case Study
Manching and Kelheim

One of the best-known oppida is the site of **Manching** in southern Germany. Excavations, conducted at the site since the 1950s, have yielded a wealth of information on late Iron Age life in central Europe. Manching is located at the conjunction of the Danube and Paar Rivers, and its fortifications enclose an area of 380 hectares (940 acres) **(Figure 24.10)**. About 200 hectares (500 acres) at the center of the site were densely occupied by a

Figure 24.10
Plan of the oppidum at Manching.

Figure 24.11
Map of the oppidum at Kelheim showing locations of the excavations and of the site's defenses.

planned community with wide streets and rectangular timber buildings. A variety of craft activities took place at Manching, including pottery making, woodworking, iron manufacture, and the production of glass jewelry. Different crafts appear to have been practiced in different parts of the site, another indication of urban planning. The large size of the oppida and the degree of urban planning seen at sites such as Manching distinguish the oppida from the earlier late Hallstatt towns.

Since the late 1980s excavations have also taken place at the oppidum at **Kelheim** in Bavaria, southern Germany, under the direction of Peter Wells of the University of Minnesota (Wells 1987, 1993). The oppidum at Kelheim is located about 30 kilometers (19 mi.) from Manching, at the confluence of the Danube and the Altmühl Rivers. Kelheim is one of the largest oppida in Europe; its fortification walls enclose about 600 hectares (1,500 acres) of land **(Figure 24.11)**. Kelheim appears to have been the site of intensive iron production at about 100 B.C. The hilltop portion of the site is pockmarked with pits that were used to obtain iron ore. Excavations were focused on an area of settlement along the Altmühl River. In addition to pottery, animal bones, and a range of iron objects, the excavations yielded enormous quantities of iron ore and slag, a by-product of iron manufacture. At Kelheim, it is estimated that 75,000 tons of iron ore were used to produce 25,000 tons of iron. The scale of iron production is unmatched in later European prehistory. In addition, it was during the late Iron Age that iron became commonly used for a wide range of specialized tools and weapons, including many specialized agricultural tools that continued to be used in Europe until the mechanization of farming in the late nineteenth and early twentieth centuries. Sites such as Kelheim supplied the raw materials for the production of those specialized iron tools.

As the archaeological evidence from Manching and Kelheim shows, the oppida represent Europe's first cities. Most of the oppida, however, fell out of use with the Roman conquest of much of western and central Europe in the first century B.C. and the first century A.D. The Romans established their own towns and cities in western Europe; sites such as Paris, London, York, and Cologne were initially established by the Romans. However, even the Roman cities were relatively short-lived. For example, long-term excavations at the city of York in England have shown that the town was largely depopulated in the fifth and sixth centuries A.D. It was not until the early Middle Ages that cities were successfully established in most of temperate Europe. It is these successful early medieval towns that are the predecessors of the towns and cities of modern Europe.

Conclusion

When compared with Mesopotamia, Egypt, and the Indus Valley, later prehistoric Europe represents a different kind of complex society. By the later Neolithic period, European agriculture had intensified dramatically through the use of the cart and the plow. In addition, regional trade networks and the beginnings of political leadership had developed by about 3000 B.C. Excavations of Early Bronze Age cemeteries have shown that by 2000 B.C. European societies were characterized by real differences in social status, political power, and material wealth. Regular long-distance trade in metals was established throughout temperate Europe during the Early Bronze Age, and the rapid development of European metallurgy suggests that metal objects were made by craft specialists. Thus, it is clear that by 2000 B.C. Europe had developed many of the characteristics that we traditionally associate with complex societies.

Urbanism, however, was a relatively late development in prehistoric Europe. The first towns did not develop until the middle of the first millennium B.C., and the first cities did not develop until the last two centuries B.C. When urban sites did appear in Europe, they were clearly related to intensive trade and commerce. The Hallstatt towns owed their existence to trade with the Greek colonies in the west, while many of the oppida were involved in commercial production of commodities such as iron.

Glossary

Bronocice. A large, later Neolithic site in Poland that appears to have been occupied over a considerable period of time. Small parts of this hilltop site were fortified, although it is unclear whether Bronocice served as a place of refuge, the seat of a small polity, or a site of ritual feasting.

Bronze Age. The European age dated to between 2300 B.C. and 800 B.C. During the Early Bronze Age, bronze began to replace stone as a raw material for tools and weapons. Bronze Age societies in Europe are characterized by the appearance of significant differences in status, power, and wealth between individuals.

Bush Barrow. An Early Bronze Age burial under a tumulus, or earthen mound. The site, located near Stonehenge in southern Britain, produced a range of metal items, including bronze and copper daggers and gold clothing ornaments.

Chiefdoms. Societies ruled by a chief or leader, but that lack a permanent government or bureaucracy.

Clientship. Patron-client relations that are established between people of unequal status and wealth. The patron provides certain material goods to the clients, while the clients provide labor and loyalty to the patron. Clientship was a fundamental organizing principal of late Iron Age society in Europe.

Dölauer-Heide. A late Neolithic fortified site in Germany where a complex series of ditches and banks encloses an area of 25 hectares (about 62 acres).

Hallstatt. The first half of the European Iron Age (ca. 800 to 450 B.C.). During the later part of the Hallstatt period, commercial towns such as the Heuneberg were established in west central Europe. These towns appear to have been engaged in extensive trade relations with the Greek colony of Massilia (Marseille).

Heuneberg. One of the early trading towns of the late Hallstatt period, located near the Danube in southern Germany. The site appears to have been engaged in trade with the Greek colony of Marseille.

Iron Age. The European age that begins with the replacement of bronze by iron in the manufacture of tools and weapons (ca. 800 B.C.) and ends with the Roman conquest of much of western Europe in the first century B.C. and the first century A.D. It is during the Iron Age that the first towns and cities appear in temperate Europe.

Kelheim. A large (approximately 600 hectares [1,500 acres]) Iron Age oppidum located in Bavaria in southern Germany. Recent excavations at the site have shown that large quantities of iron were being produced at Kelheim during the late La Tène period.

La Tène. The later part of the European Iron Age, approximately 450 B.C. to 0 B.C. The period is named after the type site in Switzerland where numbers of decorated metal artifacts were recovered in the nineteenth century. La Tène art style is associated with people whom the Greeks and Romans called Celts.

Leubingen burial. A burial site in eastern Germany that includes two individuals who were interred in an oak chamber under a mound of stone and earth. The grave goods included a diverse array of gold and bronze objects, while most other Early Bronze Age burials include only pottery vessels.

Manching. An oppidum site located in southern Germany at the confluence of the Danube and Paar Rivers. The site covers an area of 380 hectares (940 acres) and is surrounded by a fortification wall. Long-term excavations at the site have revealed a planned street layout and evidence for extensive craft production.

Oppida. Urban sites that appear in temperate Europe in the last two centuries B.C. They are generally large, fortified sites and appear to have served a variety of functions—as political capitals, centers of craft production, places of refuge, and possible residences of a landed elite.

Rudna Glava. A late Neolithic copper mining site located in northeastern Serbia (formerly Yugoslavia). At Rudna Glava miners followed seams of copper ore up to 20 meters (65 ft.) below ground and used rapid heating and cooling to extract the copper ores from the surrounding rocks.

Varna. A fifth-millennium B.C. burial ground located near the Black Sea in Bulgaria. Some of the 281 burials included large numbers of copper and gold objects, while others included very few grave goods.

Further Reading

Bogucki, P. I.
1988. *Forest Farmers and Stockherders: Early Agriculture and Its Consequences in North-Central Europe.* Cambridge: Cambridge University Press.
The second half of this useful book focuses on the later, or consequent, Neolithic in central Europe. Bogucki's focus on the relationship between human societies and their environments makes this a particularly valuable overview of Neolithic Europe.

Bogucki, Peter, ed.
1993. *Case Studies in European Prehistory.* Boca Raton, FL: CRC Press.
Several case studies in this volume focus on later Neolithic, Bronze Age, and Iron Age sites in temperate Europe. The case studies not only present new data on recent excavation projects, but also focus on the ways archaeological research projects develop over time. By reading these case studies, students can begin to understand both the intellectual and the personal sides of archaeological research.

Cunliffe, B., ed.
1998. *Prehistoric Europe: An Illustrated History.* Oxford and New York: Oxford University Press.
This textbook provides an overview of European prehistory from the Paleolithic through the Roman period. The individual chapters are written by specialists.

 ## Other Bibliography

Bintliff, J.
1984. Iron Age Europe, in the Context of Social Evolution from the Bronze Age through to Historic Times. In *European Social Evolution,* edited by John Bintliff, pp. 157–225. Bradford, England: University of Bradford.

Boardman, J.
1980. *The Greeks Overseas: Their Early Colonies and Trade,* 3d ed. London: Thames and Hudson.

Champion, T., C. Gamble, S. Shennan, and A. Whittle
1984. *Prehistoric Europe.* Orlando, FL: Academic Press.

Cunliffe, Barry
1979. *The Celtic World.* New York: McGraw-Hill.

Jovanovic, B.
1980. The Origins of Copper Mining in Europe. *Scientific American* 242 (5): 152–167.

Kimmig, W.
1975. Early Celts on the Upper Danube: The Excavations at the Heuneberg. In *Recent Archaeological Excavations in Europe,* edited by R. Bruce-Mitford, pp. 32–64. London: Routledge Kegan Paul.

Klein, J., J. C. Lerman, P. E. Damon, and E. K. Ralph
1982. Calibration of Radiocarbon Dates: Tables Based on the Consensus Data of the

Workshop on Calibrating the Radiocarbon Time Scale. *Radiocarbon* 24 (2): 103–150.

Milisauskas, S., and J. Kruk

1993. Archaeological Investigations on Neolithic and Bronze Age Sites in Southeastern Poland. In *Case Studies in European Prehistory,* edited by Peter Bogucki, pp. 63–94. Boca Raton, FL: CRC Press.

Renfrew, Colin

1972. *Before Civilization: The Radiocarbon Revolution and Prehistoric Europe.* Cambridge: Cambridge University Press.

Wells, P. S.

1980. *Culture Contact and Culture Change: Early Iron Age Central Europe and the Mediterranean World.* Cambridge: Cambridge University Press.

1984. *Farms, Villages, and Cities: Commerce and Urban Origins in Late Prehistoric Europe.* Ithaca, NY: Cornell University Press.

1987. Industry, Commerce, and Temperate Europe's First Cities: Preliminary Report on 1987 Excavations at Kelheim, Bavaria. *Journal of Field Archaeology* 14: 399–412.

1993. *Settlement, Economy, and Cultural Change at the End of the European Iron Age: Excavations at Kelheim in Bavaria, 1987–1991.* Ann Arbor, MI: International Monographs in Prehistory, Archaeological Series No. 6.

Whittle, A.

1996. *Europe in the Neolithic: The Creation of New Worlds.* Cambridge: Cambridge University Press.

Part VIII

How Did Cities and States Develop in the New World?

Cities, states, and empires developed independently in both the New World and the Old World. Part VIII of the text examines how and why complex societies developed in several regions of the New World. Beginning with the establishment of permanent agricultural villages, we chronicle in detail the process of urban development and state formation in both Mesoamerica (Chapter 25) and Peru (Chapter 26). Particular emphasis is placed on the unique environments of these regions. We also examine alternative paths to cultural complexity, focusing on eastern North America (Chapter 27). The concluding chapter examines the future of archaeological research, including the destruction of archaeological sites through looting, development, and warfare. We consider the role that the Native American Graves Protection and Repatriation Act (NAGPRA) will have in the future of archaeology in the United States.

Chapter 25

Complex Societies in Mesoamerica

Introduction

In 1519 the Spanish conquistador Cortez and his followers were the first Westerners to lay eyes on the Aztec capital **Tenochtitlán** in the Valley of Mexico. This native American city, home to perhaps 300,000 people, was centered on an island within Lake Texcoco in central Mexico **(Figure 25.1)**. To European eyes, Tenochtitlán would have teemed with people; the Aztec capital was far larger than most of the contemporary cities of Europe. The center of the city was reached by three causeways from the mainland and was dominated by a great pyramid topped by twin temples dedicated to the Aztec gods of war and rain. Nearby, an enormous rack of skulls provided mute testimony to the thousands of human sacrifices that were regularly performed for the Aztec gods. The temples and plazas of the central precinct were surrounded by the palaces of the Aztec emperors, including the palace of the emperor Moctezuma II, who would lose his kingdom to Cortez and his followers. Tenochtitlán was not just a political and military capital; it was also a center of commerce and craft activity. The Aztec capital was home to specialist potters, feather workers, and metalworkers, as well as the farmers whose surplus agricultural products supported the craftsworkers and merchants (Willey 1966: 156–159). The Aztecs, however, were only the latest in a long series of complex, urban societies that had

Figure 25.1

Sixteenth-century Spanish view of the Aztec capital of Tenochtitlán.

developed in Mexico and the adjacent regions of Central America during pre-Columbian times. In this chapter we will trace the development of those societies in the region that archaeologists call **Mesoamerica.**

Mesoamerica is a geographical term that describes the region extending from western Honduras, Nicaragua, and northwest Costa Rica in the south to Mexico, excluding the northern deserts in the north (Figure 25.2). It therefore includes most of Mexico, Guatemala, Belize, El Salvador, western Honduras, western Nicaragua, and the northwestern portion of Costa Rica. The region exhibits marked variations in climate, geography, and soils, ranging from the cool, temperate highlands of central Mexico to the rain forests of the Petén region of northern Guatemala. This varied region was home to some of the most highly developed complex societies in the Americas. In tracing the development of complex societies in various parts of Mesoamerica, we will examine how the urban, state-level societies that were encountered by Cortez developed from the simple agricultural villages that arose in this region during the earlier Holocene. The earliest complex societies appear during the **Formative (or Preclassic) period** in Mesoamerica (approximately 2000 B.C. to A.D. 250). It is during this period that we see the appearance of the earliest monumental architecture and sculpture in Mesoamerica and the beginnings of urbanism in the region.

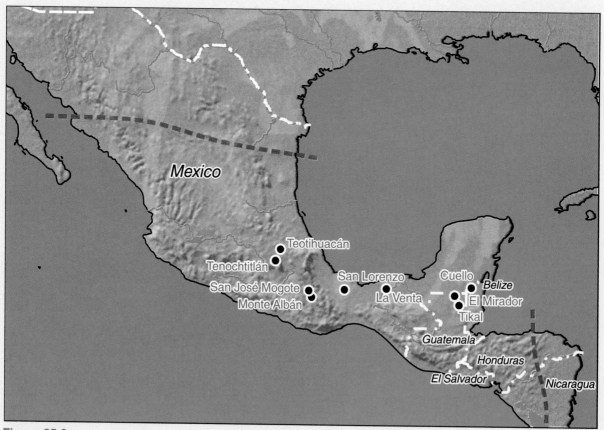

Figure 25.2

Map of Mesoamerica showing the geographical limits of the region and the major sites discussed in the chapter.

Olmec Beginnings

The study of the development of complex societies in Mesoamerica usually begins along Mexico's southern Gulf coast (see Figure 25.2). The Gulf coast was home to people known to archaeologists as the **Olmecs,** although we do not know what they called themselves. The name Olmecs, which means "rubber people," comes from the word *Olmeca,* used by the Aztecs to refer to the people who lived in the Gulf coast region at the time of the Spanish conquest. However, there is no clear evidence for continuity between the Olmecs of the Formative period and the Olmeca of Aztec times. The Olmecs of the Formative period have fascinated scholars throughout the twentieth century because they created Mesoamerica's earliest monumental art. In particular, they carved enormous human heads weighing up to 25 tons from basalt blocks **(Figure 25.3)**. The Olmecs also created the earliest monumental architecture in Mesoamerica.

Olmec sites are located in a rich, low-lying area along Mexico's southern Gulf coast, an area traversed by three major rivers and their tributaries. Abundant water for maize agriculture is provided by two rainy seasons—the first extending from June to November, the second from January to February. Periodic flooding enriches the soil along the riverbanks (Soustelle 1985: 23). Farming villages were established in the Olmec region as early as 2250 B.C. (Rust and Sharer 1988). In addition to its agricultural potential, the southern Gulf coast was home to many species of wild game, including deer, tapirs, monkeys, pheasants, and iguanas, and its lakes and rivers provided early farmers with fish and shellfish. In short, the Olmec region was rich in subsistence resources and could have provided the food surplus necessary to support nonagricultural labor and trade.

Excavations at Olmec sites have focused largely, though not exclusively, on sites that have produced monumental stone sculpture. The largest of these sites, which have been termed ceremonial centers, have yielded monumental stone sculpture and public architecture, as well as evidence for status differences between elites and commoners. They should not be seen as empty ceremonial centers, but they do not appear to have housed large urban populations. The earliest of these centers is the site of **San Lorenzo,** which sits atop a large (1,000 by 500 meters [3,300 by 1,650 ft.]) plateau overlooking the Rio Coatzacoalcos. Excavations at San Lorenzo revealed the presence of Olmec-style ceramics at the site as early as 1150 B.C. (3100 B.P.). In addition, excavations in the 1960s revealed 35 carved stone monuments (2 had been recovered earlier). Recent excavations at the site, under the direction of Ann Cyphers, have shown that many of the monumental stone heads stood on prepared floors and that one of the tabletop altars at the site had been located within a walled enclosure (Grove 1997: 70). Cyphers has also identified many additional stone monuments, bringing the total to well over 80 (Grove 1997: 71). Workshop

Figure 25.3

A carved Olmec head, San Lorenzo, Monument 1.

areas for the manufacture and recycling of stone monuments have also been identified.

What kind of a society produced these enormous heads and other stone sculptures? The limited evidence available suggests that Olmec society was a nonegalitarian one populated by both elites and commoners. Items such as greenstone jewelry and polished iron mirrors, whose raw materials were obtained through long-distance trade, have been identified as possible markers of elite status. In addition, the recent excavations at San Lorenzo have revealed marked differences in house construction that may reflect differences in status and wealth. The larger houses (presumably the elite residences) are built on top of large clay platforms, while the humbler houses of the commoners are simple wattle-and-daub structures with earthen floors.

San Lorenzo appears to have played an active role in riverine trade. Three raised causeways that run inland from the river have been interpreted as wharves or docks associated with this trade. It is not clear whether rivers or overland routes were used to transport the large stone blocks used to manufacture the monumental heads to the ceremonial center of **La Venta,** because geological uplifting has changed the course of several rivers in the Olmec region. Geological changes may have also been responsible for the decline of San Lorenzo at about 800 B.C. by changing the course of the rivers on which San Lorenzo's trade depended.

The site of La Venta emerged as a leading ceremonial center between about 800 and 400 B.C. Although the site may have been established as early as San Lorenzo, evidence for the earliest phases of occupation is limited (see Grove 1997 for a review of the chronological issues surrounding Olmec sites). La Venta is located on a small swamp island in the Tabasco region of Mexico. Because petroleum was discovered in the La Venta region in the first half of the twentieth century, many parts of this important Olmec site were destroyed when an oil pipeline was cut through it. Archaeological excavations conducted at La Venta since the early 1940s have revealed evidence for monumental public architecture, including a low, rectangular earthen mound 32 meters (105 ft.) high and measuring 70 by 120 meters (230 by 390 ft.)

at the base; several other mound complexes; a carefully laid out plaza; and mosaic pavements of serpentine blocks **(Figure 25.4)**.

The large Olmec centers such as San Lorenzo and La Venta stood at the apex of a settlement system that also included about a dozen smaller ceremonial centers with just a few stone monuments and large numbers of agricultural villages and hamlets that must have supported those centers. While the large Olmec centers have yielded evidence for craft production and monumental public construction, they do not appear to have housed large urban populations. Moreover, there is no evidence to suggest that the Olmec region was politically unified under a single ruler or king. The early appearance of monumental art and architecture in the southern Gulf coast region led some scholars to see the Olmecs as a kind of "mother culture" for later complex societies throughout the Mesoamerican region. The true picture is probably far more complex. As we shall show in this chapter, complex societies began to develop during the Formative period in a number of different geographical regions of Mesoamerica. These areas were all engaged in trade and contact with one another, just as contacts existed between the early complex societies of the Old World. The Olmec should perhaps be seen as a "sister culture" to the other early complex societies of ancient Mesoamerica (Grove 1997: 54). One of those other regions is the Oaxaca Valley, home to one of Mesoamerica's earliest urban centers.

Early Urbanism in Oaxaca

The Oaxaca Valley lies in the center of Mexico's southern highland region, a mountainous zone located south of the Olmec heartland (see Figure 25.2). The three-armed Oaxaca Valley **(Figure 25.5)** contains 1,500 square kilometers (580 sq. mi.) of arable land, the largest expanse of farmland in the southern highlands (Blanton et al. 1993).

Farming communities were established in the Oaxaca Valley by 1500 B.C. The villagers raised maize, avocados, beans, and squash, and most communities included fewer than 10 wattle-and-daub houses. One larger village, **San José Mogote,** has been discovered. This village covered 7 hectares (17 acres), over

Figure 25.4

Plan of the main architectural monuments at the Olmec center of La Venta.

two times the size of any other contemporary settlement. This site also included some evidence for nonresidential, public construction in the form of an open area that was set off from the residential portion of the site by a double line of posts. Although this feature contained no structures, it was aligned slightly (8°) west of true north, like much of the later public architecture in the Oaxaca Valley (Blanton et al. 1993: 56–57). This open area soon fell out of use and was replaced by a series of rectangular structures with altarlike platforms running along the southern interior wall. These struc-

tures were also oriented 8° west of true north and appear to have been centers of ritual activity, constructed by a society that was largely egalitarian. Neither the houses nor the burials provide evidence for marked differences in social status and material wealth. However, the presence of the ritual structures does reflect some degree of incipient leadership, since labor and resources would have had to be mobilized to construct and maintain the buildings.

After 1150 B.C. there is evidence for significant social, economic, and demographic change in the Oaxaca Valley. The town of

Figure 25.5

Map of the Oaxaca Valley region showing locations of sites mentioned in the chapter.

San José Mogote expanded to 70 hectares (173 acres), while the remainder of villages in that arm of the Oaxaca Valley were no larger than 2 hectares (5 acres). At San José Mogote there is evidence for the production of magnetite mirrors, prestige items that were traded as far away as the Gulf coast. Both burials and houses began to reflect significant social and economic differences. For example, at San José Mogote some individuals were buried without grave goods, while others were interred with such items as finely crafted ceramic vessels, jade earspools, shell ornaments, and items made of magnetite (Blanton et al. 1993: 61). San José Mogote may have been the seat of a chiefdom that controlled part of the Oaxaca Valley. In many ways, the level of social and political development seen at San José Mogote parallels the kinds of societies that developed at the same time in the Olmec area.

The political and social landscape of the Oaxaca Valley changed with the founding of a new regional capital at **Monte Albán** at about 500 B.C. Monte Albán is strategically lo-

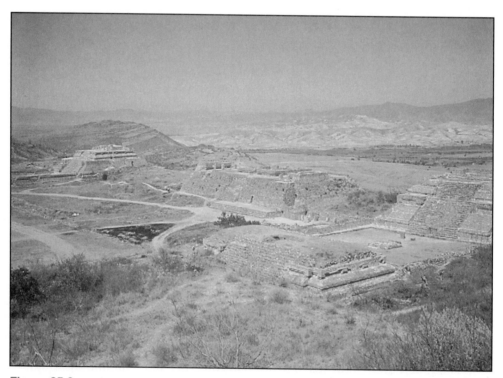

Figure 25.6

View of the Oaxaca Valley from Monte Albán showing its strategic location in relation to the surrounding countryside.

cated on a hilltop in the very center of the Oaxaca Valley (see Figure 25.5). Although Monte Albán lacks water sources and is surrounded by marginal agricultural land, its hilltop location provides views of the Oaxaca Valley in all directions **(Figure 25.6)**. Unlike San José Mogote, which had developed as a head town for a portion of the Oaxaca Valley, Monte Albán developed as a political and military capital for the entire Oaxaca Valley. Residential housing in Monte Albán was located in three distinct neighborhoods, but the central Main Plaza lacked residential settlement even in the earliest phases. Carved stone sculptures from the Main Plaza appear to depict opposing military leaders who had been brought back to Monte Albán to be tortured and killed.

The site grew rapidly to an estimated population of 5,000 inhabitants in less than 200 years. Population also grew in the rural areas surrounding Monte Albán, leading to an increase in the settlement of the hilly piedmont regions surrounding the capital. By 200 B.C. the population of Monte Albán had risen to about 17,000 people, and the piedmont regions surrounding the capital had become even more densely occupied. Archaeological evidence also suggests that administrative activity, one of the characteristics of a state level of political organization, expanded during the later first millennium B.C. Much of the population growth that took place outside the Monte Albán region was centered at secondary administrative centers rather than rural villages. The secondary centers had larger populations than the small, rural villages and included public architecture, such as platforms, mound groups, and possibly ball courts. Ball courts are found throughout many parts of prehistoric Mesoamerica. The ball games were ritualized contests between two teams that involved the use of a small, hard rubber ball.

The costs of the construction and maintenance of Monte Albán and the secondary administrative centers as well as the support of an expanding nonagricultural population must have been financed through the production of a substantial agricultural surplus. This would have placed a significant burden on the rural farming population, especially those living in the agriculturally risky piedmont re-

gions. The first evidence for irrigation in the piedmont regions appears shortly after 500 B.C., indicating that farmers may have shifted toward the production of two or three crops per year (Blanton et al. 1993: 74). This agricultural intensification is accompanied by an intensification in the production of crafts such as pottery.

After about 200 B.C., the rulers of Monte Albán appear to have focused their energy on external conquests rather than internal administration. A possible military outpost has been identified approximately 100 kilometers (62 mi.) northeast of Monte Albán. In the capital itself, a distinctive structure (Structure J) was added to the southern part of the Main Plaza. Its carved slabs depict conquests of places outside the valley itself.

Within the Oaxaca Valley, the population of Monte Albán, and especially that of the surrounding piedmont region, appears to have declined. Agricultural settlements shifted to the richer alluvial areas and away from the more risky piedmont zones. Monte Albán, however, remained the largest urban center within the Oaxaca Valley. Public construction, possibly financed through external conquest, continued and expanded within the capital. Construction of large, defensive walls around Monte Albán was completed, and the process of leveling the entire Main Plaza, an area the size of six football fields, was begun.

Monte Albán's imperial expansion was relatively short-lived. After A.D. 300, Monte Albán's military conquests decreased dramatically, and it may have lost many of its former territories and tributaries as a result of the expansion of the urban state of **Teotihuacán,** centered in the Valley of Mexico. (The archaeological history of Teotihuacán is described in detail below.) The complex interrelationship between Oaxaca and Teotihuacán illustrates that no single region in Mesoamerica may be studied in isolation. As in the Old World, early complex societies interacted with one another in a number of different ways, some peaceable and some hostile.

The loss of Monte Albán's empire was accompanied by an internal reorganization, marked by the rapid expansion of many of the secondary administrative centers within the valley. The formation and expansion of new secondary and smaller tertiary centers fostered continued agricultural expansion within the Oaxaca Valley. After A.D. 500 much of the population growth centered on Monte Albán and its immediate vicinity. The capital's population approached 25,000 during the middle of the first millennium A.D. The Main Plaza was surrounded by public buildings, including temples, mounds, and the residence of the rulers of the city. Craft production was centered in Monte Albán and other major centers, and it appears to have been tightly controlled by the ruling elite.

Monte Albán was unable to maintain tight political and economic control over the Oaxaca Valley in the later part of the first millennium A.D. At that time Monte Albán's population was dramatically reduced to about 4,000 people, and it appears to have been just one of several competing urban centers in the Oaxaca Valley. The collapse of Monte Albán is mirrored by the collapse of a number of complex urban societies in Mesoamerica in the later first millennium A.D. The possible causes for these urban collapses will be discussed in greater detail below.

Teotihuacán and the Valley of Mexico

The development of urbanism and state formation in the Oaxaca Valley is paralleled in many ways by developments in the Valley of Mexico. Located in the central highlands of Mexico, the Valley of Mexico covers a 120-by 70-kilometer (75- by 43-mi.) area that lies over 2,000 meters (6,600 ft.) above sea level. Portions of the valley bottom were covered by a series of marshy, interconnected lakes that provided fish, waterfowl, and other resources. The lakeshore plains provided valuable agricultural lands, and during the later pre-Columbian periods intensive methods were developed to cultivate many of the low-lying, marshy areas as well.

The Valley of Mexico is one of the most intensively studied archaeological regions in the world. Systematic archaeological surveys have been conducted over 5,000 of its approximately 7,000 square kilometers (2,700 sq. mi.) (Blanton et al. 1993: 106). In addition, detailed archaeological survey and excavation, much of it under the direc-

tion of Rene Millon (Millon 1981; Millon et al. 1973), has been conducted within the city of Teotihuacán itself. These data allow archaeologists to study the rise and fall of Teotihuacán in relation to changes in human settlement throughout the Valley of Mexico.

While the presence of small, permanent villages occupied by pottery-making farmers can be traced back to 1400 B.C., this section will focus primarily on the development of the city and state of Teotihuacán. The Teotihuacán region (see Figure 25.2), in the northern part of the Valley of Mexico, was an attractive area for human settlement for two reasons. First, it was located at the head of a series of springs that could have been used for irrigation. Second, and more important, Teotihuacán was located near important deposits of obsidian, or volcanic glass, an excellent raw material for the manufacture of stone tools, and one that was traded throughout Mesoamerica. The earliest settlement of Teotihuacán, dating to about 200 B.C., is a series of villages, one of which may have specialized in obsidian manufacture. By the end of the first century B.C., settlement extended over 8 square kilometers (3 sq. mi.), suggesting a population of at least 20,000 individuals (Blanton et al. 1993: 122). At the end of the first millennium B.C., Teotihuacán was one of two major urban centers in the Valley of Mexico. The other was Cuicuilco, located in the southern end of the valley. However, a series of volcanic eruptions in the first millennium A.D. eventually buried Cuicuilco, and Teotihuacán emerged as the dominant political center in the Valley of Mexico in the first century A.D.

During the first century A.D. the population of Teotihuacán grew to an estimated 80,000 persons spread over an area of approximately 20 square kilometers (8 sq. mi.). This phenomenal growth rate was undoubtedly a result of immigration from the countryside as well as local population growth. During the first two centuries A.D., Teotihuacán was laid out along a precise grid aligned 15.5° east of true north (Figure 25.7). The main north-south street, now known as the Avenue of the Dead, is intersected by a major east-west street, dividing the city into quadrants (Millon 1967). In the early first millennium A.D. approximately 20 temple

Figure 25.7

View of Teotihuacán looking south, showing the Pyramid of the Moon, the Pyramid of the Sun, and the Avenue of the Dead.

complexes lined the Avenue of the Dead. This investment in public architecture is dwarfed, however, by the construction of the Pyramid of the Sun, a stone-faced structure 70 meters (230 ft.) high, with a total construction volume of 1 million cubic meters of fill. Construction of the smaller Pyramid of the Moon (see Figure 25.7) was also initiated at that time, as was the construction of the Ciudadela, a group of four platforms enclosing a plaza that could have held 100,000 people. The Ciudadela is located at the intersection of the main north-south and east-west streets; its geographical position certainly reflects its political and/or religious importance. In addition to these civic and religious structures, residences of the ruling elite and nobility were also located along the Avenue of the Dead. The Great Compound, which served as the city's major marketplace, was constructed at a somewhat later date.

By A.D. 200 Teotihuacán had clearly established itself as the center of religious, political, and economic activity in the Valley of Mexico. Most of the valley's specialized craft activities were centered at Teotihuacán, and there is evidence for increasing specialization in both obsidian manufacture and pottery production. Secondary administrative centers were only about 5 percent of the size of Teotihuacán and contained limited public architecture (Blanton et al. 1993: 129). During the mid-first millennium A.D. Teotihuacán and the area immediately around the city continued to grow, drawing population from other parts of the Teotihuacán valley. The city itself reached a population of 125,000, and the area within 30 kilometers (19 mi.) of the capital housed an additional 65,000 people (Blanton et al. 1993: 129, 134). These demographic trends parallel those seen in Sumer (southern Mesopotamia) during the Early Dynastic period (third millennium B.C.) when the earlier widespread rural settlement was progressively replaced by a smaller number of large urban centers such as Uruk (Adams and Nissen 1972: 12).

What was urban life like in Teotihuacán, and why were residents attracted to the city and its immediate hinterland? The residents of Teotihuacán lived in multifamily compounds housing 60 to 100 persons and surrounded by high walls. Most of the city's obsidian production was carried out within the residential compounds, and it is estimated that perhaps 25 percent of Teotihuacán's population was engaged in craft activities. Approximately 600 workshops have been identified in the city. Groups of residential compounds were oriented around temple complexes; these larger units appear to represent *barrios,* or neighborhoods. In some cases specialized occupations or crafts were centered within the *barrios.* Ceramic evidence indicates that one *barrio* was occupied by people from Oaxaca whose descendants lived in Teotihuacán for generations, although the role that they played in the day-to-day life of Teotihuacán is unclear. Perhaps they functioned as traders or diplomats.

At the height of its power in the middle of the first century A.D., the Teotihuacán state controlled all the Valley of Mexico; it also controlled some centers outside the valley and had widespread contracts throughout Mesoamerica. At A.D. 500 Teotihuacán was one of the largest cities in the world. As is the case for many complex societies, Teotihuacán's success was not to last. Its foreign influence was weakening by A.D. 600, and the city itself appears to have declined rapidly at about A.D. 750. The population was reduced to about 30,000, and there is evidence for widespread destruction of buildings (and sometimes people), especially along the Avenue of the Dead. Fires were set deliberately to destroy the city center and its civic and religious buildings. It is not clear whether this destruction was carried out by a foreign military power or whether it represents an internal revolt against the political establishment. It is interesting to note, however, that the subsequent residents of Teotihuacán avoided reusing the civic and religious architecture in the city center, suggesting that the victors "wanted to dissociate themselves from these buildings and their political and religious symbols" (Blanton et al. 1993: 135). It is also important to emphasize that the destruction of Teotihuacán's center is nearly contemporaneous with the fall of Monte Albán, which suggests that the period around A.D. 750 was one of major political turmoil in Mesoamerica generally. It is possible to compare this situation in a very general way to the decline of the Western Roman Empire in the fifth century A.D. Unified Roman political authority in areas such as Britain, Gaul, and Spain was replaced by a series of smaller barbarian kingdoms, and many symbols of Roman political authority,

such as the major urban centers, declined dramatically at that time.

As we shall see below, the later first millennium A.D. was also a period of dramatic change in Mesoamerica's eastern lowlands. However, we must begin by examining the rise of what was perhaps Mesoamerica's greatest urban society, that of the Classic Maya of the eastern lowlands.

The Beginnings of the Classic Maya

The ancient Maya inhabited a unique and environmentally diverse region in the southeastern part of Mesoamerica **(Figure 25.8)**. Most sites are located in the lowland areas of the Petén-Yucatán peninsula, areas that today include Belize as well as northern Guatemala, northwestern Honduras, and southern Mexico. The peninsula is, in fact, a limestone shelf that extends outward into the Gulf of Mexico and the Caribbean Sea. Unlike the relatively arid regions of Oaxaca and the Valley of Mexico, the southern portion of the Petén-Yucatán peninsula may receive as much as 250 centimeters (100 in.) of rainfall per year. Rainfall decreases as one moves northward, and the northern portions of the Yucatán may receive as little as 50 centimeters (20 in.) of rainfall per year. Most of the rain falls during the season from May to October. The vegetation of the peninsula closely mirrors the rainfall patterns. The southern lowlands are covered by a monsoon forest dominated by huge mahogany trees; in a few areas of extremely high rainfall, a true rain forest exists. (Unlike the trees in a true rain forest, the trees in a monsoonal forest lose their leaves during the dry season.) Much of the rain forest and monsoon forest has been deforested in the past few decades, especially in Mexico. The vegetation changes to low, thorny jungle as one moves into the drier northern lowlands, and the most northerly areas of the Yucatán are covered with arid scrub vegetation.

Additional Maya sites have been identified in the highland regions to the south of the Petén-Yucatán peninsula. The highland areas lie above 305 meters (1,000 ft.) in elevation and are dominated by volcanic peaks, some as high as 4,000 meters (13,000 ft.). Vegetation varies with altitude; grasses and

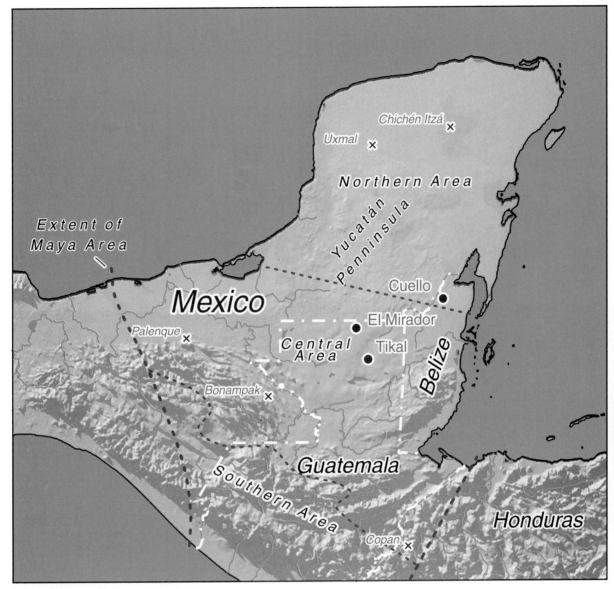

Figure 25.8

Topographic map of the Maya area showing the major sites and landforms.

pines are found in the higher elevations, while oaks trees are found at lower elevations with adequate moisture.

As in other areas of the world, the beginning of farming was critical to the development of complex societies. Early farming villages appear in Chiapas, Mexico, and the adjacent areas of Guatemala by about 2000 B.C. (Clark and Blake 1994). However, early farming villages do not appear in the Maya lowland regions until nearly a millennium later. These early farming villages were undoubtedly based on a method of shifting cul-

tivation known as swidden or slash and burn. In the slash-and-burn method, the vegetation is cleared from an area of forest and burned. The field is used for only a few seasons and then abandoned, allowing the natural vegetation to regrow and the soil's fertility to be restored. The initial appearance of pottery-using farmers marks the beginning of the **Preclassic** (or Formative) **period** (ca. 2000 B.C.) in the Maya area. The Preclassic period continues to A.D. 250, when dated inscriptions first appear in the lowland Maya areas. During earlier phases of

Figure 25.9

Reconstruction of the Late Preclassic architecture at El Mirador in Guatemala.

the Preclassic, the Maya areas were populated by small agricultural villages. One of
the earliest known villages in the Maya lowland areas is the site of **Cuello** in Belize
(Hammond 1991; Hammond et al. 1995).
The initial occupation at Cuello dates to
1200 B.C. A long-term program of excavation
at the site, which began in 1975 and concluded in 1993, has revealed a long sequence
of mud- and plaster-floored houses and their
associated yards from the Middle Preclassic
period (1200 to 400 B.C.). The Cuello excavations have also revealed 180 burials. Those
earlier than 900 B.C. contain no grave goods;
after 900 B.C. pottery vessels were included
in graves.

In the Late Preclassic (400 B.C. to A.D. 250)
Maya society changed from a simple, village
agricultural society to an emerging complex
society. During that period monumental architecture—pyramids, platform mounds,
and temples—appeared at a number of sites,
indicating that certain individuals or groups
of individuals had control over the large
amounts of human labor needed to construct those monuments. One example is the
Late Preclassic site of **El Mirador** (Fig-

ure 25.9), in the swampy northeast Petén
about 360 kilometers (225 mi.) north of
Guatemala City (Matheny 1986, 1987). The
site includes two areas of monumental architecture that are connected by a causeway.
The east group includes a 70-meter (230-ft.)
high pyramid and its associated platforms,
while the west group includes the 55-meter
(180-ft.) high Tigre pyramid, which has an
estimated volume of 380,000 cubic meters
(Coe 1993: 67) and faces the rising sun.
Causeways extend outward from this Preclassic urban center, and it is likely that El
Mirador controlled trade with the Yucatán to
the north and with the Maya highlands and
the Pacific coast to the south.

In addition, late Preclassic tombs from
the site of **Tikal** in Guatemala reflect increasing social, political, and economic inequality.
One of the most intriguing is Tomb 85. The
burial was placed in front of what was
then the central temple on Tikal's acropolis
and enclosed in a vaulted tomb. The body
was bundled in textiles and buried in a
seated position. The skull and thighbones
had been removed from the body. The reason the skull and femurs are missing is not

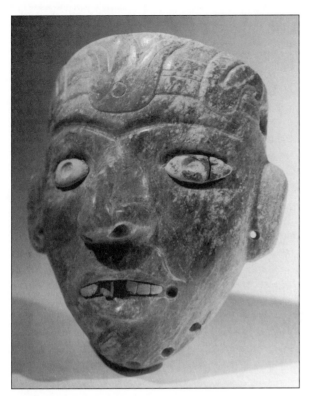

Figure 25.10

Greenstone mask from Tomb 85, Tikal.

clear. Was the deceased a victim of battle whose body had been mutilated and subsequently recovered by relatives (Coe 1993: 64), or were the bones removed by grieving family members and retained as keepsakes (Culbert 1993: 49)?

Whatever the reason for this unusual burial, it is clear that this was the final resting place of a high-ranking man. His skull had been replaced by a greenstone mask **(Figure 25.10)**, and he was accompanied by 26 finely made ceramic vessels, 4 of which had been manufactured in the Guatemalan highlands, 320 kilometers (200 mi.) away. The burial dates to the early first century A.D., and its contents and position show that distinct social and economic inequalities had developed by the Late Preclassic period.

One question that has plagued archaeologists for years is the problem of how swidden farming could have provided a sufficient agricultural surplus to support the urban centers, such as Tikal and El Mirador, that

were clearly well established by Late Preclassic times. More intensive agriculture systems must have played a role in supporting those cities, and the systems are likely to have been established by Late Preclassic times. Agricultural yields could have been increased in several ways. In the lowland areas, however, the most likely means was the use of raised fields. In swampy areas, such as those that surrounded El Mirador, canals were used to drain the fields after the rainy season or to raise the fields above the water level.

The Classic Maya

The beginning of the **Classic period** (ca. A.D. 250 to 930) is marked by the appearance of dated monuments in the southern lowlands. These dated monuments have been crucial to the chronology and interpretation of Classic Maya archaeology. The Maya used two different calendar systems: the Calendar Round and the Long Count. The Calendar Round was also used by many other Mesoamerican peoples. It was made up of two cycles—a 260-day cycle that combined 20 named days with the numbers from 1 to 13 and a 365-day cycle that included 18 named months of 20 days with 5 unlucky days at the end of the cycle. A specific combination of named days would occur only once every 52 years. The Long Count was a day-by-day count that started in 3114 B.C. (long before the Maya). Maya dated monuments also bear written inscriptions, and the recent decipherment of the Maya script has opened a new chapter in Mesoamerican archaeology (see the Archaeology in Practice box).

The Classic period is conventionally divided into an Early Classic (ca. A.D. 250 to 600) and a Late Classic period (ca. A.D. 600 to 830). Influence from and contact with Teotihuacán is seen clearly in the Early Classic but not in the Late Classic period, owing to the collapse of the Teotihuacán state in the late mid-first millennium A.D. A Terminal Classic period (A.D. 830 to 930) has recently been defined. During this final phase, many of the Maya cities of the southern lowlands appear to collapse dramatically.

Archaeology in Practice

Archaeology and History: The Evidence from the Mayan Inscriptions

The Maya differ from most other complex societies in the New World because they used an elaborate and well-developed writing system. Most inscriptions are preserved on stelae (upright carved stone slabs) and on architectural monuments, but some inscriptions have also been recovered from pottery vessels. The Maya also produced books written on bark paper, but only four of them have survived to modern times. Many were burned by early Spanish clerics who considered them the products of heathenism and therefore deserving of destruction. What remains today is only a small fraction of the once rich literary record of the Maya.

One of the most important developments in Mayan archaeology in the past 20 years has been the gradual decipherment of the Mayan writing system. As recently as 40 years ago, about all that could be identified from Mayan inscriptions were their dates. Two discoveries were of primary importance for the decipherment of the ancient Mayan script. The first was the realization that the inscriptions detailed actual political histories (Proskouriakoff 1960); the inscriptions were not simply abstract religious and astronomical texts. The second realization was that the Mayan language was logosyllabic, rather than alphabetic (see the Archaeology in Practice box in Chapter 22). That is, some glyphs represent a single idea, while others represent a syllable, a consonant-vowel combination. For example, the Mayan word *balam,* meaning "jaguar," may be written in two different ways: as a picture of a jaguar (Figure 25.11) or by using the glyphs for the *ba, la,* and *ma* (the final *a* is silent). The decipherment process has been aided by the fact that languages closely related to ancient Mayan are still spoken in many parts of Mesoamerica today. As a result of painstaking epigraphic (epigraphy is the study of inscriptions) research, most of the Mayan syllabary has been reconstructed, and it is estimated that about 85 percent of the known inscriptions can be read with some degree of certainty.

How has the decipherment of the Mayan writing system changed our view of the Maya, and how does the information revealed in the texts differ from the kinds of data that have been recovered through archaeological excavation and survey? The inscriptions focus on the highest levels of Mayan society. They record important events, such as births, marriages, and deaths, in the lives of the ruling families of the Mayan urban centers. The decipherment of the glyphs has allowed archaeologists to reconstruct king lists and the dynastic history of the main urban centers (see, for example, Schele and Freidel 1990). The ruling families of the Mayan cities "had been intricately connected through marriages and alliances and had continually jockeyed for position in relation to one another and for control and influence over lesser sites" (Culbert 1985: 44).

While the inscriptions detail the Machiavellian intrigues of the Mayan ruling classes, the lives of the Mayan lower classes can be explored only through archaeology. In addition to providing information about day-to-day life, archaeology has shed light on urban settlement patterns, Maya subsistence and diet, population dynamics, and craft activities—subjects that are not addressed in the inscriptions. The synthesis of archaeological and historical data has allowed archaeologists to paint a richer and more well-rounded picture of ancient Maya society. The decipherment of the texts has allowed scientists to envision the individual actors who peopled the highest levels of Maya society; archaeological data have allowed scholars to understand the socioeconomic context in which those individuals' actions took place.

Logographic

Balam / Jaguar

Phonetic

ba-la-ma

Figure 25.11

The Maya glyphs for the word balam, *meaning "jaguar."*

Tikal

Major archaeological projects involving both excavation and archaeological surveys have been conducted at a number of Maya urban centers. One of the most well studied is the important Maya city of Tikal in Guatemala. Tikal was the subject of a long-term archaeological research project (1956 to 1971) under the direction of William Coe (1988) of the University of Pennsylvania; Guatemalan archaeologists have conducted more than 10 years of research since the end of the University of Pennsylvania project.

One of the most important tasks undertaken by the Tikal project was the preparation of a map of the structures identified within a 16-square kilometer (6-sq. mi.) region centered on Tikal's Great Plaza (Figure 25.12). (The late Preclassic burial [Tomb 85] discussed above is located in the acropolis on the north end of the Great Plaza.) Later surveys mapped an additional 20 square kilometers (8 sq. mi.) beyond the central map. These surveys have revealed that Tikal was a densely populated urban center during Classic times. During Late Classic times it is estimated that Tikal housed 62,000 people (Culbert et al. 1991).

While archaeologists have debated the nature of ancient Maya political organization, it is clear from both archaeological and historical evidence that the Maya lowlands were never politically unified. The inscriptions clearly demonstrate that competition between the Maya urban centers was a fact of

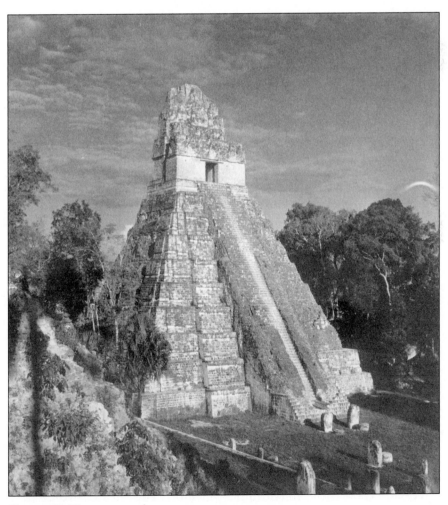

Figure 25.12
Temple 1, part of the central plaza at Tikal.

Maya political life. During the Late Classic period, it is likely that four or five major Maya urban centers, including Tikal, controlled the surrounding minor towns and cities to form a small number of competing states (Marcus 1993). Competition between these major urban centers, expressed in intensive monument-building programs during the Late Classic, may have played a role in the collapse of the Classic Maya in the southern lowlands.

The Collapse of the Classic Maya

The collapse of the Classic Maya (Culbert 1973, 1988) is an issue that has intrigued scholars for decades. After about A.D. 750 the political landscape of the southern lowlands was changing; the large states of the earlier Late Classic period appear to have fragmented into a series of smaller polities. The political instability in the southern lowlands at that time mirrored the situation in the Valley of Mexico and the Oaxaca Valley. In the southern lowlands, however, the political changes are mirrored by dramatic demographic shifts. By the Terminal Classic period, the population of the southern lowland Maya sites had declined by at least two-thirds from its eighth-century peak (Culbert 1993: 118). By the end of the Terminal Classic (ca. A.D. 930), only small, remnant populations remained in the southern Maya lowlands. What factors could have led to the political and demographic collapse of this vibrant, complex society?

One critical factor in the collapse may have been an increasing instability in the relationship between a growing population and the available agricultural resources. The agricultural products were needed both to feed that population and to provide the surplus that supported the growing elite class and its increasing desire for monumental public construction. Population growth may have been a two-edged sword for the Classic Maya. During the Late Preclassic and Early Classic periods, a growing population would have provided more labor for agricultural activities and public construction. By the end of the Late Preclassic period, however, Maya lowland populations had reached the maximum levels that could be supported by long-fallow slash-and-burn agriculture (Culbert 1988). In-creasingly intensive methods of farming had to be used to support the growing population. While intensive agricultural methods may have increased yields in the short term, in the long term they may have led to the loss of soil fertility and to soil erosion. Long-term environmental degradation, when combined with short-term risk factors such as crop diseases, variations in precipitation, and even human disease epidemics, may have led to the demographic collapse that occurred in the southern lowlands in the Terminal Classic period.

It is important to emphasize that the Maya did not disappear at the end of the Terminal Classic period. While the urban sites in the southern lowland area were depopulated and never reoccupied, a number of Maya urban centers were established in the northern Yucatán during the **Postclassic period** (A.D. 930 to 1519). People speaking languages related to ancient Maya continue to inhabit the northern lowlands, the Yucatán, and many areas of highland Guatemala and southern Mexico. Today over 4 million people still speak some form of Maya language.

The Postclassic Period in Mesoamerica and the Rise of the Aztec Empire

The reconstruction of the political, economic, and demographic history of Mesoamerica in the Postclassic period (ca. A.D. 900 to 1500) is a complex process involving the use of archaeological data from survey and excavation as well as historical sources such as the accounts of the Spanish conquistadors. While a detailed history of Mesoamerica during the Postclassic period is beyond the scope of this text, we will conclude this chapter where we began, with an account of the rise of the Aztec Empire, the greatest empire in pre-Columbian Mesoamerica.

The Aztec rise to power was as dramatic as its fall at the hands of the Spaniards. The Aztecs, or Mexica, were a small group of people who entered the Valley of Mexico from the north in the fourteenth century and established their capital at Tenochtitlán, which was then an undesirable, insect-ridden swamp. The Mexica were "despised by their neighbors as backward northern barbarians" (Conrad and Demarest 1984: 11). The Mexica made their living by exploiting Lake Texcoco's resources, by selling themselves as mercenaries, and by establishing a market in Tenochtitlán. "Through cunning and generally shabby behavior they eventually established themselves and their island city . . . as a force to be reckoned with" (Blanton et al. 1993: 148).

The Aztec conquest of much of central and southern Mexico was both a military and a commercial juggernaut. The Mexica combined guile and military prowess with intensive trading activity in the conquered provinces. The initial successful conquest of the nearby provinces fueled attempts to conquer areas that were progressively farther from Tenochtitlán. At the time of the Spanish conquest, the Mexica found themselves fighting farther and farther from home. The Aztec policy, however, continued to be one of expansion rather than consolidation (Conrad and Demarest 1984: 185). They had created an empire that they could no longer successfully administer. It is at that point that Cortez and his band of followers arrived on the scene. The political impact of the Spanish conquest of Mexico was dwarfed by the demographic impact of the diseases that the Europeans introduced. Native Mesoamerican peoples lacked immunities to Old World diseases such as measles, mumps, and smallpox. These imported diseases decimated the population of Mesoamerica in a way that European military activities never could.

Conclusion

During the first millennium B.C. and the first millennium A.D. complex, urban societies developed in a number of different regions in Mesoamerica, including the Oaxaca Valley, the Valley of Mexico, and the Maya lowlands. These developments cannot be examined in isolation. The societies interacted with each other through trade, warfare, and other forms of cultural contact. The New World states shared many characteristics with the complex societies of the Old World, including long-distance trade in luxury items, a class-stratified society, and the concentration of military power in the hands of the ruling classes. The recent decipherment of the Mayan script has shed new light on the political dynamics of one of these complex societies.

 Glossary

Classic period. The period (ca. A.D. 250 to 930) that coincides with the florescence of lowland Maya culture. The beginning is marked by the appearance of dated monuments in the southern lowlands. The Classic period ends with the collapse of many Maya urban centers in the southern lowlands.

Cuello. A Preclassic farming village in Belize, where excavations have revealed a long sequence of mud- and plaster-floored houses and their associated yards from the Middle Preclassic period (1200 to 400 B.C.).

El Mirador. A major Preclassic Maya urban center located in northeastern Guatemala. The site has yielded evidence of two monumental architectural complexes and may have controlled long-distance trade in the region.

Formative (or Preclassic) period. The period (2000 B.C. to A.D. 250) during which the earliest complex societies in Mesoamerica appear. During this period we also see the appearance of the earliest monumental architecture and sculpture in Mesoamerica and the beginnings of urbanism in the region. The beginning of the period is marked by the appearance of pottery-using agriculturalists in Mesoamerica.

La Venta. The site in southern Mexico that emerged as a leading Olmec ceremonial center between about 800 and 400 B.C.

Mesoamerica. A geographical term that describes the region extending from northwest Costa Rica to Mexico south of the northern deserts. This region was home to some of the earliest complex societies in the Americas.

Monte Albán. The urban capital of the state that developed in the Valley of Oaxaca between about 500 B.C. and A.D. 750.

Olmecs. The people that inhabited the southern Gulf coast of Mexico during the Formative period. Their ceremonial centers include monumental architecture and sculpture (huge stone heads). While the Olmecs were traditionally considered Mesoamerica's "mother culture," they now appear to be just one of a number of early complex societies that appear in Mesoamerica during the Formative period.

Postclassic period. The period (A.D. 930 to 1519) that begins with the collapse of the Classic Maya in the southern lowlands and ends with the Spanish conquest of Mexico in 1519.

Preclassic period. An alternative name for the Formative period, most commonly used in the Maya areas of Mesoamerica.

San José Mogote. A Formative village in the Oaxaca Valley that has yielded early evidence for public architecture.

San Lorenzo. The earliest of the large Olmec ceremonial centers, overlooking the Rio Coatzacoalcos. Excavations at San Lorenzo revealed the presence of Olmec-style ceramics at the site as early as 1150 B.C. as well as numerous large, stone, carved heads.

Tenochtitlán. The Aztec capital, located on an island in Lake Texcoco in the Valley of Mexico, established in the fourteenth century.

Teotihuacán. The city in the Valley of Mexico that was the political, economic, and religious capital of the valley from 200 B.C. to A.D. 700.

Tikal. A major Maya urban center in Guatemala that has been the focus of intensive archaeological research since the 1950s. At its height in Late Classic times Tikal was home to 62,000 people.

 Further Reading

Blanton, Richard E., Stephen A. Kowalewski, Gary M. Feinman, and Laura M. Finsten
    1993. *Ancient Mesoamerica: A Comparison of Change in Three Regions,* 2d ed. Cambridge: Cambridge University Press.
    This useful volume compares the development of complex societies in three different regions of Mesoamerica—the Valley of Mexico, Oaxaca, and the Mayan area. This book is highly recommended for the more advanced reader.

Coe, Michael
    1993. *The Maya,* 5th ed. New York: Thames and Hudson.
    This standard introduction to Maya archaeology is now in its fifth edition. Although it has been substantially revised, this book is beginning to show its age. Note, however, that the illustrations are beautiful.

Culbert, T. Patrick
    1993. *Maya Civilization.* Washington, DC: Smithsonian Books.

Culbert is one of the foremost experts on the question of the collapse of the classic Maya in the southern lowlands. He has written a well-illustrated and readable introduction to Mayan civilization, which is strongly recommended.

Marcus, Joyce, and Kent V. Flannery
    1996. *Zapotec Civilization: How Urbanism Evolved in Mexico's Oaxaca Valley.* New York: Thames and Hudson.
    An up-to-date and readable account of the development of urbanism in Oaxaca.

Smith, Michael E.
    1997. Life in the Provinces of the Aztec Empire. *Scientific American* 277 (4): 76–83.
    Smith provides a well-illustrated and up-to-date account of life in the Aztec provinces based on recent excavations of two rural sites and the city of Yautapec. For an older, but very readable, account of urban life in Teotihuacán, Millon's (1967) early account of his research at the site (also published in *Scientific American*) is recommended as well.

 Other Bibliography

Adams, R. M., and H. J. Nissen
    1972. *The Uruk Countryside: The Natural Setting of Urban Societies.* Chicago: University of Chicago Press.

Clark, J. E., and M. Blake
    1994. The Power of Prestige: Competitive Generosity and the Emergence of Rank Societies in Lowland Mesoamerica. In *Factional Competition and Political Development in the New World,* edited by E. M. Brumfiel and J. W. Fox, pp. 17–30. Cambridge: Cambridge University Press.

Coe, William
    1988. *Tikal, a Handbook of the Ancient Maya Ruins,* 2d ed. Philadelphia: University of Pennsylvania Museum.

Conrad, G. W., and A. A. Demarest
    1984. *Religion and Empire: The Dynamics of Aztec and Inca Expansionism.* Cambridge: Cambridge University Press.

Culbert, T. Patrick, ed.
    1973. *The Classic Maya Collapse.* Albuquerque, NM: University of New Mexico Press.

Culbert, T. Patrick
    1985. The Maya Enter History. *Natural History* 85 (4): 42–49.
    1988. The Collapse of Classic Maya Civilization. In *The Collapse of Ancient States and*

Civilizations, edited by N. Yoffee and G. Cowgill, pp. 69–101. Tucson: University of Arizona Press.

Culbert, T. P., L. J. Kosakowsky, R. E. Fry, and W. A. Haviland
1991. The Population of Tikal, Guatemala. In *Precolumbian Population History in the Maya Lowlands,* edited by T. P. Culbert and D. S. Rice, pp. 103–121. Albuquerque: University of New Mexico Press.

Grove, David C.
1997. Olmec Archaeology: A Half Century of Research and Its Accomplishments. *Journal of World Prehistory* 11: 51–101.

Hammond, Norman
1991. *Cuello: An Early Maya Community in Belize.* Cambridge: Cambridge University Press.

Hammond, Norman, Amanda Clarke, and Sara Donaghey
1995. The Long Goodbye: Middle Preclassic Maya Archaeology at Cuello, Belize. *Latin American Antiquity* 6 (2): 120–128.

Marcus, Joyce
1993. Ancient Maya Political Organization. In *Lowland Maya Civilization in the Eighth Century A.D.,* edited by J. A. Sabloff and J. S. Henderson, pp. 111–171. Washington, DC: Dumbarton Oaks.

Matheny, Ray T.
1986. Investigations at El Mirador, Petén, Guatemala. *National Geographic Research Reports* 2 (3): 332–353.
1987. El Mirador: An Early Maya Metropolis Uncovered. *National Geographic,* September: 317–339.

Millon, Rene
1967. Teotihuacán. *Scientific American* 216 (6): 38–48.
1981. Teotihuacán: City, State, and Civilization. In *Supplement to the Handbook of Middle American Indians, Vol. 1: Archaeology,* edited by J. A. Sabloff, pp. 198–243. Austin: University of Texas Press.

Millon, Rene, B. Drewitt, and G. Cowgill
1973. *Urbanization at Teotihuacán, Mexico, Vol. 1: The Teotihuacán Map.* Austin: University of Texas Press.

Proskouriakoff, T.
1960. Historical Implications of a Pattern of Dates at Piedras Negras, Guatemala. *American Antiquity* 25: 454–475.

Rust, W. F., and R. J. Sharer
1988. Olmec Settlement Data from La Venta, Tabasco, Mexico. *Science* 242: 102–104.

Schele, Linda, and David Freidel
1990. *A Forest of Kings: The Untold Story of the Ancient Maya.* New York: William Morrow.

Soustelle, Jacques
1985. *The Olmecs: The Oldest Civilization in Mexico,* translated by Helen R. Lane. Norman: University of Oklahoma Press.

Willey, Gordon
1966. *An Introduction to American Archaeology, Vol. 1: North and Middle America.* Englewood Cliffs, NJ: Prentice-Hall.

Chapter 26

Cities, States, and Empires in the Andes

Introduction

As noted in the previous chapter, Western diseases introduced by the Spanish conquistadors had a devastating impact on the native populations of Mesoamerica. Old World diseases such as smallpox had an equally disastrous effect on the native inhabitants of South America. American history books tell us that Francisco Pizarro and a small band of 260 mercenaries conquered Peru for the Spanish crown in 1532. The Spaniards tricked the **Inca** emperor, held him for ransom, and subsequently killed him and marched into the Inca capital city of **Cuzco.** What high school history books do not tell us is that six years before the Spanish conquest, the population of highland South America had been decimated by an epidemic of smallpox, a disease to which the native South Americans had no natural immunity. This epidemic spread southward from Mesoamerica, where the Spaniards had already conquered Mexico. The disease not only killed large numbers of people in South America, but also threw the Inca empire into political turmoil. These circumstances made it possible for Pizarro's small band of mercenaries to conquer the great Inca Empire.

At the time of the Spanish conquest the Inca Empire stretched from southern Colombia and Ecuador in the north to northern Chile and highland Argentina in the south **(Figure 26.1)**. The Inca domain extended over 5,500 kilometers (3,500 mi.) of Andean territory, including coastal deserts and high mountains, reaching eastward to the borders of the rain forest. The Inca Empire, the largest empire of the prehistoric New World, was, however, only the last in a long series of states and empires that developed in Peru and the adjacent areas of South America during pre-Columbian times. In this chapter, we will examine the development of cities and states in highland South America, beginning with the small agricultural villages that developed in highland and lowland South America more than 5,000 years ago.

Environmental Background

It is impossible to understand the development of complex societies in the Andes without understanding the varied environments of Peru and the surrounding countries of highland South America. Environmental extremes played a crucial role in shaping farming practices in this region. The coast of Peru is one of the world's driest deserts. In most areas, no appreciable rain falls throughout the year. The coastal areas, however, are covered with a thick fog for approximately six to eight months of the year. In the areas of dense winter fogs, some grasses and bushes can survive on trapped and condensed moisture, producing **lomas** (fog meadows), which can support animals such as foxes, lizards, birds, and snails (Lanning 1967: 10). The coastal waters are home to a rich variety of marine life, including both small and large fishes, water birds, and shellfish. The dry coastal desert is transected by approximately 40 rivers, which run from east to west **(Figure 26.2)**. The rivers are fed by summer (December to March) rains in the highlands, but the smallest will run dry during the winter. Agriculture is possible in the coastal desert areas only through the use of irrigation.

The Andes mountains form the backbone of South America. The Andes are divided

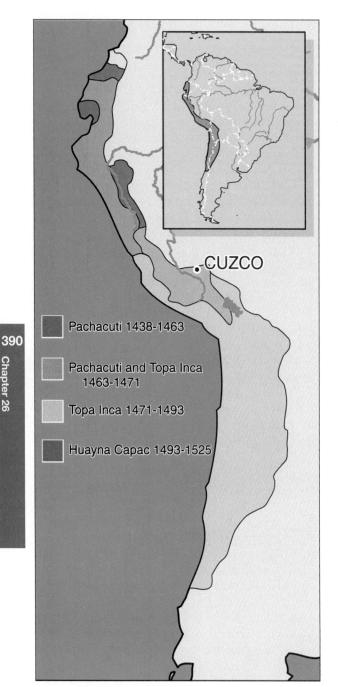

Figure 26.1

Map of South America showing modern political boundaries and the extent of the Inca Empire at its height.

Pachacuti 1438-1463

Pachacuti and Topa Inca 1463-1471

Topa Inca 1471-1493

Huayna Capac 1493-1525

Figure 26.2

Map showing major landforms and the sites mentioned in this chapter.

into several parallel chains of mountains by a series of rivers that run north-south. The river valleys were suitable for agriculture, and some of the lower slopes also could be farmed with the help of terracing and irrigation. Additional farmland was located in the **altiplano,** the high flatland surrounding Lake Titicaca, which straddles the border between Peru and Bolivia. High plateaus, called **puna,** were occupied up to elevations of 5,000 meters (16,000 ft.). These areas were used primarily for grazing livestock—herds of llamas and alpacas that provided meat, wool, and transportation for Andean farmers **(Figure 26.3).**

Herding, Farming, and Fishing: The Economic Background to the Emergence of Complex Societies in Peru

In Chapter 19, we noted that the highlands of Peru were one of a number of centers for plant domestication in the New World. Crops such as the potato and the grain

Figure 26.3

A Moche stirrup-spout bottle showing a llama carrying jars in its saddlebags. Llamas were used for transportation, for food, and for fibers throughout much of Peruvian prehistory.

quinoa were initially cultivated in the Andean highlands. Early herders and farmers in the highlands made use of the verticality of the highland environment by using different elevations for different purposes. Plant cultivation took place at lower elevations in the valley bottoms, while the high plateaus, or puna, were used primarily for grazing llamas and alpacas. The diverse geography of the Andean region, however, led to radically different subsistence systems in different parts of Peru.

In the coastal areas, the rich marine life may have supported sedentary foraging communities even before the beginnings of farming in the region (Moseley 1975b). The transition to sedentism can be seen at the site of **Paloma,** located approximately 4 kilometers (2.5 mi.) from the sea behind San Bartolo Bay in Peru. The site was occupied between 4500 and 3000 b.c. Although Paloma was initially occupied by mobile hunter-gatherers, the inhabitants eventually became sedentary, occupying small circular houses. Studies of the faunal remains recovered from the site indicate that Paloma's residents consumed a diet that was dominated by small fish, such as sardines and anchovies. Remains

of small quantities of cultivated plants have also been found in the trash middens at Paloma. Squash, beans, and gourds were undoubtedly cultivated in the local streambeds after their annual flooding. The site itself is located in the lomas, or fog meadows, rather than along the coast. The lomas areas would have provided wood for cooking and heating. The location of this site within the lomas region indicates that while the sea provided the vast majority of the foodstuffs consumed at Paloma, plant materials played a critical role in the economy because of their importance for fuel and for fiber for fishing line and netting.

After 3000 b.c., plants and plant cultivation came to play an even more central role in lowland subsistence in Peru. Cultivated food plants included beans squash, fruits, and peppers; however, the industrial cultigen cotton played an even more important role in the economy. Cotton could be used for fishing nets and lines, as well as for textiles. Cultivated gourds could also be used for containers and as floats for fishing lines and nets. The period between 3000 b.c. and 1800 b.c. is sometimes referred to as the Cotton Preceramic period because of the increasing importance of cotton cultivation in the coastal economy (Moseley 1992: 104). The term **Preceramic** indicates that this period antedates the introduction of pottery to the Peruvian lowlands; pottery was introduced to the coastal regions about 1800 b.c.

During the Preceramic period, public ceremonial architecture appears for the first time in the coastal regions of Peru. Between 3000 and 2500 b.c. large, raised platform mounds were constructed at a number of sites along the central Peruvian coast. These large platforms would have been used for religious or ceremonial purposes. The raised structures were constructed by filling in and burying earlier ground-level buildings with rubble. The rubble was placed into large, open reed containers, and the fill and container were placed inside the building to be filled. This technique allowed for the work to be divided into repetitive tasks, so that the large amounts of labor required could be coordinated (Moseley 1992: 110). By maintaining a standardized unit of fill, the builders could more easily estimate the amounts of fill necessary to bury the buildings and raise the platforms (Pineda 1988: 79). The construction of these large mounds indicates that certain individuals or groups controlled large quantities of labor, evidence that social differentiation was already present in Peru during the late Preceramic period.

The site of **Río Seco** is typical of the larger Preceramic sites. The site covers 11.8 hectares (29.2 acres) and includes two major platform mounds that were built by in-filling rooms. The mounds measure 10 to 15 meters (33 to 49 ft.) in diameter and stand 3 meters (10 ft.) in height. Río Seco also includes the remains of a large number of small dwellings that were probably covered with thatch or mats. Differences in the sizes of the houses may reflect some degree of social differentiation.

Initial Period

The beginning of the **Initial period** (1800 to 900 B.C.) is marked by the appearance of pottery, which could be used to store, cook, and brew agricultural produce. During the Initial period, farming came to play a more central role in the Peruvian economy. While Preceramic farmers had focused on cotton and gourds, which were used primarily for nonfood purposes, during the Initial period domesticated food plants become increasingly important in the diet. Maize, which was initially domesticated in Mesoamerica, is found only rarely at coastal Preceramic sites and played only a minor role in the diet at the sites where it is found. Maize is far more common at lowland Initial period sites, along with other cultivated plants, including squash, peppers, lima and kidney beans, peanuts, avocados, and guavas (Pineda 1988: 82). The mastery of irrigation techniques made farming possible in the coastal desert areas. Populations moved inland from the coast to areas along the river valleys that could be easily irrigated.

The population growth that resulted from the spread of irrigation agriculture is reflected in the construction of larger ceremonial architectural complexes located farther from the Pacific coast. The largest and most impressive of these is the site of **Sechín Alto (Figure 26.4)**, located in the lower Casma River Valley. Work was begun on this ceremonial complex by 1400 B.C. The central structure, a stone-faced platform mound, stands 40 meters (131 ft.) high and measures 250 by 300 meters (820 by 980 ft.) at its base. Five large plazas lie in front of the main platform, covering an area of 400 by 1,400 meters (1,300 by 4,600 ft.). Studies based on aerial photographs suggest that the whole Sechín Alto complex covers an area of 300 to 400 hectares (740 to 990 acres) of the valley plain (Pineda 1988: 87). Clearly, a significant agricultural surplus must have been mobilized to support the labor needed to construct this massive complex.

Figure 26.4

Plan of Sechín Alto, lower Casma River Valley, showing main platform mound and associated plazas.

How was this surplus mobilized? Initial period burials provide relatively little evidence for personal wealth or hereditary rule. Decision making and governance appear to have been vested in offices such as the priesthood, rather than in individuals (Moseley 1992: 140). Monumental construction centered on the building of large platform mounds and temples. The priesthood may have been particularly important in integrating early farming communities in Peru. If the priesthood used its religious power to gain control over the labor force, it would be able to reaffirm and increase that power by constructing ever larger and more grandiose public monuments (Pineda 1988: 94).

The Early Horizon and the Chavín Cult

The **Early Horizon** (approximately 900 to 200 B.C.) is traditionally defined as the period when artistic influences from the site of **Chavín de Huántar** in the Peruvian highlands spread across much of central and northern Peru. The site includes both residential areas housing an estimated 2,000 to 3,000 individuals (Burger 1984: 247) and a complex of monumental stone buildings known as the Castillo. The Castillo was formed out of two U-shaped structures known as the Old and New Temples **(Figure 26.5)**. The most striking feature of Chavín de Huántar is its monumental stone sculpture, which features both a unique style and a distinctive iconography. The cayman, a South American relative of the alligator, is the most important animal represented in these sculptures. A humanlike figure known as the Staff God carried a staff in each hand and had projecting canine teeth and claws **(Figure 26.6)**.

While monumental stone sculpture is uncommon outside the Chavín de Huántar area, similar designs and iconography are found on pottery and textiles from other parts of Peru. The spread of this art and iconography over large areas of northern and central Peru appears to represent the expansion of a regional religious cult (Burger 1988). The expansion of the Chavín cult can be compared to the spread of early Christianity across the late Roman Empire in the first few centuries A.D. What is even more important than the spread of the Chavín cult itself is that the diffusion of this religious cult was accompanied by the spread of a number of important technological changes in textiles and metallurgy. These changes include such innovations as the use of camelid (llama and alpaca) hair in cotton textiles, textile painting, and the use of

Figure 26.5
The New Temple (part of the Castillo) at Chavín de Huántar, Peru.

Figure 26.6

An example of Chavín art: the Raimondi stone from Chavín de Huántar showing the Staff God.
Drawing courtesy of John H. Rowe.

the heddle loom in place of finger weaving in textile production. Innovations in metallurgy that appear at this time include soldering, which allowed workers to create large, three-dimensional pieces, and the production of gold-silver alloys (Burger 1988: 129–130). These technological innovations laid the foundations for later developments in craft production.

In addition, the spread of this cult and these technologies may have linked across a wide geographical area ethnically distinct communities that previously had little communication with one another. Archaeologically, this communication can be seen in an increase in long-distance trade. For example, nearly all the obsidian recovered from Chavín de Huántar came from the site of Quispisisa, 750 kilometers (470 mi.) to the south (Burger 1988: 132). The increasing use of llamas as pack animals may have played a critical role in this expanded trade. While llamas were initially domesticated in the southern highlands of Peru by the third millennium B.C., they were not widely used in northern Peru until the Early Horizon. Llamas may have played a critical role as pack animals in transporting raw materials and exotic goods over long distances (Miller and Burger 1995).

The Early Intermediate Period

The Chavín cult was a relatively short-lived phenomenon. The period that followed the Chavín, or Early Horizon, is termed the **Early Intermediate period** (ca. 200 B.C. to A.D. 600). This period sees the abandonment of many ceremonial centers associated with the Chavín cult. New construction ceases at the site of Chavín de Huántar itself. The unity of the Early Horizon is followed by a period of diversity when various regions of Andean South America develop in very different ways. In some regions there is evidence for the emergence of states, while in others no such central authority exists. Moreover, the emergence of complex societies in Peru is not a linear process in which progressively larger kingdoms and states develop, culminating in the emergence of the Inca empire. In some periods we see a limited number of powerful states, while in others, including the Early Intermediate period, we see a larger number of smaller polities. In the following sections

Figure 26.7

Detail of the Hoover mantle from the Paracas necropolis.

we will examine two very different cultures of the Early Intermediate period: the Nasca culture of the southern Peruvian coast and the Moche, or Mochica, culture of the northern coastal region.

The Nasca of the Southern Coast

The southern coastal region, centered on the Nazca and Ica River Valleys, is well known for its artistry in ceramics and tex-

tiles. One of the finest collections of textiles comes from the **Paracas** necropolis, or cemetery. This site, which was excavated by Julio C. Tello in 1929, is made up of a cache of 429 mummies, which were wrapped in cloth and piled in an abandoned house on the Paracas peninsula. In addition to the cloth, the mummies were accompanied by food, ceramic vessels, and other grave goods, such as beautifully embroidered headbands, mantles **(Figure 26.7)**, loincloths, turbans, ponchos, tunics, and

Archaeology in Practice

The Preservation of Organic Materials

Organic materials can be broadly defined as the remains of living things—plants and animals. Organic materials were often used by ancient societies, not only as foods, but also for a range of craft and construction activities. Ancient peoples regularly made use of wood, animal skins, sinew, horn, antler, and bone. Matting, cordage, and textiles were made from a variety of plant and animal fibers, including reeds, flax, cotton, wool, and hair.

Bone is one of the most durable of all organic materials because it is composed of both mineral and organic matter. Animal bones survive poorly in acid soils (pH of 6 or less), which rapidly dissolve the mineral component of bone. Once the mineral component of bone is destroyed, the organic component is then broken down by bacteria. In neutral or alkaline soils, the mineral component of bone can survive unchanged for thousands of years, even though the organic component may be quickly destroyed by bacteria (Rackham 1994: 19). As a result, animal bones are among the most common finds in many archaeological sites.

Other organic materials, including skins, hides, and plant and animal fibers, decay rapidly in most environments. Biological agents of decay, such as bacteria, fungi, and insects, can destroy buried textiles, hides, and matting in a matter of months or years. Organic materials such as textiles can survive only in burial contexts that inhibit the action of bacteria, insects, and fungi. Waterlogging and extreme desiccation can inhibit the action of these biological agents of destruction.

Waterlogging provides an anaerobic environment (an environment lacking in oxygen), which inhibits bacterial action. As we saw in Chapter 15, waterlogged Mesolithic sites in Europe have yielded remains of wooden canoes, paddles, and other organic artifacts that are rarely preserved archaeologically.

Extreme desert conditions will also inhibit the activity of bacteria, fungi, and insects. Such dry conditions exist in Egypt in the Old World and along the Peruvian coastal desert in the Americas. The extreme dryness of the Peruvian coast has resulted in the preservation of a unique series of textiles made of cotton and camelid (llama and alpaca) hair. These unusual preservation conditions have allowed archaeologists to study both the technology of weaving (Figure 26.8) and the design motifs on the textiles themselves.

---

skirts (Paul 1990). The burials from the Paracas necropolis are dated to the late part of the Early Horizon and the early part of the Early Intermediate period; radiocarbon dates range from 300 B.C. to A.D. 200 (Silverman 1991: 351). The dry, desert conditions that exist on the Peruvian coast allowed these finely made textiles to be preserved from antiquity (see the Archaeology in Practice box).

The embroidered designs on the Paracas textiles show remarkable similarities to the images painted on later Nasca pottery. The art, technology, and iconography of the Paracas culture clearly had an influence on the subsequent Nasca culture, but the nature of the relationship between the two cultures remains unclear (Silverman 1991: 351). Part of the problem is that the pottery that was found in association with the Paracas textiles is generally unpainted (Paul 1991: 25).

The **Nasca** culture, known for its beautiful ceramics and textiles, developed on the south coast of Peru during the Early Intermediate period. The most important Nasca center, **Cahuachi,** has often been seen as the capital city of the Nasca polity. The site covers an area of 150 hectares (390 acres) and includes more than 40 mounds. Recent research at Cahuachi, however, has shown that the center was a ceremonial, not a major urban, center (Silverman 1993). Excavations at the site have yielded little evidence for defensive works, permanent residences, and day-to-day activities (Silverman 1993: 300). The mounds

Figure 26.8

Restored archaeological loom from the Chancay Valley in Peru.

at the site appear to be temple mounds, rather than elite residences. Cahuachi appears to have served as a center of pilgrimage and ritual. It never developed into a true city with a substantial residential population engaged in nonsubsistence activities.

Nasca artisans are world-famous for their ceramics **(Figure 26.9)** and their textiles, a fact that has led to the extensive looting of many Nasca sites (see Chapter 28). The Nasca textiles include large quantities of alpaca hair, indicating that extensive trade relationships were maintained with the highland regions of the Andes (Conklin and Moseley 1988: 155). While Nasca sites share common styles of pottery, textiles, and other aspects of material culture, the question of whether the Nasca es-

tablished a state level of political organization remains an open one. Although the Nasca were clearly a complex society, with differences in access to social status, political power, and material wealth, the evidence for the centralization of political power in the Nasca region is limited.

The Mochica State on the North Coast

At a superficial level the **Mochica, or Moche,** culture of the north coast of Peru shows some similarities to the Nasca of the south coast. The Mochica were skilled craftworkers in both pottery and metals. Moche metal production built on the innovations

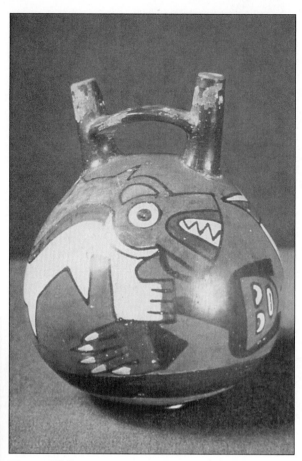

Figure 26.9
A richly decorated Nasca ceramic vessel.

Figure 26.10
A Mochica portrait vessel.

that appeared during the Early Horizon. The Mochica made use of silver and copper in addition to gold, and they alloyed metals and occasionally cast copper (Donnan 1978). Moche potters used molds to produce high-quality ceramics, such as their portrait vessels, which are realistically painted to represent distinctive individuals **(Figure 26.10)**.

While the Moche and the Nasca both produced high-quality ceramics and other crafts, the degrees of urbanism and political integration in the two regions were very different indeed. Unlike the Nasca ceremonial center of Cahuachi, the Moche capital at **Cerro Blanco** in the Moche Valley appears to have been a political capital and urban center. The capital was dominated by two major structures, the Huaca del Sol (Pyramid of the Sun) and the smaller Huaca de la Luna (Pyramid of the Moon). As can be seen in **Figure 26.11**, the

Huaca del Sol is a multilevel platform built of adobe bricks. Around A.D. 500 it would have been surrounded by elite residences, workshops, and extensive cemeteries for the nobility. The Huaca del Sol appears to have served as a palace and mausoleum for Moche leaders. The Huaca de la Luna, on the other hand, lacks domestic rubbish and was decorated with murals. It appears to have served as a ritual center. Archaeological finds from the Moche area indicate that the Moche capital was a center of specialized craft production for both ceramic and metal objects. By A.D. 500 the Moche capital had developed into a "functionally complex and differentiated settlement with a substantial resident population" (Shimada 1994: 97).

There is abundant evidence for social differentiation in the Moche capital and elsewhere along the northern Peruvian coast during the Early Intermediate period. Elite residences were constructed of adobe, while

Figure 26.11

The Huaca del Sol at the Moche capital of Cerro Blanco. Only a small part of the original platform structure survives. The Spanish diverted the Moche River to undercut the mound and loot its contents. The remaining portion of the Huaca del Sol measures 340 by 160 meters (1100 by 525 ft.) and stands 40 meters (130 ft.) high.

those of the lower classes were built of cane with stone foundations. Elite burials contained large quantities of sumptuary goods. Among the most impressive are the rich burials recently recovered from the **Sípan** pyramid complex in the Lambayeque Valley. These rich burials were accompanied by prodigious quantities of metal, presentation goblets, and distinctive uniforms and headdresses.

Finally, there is greater evidence for centralization of authority in the Moche region than there is in the Nasca areas to the south. Administrative centers, modeled on the Huaca del Sol and Huaca de la Luna but smaller in size, were established in many north coast valleys. At the apex of its power in the sixth century A.D., the Moche state controlled one-third of the Peruvian coast (Shimada 1994: 35). As Moseley (1992: 183) notes, "Moche represents a remarkable achievement in statecraft. For the first time the largest of coastal populations were forged together as one nation."

The Middle Horizon

The **Middle Horizon** (A.D. 600 to 1000) saw the rise of two powerful states in South America—**Tiwanaku** in the southern highlands and **Huari,** whose capital was located in the Ayacucho Valley in central Peru. These states developed at a time of profound environmental stress in the Andean areas. There is environmental evidence for a series of severe El Niño events in the sixth century A.D., which caused flooding along the normally dry coast and drought in the Andean highlands. (El Niño events are caused by a warming of the waters of the South Pacific. They can cause storms and flooding all along the Pacific coast and unusual weather patterns throughout the world. The most recent event took place in 1997.) As will be shown below, both the Huari and the Tiwanaku state appear to have been involved in innovations in agricultural technology that may be related, at least in part, to the climatic instability of the mid-first millennium A.D.

The city of Huari is located on the eastern edge of the Ayacucho Valley, at an elevation of approximately 3,000 meters (9,800 ft.) above sea level. The most intensively occupied core of the city covers an area of about 300 hectares (740 acres). The architectural remains at Huari are poorly preserved and difficult to interpret because of looting and plowing by modern farmers; virtually the entire area is dry-farmed today. The available archaeological evidence from survey and excavation indicates that the city was divided into a series of building compounds divided by walled enclosures (Isbell 1988: 168). The buildings within the enclosures were two to three stories high; within the compounds rooms were organized around courtyards, or patios. The population of Huari is estimated to have been between 20,000 and 30,000 during the Middle Horizon (Moseley 1992: 217). Huari was a large city in which a range of administrative, ceremonial, and craft activities were carried out (Isbell 1988: 173).

At the height of its power during the Middle Horizon, the Huari state appears to have exercised political control over a large area of the Peruvian highlands, and its influence extended to many areas of the Peruvian coast. The ability of the Huari state to expand beyond the Ayacucho region was based on an important administrative innovation—the development of a system of labor taxation (Isbell 1988). The state required its subjects to perform agricultural labor on state lands; in return, the Huari administrators provided the laborers with food and drink. At least three Huari provincial administrative centers have been identified by archaeologists. These centers often include barracks-like accommodations for temporary agricultural workers, storage areas for produce, and communal kitchens for the preparation of meals for the agricultural workers.

A second Huari innovation can be seen in the area of agricultural technology (Moseley 1992). During the Early Intermediate period, farming in the highlands took place at the higher elevations, where rainfall alone was adequate to support the cultivation of potatoes and other highland crops. Irrigation farming was limited to the coastal valleys and the river valley areas within the uplands. The Huari introduced terracing and irrigation agriculture to the steep mountain slopes of the highlands. The water for irrigation was drawn from elevated streams and springs, water sources that were less affected by variations in rainfall. This new agricultural technology would have been particularly important in the drought conditions that existed during the Middle Horizon.

A second, smaller state developed in the southern Andes during the Middle Horizon. Its capital city of Tiwanaku is located 15 kilometers (9 mi.) south of Lake Titicaca in Bolivia. The Tiwanaku state flourished between A.D. 400 and 1000. Its heartland was the flatland surrounding Lake Titicaca, but llama caravans provided links with distant regions in the southern highlands. Recent archaeological research has shown that the Tiwanaku state was directly involved in reclaiming for agricultural use the flat, marshy areas that surround Lake Titicaca (Kolata 1991).

Tiwanaku agriculture in the Lake Titicaca region was based on a system of raised fields. The raised fields were "large elevated planting platforms ranging from 5 to 20 m in width and up to 200 m in length" (Kolata 1991: 101) and were surrounded by canals (Figure 26.12). The canals supported aquatic plants, which were used as fertilizer for the raised fields, and also protected the fields from killer frosts, a serious problem at high elevations. The construction of the Tiwanaku raised field system depended on the creation of a regional system of canals, aqueducts, and groundwater regulation, and would have required the mobilization of a substantial labor force. Like the Huari system of irrigated terraces, the raised field system of the Titicaca basin was a highly productive agricultural system that would have required large amounts of coordinated labor for its construction and maintenance.

The Late Intermediate Period

The **Late Intermediate period** (A.D. 1000 to 1476) begins with the collapse of the

mound

field surface

canal

0   30
meters

Figure 26.12

Plan of the Tiwanaku raised field system. The house mound in the center, which dates to approximately A.D. *800 to 1000, was occupied on a seasonal basis by field guardians.*

Huari and Tiwanaku states and ends with the rapid expansion of the Inca Empire in the century before the Spanish conquest of Peru. The archaeology of the Late Intermediate period is best known from the north coast of Peru as a result of intensive archaeological excavation in the Moche Valley. During the Late Intermediate period the Moche Valley was dominated by the city of **Chan Chan,** the capital of **Chimor, or the Chimú state.** Chimor was the most powerful state of the Late Intermediate period; at its height the Chimú state controlled two-thirds of the Peruvian coast.

The central core of Chan Chan (Moseley 1975a; Moseley and Day 1982) covers an area of 6 square kilometers (2.3 sq. mi.) and may have housed between 25,000 and 30,000 people at its height (Parsons and Hastings 1988: 193). The most striking feature of the central core is a series of compounds termed *ciudadellas* (little cities) that appear to have been built by successive Chimú rulers **(Figure 26.13)**. The *ciudadellas* "combined the functions of royal entombment, elite residence, centralized storage, and closely administered redistribution" (Parsons and Hastings 1988: 193). They included a number of U-shaped rooms, which appear to control access to storage facilities. Similar U-shaped structures appear to serve administrative functions in areas conquered by the Chimú state. Oral histories recorded by the Spanish conquistadors indicate that Chimor fell to the Incas in about A.D. 1470.

MAIN CIUDADELA WALLS
OTHER WALLS
CANAL
DISUSED CANAL
WALK-IN-WELLS
PONDS

GENERAL PLAN OF
CENTRAL CHAN CHAN

0 100 200 300 400 500 600 700 800 900 1000
SCALE IN METERS

Figure 26.13

Plan of the central part of the city of Chan Chan showing the ciudadellas.

The Late Horizon

In the study of the dramatic rise to power of the Incas in Peru, archaeological evidence is supplemented by written accounts of the Spanish conquistadors. Much of the information in the Spanish chronicles is based on interviews with native oral historians. Thus, both historical data and archaeological evidence can be used to study the rise of the Inca Empire.

The **Late Horizon** (A.D. 1476 to 1532) refers to the period of Inca imperial expansion, ending with the Spanish conquest of Peru in 1532. The beginning date of 1476 refers specifically to the Incas' conquest of the Ica Valley in the southern coastal region, since the basic chronology for Peruvian archaeology was based on early research in the Ica Valley. However, Inca political expansion had begun well before the conquest of the Ica Valley. As noted in the previous section, Chan Chan and Chimor fell to the Incas about 1470, and ethnohistorical sources suggest that Inca imperial expansion began in 1438 under the Inca ruler Pachakuti. In the late fourteenth and early fifteenth centuries the Inca were one of a number of small kingdoms and chiefdoms competing for power in the southern highlands of Peru. The ethnic Incas probably numbered no more than 40,000 individuals (Moseley 1992: 9). Within a century the Inca had transformed themselves into the rulers of the largest empire in the pre-Columbian Americas. What factors made this dramatic change of fortunes possible?

A social institution that clearly played a role in the rapid expansion of the Inca state is the system of **split inheritance,** a system that can be traced back to the Chimú state (Moseley 1975a). Under the split inheritance system, a newly crowned Inca ruler inherited the title to the throne, including the rights to govern, wage war, and impose taxes. He did not inherit, however, the material possessions of the previous emperor. They were entrusted to a corporate group made up of other male heirs of the previous ruler who perpetuated the cult of the previous emperor. The new emperor was forced to acquire new possessions, that is, territories that could be taxed, to sustain a royal lifestyle, reward his supporters, and provide his male kinship group with the ability to perpetuate his cult after his death (Conrad and Demarest 1984: 118). The split inheritance system provided an ideological basis for rapid imperial expansion.

The expansion of the Inca Empire was also facilitated by a number of social institutions that had been developed by pre-Inca states in the Andean area. Foremost among those was the institution of the labor tax, or *mit'a*. The labor tax was levied on all able-bodied males and could include military service, construction of irrigation systems and terracing for agriculture, and road construction. The Inca Empire was connected by over 23,000 kilometers (14,000 mi.) of roads (Hyslop 1984: 222), which were built using the labor tax system. The Inca state also imposed agricultural taxes on men and women. Agricultural lands were divided into thirds: one-third supported the gods and religious shrines, one-third supported the Inca state, and the final third supported the local community. Produce raised on the state lands was used to provide food and drink for the many workers who toiled on behalf of the state. In addition, textile taxation was a part of Inca statecraft. Men and women were required to produce cloth and cordage from raw wool, cotton, and fiber. The finished textiles, which were collected by the government, were often used as rewards for government service.

Record keeping was critical to the administration of the Inca state. While the Inca differ from the Maya and many of the complex societies of the Old World because they lacked written records, the Inca did develop an elaborate system of record keeping based on knotted strings known as the *quipu* (**Figure 26.14**). The *quipu* was based on the decimal system; knots of different sizes, locations, sequences, and colors were used to indicate quantities (Morris 1988: 250). A simplified version of the *quipu* is still in use in the Peruvian highlands.

Conclusion

In the space of 100 years, the Inca built an empire that extended from the tropics to

Figure 26.14

A quipu, *a record-keeping device based on knotted strings that was used by the Inca.*

northern Chile and Argentina. The Incas' success in building and administering this vast empire was based on a tradition of statecraft that has deep roots in Peruvian prehistory. For example, the ability to mobilize large quantities of labor for monumental construction can be traced back to the late Preceramic and Initial periods. Systems of labor and agricultural taxation also appear to have developed in pre-Inca times. In short, "much of [the Incas'] spectacular but short-lived empire was based upon institutions that they shared with their competitors and precursors" (Conrad and Demarest 1984: 86).

Glossary

Altiplano. The high flatlands in the areas surrounding Lake Titicaca on the Peruvian-Bolivian border.

Cahuachi. The most important Nasca center during the Early Intermediate period, which covers an area of 150 hectares (370 acres) and includes more that 40 mounds. Recent research at Cahuachi has shown that this center was a ceremonial center, not a major urban center.

Cerro Blanco. The Moche capital in the Moche Valley, which was dominated by two major structures, the Huaca del Sol (Pyramid of the Sun), which served as a palace and mausoleum for Moche leaders, and the smaller Huaca de la Luna (Pyramid of the Moon), which served as a ritual center. During the Early Intermediate period, Cerro Blanco was a center of craft production and housed a substantial population.

Chan Chan. A site located in the Moche River Valley along the north coast of Peru. This vast site served as the political and administrative capital of the Chimú state during the Late Intermediate period.

Chavín de Huántar. A site in the north central Peruvian highlands whose monumental sculpture reveals a distinctive style and iconography that spread throughout many parts of Peru during the Early Horizon.

Chimor, or the Chimú state. The most powerful state of the Late Intermediate period. At its height the Chimú state controlled two-thirds of the Peruvian coastal desert.

Cuzco. The capital of the Inca Empire, located in the southern highlands of Peru.

Early Horizon. The period (approximately 900 to 200 B.C.) traditionally defined as the period when artistic influences from the site of Chavín de Huántar in the Peruvian highlands spread across much of central and northern Peru.

Early Intermediate period. A period (ca. 200 B.C. to A.D. 600) of regional diversity in Peru that begins with the abandonment of many ceremonial centers associated with the Chavín cult.

Huari. The capital city in the Ayucuchu Valley of Peru from which the Huari state was able to establish political control over a wide area of highland and coastal Peru. The development of an administrative system of labor taxation, as well as the development of new agricultural technologies, may have allowed the Huari state to expand rapidly during the Middle Horizon.

Inca. The term that refers to a small ethnic group from southern Peru. The Incas built and ruled the Inca Empire, which became the largest pre-Columbian empire in the Americas.

Initial period. The period (1800 to 900 B.C.) whose beginning is marked by the appearance of pottery. During the Initial period, farming came to play a more central role in the Peruvian economy.

Late Horizon. The period (1476 to 1532 A.D.) when the Inca empire expanded rapidly. It ends with the Spanish conquest of Peru in 1532.

Late Intermediate period. The period (A.D. 1000 to 1476) that begins with the collapse of the Huari and Tiwanaku states and ends with the rapid expansion of the Inca Empire in the century before the Spanish conquest of Peru.

Lomas. Areas of vegetation in the coastal regions that are supported by condensation from fog rather than by rainfall.

Middle Horizon. The period (A.D. 600 to 1000) marked by the rise of two powerful states in South America—Tiwanaku in the southern highlands and Huari, whose capital was located in the Ayacucho Valley in central Peru.

Mochica, or Moche. The state that arose in the north coastal region of Peru during the Early Intermediate period.

Nasca. The culture centered on the Nazca and Ica Valleys of Peru's south coast during the Early Intermediate period. Although the Nasca appear to have been a nonurban, nonstate society, they constructed a large ceremonial center at Cahuachi and are well known for their pottery and textiles.

Paloma. The site approximately 4 kilometers (2.5 mi.) from the sea behind San Bartolo Bay in Peru, occupied between 4500 and 3000 b.c. Although it was initially occupied by mobile hunter-gatherers, the inhabitants of the site eventually became sedentary, occupying small circular houses.

Paracas. The site of the necropolis, or cemetery, that was excavated by Julio C. Tello in 1929. The site includes a cache of 429 mummies, which were wrapped in cloth and accompanied by pottery and other grave goods. The burials date to the late Initial period and the early part of the Early Intermediate period. The designs on the Paracas textiles appear to have influenced later Nasca ceramics.

Preceramic. The period of Peruvian prehistory before the introduction of pottery in 1800 B.C. During the later, or Cotton, Preceramic (ca. 3000 to 1800 B.C.) domesticated cotton played an increasingly important role in the economies of the coastal regions of Peru.

Puna. The high plateaus of the Andes, which were used for grazing llamas and alpacas.

Río Seco. A site typical of the larger late Preceramic sites along the Peruvian coast. Río Seco covers 11.8 hectares (29 acres) and includes two major platform mounds, which were built by in-filling rooms.

Sechín Alto. A site located in the lower Casma River Valley. It is the largest and most impressive of a number of Initial Period ceremonial centers that were constructed along the Peruvian coast.

Sípan. The site of a recently discovered pyramid complex in the Lambayeque Valley, which has yielded a number of rich burials accompanied by prodigious quantities of metal, presentation goblets, and distinctive uniforms and headdresses. The burials date to the Early Intermediate period and are associated with the Moche culture.

Split inheritance. A social institution among the Incas that played a role in the rapid expansion of the Inca state. The split inheritance system meant that while one son of the dead emperor inherited his title, ability to make war, and authority to tax, the dead emperor's other male kin inherited his property.

Tiwanaku. The capital of the Tiwanaku state, located 15 kilometers (9 mi.) from Lake Titicaca in Bolivia, which controlled the southern highlands between about A.D. 400 and 1000.

Further Reading

Keatinge, Richard W., ed.
1988. *Peruvian Prehistory*. Cambridge: Cambridge University Press.
This is a detailed and authoritative summary of Andean prehistory for the advanced student. Each chapter is written by one or more regional experts.

Malpass, Michael A.
1996. *Daily Life in the Inca Empire*. Westport, CT: Greenwood Press.
Malpass's book is one in a series of volumes on daily life in ancient societies. It provides a very accessible introduction to day-to-day life in the Inca Empire based on both archaeological and historical sources. The beginning chapter includes a brief summary of the pre-Inca prehistory of Andean South America. The final chapter on the destruction of archaeological sites by looters and pothunters is highly recommended.

Moseley, Michael E.
1992. *The Incas and Their Ancestors: The Archaeology of Peru*. New York: Thames and Hudson.
Moseley's book is a very readable and well-illustrated introduction to the archaeology of Andean South America. He begins with the Inca empire and then provides a detailed survey of the pre-Inca prehistory of Peru.

Other Bibliography

Burger, Richard L.
1984. *The Prehistoric Occupation of Chavín de Huántar, Peru*. Berkeley: University of California Press.
1988. Unity and Heterogeneity within the Chavín Horizon. In *Peruvian Prehistory*, edited by Richard W. Keatinge, pp. 99–144. Cambridge: Cambridge University Press.

Conklin, W. J., and M. E. Moseley
1988. The Patterns of Art and Power in the Early Intermediate Period. In *Peruvian Prehistory*, edited by Richard W. Keatinge, pp. 145–163. Cambridge: Cambridge University Press.

Conrad, G. W., and A. A. Demarest
1984. *Religion and Empire: The Dynamics of Aztec and Inca Expansionism*. Cambridge: Cambridge University Press.

Donnan, C. B.
1978. *Moche Art of Peru: Pre-Columbian Symbolic Communication*. Los Angeles: UCLA Museum of Culture History.

Hyslop, John
1984. *The Inka Road System*. Orlando, FL: Academic Press.

Isbell, William H.
1988. City and State in Middle Horizon Huari. In *Peruvian Prehistory*, edited by Richard W. Keatinge, pp. 164–189. Cambridge: Cambridge University Press.

Kolata, Alan
1991. The Technology and Organization of Agricultural Production in the Tiwanaku State. *Latin American Antiquity* 2 (2): 99–125.

Lanning, E. P.
1967. *Peru before the Incas*. Englewood Cliffs, NJ: Prentice-Hall.

Miller, G. R., and R. L Burger
1995. Our Father the Cayman, Our Dinner the Llama: Animal Utilization at Chavín de Huántar, Peru. *American Antiquity* 60 (3): 421–458.

Morris, Craig
1988. Progress and Prospect in the Archaeology of the Inca. In *Peruvian Prehistory*, edited by Richard W. Keatinge, pp. 233–256. Cambridge: Cambridge University Press.

Moseley, Michael E.
1975a. Chan Chan: Andean Alternative to the Preindustrial City. *Science* 187: 219–225.
1975b. *The Maritime Foundations of Andean Civilization*. Menlo Park, CA: Cummings.

Moseley, Michael E., and K. C. Day, eds.
1982. *Chan Chan: Andean Desert City*. Albuquerque: University of New Mexico Press.

Parsons, J. R., and C. M. Hastings
    1988. The Late Intermediate Period. In
Peruvian Prehistory, edited by Richard W.
Keatinge, pp. 190–229. Cambridge: Cambridge
University Press.

Paul, Anne
    1990. *Paracas Ritual Attire: Symbols of
Authority in Ancient Peru.* Norman: University of
Oklahoma Press.
    1991. Paracas: An Ancient Cultural Tradition
of the South Coast of Peru. In *Paracas Art and
Architecture: Object and Context in South Coastal
Peru,* edited by Anne Paul, pp. 1–34. Iowa City:
University of Iowa Press.

Pineda, Rosa Fung
    1988. The Late Preceramic and Initial Period.
In *Peruvian Prehistory,* edited by Richard W.
Keatinge, pp. 67–96. Cambridge: Cambridge
University Press.

Rackham, James
    1994. *Animal Bones.* Berkeley and Los Angeles:
University of California Press/British Museum.

Shimada, Izumi
    1994. *Pampa Grande and the Mochica Culture.*
Austin: University of Texas Press.

Silverman, Helaine
    1991. The Paracas Problem: Archaeological
Perspectives. In *Paracas Art and Architecture:
Object and Context in South Coastal Peru,* edited
by Anne Paul, pp. 349–415. Iowa City: University
of Iowa Press.
    1993. *Cahuachi in the Ancient Nasca World.*
Iowa City: University of Iowa Press.

Chapter 27

Eastern North America
An Alternative Pattern
of Cultural Complexity

Introduction

At the time of initial European contact in the sixteenth and seventeenth centuries, North America was a mosaic of different cultures, languages, and ways of life. Native American peoples made a living by various combinations of hunting, gathering, fishing, and farming. For example, the Shoshoni and other native peoples of the Great Basin were mobile hunter-gatherers, moving seasonally to make use of a range of different plant and animal resources. The Natchez of the southern Gulf Coast region, on the other hand, were sedentary farmers who raised maize, beans, and squash, and supplemented their diet by hunting deer and smaller animals. The diversity of Native American cultures is so great that no single introductory textbook can begin to cover them all (but see Fagan 1995 for an introduction to North American archaeology).

In this chapter we focus on the development of complex societies in eastern North America, specifically the U.S. Midwest and Southeast, between 1000 B.C. and A.D. 1500. The complex societies that developed in eastern North America differed fundamentally from the cities, states, and empires that developed in pre-Columbian Peru and Mesoamerica. Native North Americans never built cities the size of Teotihuacán or Tenochtitlán; their polities were chiefdoms rather than states or empires. However, Native American societies in the Southeast and Midwest were characterized by significant social, political, and economic inequality. The later prehistoric inhabitants of these areas built monumental mound complexes and engaged in long-distance trade and exchange of exotic items. In many ways, the development of complex societies in North America parallels the process of cultural evolution seen in later prehistoric Europe (see Chapter 24). In both regions, archaeologists have documented the emergence of chiefdom-level societies that were characterized by significant differences in social status, political power, and material wealth. In tracing the development of cultural complexity in eastern North America, we will begin in the Early Woodland period at about 1000 B.C., a time when pottery first appeared in parts of the Midwest.

The Early Woodland Period and the Beginning of Cultural Complexity in the Midwest

As we saw in Chapter 16, by the Late Archaic period in the riverine areas of the Midwest and Southeast, Native Americans had domesticated a number of indigenous plants, including sunflowers, marsh elder, goosefoot, and gourds (Smith 1994). The cultivation of these plants began as early as 2500 B.C. They were part of a broad-based diet that also included aquatic resources such as fish, shellfish, and waterfowl, and terrestrial foods including wild mammals, wild turkeys, and wild plants.

The beginning of the Woodland period, approximately 1000 B.C., is marked by the appearance of pottery in the eastern woodlands. As it did in many other parts of the world, pottery served a variety of functions for early agriculturalists. Pottery certainly would have been useful for storing and cooking crop plants, especially since the early North American domesticates may have served as storable food reserves for the winter and early spring (Smith 1994: 197). In addition, pottery may have played an important role in the processing of wild plants such as hickory whose nuts are crushed and boiled during processing (Taladay et al. 1984).

During the first millennium B.C. cultivated plants came to play an even more important role in the economies of the Southeast and Midwest. In addition to the four indigenous domesticates, three additional plants appear to have

Figure 27.1

Map of the eastern United States showing the location of the sites mentioned in this chapter.

individuals were buried in rectangular log tombs; then the tombs were covered with earth. After the first burial was completed, other individuals were buried in or around the mounds. The largest Adena mounds were enormous. For example, the Grave Creek mound in Moundsville, West Virginia, originally stood 20 meters (66 ft.) high and contained nearly 70,000 cubic meters (92,000 cu. yds.) of earth fill (Fagan 1995: 406). The construction of these mounds would have involved large quantities of human labor, especially since the work would have been done by hand using shovels and baskets. The coordination of the labor needed to construct these huge mounds would have required some degree of leadership, and that, in turn, may indicate the beginnings of social and political inequality.

Local and interregional trade also increased during the Early Woodland period. The archaeological evidence for this increased trade comes primarily from exotic materials that are found interred with Adena Complex and other Early Woodland burials. The exotic goods are often nonutilitarian items that may have served as indicators of wealth, status, or prestige. These grave goods include crescents made from North Carolina mica, carved pipes made from Ohio pipestone **(Figure 27.2)**, and bracelets and finger rings made from copper from the region around Lake Superior. The appearance of the exotic items of exchange in Adena burials may reflect the emergence of a prestige goods economy, in which exotic and valuable items were exchanged among an emerging elite group, possibly leaders of lineages or other kinship groups. The exotic pipestone, copper, and mica objects found in Adena graves may have played the same role that early copper items played in the emerging complex societies of later prehistoric Europe (see Chapter 24). They were, in effect, status symbols of an emerging elite.

While the exchange of these exotic items may have been carried out by group leaders, the maintenance of the exchange networks may have benefited the society as a whole. It has been argued that these exchange relationships served to maintain alliances with social groups in other areas. In times of stress, such as droughts, floods, or crop failures, lineage leaders may have been able to call on their al-

been cultivated at this time: knotweed (*Polygonum erectum*), little barley (*Hordeum pusillum*), and maygrass (*Phalaris caroliniana*). The starchy seeds of these three plants have a high carbohydrate content and would have been valuable additions to the Early Woodland diet.

Also during the first millennium B.C., some of the earliest evidence for the emergence of complex societies appears in the eastern woodlands. As we have noted before, complexity is sometimes defined by inequality of access to material and human resources (McGuire 1983). In the American Midwest during the **Early Woodland period** (approximately 1000 to 200 B.C.) we see two clear indicators of increasing social and economic complexity—a growing trade in exotic, luxury items, and increasingly elaborate burial rituals. These characteristics are seen most clearly in the **Adena** cultural complex that is known from Ohio and the surrounding areas **(Figure 27.1)**.

The Adena cultural complex is best known for its elaborate burial mounds, which are found in eastern Indiana, southern and central Ohio, northern Kentucky, and western Pennsylvania and West Virginia. Important

Figure 27.2

A carved stone pipe recovered from an Adena mound, Ohio (height: about 20 centimeters [8 in.]).

lies in unaffected areas for subsistence resources. In this way, exchange of ceremonial items became a form of subsistence insurance (Brose 1979).

Complex Societies of the Middle Woodland Period: The Hopewell Interaction Sphere

The trend toward increasingly elaborate burial practices and long-distance trade in exotic items and raw materials continues during the **Middle Woodland period** (approximately 200 B.C. to A.D. 400). At that time a widespread network of trade and exchange, known as the **Hopewell Interaction Sphere,** developed throughout the entire Midwest and Southeast. The network was centered on the Ohio River Valley. As Kelly (1979: 1) notes, "In the Midwest the Hopewell interaction sphere has been conceptualized as a model

growing out of an early widespread network of long-distance trade in ceremonial goods." It is clear that this exchange network was well established by Early Woodland times, and its antecedents may date back to the Late Archaic period.

Although the Hopewell Interaction Sphere was centered in Ohio, it extended from the Great Lakes to the Gulf Coast and from the Appalachian Mountains to the Mississippi Valley and westward along the Missouri River. Many local groups within this region exchanged exotic raw materials, distinctive finished products, and ideas about mortuary rituals. The exotic raw materials included obsidian, most of which was obtained from a source in Yellowstone National Park (Hatch et al. 1990); seashells from the east coast of Florida; and silver and native copper from the Great Lakes region. Finished objects that were traded included small pottery jars and pipes **(Figure 27.3)**.

Much of what we know of Hopewellian archaeology comes from the excavation of elaborate burial mounds, especially those in the Ohio and Illinois Valleys. While the majority of Hopewellian individuals appear to have been cremated, elite individuals were placed into log-lined tombs and often accompanied by rich grave offerings **(Figure 27.4)**. Those offerings included copper ear spools, freshwater pearls, copper breastplates, and large quantities of exotic raw materials, such as western obsidian and mica from the southern Appalachians.

The elaborate Hopewellian burials clearly reflect some degree of social differentiation, but the nature of Middle Woodland society has long been a subject of debate among archaeologists. Do the Hopewell societies represent early chiefdoms with a centralized hierarchy of leaders who are set apart from the remainder of the population (Earle 1987), or are the Hopewell societies in Illinois and Ohio simply lineage-based societies whose leaders used exotic trade goods in accordance with their roles as kin-group leaders? This question is not easy to answer, and a case can be made for each point of view.

Chiefdom societies are characterized by a class of leaders whose decision-making authority sets them apart from the rest of the population. This decision-making hierarchy

Figure 27.3

A Hopewell carved stone monitor pipe in the form of a bird. The sculptured portion of the bird forms the pipe bowl, and one end of the base serves as the pipe stem.

Figure 27.4

Copper falcon from the Hopewell mound group in Ohio.

may be reflected in a hierarchy of settlement types, including both small rural sites and larger regional centers. Those who would see the Hopewellian societies as early chiefdoms argue that there is evidence for a clear hierarchy of settlement sites in the Illinois Valley during the Middle Woodland period. The small sites include farmsteads and hamlets, which were occupied by people engaged in horticulture, plant collection, hunting, and fishing. The larger sites, which are associated with floodplain mounds and contain large quantities of exotic materials, are interpreted as regional transaction centers where elite individuals engaged in the trade and redistribution of prestige goods (Streuver and Houart 1972).

While the settlement pattern data can be used to make a case for Hopewellian chiefdoms, the data from the burials themselves are somewhat more equivocal. Mature adult males are most likely to be buried in elaborate tombs with exotic grave goods. This has led some scholars to suggest that Hopewellian status was not inherited; instead, the elaborate burials reflect an individual's accomplishments during his or her lifetime (Braun 1979). The burial data suggest that there may not have been an established ruling elite during Middle Woodland times. Instead, status and decision-making authority were more volatile and dependent on the personal accomplishment of individual lineage leaders.

The network of trade and exchange that made up the Hopewell Interaction Sphere collapsed around A.D. 400. The end is marked by a curtailment in trade and mortuary ceremonialism (Tainter 1988: 15). The reasons for the collapse are unclear, and simple monocausal explanations such as climatic changes are not supported by the available archaeological evidence. Perhaps the costs of participation in the exchange system simply came to outweigh the benefits (cf. Tainter 1988). If the main benefit of the interaction sphere was the creation of alliances to mitigate against food shortages, then it is possible that people developed alternative ways of alleviating food shortfalls, such as increased food storage. What appears to have happened, however, is the disappearance of the highest levels of Middle Woodland society (Peregrine 1992: 99),

creating a Late Woodland society that was both less complex and more egalitarian.

The Late Woodland Period and the Adoption of Maize Agriculture

The adoption of maize agriculture was one of the most profound subsistence changes in all of North American prehistory. As noted in Chapter 19, maize was initially domesticated in Mesoamerica and must have been introduced to eastern North America from the outside. It is not clear, however, whether maize reached the eastern United States directly from Mesoamerica by way of the American Southwest or whether it was introduced to Florida from South America via the Antilles. Both studies of seed remains from archaeological sites and studies of human bone biochemistry (see the Archaeology in Practice box) indicate that maize first appeared in the eastern woodlands during the **Late Woodland Period** (ca. A.D. 400 to 800), but that its role in the diet was initially quite variable. Human skeletal analyses indicate that maize made up between 0 and 55 percent of the diet during the later part of the Late Woodland period. This variability may well be expected when people are beginning to experiment with a new resource. However, during the subsequent Mississippian period (ca. A.D. 800 to 1500) maize consistently made up between 40 and 55 percent of the diet (van der Merwe and Vogel 1978; Buikstra 1984: 226).

Why did the horticulturalists-fishers-hunters of the American Midwest and Southeast adopt maize agriculture? While maize cultivation certainly provided a storable, high-carbohydrate resource that may have alleviated seasonal shortages in food, the introduction of maize was a mixed blessing. Studies of human skeletons from the lower Illinois Valley (Cook 1984) indicate that childhood health worsened at the time that maize agriculture was introduced. These data have led Cook (1979) to suggest that the adoption of maize agriculture may have been a response to population growth, which would have placed increasing stress on the other available food resources. In other words, the adoption of maize agriculture may be seen as a form of subsistence intensification as a response to demographic stress.

Archaeology in Practice

The Analysis of Human Burials

As we have seen in this chapter, Adena, Hopewell, and Mississippian sites from the eastern United States have produced large numbers of human burials. Burial mounds have been of particular interest to archaeologists who study the emergence of complex societies because the construction of elaborate burial mounds can provide information about the mobilization of labor within those societies. In addition, the quantity and quality of grave goods included with individual burials can shed light on increasing social differentiation. However, the human skeletons interred in the mounds and cemeteries are themselves important sources of information about human diets and about the incidence of disease in ancient human populations.

The analysis of human skeletons generally begins with the determination of the sex and age of each individual. The pelvis is the most reliable criterion for distinguishing males from females. The female pelvis is specially adapted so that a baby can pass through the birth canal during the process of childbirth. One difference between male and female pelvises is the wider angle of the sciatic notch in the female pelvis (Figure 27.5).

Teeth are among the most valuable indicators of the age at death of a individual. In humans, as in other mammals, the milk, or deciduous, teeth erupt in a set sequence, and they are gradually replaced by the permanent teeth. While there is always some degree of individual variation, dental eruption can be used to provide quite accurate estimates of age at death for subadult individuals. For example, dentists commonly talk about the eruption of 6-year and 12-year molars. The general sequence of dental eruption is shown in Figure 27.6. For mature adults, the degree of dental wear can give a more general indication of age.

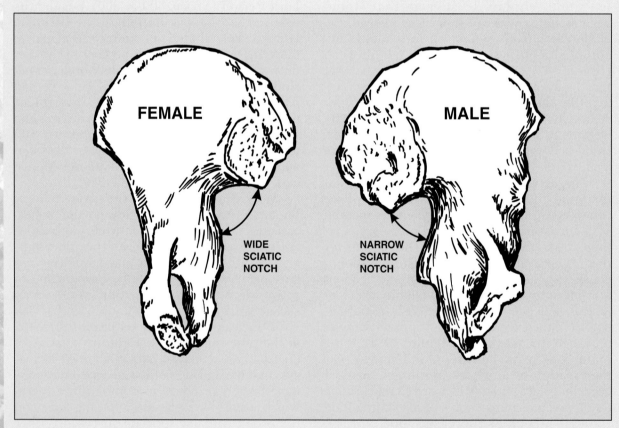

FEMALE   **MALE**

WIDE SCIATIC NOTCH   NARROW SCIATIC NOTCH

Figure 27.5
Male and female pelvises showing the wider sciatic notch in the female pelvis.

Figure 27.6
General sequence of human dental eruption.

18 months

4 years

8 years

12 years

21 years

atmosphere during the process of photosynthesis. Most native North American plants metabolize carbon in a way that discriminates against the heavier ^{13}C. Maize and other tropical grasses, however, metabolize carbon in a different way, one that does not discriminate against the heavier isotope. As a result, when Native Americans shifted from a diet of native North American plants to one that was high in maize, the amount of ^{13}C in the skeletons (indicated by rising delta ^{13}C values) increased substantially **(Figure 27.7)**. Stable isotope analysis has been a useful tool for determining when various Native American populations incorporated maize into their diets.

Studies of skeletal collections can also reveal information about the health status of prehistoric populations. However, it is often difficult to identify specific diseases or dietary deficiencies from bones alone (Larsen and Harn 1994: 223). For example, anemia (low red blood cell counts) can lead to some very specific changes in the bones of the skull. However, anemia can result both from inadequate diet and from infectious diseases that cause food to be absorbed poorly by the body. The relationship between diet, disease, and skeletal biology is therefore quite complicated. As a result, most osteologists use a variety of measures to assess the health status of past populations. These measures can be grouped into two main classes: (1) indicators of skeletal growth and development and (2) evidence of pathology or disease of the skeleton.

Archaeologists can examine the pattern of growth and development in human skeletons in a number of ways. In living populations, anthropologists assess childhood nutrition by comparing height and age. In general, well-nourished

Once the sex and age of each archaeological skeleton have been determined, a number of techniques can be used to study diet, health status, and disease in ancient human populations. Biochemical analyses have been particularly useful in the study of prehistoric diets. Among the most important techniques are those involving stable carbon isotopes (Ambrose 1987), nonradioactive forms of carbon that vary only in their atomic weight. There are two stable isotopes of carbon: a lighter and more common ^{12}C and a heavier ^{13}C. Plants obtain carbon from the

Figure 27.7

The shift to a diet based on maize farming is revealed by the changing delta ¹³C values from human bone collagen samples drawn from human skeletal materials of the Woodland and Mississippian periods in eastern North America.

INTRODUCTION OF MAIZE

children tend to be taller than poorly nourished children. Skeletal populations are somewhat different because juvenile skeletons represent only those children who failed to thrive. Cemetery samples, therefore, may include more evidence for nutritional stress than would be found in the population as a whole. Nevertheless, archaeologists often compare dental age and bone length for juvenile skeletons as a way of looking at nutritional stress in prehistoric populations.

Archaeologists can use evidence of arrested growth as an indicator of the health status of prehistoric populations. Lines of arrested growth, known as Harris lines **(Figure 27.8)**, form on the long bones when bone growth is interrupted as a result of malnutrition or disease (Goodman and Clark 1981). Similarly, defects can form in the enamel surfaces of

The Emergence of Mississippian Societies

The widespread adoption of maize agriculture provides the economic backdrop for our understanding of the emergence of complex, chiefdom-level societies in the eastern woodlands. However, it would be an oversimplification to argue that the adoption of maize cultivation *caused* the emergence of chiefdom societies in the eastern woodlands.

As we shall see, the widespread adoption of maize, which began about A.D. 800, was accompanied by other social, political, and economic changes that reflect the emergence of more complex societies.

These complex societies are described by the general term **Mississippian.** Mississippian societies are chiefdom-level societies that initially developed in the several parts of the eastern woodlands of the United States between about A.D. 750 and 1050 (Smith 1992). The question of how and why these

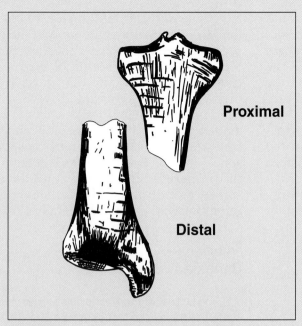

Figure 27.8

Drawing based on radiographs of a proximal and a distal tibia from a pre-Roman site in Britain, showing lines of arrested growth known as Harris lines.

the milk and permanent teeth when growth is disrupted. These enamel defects are often subject to caries. It should be emphasized that both Harris lines and tooth enamel defects are general indicators of stress that can result from malnutrition and/or infectious disease.

In addition to the osteological evidence for patterns of bone growth and development, archaeologists look for a number of bone pathologies that can provide evidence for disease. As mentioned above, anemia can cause changes to the bones of the skull, including thickening of the cranial vault and perforation of the roof of the orbit (termed *cribra orbitalia*). Bone infections, which can result from traumatic injury or from the spread of infection from the soft tissues of the body, can also provide a general indication of the health status of earlier human populations (Larsen and Harn 1994: 227). Changing frequencies of dental pathologies such as caries and antemortem tooth loss may reflect changes in diet. The shift to sticky, high-carbohydrate foods such as maize can lead to a higher incidence of tooth decay and premature tooth loss.

Despite the important information about health, diet, and disease that can be gained from the analysis of human skeletal collections, important ethical issues surround the excavation and analysis of these human remains. For years, many Native American peoples have objected to the excavation, analysis, and curation of Indian skeletal remains. Recent federal legislation, the Native American Graves Protection and Repatriation Act (NAGPRA), has required museums and other cultural institutions to return human skeletal remains and grave goods to the appropriate Native American tribes. Many prehistoric skeletons have been reburied, and more are likely to be reburied in the near future. This important issue will be treated in greater detail in Chapter 28.

chiefdoms emerged in eastern North America at that time is a complex one. As Bruce Smith (1992: 1–2) of the Smithsonian Institution has noted, "It is . . . far from clear to what degree this broadly similar process of cultural transformation was due to developmental interaction between river valley societies in transition, as opposed to their independent response to similar developmental constraints and opportunities." What is clear, however, is that this process is not the result of influences from outside the eastern woodlands; chiefdom-level societies developed independently in the eastern United States during the late first millennium A.D.

A number of scholars have suggested that the development of a prestige goods economy based on the production and exchange of luxury items manufactured from valuable, imported materials may have played a crucial role in the emergence of Mississippian chiefdoms (Peregrine 1992; Brown et al. 1992). Prestige goods were needed to arrange marriages and to form alliances. The production

417

and control of these prestige goods would have conferred both status and power to successful lineage leaders. Agricultural surpluses could have been mobilized to finance the manufacture of these prestige goods and the obtaining of exotic raw materials used to produce them. The maize-based agricultural societies of the Mississippian period were capable of generating greater surpluses than the earlier horticultural economies of the eastern woodlands.

The process of political and economic transformation initially involved competition between lineage leaders within a local area. When particular lineage leaders became successful, they may have reached out beyond the local area to form alliances with more distant lineage leaders. These distant alliances may have afforded successful leaders access to rare and exotic items that were unavailable locally. This, in turn, may have led to a process of political consolidation in which the successful leaders developed new political structures and alliances to control trade and to control manufacture and transport of prestige goods.

Mississippian Settlement and Social Organization

Mississippian sites are concentrated in the meander-belt zone of river valleys in the eastern United States. The meander belt includes the river floodplains with their oxbow lakes, seasonally flooded low areas, and the surrounding natural levees. These areas contain a variety of soil types and support a wide range of plants and animals. The Mississippians made use of fish; hunted waterfowl and terrestrial game; collected nuts, fruits, berries, and seed-bearing plants; and grew maize and other crops (Smith 1978: 483). These environments were particularly attractive to Mississippian farmers because periodic floods would have maintained the fertility of the soil, making the meander belt a naturally subsidized environment.

Mississippian sites are generally characterized by a two-tiered settlement hierarchy. Small agricultural villages and hamlets make up the bottom tier; larger administrative centers, which include platform mounds, make up the top tier of the settlement system. The

large sites serve as administrative centers for the Mississippian chiefdoms, and the mounds served as platforms for important buildings. Studies of the distribution of these administrative centers indicate that most Mississippian chiefdoms controlled territories that were no more than 30 kilometers (19 mi.) in diameter (Hally 1993). The individual territories were separated by lightly used buffer zones that were at least 10 kilometers (6 mi.) in diameter. The buffer zones may have served as military buffer zones and as reserves for wild plant foods (Hally 1993: 162).

Case Study
Cahokia

The largest of the Mississippian administrative centers is the site of **Cahokia** near East St. Louis in Illinois (Fowler 1975; Pauketat and Emerson 1997; Emerson 1997). This important site is located in a region known as the American Bottoms, near the point where the Illinois and Missouri Rivers join the Mississippi. The size and importance of Cahokia cannot be overestimated; the Cahokia site includes 120 earthen mounds that cover an area of 13 square kilometers (5 sq. mi.). Most of these mounds supported temples, council houses, and elite residences (Pauketat 1994: 5). The largest of these mounds, Monks Mound, rises to a height of 30 meters (100 ft.) and covers an area of 6 hectares (15 acres) **(Figure 27.9)**. Monks Mound, whose name derives from a brief Trappist settlement on the site, was built in stages between A.D. 900 and 1200. This 600,000-cubic meter (785,000 cu. yds.) mound is the largest pyramid in North America north of Mexico; only the Pyramid of the Sun at Teotihuacán and the Great Pyramid at Cholula in Mexico are larger (Fowler 1975: 93). It is estimated that Monks Mound would have taken about 370,000 workdays to build (Fagan 1995: 439–440). Even though the work was carried out over several centuries, the construction of this mound is a visible testament to the Mississippian chiefs' abilities to mobilize labor for public construction. "The scale of Monks Mound . . . is expressive of the overriding power of the chief and of the importance of the central hierarchy" (Dalan 1997: 100).

What kind of society was responsible for this monumental public construction? While most Mississippian societies were simple chiefdoms that controlled small territories, Cahokia and the site of

Figure 27.9

Monks Mound, Cahokia, Illinois. Monks Mound rises to a height of 30 meters (100 ft.) and covers 6 hectares (15 acres).

Moundville in west central Alabama with its 20 platform mounds were most likely centers of more complex chiefdoms. Complex chiefdoms are characterized by two or more tiers of political hierarchy. In the American Bottoms area surrounding Cahokia, there are several smaller centers that include at least one mound. These mounds may have been centers of small polities who owed their allegiance to the paramount chief of Cahokia.

How did a complex chiefdom develop at Cahokia? Pauketat (1994) has argued that the consolidation of regional chiefly authority was the result of the political actions of a small group of high-ranking individuals over a brief period around A.D. 1050. Critical to this process were the expansion of long-distance trade and the production of luxury items. The expansion of long-distance trade is seen in the increasing density of exotic chert around Cahokia at about A.D. 1050. This material was transformed into a variety of symbols and tools, including projectile points, under the patronage of Cahokia chiefs. The emergence of patron-client relations and the expansion of long-distance exchange are part of a regional political transformation. Local Cahokia elites also worked to alleviate factional disputes, dethroned local leaders, and created a divine chiefship. All these factors led to the development of a complex chiefdom centered at Cahokia.

While Cahokia clearly represents an important ceremonial site that served as the administrative center for a complex Mississippian chiefdom, the question of whether Cahokia can truly be considered urban is a far more difficult one to answer. The site is undoubtedly large, and it apparently housed a sizable population. It is estimated that about 800 hectares (2,000 acres) of the site were covered with dwellings. The number of people housed in those dwellings has been a matter of debate. Estimates have ranged from a low of 10,000 to a high of 43,000. While Cahokia was clearly home to craft specialists, including the makers of stone axes and shell beads, it is not clear that Cahokia housed the markets and other nonagricultural activities that are traditionally found in cities. Whether Cahokia represents a city or simply a large and heavily populated administrative and ceremonial center remains an open question.

Mississippian Collapse?

Cahokia's power and influence appear to have declined after about A.D. 1250, and the site had been long abandoned as a major administrative center by the time of European contact at about 1700. In the Southeast, however, many powerful Mississippian chiefdoms survived until the time of the initial European contact in the sixteenth century. The history of the entire Mississippian period (ca. A.D. 800 to 1500) is characterized by the rise and fall of local and regional chiefdoms throughout the Midwest and Southeast.

What factors could have led to the failure of individual Mississippian chiefdoms? Recent archaeological and environmental research on Mississippian chiefdoms in the Savannah River valley (the Savannah River forms the border between Georgia and South Carolina) suggests that both political and environmental factors may have played a role in the success or failure of particular chiefdoms (Anderson et al. 1995). Archaeological researchers in this region have identified 14 mound centers and over 500 small sites in the Savannah River Basin that date between A.D. 1000 and 1600. Their research indicates that the lower portion of the Savannah Basin was depopulated in the mid-fifteenth century, probably as a result of an extended period of drought. Even though favorable rainfall conditions returned in the late fifteenth century, the region was not repopulated, because the Savannah River Mississippian populations were sandwiched between two powerful complex chiefdoms—the Ocute of central Georgia and the Cofitachequi of central South Carolina—who were competing with one another for control of the region. The Savannah River area came to form a buffer zone between those two expanding polities. It is likely that similar constellations of causes are responsible for the rise and fall of chiefdoms throughout the Mississippian period.

Conclusion

The development of chiefdom societies in the eastern woodlands during the Mississippian period was the culmination of a long process of cultural change whose roots can be traced back to the Late Archaic and Early Woodland periods. In many ways, the process parallels the development of complex chiefdoms in later prehistoric Europe. In both areas, there is a clear correlation between the emergence of nonegalitarian societies and increasing long-distance and regional trade. Agricultural intensification—the introduction of the cart and the plow in Europe and the adoption of maize agriculture in the eastern woodlands—allowed progressively larger agricultural surpluses to be mobilized by emerging elites. These surpluses could be used to finance trade in exotic luxury items and to support monumental construction.

The emergence of complex societies in North America and Europe also parallels the early phases of the emergence of state-level societies in areas such as Mesoamerica, Mesopotamia, and Egypt. We will never know whether or not state-level societies would have developed independently in either North America or Europe. Contact with imperial societies—the Romans in Europe and the English and Spanish colonists in North America—forever changed the history of these two regions. In North America in particular, the introduction of epidemic diseases to which American Indians had no immunities led to a decimation of the Native American population in the Southeast in the first two centuries after European contact.

Glossary

Adena. The cultural complex, dating to the Early Woodland period, centered in southern Ohio. Adena sites include large and elaborate burial mounds. The burials often include exotic items such as pipes made of Ohio pipestone.

Cahokia. A Mississippian mounded site located near the confluence of the Mississippi, Missouri, and Illinois Rivers. The site includes 120 earthen mounds that cover an area of 13 square kilometers (5 sq. mi.). Cahokia, which reached the height of its power between A.D. 1050 and 1250, appears to have been the administrative center of a complex Mississippian chiefdom.

Early Woodland period. The period (approximately 1000 to 200 B.C.) in the eastern woodlands characterized by increasing social and economic complexity, seen in a growing trade in exotic, luxury items and in increasingly elaborate burial rituals.

Hopewell Interaction Sphere. A widespread trade and exchange network, dating to the Middle Woodland period, marked by the exchange of exotic raw materials, distinctive finished items, and ideas across the broad region of the American Midwest and Southeast.

Late Woodland period. The period (A.D. 400 to 800) during which the initial adoption of maize agriculture in the eastern woodlands took place. In comparison with the Middle Woodland societies that preceded them and the Mississippian chiefdoms that followed, Late Woodland societies in the Midwest and Southeast were relatively egalitarian.

Middle Woodland period. The period (approximately 200 B.C. to A.D. 400) during which a widespread network of trade and exchange, known as the Hopewell Interaction Sphere, developed in the eastern woodlands.

Mississippian. The term used to describe the chiefdom-level societies that developed in the Midwest and Southeast United States between A.D. 800 and 1500. Mississippian settlements are concentrated in the meander-belt zones of eastern rivers.

Further Reading

Smith, Bruce D., ed.
1992. *The Mississippian Emergence.* Washington and London: Smithsonian Institution Press.

This volume presents a number of important case studies of the emergence of Mississippian chiefdoms in various parts of the Southeast and Midwest. The concluding chapter argues that the development of a prestige goods economy may have been a critical factor in the emergence of those societies.

Other Bibliography

Ambrose, S. H.
1987. Chemical and Isotopic Techniques of Diet Reconstruction in Eastern North America. In *Emergent Horticultural Economies of the Eastern Woodlands,* edited by William F. Keegan, pp. 87–107. Carbondale: Southern Illinois University Center for Archaeological Investigations, Occasional Paper No. 7.

Anderson, D. G., D. W. Stahle, and M. K. Cleaveland
1995. Paleoclimate and Potential Food Reserves of Mississippian Societies: A Case Study from the Savannah River Valley. *American Antiquity* 60 (2): 258–286.

Braun, D. P.
1979. Illinois Hopewell Burial Practices and Social Organization: A Reexamination of the Klunk-Gibson Mound Group. In *Hopewell Archaeology: The Chillicothe Conference,* edited by D. S. Brose and N. Greber, pp. 66–79. Kent, OH: Kent State University Press.

Brose, D. S.
1979. A Speculative Model on the Role of Exchange in the Prehistory of the Eastern Woodlands. In *Hopewell Archaeology: The Chillicothe Conference,* edited by D. S. Brose and N. Greber, pp. 3–8. Kent, OH: Kent State University Press.

Brown, J. A., R. A. Kerber, and H. D. Winters
1992. Trade and the Evolution of Exchange Relations at the Beginning of the Mississippian Period. In *The Mississippian Emergence,* edited by B. D. Smith, pp. 251–280. Washington, DC: Smithsonian Institution Press.

Buikstra, J. E.
1984. The Lower Illinois River Region: A Prehistoric Context for the Study of Ancient Diet and Health. In *Paleopathology at the Origins of Agriculture,* edited by M. N. Cohen and G. J. Armelagos, pp. 215–234. Orlando, FL: Academic Press.

Cook, D. C.
1979. Subsistence Base and Health in Prehistoric Illinois Valley. *Medical Anthropology* 3: 109–124.
1984. Subsistence and Health in the Lower Illinois Valley: Osteological Evidence. In *Paleopathology at the Origins of Agriculture,* edited by M. N. Cohen and G. J. Armelagos, pp. 235–269. Orlando, FL: Academic Press.

Dalan, Rinita
1997. The Construction of Mississippian Cahokia. In *Cahokia: Domination and Ideology in the Missisippian World,* edited by T. B. Pauketat and T. E. Emerson, pp. 89–102. Lincoln and London: University of Nebraska Press.

Earle, T. K.
1987. Chiefdoms in Archaeological and Ethnohistorical Perspective. *Annual Review of Anthropology* 16: 279–308.

Emerson, T. E.
1997. *Cahokia and the Archaeology of Power.* Tuscaloosa and London: University of Alabama Press.

Fagan, Brian M.
1995. *Ancient North America: The Archaeology of a Continent,* 2d ed. London: Thames and Hudson.

Fowler, M. L.
1975. A Pre-Columbian Urban Center on the Mississippi. *Scientific American* 233 (2): 92–101.

Goodman, Alan H., and George A. Clark
1981. Harris Lines as Indicators of Stress in Prehistoric Illinois Populations. In *Biocultural Adaptation: Comprehensive Approaches to Skeletal Analysis,* edited by Debra L. Martin and M. Pamela Bumstead, pp. 35–43. Amherst: University of Massachusetts at Amherst, Department of Anthropology, Research Report No. 20.

Hally, D. J.
1993. The Territorial Size of Mississippian Chiefdoms. In *Archaeology of Eastern North America: Papers in Honor of Stephen Williams,* edited by J. B. Stoltman, pp. 143–168. Jackson: Mississippi Department of Archives and History, Archaeological Report No. 25.

Hatch, J. W., J. W. Michels, C. M. Stevenson, B. F. Scheetz, and R. A. Geidel
1990. Hopewell Obsidian Studies: Behavioral Implications of Recent Sourcing and Dating Research. *American Antiquity* 55 (3): 461–479.

Kelly, A. R.
1979. Hopewellian Studies in American Archaeology: Hopewell after Twenty Years. In *Hopewell Archaeology: The Chillicothe Conference,* edited by D. S. Brose and N. Greber, pp. 1–2. Kent, OH: Kent State University Press.

Larsen, C. S., and D. E. Harn
1994. Health in Transition: Disease and Nutrition in the Georgia Bight. In *Paleonutrition: The Diet and Health of Prehistoric Americans,* edited by K. Sobolik, pp. 222–234. Carbondale: Southern Illinois University Center for Archaeological Investigations, Occasional Paper No. 22.

McGuire, R.
1983. Breaking Down Cultural Complexity: Inequality and Heterogeneity. In *Advances in Archaeological Method and Theory,* vol. 6, edited by M. B. Schiffer, pp. 215–258. Orlando, FL: Academic Press.

Milner, G. R.
1986. Mississippian Period Population Density in a Segment of the Central Mississippi River Valley. *American Antiquity* 51 (2): 227–238.

Pauketat, T. R.
1994. *The Ascent of Chiefs: Cahokia and Mississippian Politics in Native North America.* Tuscaloosa: University of Alabama Press.

Pauketat, T. R., and T. E. Emerson, eds.
1997. *Cahokia: Domination and Ideology in the Mississippian World.* Lincoln and London: University of Nebraska Press.

Peregrine, P. N.
1992. *Mississippian Evolution: A World-System Perspective.* Madison, WI: Prehistory Press, Monographs in World Archaeology 9.

Smith, Bruce D.
1978. Variation in Mississippian Settlement Patterns. In *Mississippian Settlement Patterns,* edited by B. D. Smith, pp. 479–503. New York: Academic Press.
1992. Introduction: Research on the Origins of Mississippian Chiefdoms in Eastern North America. In *The Mississippian Emergence,* edited by B. D. Smith, pp. 1–8. Washington, DC: Smithsonian Institution Press.
1994. *The Emergence of Agriculture.* New York: Scientific American Library.

Streuver, S., and G. L. Houart
1972. An Analysis of the Hopewell Interaction Sphere. In *Social Change and Interaction,* edited by E. Wilmsen, pp. 47–79. Ann Arbor: University of Michigan, Museum of Anthropology, Anthropological Papers No. 46.

Tainter, Joseph A.
1988. *The Collapse of Complex Societies.* Cambridge: Cambridge University Press.

Taladay, L., D. R. Keller, and P. J. Munson
1984. Hickory Nuts, Walnuts, Butternuts, and Hazelnuts: Observations and Experiments Relevant to Their Exploitation in Eastern North America. In *Experiments and Observations on Aboriginal Wild Plant Food Utilization in Eastern North America,* edited by P. J. Munson, pp. 338–359. Indianapolis: Indiana Historical Society Prehistoric Research Series, Vol. 6, No. 2.

van der Merwe, N. J., and J. C. Vogel
1978. ^{13}C Content of Human Collagen as a Measure of Prehistoric Diet in Woodland North America. *Nature* 276: 815–816.

Chapter 28

The Future of Archaeology

Introduction

In this book we have shown how archaeology can be used to trace the development of human societies, beginning with our earliest stone tool-making ancestors, the early members of the genus *Homo,* and continuing to the present day. We have examined the evolution of human behavior, the appearance of modern humans and their colonization of the globe, the beginnings of agriculture, and the development of cities and states. In addition, the Archaeology in Practice boxes have explored some of the techniques used by archaeologists in the study of the past. In our review of over 2 million years of human prehistory, it is clear that many important archaeological questions remain unanswered. For example, the discovery of the Monte Verde site in Chile has documented a pre-Clovis occupation of the Americas, but we still do not know when and how the first people reached the New World. Our ability to answer these questions depends on the preservation of our archaeological heritage. In this chapter, we will examine the effects of looting, development, and warfare on the archaeological record. We will also consider the effects of the **Native American Graves Protection and Repatriation Act (NAGPRA)** on the future of archaeology in the United States, and the broader relationship between archaeology and nationalism in the post–cold war world.

The Destruction of Archaeological Sites

The greatest threat to archaeology's future is the continued destruction of archaeological sites by looting, development, and warfare. For every site that is excavated by an archaeologist, many others are damaged, looted, or destroyed by other human activities. As the earth's population continues to increase, the potential for damage to archaeological resources increases dramatically.

The sweeping destruction of lives and property that is the result of warfare can also damage and destroy archaeological sites, and the precious collections and records of past research may be lost as well. Many such losses followed the ravages of the Second World War; the disappearance of the Zhoukoudian *Homo erectus* fossils is a striking example. Recently, many important Sumerian archaeological sites may have been damaged by bombing during the Persian Gulf War.

As the world's population grows, many former agricultural lands have been converted to residential and commercial use. The construction of housing developments, industrial parks, and shopping malls has led to the discovery of archaeological sites, but too often, also to their destruction. One of the greatest dangers to archaeological sites, however, is looting—the theft of artifacts from archaeological sites. When looters steal an object from an archaeological site, its context is destroyed and its associations are lost. Without context and association, artifacts have little value for the study of the past. While looting continues in almost every country on earth, nowhere has the effect of looting been more devastating than in Peru (see Malpass 1996: chap. 8). As Helaine Silverman (1993: xii), the excavator of the important Nasca ceremonial center of Cahuachi (see Chapter 26), has noted, "Much of what we could have known [about the Nasca capital of Cahuachi] is lost to archaeologists because of the destruction wrought by massive illicit excavations at the site over the past century." **Figure 28.1** is a photograph of Cahuachi showing the massive looting that has taken place at this important Peruvian site.

Although the destruction that has taken place at Cahuachi is a graphic demonstration of the damage that looters can do to archaeological sites, looting is not just a Peruvian problem. In the United States, archaeological sites located on private land have very limited

Figure 28.1

Aerial photograph of the Nasca site of Cahuachi in Peru showing the massive looting that has taken place at the site. The many holes at lower left are looters' pits.

protection. Archaeological sites on state and federal lands are protected by state and federal antiquities laws. One such law is the **Archaeological Resources Protection Act (ARPA),** which protects archaeological sites on federal properties such as national parks and national forests. Many states have enacted laws to protect burials found on private lands. For the most part, however, landowners are free to damage or destroy sites on their property without regard for the important historical information that might be lost through those actions.

Despite the laws that are designed to protect our nation's archaeological heritage, every year federal authorities arrest looters who are engaged in stealing part of our nation's past. Two flagrant examples have been described in detail in the *SAA Bulletin,* a publication of the Society for American Archaeology. In Oregon, three individuals were convicted of looting the Lava River cave site, a Native American site in the Deschutes National Forest, in 1989. Two of the defendants were fined $1,000, and the third was required to perform 100 hours of community service. In looting this prehistoric site, the perpetrators stole artifacts and destroyed both their archaeological context and important environmental information. Since each archaeological site is unique, the looters damaged an irreplaceable part of the American past.

An even more flagrant violator of American antiquities laws was recently convicted of looting a site in the Southwest. A man from Utah was sentenced to 6½ years in federal prison and ordered to pay $5,510 in reparations for using a helicopter to loot an Anasazi site in the Canyonlands National Park. The looter's unrepentant attitude, his prior conviction for an ARPA violation, and his desecration of several Native American graves, including the grave of a small child wrapped in a ceremonial blanket, led to the stiff sentence and fine.

The preservation of our nation's past, however, depends on more than just the vigorous enforcement of laws against looting. It requires public education. Americans must recognize that the removal of any piece of cultural property from federal lands is both immoral and illegal. When entering our national parks and forests, tourists must be advised to take only photographs and leave only footprints. Only through greater public awareness can this country's rich archaeological heritage be preserved for future generations.

In the Utah case just described, a looter received a stiff fine and a lengthy jail sentence for excavating and looting Native American burials in a national park. As we shall see in the following section, national laws regarding the excavation and display of American Indian skeletal materials have changed significantly in the past 10 years, and those changes have important implications for archaeologists working in the United States.

The Native American Graves Protection and Repatriation Act

Through much of the nineteenth and twentieth centuries, archaeologists have excavated and collected the material remains of Native Americans. A multitude of Native American sites, including burial mounds and cemeteries, have been excavated, and both the artifacts and human remains within them have been transferred to university collections and museums. Large-scale federal development and survey projects during the Great Depression and continuing through the 1970s greatly swelled the numbers of sites excavated and resulted in large collections of Native American objects as well as human remains held in museums. The actual number is not known, but more than 100,000 Native American whole or partial skeletons may be held in museum storage across the United States.

For most archaeologists the intent of such investigations was surely the advancement of knowledge about early humans in the Americas. Unfortunately, few excavators took into consideration the fact that the people whose remains they were studying had living descendants. Native Americans observed that the remains of those they regarded as their ancestors were not accorded the level of respect given to European burials. Over the years many Native Americans have come to be distrustful of archaeology and the motivations of some archaeologists. Some Native Americans see in archaeology an effort to dispossess them of their traditional cultural history. In the past, Native Americans have sometimes fallen victim to the misrepresentation of archaeological findings to denigrate the cultural achievements of Native Americans and thus to justify their displacement from their lands by Europeans.

In 1990, more than 20 years of activism resulted in Congress's passing the Native American Graves Protection and Repatriation Act (NAGPRA), which requires that Native American human remains, ceremonial objects, and objects of cultural patrimony be returned to the Native American tribes. The law applies to all such remains or objects on Indian lands, under federal control, or held by institutions receiving federal funds. NAGPRA also requires that the appropriate Native American groups be consulted before excavations that will remove cultural objects from federal lands are permitted.

A few archaeologists have expressed their concern that the new federal laws will stifle future archaeological research in the United States (see the Kennewick case study on the next page). The authors of this text believe that this need not be true. In the short term, the process of identifying and classifying the vast holdings of Native American artifacts and human remains now in museums for their return to the appropriate tribes has in itself stimulated much new research. Before the passage of NAGPRA, only about 30 percent of the Native American skeletons in museum collections now subject to that law had been studied by bioarchaeologists. Today that figure approaches 100 percent (Rose et al. 1996). In the long run, many Native American groups are becoming interested in establishing museums of their own and in participating in and conducting their own archaeological research on their ancient past. It is incumbent on the existing scholarly community to incorporate these new members into the fabric of American archaeological research. Prehistoric archaeological research will continue and will be better informed through the participation and insights of the prehistoric peoples' physical and cultural descendants. As Ferguson (1996: 74) notes: "Archaeologists and Native Americans are moving beyond the contentious rhetoric of the 1970s and 1980s. Together, they are forging new partnerships to change archaeology so it is more acceptable and relevant to the descendants of the people who produced the archaeological record many archaeologists study."

Case Study
Kennewick Man

As we have seen, NAGPRA has required museums and educational institutions to develop inventories of Native American artifacts and skeletal remains. It has resulted in the repatriation of human burials and other cultural property to Native American tribes. The application of NAGPRA, however, has not been without controversy, especially when the act has been applied to very ancient skeletal materials. The case of the so-called Kennewick man illustrates the nature of this controversy. (See Slayman 1997 for a review of the issues.)

On July 28, 1996, a human skeleton was discovered in the bed of the Columbia River by two spectators at an annual hydroplane race in Kennewick, Washington. The county coroner asked anthropologist James Chatters to investigate the discovery. Nineteenth- and twentieth-century artifacts were found near the body, and the skeletal remains were initially thought to be of modern date. Chatters received a permit from the Army Corps of Engineers to continue collecting at the site, which was located on federal land, and he uncovered additional bones there.

The nearly complete Kennewick skeleton is the remains of a male who was between 175 centimeters and 178 centimeters (5 ft. 9 in. and 5 ft. 10 in.) tall. The teeth, skull, and pelvis suggest that this man was between 40 and 55 years of age at the time he died. Chatters initially identified this individual as Caucasian, rather than Native American, on the bases of the shape of his skull and his body proportions. Since a stone projectile point (arrowhead) was imbedded in the Kennewick man's pelvis, Chatters thought that the skeleton might represent an early European colonist. However, CAT scans of the pelvis showed that the projectile point was an ancient type that was in use between about 4,500 and 9,000 years ago. In addition, a radiocarbon date from one bone fragment suggested that it was between 9,200 and 9,600 years old.

The Army Corps initially determined that the skeleton must be Native American and therefore subject to the provisions of NAGPRA. Five Native American tribes in the area have claimed the skeleton, including the Umatilla, whose traditional hunting, fishing, and plant-gathering grounds include the place where the Kennewick skeleton was found. The Umatilla and the four other tribes who also claim the skeleton share ancient oral traditions (Minthorn 1996). They also share religious beliefs that dictate that human remains should be reburied as soon as possible. The Umatilla do not believe that the Kennewick skeleton is Caucasian, and they claim him as an ancestor.

In 1996 when the Army Corps of Engineers decided to repatriate the Kennewick skeleton under the provisions of NAGPRA, a group of eight scientists filed suit against the corps to prevent the repatriation of the bones. They argued that the Army Corps did not have sufficient evidence to show that the Kennewick man was affiliated with any of the five Native American tribes who claimed him. Furthermore, they claimed that additional studies were needed to determine whether the Kennewick man was, in fact, Native American and therefore subject to the provisions of NAGPRA. The scientists petitioned the court to allow DNA tests and analysis and measurement of the bones and teeth of the Kennewick skeleton. A critical issue raised by the Kennewick controversy is whether NAGPRA's provisions can be stretched back to early prehistory and the effect that NAGPRA may have on the study of early North American prehistory (Slayman 1997).

In early 1999, a team of physical anthropologists, archaeologists, curators, and conservators headed by Dr. Francis P. McManamon of the National Park Service conducted an initial detailed examination of the Kennewick human remains (McManamon 1999). Prior to these examinations, the interdisciplinary team consulted with tribal representatives and with the plaintiffs in the lawsuit. The initial studies conducted by the interdisciplinary team were nondestructive; no skeletal material was destroyed during the process. The team inventoried the human remains, measured the bones and teeth, and recorded nonmetric data that may provide evidence for the health and way of life of the individual in question. In addition, the team analyzed the soil sediments and projectile point associated with the Kennewick skeleton. These analyses were intended to help determine whether the Kennewick remains are subject to NAGPRA.

In January 2000, the Department of the Interior released the results of these studies. Following a detailed series of metrical and statistical comparisons (Powell and Rose 1999), the researchers concluded that the Kennewick skeleton did not closely resemble any modern population, including both modern Native Americans and Europeans. The most closely related human groups were certain Polynesian islanders and the Ainu, a native Japanese group with South Asian affinities.

On the other hand, the Kennewick skeleton bears a resemblance to Archaic skeletons from the Great Basin and from the eastern woodlands. Additional direct radiocarbon dating of the skeleton has indicated that the Kennewick bones are more than 9,000 years old—sufficient time for a population similar to Kennewick to have evolved and changed, and possibly to be ancestral to modern Native Americans. However, only a detailed study of human remains from the region, spanning the 9,000 years of change (data that are not currently available), could conclusively demonstrate such a direct biological relationship (Powell and Rose 1999). Attempts to extract sufficient DNA from the Kennewick bones to assess possible biological relationships have not been successful.

To help resolve the thorny question of who will be the final possessor of the Kennewick skeleton, a cultural affiliation study has been conducted, which considered the archaeological, traditional historical and ethnographic, linguistic, and bio-archaelogical evidence (Department of the Interior 2000). While this study could not demonstrate direct cultural continuity from the time of Kennewick through to modern Native Americans in the region, neither could such continuity be disproved. The great antiquity of the Kennewick remains make it clear that they do not derive from any modern, non-American group. Therefore, they are considered Native American, as defined by NAGPRA (McManamon 2000). On the basis of this evidence, the Secretary of the Interior determined, on September 21, 2000, that the Kennewick remains should be returned to the Native American people (Babbitt 2000).

 Archaeology and Nationalism

Native Americans' desire to retain control over their cultural heritage parallels similar trends around the world. Many nations, notably in eastern Europe, the Middle East, and Africa, have moved toward developing their own culture histories and archaeology. Locally and nationally sponsored archaeological research, educational programs, and museums can do much to bolster peoples' awareness of their cultural history. The results of archaeological research can expand the time depth of local histories and serve to support and enrich peoples' concept of cultural, eth-

nic, or national identity. Clearly, there are both positive and negative sides to archaeology's power in this respect. On the one hand, the open-minded sharing of archaeological knowledge and insights among locally oriented scholars and with the scholarly community and public at large can go far toward promoting interethnic and intercultural understanding. On the other hand, as Native Americans have found to their detriment, the findings of archaeology can be cited, or distorted, to support a one-sided political or social agenda.

Perhaps the most flagrant example of the distortion of archaeological interpretations to support a political agenda is the use of archaeology by the Nazis during World War II (Figure 28.2) (see also Arnold 1990, 1992). Under the Nazis, archaeology became entirely ethnocentric, focusing on the German peoples and attempts to identify them from prehistoric and early historic sites. Journal titles were changed to reflect German archaeology's nationalistic bias. For example, in 1934 the *Zeitschrift für Vorgeschichte (Journal of Prehistory)* became the *Zeitschrift für Deutsche Vorgeschichte (Journal of German Prehistory)*. Most distressingly, prehistoric data were distorted to justify Germany's claims to Czech and Polish lands.

A less well known example is the history of interpretation of Great Zimbabwe, a complex of stone ruins located near the modern town of Masvingo in Zimbabwe (Figure 28.3). In the late nineteenth and early twentieth centuries, British colonists were reluctant to accept that these impressive ruins had been constructed by black Africans. The ruins were seen as the work of northerly (i.e., non-black) peoples and variously identified as the lost palace of the Queen of Sheba and a Phoenician colony. Although detailed archaeological work carried out in the 1920s had shown that the ruins had been constructed by Africans during the Middle Ages, the myth that Great Zimbabwe had been constructed by whites was maintained until quite recently for political reasons. In 1965 Southern Rhodesia (now called Zimbabwe) declared its independence from the British Empire and established a white supremacist government under Ian Smith that lasted until 1980. Whites, who made up less than 10 percent of

Figure 28.2

Textbook used in German schools during the World War II period. The picture shows a Linear Pottery village and the title, as translated, reads "five thousand years Germany" (emphasis added). (After Jörg Lechler.)

Rhodesia's population, needed to denigrate native Africans' achievements to justify their claim to the region. The whites were concerned that the ruins would become a symbol of African achievement and heritage for blacks who were struggling for majority rule. As a result, the Ian Smith government issued a secret memorandum forbidding any official publication from stating that the Great Zimbabwe ruins were the product of African craftsmanship and engineering (Trigger 1989: 134; see also Phillipson 1993). Since independence, of course, Great Zimbabwe has become an important symbol of the Africans' cultural heritage and has given its name to the independent state of Zimbabwe.

The postcolonial, post–cold war world is fraught with ethnic rivalries in such areas as the Middle East, the former Yugoslavia, Northern Ireland, and southern Africa. The challenge for archaeology is clear. Archaeology must be used as an instrument for the

Figure 28.3

Monumental stone ruins at the site of Great Zimbabwe. Recent archaeological research indicates that the most elaborate stone buildings were built between the thirteenth and fifteenth centuries A.D. The site served as a center of political authority and trade.

appreciation of both cultural diversity and our common human heritage, not as a tool of political and cultural domination. As Kohl notes:

> Ethical standards for accepting or rejecting nationalist uses of archaeology may vary in specific cases, but they should ideally satisfy the following three criteria: (a) the construction of one group's national past should not be made at the expense of others'; (b) all cultural traditions should be recognized as worthy of study and respect; and (c) the construction of a national past should not be made at the expense of abandoning the universal anthropological perspective of our common humanity and shared past and future. (1998: 243)

Some Final Thoughts on the Future of Archaeology

Preserving the past for the future is not an easy task. As we have tried to show in this textbook, archaeological research is both painstaking and expensive. Archaeological excavation is supported by both public funds and private benefaction. For this support to continue, archaeological research must bene-fit the public at large. Archaeologists cannot simply report their research to small groups of like-minded colleagues at scholarly conferences. The results of archaeological research must be presented to a variety of audiences, including the entire archaeological community, students, and the general public. Advances in communications such as the Internet and the World Wide Web will make the dissemination of archaeological information easier. Communication is critical to archaeology's future, for the preservation of the past depends on public education.

Glossary

Archaeological Resources Protection Act (ARPA). Law that protects archaeological sites on federal properties such as national parks and national forests.

Native American Graves Protection and Repatriation Act (NAGPRA). Law requiring that Native American human remains, ceremonial objects, and objects of cultural patrimony be returned to the Native American tribes.

Further Reading

Arnold, Bettina
　1992. Germany's Nazi Past: How Hitler's Archaeologists Distorted European Prehistory to Justify Racist and Territorial Goals. *Archaeology,* July/August, pp. 30–37.
　This article provides a detailed study of how European prehistory was distorted to fit the political goals of the Third Reich.

Malpass, Michael A.
　1996. *Daily Life in the Inca Empire.* Westport, CT: Greenwood Press.
　This popular introduction to the Inca Empire includes an excellent final chapter that addresses the problem of looting at Peruvian sites and the need to preserve our archaeological heritage.

Minthorn, Armand
　1996 Human Remains Should Be Reburied. Available on the Internet at http://www.umatilla.nsn.us/kennman.html
　This article presents the Umatilla view of the Kennewick controversy, arguing that these human remains should be reburied as soon as possible.

Slayman, Andrew L.
　1997. A Battle over Bones. *Archaeology* 50 (1): 16–20, 22–23.
　This article provides a clear and readable summary of the Kennewick controversy. It is also available on the Internet at http://www.archaeology.org/9701/etc/special report.html

Other Bibliography

Arnold, Bettina
　1990. The Past as Propaganda: Totalitarian Archaeology in Nazi Germany. *Antiquity* 64 (244): 464–478.

Babbitt, Bruce
　2000. Letter from Secretary of the Interior Bruce Babbitt to Secretary of the Army Louis Caldera Regarding Disposition of the Kennewick Human Remains. September 21, 2000. Available at http://www.cr.nps.gov/aad/kennewick

Department of the Interior
　2000. Cultural Affiliation Report. Available at http://www.cr.nps.gov/aad/kennewick

Ferguson, T. J.
　1996. Native Americans and the Practice of Archaeology. *Annual Review of Anthropology* 25: 63–79.

Kohl, Philip L.
　1998. Nationalism and Archaeology: On the Constructions of Nations and the Reconstructions of the Remote Past. *Annual Review of Anthropology* 27: 223–246.

Lechler, Jörg
　1937. *5000 Jahre Deutschland: Germanisches Leben in 700 Bildern,* 2d ed. Leipzig: Curt Kabitzsch Verlag.

McManamon, Francis P.
　1999. K-man Undergoes Complete Physical. *Anthropology Newsletter* 40 (8): 3, 22.
　2000. *Determination That the Kennewick Human Skeletal Remains are "Native American" for the Purposes of the Native American Graves Protection and Repatriation Act (NAGPRA).* Archeology and Ethnography Program, National Park Service, Department of the Interior, Memorandum, January 11, 2000.

Phillipson, David W.
　1993. *African Archaeology,* 2d ed. Cambridge: Cambridge University Press.

Powell, Joseph F., and Jerome C. Rose
　1999. *Report on the Osteological Assessment of the "Kennewick Man" Skeleton (CENWW.97. Kennewick).* Archeology and Ethnography Program, National Park Service, Department of the Interior.

Rose, J. C., T. J. Green, and V. D. Green
　1996. NAGPRA Is Forever: Osteology and the Repatriation of Skeletons. *Annual Review of Anthropology* 25: 81–103.

Silverman, Helaine
　1993. *Cahuachi in the Ancient Nasca World.* Iowa City: University of Iowa Press.

Trigger, Bruce G.
　1989. *A History of Archaeological Thought.* Cambridge: Cambridge University Press.

SAA Bulletin Website
　1996. ARPA Violator Draws Record Sentence. *SAA Bulletin* 14 (1). Available on the Internet at http://www.anth.ucsb.edu/SAABulletin/14.1/SAA15.html
　1996. Lava River Cave Looters Convicted. *SAA Bulletin* 14 (1). Available on the Internet at http://www.anth.ucsb.edu/SAABulletin/14.1/SAA16.html

Credits

Line Art Credits

Chapter 1

Figure 1.3. Nuremberg Chronicle of 1493. **Figure 1.4.** Jones, Inigo, 1655. *The Most Notable Antiquity of Great Britain, vulgarly called Stonehenge, Restored.* **Figure 1.5.** Frere, John, 1800. Account of Flint Weapons discovered at Hoxne in Suffolk. *Archaeologia* XIII, pp. 204–205.

Chapter 2

Figure 2.4. Courtesy of Prof. S. Milisauskas (*European Prehistory* 1978) and Dr. P. Bogucki. **Figure 2.8.** ©1956 Time Inc. Reprinted by permission.

Chapter 3

Figure 3.1. Topography: These data are distributed by the EROS Data Center Distributed Active Archive Center (EDC DAAC), located at the U.S. Geological Survey's EROS Data Center in Sioux Falls, South Dakota. **Figure 3.4.** Topography: These data are distributed by the EROS Data Center Distributed Active Archive Center (EDC DAAC), located at the U.S. Geological Survey's EROS Data Center in Sioux Falls, South Dakota. **Figure 3.10.** Reproduced courtesy of Prof. F. Grine. **Figure 3.12.** After Aitken, M. J., 1990: *Science-Based Dating in Archaeology*, p. 121. London and New York: Longman. **Figure 3.14.** After Aitken, M. J., 1990: *Science-Based Dating in Archaeology*. London and New York: Longman and Butler, Robert F., 1992: *Paleomagnetism: Magnetic Domains to Geologic Terrains*. Boston: Blackwell Scientific Publications. **Figure 3.15.** Reproduced with permission of Masson. **Figure 3.17.** After Brain, C.K., 1981: *The Hunters or the Hunted? An Introduction to African Cave Taphonomy*, Figure 220. Chicago: University of Chicago Press.

Chapter 4

Figure 4.2. After Leakey, M., 1971: *Olduvai Gorge, Vol. 3.* Cambridge: Cambridge University Press. **Figure 4.3.** Redrawn from Leakey, M., 1971: *Olduvai Gorge, Vol. 3.* Figure 9. Cambridge: Cambridge University Press. Reprinted with the Permission of Cambridge University Press. **Figure 4.6.** After Isaac, G. L., 1983: Bones in Contention: Competing Explanations for the Juxtaposition of Early Pleistocene Artifacts and Faunal Remains. In *Animals and Archaeology: 1. Hunters and Their Prey,* edited by J. Clutton-Brock and C. Grigson, p. 14. Oxford: British Archaeological Reports, International Series 163. **Figure 4.9.** Redrawn from Leakey, M., 1971: *Olduvai Gorge, Vol. 3,* Figure 7. Cambridge: Cambridge University Press. Reprinted with the Permission of Cambridge University Press.

Chapter 5

Figure 5.1 a and b. Redrawn from Bordes, F., 1984: *Leçons sur le Paleolithique, Volume 3,* Figures 114 and 115. **Figure 5.1 c.** Copyright 1966 by the Israel Academy of Sciences and Humanities. All rights reserved. **Figure 5.3.** Skertchley, S.B.J., 1879: On the Manufacture of Gun Flints. *Memoir of the Geological Society of England and Wales.* **Figure 5.8.** Topography: These data are distributed by the EROS Data Center Distributed Active Archive Center (EDC DAAC), located at the U.S. Geological Survey's EROS Data Center in Sioux Falls, South Dakota.

Chapter 6

Figure 6.1. Topography: These data are distributed by the EROS Data Center Distributed Active Archive Center (EDC DAAC), located at the U.S. Geological Survey's EROS Data Center in Sioux Falls, South Dakota. **Figure 6.3.** Topography: These data are distributed by the EROS Data Center Distributed Active Archive Center (EDC DAAC), located at the U.S. Geological Survey's EROS Data Center in Sioux Falls, South Dakota. **Figure 6.7.** Redrawn from Bordes, F., 1984: *Leçons sur le Paleolithique, Volume 3,* Figure 167. Paris: CNRS Editions. **Figure 6.9.** Redrawn from Bordes, F., 1984: *Leçons sur le Paleolithique, Volume 3,* Figures 16 and 30. Paris: CNRS Editions. **Figure 6.12.** Reproduced with permission of Academic Press. Ltd. From Villa, P., 1990: Torralba and Aridos: Elephant Exploitation in Middle Pleistocene Spain. *Journal of Human Evolution* 19: p. 300, Figure 1. Copyright 1990.

Chapter 7

Figure 7.1. Topography: These data are distributed by the EROS Data Center Distributed Active Archive Center (EDC DAAC), located at the U.S. Geological Survey's EROS Data Center in Sioux Falls, South Dakota. **Figure 7.4.** From *In Search of the Neanderthals* by Christopher Stringer and Clive Gamble, published by Thames and Hudson, Inc., New York. **Figure 7.6.** After Bordes, F., 1972: *A Tale of Two Caves,* Figure 31. New York: Harper and Row. **Figure 7.8.** Redrawn from Phillipson, D.W., 1992: *African Archaeology,* 2nd ed. Figure 4.2. Reproduced with permission of Cambridge University Press.

Chapter 8

Figure 8.3. After Clark, J.D., 1970: *The Prehistory of Africa,* Fig. 50. **Figure 8.4.** Reprinted with permission from Yellen, J.E., et al., 1995: A Middle Stone Age Worked Bone Industry From Katanda, Upper Semliki Valley, Zaire, Figure 1, p. 555. *Science* 268, 28 April 1995. Copyright 1995 American Association for the Advancement of Science.

Smith, Bruce, D., 1989, Origins of Agriculture in Eastern North America. *Science* 246: 1570 and Ambrose, F., 1987, Chemical and Isotopic Techniques of Diet Reconstruction in Eastern North America, in *Emergent Horticultural Economies in the Eastern Woodlands*, edited by W.F. Keegan, pp. 87-107. Carbondale, IL: Southern Illinois University Center for Archaeological Investigations, Occasional Paper No. 7. **Figure 27.8.** Reproduced courtesy of D. R. Brothwell.

Text Permissions

Chapter 16. Quote from G. Nicholas. Reproduced with permission of Mary Ann Levine and G. Nicholas.
Chapter 27. Quote from C. S. Larsen. With permission, from the *Annual Review of Anthropology*, vol. 24, ©1995 www.AnnualReviews.org.
Chapter 28. Quote from P. Kohl. With permission, from the *Annual Review of Anthropology*, vol. 27, ©1998 www.AnnualReviews.org.

Photo Credits

Chapter 1
Figure 1.1. Hinterleitner/Gamma Liaison. **Figure 1.2a.** South Tyrol Museum of Archaeology, Bozen, Italy, www.iceman.it, photo Marco Samadelli. **Figure 1.2b.** South Tyrol Museum of Archaeology, Bozen, Italy, www.iceman.it, photo Marco Samadelli.

Chapter 2
Figure 2.1. John Milner & Associates. **Figure 2.2.** Pam Crabtree. **Figure 2.3.** Pam Crabtree. **Figure 2.6.** ©2000, Trustees of Princeton University. **Figure 2.7.** Peabody Museum, Harvard University.

Chapter 3
Figure 3.2. Donald Johanson/Institute of Human Origins. **Figure 3.3a.** Transvaal Museum. **Figure 3.3b.** Transvaal Museum. **Figure 3.5.** Des Bartlett/Photo Researchers. **Figure 3.6.** Cleveland Museum of Natural History. **Figure 3.7.** Prof. Tim White. **Figure 3.8.** John Reader/Science Photo Library/Photo Researchers. **Figure 3.9.** Alan Walker, Johns Hopkins University/National Museums of Kenya, Kalakol account. **Figure 3.13.** Courtesy Shari A. Kelley. **Figure 3.16.** David L. Brill.

Chapter 4
Figure 4.1. Jane Goodall/National Geographic. **Figure 4.7.** Dr. R. Potts, Human Origins Program, Smithsonian Institution. **Figure 4.8.** Dr. R. Potts, Human Origins Program, Smithsonian Institution.

Chapter 5
Figure 5.4. Giancarlo Ligabue, Centro Studi Ricerche Ligabue, Venice. **Figure 5.6.** Kathy Schick, Center for Research into the Anthropological Foundations of Technology, Indiana University. **Figure 5.7.** Kenneth Garrett. **Figure 5.9.** Photo Douglas Campana reproduced courtesy of Prof. O. Bar-Yosef, Anthropology Dept., Harvard University. **Figure 5.10.** N. Goren-Inbar.

Chapter 6
Figure 6.2. American Museum of Natural History, Dept. of Library Services, Neg. No. 319781, Photo Alex J. Rota. **Figure 6.5.** American Museum of Natural History, Dept. of Library Services, Neg. No. 335795. **Figure 6.6a.** American Museum of Natural History, Dept. of Library Services, Neg. No. 315447, Photo Charles H. Coles. **Figure 6.6b.** American Museum of Natural History. **Figure 6.8.** Javier Trueba/Madrid Scientific Films. **Figure 6.11.** Courtesy F. Clark Howell

Chapter 7
Figure 7.5. Pam Crabtree. **Figure 7.7.** Courtesy Ofer Bar-Yosef, Harvard University.

Chapter 8
Figure 8.2. John Reader/Science Photo Library/Photo Researchers, Inc. **Figure 8.5.** The Natural History Museum, London. **Figure 8.6.** Instituto Português de Arqueologia.

Chapter 9
Figure 9.1a. By permission of Guillermo L. Mengoni. **Figure 9.1b.** By permission of Alan Outram. **Figure 9.3.** Daniel E. Lieberman, Dept. of Anthropology, George Washington University. **Figure 9.4.** Photo Douglas Campana reproduced courtesy of Prof. O. Bar-Yosef, Anthropology Dept., Harvard University.

Chapter 10
Figure 10.4. Centre National de la Recherche Scientifique. **Figure 10.5.** Pam Crabtree. **Figure 10.6.** Olga Soffer, University of Illinois at Urbana-Champaign.

Chapter 11
Figure 11.2. Jean Vertut, courtesy of Yvonne Vertut, Paris. **Figure 11.3.** Randall White. **Figure 11.4.** Erich Lessing/Art Resource, NY. **Figure 11.5.** Musee de l'Homme, Photo J. Oster. **Figure 11.6.** Jean Vertut, courtesy of Yvonne Vertut, Paris. **Figure 11.7.** Reunion des Musees Nationaux/Art Resource, NY. **Figure 11.8.** Art Resource, NY. **Figure 11.9.** Jean Vertut, courtesy of Yvonne Vertut, Paris. **Figure 11.10.** Dr. David W. Phillipson, Cambridge, U.K.

Chapter 13
Figure 13.7. Courtesy Vance Haynes.

Chapter 14
Figure 14.1. Irven DeVore/Anthro-Photo. **Figure 14.2.** John Eastcott/Yva Momatiuk/Woodfin Camp & Associates.

Chapter 15
Figure 15.4. Photo courtesy David Perry. **Figure 15.6.** Courtesy Peter Rowley-Conwy and the Vale of Pickering Research Trust.

Chapter 16
Figure 16.3. National Museum of the American Indian, Smithsonian Institution, Photo David Heald [T134512D + T134513]. **Figure 16.4.** Special Collections Department, University of Nevada, Reno Library, Lorenzo Creel Collection P89-32/81. **Figure 16.5.** Special Collections Department, University of Nevada, Reno Library, Lorenzo Creel Collection P89-32/82. **Figure 16.6.** Special Collections Department, University of Nevada, Reno Library, Lorenzo Creel Collection P89-32/84. **Figure 16.7.** Courtesy Stuart Streuver and Felicia Holton. **Figure 16.8a.** Kristen Gremillion, Ohio State University. **Figure 16.8b.** Kristen Gremillion, Ohio State University. **Figure 16.8c.** Kristen Gremillion, Ohio State University.

Chapter 18
Figure 18.5. Photo courtesy of Prof. Gil Stein, Northwestern University. **Figure 18.7.** Courtesy Prof. Ofer Bar Yosef, Anthropology Dept., Harvard University and Peabody Museum, Harvard University.

Chapter 20
Figure 20.2. Ancient Art and Architecture Collection Ltd./Bridgeman Art Library. **Figure 20.3.** Ashmolean

Museum, Oxford, U.K./Bridgeman Art Library. **Figure 20.8.** American Museum of Natural History, Photo by H. Millou, Neg. No. 39604. **Figure 20.9.** Dr. Denise Schmandt-Besserat, University of Texas at Austin.

Chapter 21
Figure 21.5. Joan Oates, Cambridge, U.K. **Figure 21.8.** University of Pennsylvania Museum, Philadelphia, Neg. #S4-143183. **Figure 21.9.** University of Pennsylvania Museum, Philadelphia, Neg. #G8-8645. **Figure 21.13.** The Oriental Institute of the University of Chicago. **Figure 21.14.** British Museum. **Figure 21.16.** British Museum. **Figure 21.17a.** University of Pennsylvania Museum, Philadelphia, Neg. #G8-8344. **Figure 21.17b.** University of Pennsylvania Museum, Philadelphia, Neg. #B170725.

Chapter 22
Figure 22.3. Richard Meadow. **Figure 22.4.** Pam Crabtree. **Figure 22.5.** Archaeological Museum, New Delhi, Delhi, India/Scala/Art Resource, NY. **Figure 22.6.** Courtesy Asko Parpola. **Figure 22.10.** Borromeo/Art Resource, NY. **Figure 22.11.** Pam Crabtree. Reproduced courtesy of the Rojdi excavations, directed by Prof. Gregory Possehl, University of Pennsylvania, and funded by the National Science Foundation. **Figure 22.12:** Borromeo/Art Resource, NY. **Figure 22.13.** Karachi Museum/Borromeo/Art Resource, NY. **Figure 22.14.** Courtesy Bridgit Allchin.

Chapter 23
Figure 23.1. Douglas Campana. **Figure 23.2.** The Griffith Institute, Ashmolean Museum, Oxford, U.K. **Figure 23.3.** Art Resource, NY. **Figure 23.4.** Douglas Campana. **Figure 23.6.** British Museum. **Figure 23.7.** Petrie Museum of Egyptian Archaeology, University College London. **Figure 23.8.** Petrie Museum of Egyptian Archaeology, University College London. **Figure 23.13.** Petrie Museum of Egyptian Archaeology, University College London. **Figure 23.14.** Hirmer Fotoarchiv. **Figure 23.16.** Laurie Flentye. **Figure 23.17.** Douglas Campana.

Chapter 24
Figure 24.1. L.H. Jawitz/The Image Bank. **Figure 24.7.** Wiltshire Heritage Museum, Devizes, U.K. **Figure 24.8.** Historisches Museum der Pfalz, Speyer, Germany, Photo, Kurt Diehl.

Chapter 25
Figure 25.3. Robert Frerck/Odyssey/Chicago. **Figure 25.6.** SEF/Art Resource, NY. **Figure 25.7.** Robert Frerck/Odyssey/Chicago. **Figure 25.10.** University of Pennsylvania Museum, Philadelphia, Neg. #62-4-972. **Figure 25.12.** University of Pennsylvania Museum, Philadelphia, Photo, William Coe, Neg. #65-4-1094.

Chapter 26
Figure 26.5. Richard Burger, Yale University. **Figure 26.7.** Hoover Presidential Library-Museum, West Branch, Iowa. **Figure 26.8.** American Museum of Natural History, Neg. No.329715. **Figure 26.9.** Prof. Donald Proulx, Univ. of Massachusetts. **Figure 26.10.** The Art Institute of Chicago. **Figure 26.11.** Servicio Aerofotografico Nacional, Lima, Peru. **Figure 26.14.** American Museum of Natural History, Neg. No.325190.

Chapter 27
Figure 27.2. Ohio Historical Society. **Figure 27.3.** Ohio Historical Society. **Figure 27.4.** National Park Service, U.S. Dept. of the Interior. **Figure 27.9.** Art Grossman/Cahokia Mounds Museum Society.

Chapter 28
Figure 28.1. Helaine Silverman, University of Illinois at Urbana-Champaign. **Figure 28.2.** Photography courtesy of Prof. Bettina Arnold, based on *5000 Jahre Deutschland: Germanischen Leben in 7000 Bildern* by Jeorg Lechler, 1937, Leipzig: Curt Kabitzsch Verlag. **Figure 28.3.** Dr. David W. Phillipson, Cambridge, U.K.

Index